Cinema 16

*Documents Toward a
History of the Film Society*

In the series

Wide Angle Books

edited by Erik Barnouw, Ruth Bradley, Scott MacDonald, and Patricia Zimmermann

Cinema 16

Documents Toward a History of the Film Society

Scott MacDonald

TEMPLE UNIVERSITY PRESS
Philadelphia

Temple University Press, Philadelphia 19122
Copyright © 2002 by Temple University
All rights reserved
Published 2002
Printed in the United States of America

♾ The paper used in this publication meets the requirements of the American National Standard for Information Sciences—Permanence of Paper for Printed Library Materials, ANSI Z39.48-1984

Library of Congress Cataloging-in-Publication Data

Cinema 16 : documents toward a history of the film society / [edited by] Scott MacDonald.
     p. cm. — (Wide angle books)
 Includes numerous letters to and from Amos Vogel, director of Cinema 16.
 Includes bibliographical references and index.
 ISBN 1-56639-923-8 (alk. paper) — ISBN 1-56639-924-6 (pbk : alk. paper)
  1. Vogel, Amos. 2. Cinema 16 (Society : New York, N.Y.). 3. Cinema 16 (Society : New York, N.Y.)—History. 4. Cinema 16 ((Society : New York, N.Y.)—History—Sources.
  I. MacDonald, Scott, 1942– . II. Vogel, Amos. Correspondence. Selections. III. Series.

PN1993 .C5194 2002
791.43'06'07471—dc21
                                                      2001034069

Contents

List of Illustrations	*xi*
Acknowledgments	*xv*
Introduction	*1*
An Interview with Amos Vogel	*37*
An Interview with Marcia Vogel	*63*
An Interview with Jack Goelman	*71*
The Documents	
Letter to Frank Stauffacher from Amos Vogel (Vogelbaum), 9/1/47	*77*
Letter to Amos Vogel (Vogelbaum) from Frank Stauffacher, 9/20/47	*79*
Conversation with Cecile Starr, 12/19/00	*81*
Letter to Frank Stauffacher from Amos Vogel, 10/2/47	*84*
Letter to Frank Stauffacher from Amos Vogel, 10/16/47	*85*
Program Notes by Amos Vogel for Cinema 16's First Program, November 1947	*86*
Archer Winsten, "Cinema 16's Project Starts Auspiciously," *New York Post*, November 6, 1947	*89*
Letter to Amos Vogel from Kenneth Anger, 11/20/47	*90*
Letter to Sidney Peterson from Amos Vogel, 11/28/47	*91*
Archer Winsten, "Cinema 16's Fast Start Continues for 2nd Bill," *New York Post*, 12/4/47	*92*
Letter to Amos Vogel from Gregory Markopoulos, 12/6/47	*93*
Letter to Amos Vogel from Sidney Peterson, 12/12/47	*95*
Letter to Robert Flaherty from Amos Vogel, 12/17/47	*97*
Letter to Kenneth Anger from Amos Vogel, 12/17/47	*98*
Letter to Amos Vogel from Joseph Cornell, 1/19/48	*99*
Letter to Robert Flaherty from John Grierson, 1/27/48	*100*
Letter to Amos Vogel from Kenneth Anger, 2/13/48	*102*
Program Announcement: Spring 1948	*102*
Letter to Amos Vogel from Joseph Cornell, 6/22/48	*104*
Letter to Amos Vogel from Sidney Peterson, 6/25/48	*105*
James Agee, Review in *The Nation*, 7/3/48	*107*

Letter to Amos Vogel from Gregory Markopoulos, 7/8/48	*108*
Letter to Robert Flaherty from Amos Vogel, 11/8/48	*110*
Program Announcement, Fall 1948	*111*
Program Announcement, Spring 1949	*112*
Program Notes by James Broughton for *Mother's Day*, Shown on March 9, 1948	*115*
Letter to Amos Vogel from Jordan Belson, 3/18/49	*116*
Letter to Amos Vogel from James Broughton, 3/25/49	*118*
Letter to Amos Vogel from Joseph Cornell, 4/9/49	*119*
Letter to James Broughton from Amos Vogel, 4/12/49	*120*
Letter to Amos Vogel from Frank Stauffacher, Circa 4/49	*122*
Letter to Amos Vogel from Sidney Peterson, 5/23/49	*124*
Letter to Amos Vogel from Gregory Markopoulos, 5/31/49	*125*
Letter to Gregory Markopoulos from Amos Vogel, 6/8/49	*126*
Letter to Amos Vogel from Frank Stauffacher, 7/15/49	*127*
Mr. Harper, "The Only Path," *Harper's*, 7/49	*128*
Amos Vogel, "Film Do's and Don'ts," *Saturday Review*, 8/20/49	*130*
Program Announcement, Fall 1949	*133*
Archer Winsten, "Cinema 16 Begins Its Third Season," *New York Post*, 9/14/49	*135*
Letter to Amos Vogel from Frank Stauffacher, 10/17/49	*137*
Letter to Frank Stauffacher from Amos Vogel, 11/15/49	*138*
Letter to Gregory Markopoulos from Amos Vogel, 12/15/49	*140*
Program Announcement, Spring 1950	*141*
Program Notes by Arthur Knight for Arne Sucksdorff's *Valley of Dreams* and *A Divided World*, Shown in March 1950	*143*
Program Notes by Parker Tyler for Sidney Peterson's *The Lead Shoes*, Shown in May 1950	*145*
Letter to Amos Vogel from Parker Tyler, 5/11/50	*147*
Letter to Amos Vogel from Joseph Cornell, 6/3/50	*148*
Letter to Amos Vogel from Gregory Markopoulos, 6/13/50	*148*
Letter to Gregory Markopoulos from Amos Vogel, 9/18/50	*149*
Letter to Amos Vogel from Gregory Markopoulos, Circa 9/50	*150*
Program Announcement, Fall 1950	*151*
Letter to Amos Vogel from Sidney Peterson, 10/21/50	*154*
Letter to Amos Vogel from Frank Stauffacher, 1/6/51	*156*
Program Announcement, Spring 1951	*158*
Letter to Amos Vogel from Frank Stauffacher, 5/4 and 5/29, 1951	*160*
Letter to Amos Vogel from Kenneth Anger, 6/23/51	*163*

Letter to Amos Vogel from Hans Richter, ?/?/51	*164*
Program Announcement, Fall 1951	*165*
Program Announcement, Spring 1952	*168*
Program Notes Compiled from Various Authors for Georges Franju's *The Blood of the Beasts* and Kenneth Anger's *Fireworks*, Shown in May 1952	*171*
Parker Tyler, "*Rashomon* as Modern Art," Cinema 16 Pamphlet (1952)	*175*
Letter to Amos Vogel from Jean Renoir, 8/11/52	*182*
Program Announcement, Fall 1952/Spring 1953	*183*
Letter to Amos Vogel from Kenneth Anger, 12/8/52	*187*
Letter to Amos Vogel from Kenneth Anger, 1/31/53	*190*
Letter to Scott MacDonald from George Stoney, 3/22/01	*192*
Program Announcement, Spring 1953	*193*
Letter to Kenneth Anger from Amos Vogel, 4/23/53	*195*
Program Announcement, Fall 1953/Spring 1954	*196*
"Poetry and the Film: A Symposium" (with Maya Deren, Willard Maas, Arthur Miller, Dylan Thomas, Parker Tyler), 10/28/53	*202*
Program Notes by Amos Vogel in Response to Survey of Cinema 16 Membership, Fall 1953	*213*
Conversation with Robert Kelly, 12/19/00	*218*
Program Notes by Dr. Rene A. Spitz for *Grief*, Shown in January 1954	*220*
Letter to Amos Vogel from Willard Maas, 1/6/54	*222*
Letter to Amos Vogel from Kenneth Anger, 2/23/54	*223*
Program Announcement, Spring 1954	*225*
Letter to Cinema 16 from T.S. and Response by Amos Vogel, from May 1954 Program Notes	*226*
Letter to Amos Vogel from Gerd Stern, 5/9/54	*227*
Letter to Amos Vogel from Kenneth Anger, 5/19/54	*228*
Letter to Amos Vogel from Gerd Stern, 5/24/54	*230*
Letter to Kenneth Anger from Amos Vogel, 5/24/54	*231*
Letter to Gerd Stern from Amos Vogel, 6/1/54	*232*
Letter to Amos Vogel from Harry Partch, 6/3/54	*233*
Letter to Amos Vogel from Kenneth Anger, 7/9/54	*234*
Letter to Kenneth Anger from Amos Vogel, 8/19/54	*236*
Letter to Amos Vogel from Kenneth Anger, 8/28/54	*237*
Letter to Amos Vogel from Luis Buñuel, 9/17/54	*239*
Letter to Kenneth Anger from Amos Vogel, 9/21/54	*240*
Program Announcement, Fall 1954/Spring 1955	*241*
Letter to Amos Vogel from Kenneth Anger, 11/26/54	*246*

Letter to Madeline Tourtelot from Amos Vogel, 1/11/55	248
Transcript of Tape Recording Made by King Vidor and Played at Cinema 16 on 2/1/55 at screening of *Hallelujah*	249
Letter to Amos Vogel from Kenneth Anger, 2/11/55	252
Letter to Kenneth Anger from Amos Vogel, 2/18/55	253
Letter to Amos Vogel from Kenneth Anger, 3/1/55	254
Program Announcement, Spring 1955	255
Letter to Amos Vogel from Kenneth Anger, 4/27/55	257
Letter to Kenneth Anger from Amos Vogel, 5/3/55	258
Amos Vogel, "Cinema 16 and the Question of Programming," *Film Culture*, no. 3 (1955)	259
Letter to Barbara Stauffacher [Solomon] from Amos Vogel, 8/22/55	262
Program Announcement, Fall 1955/Spring 1956	263
Letter to Amos Vogel from Samson de Brier, 9/1/55	267
Letter to Samson de Brier from Amos Vogel, 9/12/55	270
Letter to Amos Vogel from Kenneth Anger, 10/15/55	271
Letter to Madeline Tourtelot from Amos Vogel, 11/8/55	271
Letter to Amos Vogel from Madeline Tourtelot, 11/11/55	272
Letter to Amos Vogel from Willard Maas, 1/9/56	273
Program Announcement, Spring 1956	275
Conversation with Carmen D'Avino, 2/16/85	276
Letter to Amos Vogel from Stan Brakhage, 3/27/56	278
Program Notes by Stan Brakhage for *Reflections on Black*, Shown in April 1956	280
Letter to Kenneth Anger from Amos Vogel, 4/23/56	282
Letter to Amos Vogel from Fred Zinnemann, 6/6/56	283
Program Announcement, Fall 1956/Spring 1957	287
Letter to Amos Vogel from Kenneth Anger, 2/19/57	288
Program Announcement, Spring 1957	290
Program Notes by Amos Vogel for Roberto Rossellini's *The Flowers of St. Francis*, Shown in February 1957	290
Letter to Amos Vogel from Stan Brakhage, 3/25/57	293
Letter to Kenneth Anger from Amos Vogel, 4/27/57	294
Letter to Amos Vogel from Stan Brakhage, 5/13/57	295
Letter to Amos Vogel from Stan Brakhage, 7/28/57	297
Conversation with Stan Brakhage, 11/30/96	298
Program Announcement, Fall 1957/Spring 1958	300
Letter to Stan Brakhage from Amos Vogel, 10/11/57	306
Letter to Amos Vogel from Stan Brakhage, 10/21/57	307

Letter to Amos Vogel from Kenneth Anger, 10/29/57	*311*
Letter to Amos Vogel from Stan Brakhage, 11/1/57	*312*
Letter to Stan Brakhage from Amos Vogel, 11/4/57	*314*
Letter to Amos Vogel from Stan Brakhage, 11/8/57	*316*
Letter to Kenneth Anger from Amos Vogel, 11/27/57	*317*
Letter to Amos Vogel from Stan Brakhage, 12/2/57	*318*
Letter to Amos Vogel from Lindsay Anderson, 12/14/57	*320*
Letter to Amos Vogel from Kenneth Anger, 1/8/58	*323*
Letter to Lindsay Anderson from Amos Vogel, 2/3/58	*324*
Program Notes by Gideon Bachmann for Benjamin Christensen's *Witchcraft Through the Ages*, Shown in February 1958	*327*
Program Announcement, Spring 1958	*332*
Letter to Amos Vogel from Agnes Varda, 6/30/58	*334*
Amos Vogel, "The Angry Young Film Makers," *Evergreen Review*, November/December 1958	*336*
Program Announcement, Fall 1958/Spring 1959	*345*
Program Notes by Siegfried Kracauer for Fritz Hippler's *The Eternal Jew*, Shown in November 1958	*351*
Conversation with Melvin Van Peebles, 1/18/01	*354*
Program Announcement, Spring 1959	*356*
Archer Winsten, "Rages and Outrages," *New York Post*, 3/2/59	*357*
Jonas Mekas, "Movie Journal," *Village Voice*, 9/16/59	*359*
Program Announcement, Fall 1959/Spring 1960	*360*
Conversation with Ed Emshwiller, 1/4/85	*367*
Letter to John Cassavetes from Amos Vogel, 11/17/59	*369*
Letter to John Cassavetes from Amos Vogel, 11/20/59	*372*
Letter to Amos Vogel from John Cassavetes, 1/19/60	*373*
Program Announcement, Spring 1960	*374*
Program Announcement, Fall 1960/Spring 1961	*376*
Program Notes Compiled by Amos Vogel for the 1960 Creative Film Awards Presentation in January 1961	*382*
Conversation with Robert Breer, 12/19/00	*386*
Letter to Amos Vogel from Joseph Campbell, 10/10/61	*388*
Program Announcement, Spring 1961	*389*
Program Announcement, Fall 1961/Spring 1962	*390*
Dwight Macdonald, "Some Animadversions on the Art Film," *Esquire*, 4/62	*395*
Amos Vogel, "Riposte from Cinema 16," *Esquire*, 9/62	*401*
Conversation with P. Adams Sitney, 5/20/00	*403*

Program Announcement, Fall 1962/Spring 1963	405
Letter to Friends of Cinema 16 from Amos Vogel, 2/63	411
Nat Hentoff, "Last Call for Cinema 16," *Village Voice*, 2/21/63	413
Conversation with Jonas Mekas, 5/24/85	416
Archer Winsten, "Rages and Outrages," *New York Post*, 3/11/63	418
Final Cinema 16 Distribution Catalog Film Listings, 1963	419
Letter to Amos Vogel from Stan Brakhage, 11/66	427
Amos Vogel, "Thirteen Confusions," *Evergreen Review*, 7/67	428
Amos Vogel, "The Eternal Subversion," from *Film As a Subversive Art* (New York: Random House, 1974)	435
Amos Vogel, "Foreword" to the New German Edition of *Film As a Subversive Art* (Vienna: Hannibal Verlag, 1997)	437
Index	439

List of Illustrations

Illustration 1. The Cinema 16 "Statement of Purposes." 6

Illustration 2: A portion of the audience at the Hunter Playhouse, where Cinema 16 presented programs during the spring and fall of 1948. 7

Illustration 3: A still from Georges Franju's *The Blood of the Beasts* (1949). 12

Illustration 4: The packed house at the Hitchcock event, March 28, 1956, at the Central Needle Trades Auditorium. 15

Illustration 5: First program announcement and ticket to the Children's Cinema with drawing by Maurice Sendak. 21

Illustration 6: Brochures for the N.Y.U. and New School film courses offered in conjunction with Cinema 16. 22

Illustration 7: Carmen D'Avino accepts a Creative Film Foundation award presented by Salvador Dali. 23

Illustration 8: Ben Moore accepts a Creative Film Foundation award from Willard Maas, Tennessee Williams, and Joseph Campbell. 24

Illustration 9: Maya Deren in *Meshes of the Afternoon* (1943) by Deren and Alexander Hammid. 41

Illustration 10: The sixteen-hundred-seat Central Needle Trades Auditorium (later known as the Fashion Industries Auditorium). 43

Illustration 11: *Dreams That Money Can Buy* (1947) by Hans Richter. 46

Illustration 12: Still from *The Door in the Wall*, illustrating the "Dynamic Frame Technique." 50

Illustration 13: Stan Brakhage, Bruce Conner, Carmen D'Avino, Shirley Clarke, Stan Vanderbeek, Walter Hoellerer, Amos Vogel, and Ed Emshwiller in Berlin in 1960. 51

Illustration 14: Gregory Corso and Allen Ginsberg in *Pull My Daisy* (1959) by Robert Frank. 56

Illustration 15: Three invitations to join the Cinema 16 Film Society. 59

Illustration 16: Alfred Hitchcock at Cinema 16 on March 29, 1956. 60

Illustration 17: The Anthology Film Archives Selection Committee: Ken Kelman, James Broughton, P. Adams Sitney, Jonas Mekas, Peter Kubelka. 61

Illustration 18: The logo of the Collective for Living Cinema. 62

Illustration 19: Amos and Marcia Vogel, as they appeared in *Mademoiselle* in March 1955. 64

List of Illustrations

Illustration 20: *Song of Ceylon* (1934) by Basil Wright.	66
Illustration 21: Jonas and Adolfas Mekas in 1953, from Jonas Mekas, *Lost Lost Lost* (1976).	68
Illustration 22: The Central Needle Trades Auditorium.	73
Illustration 23: The certificate presented to the filmmaker of each film shown at Cinema 16.	74
Illustration 24: Program announcement, November 1947.	86
Illustration 25: Program announcement, December 1947.	94
Illustration 26: Sidney Peterson.	96
Illustration 27: Program announcement, January 1948.	100
Illustration 28: Draft of letter by Robert Flaherty to be used to establish a list of sponsors for Cinema 16.	101
Illustration 29: *The City* (1939) by Willard Van Dyke and Ralph Steiner.	104
Illustration 30: *Land without Bread* (1932) by Luis Buñuel.	113
Illustration 31: *Night Mail* (1936) by Basil Wright.	115
Illustration 32: *Improvisation No. 1* (1948) by Jordan Belson.	118
Illustration 33: *Mother's Day* (1948) by James Broughton.	122
Illustration 34: Frank Stauffacher and James Broughton filming *Mother's Day*.	124
Illustration 35: Detail from *New Earth* (1934) by Joris Ivens.	134
Illustration 36: *The Lead Shoes* (1949) by Sidney Peterson.	146
Illustration 37: *The Plow That Broke the Plains* (1936) by Pare Lorenz.	153
Illustration 38: *Sausalito* (1948) by Frank Stauffacher.	156
Illustration 39: Program announcement, fall 1951.	165
Illustration 40: Photographic evocation of Kenneth Anger's *Fireworks* (1947).	173
Illustration 41: Cover of *Cinema 16 Pamphlet One*.	175
Illustration 42: Program announcement, fall 1952/spring 1953.	183
Illustration 43: *The Quiet One* (1948) by Sidney Meyers.	186
Illustration 44: Program announcement, fall 1953/spring 1954.	197
Illustration 45: *The Magnificent Ambersons* (1942) by Orson Welles.	200
Illustration 46: *L'Atalante* (1934) by Jean Vigo.	201
Illustration 47: Dylan Thomas, Arthur Miller, Willard Maas, Parker Tyler, Amos Vogel, and Maya Deren at the Cinema 16 symposium "Poetry and the Film," held in October 1953.	203
Illustration 48: Photographic evocation of Kenneth Anger's *Inauguration of the Pleasure Dome* (1954).	224
Illustration 49: Kenneth Anger.	235
Illustration 50: Luis Buñuel in *Un Chien Andalou* (1929).	239
Illustration 51: Program announcement, fall 1954/spring 1955.	241
Illustration 52: *Earth* (1930) by Alexander Dovzhenko.	245

Illustration 53: Fred Zinnemann and Amos Vogel at Cinema 16, spring 1956.	*247*
Illustration 54: *Hallelujah* (1929) by King Vidor.	*250*
Illustration 55: Program announcement, fall 1955/spring 1956.	*263*
Illustration 56: Alfred Hitchcock and Amos Vogel at Cinema 16.	*268*
Illustration 57: Carmen D'Avino in his studio in New York.	*277*
Illustration 58: *Reflections on Black* (1955) by Stan Brakhage.	*281*
Illustration 59: Program announcement, fall 1956/spring 1957.	*283*
Illustration 60: *The Flowers of St. Francis* (1950) by Roberto Rossellini.	*291*
Illustration 61: Marie Menken at work.	*299*
Illustration 62: Program announcement, fall 1957/spring 1958.	*301*
Illustration 63: *Gold Diggers of 1933* (1933) by Busby Berkeley.	*303*
Illustration 64: Stan Brakhage at his home in the mountains above Boulder, Colorado.	*308*
Illustration 65: *O Dreamland* (1953) by Lindsay Anderson.	*322*
Illustration 66: *Witchcraft Through the Ages* (1922) by Benjamin Christensen.	*328*
Illustration 67: *Man of Aran* (1934) by Robert Flaherty.	*333*
Illustration 68: Amos Vogel with Agnes Varda, Richard Roud.	*335*
Illustration 69: Program announcement, fall 1958/spring 1959.	*345*
Illustration 70: *The Big "O"* (1959) by Carmen D'Avino.	*349*
Illustration 71: *Pandora's Box* (1929) by G. W. Pabst.	*351*
Illustration 72: Program announcement, fall 1959/spring 1960 season.	*360*
Illustration 73: *All My Babies* (1952) by George Stoney.	*363*
Illustration 74: *Freaks* (1932) by Tod Browning.	*365*
Illustration 75: *Shadows* (1960) by John Cassavetes.	*371*
Illustration 76: Program announcement, fall 1960/spring 1961.	*377*
Illustration 77: *A Movie* (1958) by Bruce Conner.	*381*
Illustration 78: Program announcement, fall 1961/spring 1962.	*391*
Illustration 79: *The Sun's Burial* (1960) by Oshima Nagisa.	*391*
Illustration 80: *Guns of the Trees* (1960) by Jonas Mekas.	*399*
Illustration 81: P. Adams Sitney in December 1963, with Jack Smith, George Fenin, Gregory Markopoulos, and Andy Warhol.	*403*
Illustration 82: Program announcement, fall 1962/spring 1963.	*406*
Illustration 83: Opening page of Amos Vogel's letter asking the Cinema 16 membership for financial assistance.	*411*
Illustration 84: The four Cinema 16 distribution brochures.	*420*
Illustration 85: Amos Vogel with John Lennon and Yoko Ono.	*435*

Acknowledgments

I MUST ACKNOWLEDGE the consistent, generous support of this project by Amos and Marcia Vogel, who never seemed to tire of what must have seemed my endless questions. Without the Vogels' generosity in granting me unlimited access to the Cinema 16 files and permission to reprint letters and other materials relating to Cinema 16, this book would not have been possible.

My deep appreciation also to Jack Goelman, to Richard Herskowitz (for assembling Vogel's program notes and lists of the films/filmmakers Vogel presented at Cinema 16), to Stephen J. Dobi (for his useful Ph.D. thesis on Cinema 16), and to David James for his valuable comments on the manuscript. Many people have assisted me in tracking down materials and information: thanks especially to Ruth Bradley, Robert Haller, Jonas Mekas, John Pruitt, P. Adams Sitney, Lorna Lentini, and William Sloan.

I am grateful to two exhibitors for providing me with the opportunity, during my early research into Cinema 16, to explore some of these films and to present them publicly in New York City. Karen Cooper allowed me to present a Cinema 16 retrospective at Film Forum in 1986; and Jonas Mekas and Robert Haller provided me with the opportunity to present a seventeen-program Cinema 16 retrospective during April 1994 at Anthology Film Archives.

In my efforts to adapt to the digital era, I have been fortunate to have the assistance of my wife, Patricia Reichgott O'Connor, and of two capable, patient typists: Carol Fobes, with whom I have worked for years, and Elizabeth Spaziani.

Special thanks to two of my fellow editors on the Wide Angle Books series—Ruth Bradley and Patricia R. Zimmermann—for their collegiality and support; and to Micah Kleit, for his support of the Wide Angle project itself.

Introduction

FROM THE END of 1947 until mid-1963, the New York City cultural scene was energized by Cinema 16, the most successful and influential membership film society in North American history. At its height, Cinema 16 boasted seven thousand members, who filled a sixteen-hundred-seat auditorium at the High School of Fashion Industries (in Manhattan's garment district) twice a night, as well as two and sometimes three five-hundred-seat first-run theaters at various Manhattan locations, for monthly presentations. These audiences were presented with a very wide range of film forms, often programmed so as to confront—and sometimes to shock—conventional expectations. Amos Vogel, first with his wife, Marcia Vogel, and later with assistant Jack Goelman, looked at hundreds of films annually, choosing and arranging fall and spring series of events that were meant to function as critiques of the conventional cinema and of conventional relationships between filmmakers, exhibitors, and audiences. Instead of accepting moviegoing as an entertaining escape from real life, Vogel and his colleagues saw themselves as a special breed of educator, using an exploration of cinema history and current practice not only to develop a more complete sense of the myriad experiences cinema makes possible, but also to invigorate the potential of citizenship in a democracy and to cultivate a sense of global responsibility.

By the 1950s, Cinema 16 was not just a thriving exhibitor but an important distributor of films not available from established distribution companies, and a crucial model for a nationwide network of smaller film societies. Further, Cinema 16's large, vociferous audiences became an inspiration for a generation of independent filmmakers whose work traveled this network of alternative screening venues. By the early 1960s, various factors conspired to undermine Cinema 16's financial viability. Nevertheless, the film society remains noteworthy, both as a major historical contribution to film awareness in the United States and as a potential model for film/video exhibition. During periods when financial resources for alternative exhibition are rare, it is well to remember what one small organization devoted to the broadest sense of cinema was able to accomplish in the era before government grants for film exhibition were even a fantasy.

Backgrounds

While its longevity and the scope of its activities made Cinema 16 a new and remarkable phenomenon in the postwar American film scene, the organization—and Vogel's approach to programming, which gave the organization its energy—had historical precedents in Europe and on the North American continent. The ciné-club movement was underway in France by the early 1920s.[1] The first formally organized French ciné-club, C.A.S.A. (Club des amis du septième art), was formed in 1920, originally as a discussion group, though it soon began to present private screenings to members. Club Français du cinéma was formed in late 1922 or early 1923 by critic Leon Moussinac "to defend filmmakers as artists . . . and to attack the restrictions of the commercial industry."[2] One dimension of this agenda was an alternative film series. C.A.S.A. and Club Français du cinéma subsequently merged and began an extensive schedule of monthly public screenings of revivals of impressive but underappreciated earlier films and premieres of new films, including avant-garde work (Dudley Murphy and Fernand Leger's *Ballet méchanique* [1924], for example), and political films rejected by commercial distributors or the censors (Eisenstein's *Potemkin* [1925], for example)—precisely the types of film that were to become Cinema 16 staples. Ciné-club activity proliferated throughout France in the 1920s, and while the audience for ciné-club events remained limited—Richard Abel describes it as an elitist audience "of artists, intellectuals, cinéphiles and (to use an unflattering label from the period) 'boisterous snobs'"[3]—the growing enthusiasm for a broader spectrum of cinema led to Germaine Dulac's formation of the Federation Française des Ciné-Clubs in 1930, the first national film organization of its kind.[4]

The film society movement spread quickly throughout Europe, in some instances with considerable success. Most notably, perhaps, the London Film Society was established in 1925 so that the organizers could insist on "the principle of selection and serious study from the widest possible range of film material."[5] From the beginning, the London Film Society offered members programs of remarkable breadth, combining avant-garde films, scientific films and other types of documentaries, classic shorts and features, and commercial films of distinction from around the world—an eclectic format that lasted through fourteen seasons, until April 23, 1939.[6] When the British Federation of Film Societies was re-formed after World War II, it had 46 members (down from before the war) and quickly grew to 267 member societies in 1955.[7]

In the Netherlands, Filmliga began presenting regular programs in 1927 (using a programming strategy much like Cinema 16's), and supporting its activities with a journal, *Film Liga*, which published discussions about Filmliga programs. According to Tom Gunning, "The whole set-up of the Filmliga informed its audience that these screenings were not ephemeral viewings serving to pass the time" but, rather, "important and unique events, scheduled once a month like a cultural event, in contrast to the consumer friendly continual showings of commercial theaters."[8] In general, Filmliga presentations reflected the widespread assumption during the 1920s that both avant-garde film and what we now call documentary film offered alternatives to studio-bound commercial films and thus belonged together—an assumption that was at the heart of Vogel's Cinema 16 programming.

On this continent, film society movements took a bit longer to form, but by 1936 the National Film Society of Canada was already in existence, promoting the formation of new film societies across Canada. According to Germaine Clinton, writing in 1955:

> In Canada . . . the center of genuine interest in the film as art has always been in the film societies. Since the first world war, the visual education field has been constantly expanding and in the years between the wars the resulting growth in film sophistication came to flower in an active film society movement. Spread across thousands of miles of territory, often with hardly any supply of film, societies were started, grew, and prospered. In Edmonton, the film society grew out of the work of H. P. Brown at the University of Alberta; in Vancouver it was founded by a group of enthusiasts who ended up scouring the distributors of the world for unique films to look at.[9]

The Vancouver group seems to have been particularly successful; the Vancouver Film Society had a membership of two thousand at one point during the mid-1930s and showed "programs of great intrepidity."[10] Canadian film society activity was halted by World War II but resumed once the war was over. In December 1953, a film society division of the Canadian Film Institute was formed; in 1955, it became the Canadian Federation of Film Societies.

Perhaps because of the power and prestige of the Hollywood film industry, film society activity developed more slowly in the United States than in Europe and Canada. But before the film society movement developed momentum in the United States, interest in alternatives to commercial movie houses did produce a short-lived art house movement. The crucial figure here seems to have been New Yorker Symon Gould, who organized screenings for the newly founded Screen Guild and then began the nation's first regular art film programming, in March 1926, at the Cameo Theater in New York City. These screenings, which focused on European and classic American features, were sponsored by the International Film Arts Guild. In 1929 Gould opened the Film Guild Cinema on Eighth Street, designed by Frederick Kiesler, who claimed it was "the first one-hundred percent cinema in the world."[11] The inaugural screening at the Film Guild Cinema included two avant-garde shorts—*The Fall of the House of Usher* (James Sibley Watson and Melville Webber, 1928) and *Hands* (Stella Simon, 1928)—and a Russian feature, *Two Days* (1927). The art theater movement spread thinly across the country during the late 1920s, then seems to have petered out during the 1930s. It was not until after World War II that a substantial American film society movement developed.[12] The leader of this movement—and, indeed, its central achievement—was Cinema 16.

During 1947, as the Vogels were developing the concept of Cinema 16 and getting their project under way, their efforts were inspired not only by their general awareness of European film societies (and by Vogel's experience of film society screenings in his native Vienna in the 1930s), but also by several American film programs. The daily film presentations at the Museum of Modern Art, which had begun in 1939, were of particular importance. Indeed, Marcia Vogel remembers rushing to meet Amos at five o'clock screenings, and witnessing his growing realization that there might be a larger market for the classics and documentaries the museum was showing.

By the mid-thirties, the Museum of Modern Art—as a result of the efforts of the museum's first director, Alfred H. Barr—was creating a library with a mandate to preserve and exhibit (and subsequently distribute) a broader range of films than was commercially viable in the United States. Iris Barry, one of the major figures in the London Film Society, was the MoMA Film Library's first film curator.[13] In 1936, the Museum of Modern Art Film Library began circulating films to colleges and museums nationwide and in 1937 created the first college credit course in film at an eastern university (Columbia), a course that included lectures by Alfred Hitchcock, Luis Buñuel, Joris Ivens, and others whose work and presence would be important at Cinema 16.[14] Later on, once Cinema 16 was underway, Richard Griffith, then director of the museum's film department, helped the Vogels in various ways. For example, Griffith got Vogel together with Robert Flaherty, who assisted in Cinema 16's original membership drive.

Another set of programs that was important for the Vogels was the Art in Cinema screenings instigated by Richard Foster and Frank Stauffacher and presented, beginning in 1946, at the San Francisco Museum of Art. (After 1947 Stauffacher programmed and ran Art in Cinema himself, with help from volunteers and later from his wife, Barbara Stauffacher [Solomon].) Art in Cinema specialized in avant-garde film. The first Art in Cinema series surveyed the European avant-garde film of the 1920s and 1930s, and then, having developed a historical context, introduced audiences to historical and contemporary American avant-garde work. As would be true of Cinema 16, Art in Cinema's success in attracting hundreds of enthusiasts to its screenings provided an audience for fledgling filmmakers like Harry Smith, Jordan Belson, and Stauffacher himself. As Belson said later, "If that outlet had not been there, there wouldn't have been any incentive to make films. Might as well paint."[15] The success of Stauffacher's Art in Cinema programs in raising consciousness about alternative cinema can be measured not only by the fact that the series continued until the early 1950s, but also, perhaps, by the continued prominence of San Francisco as a center for avant-garde filmmaking during subsequent decades. Art in Cinema seems to have been the first set of programs—at least on this continent—to demonstrate that, taken together, the various forms of avant-garde filmmaking form a reasonably coherent, ongoing, alternative film history.

A final influence on the early moments of Cinema 16 occurred closer to home. Beginning in 1946, Maya Deren—filmmaker, critic, and apologist for an American independent cinema—began to show her films to audiences at the Provincetown Playhouse, the Greenwich Village home for new theater established by Susan Gaspell and Eugene O'Neill. Between February 18, 1946, and May 6, 1947, Deren screened her *Meshes of the Afternoon* (co-made with Alexander Hammid, 1943), *A Study in Choreography for Camera* (by Deren and Tally Beatty, 1945), and *At Land* (1944) to 3,243 paying customers, Amos and Marcia Vogel among them.[16] Vogel remembers:

> There was *a point* in my life when I saw Maya's films for the first time at one of those showings, and . . . it was a tremendous experience. I'll never forget it. . . . I was very impressed with the way she handled the whole thing. It didn't seem to be a fly-by-night operation. Money was not the primary concern obviously. She made it very clear in her program notes . . . that you had to be silent during the films, and I think it said something about late-comers not being admitted. . . . It was very well organized. The projection worked fine; the films looked good, in addition to being good films. I realized that there was something there that to me was far more important than the so-called "best" Hollywood films.[17]

Deren's importance for the Vogels is suggested by the fact that the earliest Cinema 16 presentations were held at the Provincetown Playhouse; and Deren was later to be involved with Cinema 16 as the founder of the Creative Film Foundation, a collaboration with Cinema 16 that from 1956 to 1961 presented annual awards to independent filmmakers.

The Formation of Cinema 16

Cinema 16 was incorporated in November 1947. The signatories on the Certificate of Incorporation were Amos and Marcia Vogel, Robert Delson (a civil-liberties lawyer who remained Cinema 16's lawyer for years), David Diener (Marcia Vogel's brother), Rene and Ralph Avery (close friends), and Samuel Vogel (Vogel's father). On the Certificate of Incorporation, the three nonprofit purposes of the corporation were defined:

(a) To promote, encourage, distribute and sponsor public exhibition of documentary, sociological, educational, scientific and experimental motion pictures, and to further the appreciation of the motion picture as an art and as a social force.
(b) To advance the science and technique of the production and distribution of documentary, sociological, educational, scientific and experimental motion pictures; to further the production of such films by amateurs; and to encourage the production of feature-length film classics.
(c) To foster interest in and to promote the establishment of motion picture theaters in the principal cities of the United States for the public exhibition of documentary, sociological, educational, scientific and experimental motion pictures.

These goals were detailed in the broadside, "Statement of Purposes" (Ill. 1), which was presented to members and potential members beginning in 1948.

It is evident in the language of the "Statement of Purposes" that Vogel did not see his project as marginal in any way; his goal was to service a "vast potential audience." This determination to provide a public service in the broadest sense had instigated Vogel's attempt to build a community of citizens who would support Cinema 16 not with donations—Cinema 16 was to be self-supporting and entirely independent—but by their presence as members and by their general enthusiasm for the film society's activities. Robert Flaherty agreed to serve as chair of the Committee of Sponsors, and his letter to prospective sponsors (see p. 101) resulted in the list of names in the column on the left edge of the statement—a list that includes such movers and shakers of the New York cultural scene as W. H. Auden, Leonard Bernstein, Van Wyck Brooks, Eddie Cantor, John Dos Passos, Oscar Hammerstein II, John Huston, Yehudi Menuhin, Gilbert Seldes, and Eli Willis, none of whom was identified with avant-garde or documentary film. In recent years organizations devoted to avant-garde exhibition, and even to documentary exhibition, seem to see their precarious tenure on the periphery of cultural life as a necessary evil, and what communities they *are* able to develop are often made up of people who accept, sometimes even fetishize, social marginalization. Vogel had a level of faith in his project that led him, from the outset, to do whatever he could to situate Cinema 16 within the mainstream of New York City cultural life. His success in doing so is evident not simply in the Committee of Sponsors, but in the many accomplished thinkers, writers, and artists who became members of the film society.

However, despite Vogel's success in developing a sense of community around his activities, Cinema 16 was forced to evolve, and quickly, in order to have any hope of accomplishing its goals. While the Vogels understood enough about what they were doing to become a corporation, their business acumen was limited. Cinema 16's first screening was successful well beyond their expectations. Vogel remembers, "It was a huge, smashing, immediate success. We had to repeat this first program for *sixteen* evenings!" (Unless otherwise indicated, all quotations by Amos Vogel, Marcia Vogel, and Jack Goelman are from the three interviews that follow this introduction.) As a result, he and Marcia invested the thousand dollars they had received as wedding presents in the second program, which was turned into a disaster by a blizzard: "Four people showed up at the theater: myself, Marcia, the projectionist, and some crazy person who came through the snow." Broke and befuddled about what to do next, the Vogels realized that all was not lost only when Samuel Vogel explained to his son and daughter-in-law how to use credit to keep a business viable during lean times.

The combination of the need to put Cinema 16 on a reasonably stable financial footing—stable enough to allow the Vogels to devote themselves full-time to the project—

Statement of Purposes:

Amos Vogel
Executive Secretary

Committee of Sponsors:

Robert J. Flaherty
Chairman

Erica Anderson
Kenneth Anger
W. H. Auden
Paul Ballard
Jean Benoit-Levy
Leonard Bernstein
A. A. Brill
Van Wyck Brooks
Henry Seidel Canby
Eddie Cantor
Theodore R. Conant
Jo Davidson
Robert Delson
John Dos Passos
Ernestine Evans
David Flaherty
Waldo Frank
John Gassner
Robert Gessner
John Grierson
Richard Griffith
John Gunther
Oscar Hammerstein, II
Natalie Hays Hammond
Curtis Harrington
Walter E. Harris
Robert P. Heller
Bryn J. Hovde
Elizabeth Hudson
John Huston
Horace M. Kallen
Arthur Knight
Dr. Siegfried Kracauer
Albert Lewin
Roy Lockwood
Mary Losey
Len Lye
Arthur L. Mayer
Allan McNab
Yehudi Menuhin
Gjon Mili
Pierre Monteux
Seymour Peck
Erwin Piscator
Carl Pryer, Jr.
Philip Rahv
Man Ray
C. R. Reagan
Jean Renoir
Elmer Rice
Hans Richter
Paul Rotha
Juliet Barrett Rublee
Edward R. Sammis
Gilbert Seldes
Elie Siegmeister
Mark Starr
Frank Stauffacher
Roy E. Stryker
Deems Taylor
Francis Thompson
Parker Tyler
Margaret Valiant
Helen Van Dongen
Gordon R. Washburn
Eli Willis
Archer Winsten
Basil Wright

CINEMA 16 is a cultural, non-profit organization devoted to the presentation of outstanding 16mm documentary, educational, scientific and experimental films.

CINEMA 16 endeavors to serve a double purpose. By its screening of superior and avant-garde films, it will contribute to the growing appreciation of the film as one of the most powerful art forms. By its screening of documentary as well as scientific and educational pictures, it will provide its audience with a more mature realization of the nature of this world and of its manifold problems.

The complexities of industrial society, the contraction of the world into an interdependent whole, the advance of modern science and technique impel modern man toward greater knowledge and a more profound understanding of his world.

It is to the credit of the documentary film makers that they have attempted to provide this knowledge and understanding. Together with the scientific, educational and experimental film producers, they have given us a comprehensive as well as scientific and educational interpretation of life. Unadorned and free of Hollywood tinsel, they have recreated the stark reality, the poignancy, the brutality of life. By their cinematic dissemination of knowledge about other cultures and peoples, as well as topical social problems, they have aimed at greater international and interracial understanding and tolerance.

Yet their creations are gathering dust on film library shelves, where a vast potential audience — numbering in the millions — can never see them. Shall this audience continue unaware of these hundreds of thought-provoking, artistically satisfying and socially purposeful films?

It is the aim of CINEMA 16 to bring together this audience and these films. CINEMA 16 will thereby advance the appreciation of the motion picture not merely as an art, but as a powerful social force.

SPECIFICALLY:

1. CINEMA 16 will screen at regular intervals outstanding documentary, factual and sociological films. It will present the classics of a Flaherty, Grierson, Ivens and Cavalcanti as well as newest releases dealing with the life of man, be he a Navajo Indian, a Southern sharecropper, a Trappist monk or a "displaced" human being.

2. CINEMA 16 will screen superior educational and scientific films, hitherto made use of only by schools and the medical profession. It will show films dealing with psychology and psychiatry, biology and chemistry, art appreciation and literature. It will present newest releases in micro-photography as well as such classics as Professor Pavlov's film on conditioned reflexes.

3. CINEMA 16 will screen the best in experimental and avant-garde films. It will show expressionist, surrealist and abstract films, presenting such pioneers as Fernand Leger, Man Ray, Watson-Webber, Maya Deren.

4. CINEMA 16 will encourage the production of new amateur and professional documentary and experimental films. First, it will provide an audience for new releases of special interest by both exhibition and distribution. Secondly, by sponsoring film contests, it will provide recognition to individual film producers. Thirdly, by purchases and rentals of prints, by establishing regular booking circuits in various cities for films of this type, it will provide funds for amateur and professional producers to help them carry on their work.

5. CINEMA 16 will invite well-known directors, producers and cinematographers to lecture before its audiences and to participate with them in forums on motion picture appreciation and technique.

6. CINEMA 16 will at all times encourage the presentation of foreign masterpieces of the documentary and experimental screen. The American public must be made aware of the truly international aspects of the fact and art film movement.

7. The final goal of CINEMA 16 is the creation of permanent "CINEMA 16" movie houses in the major cities of the nation, in which the documentary and experimental film will for the first time find a proud home of its own. The existence of such theatres in England and France testifies to the feasibility of this plan.

CINEMA 16 is determined to bridge the gap which exists between documentary film production and the people. By bringing purposeful films to the general public, film groups, labor unions and schools, CINEMA 16 will contribute to a greater realization of the problems facing man in the atomic age.

cinema 16

Incorporated as a non-profit cultural society under the educational laws of the State of New York
59 park avenue, new york 16, n. y.

Illustration 1. The Cinema 16 "Statement of Purposes."

Illustration 2. A portion of the audience at the Hunter Playhouse, where Cinema 16 presented programs during the spring and fall of 1948.

and the New York City and New York State censorship regulations in place in the late 1940s necessitated a decision to make Cinema 16 a membership film society. By offering screenings exclusively to members, the Vogels could in effect charge admission to all their events in advance (once Cinema 16 was a membership society, tickets to individual events could no longer be made available), which allowed them not only to stay solvent, but also to be more creative with programming.

Also, membership societies could not be the victims of prior censorship. In my interview with him, Vogel describes some of the more absurd results of the censorship system during the months before Cinema 16 became a membership society, when any film shown to the public had to be passed on by the Censorship Board. Members of a film society, however, could see a much broader range of film activity than could the general public, since the films shown at membership societies were only seen by the Censorship Board in the unlikely event that a member complained to the board that a film was obscene. Indeed, it seems clear now that one of the film society's central lures was this access to what would have seemed outrageous in conventional movie houses—for example, Kenneth Anger's *Fireworks* (1947), a courageously explicit psychodrama about a young homosexual's sadomasochistic fantasies, which Cinema 16 showed in 1952 and again in 1953, and Stan Brakhage's *Loving* (1957), a romantic portrait of lovers Carolee Schneemann and James Tenney, shown in 1958.

Whatever the precise set of urges that brought members to Cinema 16 screenings, the film society's membership grew quickly, from several hundred in 1947 to seven thousand in the early 1950s.

Programming at Cinema 16

Vogel's announced commitment to the broadest spectrum of cinema he could assemble was enacted in his programming from the beginning. Of course, conventional commercial movie houses in the 1940s also presented audiences with a variety of films—a newsreel, a cartoon, a feature narrative—but the goal of this highly conventionalized and regularized "variety" was always the same: simple entertainment with a touch of current events awareness. Vogel's primary goal was not entertainment, but pleasurable, exciting education: "A film society functions as a viable entity only if it both expresses and satisfactorily fulfills an existing need: to provide a forum and showcase for an increased awareness and appreciation of film as a medium of art, information, and education."[18]

Vogel's focus on education informs his "Statement of Purposes." Vogel seems always to have assumed that Cinema 16 screenings would include both avant-garde film and various forms of documentary, but his primary emphasis, throughout the statement, is on documentary. Avant-garde film might be educational in the general sense that it reveals to audiences the wide variety of forms cinematic expression makes possible, but the full range of documentary, scientific, and educational films offers the viewer "greater knowledge and a more profound understanding of his world," and "greater international and interracial understanding and tolerance." In order to develop a Cinema 16 community, Vogel recognized that he needed to emphasize those aspects of his activities that could be understood by people with no particular commitment to cinematic experiment or to avant-garde film. Having established Cinema 16's educational mission, however, Vogel quickly developed a programming practice that went far beyond conventional assumptions about education through film.

Cinema 16 presented what Vogel judged the most interesting, informative, and challenging instances of those many forms of film produced in North America and abroad that were not available to general audiences in commercial theaters, or anywhere else. Nearly every type of film other than first-run, big-studio Hollywood features and newsreels was regularly exhibited. As often as feasible, screenings at Cinema 16 were premieres. In fact, Cinema 16 was one of the first, if not *the* first, American exhibitor to present the work of Robert Breer, John Cassavetes, Shirley Clarke, Bruce Conner, Joseph Cornell, Brian DePalma, Georges Franju, Robert Gardner, John Hubley, Alexander Kluge, Jan Lenica, Richard Lester, Norman McLaren, Jonas Mekas, Nagisa Oshima, Yasujiro Ozu, Sidney Peterson, Roman Polanski, Alain Resnais, Tony Richardson, Jacques Rivette, Lionel Rogosin, Carlos Saura, Arne Sucksdorff, Francois Truffaut, Stan Vanderbeek, Melvin Van Peebles, Agnes Varda, and Peter Weiss. And while a good bit more research will be necessary before we can be entirely sure which Cinema 16 screenings were premieres, it seems likely that Cinema 16 was responsible for more American premieres of experimental and educational films than was any other organization.

Vogel's concern with using film to enlighten, rather than simply to entertain, was evident in the programming itself, and in Vogel's commitment to helping audiences develop contexts for the films he presented. Vogel's programming principles were clear from the beginning. Most obviously, he was committed to variety. Cinema 16's first program included *Lamentations* (1943), a dance film with Martha Graham; *Monkey into Man* (1938), a documentary on primate behavior, directed by Stuart Legg and supervised by Julian Huxley and S. Zuckerman; *The Potted Psalm* (1946), James Broughton and Sidney Peterson's avant-garde psychodrama; and two animations—*Boundarylines* (1945), Philip Stapp's polemical cartoon on boundaries between people, and *Glens Falls Sequence* (1946), an abstract work by Douglas Crockwell, made by painting designs on several movable layers of glass. The second program included *The Feeling of Rejection* (1947), a psychological study of the effects of childhood emotional ties on the behavior of adults; *Five Abstract Film Exercises* (1941–1944), abstract animations by John and James Whitney; *And So They Live* (1940), John Ferno's documentary on the lives of an Appalachian family; and *Hen Hop* (1945) and *Five for Four* (1945), two animations by Norman McLaren made by painting and scratching directly on film, frame by frame.[19]

As varied as Vogel's first two programs were, his selections reveal certain general tendencies. For one thing, all the films in both programs can be seen as supplying evidence about what is usually termed individual personal expression. From the very beginning, Vogel was determined to demonstrate that there is an alternative to industry-made cinema, an alternative that is in touch with the practical and spiritual lives of individuals, whether these lives are represented by committed documentarians or expressed in abstract or psychodramatic imagery. For Vogel, film going was more than a process of experiencing, over and over, the particular codes of genre film, or of worshipping the physical beauty or the dramatic ability of the stars; it was a means of getting in touch with the immense and fascinating variety in the ways people live and with the myriad ways in which individuals express their inner struggles. There was also an economic dimension to Vogel's selections. It is most obvious in *And So They Live*, in Ferno's respect for the dignity of the impoverished Appalachians he documents, but it is also implicit in the relatively inexpensive level of production used in making all the films. One of the aspects of 16 mm that particularly interested Vogel—it helps to account for the focus on 16 mm reflected in Cinema 16's name—was its potential for democratizing the cinematic representation of individuals and social life, and for expressing the problematic realities of class. Of course, 16 mm cameras and film weren't cheap, but from Vogel's point of view, the smaller gauge was at least a step in the right direction.

Those who attended Cinema 16's opening shows could not have left, as most viewers leave commercial films, with the film adventure complete and clear and their attitudes reconfirmed. As Vogel and his collaborators well knew, the puzzling films on the program—*The Potted Psalm*, most obviously (almost half the two-page program note for the opening screening was devoted to the Broughton/Peterson film: see pp. 88–89)—and the troubling social realities demonstrated in *And So They Live* and *The Feeling of Rejection* can only have undercut whatever expectations of narrative and emotional resolution viewers had brought with them from their more conventional film experiences.

Once Cinema 16 had become an established film presenter, specific programs were designed well in advance. Working with assistant Jack Goelman (and often with Marcia Vogel's advice), Vogel would preview films and decide which films should be screened during each coming year's programs. At first, Vogel needed to search out films in catalogues and by word of mouth. But as Cinema 16's reputation grew, filmmakers sought Vogel out.[20] In Cinema 16's later years, Vogel regularly attended European film festivals, searching for films to show in New York. "When we were ready to do the programs," Goelman remembers, "we used a system of index cards. We would lay a deck of cards on the table and play around with them. The problems sometimes started *after* we saw the films and knew we wanted to show them. What is a program? What six films would go together? What about the order of the six? Why would a certain film open a program? Why would a certain film close it? It was fascinating because it was all theoretical."

To some degree, the answer to the question of how to arrange the films within an individual program, and the larger issue of how to design a season-long series of programs, was a function of Vogel's (and Goelman's) politics. Vogel had considered himself a political person, a leftist, long before he came to the United States. During the years before he fled Austria, he had planned to join a kibbutz in what is now Israel, "to build a communal settlement where nobody would own land or private property, and all income would be shared—a real participatory democracy." As the events of the 1930s transpired, Vogel found it impossible to get to Israel, first because of bureaucratic and political difficulties, and later on because he found Israel's movement in the direction of a Jewish state, rather than a binational Arab-Jewish state, ideologically unacceptable.

Once Vogel was established in New York, his desire to function as a political person expressed itself through Cinema 16. Of course, implicitly, the very existence of Cinema 16 functioned as a politicized critique of commercial exhibition—of its predictable subject matter and format and of its conservative tendencies. A more fundamental dimension of Cinema 16's politics, however, was implicit from the beginning, in Vogel's (and later Vogel's and Goelman's) arrangement of the films he chose for individual programs. While some programs or parts of programs revealed particular political positions on specific issues, individual programs and seasonal series were usually structured as if each were a meta-film meant to confront the audience in a manner reminiscent of Sergei Eisenstein's dialectic editing. For Eisenstein, arranging successive shots so that their graphic and conceptual collisions would instigate viewer engagement was a means of providing cinematic interventions into the status quo reflected by and ministered to by traditional entertainment film, and of confirming and expanding cultural revolution. Similarly, at Cinema 16 presentations, one form of film collided with another in such a way as to create maximum thought—and perhaps action—on the part of the audience, not simply about individual films but about film itself and about the social and political implications of its conventional (or unconventional) uses. This similarity to Eisensteinian dialectic is more than accidental; Vogel and Goelman were great admirers of the Russian filmmaker.

Of course, the dialectic within individual programs was extended by the arrangement of each season's set of programs into a series. Indeed, even when Cinema 16 began to present programs organized around very specific topics, the comparative regularity of these programs contributed to the meta-dialectic that characterized the overall history of the film society's offerings. Similarly, the presentation, from time to time, of a classic feature, rather than a grouping of several shorter works, eliminated dialectic on one level merely to enhance it on another.

While dialectically "edited" monthly presentations remained Cinema 16's mainstay until the film society's final years, by the early 1950s a second form of programming was becoming increasingly significant, what Cinema 16 program announcements called "Special Events." The first special event occurred during the fall 1948 season: a special holiday evening with Norman McLaren. But by 1952 special events were being announced in brochures as a separate listing from the regularly scheduled, dialectically arranged programs. Vogel's interest in hosting special events in addition to his regular programming was a function of a number of concerns. For one thing, while Cinema 16 was regularly presenting films that could be counted on to surprise or offend the sensibilities of many audience members, Vogel was determined to program films likely to go so far beyond the limits of many members' tastes that special screenings, apart from the regular presentations, seemed called for.

The fall 1951 brochure announced several upcoming special events to be presented at the Central Needle Trades Auditorium only (by this time regular programs were presented at both the Central Needle Trades Auditorium and at the Paris Theater uptown). They included *Childbirth-Normal Delivery* and other medical and surgical films; a breakthrough avant-garde film, Kenneth Anger's *Fireworks* (1947); and an unusually visceral documentary, Georges Franju's *Blood of the Beasts* (*Le sang des bêtes*, 1949). The April 1952 program notes explained that *Fireworks* and *Blood of the Beasts* "are, in our opinion, among the most important short films made in the last few years. *Fireworks* is a cinematic recreation of a nightmare and is shocking both in its frankness and in its scenes of physical violence. *The Blood of the Beasts*, unqualifiedly a masterpiece, takes us inside the French slaughterhouses." In later years, other controversial films—*Witchcraft Through the Ages* (Benjamin Christensen, 1922), for example, and *The Eternal Jew* (a Nazi propaganda film by Franz Hippler, 1940)—were shown as special events.

The separate special-events scheduling also allowed Vogel the leeway to arrange events that didn't fit comfortably within the regular schedule. From time to time, Cinema 16 hosted distinguished commercial directors at one-time special evenings: Hitchcock, for instance, Fred Zinnemann, Stanley Kramer, Robert Wise, and King Vidor (when Vidor was unable to attend a scheduled screening of *Hallelujah* [1929], he sent a tape for Vogel to play for the audience—the transcript of the tape is reproduced on pp. 250–53). In other instances, the film society presented symposia on particular topics of interest to members. The fall 1953 schedule announced a symposium called "Poetry and the Film" for October 28, with a panel of distinguished guests: Maya Deren, Willard Maas, Arthur Miller, Dylan Thomas, and Parker Tyler. "Are You Really Against Censorship?" was scheduled for February 25, 1959, with special guest Ephraim London, the civil-liberties lawyer who had argued the case of Roberto Rossellini's *The Miracle* (1948) before the courts.

The special events schedule also allowed Vogel to program long films more often, including revivals of classic features, such as Erich von Stroheim's *Greed* (1923), Vidor's *The Crowd* (1928), Todd Browning's *Freaks* (1932), Mervyn LeRoy's *Gold Diggers of 1933* (1933), and Orson Welles's *The Magnificent Ambersons* (1942), and unusual features from around the world, for example, *Chandra Lekha* (directed by S. S. Vasan, 1953), "India's first million dollar musical," and *Latuko* (directed by Edgar McQueeny, 1952), a feature-length Museum of Natural History anthropological documentary banned by the censors in its entirety because of the nudity of the aborigines. Other

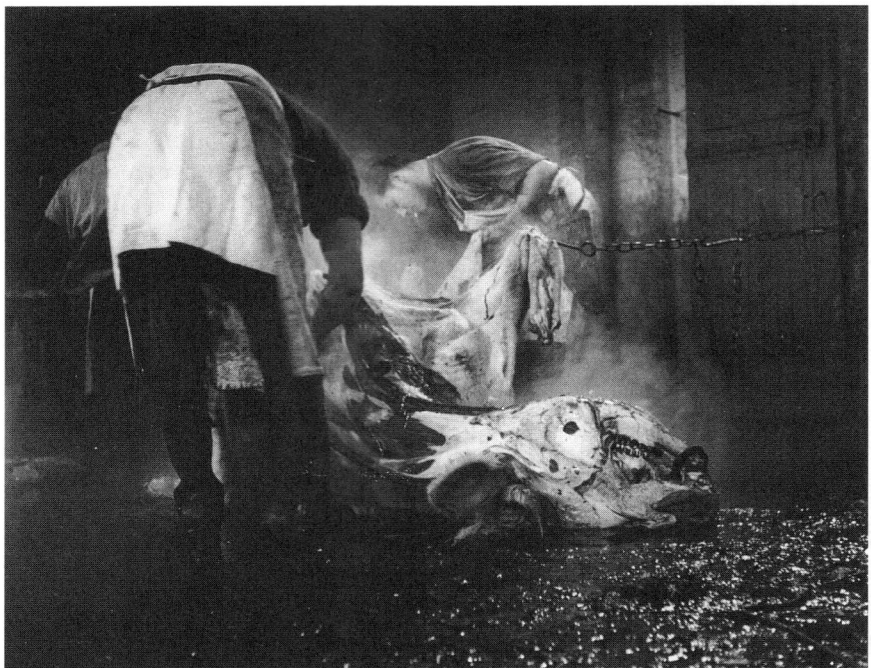

Illustration 3. A still from Georges Franju's *The Blood of the Beasts* (1949), which had its American premiere at Cinema 16.

special events were evenings of short films chosen thematically. "Voyages into the Subconscious" (presented April 21, 1954) included Peterson's *The Lead Shoes* (1940), Broughton's *Mother's Day* (1948), Willard Maas's *Geography of the Body* (1943), Crockwell's *Glens Falls Sequence,* and Curtis Harrington's *On the Edge* (1949); "The Search for Love" (April 26, 27, 1955) included Harrington's *Fragment of Seeking* (1946), Robert Anderson's *The Feeling of Hostility* (1947), Broughton's *Four in the Afternoon* (1951), Maas and Ben Moore's *The Mechanics of Love* (1955), and Gregory Markopoulos's *Psyche* (1947). The annual winners of the Creative Film Awards and the Robert J. Flaherty Awards (both discussed later) were also presented as special events.

In Cinema 16's final years, the distinction between regular offerings and special events became increasingly blurred. Features were more frequently included in the regular series, as were programs of short films arranged thematically; there were programs titled "First Films," for example, as well as programs called "Love in the City" and "Trance, Ritual and Hypnosis," and several programs of prize-winning films from other countries. Until the end, however, Vogel remained committed to the widest possible spectrum of film.

From the beginning, Cinema 16 screenings were accompanied by program notes, in many cases supplied by such distinguished critics and scholars as William K. Everson, Richard Griffith, Arthur Knight, Siegfried Kracauer, and Parker Tyler. These notes provided historical background and raised theoretical issues. In the early 1950s, Vogel considered expanding his educational mission to include the publication of important essays on film. And though only one essay was published by the film society—

Parker Tyler's discussion of Akira Kurosawa's *Rashomon* (1950), Cinema 16 Pamphlet Number 1 (see p. 175–83), Cinema 16 maintained its commitment to serious program notes throughout the 1950s and 1960s. Of course, this commitment to education was also evident in the film society's sponsorship of special events such as the symposium "Poetry and the Film" and the presentation "Are You Really Against Censorship."

If the regularity of commercial film exhibition from the 1940s through the 1950s can be said to reflect American society in one of its more conservative periods (the specters of the House Un-American Activities Committee and the McCarthy hearings hover over much of the period during which Cinema 16 was active), Vogel's alternative, firmly grounded in the assumption that we need to know more about the world and to learn to function as global citizens, was a way of advocating change and—at least in theory—of enhancing his audience's capacity to make necessary social and political improvements. In principle, Vogel embraced many economic levels of film production, as well as all nationalities; each Cinema 16 program and seasonal series functioned as a microcosm of this idea. This comparatively international approach had obvious political implications, especially during a period when anything outside mainstream American culture seemed alien, even subversive, to large numbers of Americans.

Reception

One of Vogel's most remarkable accomplishments at Cinema 16 was to sustain his programming dialectic, year after year, with a very large audience in a more-or-less public arena. In fact, it seems very doubtful that in any other instance in the history of film—certainly in American film history—such large audiences have regularly attended film programs of such diversity. Of course, the Cinema 16 audience was not a cross section of the United States, or even of New York City, though a wide variety of people attended Cinema 16 screenings. People could not come in off the street and attend a program unless they became members, and while a year's membership was not expensive, it was well beyond what some could pay. Originally a $10 fee admitted a member to eight monthly screenings and to infrequent special events; the price of membership gradually rose—as did the number of events it paid for—to a top rate of $16.50 in 1960–1961 (this in an era when admission to a neighborhood commercial movie house ranged upward from 25 cents). The one thing we do know about this audience is that its members read the Sunday *New York Times*; annual programs were announced in a *Times* ad that generated the majority of membership requests.

At various times, Vogel distributed questionnaires in order to learn something about the Cinema 16 membership. A program note for the fall of 1953 announced the results of that season's questionnaires: 55 percent of those responding were between twenty-one and thirty years old, 23 percent between thirty-one and forty, 18 percent over forty, 4 percent under twenty; 75 percent of those responding were college graduates; 41 percent were "professionals or professionally employed"; 14 percent were in business, 8 percent had clerical or sales jobs, 17 percent worked in the arts, advertising, or publicity, 6 percent were skilled workers, 5 percent were housewives. The questionnaires—as well as viewer response during and after screenings—also revealed that Vogel's audience had varied ideas of what kinds of programming Cinema 16 should be doing.

The April 1951 questionnaire results indicate that while 31 percent of members responding were happy with the current balance between documentary and experimental films, 42 percent wanted Vogel to show more documentaries and fewer experimental films, and another 15 percent wanted fewer documentaries and more experimental films.

While such feedback interested Vogel (and, presumably, Cinema 16 members; many of the results were included in the monthly program notes), he was not committed to changing his programming as a result of his audiences' preferences. Indeed, his mission as programmer frequently required him to show films he knew audiences would have problems with; and one can only assume that whatever their announced feelings about specific films or kinds of film, Cinema 16 members were generally intrigued by their very *inability* to control what Vogel would show them, by their knowledge that Vogel was committed to the idea of using film—in a phrase he was later to employ as the title of a book—as a subversive art. Even if audience members didn't enjoy particular films, they knew that they were privileged to see films almost no one else got to see. Indeed, many of the films Vogel showed are no longer in distribution; one can presume that without Vogel, we have lost access to much interesting work. Of course, Vogel chose to show many films that look unimpressive today. But his dialectical programming offered audiences an opportunity to test the limits of their taste and their understanding in what amounted to a community forum.

In recent years, film audiences have become very specialized. Opportunities for people to be confronted with types of film they would not consciously pay to see are very few. But, from all accounts, large segments of the Cinema 16 audience were regularly entertained, outraged, and bored by turns; and they could be counted on to vociferously demonstrate their approval or disapproval during and after screenings. Carmen D'Avino remembers that the Cinema 16 audience was "marvelous": "They'd boo; they'd walk out; they'd scream for joy. It was a volatile and beautiful audience to present anything to. I was thrilled to have work shown at Cinema 16" (see "Conversation with Carmen D'Avino" on pp. 278–80). Of course, by all accounts, D'Avino was a favorite of the Cinema 16 membership, which could affect filmmakers in more negative ways. Ken Jacobs, who attended as many Cinema 16 screenings as he could afford—"Cinema 16 was very cheap, but I was *that* broke"—recalls:

> I wasn't always so happy with the Cinema 16 audience. I saw *The Wonder Ring* [1959, by Stan Brakhage] on a program about the Third Avenue El. The other two movies about the El were terrible, and then Brakhage's gem comes on. And the audience (which I saw mostly as people looking to pilfer the films, use them in advertising) hated it, talked during it, *booed* it! Usually I just stared at the audience, but this time I got into a verbal fight with them. At the time, I was not only hotheaded, I could be physical—though I don't think it happened in that instance.[21]

Cinema 16 was, above all, a large public forum in which individuals could regularly measure their personal sensibilities against those of many other individuals. The dialectical premise of Vogel's programming, in other words, extended into the audience.

Because Cinema 16 was a membership film society that presented programs generally made up of a variety of kinds of short films that were not available elsewhere, press coverage of the films shown at Cinema 16 was limited. The film society had a friend in Archer Winsten, who reviewed the first program for the *New York Post* (predicting that if Cinema 16 can find more films like the "masterpiece" *Monkey into Man*, "its success will be sensational") and continued to support the film society until its demise (see Winsten's "Rages and Outrages" column from March 11, 1963). But generally, the reviews that Vogel's efforts were able to generate were little more than announcements of a given season's upcoming programs.

In at least one instance, however, Cinema 16 came under a somewhat more sustained attack. Writing for *Esquire,* Dwight Macdonald (see pp. 398–404) argued that regardless of Vogel's impassioned claims to the contrary, the "art films" presented at Cinema 16 were simply not "aesthetically enjoyable"—and therefore not really art at all: "From Griffith to Antonioni, all the great films—with only a few exceptions, such as Cocteau's *Blood of a Poet* [1930] and Vigo's *Zero de conduite* [1933]—have been aimed directly at the box office." Macdonald wonders "just who its [Cinema 16's] four thousand devotees are. Masochists? Psychiatric social workers on a busman's holiday? Whoever they are, they have taken a lot of punishment." Vogel's response, in a letter printed in the subsequent issue of *Esquire* (see pp. 404–5), attacks Macdonald for his "defense of the commercial cinema": "Art and experimentation . . . are only incidentally 'entertaining' and we have never claimed to exist for the sake of entertaining our members; we leave this to the neighborhood houses." Aside from this minor public skirmish with Macdonald, however, Vogel received rather minimal press response, considering the longevity and the ambition of Cinema 16. Indeed, as my interview with him reveals, Vogel continues to be haunted by the question of what might have happened had there been more response from the press.

Illustration 4. The packed house at the Hitchcock event, March 28, 1956, at the Central Needle Trades Auditorium (the walls of which had been decorated in the 1930s by WPA artists).

Cinema 16 as Distributor

While the presentation of varied programs of difficult-to-see films was the central activity of Cinema 16 from 1947 until 1963, a number of other activities were instituted by the film society. By far the most significant of these was Vogel's entry into film distribution. Individual titles of films available from Cinema 16 began to be listed in program notes at the beginning of 1948. In general, the types of films Vogel chose to distribute tended to echo the types of films he exhibited at Cinema 16; but because the distribution of most forms of avant-garde cinema was less developed than the distribution of documentaries or of educational shorts, Vogel increasingly committed himself where he could make the most substantial contribution. The first films distributed by Cinema 16 were Leonard Stark's *This Day* (1947), "a sensitive film poem on the horror and futility of war"; animator Francis Lee's *1941* (1941), in which "violent color, swiftly changing compositions and a brilliant musical score portray the impact of war [in this case, the Japanese attack on Pearl Harbor] on the artist"; and Lee's *The Idyll* (1948), another abstract animation; Sara Kathryn Arledge's *Introspection* (1947?), "a series of bold experiments in film-dance, fundamentally different from stage choreography"; and Hy Hirsh and Sidney Peterson's *Horror Dream* (1947), "a choreographic interpretation of a dancer's anxiety before starting her theater routine. Choreography by Marian Van Tuyl, accompanied by John Cage's sophisticated 'noise' music." Even in these early avant-garde offerings, Vogel's dual commitment to formal experiment and social awareness is obvious.

By 1951 Cinema 16 was publishing a foldout brochure entitled "20 Experimental/Rental Films from Cinema 16." While some of the films Vogel chose to distribute are no longer widely known (several are no longer in distribution), others were to become landmarks in the postwar explosion of avant-garde filmmaking. Cinema 16's first catalogue listed Lee's *Le Bijou* (1947), *1941*, and *The Idyll*; Broughton and Peterson's *The Potted Psalm*; Peterson's *The Cage* (1947) and *Horror Dream*; the Whitney brothers' *3 Abstract Film Exercises* and *Film Exercises No. 4 & 5* (1943–1945); Gregory Markopoulos's *Psyche, Lysis,* and *Charmides* (all 1948); Stark's *This Day;* Andre Michel's *La Rose et la Reseda* (1945; shown at Cinema 16 in an English version as *The Rose and the Mignonette*); Arledge's *Introspection;* Norman McLaren's *Fiddle De Dee* (1947); Maas's *Geography of the Body;* Jordan Belson's *Improvisation No. 1* (1948); Crockwell's *Glens Falls Sequence;* Emlen Etting's *Poem 8* (1933); and Hugo Latletin's *Color Designs No. 1.* The first catalogue was expanded by the Winter 1951 Supplement, which listed thirty-one films, including Anger's *Fireworks,* Broughton's *Four in the Afternoon* and *Loony Tom, the Happy Lover* (1951), and Peterson's *The Lead Shoes, The Petrified Dog* (1948), and *Mr. Frenhofer and the Minotaur* (1949), as well as several documentaries—Paul Rotha's *Shipyard* (1935), the U.S. government's *The Atom Strikes* (1946), and the time-lapse film *Power of Plants* by Paul F. Moss and Thelma Schnee.

The second catalogue, also a brochure (entitled "CINEMA 16 Poetic Surrealist Abstract Experimental Films"), included forty-eight listings (Broughton's *Mother's Day* [1949] and Franju's *Blood of the Beasts* among them). The third catalogue, published in spring 1956, was a twenty-one- page booklet entitled "A Catalogue of the Experimental Cinema"; it included ninety-nine separate listings. The final catalogue, published in 1963, presented forty-seven pages of listings of mostly avant-garde films (including a good many experimental animations), several documentaries, and a number of American and European classics: Robert Bresson's *Pickpocket* (1959), Chaplin's *Easy Street* (1917) and *The Immigrant* (1917)—more than two hundred films by more than a hundred filmmakers. The films were rented by other film societies, by art museums, colleges, religious and cultural organizations, libraries, medical schools, and a variety of other groups.

An examination of Vogel's records reveals the growth of a network of venues and individuals that exhibited alternative forms of cinema. In the early years of the film society's distribution efforts, specific renters are listed on the statements Vogel sent to filmmakers. By the end of 1957, however, the statements indicate only the location of the renting organization. The successive statements chart the trajectory of popularity for particular films. Kenneth Anger's *Fireworks*, for example, was rented three times at the end of 1951 (by a Mr. Sanft in New York City, by the Illinois Institute of Technology, and by Raymond Rohauer for the Coronet Theater in Hollywood); six times in 1952 (three times by Rohauer, by Christopher Bishop in Connecticut, by a Mr. Olkinetzki in Oklahoma, and by an unnamed New Yorker); eighteen times in 1953 (four times by the Society for Cinema Arts in California, by a Dr. Semans in Atlanta, by the U.S. Naval Hospital in Portsmouth, Virginia; by Antioch College, the University of Chicago, the University of Pennsylvania, Middlebury College, and the University of Wisconsin; twice by Jonas Mekas, by the Peninsula Film Society [California], the Long Beach Film Society [New York], the Wilmington Film Society [North Carolina], and by unnamed individuals in New York City and Highland Park, Illinois); six times in 1953 (by Western Reserve University, by Cinema 53 in Bellingham, Washington, by the Film Society of Denver, by the Lee Memorial Journalism Foundation in Lexington, Virginia, by Colonial Williamsburg, and by William Dalzell in Pittsburgh); eight times in 1954 (by the A. I. Dupont Institute in Wilmington, Delaware, by Contemporary Films in New York City, by J. K. Sours at the University of Wichita, by C. B. MacKirahan at the Lake Placid Public School in Lake Placid, New York, by the Independent Filmmakers Association, by the University of Alaska, by Mrs. J. Kummer of Midland, Michigan, and by Mr. C. Grohe in Palo Alto, California); seven times in 1956; ten times in 1957; twenty-one times in 1958; sixteen times in 1959; and twenty-seven times in 1960. *Fireworks* rented for $15 a screening, though from time to time, Vogel would negotiate a special reduced rate of $12.75 or $13.50; a second screening cost an additional $7.50. Anger received 50 percent of the total rentals. Of course, one can only wonder how some of the renters—the U.S. Naval Hospital, Colonial Williamsburg, the Dupont Institute, Stock Shots to Order in New York (1957)—used Anger's remarkably candid film.

When Cinema 16 ceased distributing films in 1963, Vogel made an arrangement with Barney Rosset at Grove Press. In keeping with Vogel's previous contractual arrangements, filmmakers were offered exclusive contracts with Grove; if they wanted to distribute their work cooperatively, they would be on their own. While some Cinema 16 filmmakers went with Grove, many others decided to take their chances elsewhere.[22]

Cinema 16 and the New American Cinema

While Cinema 16 quickly became the leading distributor of avant-garde film in North America, its methods of operation differed from those of the most important present-day North American distributors of such films (Canyon Cinema in San Francisco, the Film-makers' Cooperative in New York, and the Canadian Filmmakers Distribution

Centre in Toronto), where the filmmakers determine which of their films will be available to film renters. As Vogel explained in his introduction to the 1963 catalogue, "No attempt is made in this catalogue to either include all independent filmmakers or to include all the work of any one particular filmmaker; quality and originality remain the sole criteria of selection." In one respect, Cinema 16's distribution was set up along the lines of commercial distributors of the time: Vogel chose the films he wanted to work with, offered filmmakers exclusive contracts for the distribution rights, and to the extent that Cinema 16's means allowed, promoted the films among potential renters. In another respect, distribution by Cinema 16 differed fundamentally from commercial distribution since profits did not accrue to the Vogels; Cinema 16 was a nonprofit organization.

While Vogel's policies as exhibitor and distributor had a major impact on the field of avant-garde film, these policies were also, increasingly, a cause for frustration among some avant-garde filmmakers. On September 28, 1960, a meeting of what became known as the New American Cinema Group was called by Lewis Allen and Jonas Mekas, in large measure to consider alternative forms of distribution and exhibition for a variety of new, alternative forms of film.

Even after the New American Cinema Group had begun meeting, Mekas—who in retrospect seems to have been the group's prime mover—would continue to support Vogel's work, at least in print. In his September 14, 1961, "Movie Journal" column in the *Village Voice*, Mekas bemoans the fact that while European features are finding American theatrical venues, "the avant garde of cinema is as homeless as ever," and he describes Cinema 16 as the one exception:

> Meanwhile, as always around this time, I feel it is my duty, both as a critic and as a member of the public, to praise Cinema 16. This unique film society, alone and by itself (and I think it's time that some of the foundations came to its assistance), is trying to do a giant's job, the job that really should be done by our art theatres: to provide the showcase for the avant garde of cinema. It doesn't take much wisdom or daring to revive good old films, but it takes courage and intelligence to see and introduce the best of the new and unknown.
>
> This year Cinema 16 is coming in with another series of new and old films that you can't see anywhere else....
>
> By the way, this is the 15th anniversary of Cinema 16—so don't forget the birthday cake and the candles.

If in retrospect it may seem implicit that Mekas wishes Vogel would place an even greater emphasis on new avant-garde work, it is also obvious in Mekas's subsequent description of Cinema 16's upcoming 1961–1962 season (which included Mekas's own *The Guns of the Trees* [1960], Robert Frank's *The Sin of Jesus* [1961], and Ron Rice's *The Flower Thief* [1961]) that films now identified with the New American Cinema were playing a substantial role in Cinema 16 programming.

Nevertheless, for the New American Cinema Group, the idea that Vogel would continue to be the sole arbiter of which avant-garde films would be available and the primary arbiter of how they were presented was no longer tenable. After a series of discussions, the group became determined to distribute their films through a cooperative, nonexclusive system in which the filmmakers would decide which of their films would be distributed and would be paid directly the bulk of the money earned from rentals. Vogel's contracts called for a standard fifty-fifty split of rental revenues; the New York Cooperative returned 75 percent of rental revenues to the filmmakers. By 1962 the

Film-makers' Cooperative was publishing its own catalogue and was suggesting to catalogue readers that they offer programs of avant-garde films dedicated to individual film artists, "instead of booking, as it is usually done, potpourri programs"—a clear reference to the kind of programming that had become the mainstay of Cinema 16.[23]

Vogel was understandably upset by the New American Cinema Group's actions—and in particular, by the fact that, despite his contributions to the field, he had not been invited to be part of the new group—and though Cinema 16's distribution activities continued for several years after its exhibition program ended, the competition from the Film-makers' Cooperative may have cut into his rentals. Further, Vogel came to feel that the New American Cinema Group's "proudly proclaimed policy of showing, distributing, and praising every scrap of film" was self-defeating: "It may be essential to show every single film to filmmakers at internal, workshop screenings so that they can see each other's work; it is suicidal if this is done with general audiences.... Unable to judge the works in advance or to rely on somebody else's judgement (since no selection takes place), they ultimately decide to stay away or to stop renting films."[24]

Essentially, the arrival of the New American Cinema and the Film-makers' Cooperative reflected a change in focus. Vogel was, above all, an audience builder, a teacher, and a political motivator. For him, the challenge was to use the widest articulation of film practice as a means of invigorating viewers' interest in cinema and their willingness to use what they learned at Cinema 16 in their everyday lives as citizens of the United States and the world. The focus of the New American Cinema Group was not the audience, but the filmmakers. While the Film-makers' Cooperative certainly hoped programmers would rent the films they distributed, they were less concerned with audience size than with the integrity of individual film artists' cinematic visions. From the New American Cinema Group's point of view, Vogel's programming privileged *his* vision at the expense of the increasingly articulated visions of the filmmakers. Mekas and the others were gambling that while audiences for avant-garde film might be smaller than Vogel's audiences, these smaller groups would grow enough to sustain the field without compromising the films and the filmmakers.

From our current vantage point, it seems unfortunate that Cinema 16 and the New American Cinema Group could not find a way to combine their efforts. Vogel had proved himself a remarkable programmer, capable of generating large audiences for unusual films. Over the years, the New American Cinema Group's approach of showing programs of works by individual film artists has also proved its value—especially for that relatively small group of viewers who have already developed an interest in avant-garde film. Working together, Vogel and Mekas might have generated a two-tiered system of exhibition. Whatever we may feel the value of collaboration might have been, however, Vogel, Mekas, and the others were unable to compromise in ways that would allow them to function synergically.

Cinema 16's Other Activities

During the years that Cinema 16 was in operation, Vogel and his colleagues were involved in a number of activities in addition to choosing and presenting the film society's regular film series and special events, and putting some of the films they admired into distribution. In general, these activities reflect Vogel's commitment to enlarging the general awareness of film on the part of Cinema 16's membership, though in some cases, Vogel assisted filmmakers in completing works he was interested in screening at Cinema 16. Perhaps the most influential of these instances involved the film that came to be known as *Weegee's New York* (1954). By the late 1940s, Weegee (Arther Fellig) was a nationally known photographer; his clear-eyed observation of New Yorkers was popular among the Cinema 16 membership. Weegee himself was a Cinema 16 member, and when Vogel discovered that he had been recording film imagery, he became enthusiastic about the possibility of showing Weegee's film work. As Vogel remembers, Weegee had no sense of how to edit the considerable body of film imagery he had recorded (Vogel remembers two 1600-foot reels) and no particular interest in learning. Not to be denied the pleasure of presenting Weegee-as-filmmaker, Vogel edited the footage himself, supplied the opening credits ("Cinema 16 Presents Weegee's New York"/"A Travelogue with a HEART"/"Photographed by WEEGEE") and the titles of the two sections of the finished film ("New York Fantasy" and "Coney Island"), and saw to the production of the musical track that accompanies the visuals.[25] The result was one of the most under-recognized films of the 1950s (under-recognized *now*; *Weegee's New York* was popular at Cinema 16 and at film societies around the country), and perhaps one of the more influential films Cinema 16 premiered. The film's visuals seem an obvious inspiration for a set of New York City symphonies produced during the 1960s, including Francis Thompson's *N.Y., N.Y.* (1957), Marie Menken's *Go! Go! Go!* (1964), and Hilary Harris's *Organism* (1975); and its use of already popular records to accompany the visuals of "Coney Island" predates Kenneth Anger's recycling of rock songs in *Scorpio Rising* (1963).

Vogel's contribution to Cinema 16's presentation of scientist/photographer Roman Vishniak's microphotography, on the other hand, was, he says, "one of my worst experiences at Cinema 16."[26] Having discovered that, in addition to his other activities, Vishniak had made scientific films—"the most gorgeous footage of its kind I've ever seen"—Vogel was excited about presenting the material to the Cinema 16 membership but was worried that seeing this semi-abstract microphotography in silence might be confusing. He asked Vishniak to tape-record a personal commentary to accompany the imagery, and Vishniak obliged. But as the screening neared, Vogel realized that because of the vagaries of the electric current available in the auditorium, he was unable to keep Vishniak's detailed remarks in synch with the images on the screen: "I was behind the screen, stopping the recorder when it got ahead of the images (and throwing the auditorium into sudden total silences) . . . and sweating bullets. It was impossible, and I'm sure Vishniak must have been upset—though at the end the presentation received tremendous applause. Amazing and wonderful—but exhausting!"

Other Cinema 16 activities provided the membership with screenings of films that even Vogel, with all his enthusiasm, could not access. In spring 1956, and again in 1957 and 1958, Vogel collaborated with James Card, curator of film at the George Eastman House, to take busloads of Cinema 16 members to Rochester for weekend-long immersions in classic films from the Eastman House archives.[27] Also in the spring of 1958, Vogel arranged an excursion to Canada for those members who wanted to see Chaplin's *A King in New York* (1957), when that film was kept out of the United States.

Vogel also attempted to interest a much younger audience in a wider variety of films. During the spring and fall of 1958, two series of films for children ages four to eight were developed by Vogel and Peretz Johnnes and presented at the Beekman Theater (Sixty-sixth Street and Second Avenue). The children saw mixed programs of documentaries, experimental films, animations, and recent and classic live-action narratives.[28] According to Vogel, "Most of the stuff that was considered good children's films we knocked out. We would take films that weren't considered children's films; we made them into children's films. And the children loved the avant-garde abstract films. We didn't show them [Sidney] Peterson, that would have been silly, but my god, other things they just loved, absolutely adored."[29] The children's programs were sold out.

Several college courses were developed in collaboration with Cinema 16, first at N.Y.U. in 1950–1951 (a course in avant-garde film, designed by Vogel and George Amberg), and subsequently at the New School ("Film and Reality" and "New Frontiers for Film," both taught by Arthur Knight in 1954–1955; and "The Film and Its Related Arts," taught by Knight during 1955–1956).

For most filmmakers, the very opportunity to have films presented at Cinema 16 was an honor, but Vogel was also interested in providing special recognition to filmmaking accomplishments of particular significance. During the 1950s, Cinema 16 was involved in two sets of awards for distinguished filmmaking, in the two areas to which Vogel was most fundamentally committed as a programmer: avant-garde film and documentary.

From 1956 until 1961, the Creative Film Awards were presented at Cinema 16 as a collaboration with the Creative Film Foundation, a nonprofit organization run by Maya Deren as a way of supporting independent filmmaking.[20] The Creative Film Awards provided public recognition and cash prizes for achievements in avant-garde film. Winning films were presented at a Cinema 16 special event in the spring by guests of honor—Joseph Campbell, Salvador Dali, Lotte Lenya, Arthur Miller, Kurt Seligman, Tennessee Williams, and so on. The Creative Film Awards ceased when Deren died in 1961. The Robert J. Flaherty Awards for the best documentaries of the year were not formally a collaboration with Cinema 16, though Vogel was on the jury and the winning films were shown annually at Cinema 16.[31]

Illustration 5. First program announcement and ticket to the Children's Cinema developed by Vogel and Peretz Johnnes and presented in the spring and fall of 1958—with drawing by Maurice Sendak.

Courses for Adults

Volume 1   August 23, 1950   Number 9

New York University—The Division of General Education in co-operation with Cinema 16 Announces a New Course

NEW FRONTIERS IN THE CINEMA

For the public interested in the motion-picture as an art form: Fee $25.00

INTRODUCING THE CINEMA 16 FILM CENTER AT THE NEW SCHOOL

In response to repeated requests from Cinema 16 members for a Center where outstanding films can be examined and discussed from an aesthetic and social viewpoint, Cinema 16 is proud to announce the establishment of such a Center at—and in cooperation with—The New School, 66 West 12th Street, New York City. Under the joint direction of Arthur Knight, film critic and historian, and Amos Vogel, Executive Secretary of Cinema 16, the Center will present two series of screenings in the intimate New School Auditorium on alternate Thursday nights commencing December 9th and December 16th respectively. You may enroll for either or both series. Registration is limited to the capacity of the hall. A special discount on course fees is available to Cinema 16 members (see below).

Illustration 6. Brochures for the N.Y.U. and New School film courses offered in conjunction with Cinema 16.

The Impact of Cinema 16

By 1963 a variety of factors conspired to bring an end to Cinema 16's exhibition program. The central factor was financial; the modest cost of a Cinema 16 membership was no longer enough to keep the organization's activities afloat, and yet it was high enough that Vogel felt he could raise it no further. Vogel seems not to have been interested in soliciting wealthy benefactors for assistance, apparently because he did not trust that money raised this way would allow him to continue to operate with the degree of independence that had become the keystone of Cinema 16. And, of course, in 1963 there was no National Endowment for the Arts or New York State Council on the Arts to which he could apply for grants. Cinema 16 was faced with increasing costs, and with competition—from new art theaters devoted to recently released foreign features; from TV, which was beginning to show some of the kinds of scientific film that had been a Cinema 16 staple; from college classrooms (by the 1960s many universities were developing film courses); from independent screening spaces inter-

Illustration 7. Carmen D'Avino accepts a Creative Film Foundation award presented by Salvador Dali.

ested in presenting avant-garde film; and even from the commercial cinema, for as censorship restrictions disappeared, Hollywood was increasingly able to siphon off the interest in the risqué that had been important for some Cinema 16 members. In the end, Vogel and his colleagues could see no way to proceed.

As the final Cinema 16 season drew to a close, Vogel did some rough calculations and concluded that some 188,000 individuals had come to Cinema 16 screenings during the film society's sixteen-year history (obviously most people came over and over, so Vogel's number does not approximate the number of people who attended screenings, only the total attendance). And he concluded, again very roughly, that some two million people had seen films distributed by Cinema 16 (he estimated that two hundred people per screening saw ten thousand individual rentals). Without a more thorough investigation of who these people were, one cannot make sensible deductions from these numbers, even if they are accurate; but, given the unusual nature of the films screened at and distributed by Cinema 16, I find it difficult to imagine that substantial numbers of those who attended were not strongly affected by Vogel's work.[32]

We do know that many important figures in the arts and entertainment—Marlon Brando, Steve Allen, Henry Morgan, Burl Ives, Jerome Robbins, Susan Sontag, Gian-Carlo Menotti, Ad Reinhardt, Joshua Logan, Meyer Shapiro, Joseph Campbell, Norman Mailer, Lotte Lenya, Agnes de Mille—attended screenings. And we know that many of those who were, or were to become, the movers and shakers in the New York

Illustration 8. Ben Moore accepts a Creative Film Foundation award from Willard Maas *(center)*, Tennessee Williams *(left)*, and Joseph Campbell *(behind Maas)*.

film scene were regular members. Jonas Mekas and P. Adams Sitney, who became leading spokespeople for North American avant-garde cinema in the 1960s and early 1970s, were two of Cinema 16's most devoted members. In fact, Mekas claims to have attended "absolutely every screening, I would say, of the so-called experimental films in Cinema 16's whole existence. It became my Sunday church, my university."[33]

Again, there is no easy way to determine the extent of Cinema 16's influence on particular members, but as early as 1950, in response to Vogel's request for a letter of introduction to film people in Europe, Siegfried Kracauer could comment:

> I welcome this opportunity to tell you that in my opinion your CINEMA 16 is one of the living forces in a field which had been badly neglected before you took over. You have created this unique organization out of nothing and you have shown us, within its framework, a great number of educational, scientific, experimental and socially interesting documentaries which we would have never seen were it not for your untiring initiative. Through your activities many young people who confused films with Hollywood films and perhaps were fed up with them, have for the first time realized the inherent potentialities of the medium. Whenever I attended the screenings of CINEMA 16, I felt elated about the intensity with which a huge audience watched the spectacles you offered them—films in a daring mood, films with a serious purpose. You yourself are an educator, and your own passion for the cinema is contagious.[34]

The fact that Cinema 16 was providing a regular audience for avant-garde film gave a number of filmmakers the impetus to pursue unconventional kinds of work. Ed Emshwiller remembers that he "would go to Cinema 16 and see some animation or some surrealist movies, and I would go home and try the same thing. Later on, I decided I was going to make a real movie. I took it to Amos and said I'd like to be considered for one of the annual experimental film awards he and Maya Deren did. The film [*Dance Chromatic*, 1959] was considered by the group and got the top award. I was so delighted: it just started me" (see pp. 369–71). Emshwiller went on to make an extensive body of film and became for a time a roving goodwill ambassador for avant-garde film, and subsequently one of the nation's pioneer video artists, as well as an influential educator (and dean at the California Institute of the Arts) and one of the original board members of ITVS (the Independent Television Service).

Probably the best evidence of Cinema 16's importance in film production, especially of avant-garde films, is clear in the voluminous correspondence between Vogel and such filmmakers as Kenneth Anger, Gregory Markopoulos, and Jordan Belson. In many cases, young filmmakers were already looking forward to a screening at Cinema 16 before they had begun the film they hoped Vogel would show. The fact that some filmmakers were shown more often than others, and that a few became regulars (Anger, Stan Brakhage, James Broughton, Carmen D'Avino, Curtis Harrington, Julian Huxley, Norman McLaren, Sidney Peterson, Hans Richter, Joseph L. Stone, Willard Van Dyke, and Herbert Vesely, most obviously), implicitly established a canon of independent cinema that subsequent generations of programmers have debated and revised.

Another area where Cinema 16's influence seems clear is in the development of a network of film societies in the United States. Cecile Starr's *Film Society Primer* includes essays contributed by film society directors from across the country, and as one reads these essays, the influence of Cinema 16's programming becomes a motif. Most of the film societies discussed were formed in the late 1940s and early 1950s, after Cinema 16 was already a success, and the relationships between the new organizations and Cinema 16 were often quite direct.[35] Cinema 16's influence was both general (the fledgling film societies imitated Cinema 16's basic mission and approach) and specific (cinema societies rented the films Cinema 16 distributed).

By the 1960s, the film exhibition and distribution terrain was changing rapidly, but there are instances even now where active programmers reveal a debt to Vogel and Cinema 16. Karen Cooper, director of New York's Film Forum, presents diverse programs that bear some resemblance to Vogel's. For Cooper, the Vogels were the pioneers whose work "certainly preceded Film Forum's."[36] During Richard Herskowitz's recent tenure as president of International Film Seminars (the organization that sponsors the annual Robert Flaherty Seminar), the Flaherty seminars combined documentary and avant-garde filmmaking in a mix that is quite reminiscent of Cinema 16.[37] Herskowitz was Vogel's teaching assistant for a time at the University of Pennsylvania, and as his master's thesis project, he assembled the Cinema 16 programs and developed listings of the films and filmmakers screened. Throughout Herskowitz's years as a member of the board of International Film Seminars and as its president, his central programming mission was to expand the seminars' inclusion of avant-garde film and to achieve a dialectic diversity akin to what he discovered in the Cinema 16 programs. Subsequent Flaherty presidents have confirmed the Flaherty's interest in the kind of programming Vogel was known for. Indeed, Vogel himself presented a program of Cinema 16 films at the second Flaherty seminar in 1956.[38]

After Cinema 16 ceased programming, Vogel continued to press for a broader cinematic awareness. He became one of the cofounders (with Richard Roud) of the New York Film Festival and was the festival director from 1963 to 1968. He also directed the film department at Lincoln Center from 1964 to 1968, where he curated several film series and festivals. For a time, Vogel was given to hope that Lincoln Center would provide a space where Cinema 16's activities could continue on an expanded basis (Vogel worked on plans for a full-fledged film center at Lincoln Center for several years), but this didn't pan out. Vogel has also served as a jury member and has been an invited guest at many international film festivals. And he taught film history and film aesthetics at the Pratt Institute, the School of Visual Arts, New York University, and Harvard, and until 1990, at the Annenberg School of Communications at the University of Pennsylvania.

He also continued to write about film for various journals (the *Village Voice* and, later, *Film Comment*), in some cases exploring and expanding the thinking about programming and exhibition that underlay Cinema 16's success. He wrote *Film As a Subversive Art* (New York: Random House, 1974), a fascinating encyclopedia of the more "subversive" films he had shown at Cinema 16 (the book is dedicated "To Marcia, Steven, Loring—and Cinema 16"), as well as of more recent instances of politically, morally, and formally subversive work. *Film As a Subversive Art* is a culmination of the thinking that fueled Cinema 16—on at least two levels.

Most obviously and generally, *Film As a Subversive Art* sees a wide range of films as fundamentally united in their commitment to subverting "existing values, institutions, *mores*, and taboos—East and West, Left and Right—by the potentially most powerful art of the century." Indeed, Vogel argues that cinema going is essentially subversive: "Subversion in cinema starts when the theatre darkens and the screen lights up. For the cinema is a place of magic where psychological and environmental factors combine to create an openness of wonder and suggestion, an unlocking of the unconscious."[39] The subversion offered by the films discussed and illustrated in Vogel's subsequent chapters works in a wide range of ways, too many to detail here. But *Film as a Subversive Art* suggests that the educational focus of Cinema 16 probably always implied that the more fully we are aware of events, both external "political" events and internal "psychological/aesthetic/spiritual" events, the more we will realize where and when we need to commit ourselves to the improvement of our social and psychological structures in the interest of a more thoroughly humane and progressive world.

The other level of *Film As a Subversive Art* that reflects Vogel's thinking at Cinema 16 is the very nature of that volume, which—quite unlike more standard scholarly books on cinema—depends both on expository texts and on illustration. Indeed, whatever challenges to the intellect are offered by Vogel's discussions of cinematic subversion seem far outweighed by the impact and implications of the variety and extent of the imagery, and by its frequent shock value (which has not appreciably diminished in the intervening decades). As one turns the pages of *Film As a Subversive Art*, there is no telling what will be revealed next and how it will relate to what we think we know about film history. Ultimately, Vogel saw himself in the service of both his audience and of the films he chose to show; in *Film As a Subversive Art* the texts provide contextualization for the reader, but the imagery from the films is allowed to speak for itself.

The Design and Purpose of *Cinema 16:*
Documents Toward a History of the Film Society

This introduction is followed by an interview with Vogel in two parts—the first recorded and edited when I was first researching Cinema 16, the second recorded and edited later and informed by the weakening of government financial support for alternative cinema exhibition across the country—and by interviews with Vogel's principal collaborators, Marcia Vogel and Jack Goelman. The body of *Cinema 16: Documents Toward a History of the Film Society* is composed of letters to and from Vogel; excerpts from the Cinema 16 program notes; instances of the reception of Cinema 16's activities in the press; edited transcripts of conversations I have had with people who had firsthand experience with Cinema 16; essays written by Vogel explaining the theory behind his programming and reporting on what his experiences as a programmer had taught him; essays published by or about Cinema 16; and a complete listing of Cinema 16's programs, exactly as they were announced to the membership in the film society's brochures. After lengthy consideration, I decided to present these materials chronologically, in the hope that chronological organization provides the most accessible sense of the evolution of Cinema 16 as an institution and of the day-to-day life of the film society.

Vogel's files include thousands of letters; indeed, throughout the history of Cinema 16, and ever since, Vogel has been remarkably careful in collecting and organizing the documentation of Cinema 16. This volume has space for only a sampling of Cinema 16 correspondence, and I have chosen particular letters for two primary reasons. First, I have included letters that seem especially revealing about the development of Cinema 16 and about the kinds of interchange Vogel had with filmmakers (it was virtually always Vogel who corresponded with filmmakers). Second, I have chosen letters that seem important in a film-historical sense, for example, letters to and from important filmmakers that reveal dimensions of those makers' attitudes and of their work as it was being produced. Whenever it has seemed useful, I have honored an ongoing interchange between a particular filmmaker and Vogel, so as to create a sense of the give and take between an increasingly prestigious exhibitor/distributor and an emerging filmmaker.

In all cases, the letters are presented without correction; whatever idiosyncrasies of spelling, usage, or grammar are evident in the original documents have been maintained (at least to the extent that replication is possible in print). My assumption is that the manner in which the various correspondents communicated reveals dimensions of the writers and their era not completely evident in the stated content of their letters. However, in the interest of avoiding distraction and confusion in the text, we have developed an overall format for the letters—that is, we use consistent block paragraphing with a double space between paragraphs, signatures are always presented on the bottom left, and so on—regardless of the particulars of the original letters, and we have used conventional spacing after punctuation. The notation "[hw]" means "handwritten"; it is used to indicate which letters and portions of original letters (or the copies I had access to) are handwritten.

Program notes were available at every Cinema 16 event. In most cases, they were assembled from previously published material, but sometimes they were written specifically for Cinema 16 presentations by Vogel himself or by noted scholars and critics. I have included a sampling of program notes written by Vogel and others on the occasion of particular Cinema 16 events. Press response to Cinema 16 was never as consistent or as extensive as Vogel might have liked. My selections include reviews of early Cinema 16 series, the well-known attack on Cinema 16 by Dwight MacDonald and Vogel's response, and press reaction to Cinema 16's demise.

Over the years, I've had occasion to talk with many people who have memories of Cinema 16 and the Vogels, and in some instances I've recorded conversations with these people. *Cinema 16: Documents* includes a number of these conversations, each presented at a point in the overall chronology of Cinema 16 where it seems of particular relevance, regardless of when I recorded the conversation. My choices of conversations to include are not simply a function of my desire to honor the good work Cinema 16 did. There were certainly people—members and nonmembers—who were not entirely happy with Cinema 16; and of course individual members had a wide variety of relationships with the film society and with Vogel. The several conversations reproduced here are meant to expand the reader's sense of the many ways individual film-interested people could relate to the activities of Cinema 16.

Several essays by Vogel are included in *Cinema 16: Documents*. In some instances during the years that Cinema 16 was operating, Vogel took the opportunity to explain the workings of the film society, the thinking behind it, and—in the case of "The Angry Young Filmmakers"—international research he had pursued as Cinema 16's director. I have included a sampling of such essays. But even after Cinema 16 was no longer presenting programs, Vogel continued to draw conclusions on the basis of his Cinema 16 experiences and to deploy these conclusions in the ongoing discourse about cinema in general and about avant-garde film in particular. I have included a few instances of Vogel's writing after 1963, essays that reveal or expand on the thinking that fueled Cinema 16.

Finally, we have reproduced the semiannual announcements of Cinema 16 events, beginning with the broadsides announcing the first three presentations, and concluding with Cinema 16's final season. The form of the program announcements evolved over the years. Each of the first three programs was announced by an individual broadside. The spring 1948, the fall 1948, and the spring 1949 series were announced with 8½-by-14-inch colored flyers. Beginning with the fall 1949 series and continuing through the spring 1952 series, events were announced with increasingly professional-looking seasonal brochures. From fall 1952 through spring 1961, the fall brochures listed an entire year's events (that is, all the events planned for the fall and the following spring) and were supplemented by brochures reannouncing the spring events (including, at times, revisions in the original programming). The 1961–1962 and the 1962–1963 seasons were announced by individual brochures with no spring supplements. There was often overlap between the program announcement for fall/spring and the announcement for spring; we have tried to minimize the repetition of information while maintaining a sense of Cinema 16's calendrical rhythm.

The program announcements provide the best sense of Vogel's programming theory in action. The films announced and the blurbs describing them present the final results of the research and debate that went on year round at the Cinema 16 offices. However, these announcements do not always predict exactly what films were shown on a particular date, since a variety of factors could result in last-minute changes in scheduling. Probably the best way to determine exactly which films were shown and when would be to examine the Cinema 16 program notes, which were done closer to the specific screenings, and the Cinema 16 rental receipts (all these materials are available in Vogel's files). For purposes of this volume, I have been satisfied to detail what Vogel *planned* to show.

In presenting the texts of the program announcements, we have included only the films and the blurbs about them. In the interest of avoiding clutter in an already complex manuscript, we have not included the various categorizations that Vogel sometimes used in the brochures to identify the types of films listed: for example, "The Scientific Film: U.S.," "The Poetic Film: France," "The Art Film: Belgium," "Recent Danish Experimental Films," "A Special Cinema 16 Presentation," and so on. In some instances slight rearrangements of the texts on the program announcements have seemed useful for clarity.

In general, the documents included in *Cinema 16: Documents* speak for themselves, sometimes with considerable eloquence; but I have also provided context for the documents—in the form of notes and parentheses—that may be useful, especially for those unfamiliar with the pivotal role of Cinema 16 in American independent film history or with avant-garde filmmaking in the 1940s and 1950s.

Of course, while this project attempts to reveal something of the remarkable scope of Cinema 16's activities and contributions, it can make no pretense of being a complete, or even a thorough, exploration of the film society. At most, I provide a lure toward a remarkable moment in the institutional history of independent film—a lure that, I hope, will attract other scholars.[40]

In recent years, there has been continual talk in avant-garde film circles about what is widely seen as a petering out of a movement that peaked in the mid- to late 1960s: supposedly, many moving-image makers have moved on to video and digital work, fewer interesting films are being made, and as a result, there is less audience support for alternative cinema. My sense of the situation runs counter to this interpretation: I believe the production of interesting avant-garde films has remained at a consistently high level (with, of course, relative peaks and valleys) at least since the late 1940s, and, as Jan-Christopher Horak's *Lovers of Cinema* (see note 11) has demonstrated, even the 1920s, 1930s, and 1940s deserve far more attention than they have received so far. What *has* changed in recent years is the willingness of programmers to develop screening opportunities that maximize the audience potential of a truly wide range of film practice, and to integrate independent film practice with moving-image practice in general. Few programmers are willing to take the chances or to expend the energy necessary to build a substantial public audience interested in seeing a wide range of cinema. The result is that even "successful" screening venues devoted to the forms of film Cinema 16 exhibited have limited audience support.

While we may never return to the situation Vogel found himself in during the late 1940s, where large numbers of people had almost no access to a wide range of film forms and were hungry for exposure, there is no reason that the current situation cannot improve substantially. Amos Vogel remains a most useful role model for such improvement; his energy and ingenuity as a programmer remain exemplary. My hope is that this volume will help stimulate in some of those who read it, not merely an admiration of Cinema 16, but a desire to emulate it.

As this introduction is completed in the winter of 2001, the mainstays of alternative film exhibition—the NEA and NEH, and the various regional and state arts organizations—are increasingly under attack by those attempting to tighten federal and state budgets and by doing so to restrict and police cinematic discourse. Indeed, there seems little reason to assume that alternative exhibition will receive substantial government funding in the years to come. And should such funding cease to be available, those of us committed to alternative moving-image exhibition will find ourselves financially in much the same position Vogel found himself in 1947. The general principles of Vogel's programming may again have wide utility.

Notes

Some of the Cinema 16 papers are currently at the Wisconsin Center for Film and Theater Research, 6040 Vilas Communications Hall, 821 University Avenue, University of Wisconsin–Madison, Madison, WI 53706; the remaining materials will remain with Vogel (15 Washington Place, New York, NY 10003) until his death.

1. I am indebted to chapter 3 of Richard Abel's *French Cinema: The First Wave, 1915–1929* (Princeton: Princeton University Press, 1984), pp. 250–275, for my information about the development of the French ciné-club movement in the 1920s.

2. Abel, 253.

3. Abel, 164. Abel describes one important exception to the "elitist" tendency of the ciné-club movement, Les Amis de Spartacus, a ciné-club organized in July 1927 for the purpose of creating a mass cinema movement that might have serious political impact by battling the "dictatorship of money" and working against French protectionism and American cultural colonialization. Club des Amis de Spartacus was an immense though short-lived success. On March 15, 1928, it presented the first of six months of weekly programs at the Casino de Grenelle, the largest cinema in the Fifteenth Arrondissement: "Four thousand people reportedly showed up to vie for the 2,000 available seats. . . . Within three months, membership had swelled to ten thousand" and the club was organizing in the suburbs and provinces. Club des Amis de Spartacus presented film classics, recent popular films (Robert Flaherty's *Moana* [1925], for example), and, most importantly, three banned Soviet films: *Potemkin* [1925], Pudovkin's *Mother* [1926], and *The End of St. Petersburg* [1927]. The success of Club des Amis de Spartacus in assembling a politicized audience soon resulted in such powerful attacks by anti-Communists that in October 1928, police pressure forced the organization to disband.

4. Jean Beauvais and Guy L. Coté, eds., *Handbook for Canadian Film Societies* (Ottawa: Canadian Federation of Film Societies, 1959), 10.

5. Margaret Hancock, "The Federation of Film Societies," in Cecile Starr, ed., *Film Society Primer* (Forest Hills, N.Y.: American Federation of Film Societies, 1956), 78. In his autobiography, Joris Ivens describes the formation of the Filmliga Amsterdam in 1927 for the purpose of showing political films, experimental films, and documentaries not available in commercial theaters, and that organization's surprising success: "We expected a maximum of four hundred subscribers in Amsterdam. Twenty-five hundred responded and there were demands for branches in The Hague, Rotterdam, Utrecht, Leyden, Groningen and later Harlem." See Ivens, *The Camera and I* (New York: International Publishers, 1974), 23.

6. For a complete set of the London Film Society's programs (listings of films, programs notes, organizational information), see *The Film Society Programs, 1925–1939* (New York: Arno, 1972).

7. Hancock, 78.

8. I am quoting from an unpublished manuscript by Tom Gunning titled "Filmliga: Programming an Alternative Cinema, 1927–31."

9. Germaine Clinton, "Film Societies in Canada," *Film Culture* 1, no. 2 (March–April 1955): 49.

10. Germaine Clinton, "The Canadian Federation of Film Societies," in Starr, 71–72.

11. Jan-Christopher Horak quotes Kiesler in his essay "The First American Film Avant-Garde, 1919–1945," the introduction to Horak, ed., *Lovers of Cinema: The First American Film Avant-Garde, 1919–1945* (Madison: University of Wisconsin Press, 1995), 23.

According to a letter written in March 1956, Symon Gould founded the Film Guild in New York City in 1923 and was "perhaps the first to show non-box office film in this country . . . in Broadway theaters, at the Cameo Theater, and subsequently at the theater which I built and helped design, known as the Film Guild Playhouse, which is now called the 8th Street Playhouse." A fact sheet compiled by Andrew C. McKay in 1972 claims that the opening date was October 1925. (Both the letter and the fact sheet are at the Film Study Center at the Museum of Modern Art.) McKay's fact sheet indicates that the Film Guild sponsored Sunday screenings, beginning November 22, 1925, at the George M. Cohan and Central Theaters. Regular screenings of revivals and foreign films were subsequently presented at the 549-seat Cameo Theater until the end of 1928. Films shown included Alberto Cavalcanti's *Rien que les heures* (1926), *Potemkin, Ballet mécanique, Nanook of the North* (1921), and *Moana* (1926). On either December 28, 1928, or February 1, 1929, screenings began at the five-hundred-seat Film Guild Playhouse, which was designed by visionary architect Frederick Kiesler to resemble the bellows-like interior of a still camera (the theater was called "The House of Shadow Silence"), with Grigori Stabovoy's *Two Days* (1927). The fact sheet indicates that the same film "served to open the Philadelphia branch on March 24, 1929 at the Film Art cinema (formerly the Regent Theatre)." Obviously, Gould's work is fertile ground for research. As Vogel said to me, Gould's success must have been considerable: "none of *us* actually built a theater!"

12. In *Film on the Left* (Princeton: Princeton University Press, 1981), William Alexander describes a workers' film circuit that presented programs that mixed commercial films and films produced by the Workers Film and Photo League. Garrison Films, which was the distributor for many of the Soviet revolutionary films as well as for films produced by the Workers Film and Photo League, "generously estimated its audiences among American workers and farmers in 1933 at 400,000, and in 1934 Brandon [Tom Brandon of Garrison Films] went to work on establishing film guilds and circuits in the Midwest. During the week beginning 27 October, the talkie version of Pudovkin's *Mother,* written by Mike Gold, went the rounds of workers' clubs in Detroit, along with a commercial comedy and *America Today* [1933]. The program then departed for Flint, Grand Rapids, Ann Arbor, Kalamazoo, and Berkeley—cities on Garrison Films' Michigan film circuit" (37).

In "Revolutionary Movie Production," an article in *New Theatre* (September 1934), filmmaker Ralph Steiner announces (though it is unclear where he got his figures): "The present size of the organized audience which now sees Soviet and other working class films turns that potential importance [of film] into a very real and exciting fact. Last year in 1,580 theaters, workers' groups and organizations in the United States, Canada, Mexico, Cuba, and South America, 400,000 people were entertained by, excited by, educated by, and strengthened by seeing revolutionary films. This great audience should not only be a great inspiration for filmmakers but also a definite responsibility" (22).

These workers groups were not film societies in the usual sense of the word, since the central issue for the groups was not cinema but political action, for which cinema was a useful tool. Nevertheless, when a complete history of American alternative exhibition is written, these workers' groups will require at least a substantial chapter.

13. For information about the founding of the Museum of Modern Art Film Library, see Haidee Wasson, "'Some Kind of Racket': The Museum of Modern Art's Film Library, Hollywood and the Problem of Film Art, 1935," *Canadian Journal of Film Studies* 9, no. 2 (Spring 2000): 5–29.

14. Christopher Bishop, "The Museum of Modern Art Film Library," in Starr, 59–61.

15. The complete programs of films shown during Art in Cinema's first series, along with the program notes, and essays on the history of avant-garde film by filmmakers and critics are

included in Frank Stauffacher, ed., *Art in Cinema* (New York: Arno, 1968). This volume is a reprint of the catalogue assembled by the San Francisco Museum of Art for the Art in Cinema programs.

Belson's comments are from an unpublished interview with the author, conducted July 22, 2000.

16. See VèVè A. Clark, Millicent Hodson, and Catrina Neiman, *The Legend of Maya Deren*, vol. 1, pt. 2, "Chambers" (New York: Anthology Film Archives, 1988), 328–29.

17. Vogel, in Clark, Hodson, and Neiman, 369.

18. Vogel, in "Cinema 16 and the Question of Programming," in Starr, 54–55.

19. Vogel's commitment to variety within specific presentations, a commitment he maintained throughout Cinema 16's history, is particularly reminiscent of the London Film Society's eclectic programs, though, apparently, these were not a direct influence; Vogel remembers first seeing the London Film Society programs "years after Cinema 16 started."

The London Film Society's Program 17, for example, included Viking Eggeling's *Symphonie Diagonale* (1924); Hans Richter's *Rhythmus 21* (1921); *Billy's Bible* (produced by Cricks and Martin in England, 1912); Mack Sennett's *The Face on the Bar Room Floor* (with Chaplin, 1916); *Selections Illustrating the British Polychromide Colour Process* (produced by British Polychromide, 1926–1927); footage of Tolstoy at eighty, recorded in 1908; and a feature, M. V. Strizhevski's *Taras Bulba* (1923). Program 9 was *The Battle of Plants* (produced by British Instructional Films, 1926); *Sashascopes* (examples of Alex Stewart's kaleidoscopic cinematography, 1926); *The Mating of Birds* (part of a series of films about animal life, obtained from zoological societies and the collections of scientists, 1925–1926); Chaplin's *One A.M.* (1917); D. W. Griffith's *Beyond All Law* (1912); and Robert Weine's *The Hands of Orlac* (1942). See *The Film Society Programs, 1925–1939*, 66–67, 34–35.

Vogel's earliest experiences with the film society movement occurred long before he began Cinema 16. He remembers attending the screenings of a large Viennese film society at the Urania cultural center during the early 1930s: "I saw that there were all kinds and types of film being made all over the world, not just Hollywood-type films.... I wasn't a member very long and I was a kid, you know, so it wasn't conscious or very serious. But when I think back, it obviously led to the formation of who I became." From a useful interview with Vogel in Stephen J. Dobi's *Cinema 16: America's Largest Film Society* (Ph.D. diss., New York University, 1984), 271.

Of course, the idea of creatively mixing various forms of film in individual film presentations predates the entire film society movement. Charles Musser explains that during the late 1890s, "There was a dialectical tension between unified programs built around a single event, theme or narrative and a variety format with its emphasis on novelty and diversity." Proctor's Pleasure Palace sometimes emphasized variety to the point of separating films that had a thematic relationship: "In his program at Proctor's Pleasure Palace for the week of July 11, 1898, for instance, [Eberhard] Schneider placed *Snowballing* between *Spanish Attack on an American Camp* and *Charge of American Cavalry;* then *Storm at Sea* between *Execution of a Spy, Turco-Grecian War*, and *Defense of a House, Turco-Grecian War*." See Musser, "The Eden Musee in 1898: The Exhibitor as Creator," *Film and History,* December 1981, 73–83.

20. When Robert Breer tried to get his innovative animations screened in New York in the 1950s, he was rejected by several exhibitors and distributors and finally found his way to Vogel: "He was the only one who could deal with this kind of film. Amos played the Hollywood mogul, with the cigar and his feet on the desk, but all on a modest scale.... He was supportive, but wanted to drive a hard bargain, sign a contract, exclusive this, can't do that—and didn't promise me much return. But he would show the films, and it's all I had and so it was fine: I went with Amos." Of course, other filmmakers had different impressions of Vogel—even about his cigars. Stan Brakhage remembers that "some people teased Amos about his cigars in those days; but I always especially enjoyed sitting and talking with him, accepting his cigar so that we both filled the old Cinema 16 office with a cloud of thick Vienna atmosphere together." Breer's comments are from an unpublished interview with the author conducted in 1985, Brakhage's from a letter to the author in April 1989.

21. Ken Jacobs, in Scott MacDonald, *A Critical Cinema 3* (Berkeley: University of California Press, 1998), 367. The program Jacobs refers to was presented in January 1959. "The Third Avenue El (as Seen by 3 Film Artists)" included *The Wonder Ring*, Henry Freeman's *Echo of an Era* (1958), and Kit Davidson's *Third Avenue El* (1958)—followed by Buster Keaton's *The General* (1926).

22. From the vantage point of 1990, the chance-takers seem to have come out ahead, while those who went with Grove may have been hurt in the long run by their exclusive contracts and their resulting lack of control over their films. Carmen D'Avino, for example, was one of the most admired independent animators of the 1950s, largely as a result of Cinema 16's frequent presentation of his films, but once he signed with Grove, and the rental rates for his animations were subsequently raised, his work was, for all practical purposes, out of reach for many smaller exhibitors, and his reputation suffered as a result.

23. The "First Statement of the New American Cinema Group" (*Film Culture*, no. 22–23 [Summer 1961]: 131–33) reflects the group's unhappiness with conventional distribution: "We'll take a stand against the present distribution-exhibition policies. There is something wrong with the whole system of film exhibition; it is time to blow the whole thing up.... We plan to establish our own cooperative distribution center.... The New York Theatre [I assume the New Yorker Theater is meant (Dan Talbot, who ran the New Yorker, was a member of the group)], The Bleecker St. Cinema, Art Overbrook Theater (Philadelphia) are the first movie houses to join us by pledging to exhibit our films. Together with the cooperative distribution center, we will start a publicity campaign preparing the climate for the New Cinema in other cities. The American Federation of Film Societies will be of great assistance in this work."

The listing of the members of the group who attended the first meeting includes Lewis Allen, Edward Bland, Peter Bogdanovich, Ben Carruthers, Shirley Clarke, Emile de Antonio, Edouard de Laurot, Robert Frank, Don Gillin, Walter Gutman, Harold Humes, Argus Speare Juilliard, Alfred Leslie, Gregory Markopoulos, Adolfas Mekas, Jonas Mekas, Jack Perlman, Sheldon Rochlin, Lionel Rogosin, the Sanders brothers, Bert Stern, David C. Stone, Daniel Talbot, and Guy Thomajan. While most of the members are designated as filmmakers or producers, the group also included actors, a theatrical and film lawyer (Perlman), and a theater manager (Talbot). See "The New American Cinema Group," *Film Culture*, no. 22–23 (Summer 1961): 130.

24. See Vogel, "Thirteen Confusions." "Thirteen Confusions" was originally published in *Evergreen Review*, then in Gregory Battcock, ed., *The New American Cinema* (New York: Dutton, 1967), 124–38. "Thirteen Confusions" is Vogel's most extensive comment on Jonas Mekas and the New American Cinema.

25. I spoke with Vogel about *Weegee's New York* in April 1996. Vogel had not discussed his role in the film before, because "Weegee didn't want it talked about." It is unclear exactly how the current soundtrack got to be part of the film. Vogel doesn't remember composing it himself—only that it was not Weegee's doing.

26. I spoke with Vogel about Vishniak in September 1996.

27. For a complete listing of the films screened at the three Eastman House weekends, see Appendix 5 (298–301) of Dobi's *Cinema 16*.

28. The first program (March 2), for example, was Lotte Reiniger's *The Grasshopper and the Ant* (1954), Charles and Ray Eames's *Parade* (1952), Shirley Clarke's *In Paris Parks* (1954), Len Lye's *Rainbow Dance* (1936), and Buster Keaton's *The Balloonatic* (1923). Other presentations included scientific documentaries about animal life, and in some cases feature documentaries about other cultures (*Nanook of the North*, for example).

29. See Dobi's interview with Vogel in *Cinema 16*, 276.

30. In *Points of Resistance: Women Power and Politics in the New York Avant-garde Cinema, 1943–1971* (Urbana: University of Illinois Press, 1991), Lauren Rabinovitz discusses Deren's work in organizing what was first called the Film Artists Society, in 1953–1954, as a means of consolidating "informational services on grants, film festivals, technical data, film labs, distribution, and organizations bidding for independent films" (81). In 1955 the group changed its

name to the Independent Film Makers Association, Inc. By then it had become "a monthly forum for a full-fledged social, intellectual, and professional community" (81). Vogel was a guest of the association in the fall of 1955.

In addition to her work with the Independent Film Makers Association, Deren ran the Creative Film Foundation with nominal assistance from her board, which included Vogel and various others who were connected with Cinema 16: Arthur Knight, Parker Tyler, and Lewis Jacobs, for example. See Rabinovitz, 80–85.

The Creative Film Foundation made awards from 1956 until Maya Deren's death in 1961. The 1956 awards (presented January 30, 1957, at Cinema 16) went to Hilary Harris's *Generation* (Award of Exceptional Merit), Christopher Young's *Subject Lesson* (Award of Exceptional Merit), Willard Maas and Ben Moore's *Narcissus* (Award of Distinction), Carmen D'Avino's *Theme and Transition* (Award of Distinction), Stan Brakhage's *Reflections on Black* (Award of Distinction), and Robert Breer's *Recreation* (Special Citation). In a letter to Vogel dated February 2, 1957, Anger mentions receiving a "Special Citation" for *Inauguration of the Pleasure Dome*. This award is not included in the list of award winners compiled for Cinema 16. In 1957, Herbert Vesely's *No More Fleeing*, a feature, received the only award (Award of Distinction). In 1958, awards went to Francis Thompson's *N.Y., N.Y.* (Award of Exceptional Merit), Pontus Hulten and Hans Nordenstroem's *A Day in Town* (Award of Exceptional Merit), Carmen D'Avino's *The Big "O"* (Award of Distinction), Herbert Veseley's *On These Evenings* (Award of Distinction), and Stan Vanderbeek's *What, Who, How* (Award of Distinction). In 1959, an Award of Exceptional Merit went to Ed Emshwiller's *Dance Chromatic;* Awards of Distinction went to Charles Boltenhouse's *Handwritten,* Wolfgang Ramsbott's *The City,* Rubington's *The Rose Window,* E. van Moerkerken's *Cuckoo Waltz,* and D'Avino's *The Room;* Special Citations went to Stuart Hanisch's *Have I Told You Lately That I Love You,* Shirley Clarke's *Bridges-Go-Round,* and Marie Menken's *Dwightiana.* In 1960, Awards of Distinction went to Robert Breer's *Inner and Outer Space,* Jane Belson-Conger's *Odds and Ends,* Bruce Conner's *A Movie,* D'Avino's *A Trip,* Emshwiller's *Lifelines,* and Vanderbeek's *Science Friction;* and Special Citations went to Emshwiller's *Transformation,* Richard Preston's *May 2, 1960,* and Vittorio Speich's *Metrographic.* The final (1961) award went to the films of Maya Deren, in memoriam.

31. I have not been able to obtain a complete listing of films that won the Robert J. Flaherty Award. I do know that in 1953, George Stoney's *All My Babies* won a Special Award; in 1958 John Marshall's *The Hunters* won the Robert J. Flaherty Award, while a Special Award went to Zachary Schwartz's *The Earth Is Born,* and Honorable Mentions went to Jean Louis Polidoro's *Overture* and Colin Low and Wolf Koenig's *City of Gold;* in 1960, the Flaherty Award went to *Hoffa and the Unions* directed by Al Wasserman, while Satyajit Ray's *Aparajito* won a Special Award, and Ralph Keene's *Between the Tides* received an Honorable Mention.

32. The film society's membership lists are housed at the Wisconsin Center for Film and Theater Research.

33. Mekas, in Scott MacDonald, *A Critical Cinema 2* (Berkeley: University of California Press, 1992), 82.

34. Letter to Vogel from Kracauer, May 28, 1950.

35. For example, Armine T. Wilson, who organized "Film Perspectives" in Wilmington, Delaware, explained: "In programming the major problem has been to decide how far we can go in presenting experimental films. Some of our members like them very much, but more abhor them. Our feeling however is that we do not exist only to exhibit regular movie fare twenty to forty years late. We should also serve as an outlet for non-theatrical, experimental, art and creative films.... Last summer a small subgroup of our society gave for themselves a series of five programs from the Cinema 16 catalogue at a cost of somewhat more than a good seat at a Broadway musical.... Some of the films were good, some were poor. There was a division of opinion on many of the things shown, but one thing became clear; there can be no doubt but that these films constitute a new form of art, and that anyone who wishes to become familiar with one of the most important cultural activities of his own time must (if he lives outside New York) form a society to present it" (See Wilson, "Film Perspectives," in Starr, 20–21).

36. Scott MacDonald, "Program Notes: An Interview with Karen Cooper," *Afterimage* 11, no. 4 (November 1983): 5. Cooper's admiration for Cinema 16 was expressed in a Film Forum homage that ran from May 28 until June 10, 1986. I curated this homage, choosing a program that mixed a variety of film forms reminiscent of Cinema 16's regular monthly presentations *and* several of the special-events films that caused the most stir in Cinema 16. The films shown were *In the Street* by Helen Levitt, Janice Loeb, and James Agee; *The Wonder Ring* by Stan Brakhage; *Geography of the Body* by Willard Maas; *Fireworks* by Kenneth Anger; *The Room* by Carmen D'Avino; *Living in a Reversed World* by Dr. Pacher; *Recreation* by Robert Breer; *A Divided World* by Arne Sucksdorff; and *Blood of the Beasts* by Georges Franju.

37. See Erik Barnouw and Patricia Zimmermann, eds., *Wide Angle* 17, nos. 1–4, for a listing of films presented at the Flaherty seminars.

38. As is clear in various essays included in Jan-Christopher Horak's *Lovers of Cinema*, considerable research remains to be done on the American independent scene(s) of the 1920s and 1930s.

39. Vogel, *Film As a Subversive Art* (New York: Random House, 1974), 9.

40. A good many research projects could be undertaken to further our understanding of the history and impact of Cinema 16. For example, the Cinema 16 membership lists might be explored in detail, as could the listings of film venues served by Cinema 16's distribution.

An Interview with Amos Vogel

I INTERVIEWED VOGEL in February and March 1983. An addendum was recorded in September 1995.

❖ ❖ ❖ ❖ ❖ ❖

Scott MacDonald: Tell me about your background, especially as it relates to film. Were you involved with film before you got to New York?

Amos Vogel: I lived in Vienna from the beginning of my life (in 1921) until age seventeen. At age seven or so, I got a laterna magica, complete with color slides—just like Ingmar Bergman. I was entranced. Later (I must have been ten or eleven) my father bought me a home movie projector, 9.5 mm. It came from France. It was hand cranked, not motorized. With that projector came not only the ability to make and show home movies—my father filmed family trips and so on—but also the possibility of buying films available in 9.5 mm: Krazy Kat and Mickey Mouse, Charlie Chase, Chaplin. I enjoyed running the comedies backward as well—the magic of transforming, subverting reality.

It seems to me that at a very young age I was already an avid moviegoer. I must have been, because I remember many films that I must have seen in Vienna, judging from the way the dates work out. I went to see a lot of American films as a kid, the typical Hollywood exports. I was also able to see not only Austrian films, but German films. We're talking about the period prior to 1938, so that included films made during the Nazi period, not just the German films of the late twenties or early thirties.

Furthermore, there was a film society in Vienna. It's hard for me to believe, but I must have joined at around the age of twelve or thirteen. The programs were held in a beautiful theater at the Urania, a miniature Lincoln Center in Vienna. There must have been five hundred to a thousand members per performance. And I remember all the films I saw there, and I saw quite a few: early German cinema, Russian cinema—well, in 1934, it became illegal to show Russian films, but I did see Russian films prior to that, so that must have been even prior to age thirteen. One film I remember specifically and very strongly is *Night Mail* [1936], the collaboration of Harry Watt, Basil Wright and, on the sound, W. H. Auden, Cavalcanti, and Benjamin Britten. The whole notion of documentary became important to me because of that film. And simultaneously I realized that this was really a poetic film, and I was amazed that such a boring subject—the workings of the British mail system—could be made interesting. Wright's *Song of Ceylon* [1934] was also tremendously important to me.

MacDonald: Did the film society show a variety of kinds of film?

Vogel: They showed mostly feature-length films, but they would accompany the feature with one or two offbeat shorts not available in regular theaters. I don't remember any "social" aspects to that film society, and I have no recollection of who organized and ran it. I was a kid, and I went on my own. I guess I was only interested in the films. I enjoyed going to the movies almost as much as reading books. I read extensively: American, British, and French literature in translation—Dreiser, Dos Passos, Sinclair, Twain, Whitman, Wells, Walpole, Sinclair Lewis, Gide, Zola—and German literature, in the original.

MacDonald: When did you leave Vienna?

Vogel: In the fall of 1938, six months after Hitler took over Austria. I'll never forget what I experienced during those six months. I was very lucky to be able to leave. If I had waited, undoubtedly I would be dead by now. It was very traumatic and has stayed with me all my life.

MacDonald: Did you have any money when you got here?

Vogel: No. Whatever money we did have in Vienna (my father was a lawyer and my mother a teacher—they couldn't get those jobs here) was taken by the Nazis. We even had to leave Europe on a German ship so they would get the money for the tickets.

Anyway, an uncle of mine had settled in America during the First World War and had become quite rich. This uncle sent a statement—it was called an affidavit—to the effect that he would support us for a period of time. And with that it was possible to get a visa to the United States.

MacDonald: The whole family came?

Vogel: My father, my mother, and I came. My father's sisters and my mother's mother and brothers could not come. Most of them were subsequently killed.

It was also very educational, that experience. Because America did not say, "We will accept anybody who is in trouble." They did just the opposite. America probably let in less than 3 percent of the people who wanted to come. There were quotas based on country of origin. My father was born in Poland, so we were part of the Polish quota. I don't know what the actual figures were. With the affidavit from my uncle in America, my father went to the American Consulate in Vienna and got a number. And they gave him a visa and told him we'd have to wait six months. If he had come one day later, he would have been told that he would have to wait approximately ninety years. In that *one day*, the Polish quota for the next ninety years was exhausted. That's how small the Polish quota was.

MacDonald: Did you come directly to New York?

Vogel: I had to go to Cuba to wait the six months before we could get in here. Another strange experience. Beautiful country, beautiful people. I love Cubans. But under Batista, the Cuban government was totally corrupt. I spent my time there learning English. I saw many American films during that six-month period.

MacDonald: You finally got to this country in 1939. And you started Cinema 16 in 1947. What did you do in the intervening years?

Vogel: I was not working in film at all. During my last three years in Vienna, I had become involved with a Socialist-Zionist youth group, boys and girls who wanted to go to a kibbutz in Israel—though it wasn't Israel then. We wanted to build a communal settlement where nobody would own land or private property, and all the income would be shared, a real participatory democracy. Part of that group's ideology called for a binational state, an Arab-Jewish state. It was not to be a Jewish state. I was very happy about that.

At that time, the British decided who could go into Palestine and who could not. In Austria, there had been a program, limited to young people between the ages of fifteen and seventeen. At a certain point, my entire group, including my girlfriend, got permission to go. And many of them did go; those who didn't were subsequently killed. As it turned out, I couldn't go because I was three months too old—a severe blow. When I was in Cuba, and also when I got here, I still had the definite intention to go to Palestine and rejoin that group. I tried everything; I even tried to get myself adopted by someone there. Impossible. The British wouldn't allow it. During this period, in order to prepare myself for that life, I was able to get a scholarship at an agricultural school in Georgia, one of the National Youth Administration colleges that had been started under Roosevelt to bring college-level education to the sons and daughters of farmers, primarily in the southern states, though some of the people who came from Europe were also let in. So I found myself in Haversham College in Georgia, for two years. A very strange introduction to America. I had left a country in which the park benches said, "Jews and dogs should not sit here." Here I saw drinking fountains that said, "For whites only." Later, I moved to the University of Georgia and took agriculture plus general courses in civics, history, whatever. And after that, I worked for two years on farms in New Jersey.

During this period, I became more and more disturbed about the way in which the Arab question was being handled by the Zionists. I did a lot of reading and talking to people. Finally, I came to the conclusion that not only was I *not* a Zionist and didn't want to go to Israel, but I realized I was becoming an anti-Zionist because of the Arab question. I'd prepared myself for a life I now knew I wasn't going to pursue. And I was not interested in being an agricultural laborer in the United States. The point had been a communal kind of living, not simply working on a farm. So I got a degree in economics and political science at the New School for Social Research in New York.

MacDonald: This was 1943–44?

Vogel: Right. We didn't have any money, but I got a scholarship and took all kinds of odd jobs.

During the war I worked in defense factories as an assistant tool-and-die maker. The interest in politics I had developed in Vienna continued to be very strong. I wanted to find some left-wing movement with which I could work, but I couldn't really find one. I was drawn more towards Trotskyites than Stalinists. In Vienna, I had known about the huge concentration camps in the Soviet Union, about the purges, and the trials at which leaders of the revolution were falsely accused of being Nazi spies. It's amazing to me now that *I* knew of all these things by age fifteen, and at the very time these things were occurring, while many American "radicals" only discovered them from Khrushchev's speech in the sixties!

MacDonald: When did you meet Marcia?

Vogel: In 1942, through a cousin of hers who had come from Europe on the same boat I was on. Marcia and I didn't particularly like each other. A year later, however, I met her again, and we immediately got involved—one of the best things that has happened to me in my life. Three years later we got married. The morning after our wedding night, I walked down to the hotel newsstand and saw this great big headline: NEW TYPE OF BOMB DROPPED OVER HIROSHIMA—so it's easy to remember the date of our wedding! Bad jokes have been made about that, believe me.

At the time we got married, Marcia was doing market research. She'd graduated from Queens College with a degree in sociology.

MacDonald: At what point did you two get involved with film?

Vogel: After I got my degree. I was interested in learning through film. At a certain point after I came to New York, I had become aware that there were a lot of films around, in 16 mm, which were not being shown publicly, and which were not available anywhere for me to see. I'm *not* talking solely or primarily about avant-garde films. There were always two main components to Cinema 16, avant-garde films and what might be called nonfiction films (documentaries, scientific studies, psychological studies, informational and educational films). I'd read about these films in a local newspaper, or somebody (not a film person, but a member of a union or a teacher) would mention a film to me. Once in a while I'd go to see such films at local universities. I began to find out who the distribution companies of the films were; I'd go to them and ask, "How can I see your films?" I learned it would be very expensive to rent them and that I'd have to get my own projector. I didn't have the money to do this.

It occurred to me that if I was interested in such films and couldn't see them, there must be other people in a city the size of New York who would be equally interested. Maybe I should get some of these films together and attempt to show them publicly. Maybe enough people would come to see them to pay for the film rental, and the whole thing would take care of itself.

MacDonald: How did you first learn about avant-garde film?

Vogel: I was always very interested in modern art and the avant-garde—particularly in the visual arts. I had been tremendously affected by Meyer Shapiro's magical lectures on modern art. I began to hear things about such films and to look out for them. There was a film magazine—it lasted for only three issues—called *Cinema,* run by Eli Wilenski. (I think that's what his name was in those days; years later, under the name of Eli Wilentz, he became the owner of what was the best and by far the most important bookstore in New York City, the Eighth Street Bookstore.) That magazine mentioned Sidney Peterson and James Broughton as having made one or two films that sounded very interesting—surrealist films, poetic films. It may also have mentioned Kenneth Anger. And of course, there was Maya Deren. She had begun to show films in New York and to write. I saw her films and was very impressed.

As a spare-time activity Marcia and I, and a couple of our friends, decided to see if we could get a little money together and rent the same theater that Maya Deren had rented, the Provincetown Playhouse, and put on a program of films. Next step: I went back to film distributors and convinced them to let me look at films for free on their premises because I was going to try to show them publicly afterwards, which would help them. Many agreed.

Illustration 9. Maya Deren in *Meshes of the Afternoon* (1943) by Deren and Alexander Hammid. Courtesy Anthology Film Archives.

I chose a first program and put ads in the papers. The Provincetown Playhouse had two hundred seats. We announced showings for six o'clock and eight o'clock one evening. It was a huge, smashing, immediate success. We had to repeat this first program for *sixteen* evenings! With two showings per evening! My naive but logical supposition was immediately proven correct. I have no doubt that if I had chosen other films, I would have done just as well, so long as they made for a well-rounded program. This idea worked, not because of my excellence as a programmer or anything like that, but because historical circumstances allowed Cinema 16 to fulfill a real social need.

Very quickly, we realized that planning to show films on a one-shot basis, on one evening, was not a very good idea. For the second program, we decided to expand and add weekend shows and really build the audience, so Marcia and I spent the thousand dollars we had received as wedding presents a couple years earlier on expanded advertising, including an ad in the *New York Times*. Well, that second program took place on the evening of the worst blizzard in New York history. Four people showed up at the theater: the projectionist, myself, Marcia, and some crazy person who came through the snow. We were faced with an immediate catastrophe because we had absolutely no other funds. Then my father, who knew about business, told us we could try to keep going on credit, hoping that income from the next shows would pay for what we spent and leave us with a little surplus. We were so naive that we had never even heard of doing business this way!

A second problem we ran into was even more serious, and more interesting. It started on the first evening. A somber representative of the New York State Censorship Office came to the theater and said, "You can't show this program, because your films have not been submitted to the censors and have not been approved." I said, "I don't know anything about that. I know there's some kind of censorship for Hollywood films, but what's this got to do with me?" He said, "Every film that's shown publicly in New York has to be okayed by us. You have to have a censorship seal." He could see that I wasn't a conniving businessman, but some kind of naive young guy who really didn't know. And he said, "Okay, you can show this program, but after this, you have to submit all your films to us."

I was very unhappy about this. When I began to submit films to the Censorship Office (with our second program), we ran into impossible problems. Example: part of the censorship law was that you had to submit a copy of the script. I wanted to show a French animated film for children which had a nonsense language soundtrack; I *had* no script. We had to hire a stenotypist at some fantastic sum, who came and took down "baba, booboo." Can you believe this? We didn't have the money to do that kind of thing. Secondly, we had to rent the films from the distributors early to submit them to the censors, who sat on them for at least a week. And the censors were doing me a favor by looking at the films so fast! Thirdly, some films—Peterson's and Broughton's, for example—used nudity; sometimes there was some sexy business. Well, the censors applied the same standards to us that they applied to Hollywood films. There was a film by Maya Deren and Alexander Hammid—*The Private Life of a Cat* [1945]—a beautiful documentary of their cats at home, including birth sequences, which made the censors reject the entire film as "obscene." Unbelievable!

We decided that we couldn't possibly continue this way. I'm a total enemy of censorship in all of its forms. Period. Without any reservations. To me this process was absolutely obnoxious—"obnoxious" isn't strong enough. By submitting the films to the censors, I was betraying something. We had some discussions with a civil-liberties lawyer and decided that we were going to start a private membership club. When you do that, you're not subject to censorship.

MacDonald: Did your troubles with New York State censorship end once you'd become a club?

Vogel: There's pre-censorship and post-censorship. We eliminated pre-censorship completely by becoming a film society. However, with post-censorship, the police can go into a place and say, "You *have shown* something obscene." Had I desired to show hard-core porno films at Cinema 16, I certainly would have had access to them, but we would have been closed by the police, even if we were a club. In any case, I had no desire to do that, not because I'm against porno—it just wasn't what I was interested in showing.

However, if you're a club, you're not subject to blizzards, because you collect the membership fees in advance for an entire year. If the member doesn't come, for whatever reason, you've still been paid. Of course, it also meant that we could not sell individual tickets, and later we had programs where we had to turn hundreds of people away. But you could join the night of the performance, if you paid for the entire year. The fees were very low, ten dollars a year for sixteen performances plus two free guest tickets.

I started showing films in 1947, and six months later we were an official membership film society, nonprofit and tax exempt. The government checked us out to see that we were not putting a profit into our pockets. What we were allowed to do, of course, is pay salaries. The amount of money that came in simply paid the cost of the operation, plus very reasonable salaries. In the beginning we had nothing; Marcia and I worked for weeks or months for nothing or very little. But ultimately, when it got to be good, Marcia and I together made maybe $15,000 a year.

Projectionists were another interesting problem. The union came after us immediately. They said, "This should be unionized," and I was in favor, I've always been in favor of unions. I said okay, despite the fact that they insisted on *two* high-priced union projectionists per show. But it was a unionized operation from the very first performance to the very last. I'm proud of this.

Marcia was in charge of memberships. We hired ushers, who got paid two dollars an hour, or whatever it was in those days. Very little. It was a minimal operation, always determined by the yearly budget.

MacDonald: How long were you in the Provincetown Playhouse?

Vogel: Very briefly. We grew too fast. Why have sixteen nights for two or four hundred each? It wasn't economical. Actually, the very first showing of the Cinema 16 Film Society took place at the Fifth Avenue Playhouse, also an art theater; the film was the premiere of Hans Richter's *Dreams That Money Can Buy* [1947]. After that we went to a place called the Central Needle Trades Auditorium, a huge space. And later, when we had five to seven thousand members, we had additional showings at other art theaters. A member would simply sign up for the Wednesday evening series at the Central Needle Trades Auditorium or for the Sunday morning series at a regular theater.

MacDonald: Did you have a sense of the sorts of people who came to the screenings?

Illustration 10. The sixteen-hundred-seat Central Needle Trades Auditorium (later known as the Fashion Industries Auditorium), often filled to capacity for Cinema 16 events.

Vogel: We did questionnaires, things like that. There were a lot of artists and intellectuals, and would-be intellectuals and artists. The gamut ranged from the movers and shakers on the cultural scene to schoolteachers and secretaries, people who wanted to widen their horizons. I'm continuously surprised by the well-known people who say to me, "Ah, Cinema 16, how wonderful it was!" It would be an interesting research project to go through the lists name by name and try to find out who these people are now. All the Beats came—Ginsberg and the rest. All the film people came: people who were teaching film and making films. And there were many liberal bourgeois people. It was the only place to see such films.

MacDonald: Could you apply for state or federal grants?

Vogel: There was a totally different situation in those days in respect to funding—there was none. No private foundations were interested in this sort of activity. And what really amazes me, in retrospect, is that this project ran for sixteen years without *any* outside support, dependent 100 percent on membership fees.

MacDonald: What was the process of putting the programs together?

Vogel: I looked at thousands of films to select the programs. I began to go through the catalogues of whatever distribution firms existed, and there were many. It wasn't as though I had to go into barren territory. I had more films than I could handle. But the avant-garde field had to be developed. Sidney Peterson would tell me he knew so-and-so who had made a little film, and I'd get in touch with this person. Or, having heard of Cinema 16, people would write to tell me about their films. Tens, hundreds of films began to drift in. Any film submitted to us was looked at. I had very good help with this—Jack Goelman, who worked with me. We had a rapport in questions of aesthetics, originality.

I made a folder for every film I saw, regardless of its length. While I was watching a film, I took notes, and the notes went into the folder. As of now, at age sixty-two, I have between twenty and thirty thousand folders.

An entire year's programs—sixteen different events—would be put together in advance. It might consist of two hundred or fifty films, depending on length.

MacDonald: Did you have particular things in mind when you were deciding on programs, or did you just program the films that knocked you out?

Vogel: The latter would be an honest way of putting it. I wanted films that would disturb you in some way, would add to your knowledge and make you change. The whole notion of change was very basic to Cinema 16. I've always been very involved with the idea of creating a world different from the one in which we are living. I'm very dissatisfied with *this* world. I have always considered myself to be a radical socialist, and I have always had the curious notion that even a film on cosmology or a psychological study or an avant-garde work can serve a positive function in improving the world, because it takes us away from where we are now and opens us up to new possibilities.

There was inevitably a strong subjective factor in all these decisions. Essentially you choose in terms of who you are, and who you are is, in turn, the end product of a very long prior development, including your environment, all the influences that have worked on you—your parents, your children, your school, the books you've read, even your genetic constitution. My experience with Hitler was important to me. All these things entered into the picture, obviously.

There were definitely films I did not feel were good enough to be shown. At the same time—this is an important point—there was never any attention paid to what might be called "box office." I think box office is poison. Many times in my life I've had the possibility of starting a commercial theater, but I never wanted to do it because I *knew* that if I did, I would become the prisoner of what the box office requirements were. That was another wonderful thing about having a membership set-up. I was able to present programs which I knew in advance would antagonize most of the audience. But that was okay; there were other programs they would like. People soon learned that when they went to Cinema 16, they had to expect to be displeased sometimes.

MacDonald: If you showed a program that offended people one week, was attendance down the next week?

Vogel: No. When people were offended by a program, there was usually a very small percentage who would be extremely upset. They would write us letters or call us up and say, "How dare you show this piece of shit!" If they said, "Give us our money back," we were delighted to do so. We wanted to get rid of them. We weren't going to have them tell us what to show. I showed one of the worst (that is, most powerful) Nazi propaganda films ever made, a film that to this day cannot be shown publicly, Fritz Hippler's *The Eternal Jew* [1940], which I imported from the Dutch Film Museum. The film was stopped at the border here. They wouldn't have let it in, except that Siegfried Kracauer, himself a Jewish refugee from Germany, wrote a letter to the customs people and told them I was going to have a very educational evening for which he was going to write program notes. It was allowed into the country for one showing only. There were many Jews who felt that I had done the worst possible thing by presenting that film; I'd shown a film which said Jews were as evil as rats. Those who objected could not understand why I, myself a Jewish refugee from Hitler, would want to show it.

In some instances I chose films with sex in them. In those days that alone was more than some people could abide. Kenneth Anger's *Fireworks* [1947]? It was a scandal in those days to show a film with a gay theme. The censors didn't allow it. And even though we had a private club, there were people who felt gay issues should not be talked about. I felt, why not? And I would show the films more than once. I'm a strong believer in showing essentially anything that has human and aesthetic validity and relevance. Maybe it's obnoxious to some, but there's a fighting element in me which rebels against authority and constraint. That has been true throughout my life, and it came out in my choice of films. People would come to me and say, "You know those films you showed yesterday with the red, blue, and green dots? They gave me a headache." I'd ask, "What did you take?" They'd say, "You *really* gave me a headache!" So I'd say, "If you get too many headaches, maybe you shouldn't come."

MacDonald: Did filmmakers appear with the films?

Vogel: Rarely. We did not have that tradition in those days. At every showing we did have four single-spaced pages of program notes which we produced ourselves. Even now there are not many places with program notes. I believe in program notes. I think they have to be done very carefully; you have to be very objective. You shouldn't try to impose something on the audience by having some critic say, "This film is marvelous!" But on the other hand, a lot of interesting information can appear in program notes. But, no, we did not have filmmakers come in person. It wasn't that they came to me and I refused to let them appear; the filmmakers weren't interested in coming. Filmmakers did attend our Creative Film Foundation events. But even then they were only available for questions. In retrospect, I think it would have been better had we had such programs. We did have well-known film critics and scholars from time to time, people like Parker Tyler.

MacDonald: It must have been very exciting to explore all those films and learn what people would like and how they would respond. What moments stand out?

Vogel: It *was* exciting. And it was a continuing process of feedback. Sometimes, of course, what stands out are not the high spots, but the difficulties. We had huge difficulties with the Hans Richter film [*Dreams That Money Can Buy*], because the distributor was a very crass businessman; he gave us such a hard time. I learned so much about the film business from him. One day we had the film, the next day we didn't. Then we had sent out mailings that we were going to show the film and there was a signed agreement; then they'd tell us we don't have an agreement, we don't like this arrangement. It was a very tough experience for us, but we came out okay in the end and showed the film. Richter and I became good friends. He was a great guy.

Illustration 11. *Dreams That Money Can Buy* (1947) by Hans Richter. Courtesy Museum of Modern Art Film Stills Archive.

The avant-garde was very exciting. When I saw Peterson's films and Broughton's at the very beginning of Cinema 16, I can't convey to you how I felt. They were just marvelous for me. Why is an interesting question, because as it turned out, my enthusiasm was shared by only a small portion of the audience. The majority were either against the avant-garde films or totally indifferent to them.

MacDonald: Do you have a sense why that was?

Vogel: A very simplistic way of putting it would be to say that the most difficult thing for people to take in or absorb or appreciate is a new way of seeing. There's something very comforting about dealing only with the conventional—and, of course, something extremely conservative, if not reactionary. Hollywood and television are constantly giving us things that we've already seen, both in terms of content and in terms of style. The most interesting and important avant-garde films are precisely those films that have never been done before—in content, in style, in form—and therefore are extremely difficult for most people to accept. I prefer to be upset, and one of the main criteria I use when I look at films and write my notes is unpredictability. If I can say that I don't know where a film is going or how it's going to get there—that's one of the greatest assets. I had hoped that by showing these films at Cinema 16, and by making audiences more and more familiar with them, I would develop more tolerance. I'm sure I succeeded, but only within certain limits. Always there was the complaint, especially with abstract films, "I got a headache from looking at it." They said it then; they say it now. It's obviously an ideological headache.

The main reason why I personally liked these films has to do with what I'd call "visual sensibility." I believe each person involved with culture has either a verbal sensibility, or a visual one. I was so entranced with visual modern art—paintings, photography, anything visual—that it carried over, of course, into film. When I see a Peterson film or an Andrew Noren film or an Anger, I am transfixed; I get acute sensual/sensuous pleasure from it, a pleasure I want others to feel as well. That's why I showed those films.

We had at Cinema 16 two different audiences—at least two. We had an audience that preferred documentary and nonfiction, social and political films, realistic films; and we had an audience that preferred avant-garde and experimental films. There were instances where the documentary group would say to me, "What the hell are you showing these avant-garde films for! Obviously they're frauds." "Fraud" was popular, like "It gives me a headache!" On the other hand, the avant-gardists were saying, "What the hell are you showing these documentary films for? They're hackneyed: 'realism' doesn't exist . . ." I was in the middle. For me the films all had a common denominator; they created a disturbance in the status quo.

MacDonald: I'm often surprised by the way in which people who are savvy about contemporary art, poetry, and music are still not able to accept parallel developments in film. In this sense there seems to be a gap between film and the other arts.

Vogel: Well, I'll give you one reason. When you look at a very advanced kind of modernist painting, you can decide whether you want to look for one minute or for half an hour, or just turn away. A few seconds is as much time as some people look at modern art, even when they're *interested.* Maybe I'm exaggerating: maybe it's half a minute or two minutes. With film you're a captive. The abstract or surrealist film that someone has made cannot be conveyed to you in an instant. If you've got a film that goes on for fifteen, thirty, fifty minutes—or an hour and a half, there's a kind of domination by the filmmaker over the audience.

Secondly, in other art forms—literature and painting, for example—not only has modernist work been known and accepted for a long time, but in fact modernism has been dominant; we call it *serious* literature or *serious* art. This is not true of film; in film you have the total domination of Hollywood, and Hollywood was not, is not, in the twentieth century.

But don't think for a moment that because the majority of members said in our polls that they didn't want to see avant-garde films, that I showed fewer of them. I used the polls just to get a feeling of where people were.

MacDonald: The time element is important; the audience is captive. But still it seems strange to me. I've routinely used *The Sound and the Fury* in my American literature classes, and students struggle with it, but there's never any feeling that I'm doing something terrible by assigning it. Most students admire the book. But if I show *Serene Velocity* [Ernie Gehr, 1970]—and it's a class period, so it's clear that the film can't possibly be longer than thirty minutes or so—they usually react as though I've purposely tortured them. Of course, *The Sound and the Fury* includes a narrative; reading it is largely involved with finding the conventional narrative beneath the complex form and language.

Vogel: And that gets you involved. But you can't do that with so many avant-garde films.

Now, I want to make another point. I have come to the conclusion that we are not uniformly open to new trends in all media. Let me be quite personal about this: I love avant-garde film, but I have definite difficulties with very advanced modern music. Why? There are differences between human beings and inconsistencies within us, and that's good too. I think most human beings do not represent a particular viewpoint across all media. There may be such people; if so, they are closer to a true avant-garde. But there aren't many of them. I think some of the resistance to avant-garde films is—I hate to use the word—genetic. I'm absolutely convinced that if you gave me one hundred undergraduates for two years, two courses per year, I could develop in half of them a real appreciation for what's being done in those films. But only in half.

MacDonald: A related question. I've found in programming my own film series that when I program a film, I almost always get a fairly sizable audience, but when I program a film *and filmmaker,* I get a smaller group. In my head, having the filmmaker present is an advantage, but not to most people.

Vogel: Maybe they've already had experiences with some of the filmmakers as speakers! They aren't always so wonderful. For you and me they add something (not always!), but for a more general audience, I'm not too sure.

There's only one way in which a more general audience loves the filmmaker, and that is the way we used to do it, and the way it's still being done, at the New York Film Festival. If at the end of a film which has been well received, the filmmaker is there to receive the applause, a wonderful rapport takes place between the audience and the filmmaker. But if that continues into a discussion with the filmmaker, only a certain proportion of the audience will stay, and the questions that come from the audience, I'm sorry to say, are not terribly good. As a result, the filmmaker doesn't open up sufficiently, either. But there have been exceptions, very fruitful interchanges, even with general audiences.

MacDonald: I don't remember seeing any other American film programmer present scientific films, though it seems like an obvious idea. Even now, I'm not sure I'd know how to locate quality scientific films.

Vogel: To me, it was the most natural thing in the world to show scientific films, but it took a lot of spadework to find my sources. There was an outfit called Psychological Cinema Register which had a very large collection of films primarily by medical people, psychologists, scientists. It was unusual for them to get a request from somebody on the outside. They didn't even know how to deal with it; suddenly they had to establish a policy. There was often a problem with sex. Should Cinema 16 be allowed to show a bunch of rhesus monkeys fucking?

I always went by what interested me and what involved me, feeling that there had to be others who'd be interested. I even programmed films that were only interesting for their content—films that weren't well edited, well photographed, but were absolutely marvelous in terms of what they showed. One such film—I'll never forget it—was called *Neurosis and Alcohol* [1943]. It was about cats that were made drunk and then presented with extremely frustrating situations. It was hilarious, and extremely revealing and informative about the connection between neurosis and alcohol. On the other hand, we had a film called *Monkey into Man* [1938] by Stuart Legg, who came out of the British documentary movement, a scientific (and poetic!) film about evolution, beautifully photographed and edited.

Another good example involved the work of Roman Vishniak, a famous scientist and a famous photographer. The International Center for Photography here in New York had an exhibition of his photography, which ranges from the definitive images of Polish Jews to microcinematography—some of the most marvelous imagery I've ever seen. I spent wonderful afternoons with Vishniak, preparing for the screening. All he had was footage; he did not have finished films, and we had to add the soundtracks, which he spoke on tape. Presenting his work to the public is one of the best things I've ever done.

One quote that has had a tremendous influence on me, maybe the basic one, is, in English (I first heard it in German): "Nothing human is alien to me." Marx used it—it came from the Roman philosopher Seneca, I think. It has allowed me to be tolerant of everything "because it's human." In relation to Cinema 16 this meant there was no such thing as a film that, because of its genre, let's say, would not be of interest to me. I remember Andy Sarris saying that animation is not really film, and explaining why (and I've heard others say it too). That's harebrained. I've seen some very great works of cinema art in the animated film. The same with scientific film. A few months ago I saw a film on TV, one of the Nova series I think, about spiders. I've never seen anything more fascinating, or more visual. How can you possibly ignore such work? I'm delighted that it's there, and I've always wanted to show it. And it's always worked very well, in terms of audiences.

MacDonald: Those sorts of films are on TV a lot now, but it's a shame not to see them on a big screen.

Vogel: That spider film would be wonderful in a first-run theater.

MacDonald: Did Cinema 16 do anything with modified forms of film, 3-D, or film installation?

Vogel: Very little. We showed *The Door in the Wall* [Glen H. Alvey, Jr., 1956] based on an H. G. Wells story—a film with variable-size screen images. Had there been a system that would have allowed me to show 3-D in 16 mm, I would have definitely wanted to do it. I'm extremely interested. I bought a 3-D still camera recently and I go to the Museum of Holography regularly—what a great (and mysterious) place! Cinema 16 ended before performance art and happenings, which came in during the sixties. Oh, I do remember an exception. When we premiered Willard Maas's and Ben Moore's *Narcissus* [1956] (we premiered all of Maas's films), he arrived on the evening of the premiere and said, "Where's the door to the projection room?" I said, "Over there—why?" He says, "I gotta do something." He had brought different-colored gels with him which he put in front of the lens at certain points so that the film was tinted. Very amateurish, but beautifully done.

MacDonald: When Cinema 16 was developing, were you traveling in Europe to look for films? I know you're a regular at the Berlin Film Festival.

Illustration 12. Still from *The Door in the Wall* (presented at Cinema 16 in November 1956), illustrating the "Dynamic Frame Technique."

Vogel: Not at the beginning. Later, I traveled to film festivals, and I would go to Paris and London to meet filmmakers, producers, distributors. As time went by, I brought in more and more films from abroad. I remember Agnes Varda asking me if I wanted to distribute *L'Opera Mouffe* [1956], one of her shorts. In those days she hadn't made features yet. I dealt with Georges Franju in Paris and got *Blood of the Beasts* [1949]. I dealt with Argus Films, a fascinating commercial outfit that made hundreds of shorts and also features, many of great interest.

Oh, let me tell you a story. There were supposed to be some fabulous student films being made in Poland, at this famous film school. People told me about them, or maybe I read something somewhere. I sat down and wrote a letter to Jerzy Toeplitz, the director of the school, with whom I subsequently became good friends, asking if we could get those films here, and sure enough we got them. (I had to learn about "diplomatic pouch" and about the censorship involved when you import films.) And who made these films? Roman Polanski! *Two Men and a Wardrobe* [1957] and five or six other titles.

Also, I was in correspondence with Makavejev when he was making student films in Yugoslavia, but I could never get them out. And I had all kinds of contacts with Japan. We premiered Oshima's *The Sun's Burial* [1960]. So Cinema 16 was an international enterprise.

Illustration 13. *Left to right:* Stan Brakhage, Bruce Conner, Carmen D'Avino, Shirley Clarke, Stan Vanderbeek *(seated)*, Walter Hoellerer (of the Literarisches Colloquium in Berlin), Amos Vogel, and Ed Emshwiller in Berlin in 1960 at an event commemorating the recent accomplishments of American avant-garde film, organized collaboratively by the Literarisches Colloquium and Cinema 16.

In retrospect, I sometimes wonder what would have happened if we had had real press support. In those days the *New York Times* not only had no policy of reviewing independent films, they had a critic who was an active, hostile opponent of independent cinema, Bosley Crowther, a very powerful and ignorant man. I'd invite him to every show, but he wouldn't come. Even without much press support, we had seven thousand members. Imagine what could have happened if we'd had it!

MacDonald: Just at the time when Cinema 16 was winding down, between 1959 and 1963, there was a move by a number of people—Jonas Mekas, centrally—to form a filmmakers' distribution cooperative. Your relations with Mekas at this time weren't friendly.

Vogel: No.

MacDonald: When I talked with Jonas, he said that the first day he was in the United States, he came to a Cinema 16 screening. And he was a regular after that.

Vogel: He came to all the showings. He had no money, and we always let him in. We knew of his love for film.

MacDonald: How did the rift between you occur?

Vogel: Well, first of all, there was never anything on a personal level between me and Jonas. It wasn't a situation where two friends had a falling out. I think he will verify that.

When I think back on that period, there is a very definite start to the developments you're asking about, which were for me, to be quite frank, totally unexpected. I learned that a group of people, filmmakers and other people—Dan Talbot [Talbot founded and runs New Yorker Films, a leading distributor of feature films from a variety of nations] was among them—had met in New York. I can't tell you whether they met once or several times. I assume, several times.

MacDonald: You were not an invitee?

Vogel: Absolutely not. This group then published the first manifesto of the New American Cinema. I got the manifesto in the mail, and I was astonished. Why? Two reasons. First, here was a new organization in New York which had a point of view I was totally in agreement with: they were radical, anti-Hollywood, anti-commercial, committed to independent, avant-garde forms of cinema. What else had I been doing all these years except showing that kind of work? In our original "Statement of Purposes" (which uses fancy language I now find a bit stilted), I make clear that Cinema 16 is against the "empty tinsel of Hollywood," and for free cinema, and so on. What astonished me was that I was *not* invited. I couldn't understand it. The second thing that astonished me was the list of the people involved: they were all people I knew well. I was so naive about what was happening that I went so far as to investigate why I hadn't been invited. And it became clear very quickly, that the reason I had not been invited was because I would have been precisely the *last* person to be invited. There was an attempt being made to start a new center for independent film in New York, and they didn't want the person who was the head of the other center to be in that organization. It was as simple as that. Obviously, I realize that if a new center is started, there must be a dissatisfaction with the existing center. These activities were based on dissatisfaction, even though the manifesto didn't address that question.

One thing certainly had to do with the fact that at Cinema 16 I did not have programs devoted to the work of one filmmaker. And I didn't have regular programs devoted entirely to avant-garde film, though there were such programs from time to time. There must have been a feeling on the part of some people that I should not have the power to decide which films should be shown or not shown and, later, distributed or not distributed. That's a very logical feeling. When you run an organization of exhibition/distribution, you are a gatekeeper; you open doors for certain people and close them to others—because you don't show their films.

Anyway, that was the beginning of the whole thing. We all have our interpretations of events, but I'll make the following rash statement: in my opinion, Jonas was more interested in building a Jonas empire than I was in building an Amos empire at Cinema 16. I was never a very sophisticated person about power relationships. And I was not very involved with wanting to push myself or my name. To me, Cinema 16 was a great idea, and it was wonderful that the idea gave me enough of an income so that I could continue to pursue it. And to see new films, to find new films—I loved that.

MacDonald: You don't remember any particular incidents previous to that announcement, where people approached you to do something different than you were doing, or—

Vogel: Honestly, no. I'm sorry that if people had such things in their minds, they didn't come to me. It's possible that they were afraid to. Maybe filmmakers felt that if they came to me and discussed things that ought to be changed, they might have less of a chance to have their films selected for Cinema 16. From my point of view, that would have been a ridiculous fear—my allegiance has always been more to ideas or to artistic creations than to people; I'd reject the films of people I knew and choose films by people I'd never heard of—but in retrospect I can see how someone might not feel confident about talking to me about such things.

MacDonald: Cinema 16 and the New American Cinema group both distributed films, some of them by the same filmmakers. Did you have meetings about distribution arrangements?

Vogel: That question didn't come up immediately, as far as I remember. At first they were simply proclaiming an intention. So far as I remember, there were no negotiations. There was nothing. They absolutely didn't want to deal with me. They were out to do something on their own and the hell with me.

There was an incident much later, toward the end of Cinema 16. Ely Landau (he later produced *King: A Filmed Record, Montgomery to Memphis* [1969] and other films) was trying to build himself up in the film world in those days, and he had heard about my difficulties at Cinema 16. He called me in and in the course of saying that he wanted to help me make my organization work financially, he told me that he was also in touch with Jonas, because Jonas and his group were in financial difficulties as well. This must have been around 1962, 1963. He wanted to bring us together. Jonas and I got together, and there were some talks about Landau's idea, which failed, fortunately. I don't mean "fortunately" in relation to Jonas—not at all—but in relation to Landau.

Joining with him would have been a disaster. I'm not being very diplomatic. The man had very good intentions and has done some very good things, but that idea would have been an unholy marriage of commercial interests with two nonprofit, noncommercial institutions. It wouldn't have worked. He would have taken both of us over.

MacDonald: The Film-makers' Cooperative, which grew out of Jonas's efforts, is at 175 Lexington Avenue. That was Cinema 16's address.

Vogel: After Cinema 16 failed in 1963, Jonas decided to establish the office of the Co-op on the former premises of Cinema 16. I thought it was not entirely in good taste. Jonas did a lot of things I can't forgive him for, including certain terrible things he wrote about me in the *Village Voice* at the time when we were both trying to help avant-garde cinema. One that comes to mind right off the bat was a column that began something like: "There are many people who are entirely opposed to avant-garde films because they think that they are the creations of madmen or psychotics. Such a view is represented in this country by Amos Vogel." [Vogel is referring to Mekas's comments in the *Village Voice,* April 18, 1968, subsequently included in his *Movie Journal* (New York: Collier, 1972): " 'Experimental Film is synonymous with mental delirium and the escape from reality,' writes French movie critic Marcel Martin in one of the three leading French movie journals, *Cinema 68* (N. 124), as he reviews the Fourth International Experimental Film Competition at Knokke-LeZoute. This kind of attitude is still very typically European. In the United States this mentality is represented by Amos Vogel (see his *Evergreen* article [see pp. 338–47])." That Mekas's attack is unfair seems clear from the *Evergreen* article cited, "The Angry Young Filmmakers," November–December 1958.] That was terribly hurtful to me. There's no way one can possibly defend such a statement. I sent Jonas a note and asked him to retract it, or to explain what he had in mind. Or to give me a chance to talk about it in his column. Something! No answer. No retraction. No explanation. Nothing. Jonas was important at that time. Such statements meant that anybody who didn't know me would assume I was totally opposed to avant-garde cinema, and for ridiculous reasons.

I think that while we are doing things in life, we're not always aware of what these things really mean. Ten, twenty, thirty years later, the meaning sometimes becomes obvious. When I started, almost nobody cared about avant-garde films. There was no interest in showing them or distributing them. So I got something started. When I was having my programs, people from all over the country—a little film society, a labor union, a library—would write to us asking if they could show Sidney Peterson's *The Lead Shoes* [1949] or whatever. We would sit around and say, "What should we do? Why don't we send them the film and make up some kind of rental figure; we'll keep some and send the filmmaker some. How about that?" We became distributors because no one else wanted to do it. And we had contracts with these filmmakers that called for a fifty-fifty split of the income. An ACLU lawyer who worked with all kinds of progressive causes gave us the idea of a fifty-fifty split. In those days, that was standard in any kind of film distribution arrangement. If somebody had said to me, "Split it ninety-ten, eighty-twenty," whatever, it would have been the same. I didn't know anything about it.

Then, along came the Co-op idea and a split more favorable for the filmmaker. An entirely possible idea. Of course! The intermediary, the middleman, should be cut out, right? I was a middleman. I didn't *make* the films; I only made them available.

Although, remember, Cinema 16 was a nonprofit institution. It wasn't that I was putting money into my own pocket; it would be plowed back into the institution. So the New York Co-op comes along and says: "Let's eliminate even this nonprofit middleman. We'll do everything ourselves. And *every* film that a filmmaker makes should be in our catalogue. And every filmmaker who wants to be in this catalogue *should be* in this catalogue." It was a very different idea. In some ways, it was a good idea—in retrospect, an obvious idea. But in the long run, it's raised as many questions as the kind of distribution that I ran, questions that to this day haven't been resolved. A co-op confronts the consumer with a huge catalogue, with hundreds of names and hundreds, if not thousands, of films. How should the consumer choose? The fact of the matter is that avant-garde film distribution is in a very bad way. Between 1975 and 1989, the New York Co-op didn't even have an up-to-date catalogue and may still be in financial difficulties.

Don't get me wrong, Jonas has done very important things for the American avant-garde. How could anybody deny that? He called a movement into being, pushed it, worked his ass off to make it successful. And it's had impact all over the world. But I think of him as a mixed blessing for the American avant-garde. Because while he was doing all these things, he was simultaneously doing things that, finally, prevented this movement from becoming as powerful or as influential as it should have been.

I would say that the historical catastrophe of the American avant-garde movement is precisely the fact that Jonas and I were *not* together, that Jonas excluded me at a time when I was doing a very big and very successful project in New York. Despite the fact that the American avant-garde cinema movement became known worldwide, it could not, after a while, sustain itself. And I think that could have been avoided. And a real movement could have been built.

✦ ✦ ✦ ✦ ✦ ✦

Addendum

MacDonald: When you ran Cinema 16, the film society model was the most standard way of presenting alternative film. During the sixties there was an avant-garde or underground movement or at least the illusion of one. Then in the seventies came government support for venues for alternative cinema. I'm wondering how you see the alternative film scene at this point.

Vogel: Of course, to begin with, you always have to look at the overall social scene, because avant-garde film only exists embedded within the larger scene. When we were showing films at Cinema 16, our activities coincided, roughly, with the period of the Beats, which eventually developed into the movement of the sixties. Of course, we started in 1947–1948, before the Beat era, but the very fact that films like *Pull My Daisy* [1959] were premiered at Cinema 16 shows that there was an atmosphere beyond Cinema 16, if not in the whole country, at least in the urban centers—an attitude, an atmosphere that began to be friendly towards the kinds of experimentation we were concerned with. It's true that by virtue of showing such films at Cinema 16 we helped to prepare the groundwork for such a situation. It didn't fall from heaven. But there was a larger social situation that allowed us to develop and be successful.

Illustration 14. Gregory Corso (*foreground*) and Allen Ginsberg in *Pull My Daisy* (1959) by Robert Frank. Courtesy Anthology Film Archives.

I don't find this to be true today, or even in recent years. We're in an extremely retrograde and retrogressive atmosphere at the moment—politically, culturally, in every respect—which has very serious consequences for cinema, and certainly for avant-garde cinema, since it's more oppositional than some of the other independent cinemas that are around.

MacDonald: There's irony here, though, because Cinema 16 thrived at a moment when American culture was especially conservative: the late forties and the fifties. You used the word "experimental"; do you think avant-garde cinema profited from the culturewide ideal of experiment in the sciences and in technology?

Vogel: Well, I *don't* think that the general cultural situation in the forties and fifties was worse than it is now. That's not my memory. There are many factors operating here. At the moment, there's a very tiny audience for avant-garde film, even in an urban center like New York, and there are very few places to see avant-garde film. But you have to be careful not to generalize too much. When I started, there were *no* such showings in New York, but when I did start, almost immediately I found a lot of people who were anxious to see such material and who came to screenings.

It's always a direct interaction between some kind of social agent and the surrounding social situation at the time. Frank Stauffacher [founder of the Art in Cinema series in San Francisco, and a resource for Vogel at Cinema 16] and I were such agents.

The point is that it would be a mistake to assume, well, hardly anybody is interested in this kind of film nowadays, period. That's not the case. I can *see* various things that could be done. It's very possible for me to sound old-fashioned, particularly as I get older, but I've done a great deal of thinking as to what could be done with avant-garde cinema at the present time to get it more widely seen, and the solutions I come up with aren't all that new. There were certain things done at the time of Cinema 16 that are simply not being done now. The first thing would be to try these things again and see what emerges. I'm certain that there could only be an improvement in the situation.

MacDonald: Can you be specific?

Vogel: In terms of programming, the Cinema 16 formula, in my opinion, could still be used successfully. When I say "successfully," I mean it would be more successful than the formulae used now, which consist very simply of two options: number one, you put together a number of avant-garde films by various avant-garde filmmakers and make a program out of that; or number two, you show the work of one avant-garde filmmaker as the program. As you know, at Cinema 16 there was a *mix*, an eclectic mix of documentaries, scientific films, more conventional narrative shorts, animations, and avant-garde films. When I attend the few programs available now, where you see *only* avant-garde films, in one of those two formulae, I notice two things. First, there's hardly anybody there; I'm one of maybe ten or twenty people. Of course, there are exceptions, but I'm speaking generally. Second, after seeing five avant-garde films, I myself get fidgety.

Don't get me wrong, while the backbone of Cinema 16 was the more general screenings of various types of short film by various filmmakers, I believe there *also* ought to be separate series where you concentrate on the work of particular avant-garde filmmakers. That's something I didn't do at Cinema 16, though I remember thinking of it frequently. But always I came to the conclusion that given my own personal resources, I just couldn't bring it off in addition to what I was already doing. That was done by Jonas; he was right about that. But he did it exclusively. He *only* went in that direction, which in the end created very serious questions about whether such programming can hold or build an audience. In my experience in those days (because I attended his screenings at the Charles Theater and wherever), this method did not work. Instead of an audience being developed, I noticed a decrease in the number who attended, even then.

If we had said to the Cinema 16 audience, we're now going to present an entire program to you of one avant-garde filmmaker (whoever that might be, Oskar Fischinger, Michael Snow . . .), and if I had done this again and again over the course of a year, I would have lost my membership. It was and is difficult for me to sit through an entire program of avant-garde film—and I *love* avant-garde film. Why would it be different for those who have *not* developed a strong interest in such work?

There's another issue, a very mundane-sounding issue. I'm firmly convinced that whatever kind of programming you do must have a very strong publicity component, a publicist and a promotional set-up that reaches out into the general population. Programmers must insist on adequate publicity, even if it means making a pest of yourself at the newspapers. Believe me, I know how difficult this is. I'm not a utopian. But I'm also convinced that this is not being done adequately now.

At Cinema 16, we had very attractive brochures, with a lot of information, and these were very widely available. We printed very large runs of these brochures.

MacDonald: How large?

Vogel: Maybe a hundred thousand.

MacDonald: Really? A hundred thousand!

Vogel: Of course! It was *only* out of that that we got the attendance we did.

MacDonald: What did you do with these brochures?

Vogel: Mailed them—it was very expensive. The one great privilege we had was that we were able to work with first-rate commercial art directors; I was very interested in the visual design of these brochures, and I wrote the texts. If we'd sent out ten thousand brochures, the membership would have been five hundred. All these promotional efforts—unfortunately—are absolutely necessary.

MacDonald: One of the ironies of the seventies and eighties is that once federal and state grants kicked in to support not just filmmaking but venues for exhibiting film, it took the pressure off many programmers to build audiences. The money would keep coming in, as long as we presented intelligent programming, even if nobody showed up to see the films. I hate making this argument, but in fact, your success in building audience was at least partly a product of necessity. If you *didn't* build an audience, you couldn't show films.

Vogel: Well, that's true, but on the other hand, I am much in favor of government support for the arts, so long as there are no conditions attached to the money. At Cinema 16 our lives would have been much easier and we would have been even more successful—we might have continued to exist!—had we had outside support. In many other countries, as you know, there's much greater governmental support for the arts than there is here. Anyone who studies this comes to the conclusion that in America we're like paupers when it comes to the arts. And, of course, even the tiny amount now being given will probably be cut further. But as I said, governmental support must be *entirely* without strings or any kind of censorship. Otherwise I would reject it. The ideological, political, aesthetic independence of the project is much more important to me than any support I could be getting from any outside source.

There are many exhibitors now, as then, who don't particularly care about building an audience. They're in safe little oases, and they're showing the films to their friends, and everybody likes each other's films. But it is also true that we find ourselves in an extremely negative general cultural situation that is very hostile to the avant-garde and to new ideas both in terms of style and in terms of content. Some of this has to do with the suffocating consumerism under which we are all suffering now. Television has been a horrendous influence—not because of what television is inherently, but because at the present time, it's owned by business interests. This leads to a kind of national infantilism, cultural idiotization, stupefication, which has recently become an international process. American television is dominant across the world, and it has led to the destruction of national cinemas in most of the existing production centers. So we also have to look at the question of the avant-garde in that context.

Another point, a very essential point: What *is* the avant-garde? *Who* is the avant-garde? I think there was an interesting conceptual error made by the New American Cinema group in the early sixties: namely, they excluded—either were not interested in or were opposed to—the commercial avant-garde. They even questioned whether these people *were* avant-garde. From the very beginning I had always included in my own definition of "avant-garde" people like Antonioni, and Bresson, and the early Bertolucci. Oshima. Fassbinder. You could go on and on with these names. It's a very serious error to exclude these filmmakers. I'm against commercialism as much as the next person, but at the same time, you have to realize that there are people trying to

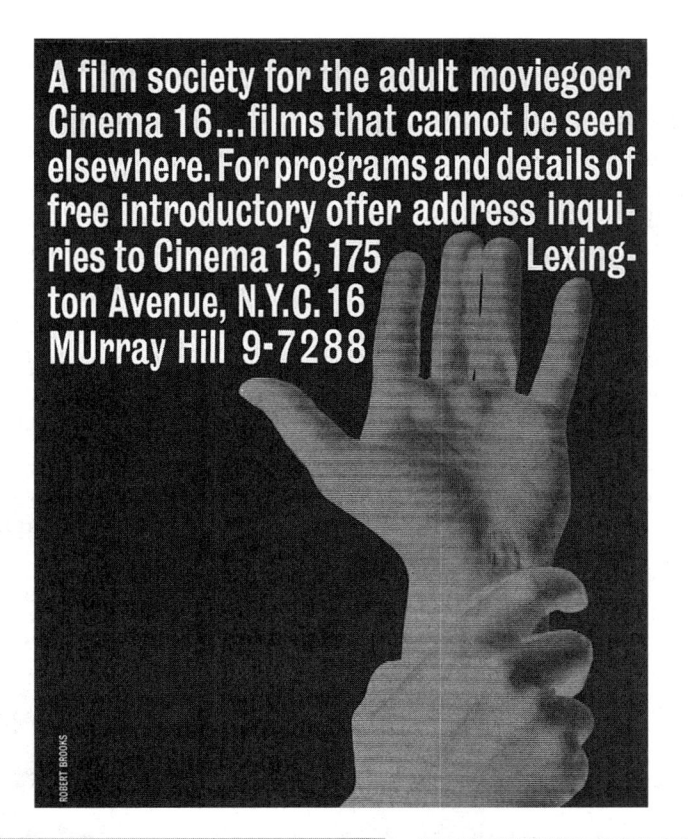

Illustration 15. Three invitations to join the Cinema 16 Film Society.

find new styles, approaches, content, even in the commercial arena, and they must not be eliminated. Sometimes their achievements—in terms of experimentation—are as important, if not more important, than those of the strictly noncommercial experimental filmmakers you and I love.

If I ran a Cinema 16 now, I would show the works of such people, along with all the other kinds of experiment. Certainly this would attract more of an audience.

MacDonald: I think I would go further than you. Most of us get into film, not through avant-garde work but through popular film experiences. I go to the movies all the time. I have never seen my interest in avant-garde film as destructive of my interest in the movies. Even at Cinema 16, you scheduled visits by Hitchcock and King Vidor.

Vogel: Commercial directors can give *us* ideas sometimes. After all, they have access to production budgets that allow them to try things no other filmmakers can.

Another controversial point—at least for some people, not for me. Video. There's much greater technical proficiency with video now than there was at the beginning,

Illustration 16. Alfred Hitchcock at Cinema 16 on March 28, 1956. Vogel had announced that Hitchcock would present a sequence from his newest film, *The Man Who Knew Too Much* (1956), scheduled for release the following June. Hitchcock surprised the audience and Vogel by screening the entire film.

and the projection facilities have improved greatly. When the average audience sees good video work well projected on a large screen, they can't even tell the difference between video and 16 mm film, or even 35 mm. Certainly, there's interesting avant-garde work going on in video. As a programmer, am I supposed to say to people who only want to work in video, I will not show your work because it's not pure cinema? I don't even know what "pure cinema" means. If you want to build audiences, you have to include the best videos, which can range from advanced avant-garde work to wonderful documentaries to music videos.

As we know, the MTV-style, one-image-after-another cutting accompanied by a very strongly rhythmic soundtrack of rock 'n roll or rap or what have you, has entered the commercial cinema. Oliver Stone is an example, both in *JFK* [1992] and *Natural Born Killers* [1995], as are current movie previews—we used to call them "trailers." Much of it is mind numbing. On the other hand, there are some people who are doing very interesting things in music videos. You can't throw the baby out with the bathwater and say all music videos are commercial and not to be taken seriously as art. What do you do with Zbigniew Rybczynski? And there are many others. *All* of these things should be part of the mix of the programming of this ideal exhibition showcase we're talking about here.

Illustration 17. The Anthology Film Archives Selection Committee (*left to right:* Ken Kelman, James Broughton, P. Adams Sitney, Jonas Mekas, Peter Kubelka), which chose the "essential cinema" at the end of the 1960s. Photograph by Steven Shore.

Illustration 18. The logo of the Collective for Living Cinema.

MacDonald: I think we need to learn from the other visual arts. For me, it's a question of where the dialectic takes place. At the major modern art museums, we can see the history of very diverse approaches that were established originally in opposition to each other; and the public, which is considerable for any major show, goes to the museum to experience the interplay of these various approaches. In the history of avant-garde film, the situation is very different. One could argue that the New American Cinema model of exhibition and distribution was a healthy response to what Cinema 16 had done. The problem is that these two approaches were set up as mutually exclusive. The Collective for Living Cinema was established, for understandable reasons, in opposition to Anthology and its essential-cinema approach rather than as a collaboration *within* a growing, larger institutional framework. [Anthology created a five-man selection committee—James Broughton, Ken Kelman, Peter Kubelka, Jonas Mekas, P. Adams Sitney—that chose a set of films they defined as the essential masterworks of film history; see Sitney, *The Essential Cinema* (New York: New York University Press and Anthology Film Archives, 1975).] Each new institution has been built on the ashes of the previous institution—and so at the end all we have is a lot of ashes.

Vogel: I understand what you mean, but I must tell you that no matter what the present situation is, despite the social factors that are operating against us and the narrowness of the existing showcases, I have a very optimistic attitude. In my opinion, the avant-garde will never die; it *cannot* die. There will always be people who want to go against whatever the current orthodoxies are, who want to strike out in new directions and find new ways of expression. When people ask me how I can be optimistic now about the possibilities for progressive politics or for subversive art, I have a saying: "I have more confidence in my enemies than I have in my friends." I'm convinced that my enemies will continue to do the most outrageously repressive things and therefore will again, inevitably, evoke a revolt on the part of those who are being kept out or kept down artificially and by force. The power of the artistic impulse that creates what we call the avant-garde *cannot* be overcome; it will always rise again.

An Interview with Marcia Vogel

MARCIA (DIENER) VOGEL was an equal partner in the founding of Cinema 16, and she remained an active partner throughout the film society's existence. She advised and assisted Amos in all areas of Cinema 16's operation, but her specialties included managing the film society's finances and audience relations. When members were angry about films, she was often the first person they approached. I spoke with Marcia Vogel in January 1985.

❖ ❖ ❖ ❖ ❖ ❖

Scott MacDonald: Some years ago when I interviewed Karen Cooper, she said that two of the main inspirations for her Film Forum were "Amos and Marcia Vogel." Usually Cinema 16 is credited to Amos.

Marcia Vogel: Amos mentioned that you were interested in the feminist angle. Several years ago, some young women (Karen Cooper was one of them) got interested in Cinema 16 and came to me and said, "How come it's Amos's Cinema 16, and not Amos and Marcia's?" They were ready to pounce. Of course, it made me think about how come it *wasn't* in both our names. And my first thought is that Amos definitely always considered us a partnership. He always wanted me to be involved. It was me who didn't want it, who felt too shy, too insecure, and never thought that I could make a good impression like he could wherever he went. And that makes me think, how come I felt like that? Part of it is definitely that I was comfortable in the role that women usually played: I was the person who helped the main breadwinner in the family pursue his career. It never occurred to me that it should be any other way. For the reason for that, I'd have to go back into my early life.

MacDonald: I guess the real question is how important your role was at Cinema 16.

Vogel: I had an important role. But I never needed or wanted public recognition.
   First of all, Cinema 16 was Amos's idea. I didn't have as much confidence in the idea as he did. When we had that first big problem with the snowstorm and didn't have any more money, and everybody said, "You should chuck the whole thing," it was Amos who was determined. I remember we were up all night that night, not sleeping, going to the penny arcades on Forty-second Street. (Amos loved to play in those penny arcades; they were very relaxing for him.) He didn't want to accept the idea that we might have to stop showing films, because he cared so much about it. In the morning, he said, "Let's see if we can't find some other way to make it work."

MacDonald: What was your role once things got going?

Illustration 19. Amos and Marcia Vogel, as they appeared in *Mademoiselle* in March 1955. Photograph by Peter Martin.

Vogel: When the operation was very small, and Cinema 16 first became a membership organization, both of us together did all the clerical work. But all the creative stuff, the ideas about what to do, were his. The practical stuff was mine. And I don't mean that in a self-deprecating way. I think Amos tends to be more interested in creative things, in ideology, than in the practicalities of life. He was not born in this country, so I had a little more New York know-how. That was where I could contribute.

So at first we did just about everything together. However, as Cinema 16 grew, more of the administrative stuff became my responsibility. Also, I did a lot of behind-the-scenes public relations work.

MacDonald: What sorts of things do you mean?

Vogel: Getting the press interested, arranging press screenings. I can't remember all the specifics, but knowing myself and the work I do now, I understand what I must have done then, too.

MacDonald: What work do you do now? [Marcia Vogel retired in 1987.]

Vogel: I'm the director of the New York City Foster Grandparent Program, which hires low-income elderly to be surrogate grandparents to needy children who are abandoned, retarded, abused, or neglected. It's a very worthwhile program that serves to help both these groups—children in need of love and individual attention and older people who need to be needed and have much love to give.

I also previewed many of the movies. At first, I really did not appreciate or understand the avant-garde films. But I learned to appreciate many of them and to see their value. It wasn't as if I didn't know about good movies, but at first this far-out stuff that Amos appreciated was too much for me. Amos and Jack Goelman sometimes joked that if I had been a member of the general public, I would never have joined Cinema 16!

MacDonald: When you were previewing films, did you and Amos then talk together and decide on programs?

Vogel: Amos and I always discussed programming together, but decisions about which films to show were made basically by Amos and Jack. Since my time did not permit me to preview everything, I was not part of the final decisions. When Amos and Jack were unsure, my advice was always sought and welcomed. My opinions and my ideas on how to handle problems were also welcomed, but not always accepted, which was sometimes a source of complaint on my part. You know, our married life was completely intertwined with our work. We ate, slept, and drank Cinema 16, often more than I cared to, but it was our commitment, and it helped to make Cinema 16 the success it was.

Oh, another thing I did: I was the person who punched the tickets. I hired my friends to be the ushers at the Needle Trades Auditorium. And whenever movies were shown that were not liked by the audience, I was the person who had to face the disapproval. I didn't like that job.

MacDonald: Do particular incidents stand out?

Vogel: One I remember was either *Night Mail* [1936] or *Song of Ceylon* [1934]—maybe it was both. I loved those films when I saw them in preview, and then half the audience walked out! It was unbearable to me. I stood there crying, because I couldn't understand why these people didn't love these movies as I did. Then there were movies like Kenneth Anger's *Fireworks* [1947]. That film moved people so much that they had to get up and leave.

MacDonald: It's still a pretty shocking film.

Vogel: Anyway, I was the front line, which was an important job and not a pleasant one.

We always prided ourselves on having an equal relationship, but our different personalities made us shape our work differently. I was always worried about finances. I took care of the checkbook, at least at the beginning, and to balance it made me very anxious. After a few years, we decided to switch that job. But I was always concerned about whether we could rely on Cinema 16 to be a source of income for us. Another thing was that I wanted to have a baby. I used to say to Amos, "You have *your* baby, but I don't have *my* baby." I wanted us to have enough money so that we could hire somebody to take my place. Finally we did, and I got pregnant, and for some reason I can't remember now, the woman we'd hired had to leave, so we were right back where we were before—only with me pregnant. But it made me realize that you can't plan to get everything in order and then have a baby. Life isn't like that. Things are

Illustration 20. *Song of Ceylon* (1934) by Basil Wright. Courtesy Museum of Modern Art Film Stills Archive.

never in order. Anyway, we managed, and it was a good idea for me to work until the last minute.

MacDonald: Were you a film buff before you met Amos?

Vogel: I began to fall in love with foreign movies when I went to college. And in those days there was only one foreign film outlet, the Apollo Theater on Forty-second Street. I went there a lot to see French films. Actually, Amos and I were first introduced to each other at that theater. And I remember Russian movies being shown at the Irving Place Theater. I saw and loved them.

Amos and I used to be big Museum of Modern Art buffs. In a way that's how Cinema 16 was born. I worked on Forty-eighth Street and he worked on Forty-seventh Street. I got out at 5:00, and he got out at 5:30. It was my job to run to MoMA and get tickets for the 5:00 show. Because of his job Amos would always be late. This was part of our dating arrangement for a long time. We enjoyed it. Then one day we said, "Why can't we see these movies at normal times?" Amos began to do some research on whether it was possible to get these films in some other way, and he began to realize that there were many movies not being shown anywhere where the public could see them. I guess he found them in catalogues. Amos has always been a collector of distribution catalogues.

We used to hand out little leaflets to get people to come. One thing we thought would be a wonderful idea would be to stand in front of the Museum of Modern Art and hand out our leaflets. We figured the people who went to the museum were the kind of people who would like to see our movies. We'd stand there in the freezing cold, handing leaflets out. Years later we found out that everybody at the museum was in an uproar about us. Probably our event wasn't posh enough looking, and we represented competition. Of course, we felt so insignificant that it never occurred to us that anybody would consider *us* competition. We were just two young kids with a good idea.

Richard Griffith, then director of the film department at the Museum of Modern Art, helped us. He was a wonderful, sad man who loved only Hollywood films. But he and Amos met, and he was the one who got Amos together with Robert Flaherty, who allowed us to use his name to get support. That was such a wonderful lucky break. We learned about getting influential names from our dearest friend, a second cousin of mine, the person who introduced Amos and me, Rene Peller (now Rene Petersen). She had a wonderful job with a fund-raising organization in New York that did jobs for big liberal and artistic causes. She told us that the most important thing to do is to get an important person to sign a letter and then send it out to everybody. We never would have thought of doing that. We used the idea to establish a list of sponsors. This helped establish our credibility, which influenced people to become members at the beginning.

MacDonald: When you look back on Cinema 16, who, other than you and Amos, were important contributors?

Vogel: My brother, David Diener, was one. He was in the movie-advertising business; he wrote movie copy for ads. We would sit around and talk about the idea of having screenings. As a matter of fact, the name Cinema 16 just popped out one time when we were together. He thought our idea was crazy, and I remember him sitting on a chair, saying, "Who would want to go to see these 16 mm movies?"—something like that, and bingo, we pounced on that number. Later, when we became a membership organization, David's unusual advertising ideas worked very well.

MacDonald: Are there specific people you remember as being particularly strong presences at Cinema 16?

Vogel: Parker Tyler, Hans Richter, Siegfried Kracauer, Marcel Duchamp, Alfred Hitchcock. And, of course, Dylan Thomas. Regulars were Maya Deren, Shirley Clarke, Anaïs Nin, Carmen D'Avino—all the avant-garde artists, painters, filmmakers, people experimenting with synthetic sound, dancers. I especially remember Willard Maas and Marie Menken. Once Willard was annoyed with us for some small infraction, and he sent us a funeral wreath. His anger was very shocking to me. He was a strange and angry man who, as I look back, I realize was addicted to drugs and alcohol. He often got very drunk at parties. Once at a party we gave, he got so drunk that he conked out on our doorstep so that people who were leaving had to step over him. It was very scary to me; I'd had no experience seeing a person so out of control.

James Broughton was an interesting person. And, of course, there was always Stan Brakhage. Stan was a beautiful young man who was very close to Maya when we knew him. Then there was some kind of split between them, and he hung around with Willard Maas. I always remember that Stan and his wife were going out to Colorado and leaving everything. They were like a pioneer couple. The last I saw them, Jane was dressed like a pioneer lady of the 1800s, in a long calico dress—a beautiful girl and pregnant. They were such an unusual couple. I think they may have left from here; I remember us waving goodbye to them. And I remember Stan coming back to

Illustration 21. Jonas (*right*) and Adolfas Mekas in 1953, from Jonas Mekas, *Lost Lost Lost* (1976). Courtesy Jonas Mekas.

visit. My two little boys found him so fascinating. He would tell them that he spoke to animals and explain exactly how, and they believed every word of it. He and Amos were close in those early years. Later there were differences between them, but now they're good friends again.

I have a feeling that Stan liked to stir up trouble. I never really liked many of his movies, but there are one or two that I think are very special, wonderful—*Mothlight* [1963], for example—and I feel grateful for having learned to appreciate them.

MacDonald: What's your feeling about the rift that developed between Amos and Jonas Mekas and the New American Cinema group?

Vogel: I'm the sort of person who thinks things can always be worked out, talked out. Jonas and Amos aren't like that. I think that maybe if those guys had been able to talk to each other, things could have been better. It seemed to me that the rift did not have to be so great, but then you know what happens: things build. First, there's one thing, and if that doesn't get cleared up, something else happens that makes both people more angry. In those days Jonas never could have generated audiences the way Amos did, because his philosophy was so different. Amos believed you had to show only the best or the most interesting; you had to work on making your audience interested. Jonas felt you should just show the films. I felt very strongly negative about Jonas having showings where everybody could bring any film they wanted to show. I thought that did a terrible disservice to the entire field. Amos had built up an audience who would be receptive to some of this stuff, and they would go to the screenings Jonas had and get completely turned off. Of course, Jonas was reacting to the fact that it all came down to Amos's taste. What about Jonas's taste?

Jonas was one of our early-on contingent of people who hung around the ticket taker's table at the Needle Trades Auditorium. He never had the money for a ticket, and I always sneaked him in. In those days, he hated the avant-garde movies but loved the documentaries. [In a conversation I recorded in February 2001, Adolfas Mekas remembered: "At the beginning Jonas and I could afford only one Cinema 16 membership, and for a couple of months we were both using the same pass: I would take it one time; he would take it the next. One night, Marcia, who took tickets at the door, said, 'I know you brothers have been cheating, and I know you have no money; go on in.' It was most embarrassing, but from then on we were both able to attend, free, through the graces of Marcia."]

MacDonald: In your opinion, why did Cinema 16 come to an end?

Vogel: I think there were several reasons, the first being economic. Inflation was high, and Amos was strongly opposed to raising membership rates because he believed that this film society was intended for a broad audience that included people unable to afford other kinds of cultural activities. In those days, there was no NEA or New York State Council on the Arts. And Amos always—rightly—kept away from corporate support because there were always strings attached which could interfere with his artistic freedom.

MacDonald: I've always assumed that part of the decision to end had to do with fatigue.

Vogel: Definitely not. We were running at a deficit, and that could not continue, but how to get out of the deficit was the issue. As I look back, I feel we should have found a way. As I remember, the pain of losing Cinema 16 was eased when Amos was asked by Lincoln Center, during those early years of his directorship, to conduct a feasibility study for the creation of a film center at Lincoln Center. For awhile we thought he could bring the substance of Cinema 16 back to life with the support of an institution, but the 1968 financial crisis at Lincoln Center aborted the idea.

An Interview with Jack Goelman

JACK GOELMAN was Vogel's paid assistant for many years. Goelman previewed films with Vogel. He had major input into the choice and arrangement of programs, and he was in charge of the projection at Cinema 16 screenings. I spoke with Goelman in February 1985.

✦ ✦ ✦ ✦ ✦ ✦

Scott MacDonald: How did you come to work for Amos at Cinema 16?

Jack Goelman: I had read about Cinema 16 in the newspapers. Amos's name was mentioned, and I thought I had known a guy by that name, so I attended one of the Provincetown showings. I saw Amos there and said hello. Then, later, when I came out of the army, I didn't know what I was going to do or wanted to do. I was already a film fan. I loved film, and I'd seen a lot of it. In my wanderings around New York, I'd found all the places that showed films, including the Apollo Theater on Forty-second Street, which then showed nothing but French and English films. And the Museum of Modern Art, which was very cheap then—twenty-five cents, I think. I discovered Eisenstein and Dovzhenko and got very excited about becoming a film editor. I was on the GI Bill and decided to go to the Institute of Film Techniques at City College, which was run by Hans Richter. It was a very peculiar film school, but I went.

Then I called up Amos and said, "I'd love to work for you." He said he had no money, and I said that I'd heard that the state would pay some money for on-the-job training. I went to my VA [Veterans' Administration] counselor, and he said they'd not only pay for my schooling, they'd also pay me to train at Cinema 16. So I sold Amos on the idea, which wasn't hard; he needed help. I did office work. There weren't seven thousand members yet, but there was a lot of paperwork to be done, letters to be answered, members to be taken care of. And the phone was ringing all the time. I worked maybe a year, but it wasn't a good year. They ran out of money and had to let me go. I got a job as an assistant editor for Affiliated Films, a very prestigious documentary film company Willard Van Dyke and Irving Jacoby were running. Nearly everybody in the film trade worked for Affiliated: Sasha [Alexander] Hammid and Sidney Myers, Ricky Leacock. It was very interesting to be there; I felt very fortunate. But that job lasted only six months, and I couldn't get another job in the film industry, so I worked as a machinist for Curtis-Wright on jet airplane engines in Jersey.

I kept in touch with Amos, and at one point he told me that things were getting better and he would like to have me back. I jumped at the chance. This time I was with him for ten years, from 1953 until the fall of 1963. I did all sorts of things. I managed the screenings at the High School of the Fashion Industries Auditorium. And I supervised the testing of the equipment, which was very important. Amos was very systematic and very thorough. He had worked out a plan to overcome any breakdowns in equipment. We had two 16 mm Bell & Howell arc projectors. The one we used would be taken apart at the end of every show. Remember, Cinema 16 didn't have a permanent home. We leased the auditorium, but that didn't mean we could leave our machines there. And we had to use them at the other theaters anyway. Amos had special packing cases built for the equipment. I think we must have had sixteen or seventeen cases. We always had two arc projectors with us, so that if we needed a piece of equipment for the projector we were using, we could use a part from the other one. There weren't a lot of 16 mm arc projectors around, so Amos felt we needed duplicates of everything, even things that wouldn't break down! We wanted to be as professional as possible, and the only way to be professional is to worry in advance about anything terrible that could happen.

The day before our Wednesday showing at the auditorium, our trucker would deliver the equipment. We would drag it up to the booth, and I would watch Norman Kessel and the other union projectionist put the equipment together. Amos had won a concession from the union to have Norman, who wasn't just a projectionist but an all-around tinkerer, who knew where to put his finger on faulty equipment and keep it running. We'd run a test with a test reel. We had a buzzer system set up. I'd go to the auditorium. The buzzer would hang down below the booth, and we had signals for focus, volume, and tone. We'd adjust things and run the equipment for twenty minutes. I would also personally check every film that we were going to show, every splice. I'd redo splices and prepare the leader so it would be short enough—we ran continuous showings, with less than ten seconds between films. Amos was a very thorough guy, and very serious about these things, and that paid off. I don't remember any really bad incidents.

MacDonald: You were also involved in choosing programs?

Goelman: Yes. Amos was always busy doing outside things. I was the inside man. We had films coming in constantly. People would come in off the street and drop off films. We would never turn anybody down. Part of my time would be spent looking at those films. If Amos was around, we'd look at them together. If he wasn't, I'd pre-screen them and sort them out and leave some sort of description for him.

MacDonald: So you knew what he would be likely to be interested in.

Goelman: I would tell him what I thought. I would say, "You must look at this," or "I'm doubtful about this," or "This is terrible." There'd be times of the year when we'd spend more time looking at films than doing anything else. The heavy screening usually was done March, April, May, June. We'd spend three days a week and sometimes weekends if we had a lot of films. I don't know how many films we'd look at in a day. I just remember films being all around the room—science films, experimental films, travel films, foreign films without subtitles. We kept notes on every film we saw, whether we liked it or not.

When we were ready to do the programs, we used a system of index cards. We would lay a deck of cards on the table and play around with them. The problems sometimes started *after* we saw the films and knew we wanted to show them. What is a program? What six films would go together? What about the order of the six? Why would a certain film open a program? Why would a certain film close it? It was

Illustration 22. The Central Needle Trades Auditorium.

fascinating because it was all theoretical. I always felt that we were into unknown territory, and there was a great deal of satisfaction in it.

MacDonald: That diversity of individual programs was—still is—very unusual.

Goelman: It's easy to program when you have a feature and a short, or three thirty-minute films, but six or seven—that's when the fun would start. We'd lay out the programs for a whole series. It was like editing a huge film. Sometimes we'd have to carry a film we liked over to the next year, if it didn't have relevance and immediacy in the series we were working on.

What I most admired about Amos was his range of feeling about film; I've never met anyone with such a broad approach.

MacDonald: Were there particular areas where the two of you tended to disagree?

Goelman: I'm sure we did. We both had our weaknesses. I remember I fell in love with *Yellow Cruise* [Léon Poirier and André Sauvage, 1934], a trip by car through Asia. Amos wasn't that excited about it, but I thought it was quite unique and that up until that time no one had really explored the travel film, except by incorporating it into another kind of film. I loved this film, but there was no information about it, so Amos said, "Okay, you write the program notes." I went to the library and dug up all sorts of things, trying to piece my ideas together. I don't know how good a film it was.

Illustration 23. The certificate presented to the filmmaker of each film shown at Cinema 16 (the original was nine by twelve inches).

And there were other films we wouldn't agree on, but I don't think we ever showed a film that I hated, or where I thought Amos had made a mistake. If we did, I don't remember it. Of course, Cinema 16 was not a democratic organization. The audience didn't decide things. But it was always a question of who *are* we? What is our relationship to the audience? What do we owe them? What do they owe us? How do we listen to them?

What I liked about Amos was that he was very definitive about what he wanted. He was the ideologue. After awhile I found I could say my piece, and Amos would listen. And we'd bring in Marcia. And Parker Tyler. We wanted people who had definitive feelings about aesthetics, but we also wanted them to be open. It worked out most of the time.

MacDonald: Did you have a sense of who the audience was?

Goelman: Well, we got the bulk of the audience from advertisements in the Sunday *Times* [see Illustration 15]. You could say that 90 percent of the people were Sunday *New York Times* readers. At one point we advertised in other places, but all the ads were keyed so we'd know which ones members would have seen, and we found out it was the *New York Times* that pulled them in. But who were those *New York Times* readers? I assume they were more literate than the readers of the other newspapers. New York had six or seven at that time.

I'm sure a lot of people were brought in because they were interested in sensationalism. We showed more nudity than most theaters did. Also, I remember that a lot of doctors came. And we had a homosexual group that liked certain kinds of film.

As far as individuals, I remember Henry Morgan coming all the time. And Steve Allen. Burl Ives was a member for years. An awful lot of celebrities. The Sunday group was interesting. Everybody in New York sleeps Sunday morning, but these people would begin the day by seeing the Cinema 16 show. Most peculiar. I would say the Sunday people were much more affluent—though I don't know exactly why I think that. Some of the Sunday people were out-of-towners who drove in from as far south as Philadelphia and Baltimore, and as far north as Boston. I think we had one person who flew in from Rochester.

I was working in a film laboratory with a guy not long ago, and he said, "P. Adams Sitney said that you used to let him take films out for free over the weekends." I said, "I did? He couldn't have been that pimply-faced kid who kept bothering me with his interest in experimental film!" And it *was* Sitney—a very intelligent, very sweet guy with an obsession. There were certain films he hadn't seen and he wanted to see them badly, but he couldn't afford to rent them. After knowing him for a number of weeks, I trusted him and let him take films home. I admired someone who would come all the way from Connecticut at such an early age to see experimental films.

MacDonald: Did you attend all the screenings?

Goelman: Yes. Part of my job was to evaluate the audience reaction. We tried to understand the audience as much as possible. I'd see these films over and over again with the different audiences, and I'd take notes on a little pad. I would write down how many people left, how much applause there was during the film and after the film. I would make a note if there was nervousness—coughing, talking—or if people seemed bored. I'd come into the office the day after the screening and immediately take out my notes on the audience, write up a report, and give it to Amos, and we'd talk about it.

The record number of people walking out must have been set the night we showed Willard Maas's *Image in the Snow* [1952]. If twelve hundred people came in that night, I'd guess that four or five hundred walked out. That's a hell of a lot of people making noise. I mean people walked out grumbling, enraged, stamping their feet, yelling, "What kind of shit is this!" On and on, one after another. Others were going "Shhh-hhh!"—they wanted to hear and see the film.

Image in the Snow wasn't the best of Willard's films, but Amos and I liked it. And we always felt that we had a job to do: we thought it was important to show independent cinema, even if the audience would have problems with it. We had two types of film showings: regular film showings, which were programs we repeated to all our audiences, and special film programs we showed only once. I think *Image in the Snow* was part of a special program of experimental films. [*Image in the Snow* was shown in November 1952 with *Time in the Sun* (1939), produced by Marie Seton from the Mexican footage of Sergei Eisenstein and Grigori Alexandrov, and *Form in Motion* (1952) by Jose Pavon. It was a regular Cinema 16 presentation, not a special event.] It was very slow going—a cemetery on a snowy day and a monologue—but I found it fascinating. I'd like to see it again; I bet it would hold up.

It's too bad Willard is dead, because *he* would have had some things to say! You couldn't tell from week to week whether Willard was a friend of yours or not. He was a little guy, stocky, with a bulldog face, and he always expressed his opinion—and more acutely when he had a few drinks, which wasn't infrequent. You'd get an earful, no matter where you were, while the show was going on or out in the lobby.

MacDonald: Were you involved in the distribution end of Cinema 16?

Goelman: Yes. Another of my jobs was to send out the quarterly reports, which we kept very accurately. I had open books. Any filmmaker who wanted to come in and look at them would be allowed to. There were the inevitable rumors that Cinema 16 was very rich. A filmmaker would come to a show and see sixteen hundred people, and he'd figure he'd earned a lot of money. He couldn't see all the costs. As I remember, Anger made more money than any other filmmaker, and yet he always felt he wasn't getting enough, which always made me laugh.

I handled all requests for film rentals. I helped people do programming. College film societies would call, and commercial theaters. General Motors had a division that did some audiovisual experimentation, and they were always interested in experimental films—I don't know for what reason. Bell Labs and Kimberly-Clark, the paper company, would rent films for their creative staffs. I'd try to be as straight as possible with the people who called. We seldom sent out films for previewing, so I had to devote a lot of time to telling people what the films were that they were renting, and to asking questions about the problems they had had. Distribution grew very slowly. What proportion of the income it was at Cinema 16 I can't remember, but there were filmmakers getting money for the first time. It was only after we took on experimental filmmakers that Brandon started distributing some of them too, and Leo Dratfield at Contemporary Films.

MacDonald: How do you account for Cinema 16's demise? I know that at one point it got too expensive for the costs of the memberships to sustain it, but with seven thousand members there must have been a way to keep it going.

Goelman: I think it was a question of Amos keeping his independence. A lot of people would have liked to have an input into Cinema 16, but I think Amos was afraid of what having a rich patron might mean, and anyway, finding such a patron would have required a lot of time and effort. The bigger the organization became, the more costly it was to service the members. It would have been fine if there had been one auditorium that held seven thousand people. But we were spread out. The cost became very high for the Sunday showings, because the theaters didn't hold that many people. As a matter of fact, Cinema 16 helped to put the Paris and the Beekman Theaters, these nice little theaters Donald Rugoff had built, on the map. Amos started at the Paris Theater, and when Rugoff was satisfied that the Paris Theater was established, he offered Cinema 16 the Beekman, and when the Beekman Theater was established, he offered Amos the Murray Hill Theater. And we had no choice: we wanted a Sunday morning showcase, and they were very attractive terms, I'm sure. But Rugoff was a cagey guy; he knew what he was doing.

In any case, we were too spread out. There were too many audiences, and they were too small. There were three Sunday morning audiences, with only five hundred or so in each audience.

It's amazing, isn't it? I'll bet an audience of "only five hundred" for an independent film screening would be a spectacular success these days!

The Documents

Letter to Frank Stauffacher from Amos Vogel (Vogelbaum), 9/17/47

Sep. 17th, 1947

Frank Stauffacher
Art In Cinema Society
San Francisco Museum of Art
San Francisco, Calif.

Dear Mr. Stauffacher,

thank you very much for your letter of Sept. 13th. The information contained in it, plus your program notes for the ART IN CINEMA showings proved to be of great help to us.

We are at the present time engaged in the setting up of a film society in New York City which—while concentrating on experimental and avantgarde films—will at the same time screen documentary and scientific shorts.

We are, as may be readily imagined, encountering the usual problems connected with the setting up of such an organisation. It is for this reason that we feel you can be of help to us in our common work and endeavor—to bring a greater awareness of the film as a powerful medium of art.

1) Film Sources; While we are fully acquainted with the facilities offered by the Museum of Modern Art, as well as various commercial distributing agencies, we find it difficult to get in touch with "contemporary" experimental film producers (most of them located on the West-coast). We also do not know where to locate some of the avant-garde classics and wonder if you could supply us with more concrete information as to how we may obtain the following pictures:

> The films of Oscar Fischinger
>   of John and James Whitney
>   of Hans Richter
>   of Viking Eggeling
> UN CHIEN ANDALOU
> THE LOVE OF ZERO
> WAXWORKS
> ARSENAL
> RAIN
> ROMANCE SENTIMENTALE

UNDERGROUND
KALEIDESCOPIO
MR. MOTORBOAT'S LAST STAND
BY THE LAW
THE CAGE
MARS

and all the Films in your Oct. 24th, 31 and Nov. 7th 1947 showing, except those that may be obtained from the Museum of Modern Art.

We do hope that we are not imposing on you by asking you for this information. We notice in this connection that you are about to start a rental library of some of these films. Needless to say we would order our films through you, or even go so far as to book entire programs of your society, if this would be agreeable to you, acknowledging the source fully in our publicity. From our vantage point, however limited a liaison between the two societies could only be of mutual benefit.

2) Organisation; Quite in keeping with your own policy, our own society will also be based on a non-profit, noncommercial basis. However, we fail to see at the present moment how expenses and staff salaries could be paid out of the sale of subscription series only. We are considering the sale of single tickets in addition to the series, but are aware that some distributing agencies are opposed to such a procedure.

After careful perusal of your operational set-up as explained in your letter and program notes, we cannot understand how your "expenses are well covered by the subscription series" unless 1) your audience runs into the thousands which it would not in New York due to the presence of the Museum of Modern Art, or 2) you have no paid staff in your society.

We should appreciate any information on this point that you would care to give us.

As we are planning to hold our first series in the near future, we should appreciate your early reply and are enclosing a self-addressed, stamped envelope for your convenience.

May we thank you once more for your kind co-operation?

Very Sincerely yours,

[Amos Vogel]

Reprinted by permission of Barbara Stauffacher Solomon.

[Stauffacher was co-founder (with Richard Foster) of Art in Cinema, the series of programs at the San Francisco Museum of Art that introduced Americans to the idea of international avant-garde cinema as a reasonably coherent, on-going tradition. He was also a filmmaker—one of those rare film artists whose commitment to their own work is equaled by their commitment to the field.]

✦ ✦ ✦ ✦ ✦ ✦

Letter to Amos Vogel (Vogelbaum) from Frank Stauffacher, 9/20/47

San Francisco Museum of Art [. . .]
20 Sept., 1947

Amos Vogelbaum
125 East 17th Street
New York 3

Dear Mr. Vogelbaum,

I'll try to answer your questions in order. First, the source list:

The films of both Fischinger and the Whitney brothers you can get through us, on 16mm, but we havn't set a reasonable rental fee for them as yet. Nor do we have dupe prints at the present time, although we can get hold of prints on short notice from them.

All of Hans Richter's work, with the exception of RYTHMUS 21 (which the Museum of Modern Art circulates), is in the possession of Richter himself, and it is all on 35mm., except for the above mentioned film—which, by the way, is not very good, and only has a certain archeological interest. It was the first—with Eggeling's—abstract film.

The Museum of Modern Art has Eggeling's SYMPHONIE DIAGONALE, but it is on 35mm. However, they are supposed to be making a 16mm print for us—I don't know if they've started it.

UN CHIEN ANDALOU is at the Museum of Modern Art. THE LOVE OF ZERO was a mistake—we couldn't get it. The announcement was based on misinformation. Apparently all prints of this are missing. WAXWORKS is at Brandon Films, Inc.,1600 Broadway, N.Y. ARSENAL and RAIN are at the M. of M.A. ROMANCE SENTIMENTALE is at Film Classic Exchange, Fredonia, N.Y., and so is UNDERGROUND. KALEIDOSCOPIO and MR. MOTORBOAT'S LAST STAND we got from the Amateur Cinema League, Inc. 420 Lexington Ave. N.Y. BY THE LAW is at the M.of M.A. You can get THE CAGE through us, and MARS, contact its creator, Reginald McMahon, 170 President Street, Passaic, New Jersey. I've written the sources for the rest, on the enclosed list.

We would be glad to rent entire programs of local experimenters, and we intend too, but we just havn't enough time to set up such a deal right at the present because our own forthcoming program is taking lots of time and preparation. Besides, I am personally engaged in shooting TRANSMUTATION for Jordan Belson, and at the same time, organizing a gallery show of stills, and trying to complete a film of my own.

Our organizational set-up here is rather vague and flexible. None of us depend upon the film showings as a means of livelihood. The project was started a year ago by Mr. Foster and myself entirely as a cultural broadening, and the fact that we felt it needed doing. We are both employed at other work outside of the Museum, and, with the exception of a certain amount of clerical work, ticket sales, bookeeping, etc. which is handled by the Museum secretarial staff—all the program planning, research, etc. is done in our spare time. This also includes trips, now and then, to Los Angeles, contacting, searching out obscure experimenters, and so forth. Frankly, it has developed into a full time job, but I hesitate to devote my full time to it because in the long run, it is hardly self-supporting.

However, as I said in my first letter, each series that we've given has certainly been self-supporting, but of course you couldn't spread the "Art in Cinema" idea too thinly, for after all there is a fairly limited audience. We manage to sell about 500 subscriptions for each series, and you can see by our subscription prices and a little multiplication, that we can thus gross way over our expenses, which hardly run over four or five hundred dollars. The profits we've devoted to better equipment, publishing the cinema book, and financing individual film-workers, with the belief that the reason there is so little good "avantgarde" work, is because it costs considerably, and there is hardly any outlet or return.

Actually, we did not ever intend to continue "Art in Cinema", as a permanent thing. In the first place, it was so successful because no one in San Francisco had ever seen this type of film before—or hardly anyone. The unusual and bizarre quality of film material was, I think, its main drawing point. But it seemed to stimulate a good deal of local experimentation, and this, combined with the general disgust felt toward ordinary commercial film entertainment, made us feel that we should continue with the showings. But there is really not much material to draw from—if we stick to our original premise. It is becoming increasingly difficult to put together a well-rounded series. The local experimentation, while very interesting, is too short and unsubstantial by itself. Our desire to set up a small rental library is entirely for the benefit of the film-makers themselves—an effort to get them better known.

One more thing. The Museum of Modern Art Film Library has just organized a complete program available for rental, consisting entirely of experimental work. It goes under the heading: "Art and The Experimental Film." You might inquire about it.

I hope this letter may be of some help to you. And I wish you good luck with your Society.

Sincerely yours,

[hw] Frank Stauffacher

Frank Stauffacher
Cinema

Reprinted by permission of Barbara Stauffacher Solomon.

[By the end of October 1947, Vogel had legally shortened his name.]

✦ ✦ ✦ ✦ ✦

Conversation with Cecile Starr, 12/19/00

[Cecile Starr has worked with non-theatrical films since 1945. Since the early 1970s, she has run a small, home-based distribution outlet that specializes in a range of experimental animation and other avant-garde films. In 1991 she was an Anthology Film Archives Film Preservation Honoree.]

MacDonald: What was your original contact with Cinema 16?

Starr: I remember it as though Amos were sitting here with me. I met Amos Vogel shortly before he started Cinema 16. He came up to see me when I was working at Columbia Teachers' College as a co-editor of a magazine called *Film Forum Review*. I was also an active member of the New York Film Council—not in my own right at first, but as a substitute for Evelyn Oelen whom I had worked for at the March of Time. I met a lot of people at the Council. At that time, there were only twenty or thirty people in New York who were involved with 16mm film, and since I was one of them, I got a call from Amos. I did not know who he was and he came up to see me and he told me he was going to start a film society for unusual 16mm film, and he wanted everybody's ideas and input. He asked a lot of questions, which I answered the best I could—it was just my second or third year of working in film too.

I told Amos that I was also going to start a film society and I did, but *my* idea of a film society and his were very different. He clearly had very big plans, and a great deal of self-confidence about making a go of it.

MacDonald: What were your plans?

Starr: My plans were on a much smaller, neighborhood scale. I lived down in the Village then, and there was a church about three blocks from me that did amateur theater in the basement, and I persuaded them to let me come in once a month and show unusual films—mostly documentaries, as I recall.

MacDonald: What did you show?

Starr: I showed *The City* and other documentaries by Willard Van Dyke and the O.W.I. [Office of War Information] Group. Willard came and spoke. I don't remember most of the films, but I do remember that I borrowed the 16mm projector from my job at Teachers' College, and I inveigled my roommate, Amy Clampitt, the poet, to come and help me set the thing up and give out programs—and to help me keep track of the finances, a percentage of which went to the church.

People paid three dollars a year and I think I did six or eight programs during the year, and several filmmakers came to speak. Some of the papers are in a special file under my name in the rare book department at Columbia University (where I taught from 1953 to 1961).

MacDonald: At a certain point you were also writing about 16mm film for the *Saturday Review*.

Starr: In 1946, 47, 48 I was writing for *Film Forum Review*, and then in 1949 I began writing for the *Saturday Review*, and I stayed there for ten years.

MacDonald: Was it an unusual to have a reviewer of 16mm film?

Starr: Very unusual. The reason I got the job is that I had seen and written about so many 16mm films in the work I was doing at the *Film Forum Review,* which was sponsored by the Institute for Adult Education at Columbia. They thought 16mm films, mostly documentaries, were going to be important in adult education.

So anyway, I had my year of lugging the projector down to the church on 13th Street and seeing how much work it *was* to do the programs. I couldn't wait until the end of the year!

But Amos went ahead and started Cinema 16 with help from Marcia and Jack Goelman and with *big* ideas and a letterhead that listed every important person in New York as his Board of Advisors, some of whom hardly knew he existed. The one person on that list who I knew very well at the time, Jim Agee, hardly ever went to the screenings and was rarely involved with Cinema 16 in any capacity I knew about; but he was reviewing films at *The Nation* at that time and was *very* influential. (Amos never asked *me* to be listed as an advisor, though I actually *did* give him my best advice. I wasn't important enough. I've always held that against him!)

So Amos went out for the big time, and he achieved it. And almost right away. At first his group was small but it was extremely influential from the very start.

MacDonald: Did you go to Cinema 16 regularly?

Starr: I went whenever I could. There was a Sunday morning event at the Paris, and when I lived in the East 70s, it was easy for me to go there; when they showed at the theater on Second Avenue in the Sixties [The Beekman] I went fairly often. I went less often to the Needle Trades theater, which was harder to get to. But sometimes there was a special event, like when Maya Deren and Cinema 16 co-sponsored a big discussion, and I went there.

At that time I wasn't especially interested in avant-garde film. But I tried to be fair. When I saw a film I didn't know how to review, I'd ask Arthur Knight to do the review: he was into the Whitney Brothers and Maya Deren. One filmmaker I'd see at Cinema 16 who I particularly did *not* like—was the husband of Marie Menken, Willard Maas. He was usually drunk when I met him, which was mostly at the parties that Amos gave, and he would attack me verbally for not reviewing his films. Amos gave a lot of parties for filmmakers. I also met Robert Breer there just after he had come back from Paris, and Carl Dreyer too, and so many others. At those parties, you certainly met the best of the New York film world, and the avant-garde.

I also met filmmakers at little receptions that the Museum of Modern Art gave for visiting filmmakers at the Rockefeller house, when Dick Griffith was curator. Another person who brought people together quite often was Rosalind Kossoff. She met filmmakers through her distribution work.

Rosalind and Tom Brandon and Leo Dratfield were the *most* important distributors of the kinds of films that Amos was showing and they also were very important in the New York scene. Rosalind had a company called A.F. Films that made and distributed English versions of French documentaries. Then she got to do American films and also took on Ismail Merchant and James Ivory, who at that time were doing short art films about Indian art. At a cocktail party she had for them, she told me, "These guys are going to be really important producers of major fiction films." And I said, "Why do you think so?" Of course, in those days most people who were making short films thought that *they* were going to be the ones to hit it big. And she said, "Well they just *are:* they have contacts, they have talent, they have money. Nothing is going to stop them." And she was right.

Rosalind also distributed the films of Ian Hugo, Anais Nin's husband, and James Broughton's first films. She very much believed in the avant-garde.

In the Thirties, Tom Brandon had been the only person distributing political films—the Russians—and by the Forties he also had dance films and art films. And then Leo Dratfield came along and took a lot of Brandon's customers away, because Brandon never bothered to pay anybody any royalties: he was a true believer in socialism who thought everything the films earned belonged to *him!* So people like Alexander Hammid and others went to Leo's Contemporary Films because Leo was basically an honest businessman who was bringing in a lot of art films and social documentaries.

These were all major people slightly before and then during the early years of Cinema 16. Leo and Brandon and Rosalind were all very active in what was called the New York Film Council, in which Amos played a relatively minor role, minor because he had much more specialized interests. The Film Council had started when the war ended, around 1945.

MacDonald: What was its function?

Starr: It helped promote the production and use of non-theatrical films of all kinds in schools, libraries, museums, government; it tried to get more money for production, to get more reviews written—that kind of stuff. It still exists.

MacDonald: You edited a small book about film societies, *The Film Society Primer* [New York: American Federation of Film Societies, 1956], in which Cinema 16 has a special place. You must have been very involved in the film society scene.

Starr: I was. Having had that little experience that led to my knowing I *didn't* want to do that kind of work gave me a real appreciation for what was involved. A lot of people wrote to me when I was at *The Saturday Review* and asked me questions about how to run a film society; and I worked part time for the Film Council of America, which had three big meetings in the middle Fifties—two in Chicago and one in New York—all three of which hosted sub-meetings of the American Federation of Film Societies. I helped organize those meetings and met many of the people who were running film societies around the country. Almost all of them acknowledged that they got their inspiration from Cinema 16. Actually, some of them were older than Cinema 16, but even many of these credited Cinema 16, which had an on-going influence.

I edited *The Film Society Primer* with the help of Carolyn Henig, who was my assistant at the New York office of the Film Council of America. I got the idea of putting ads in the back of the book to pay for the production costs. We got Shirley Clarke's husband, Bert Clarke, a *top* designer, to design the book for us. And Bob Brooks, a Madison Avenue ad man, helped too. We all worked on it for nothing. It gives a little slice of those times, fairly idealistic and volunteer-based.

My husband was a close personal friend of Amos and Marcia's before he and I married, and I was a close business friend of theirs—but I kept my distance while

I was writing and reviewing. That's just my nature. I certainly knew them well and I owe Amos quite a lot. I feel very nostalgic about that whole era. Some wonderful people were involved in the New York film scene at that time.

✦ ✦ ✦ ✦ ✦ ✦

Letter to Frank Stauffacher from Amos Vogel, 10/2/47

Oct. 2nd, 1947

Mr. F. Stauffacher
Art in Cinema Society
San Francisco, Calif.

Dear Mr. Stauffacher,

May I thank you very much for your letter of Sept. 20th which I received some days ago. Your information and kind advice were of great interest and help to us here, and your cooperation in what we hope to be a new and "flourishing" film society is very much appreciated.

We hesitate to again make demands upon your already overcrowded time schedule by asking you for further information. However, inasmuch as we intend to rent films from you, we do not see what can be done about it. May we therefore once more ask for your indulgence?

1. We wonder which of the films available through you for rental, would be recommended by you for our first showing. Perhaps you can give us an inkling of the contents of some of these pictures, or simply select the one most suitable for the purpose. We are here referring to films such as: THE CAGE, HORROR DREAM, ALL THE NEWS, TRANSMUTATION, META, FISHINGER and WHITNEY FILMS, ABSOLUTE FILMS No.2–4, and SUITE No.2

2. Please include information on rental rates, shipping charges to N.Y. (per reel, approximately), also, if you will charge us for the films while in transit.

3. We assume that there will be no objection on your part to our charging admission to defray expenses.

4. We are interested in 16 mm. films only. In this connection you might let us know if you project 16 or 35 mm. films, i.e. whether you found 16 mm projection unsatisfactory for the size of your audience or theatre.

5. We wonder just what type of publicity and advertising you need for your series. Frankly, we are surprised at your stating that total expenses per series were "four or five hundred dollars". We intended to place advertisements in various newspapers and magazines, but your experience might indicate that this is not absolutely necessary.

In the meantime, we have received your ART IN CINEMA catalog and were much impressed by it. You and Mr. Foster have done a really magnificent job—and a very much needed one. We intend to place quantity orders with you in the future for sale to our audiences.

We were also interested in learning that you were engaged in shooting TRANSMUTATION at the present moment. Do not fail to let us know when this picture will be available and also send us information or publicity releases as to content.

The enclosed prospectus will give you a clearer idea of the type of films we intend to present in New York. As you seem to be faced with the problem of a continuous supply of new pictures, perhaps it might be advisable for you to broaden your scope and include some of the other types of "serious" films. You might at first stick to your original idea of "Art" in the movies by presenting only the best in documentaries. Frankly, to us at least, films with a purpose are as sorely needed as the purely experimental ones.

Please keep us informed of the progress of your society and of your plans for the future. As we are planning for our first showings in the next few weeks, may we hear from you soon?

Thank you once more for your kind help.

Very sincerely yours,

Amos Vogelbaum
CINEMA 16

[The "prospectus" mentioned in paragraph 10 is, as Vogel remembers, the "Statement of Purposes" reprinted on p. 6.]

✦ ✦ ✦ ✦ ✦ ✦

Letter to Frank Stauffacher from Amos Vogel, 10/16/47

Oct.16th, 1947

Mr. F. Stauffacher
Art in Cinema Society
San Francisco Museum of Art
San Francisco, Calif.

Dear Mr. Stauffacher:

It might interest you to know that we are holding our first New York showings on Nov. 4th and 5th. Our program will include GLEN FALLS SEQUENCE, POTTED PSALM, BOUNDARY LINES, LAMENTATION (a dance film with Martha Graham) and MONKEY INTO MAN (a "popularly" scientific film by Julian Huxley). We are placing quite a bit of advertising and publicity with our first showings and expect them to be a success.

In this connection, we should like to ask you to send us anywhere from 50 to 100 copies of your ART IN CINEMA catalog-book on consignment, at a discount to be determined by you. We should like to introduce your excellent study to New York audiences and are confident that we could sell quite a few of them at our showings. If you care to send more, we have no objections. We suggest that you do so immediately so that they arrive here in time for the showing. Whatever remains unsold will be shipped back by us immediately.

We also wonder if you would have any objections to our quoting from your program notes in the ART IN CINEMA catalog, in relation with our publicity work and our own program notes. We would, of course, mention the source from which we took this explanatory material, in full.

We should appreciate your early reply in regard to both the above questions, as they tie in directly with our preparations for our first showing. If you are not too busy with other matters, you might also at the same time answer our letter of Oct. 2nd, in which we asked you a few other impertinent questions.

Thank you for your cooperation.

Very sincerely,

[Amos Vogel]

[The first presentation of the program Vogel describes for Stauffacher was on November 4, 1947.]

✦ ✦ ✦ ✦ ✦ ✦

Program Notes by Amos Vogel for Cinema 16's first program, November 1947

Cinema 16
Devoted to the screening of documentary and experimental films

program notes

GLEN FALLS SEQUENCE
by Douglas Crockwell

A non-objective film, concerned primarily with the intuitive expression of the artist through the play and hazard of his medium. The fluid imagery is left for each of us to interpret in his own way. Crockwell would be the last to explain the "meaning" in his work. He writes: "About 8 years ago, I set up an animation easel with the camera mounted overhead and the work area arranged much as a draftsman's desk, except that it consisted of several movable layers of glass slightly separated. The basic idea was to paint continuing pictures on these various layers with plastic paint, adding at times and removing at times. This basic process was changed from time to time with varying results and I have still made no attempt yet to stabilize the method."

Scores of artistically satisfying, socially purposeful and thought-provoking 16 mm films are gathering dust in film libraries, where interested audiences can never see them. Except for schools, social or scientific societies, these films remain unavailable to the general public. It is the aim of CINEMA 16 to bring together these films and this audience.

CINEMA 16 will screen at regular intervals outstanding documentary and sociological films of all nations. It will present superior educational and scientific, as well as experimental and avant-garde films. By providing an audience and sponsoring contests, CINEMA 16 will encourage the production of new documentary and experimental films. CINEMA 16 thereby hopes to advance the appreciation of the motion picture not merely as an art, but as a powerful social force.

●

For mail orders or information address:

cinema 16
133 mcdougal street
new york 12, new york

cinema 16

PLEASE POST

devoted to the screening of documentary and experimental films

presents the first
in a series of programs:

lamentation
Martha Graham in an outstanding film study of her interpretative dance. Original music played by Louis Horst. Introduction by John Martin, New York Times dance critic. In color.

glen falls sequence
Hand-painted color animations on glass. A non-objective experimental film by Douglas Crockwell. A vivid experience in fluid imagery. Loaned by Mr. Crockwell.

the potted psalm
A sordid and often revolting surrealist film in the French tradition. Full of unusual techniques and novel cinematographic devices, it projects a highly provocative psychological study. An outstanding experimental film written, produced and directed by Sidney Peterson and James Broughton. Music by Francean Campbell. Loaned by Mr. Peterson.

monkey into man
Professor Julian Huxley's famed scientific film on ape behavior and conduct. Just how different is man from them? Produced by Stuart Legg for Strand Films, England.

boundary lines
A unique achievement in the contemporary animated film. Novel and unprecedented color animation skillfully blended with imaginative sound and evocative music. Produced by the International Film Foundation. Its message: In this atomic age, there is no boundary behind which modern man is safe. Animation by Phillip Stapp. Music by Gene Forrell.

PROGRAM UNSUITABLE FOR CHILDREN

4 nights: tuesday, november 4th and 11th — 7:45 and 9:30 p. m.
wednesday, november 5th and 12th — 7:45 and 9:30 p. m.
provincetown playhouse · 133 mcdougal street, new york, n. y.
(1 block east of 6th avenue at 4th street · southwest corner of washington square)
admission: $1.00 (tax included) at box office—mail orders filled

Illustration 24. Program announcement, November 1947.

MONKEY INTO MAN
Supervised by Julian Huxley. Produced by
Stuart Legg for Strand Films, England.

Not by any means a truly comprehensive scientific study, this film nevertheless conveys in a popular fashion facts as to the development and habits of various types of apes. Skillful direction and interesting commentary almost succeed in transforming the film into an "entertainment" piece.

LAMENTATION
Produced by the Harmon Foundation. Photographed
by Mr. and Mrs. Moselio. Original music played
by Louis Horst. Introduction by John Martin

This masterpiece of interpretive dance is done entirely from a sitting position, with repeated close-ups, revealing Martha Graham's dance technique in great detail. Because of its interesting movements and sculptural planes, the film should prove of interest not merely to students of dance, but also to artists and sculptors.

THE POTTED PSALM
Written, produced and directed by Sidney Peterson
and James Broughton. Photography by Sidney Peterson.

Shot in San Francisco during the summer of 1946, this film undertakes a visual penetration of the chaotic inner complexities of our post-war society, heretofore the preoccupation of serious modern writers. The film medium is potentially a more natural one than literature in dealing with the sub-verbal realms of the subconscious since it is more analogous to the dream world and its imagery. But the contents of the dream world are divorced from rationality and possess a necessary ambiguity. Thus the only possible approach to a film of this sort—indeed, in a sense, to any work of art—is to accept the ambiguity without interjection of the question: Why? Since we all possess an infinite universe of ambiguity within us, these images are meant to play upon that world, and not our rational senses.

Mr. Peterson writes regarding his work: "The original scenario was discarded on the first day. Thereafter fresh scenarios were prepared at least once a week for about three months. The surviving film was cut into 148 parts. The scenarios then read like stock market reports. This pollution of literary material, finally taking a numerical form, was deliberate. What was already literary had no need to become cinematic. The resulting procedure corresponded to the making of a sketch in which, after an enormous preliminary labor of simplification the essential forms are developed in accordance with the requirements of a specific medium."

"The word PSALM comes from the Greek meaning a twitching. The obvious reference to palm in the title connotes not only the potted Victorian spirit but the tree which is the symbol of resolution overcoming calamity, a signification based on the belief that it grows faster for being weighed down."

"The necessary ambiguity of the specific image is the starting point. From a field of dry grass to the city, to the gravestone marked 'Mother' and made specific by the accident of a crawling caterpillar, to the form of a spiral, thence to a tattered palm and a bust of a male on a tomb, the camera, after a series of movements parodic of the sign of the cross, fastens on the profile of a young man looking into a store window. All these scenes are susceptible of a dozen different interpretations based on visual connections. The restatement of shapes serves the general purpose of increasing the meanings of the initial statements. The connections may or may not be rational. In an intentionally realistic work the question of rationality is not a consideration. What is being stated has its roots in myth and strives through the chaos of commonplace data toward the kind of inconstant allegory which is the only substitute for myth in a world too lacking in such symbolic formulations."

BOUNDARY LINES
Animation by Philip Stapp. Music by Gene Forrell.

This outstanding cartoon successfully combines a social message with unique color animation, provocative commentary and a distinguished musical score.

Program notes for *Glen Falls Sequence* and *The Potted Psalm* courtesy of Art in Cinema Society, San Francisco, Calif.

Information and inquiries: write Cinema 16, 509 Fifth Ave., New York 17.

✦ ✦ ✦ ✦ ✦ ✦

Archer Winsten, "Cinema 16's Project Starts Auspiciously," *New York Post*, 11/6/47

The group calling itself Cinema 16, citing scores of artistically satisfying and socially purposeful films gathering dust on film library shelves, and ambitiously proclaiming its "determination to bridge the gap between documentary film productions and the public and thereby to contribute to a greater realization of the problems facing man in the atomic age," showed its first program twice last night and the night before. It will be shown again next Tuesday and Wednesday at the Provincetown Playhouse.

Four of the five films are limited in appeal to their very special audiences.

A film interpretation of Martha Graham's dance, "Lamentation," is something for Graham enthusiasts. The non-objective color animation of "Glens Falls Sequence" will interest some but put others to sleep. "Boundary Lines," a cartoon with social content, enters into a more popular kind of thinking.

The fourth film, "The Potted Psalm," is exceedingly ambiguous for the greater part of its expressionistic length. When it emerges into the understandable, it has trouble with censors. Therefore, when and if shown at all, it is hard to predict which scenes remain and whether, taken out of context, they make sense.

The fifth, "Monkey Into Man," directed by Stuart Legg, is a masterpiece. It alone is worth a trip any time, any distance. The swinging gibbons are poetry of motion. The baboons are striking caricatures of many human attitudes. The picture as a whole is fascinating both for its brilliantly executed shots of baboons, gibbons, orang-utans and gorillas and for the well-stated human comparisons. This is a film no educated person would want to miss. If Cinema 16 can find more like it its success will be sensational.

Reprinted by permission of the *New York Post*.

✦ ✦ ✦ ✦ ✦ ✦

Letter to Amos Vogel from Kenneth Anger, 11/20/47

20 XI 1947

Dear Mr. Vogel,

I was very pleased to receive your letter informing me of your organization, Cinema 16, in New York. I certainly wish you success with your venture, and from your prospectus, I would say that your organization is exactly what is needed for the independent film movement in America. We experimental film makers are particularly indebted to such a project as yours, as it constitutes practically the only means for our works to reach the public.

Thank you for your interest in my films. I would be most happy to have my films presented by your organization. You will find enclosed the conditions of rental for these films, and I hope these are agreeable with you.

Three of my films are now available for booking: ESCAPE EPISODE, DRASTIC DEMISE, and FIREWORKS.

ESCAPE EPISODE had its premiere showing at the Coronet Theatre in Hollywood, October 26 of this year, and was presented by the Art in Cinema Society at the San Francisco Museum of Art, November 7.

This film is an experimental study in conflict of moral values, following closely the psychological state of mind of the protagonist, a young girl. The film becomes increasingly subjective in treatment as the climax is reached and the conflict is exposed, taking the audience from a solid, "real" time-space relationship in the beginning to the unreality of the mind of the protagonist at the conclusion.

DRASTIC DEMISE is a short film dealing with a subjective reaction to the end of the war. In it negative and positive film are used for their moral implication. This film has an original score for percussion instruments.

FIREWORKS, my most recently completed film, has not, as yet, been shown publicly, although it has been reviewed by several private groups, including a meeting of doctors and psychiatrists.

This film is a study in the use of the shock-image. It deals with the self-named outcast, the "wild beast" that is hunted through the night. This film is recommended only to adult audiences.

I will be glad to furnish you with additional material on these films, as well as stills, if you desire me to do so.

Again, good luck in your venture, and I am most anxious to cooperate with you in any way possible.

Sincerely yours,

[hw] Kenneth Anger

Reprinted by permission of Kenneth Anger.

✦ ✦ ✦ ✦ ✦ ✦

Letter to Sidney Peterson from Amos Vogel, 11/28/47

November 28th, 1947

Mr. S. Peterson
2437 Washington St.
San Francisco, Calif.

Dear Mr. Peterson:

Enclosed please find check for $ 112.50. We have just concluded our first program. Comments on your film, as you may have expected, ran from "go see a psychiatrist" to "a masterpiece". Pick your choice.

We are returning both of your films today. As we are booked till February, it would be senseless to keep THE CAGE here. Furthermore, the censors will not enjoy the nude, as we did. This problem could be taken care of either by re-shooting the scenes, as you wrote us about, or by presenting the film before our membership only, which we are about to recruit at the moment. Censorship laws do not apply to membership film groups. W e shall keep you informed of our plans in this connection.

CINEMA 16 never intends to appear as the arbiter of taste nor does it consider its function to consist of telling the producer what to do. However, with all due modesty and speaking only for myself, I might say that THE CAGE could only benefit by at least some cutting, if not some radical cutting. There is much repetition or slow-ness there, which perhaps to you is an integral part of the artistic whole, but to some of the onlookers, just a bit too long. I feel sorry to say this, for you probably do not intend to shorten the film, and it so happens that I consider it—at least, the second half of it—better than the POTTED PSALM. I'm sure, if it was shorter it would go over very well with audiences here. I'm equally sure that if it maintains its present length, it will not be so well liked. Please write me concerning your plans in relation to this picture.

In relation to our distributing of your films here—we are in agreement with your formula of "40% of on an adjusted rental to CINEMA 16", but would like to get a clearer idea of what you mean by "adjusted rental". Please write us on it.

By the way, some of the very small film groups around here are interested in showing your films, but are simply unable to do so on the basis of flat (and high) rentals. These groups run anywhere from 15–50 people. It would, of course, be worthwhile both artistically and "commercially", if your film was seen by ever wider circles.

For this reason, we wonder if you wouldn't consider percentage-rentals for such groups. In the long run, this arrangement could work out better for you than the flat rental one.

We are eagerly looking forward to previewing HORRORDREAM and the other films you are planning. Please send any films you have to us without delay, as we are forced to plan our programs weeks in advance. By the way, if any of your films is with sound, i.e. voices or commentary, be sure to include a copy of the script as we have to hand in a verbatim copy of all spoken words to the censors.... (we shall yet make you appreciate the fact that you live in California!)

Dance films, especially, are well-liked here in N.Y., so be sure to also send us the new one you are shooting.

Very sincerely,

Amos Vogel
for CINEMA 16
AV/md

[The first screening of Cinema 16 as a membership film society protected from censorship laws occurred on April 22, 1948, at the Fifth Avenue Playhouse; Hans Richter's Dreams that Money Can Buy *and Douglas Crockwell's* Glens Falls Sequence *were shown.]*

✦ ✦ ✦ ✦ ✦ ✦

Archer Winsten, "Cinema 16's Fast Start Continues for 2nd Bill," *New York Post*, 12/4/47

Cinema 16, an organization filling a need often talked about but never steadily met, has followed its first and remarkably successful program with a second program of comparable variety. Films never seen in commercial houses, films of documentary, educational and/or abstract value have their outings here. Twice nightly, Tuesday and Wednesday, at 7:45 and 9:30 they are shown at the Provincetown Playhouse on MacDougal Street.

The current program offers two films which avoid anything remotely familiar. The first, "Abstract Film Exercises" by John and James Whitney, is well named. In default of comprehension the most literal minded will have to admit the eyes are greatly exercised. The sound track, created by ingenious management of a light beam, resembles rhythmic static with spiritualistic overtones. Probably a taste must be developed for this sort of thing. Probably this sort of thing, in fact, needs to be developed a little more too.

The second item without visible parentage is Normal McLaren's color animations inviting Canadians to buy war bonds, etc. This is clearer and correspondingly less open to stimulating and fresh interpretations on the part of each new viewer.

The Canadian Film Board's first film in its series, Mental Mechanisms, is shown under its title, "The Feeling of Rejection." Since this film has already been hailed by the writer as a victory of the subject, there is no call to repeat the analysis of plain, unadorned picture-making greatly enhanced by a story of wide and vital application.

The final film, "And So They Live," made seven years ago in the southern mountains by John Ferno, shows the poor farmer's family at breakfast, in school, and again at home. It is a picture of stark beauty and ugliness. It contains the truth of a certain kind of existence, at the same time plumbing the abysmal ignorance of the mountaineers, often described, but rarely seen with intimacy such as this.

The strength of Cinema 16 programs thus far has been that they have thrown a wide net of taste. No matter how much more cleverly "The Feeling of Rejection" could have been made, the important fact is that it has been made, and that it can be seen by the wide public, not merely as an illustration for a psychiatrist's lecture. On the other hand, the filmic artistry of "And So They Live" is a sufficient comment in itself on these truncated lives. And if abstractions, in some unimaginative cases, do no more than whet the appetite for bone, meat and gristle of the fact film, they have functioned as efficiently as many a fiction powder puff in the major movie palaces.

Reprinted by permission of the *New York Post*.

Letter to Amos Vogel from Gregory Markopoulos, 12/6/47

My dear amos vogel,

Thank you for yours of december the fifth, and all therein.

To begin with there will be no need to send any of the films to me, as I shall be unable to proceed with my plans for a film showing here in Toledo due to the censors.

I do not wish to distress you, but I was under the impression that the English returned the silent print of PSYCHE. I wonder what we can do about getting it back, if anything?

Concerning the contents of my very last letter to you, it was written under great verbal pressure from sources which i had to obey; namely my parents who have virtually financed all of my films; and of course I cannot make them understand that I am only interested in making the films, and really care very little as to what they might make.(I suppose I should be interested in money!)

There is no point in writing a long letter; Cinema 16 and I shall continue to understand each other as we have done so,in the future. You have had my full cooperation and shall continue to have it.

With all very good wishes for the season, and perhaps Cinema 16 can be the perfect foundation for a school of cinema which i have wanted to create someday,

[hw] Gregory J. Markopoulos

[hw] 12/6/47

Reprinted by permission of the Estate of Gregory J. Markopoulos/ Courtesy Tenemos, Inc.

cinema 16

devoted to the screening of
documentary and experimental films

presents the second
in a series of programs:

the feeling of rejection

The much-discussed psychological study of the effects of childhood's emotional ties upon the behavior of an adult. The authentic case history of a twenty-three year old girl forms the basis for this "unique film" (New York Times).

five abstract film exercises

by John and James Whitney (Guggenheim fellowship, 1947). Brilliant color images and experimental sound, synthetically produced, create a strikingly unified sensory experience of "visual music". Loaned by Mr. Whitney.

and so they live

John Ferno's powerful and moving commentary on the lives of simple people. An outstanding example of documentary film making. Produced by the Educational Film Institute of New York University. Music by F. Groen.

hen hop
five for four

These two excitingly different color animations by Norman McLaren were created by painting directly on the negative film, frame by frame. Mr. McLaren has used exuberant jazz and folk music to provide a delightful background.

PLEASE POST

program
2

The public's overwhelming response to CINEMA 16's first program has given concrete proof of the viability of its original idea: to provide a permanent home for the documentary and experimental film. With fourteen performances of its first program sold out in advance, CINEMA 16 is proudly confident that it has reached an audience less interested in the barren tinsel of Hollywood than in a truthful interpretation of life by either realistic or experimental cinematic methods.

In continuing to present artistically satisfying and socially purposeful 16 mm films to the general public at regular intervals, CINEMA 16 hopes to contribute to the growing appreciation of the motion picture both as an art and as a powerful social force.

●

For mail orders or information address:

cinema 16
133 mcdougal street
new york 12, new york

6 nights: tuesday, december 2nd, 9th and 16th — 7:45 and 9:30 p. m.
wednesday, december 3rd, 10th and 17th — 7:45 and 9:30 p. m.
provincetown playhouse . 133 mcdougal street, new york, n. y.
(1 block east of 6th avenue at 4th street • southwest corner of washington square)
admission $1.00 (tax incl.) at box office — mail orders filled.

Illustration 25. Program announcement, December 1947.

Letter to Amos Vogel from Sidney Peterson, 12/12/47

2437 Washington street
San Francisco, California

December 12th, 1947

Dear Mr. Vogel:

Thank you for the check. From what I can gather NY reactions to The Potted Psalm were very similar to reactions elsewhere in the country. Thanks too for your personal reactions to The Cage. The general point as to the need for some cutting is, I think, well taken. I have been considering some changes for quite a while and will probably make them when cutting in the new material which will supplant the nude. That material was shot some time ago and I will get around to substituting it shortly. Incidentally, since you have previewed The Cage (the substitutions will be of the same general quality as the rest of the film) do you intend to book it in February—since you are booked until then? I ask because I think it is only fair that you should have first wack at it if you want it and your letter of Nov. 28th is ambiguous as to specific intent. I have had several requests for the film from NY and do not feel that I can hold it for you beyond February. Will you please reply by return mail?

By an adjusted rental I mean rentals adjusted to the circumstances of showing. The details would have to be ironed out in a specific agreement. In effect I merely meant adjusted to the market. Obviously small groups cannot afford flat rentals unless they are so low as to be ridiculous from the point of view of the unsubsidized producer. An enormous amount of film is practically given away for all sorts of reasons. It is almost impossible to establish a just rental fee on the comparative basis. I think a percentage-rental is probably the best deal for small groups. Percentage on the net with a minimum based on the cost of a print divided by the probable number of showings a print is good for plus something for art and the cost of production plus an equivalent amount which shall be forty percent of the whole and represent the distributor's cut. Obviously there are occasions on which the minimum would be waived. A guarantee of an equivalent value in publicity might be considered. Etc. It sounds more complicated than it would be. The minimum cannot, of course, be so low that forty percent of it would not pay you for handling it. On the other hand you might consider the value to Cin 16 of being a distributing center for small groups. The only percentage setup I know of out here is the SF Dance League which gives 90 per cent of the net. This is, I know, extremely liberal. I think there might be, perhaps, a sliding percentage scale, depending upon the size of the group. A very small group would pay a slightly higher percentage. I'll do a breakdown on The Potted Psalm and send you some exact figures to mull over.

I'll have a print of HORRORDREAM back from Los Angeles in a day or two and I'll send it along.

Incidentally, it will give you, if you do not already have it, some idea of the financial problem on the productive end to know that the current estimating on ordinary commercial 16mm production, educational shorts and the like, by small producers is on the basis of $2,000 per minute. That can be cut and recut and has been

Illustration 26. Sidney Peterson. Courtesy Anthology Film Archives.

in my productions drastically. By throwing out any profit and performing practically all the labor oneself. One obvious reason for the lack of sustained experimental production in the 16mm field is not simply the lack of profit but the patent charity in giving away not only labor but an actual capital investment. If the whole thing is ever to achieve a sound basis obviously every break has to be given the exhibitors and the distributors. In return, I think, the exhibitors and distributors have got to think of ways of making the hire at least partially worthy of the laborer. Grants and the like are all very well but they solve the problem only for particular films. Etc. It isn't a simple business.

Sincerely,

[hw] Sidney Peterson

Sidney Peterson

Reprinted by permission of Sidney Peterson.

❖ ❖ ❖ ❖ ❖ ❖

Letter to Robert Flaherty from Amos Vogel, 12/17/47

December 17, 1947

Mr. Robert Flaherty
222 West 23 Street
New York City

Dear Mr. Flaherty:

Continued pressure of work has prevented me from getting in touch with you any sooner, as I should have. The day by day operation of CINEMA 16 and its unexpectedly great success have imposed heavy personal burdens on me, which I had not fully anticipated.

You will recall that at our first meeting with Mr. Griffith you had been kind enough to agree to sponsor our project. In this connection, Mr. Griffith has now suggested that you may be willing to be the honorary chairman of a Sponsors Committee to be organized at a this time, with himself or Mr. Howe serving as the Vice Chairman. Needless to say, I would feel very happy and honored if you will accept. Sponsorship will be honorary and will not, of course, entail any obligation as to time or actual services.

I am anxious to send out a letter inviting prominent persons in the film and art world to also become sponsors of CINEMA 16. This letter would go out over the signature of the chairman of the Sponsors Committee. Would you let us send out about fifty letters over your signature to a list that would first be submitted to you for approval? I am taking the liberty of enclosing a suggested draft for such a letter. We would, of course, take care of all technical and clerical details.

I have discussed in detail the formation of such a Sponsors Committee with Mr. Griffith and if there are any questions you might have in reference to it, to CINEMA 16 or this mailing, both he and myself will be happy to discuss them with you.

We also would like to welcome you at the Provincetown Playhouse to what will be the final showings of our second program next Tuesday and Christmas Eve. As you know, we are presenting: 1. "The Feeling of Rejection"—Canadian Film Board; 2. John Ferno's "And So They Live"; 3. Two Animations by Mr. McLaren; 4. Five Abstract Film Exercises. I am hoping to see you there.

Very sincerely,

Amos Vogel

P.S. I shall phone you in reference to this letter sometime Friday.

AV/ms

❖ ❖ ❖ ❖ ❖

Letter to Kenneth Anger from Amos Vogel, 12/17/47

December 17, 1947

Mr. Kenneth Anger
Hollywood
California

Dear Mr. Anger:

We were very surprised to hear that you had sent your films out to us on November 24th. Undoubtedly due to the heavy holiday mail (it has tied up all our correspondence in knots), your films never reached us until a few days ago. We previewed them immediately and returned them to you by Railway Express on Monday. We do hope that no inconvenience was caused by this delay in the mails.

As to your films, we are considering "Escape Episode" for one of our future showings, but cannot at the present moment give you any definite dates. It would most probably be some time in the Spring.

As you can imagine, "Fireworks" could not possibly be shown to the general public, but we are considering exhibiting it at a later date before our membership division which is about to be established. Censorship would not interfere with membership showings.

In regard to the purchase of your films, we consider your desire to retain all rights to films entirely justifiable. At the same time, some of the other local film groups might wish to purchase (as we might too) some of your films and yet present them publicly. Your letter is not entirely clear on this point. We assume that in the case of such a bona fide film group, you would not object.

In reference to our distributing your films, we would suggest your making us a definite proposal as to the percentage basis on which sales and rentals would be worked out between us. We are thinking of putting out a catalogue of experimental films in the near future and it definitely would be of interest to you to thereby broaden your area of operations.

Please send us your "Drastic Demise" as soon as it becomes available. Undoubtedly the mail situation will have been straightened out by that time so that the film will be returned to you without delay.

Thank you for your continued cooperation.

Sincerely,

CINEMA 16
Amos Vogel

av/rps

Letter to Amos Vogel from Joseph Cornell, 1/19/48

3708 Utopia Parkway
Flushing, NY.
January 19, 1948

Dear Mr. Vogel,

Replying to your letter of the sixteenth instance, I have a certain amount of interesting screen classics varying from a fifty foot Kinetoscope subject to a nine reel version of "Merry-Go-Round" partially directed, as you know, by von Stroheim, as well a print of the last picture in which Lubitsch acted, "Sumurun", both of which pictures are extant only in my collection (so far as I know, or at least available on 16 mm. in decent condition.)

There are considerations of just how interested you might be in the films regarding making up a full list. At the present time the preparation of a program for a showing with all that this entails(I use hand-picked records for full running time) I like to feel is worth $25–$60 a showing. As for out-right sale I have not gone in for that as yet except to private collectors.

I am strongest in the French primitives and think that this genre of program would be the best to offer first as it has stood the test of showings already so well. A Chaplin supplements it.

Sincerely yours,

[hw] Joseph Cornell

Joseph Cornell

[in lower left margin, typed vertically]
Mr. Amos Vogel
Studio 16
59 Park Avenue
NYC.

Reprinted by permission of the Archives of American Art.

✦ ✦ ✦ ✦ ✦ ✦

Letter to Robert Flaherty from John Grierson, 1/27/48

UNITED NATIONS EDUCATIONAL,
SCIENTIFIC & CULTURAL ORGANIZATION
19, Avenue Kléber
PARIS-16e

27th January 1948.

Mr. Robert Flaherty
Chelsea Hotel,
West 23rd Street
NEW YORK.

Dear Bob,

Who the hell is writing your letters? I mean particularly the January 9th one. There is not a sentence in it that sounds like you had touched it with a ten-foot pole. What do you mean by "I need not point out...", "I would consider it a privilege...", "is contribution to the advancement of the motion picture as a medium of art and of social documentation.", "Their work is endorsed by and they are closely collaborating with...", not to mention "perspectives and goals."

But this only by the way. If my name is any use to you, please use it. On the other hand, consider carefully if it may not put you into the dirty red!

Yours,

[hw] John Grierson

John Grierson

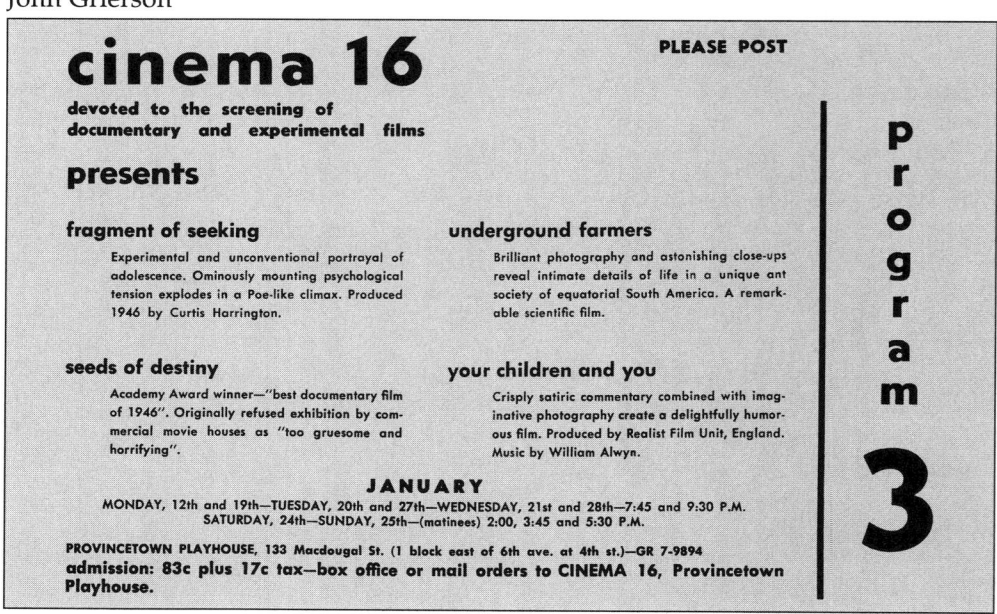

Illustration 27. Program announcement, January 1948.

R.F.

All of us have felt and discussed on many occas the need for a perm doc f theatre wh would present outstandg fact and info f to the gen publ.

I am happ to tell y th such an org has at last been set up and for the past months jhas been successfully presentg f of this nature to NY audiences. Incorp as a cult nonprof organiz,w offices at 59 Park Ave,NYC,C16 has to date given more than thri ty performances at the PP,where it presented to capac houses f such as Monkey,by Julian H,M Grahams Lament,John Fernos And so they liv,the CFB Feelg of Rejex,and sev experim f such as 5 Abstract abd Crockwells Glens Falls. Their work is endors by and they are closely collabora w the NBR.The enclosed prospect will giv y addit info on their perspex and goals.

I need not point out the urgent need filled by such an organize. By its screeng of artis satisfyg and soc purposful f,C 16 is contrib to th advanc of the m p as a med of art and of soc ducument.

I am servg as chairman of the Comm of Spons of C 16 and I would consid it a privilg thave y join me on this committ.Sponship is honarary and will not entail any oblig on y part. Will you let me know on the enclos card th I can includ y name among those of toher promin citiz who have agreed to spons C 16 with me bec of their interest in the advanc of the m p as a social force as well as an artistic medium.

soncerely,

Illustration 28. Draft of letter by Robert Flaherty to be used to establish a list of sponsors for Cinema 16.

❖ ❖ ❖ ❖ ❖ ❖

Letter to Amos Vogel from Kenneth Anger, 2/13/48

[hw]
February 13, 1948

Mr. Amos Vogel
Cinema 16
New York City

Dear Mr. Vogel,

I appreciated your letter of February 7 very much.

Please be assured that I am holding <u>Escape Episode</u> for your New York showing—that your showing will be the "first" in New York, and that a sound print of the film is being held available for you.

A sound print of <u>Fireworks</u> will be ready for your membership showing at whatever time you are ready for it.

I have several film projects which need immediate action, but have been completely tied up due to lack of funds, so the earliest possible showing of my films would certainly be appreciated.

Continued Success!

Yours very sincerely,

Kenneth Anger

c/o Joana Zweigart
4 Harwood Alley
San Francisco 11
Calif.

Reprinted by permission of Kenneth Anger.

❖ ❖ ❖ ❖ ❖ ❖

Program Announcement, Spring 1948

April 22nd, 1948

Dreams That Money Can Buy (Hans Richter)
A special preview of this oustanding feature-length surrealist film for members of Cinema 16. Based on ideas of Leger, Ernst, Duchamp, Calder and Man Ray, with music by Milhaud, Bowles, Cage, lyrics by Latouche.

May 12th, 1948

Wind from the West
A captivating and unusual film by Arne Sucksdorff.

Balloons: Aggression and Destruction Games
Fascinating experiments with children. Produced by Department of Child Study, Vassar College.

Death Day (Eisenstein)
A brilliant pictorialization of a macabre Mexican holiday.

The World Is Rich (Paul Rotha)
A strong and often bitter presentation of one of mankind's basic problems: the conquest of hunger. Released by Film Alliance of America for BIS through Brandon Films, Inc. Produced by Films of Fact, Ltd.

Speaker: Willard Van Dyke

June 2nd, 1948

Round Trip
Foreign trade becomes an exciting adventure in this unique film. Produced by Stuart Legg, The World Today, for Twentieth Century Fund.

First Steps 1948 Academy Award Winner
The fight against cerebral palsy. A Frederick House production for U. N.

Weegee's New York
The famed press photographer creates a vividly impressionistic feature-length study of the metropolis, combining documentary and experimental techniques. ("I am very excited about this film. Weegee has the eye of a Balzac." Robert Flaherty, "Nanook")

The City (Van Dyke-Steiner)
This classic provides a striking counter-point to Weegee's film.

Speaker: Weegee

June 23rd, 1948

The Idyl (Francis Lee)
1941 (Francis Lee)
Two excursions into the dreamland of color, with music by Stravinsky and Debussy. (Mr. Lee has just been awarded a Guggenheim fellowship.)

One Second in the Life of a Humming Bird
Henry M. Lester's high-speed camera expands each second into three minutes of breath-taking film adventure, revealing secrets never before seen by the human eye.

Fiddle-De-Dee
A color phantasy, hand-painted on film by Norman McLaren.

Illustration 29. *The City* (1939) by Willard Van Dyke and Ralph Steiner. Courtesy Museum of Modern Art Film Stills Archive.

Films by Maya Deren:
Meshes of the Afternoon
A Study in Choreography for Camera
Ritual in Transfigured Time

Speaker: Maya Deren on "The Form of Film"

✦ ✦ ✦ ✦ ✦ ✦

Letter to Amos Vogel from Joseph Cornell, 6/22/48

3708 Utopia Parkway
Flushing, New York
June 22, 1948

Dear Mr. Vogel,

In accordance with my promise to you please find enclosed a list of subjects available for the most part for immediate delivery(that is, printing time) for outright sale, and if enough business might develop to take a few things to the lab at one time.

Will you kindly let me know what figure you would like to place on this type of film and also your commission, in the event that the subjects appeal to you. Even should they require a projection (for some subjects) I'd like to get an inkling of the arrangements as a basis for considering how much time I could give to them, their development, etc.

The furniture reels I'd appreciate your help with; I'd let them go for anything at all.

I got some avant-garde projects out of the cellar trunk yesterday and was surprised to find that I'd all but completed one some years ago even to the obtaining of a negative of the rough cutting, and a print. But this needs some attention along with the semi-completed. These were all started before the war years since which valuable time has been lost in not acquiring miscellaneous pieces of stock shots from various sources. This may possibly prove an insurmountable obstacle toward the completion of the half dozen projects; but I hope not, for I am greatly stimulated at the moment, especially with the chances of keeping at least a couple away from the esoteric which so strongly permeates the average avant-garde.

I was happy that there was at last an opportunity for you to get an idea of my collection and its possibilities last week.

Very sincerely,

[hw] Joseph Cornell

Joseph Cornell

Mr. Amos Vogel
Cinema 16
New York, NY.

Reprinted by permission of the Archives of American Art.

✦ ✦ ✦ ✦ ✦ ✦

Letter to Amos Vogel from Sidney Peterson, 6/25/48

June 25, 1948

2437 Washington street
San Francisco, California

Dear Mr. Vogel:

There is nothing mysterious about my continued silence. Overwork and illness—I've been in and out of a hospital—account for most of it. The rest is entirely due to the inertia provoked by both the foregoing. I replied to your telegram about the French Congress the day I received it. By wire. I left San Francisco the next day and have been gone a week. There is no indication here that a telegram has been received during that time, so I suppose you must mean the one referring to the Congress. I'm sorry you didn't get my answer, which was to the effect that you should go ahead and send the film. It didn't occur to me that you had delayed about it so there is no misunderstanding on that score. Nor, I think, on any other score. So much for the private part of your westcoast "public relations." Frankly, the situation in regard to exhibiting is somewhat touchy out here—I think largely as a result of a confusion of purpose among the producers of film. There are, for instance, producers who are looking purely, or almost purely, for museum presentation. They think, perhaps, entirely in terms of prestige and subsidy. Other, perhaps too exclusively aware of the difficulties and expenses of production, regard typical rentals as too low. Others are relatively indifferent to any presentation. There are, in short, all kinds of attitudes which typically prevail in a field where there is little production and an even more constricted market. They constitute a disease for which there is a single cure—more production and a wider market. All this is very general. A specific notion that I have run into out here is that you are trying to corner the 16mm experimental film supply. The people who have this notion are not concerned with the conditions necessary to your existence. They regard a competitive exhibiting situation as essential for the producer. Etc. You can dream up these things for yourself. I don't think that they are serious, and, as I said, there is a single cure—more distribution. As for the Creative Film Associates. I am not associated. If I should become associated I should certainly let you know, since it is, to date and so far as I know, an association for distribution purposes. My correspondence on the subject has been with Harrington. It is my impression that Harrington and Anger are most deeply involved. As you say, their aims are similar to yours. I have neglected writing to them for the same reason that I have been negligent in not communicating with you. So I don't really know a lot about it. They were both up here a few months ago and we discussed the problems of distributing from the producers' points of view and I certainly gave the idea of the Associates my blessing for what it was worth. I haven't had time to go into it further.

Make your own date for HORROR DREAM and I'll send you the print when you need it. It's the only one I have at the moment. I'm planning to make a package of dance film and will get another print for that. I've got three more dance films in color with tracks shot but not yet cut. They should all be ready for release in a month or so. All three promise to be as good or better than HORROR DREAM. Together they'll run about fifty minutes. Two of them were shot with State funds so I have to iron out the distributing rights before there is any question of conferring them upon you. Time enough for the options when they're ready for release. I'm doing a documentary about an art school for the California School of Fine Arts. Mr. Hirsh, with whom I shot THE CAGE and all the dance film, is doing the photography for this one too. If it looks as though it should interest you I'll tell you about it later. Also we are shooting a long sound film this summer as the first production of a new company. By long I mean something less than one hour. It's got a good story. The script is exciting. It should be a good film. I'll tell you more about that later too.

I'm returning the contract signed and with rental rates filled in but without a continuing option on films about to be completed for the general reason that the question of full rights has still to be ironed out.

Incidentally have you had any inquiries about film as a result of the spread in the May US Camera? I haven't.

I should add to the above—to keep you fully informed—another school film this Fall; probably similar to THE CAGE. If the company deal works as planned we shall be producing more film more regularly. A few major works per annum and a flock of shorts is the general plan. Experimental and documentary. I haven't been worrying about your bill. I'm only sorry it isn't larger.

Sincerely,

[hw] Sidney Peterson

Sidney Peterson

Reprinted by permission of Sidney Peterson.

❖ ❖ ❖ ❖ ❖ ❖

James Agee, Review in *The Nation*, 7/3/48

Cinema 16, a film society founded in New York last fall, is not exclusively devoted to 16mm. films. The idea is to show the best of the various kinds of documentary, pedagogical, experimental, and (sometimes) censorable movies which don't ordinarily get a showing in theaters, not even in the little theaters. Some of them do get shown around, more or less, in union halls, parish houses, schools; some others, I imagine, by societies of amateur movie-makers, or in the homes of friends, or, in a sort of extension of shop talk, among the people who made them in the first place. But in general the people who make such pictures have to work against the discouraging assumption that their work will never be seen by most of the people who might be most interested; let alone by a general audience. And, on the other hand, those who might like to see such films seldom get a chance to. The only way I can imagine of getting these people and the films and their makers into any kind of healthy reciprocal acquaintance is through just this kind of subscription plan. There, I gather, the difficulties only begin: some of the distributors or owners of these movies refuse to "cooperate" at all; others make it as hard as possible rather than as easy as possible. But all this is likely to loosen up with time, and already a great deal of work, good and bad, is available.

So far as I know, Cinema 16 is the only society of its kind in the country. I only hope the idea will spread. I only wish it might spread well beyond the big key cities; for I have some idea how many interested people there are in smaller cities and small towns who never get a chance to see such films as these, or European films either. But in many communities there are probably so few of these people that they doubt they can ever develop or support any kind of subscription plan. Another difficulty is that at any distance from New York it becomes very hard to know whom to write to for information about available films, or how to begin. Alex Vogel, of Cinema 16, tells me that he has had between twenty and thirty inquiring letters from various parts of the country; so the spread is already beginning. The society will be glad to hear from anyone who is interested. The address is Cinema 16, 59 Park Avenue, New York 16.

All that is unfortunate about movies doesn't, of course, begin and end with Hollywood and the general Hollywood audience. One of the biggest mistakes that can be made and one which appears to be made remarkably often, is to assume that uncommercial or relatively uncommercial motives guarantee a good film or a good minority audience for it. Instead, such motives guarantee special temptations and liabilities, as grave at least as those imposed by rankest commercialism. Only too many documentaries make the very word a synonym for dullness. Only too much of the pedagogical and social content boils down to special pleading, dishonest thinking and perception, and again dullness. Only too often the experiments were not fundamentally experimental any more when movie people first borrowed them from other arts and to some extent from science back in the 1920s. And there are inevitable drawbacks about his kind of showing which so exclusively assembles the specially interested: the danger of a kind of churchy smell to the whole business which seems to me essentially much more hostile to vigorous work and vigorous enjoyment and criticism than the good honest stench of the average movie theater—the odor, if not of sanctity, of cold, arrogant, uncritical self-righteousness in the audience, in the pictures, and in those who make them. But that can't be helped, certainly not at this stage of the game anyhow. And it isn't by any means all you get. Some of the most honest, selfless, and talented people in movies work on such pictures; some of the best that can be hoped for will come from them if from anyone; and the audience is by no means all churchy. After all, there are a good many people who honestly enjoy movies, know the difference between good work and bad, and care a great deal about the difference. They are the people I hope, and assume, who will be most interested to learn more about Cinema 16.

Reprinted by permission of *The Nation*.

✦ ✦ ✦ ✦ ✦ ✦

Letter to Amos Vogel from Gregory Markopoulos, 7/8/48

[hw] 7/8/48

Dear Mr. Vogel:

Were my two new films seen with or without music?

As to the preview; it would be best if the films were returned to me, until the date of the preview. You may keep the wire recording of the music or send it on also. Permit me, also to ask whether you were going to consider showing the complete trilogy this coming fall? or were you going to show each film seperately on different occassions. I thought if you showed the film at one complete showing of the trilogy, then the rental price would, by rights not be as high as if each part were shown seperately.

Now as to my getting prints of LYSIS and CHARMIDES made. I am afraid that is almost impossible, although I shall make every effort to do so. In as much as I am working on a costly sound film at the present, and unfortunately cannot cancel it for a while, for i am leaving toledo soon, I see very little hope of having those prints made. I did think though, that perhaps, it would be possible for you to advance me some funds (Of course I do not know what the ultimate price is to be, etc. .) from the New York showing of PSYCHE as it stands now, to be held in September? Perhaps if not enough funds for both films, just for one, and I could see what might be done about getting a print made for the other. All my prints thus far have been made at Eastman, in Rochester New York, except one. I hope this is not too presputious of me.

I wish to inform you also, that my new sound film has definitely been baptised "UN DEUIL PERPETUEL". The shooting will be finished very shortly now; but the task of getting a sound composite of the film, remains.

If it is one thing I do not like to do, it is to discuss my own work after it has just been completed. The name LYSIS is taken actually from a dialogue of Plato of the same title. LYSIS though, has another meaning, besides that of a common name. It means a complete dissolving and curing of any task or problem. A complete dissolving into nothing. LYSIS is actually a poem on celluloid, that is why it moves so slowly, for it is the contents of each scene which last on the screen much longer than a normal scene would, that cause the spectator to give his own feeling forth, mentally. A beings thought, one thought, dissolves into an unknown, but completely populated universe of phantoms, if you will. LYSIS might even be called a complete seduction, as one person has mentioned; a complete seduction of an audience who are made to deal with perverted or homosexual types. But unless the audience is following the film closely, and has followed PSYCHE closely, they most probably will not discover the film, and the film will not discover them. If they do not grasp the opening idea of a stairical, but symbolistic birth then they most probably will be lost. But in defense of those that see the film, I could not expect them to understand it at one showing, except in rare cases, would a complete cycle be created. May I also point out the green leaves in the end. And my I also point out that the complete clue for the trilogy is, and is for each part of the trilogy in the name, "DU SANG DE LA VOLUPTE, ET DE LA MORT". CHARMIDES is a completing statement for the trilogy itself. CHARMIDES is the very simplest one of the three films, for it can be followed very easily, taking for granted of course, that my audience has been thinking; thinking in terms of truth and beauty. The meaning is there, the atmosphere is there. The audience need only be there!

Do let me know how much my share of the costs shall be for the press preview, for I should like to send them to you and get them out of the way. Thank you for getting CHARMIDES vaporated for me. And there is no need to splice the titles in, since the film is being returned.

May I aslo suggest that if we do not hear from ENGLAND within two weeks, that we ask them to return the print of PSYCHE that they now have in their possession, because after all I think I have been more than generous with that particular print.

I shall check on the long stretches in the film, but to be truthful, I doubt very much whther I shall make much change.

I shall look forward to hearing from you on things mentioned herein, at your conveninec. And if my comments are not suffieceint, you might add to them, or perhaps

I shall; I have been meaning to ask that you send me a copy each time, of any comments which you might make or give away regarding my films or work, so that I may have a copy of them in my files.

Remaing with best wishes,

[hw] Gregory J. Markopoulos

Markopoulos, gregory j.,
523 Bush,
Toledo,11,Ohio.

CINEMA 16,
AMOS VOGEL,
NEW YORK CITY.

> Reprinted by permission of the Estate of Gregory J. Markopoulos/ Courtesy Tenemos, Inc.

✦ ✦ ✦ ✦ ✦ ✦

Letter to Robert Flaherty from Amos Vogel, 11/8/48

November 8, 1948

Dear Bob Flaherty,

I am very happy to be able to reciprocate in our own small way for all the kind help and assistance you have given us in the past. Without it, we would not have been able to grow into what we are today—a showcase for the best documentary and informational films.

Our mailing house has already begun to address the envelopes but the actual mailing cannot begin until the cards to be enclosed into the envelopes have been delivered to them. They have not received them as yet. The envelopes will be addressed by hand, which will help to make it look more like a personal invitation than if they had been addressed by typewriter.

I shall keep you informed as to the actual time of mailing. In the meantime, I am enclosing a bill that covers actual addressing and mailing costs,as well as postage for 9000 envelopes.

I do hope that this mailing will be very successful,and on the basis of the lists we have provided—they are our very best lists, including all members—we are confident that it will be.

Very sincerely,
Amos Vogel

November 8, 1948

INVOICE

9000 envelopes addressed, stuffed sealed,
   stamped and mailed. (at $ 15 per M) $135.00

9000 3¢ stamps $270.00

      $405.00

✦ ✦ ✦ ✦ ✦ ✦

Program Announcement, Fall 1948

September 29th, 1948

The Feeling of Hostility
Second in an unusual series of films based on actual case histories. Produced in cooperation with the Allen Memorial Institute of Psychiatry.

Aristide Maillol
This poetic French art film by Jean Lods features the famed artist's sensuous sculptures. A moving and last film record of Maillol at work. Music by Roger Desormais.

Poverty in the Valley of Plenty
A timely and bitter film on the Di Giorgio strike, now in its eleventh month. Produced by the Hollywood AFL film council.

The Private Life of a Cat
Alexander Hammid's ("Forgotten Village") tender and sensitive documentary film. Rejected by censorship for showings to the general public.

October 27th, 1948

Psyche
A cinematic stream-of-consciousness poem, based on Pierre Louys' novel. Produced, directed and photographed by Gregory Markopoulos. In color.

New Faces Come Back
A film that shocks into compassion. Plastic surgery "rehabilitates" horribly maimed RAF fliers.

Henry Moore
A Cinema 16 premiere, featuring the work of one of the great contemporary artists. Music by Vaughan Williams. Commentary by James Johnson Sweeney. Moore himself discusses his "Shelter drawings" executed during the London Blitz. A Falcon Films Production.

The Story of the Bees
Amazing photographic techniques reveal the wonders of another world. Grand Prize at Cannes 1946: "The World's Most Outstanding Educational Film." Distributed by United World Films.

November 24th, 1948

Le Chien Andalou
One of the classics of surrealism. Produced by Luis Bunuel and Salvador Dali. A brilliant and disturbing film experience.

The Puritan
The famed controversial French film by Jeff Musso, based on the novel by Liam O'Flaherty, with Jean-Louis Barrault and Viviane Romance. Rejected by censorship for general public exhibition. Psychological drama of a religious fanatic who is driven to murder by his convictions. Distributed by Brandon Films.

December 22nd, 1948

This Day
Experimental film by Leonard Stark. A sensitive cinematic comment on the horror and futility of war.

Housing Problems
Produced by Arthur Elton and Edgar Anstey. One of the most famous of all documentaries, featuring unrehearsed interviews with slum dwellers.

Special Cinema 16 Holiday Presentation:

AN EVENING WITH NORMAN MCLAREN

The famed Canadian creator of *Fiddle-de-dee* and *Hen Hop* will be present to discuss his new experimental animations and color abstractions:

A) *Hoppity Pop, Loops, Dots, Boogie Doodle*
B) *Automatic Drawing* and *Synthetic Sound Experiments*.

<u>No camera</u> and <u>no musical instruments</u> are used for these sensational new sound films.

✦ ✦ ✦ ✦ ✦ ✦

Program Announcement, Spring 1949

February 2nd, 1949

What is Modern Art?
A provocative introduction to a controversial topic, featuring paintings by Van Gogh, Picasso, Mondrian, Dali, etc. With Vladimir Sokoloff and Neva Patterson. Directed by Felix Brentano for Reichof Productions. Script Consultants: Ben Shahn, George Biddle, Betty Chamberlain. In color.

Neurosis and Alcohol
The artificial inducement of neuroses in cats, and their temporary alleviation by alcohol.

Steps of the Ballet
How the arts of dancing, music and painting are combined in creating a new ballet. Produced by Alexander Shaw. Directed by Muir Mathieson. Music by Arthur Benjamin, performed by the London Philharmonic Orchestra.

The Window Cleaner (Jules Bucher)
A sensitive sketch of New York and its people, as seen by the man who keeps its windows clean.

Indonesia Calling (Joris Ivens)
The producer of the *Spanish Earth* presents a stirring film commentary on Indonesia's struggle for independence. Produced for the Waterfront Unions of Australia.

March 9th, 1949

Human Growth
The widely acclaimed Eddie Albert film on sex education for children, produced for the University of Oregon. "An epoch-making movie!" (LIFE)

Land Without Bread (Luis Bunuel)
This powerful account of abject poverty and human degradation in Spain is a unique socio-anthropological document.

Illustration 30. *Land without Bread* (1932) by Luis Buñuel. Courtesy Museum of Modern Art Film Stills Archive.

Mother's Day (James Broughton)
A sardonic and poetic comment on childhood, told in psychological symbols and visual metaphors. A sophisticated "take-off" on the "I remember Mama" type of family history. Photography by Frank Stauffacher. Music by Howard Brubeck, played by the San Francisco Symphony Orchestra.

Speaker: Parker Tyler: How to Look at An Experimental Film

Does the spectator "lag" behind the experimental film maker or vice versa? Mr. Tyler, well-known author and motion picture critic, will discuss difficulties in the way of comprehending the Experimental Film and indicate a technique of appreciating it.

April 13th, 1949

Crystallization
Nature's ever-changing 'abstractions' are revealed in these unique microscopic studies of the process of crystallization.

Picking Peaches
Once again the unforgettable Harry Langdon cavorts with the luscious Sennett Bathing Girls...

2 CONTROVERSIAL FILMS
Men Against Money United Electrical Workers, CIO
An indictment of Big Business

Crossroads of America Research Institute of America
An indictment of the Communists.

These hard-hitting films indicate the possibilities of the screen as a propaganda medium.

Night Mail (John Grierson)
One of the great masterpieces of the poetic cinema, featuring unprecedented use of sound by Cavalcanti, and commentary in verse by W. H. Auden. Produced by Grierson, directed by Basil Wright. Music by Benjamin Britten.

May 18th, 1949

Tjurunga
An astounding glimpse into the intimate lives of stone age survivors in our time. In color.

2 EXPERIMENTAL DANCE FILMS
Horror Dream (Sidney Peterson)
Accompanied by John Cage's percussive score, this film visualizes the anxiety dreams of a dancer. Choreography by Marian Van Tuyl. In color.

Introspection (Sara Kathryn Arledge)
A new departure in the cinematic presentation of dance, differing fundamentally from stage choreography. In color.

Illustration 31. *Night Mail* (1936) by Basil Wright. Courtesy Museum of Modern Art Film Stills Archive.

An Experimentally Produced Social Problem in Rats (Yale University)
A group of rats find a unique (and disturbing) solution to an artifically created problem.

The River (Pare Lorentz)
This masterpiece of the American screen features an outstanding musical score by Virgil Thompson; Lorentz' now classic lyrical commentary; and beautiful photography by Willard Van Dyke, Stacey Woodard and Floyd Crosby.

✦ ✦ ✦ ✦ ✦ ✦

Program Notes by James Broughton for *Mother's Day*, Shown on March 9, 1949

The Contemporary Experimental Film: James Broughton: MOTHER'S DAY
Written and directed by James Broughton, assisted by Kermit Sheets. Photography: Frank Stauffacher. Music by Howard Brubeck. (22 minutes)

"This is a playfully nostalgic family album which attempts to recapture some of the pictorial atmosphere in everyone's emotional world of growing up. In exploring certain images of childhood recollection, I wished to visualize that tell-tale realm wherein both the imagined and the actual operate with equal intensity. So that, as with all emotionalized memory, this incomplete family history contains as much distortion as truth, as much dream as fact. It can be interpreted on many levels—as a personal history, a period piece, a nostalgic game, a malicious rhapsody on the Oedipal complex and so on—I would rather not insist upon its being looked at or labeled in any one specific way. I should much prefer that it evoke for each spectator whatever he wants to find in it or in himself. Hence what little I have to say about the film is merely suggestive of an approach, or is tangential to its theme and mood.

Every child's mother who was once a child is usually obliged to grow up and to alter her toys. But very often there are certain cherished old playthings—a window, a mirror, a scrapbook—which she wishes she could refuse to alter. And she may also regret in each new picture-game of her children how the play of their reflections alter her. Images like these tend to provoke a rather askew nostalgia.

However much she may desire her mirror to tell her she is still a princess, she can see for herself how fairy tales go awry. She may even grow into a kind of witch-queen, when she can no longer play the fairy godmother with her children's own fancies. To say nothing of their father becoming a real ogre, who likes to order all the windows shut.

And if she wants her children to keep her scrapbook, and to illustrate it, they seldom picture it the way she sees it. Or they merely find it diverting. For as they grow up to the mirror, they open their own windows. And when they overtake her toys and begin to collect her into their own souvenirs, she may be left unwillingly to repicture her scrapbook.

For her favorite bedtime story is apt to remain: 'Once upon a time there was a very beautiful and refined girl who had a great many suitors. But she married the wrong one. Then she had a great many children and she did not know what to do with them either.'"

James Broughton

Reprinted by permission of James Broughton.

✦ ✦ ✦ ✦ ✦ ✦

Letter to Amos Vogel from Jordan Belson, 3/18/49

March 18, 1949

Mr. Amos Vogel
Cinema 16
59 Park Ave.
New York 16, N.Y.

Dear Mr. Vogel,

I am pleased that you found my film of some value, and I write to thank you for taking the trouble to write me your impressions of the film. The film is still in the mails, I have not received it yet, and I will send it on to you whenever you feel that you want to program it.

Your proposal to distribute the film for me meets with my approval, would you further communicate with me in this regard. I do not know the procedure of how you go about this. Am I to supply you with copies of my film as you need them? Or do you supply the prints of the film? Or do I sell you a print? Will you please write and tell me exactly the plan of distribution that you have in effect.

I do think that $10.00 is not too much to ask for rental on my film when it is to be shown to a large audience. The rental amount for showings to smaller audiences I will leave up to you, you undoubtedly have greater experience in this matter than I.

I feel you should know that I am primarily a painter and that film serves me, at this time, only as an extra interest. I am not the least convinced that the abstract film is the ultimate art form, in fact the work that I have done with films have has shown me the boundless wealth of experience and joy that painting may possess. I have been, however, considering now for some time making another film. Its appearance and concept (and sound track) are quite clear in my mind, but I am reluctant to begin work on it at this time without the financial aid that I will need to allow me to work on it in a secure and uninterrupted manner. The film will be in color which will of course make it much more expensive to produce than the black and white. I am negotiating with Hilla Rebay of the Guggenheim Foundation (Museum of Non-Objective Painting) in this regard. Well, more truly, I am trying to get her to send me a yearly income so that I can continue painting with a reasonable amount of security; and should I receive such an income I would try to find time to make this film that I have in mind, at which time I will be glad to send it to you, unless of course Miss Rebay insists upon exclusive rights to whatever I produce. I believe Mr. Fischinger had some similar arrangement with her. You may be interested to know, incidentally, that I have a large painting on exhibit currently at the Museum of Non-Objective Painting and you may like to see it if you should be out that way. I suspect that this Museum is generally overlooked by persons in New York because of an exclusive and high-flown attitude that it effects. Do you find this to be the case? I know that the Museum possess many fine Non-objective films, but I don't know if they are available to shown anywhere than at the Museum.

I was about to send you a stack of original drawings from my film, but decided against it without some assurance from you that they would be returned to me. I will be glad to send them to you if you can make arrangements to have them photographed <u>in reverse values</u> and then sent back to me. You see, the drawing are black on white cards and I photographed them with reversal film to obtain the desired black background. I feel the drawings would be better (if they were included in a wall display or printed in a catalogue) if they are seen as white shapes on a black background. If you would undertake to do this; I believe it is very simple and inexpensive, Frank Staufacher did this for the Art in Cinema shows. I possess absoulutey no photographic equipment or I would certainly do it for you. If you are reclutant to do this I will send you a few drawings. If it can be promised that they would be returned to me. If you made the suggested negative prints you would be most welcome to keep the prints for whatever purpose you desire.

Illustration 32. *Improvisation No. 1* (1948) by Jordan Belson—*not* shown at Cinema 16. Courtesy Jordan Belson.

Many thanks for your interest and encouragement, and I shall expect to hear from you in regards to distributing my film and whatever other matter occurs to you.

Sincerely yours,

[hw] Jordan Belson

Reprinted by permission of Jordan Belson.

❖ ❖ ❖ ❖ ❖ ❖

Letter to Amos Vogel from James Broughton, 3/25/49

THE CENTAUR PRESS
1724 Baker Street
San Francisco 15, California

25 March 1949

Dear Amos Vogel:

I want to thank you warmly & fully for your many kindnesses to me while I was in New York, and for all your labors on behalf of MOTHER'S DAY. I still look back on that evening with a certain amount of distaste and amazement; we are fortunate here not to have to cope with audiences like yours for fortunately they only exist in New York. I suppose I should be gratified that my film stood up as well as it did under the circumstances. However, in reporting to the other film-producers here I have made it clear that your New York showings are not necessarily to be confused (I assume) with your plans for general distribution.

Just after I saw you, on the day I left New York, I had an interview with Rosalind Kossoff of A. F. Films which had been arranged for me by the Museum of Modern Art. Miss Kossoff made me a splendid offer for distribution of MOTHER'S DAY, with immediate and very wide promotion and circulation on most reasonable and cooperative terms, and so I agreed to give A. F. Films exclusive rights to the film and I will sign with them. This came as a most unexpected last-minute stroke of luck, for I think it will bring me a quicker return and allow me to proceed with production of new films much more rapidly. I regret that I did not have opportunity to inform you of this sooner; I am only now catching up with all that happened and all that has accumulated on my desks here.

There is, of course, a special situation involved with A. F. that does not conflict with what you outlined to me as your plans for circulating a group of experimental films. Miss Kossoff is not, as you are, interested in the whole body of experimental film; she thinks MOTHER'S DAY a good movie in its own right, however specialized, and will push it on its own. It is unlikely that many of the other films from this area would appeal to her on these same terms, if only for their lack of certain professional requirements—such as sound-tracks, original music, etc. And certainly she has no intention nor inclination to form programs and such.

So again I send you my good wishes and greetings and my genuine gratitude for your cooperation; and I hope that MOTHER'S DAY did not alienate too many of your customers.

Very sincerely,

[hw] James Broughton

Reprinted by permission of James Broughton.

✦ ✦ ✦ ✦ ✦ ✦

Letter to Amos Vogel from Joseph Cornell, 4/9/49

3708 Utopia Parkway
Flushing, New York

April 9, 1949

Dear Mr. Vogel,

Replying to your letter of the thirty first of March I am interested in your proposal of presenting a "fifty five minute program at one time" but more on the basis of the films(the first group especially which is a tried and tested unit) standing on their own rather than being named from my own collection. At least with this point subordinated for the time being.

Concerning an "idea of what rentals" should be charged this is something a little difficult to set a definite figure upon. I have received up to a hundred dollars an evening privately(appearing only to supervise my selection of music and not having the details of projection to consider). I feel that a program should bring me some kind of scale price such as you remunerate others bringing a similar type of program to your group.

There may be a possibility of getting into a small group of "avant-garde" things which I started before the war. This is one reason why I'm not too strong about being labeled with only old pictures. However the present preoccupation with films is the old timers, and if CINEMA 16 is seriously considering something I hope that I may hear from you soon, for there are other possibilities that must be considered to get beyond limited showings which do not always warrant the demands of time and energy and expense put into these showings.

There is a "possibility of renting or selling these things to others" but at the moment not the prize things such as you itemize in your letter. What is available was listed in the misfiled letter which you say you finally located.

In any event I should look forward to working out some interesting things with CINEMA 16, if you wish, in the same adventuresome spirit that has characterized my whole activity in this field. Nothing should be regarded as too rigid as things are dusted off from the trunks and found to contain many surprising and delightful possibilities.

Sincerely yours,

[hw] Joseph Cornell

Mr. Amos Vogel
Cinema 16

Reprinted by permission of the Archives of American Art.

[Cinema 16 presented "Early Films from the Unique Collection of Joseph Cornell" in December 1949: "We sweated blood during that entire performance, because the films were brittle and broke continually. Also, some films had unusual sprocketholes, which threw the projectionist. I remember thinking, 'Never again!'
 I loved Cornell's boxes, and one day he offered to sell me boxes at a hundred dollars each. I didn't have a hundred dollars and missed my chance—imagine what they'd be worth now!" (Vogel in conversation with the author, 6/14/01)]

✦ ✦ ✦ ✦ ✦ ✦

Letter to James Broughton from Amos Vogel, 4/12/49

April 12, 1949

Mr. James Broughton
1724 Baker Street
San Francisco 15, Cal.

Dear Mr. Broughton:

I was somewhat surprised about your signing with A. F. Films without in any way discussing this matter with me. I hope this does not sound presumptuous, but I felt that an informal relationship had been established, according to which all of us were freely working together "for the good of the experimental film", and where such prior discussion would have been self-evident.

Miss Kossoff and I are on the best of terms, and, having the highest respect for the type of work she has done for the 16mm film, I can only wish you the best of luck. Could you perhaps tell me on what basis you are working with her? Needless to say, I would treat this information in a confidential manner.

I also feel that although you were in a sense the West Coast "ambassador", destined to carry news from and to California, you are apparently under some misapprehension as to the situation here, which I would like to do away with.

1. The show which you attended in New York was <u>not</u> typical of Cinema 16 shows. We have shown a great many experimental films before, and have had speakers before, and there has never been an incident such as occurred at the showing you attended. In fact, subsequent comments from "true" experimentalists in the audience indicate very strongly that the failure of the microphones, as well as Parker's rapid delivery of a paper rather than a speech, were at least as much to blame for the situation as all the other factors (we had a very successful show with Miss Deren, who, you may be sure, did not take a conciliatory attitude).

2. In any case, our shows are, as you yourself say, <u>not</u> to be confused with our distribution plans. They are entirely separate, and films distributed by us will obviously only reach the audience which is interested in them.

3. If any one of our members was "alienated" by your film, he does not belong into Cinema 16, and we will not accommodate ourselves to him. In fact, we will encourage him to leave the organization. Is this clear?

I would appreciate if you would clarify the above points to any one on the West Coast who may ask you. I don't think that misunderstandings should exist between us and California.

Very sincerely yours,

Amos Vogel

AV/jnp

P.S. With the deadline for Parker's article in Theatre Arts two days away, and with neither Parker nor Miss Kossoff having stills of your films in their possession, I was pleased to make our stills of the film available to them.

A. V.

✦ ✦ ✦ ✦ ✦

Illustration 33. *Mother's Day* (1948) by James Broughton. Courtesy Museum of Modern Art Film Stills Archive.

Letter to Amos Vogel from Frank Stauffacher, Circa 4/49

San Francisco Museum of Art [...]

Dear Amos,

I have not had a chance to answer your letter of March 3, having not been at the Museum regularly during the past few weeks. I've been engaged on several film projects, and eventually hope to break into the business of advertising films.

In regard to your question about how the recent Art in Cinema showings have been faring—I am glad to say that they were enormously crowded, and apparently very satisfactory to the general audiences. As you know, these last two programs consisted of recent experimental work only—no famous old films, etc. I was skeptical of this venture, but it has even proved, perhaps, more energizing than the type of program on the regular series. As for the future—I can't say. Each time I anticipate a new series I am hopelessly pessimistic; but our following seems to grow.

You don't have to apologize for your long silence due to work. I know what a job it is to put on this sort of thing, and how much more it must be in your case. And the battles one puts up with.

From Broughton I've had only cursory word which seemed to indicate he didn't like the reception M. D. got at your showing. I am always struck by the huge divergence in audience reactions to what a film ought to be, and what an audience likes. A good example is Richter's DREAMS THAT MONEY etc. It ran months in N. Y. but only two weeks here in S. F. It just didn't take at all here. Nor in Los Angeles. Yet a film like SYMPHONIE PASTORALE played here four months. LA BELLE ET LA BETE, just as long. As far as your and my showings are concerned, it must be a difference in audience. In my effort to keep the films of Art in Cinema on a liberal aesthetic par with the rest of the modern art that is hung on the walls here, and on a par with the presentations of the San Francisco Symphony Orchestra which holds forth next door at the Opera House, the keynote has been strictly just what it says: Art in cinematic form; the cinema as art. If I get too ideological or partisan you can bet the audience will no longer remain the liberal and highly discriminating one it is. I've got to keep these films in line with the Museum's attitude towards all other manifestations of art. Its rather like walking a tightrope. A film like Etting's Oramunde was laughed off the screen here. Dovjhenko's Arsenal was considered one of the best we've ever shown. Window Cleaner was a flop here; someone said it was like a John Nesbit. A film like the very excellent Brotherhood of Man would be condemned only on the basis of its soap-box oratory—soundtrack—not because of its great message—but its "preachiness"—Yet in the case of Dovjhenko's wonderful film, although it drips with flag-waving in the case of the Ukrainian revolt, it is clearly one of the masterpieces of the silent film-as-art. At any rate, I am discussing the wide difference in audience groups. It is really amazing, and I have no satisfactory answer to it.

I do hope you can continue on and help widen the field for the independent experimenter. Hollywood seems to be getting caught with its pants down; this could become the Age of Reason for the film as a mature medium of communication and expression. But it needs a big and liberal hearing for its small, kicked-around experimenters. The cost of production which results in necessary higher rentals for these films is, as you say, a hitch, but perhaps this can be adjusted with the growth of interest.

Both Dorsey Alexander's films and my film are out on a showing down South. Dorsey has three of them, beside his old BIRTH OF A SPHERE. I'll send them to you when I get them back. I have not seen Belson lately, and you'll have to write him for a print of TRANSMUTATION. The other information is enclosed.

Have you come across anything new in our line? I have a line up on quite a bit of material, but am not at all sure yet, and much of it is from second-hand sources, so I can't be sure.

Best of luck;

Sincerely,

[hw] Frank

Reprinted by permission of Barbara Stauffacher Solomon.

[No date is indicated on this letter, but—given that the Broughton show referred to occurred in March 1949—April seems a likely date for Stauffacher's letter (see also the letters between Vogel and Broughton on 3/25/49 and 4/12/49).]

✦ ✦ ✦ ✦ ✦

Illustration 34. Frank Stauffacher (*left*) and James Broughton filming *Mother's Day.*

Letter to Amos Vogel from Sidney Peterson, 5/23/49

May 23 1949
San Francisco, California

Dear Mr. Vogel:

Thanks for the check to The Petrified Dog and the Clinic of Stumble. I agree that I can do a little more cutting on The Pet. Dog. Incidentally, while I am very aware that the spectator is stirred up a bit and antagonized, it <u>doesn't</u> make me particularly happy. In this case the effect is incidental to the purpose. My feeling is that there are certain things that can only be reached through the nightmare and if the spectator sticks at the nightmare, I'm sorry, I don't enjoy his discomfort, on the other hand I see no other way of doing what I wanted to do, at least in this case....

In the Clinic I find the disintegration of imposed image and main action at least as interesting as their integration. If the thing had come off completely you would not have distinguished superimposition from main action... the dance, in a sense, gets in the way of the formal value of the film. One tends, no doubt, to try to follow it and see the superimposition as a kind of commentary. Sometimes it's a commentary and sometimes it isn't. Next time you see it try looking at the "superimposition" as though IT were the main action and the dance, the smaller figures, a mere thread of continuity constantly referring to the other images as carrying the burden of meaning if not of sense.... Good Lord no, I don't mind your mentioning good, bad and indifferent points about my films! As you say we are all together and I am not interested in being flattered.

About Belgium: The only extra prints I can send you are The Potted Psalm and The Cage, which I will do. I suggest that you send The Potted Psalm, The Cage and Clinic of Stumble. Three's enough. That'll leave you with prints of The PP, The Cage and Horror Dream. I have to have the print you have of The Petrified Dog back here for a little bit and will then return it to you. It's got to be shown at the end of the semester at the school here. Along with the new film, Mr. Frenhofer and the Minotaur, which is a (again) surrealist version of Balzac's story. At the moment I think it's the best of the lot. I'll send it along to you sometime this summer. Incidentally I'm running the film workshop here this summer session so that means another film. Don't know what yet. This Fall I'm doing a long documentary of (of all things) Persian students on the west coast; at the moment this is confidential. Also, this summer, some psychiatric documentary intended primarally for teaching purposes in medical schools but which may turnout to be something for you too.... Anyway will you take care of the three films for Belgium and send me back The Petrified Dog and I'll send The Cage and The Potted Psalm along.

Sincerely,

[hw] Sidney Peterson

Sidney Peterson

PS. Glad you had a pleasant chat with Mrs. Campbell. Together we constitute a new film company, CP Films. We expect to get rolling this Fall with a continuing schedule. Experimental, documentary and what have you.

SP

[hw] PPS: I'll send a contract along shortly: There are one or two points I want to think over. S.P

Reprinted by permission of Sidney Peterson.

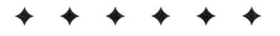

❖ ❖ ❖ ❖ ❖ ❖

Letter to Amos Vogel from Gregory Markopoulos, 5/31/49

[hw] 5/31/49

Dear Amos,

In answer to your letter of the 27th, I regret that I do not have another copy of LYSIS. I checked with the film valot and the exact footage of the film is 925', at appr. $ .125 a ft. or about $106.63. I have no funds to pay for the print, or I would consider it. If you think of any other solution, I should be happy to hear of it. Nevertheless, when do you need the print?

You see, Amos, I am one of those few film experementalist, that give all they have towards the making of the films. There are four of us in Los Angeles, each going our own way in making these films. But for us it is not just an experemental film, it is more than that, it is, each film, a step towards our goal of being someday the first film poets or creators of this country. That is the way I feel about it, and I know the other three expermentalists feel the same way about it. I am the first to make such a statement, in an effort to make you understand that which we are striving to do, <u>in each our own way</u>. <u>Confidentially; please:</u> the others I speak of are Curtis Harrington, Chester Kessler, Kenneth Anger, and my self.

At the moment, I must get together such a pathetic sum: $575.00 to finish my 35mm. film. To make you realize further: when I began THE DEAD ONES, I had no funds whatsoever. I merely talked one of the companies into letting me have some black and white film (surplus) for a time. They finally agreed. The film was developed at Consolidated, only because I begged them to do so, with each film footage that I shot, bit by bit. The camera was practically shanghaied from Goldwyn Studios. Need I say more! but my work continues; and others struggle along also.

As to Objectif 49, I am waiting for a letter of theirs, and we shall see. At any rate the film THE DEAD ONES will be sent to you first for showing, before it is sent abroad.

If I manage to talk the film lab. in making a print of Lysis, or procure the necessary money, I'll ship it to you air-express, the moment it is finished. Or you let me know of any ideas.

Cordially,

[hw] Gregory J. Markopoulos

Reprinted by permission of the Estate of Gregory J. Markopoulos/ Courtesy Tenemos, Inc.

✦ ✦ ✦ ✦ ✦ ✦

Letter to Gregory Markopoulos from Amos Vogel, 6/8/49

June 8, 1949

Dear Gregory Markopoulos,

your last letter once again showed me the so difficult and often unbearable conditions under which experimental film producers operate. I only wish we could help you more than what we are already doing. Needless to say, through our activities both in exhibition and distribution, we are increasing knowledge and awareness of those films, and are opening up wider possibilities for the future. But we must all be patient.

If you were a documentary film producer, you may have more opportunities to get money for your work, but then again, you would almost inevitably have to prostitute your artistic talent in order to make sponsored films for button manufacturers or whiskey firms. In short, film, as everything else, is a commodity in our money-mad society, and is subject to the same laws as others. It remains difficult, if not often impossible to carry on independent artistic activity inspite of all the odds. You and your friends are to be congratulated for your tenacity and determination to remain free of prostituting agreements.

I have no other solution on LYSIS, but as long as rentals do not pick up (and they cannot be expected to during the summer, inspite of the catalog which will be ready within 3-4 weeks) I cannot suggest to you to spend $ 100 just to have another print of it. We'll just have to see that Belgium returns the print soon.

Sincerely,

[Amos Vogel]

✦ ✦ ✦ ✦ ✦ ✦

Letter to Amos Vogel from Frank Stauffacher, 7/15/49

San Francisco Museum of Art [...]

July 15, 1949

Dear Amos,

Sorry for such a long delay in answering you. It was because I've been away from the film-showing matters for quite awhile. But now that the Fall is approaching, I'm back at it again, trying to arrange a new series—and answer letters by now criminally overdue. To get immediately to your questions, I'll answer them in order: Hal McCormick's address is 2074 17th Ave., S.F. 16. He spends most of his time over at the University of Cal. and I do not see him very often. Martin Metal gave me your letter to him, and asked me to answer for him. He says that you may use COLOR whenever you wish on your Fall program. As for distributing it, you can do so, the only hitch at this time being that he does not have enough money to make another print, and besides, the original of this film is in the possession of The Institute of Design, Chicago, who financed the making of it when he was a member of their faculty. He has since broken relationship with them, and so only has this one print. That brings up the question of who actually has the rights to it. He feels sure they would not react, although you could possibly get direct response from them. Try writing them. If no reaction, then perhaps he could do something. The only thing as far as signing a contract with you goes is that he does not wish to give you an exclusive right to its handling as there are often small groups showings of these films around in this region, and they are supplied by odds and ends that are available at the moment from us here at the Museum. There is no set rental fee for the films. Like a physician's fees, they are set at what the traffic will bear— sometimes nothing.

Metal and I are working on another film made in conjunction with his classes at City College, and it should be ready easily by Fall. I'll let you know. I hesitate to give you carte blanche on it because it may turn out to be a lemon, as they sometimes do. It will be called FORM EVOLUTION.

As for ZIGZAG, you are welcome to use it on your Fall program. I've been asking $5.00 rental for it. Glad you liked it. You could handle its distribution if you wished, only that same stipulation as above holds. Of course I'll have to get other prints, and add an "end" title to it (which it does not now have). If you wish notes, releases, etc. on it, those I could send.

I am definitely interested in renting Hugo Lateltin's COLOR DESIGNS #1 upon your recommendation, and the date would be Sept. 30. Let me know the rental, and whether or not it will be possible to have for that date. Also, I will finally capitulate and ask for Etting's POEM 8. If I could get this, I would like to have it for Sept. 23. I say this because our series this year will only be four weeks, starting on the 23rd of September. I do want to see the Etting film before I show it—so by having it here by the 23rd, I could look at it, and place it for showing the following week—the 30th. If you needed it back at that time I could send it air express. Could all this be done? Do you have any descriptive material on GEOGRAPHY OF THE BODY? Also, send me your catalogue when it becomes available, for at the last minute I would probably need other items.

That showing which Broughton attended must have been an exception because I hear nothing but successful reports from all your subsequent programs. Anyhow, I understand the problem of putting on the sort of film fare that you do in a large place like N.Y.—it is terribly difficult handling certain attitudes in the audience, in fact impossible.

There are a lot of local films in production. Peterson has a new one—the best he's made so far, I think. I myself have one about half finished, a kind of personal documentary of a place. I intend having it finished by the Fall. It is held up by lack of money for a sound track. The track will be a rather important factor in the whole, and so I'm waiting till I scrape enough together. It will be called SAUSALITO.

That's about it. Again, pardon my tardiness. I'll be more prompt now that I'm working around a typewriter more.

Sincerely yours,

[hw] Frank Stauffacher

Frank Stauffacher

Reprinted by permission of Barbara Stauffacher Solomon.

✦ ✦ ✦ ✦ ✦ ✦

Mr. Harper, "The Only Path," *Harper's*, 7/49

At the Central Needle Trades Auditorium on West 24th Street, in one of New York's several industrial high schools, enormous fresco murals of exploited immigrants and early heroes of trade unionism look down from the walls on one of the most remarkable audiences in the city. Here, on a summery evening in early May, was held the eighth and last showing in the season of Cinema 16, a non-profit cultural society incorporated under the educational laws of the state "to further the appreciation of the motion picture as an art and as a social force." The several thousands who were present that evening—they filled the auditorium for two complete performances—will thus have to wait until fall to put up ten dollars apiece for another eight programs of non-commercial films that fall under the general headings of educational, artistic, experimental, scientific, or forbidden the public by censorship.

Since Cinema 16 is less than two years old, and since it has neither advertised extensively nor received wide publicity, not the least remarkable thing about the audience is its size. Before I first went to one of the programs, I remembered having heard Cinema 16 described as "a few people who are interested in film," and I foolishly expected this to mean several hundred—about as many, perhaps, as would fill the Provincetown Playhouse on Macdougal Street, where Cinema 16 began. That a tiny group of movie enthusiasts should grow so quickly is in part a tribute to the Society's sensible programming, but it is also specific and inescapable evidence of the natural enthusiasm for the national art form that no number of bad movies will ever dampen out. Quite the reverse, in fact. After one evening's performance, I asked Siegfried Kracauer, one of the most penetrating film critics in the country and a mainstay of Cinema 16, what was the secret of its success. "Every time Hollywood makes a picture," he said, "more people come in here."

Cinema 16—the sixteen stands for sixteen millimeter—provides its members not only with the eight closed performances but also with lectures, forums, and discounts on tickets at selected foreign film houses, on film and photographic books, on camera merchandise, and on rental equipment and films and an information service on all American films that fall within the area of its interest. This, according to Amos Vogel, the society's founder, moving spirit, and executive secretary, is one of his most exacting jobs. "There are plenty of these films around and being made," he says, "the only problem is to find them—then look them over and winnow out the best. I don't believe, though, that there's one worth mentioning that we don't know about." An average program, along with something as conventional as the Riethof Production's trailer for Modern Art, is just as likely to include a silent film made at the University of Pennsylvania of the effect of alcohol on cats, plus a documentary on Indonesian independence made by a maritime union in Australia, and a humorous short subject about washing the windows of the Empire State Building.

But if you go to Cinema 16 in the fall, or if you are ever prompted to start a film society on your own elsewhere, don't spend all your time watching the movies: watch the audience. Perhaps it was the proletarian surroundings of the showing in May, or the fact that on this evening one of the films was Pare Lorentz' "The River," that made me conscious of how far the enthusiasts of the twenties and thirties have come toward maturity, but at least I am certain that I have never seen so intelligent a cross-section of class and race. Interest in film apparently does not generate the introspective refinements that clutter up chamber music, ballet, or the opera; whatever draws people together in the quality of the dancing images on the screen is a Leveler of a very new kind, for it levels up. "I shall be content to assert," wrote John Grierson in the *Hollywood Quarterly*, "that it is a basic tenet of documentary theory that the primary search is not for beauty, but for the fact of the matter, and that the fact of the matter is the only path to beauty that will not soon wear down." Perhaps it is also a definition of the Cinema 16 audience that they would agree with him.

Reprinted by permission of *Harper's*.

✦ ✦ ✦ ✦ ✦ ✦

Amos Vogel, "Film Do's and Don'ts," *Saturday Review*, 8/20/49

The experiences I have had since helping to found an organization in New York called "Cinema 16" prove, it seems to me, that with ingenuity, perseverance, knowledge of films, and luck, anyone can operate a film society. A non-profit membership organization presenting unusual documentary and experimental films, Cinema 16 has acquired more than 2,000 yearly members since it was founded in 1947, making it the largest film society in the country. Started by people with enough confidence in the non-fiction film to believe that there must be a larger potential audience for them than those consisting of school children, members of women's clubs, and hospital inmates, it aims at the "glorification" of the fact film. Its programs read like a "Who's Who" of many of the best fact and avant-garde films, contemporary as well as classic, and its activities have been reported locally and nationally in major newspapers, magazines, and on the air. Members are drawn from seven states, and include teachers, artists, workers, program directors, film producers, and businessmen. Sponsors include Robert Flaherty, Richard Griffith, Paul Rotha, Jean Benoit-Levy, Dr. Siegfried Kracauer, Arthur Knight, Mary Losey, Hans Richter, John Huston, and Jean Renoir.

Activity of any kind is impossible without the committing of errors. Nevertheless, if you are determined to run a local film society—and go ahead you should—here is some information to help you avoid obvious mistakes.

It is a catastrophic fallacy to assume that running a film society involves nothing more than an idealistic concern with good films, coupled with their lackadaisical presentation to willing audiences. On the contrary, the individual brave enough to venture into this troublesome field, must be—no matter what the size of the society—an organizer, promoter, publicist and copywriter, businessman, public speaker, and artist; a conscientious, if not pedantic, person versed in mass psychology. He must have roots in his community. And he must know a good film when he sees it.

Thus you need film sources and film evaluation. The two are distinct. More often than not, you will have neither time nor money to preview films. Distributors' catalogs are not always objective guides. Many catalogs overlap, rental rates vary with various distributors. It is therefore best first to get the two basic master catalogs available: "The Educational Film Guide" (H. W. Wilson Co., 950 University Avenue, New York); and "The Blue Book of 16mm. Films" (Educational Screen, 64 East Lake Street, Chicago). Both list practically all presently available 16mm. films and their sources, from whom you may obtain further catalogs. "The Educational Film Guide" features more detailed evaluations. "The Educator's Guide to Free Films" (Educator's Progress Service, Randolph, Wis.) lists a great number of free films. New York's Museum of Modern Art Circulating Film Library (11 West 53rd Street, New York) has the finest and most comprehensive collection for film societies, with use of their film restricted to bona-fide membership and non-profit organizations. Scientific films (restricted to special groups) are obtainable from the Psychological Cinema Register (Pennsylvania State College, State College, Pa.); experimental and avant-garde films from Cinema 16 (59 Park Avenue, New York).

For information and reviews of new releases you will find it important to subscribe to leading 16mm. magazines, such as *Film World* (6047 Hollywood Blvd., Los Angeles, Cal.); *Film News* (13 East 37th Street, New York); *Educational Screen* (64 East Lake Street, Chicago Ill.). Get back numbers of the *Film Forum Review* (Institute of Adult Education, Teachers College, Columbia University, New York) which—together with the *Saturday Review of Literature*—has presented some of the most mature evaluations of 16mm. films. Get the EFIA evaluations, on 3 x 5 cards, by joining The Educational Film Library Association, at 1600 Broadway, New York.

Do not think it easy to get an audience just because you have a film that you alone know to be good; you must let your fellow man know that it is worth his while to see it. Neither must you assume that an audience of twenty is your "maximum." Publicize your show in local newspapers by sending them announcements and news stories. Fire your local movie critic with the importance of your project. Give storekeepers a pass as they will display your window cards. Send program announcements to all organizations, schools, and clubs for display on their bulletin boards. If you show a film on Greece, for example, send special announcement and block tickets to local Greek organizations. Do the same with your parent-teacher groups when you have a film on child education. Contact your radio or TV station; they will help if you can show that you are performing a community service.

Names and addresses are your greatest assets. Get names from clubs, camera clubs, women's, parent-teacher, YMCA, and labor groups. Mail copies of your program to them. Build up your own mailing list. Never let anyone see a show without getting his name. Hand out interest blanks or offer a special incentive so you will get the names. If your budget allows it, run a neatly designed small ad in your paper with a coupon for name and address.

After you have found an audience, you must learn to hold it by proper programming. This is where you are on your own. If you haven't the "feel" for balanced programs, you will fail. The science of programming cannot be taught; it requires psychological insight into the likes of other people and continuing contact with your specific audience to permit you to correct yourself as you go along. Five excellent and serious social documentaries may produce one very bad program. You must lighten programs by humorous shorts, dance or music films, cartoons. A color short brightens any program, and if presented at the end, often provides a much-needed fillip. A variety of films is usually preferable to an entire evening of one subject. If yours is a functional program, centered around documentaries on, say, atomic energy, variety can be introduced by a cartoon ("One World or None").

Never overpower your audience with too many or too "heavy" films; moderation and variety will make them come back for more the next time.

Carelessness and amateurishness are the bane of the 16mm. industry.

Portable equipment and low film rentals have enabled unqualified individuals to "slap together" a program, present it one night—thus setting back 16mm. in the particular community for another five years. It is an error to assume that a good film will "go across" no matter how it is presented. Showmanship is one of the first prerequisites of a successful film society.

Before you show, test your auditorium for acoustics, comfortable heating arrangements, proper electrical connections. Check or provide shades to keep all light from entering. If possible, use curtains or black fabric to mask off the screen to prevent the usual "naked" 16mm. screen, complete with tripod, from impressing your audience with the amateurishness of the performance. If there is no booth, place the projector above the heads of the audience where its noise will be least audible. If you have a booth, arrange for a 50¢ buzzer and code system to communicate with the projectionist who is almost as important to your show as a good film. Check and clean your prints; if possible, splice them onto larger reels, reducing work at the performance, and lending it greater professional flavor. Test your projector. If you rent one, and have no time to check it, don't run your show. You will still keep more good-will than by exposing your audience to the horrors of an improperly working machine, while damaging prints at the same time.

During the show, keep all the doors closed. Ask the projectionist to move quietly and, if he has brought his family to watch him, to wait to discuss personal matters until after the show. Check and correct your sound constantly (sound level varies greatly on 16mm.); watch for focusing, framing, and dirt in the aperture. Be sure not to flash the leader on the screen.

In general, remember that you are a missionary for a wider use of 16mm. films and that you should try approximating professional theatre standards, with the possible exception of providing popcorn or exhibiting insipid films. For further information, get "The Projectionist's Manual" (Educational Film Library Association, 1600 Broadway, New York) or "Projecting Motion Pictures in the Class Room" (American Council on Education, 744 Jackson Place, Washington, D.C.).

Legal matters are often important. Consult a lawyer, ask him to serve on your board if you have no money to pay him. Find out about fire regulations, licenses, censorship regulations.

Whatever you do, be prepared for much work, unexpected and recurrent headaches, no remuneration—except the deep satisfaction that comes from accomplishing a very much needed job: that of bringing socially purposeful and artistically significant films to more and more people.

Reprinted by permission of *Saturday Review*.

✦ ✦ ✦ ✦ ✦ ✦

Program Announcement, Fall 1949

October 1949

Over Dependency
Third in an unusual series of films based on actual psychiatric case histories. Produced in cooperation with the Allen Memorial Institute of Psychiatry.

Development of the Chick Embryo
Julian Huxley's unique film study of the origin of life. Startling micro-photography reveals the mysteries of embryonic development

Poem 8
The film as a medium of poetry: Symbolic interpretation of a man's love life seen entirely through the protagonist's eyes. Produced by Emlen Etting.

The Assassination of King Alexander of Yugoslavia
This remarkable film record takes you "behind the scenes" of movie production in showing both the edited version as presented in theatres, as well as all original, uncut footage shot of this dramatic event.

Picture in Your Mind
Philip Stapp's unorthodox experimental animations make this film and its social message a provocative visual experience. International Prize Winner at 1949 Film Festival in Belgium. Music by Gene Forrell.

November 1949

No Credit
Colorful modeling clay comes to life in a charmingly informal and spontaneous film experiment. Produced by Leonard Tregillus and Ralph Luce.

Feeling All-Right
A forthright and dramatic film about syphilis performed entirely by Negro actors. Music by Louis Applebaum ("Lost Boundaries").

Bharatnatyam
Exciting film record of a classical Indian dance with close-ups of its complex gesture language. Produced by Ezra Mir.

Explosions on the Sun
A spectacular portrayal of turbulent solar disturbances, never before captured on film. Photographed at Harvard Coronograph Station by Professor D. H. Menzel. "A remarkable, awe inspiring motion picture...the first of its kind!" (*The N. Y. Times*)

Light Reflections
Multicolored transparent plastics create a fantastic abstract ballet, accompanied by an unusual musical score. Produced by the noted American painter and sculptor, James Davis.

New Earth
Joris Ivens' starkly dramatic documentary classic is a masterpiece of the cinema. This is the complete, uncut version, seldom shown because of its uncompromising social realism.

Illustration 35. Detail from *New Earth* (1934) by Joris Ivens. Courtesy Museum of Modern Art Film Stills Archive.

December 1949

3 Recent Experimental Films: U.S.

Dime Story by Dorsey Alexander
The wonders of the Ten Cent Store: Hundreds of fascinating objects comes to riotous life in this delightful experimental film. In color.

Le Bijou by Francis Lee
The perilous adventures of a colorful jewel representing the artist in search of creative fulfillment. Lee is a Guggenheim fellow for his work in films.

Geography of the Body by Willard Maas
An analogical pilgrimage of the terrors and splendors of the body as the undiscovered, the mysterious continent. Commentary by the British poet George Barker.

Children Growing Up with Others
Hidden cameras reveal an unstaged portrayal of childhood in this charming yet thought-provoking psychological film.

Early Films from the Unique Collection of Joseph Cornell
The magic, free abandon and creative imaginativeness of the early cinema are fully revealed in these unique and charming films, some of them not seen for 30 years. This medley of slapstick at its unspoiled best, unbridled trick photography, Gallic wit and unconscious avant-garde techniques includes: 3 Melies Magic shorts, *A Detective's Tour of the World, Hanky Panky Cards, Metamorphosis, The Automatic Moving Co.* and others.

January 1950

Valley Town
This powerful and deeply moving portrayal of unemployment is a documentary film classic. Produced by Willard Van Dyke, it has an outstanding musical score by Marc Blitzstein.

Hypnotic Behavior
Produced at Bucknell University for the Psychological Cinema Register. A subject in deep hypnosis experiences hallucinations, regressions to childhood, "blindness," and post-hypnotic disorientation.

Thomas Benton...The Making of a Mural
The camera catches a noted artist at work. Impressive close-ups clearly reveal his technique. In color.

The Petrified Dog
This violent surrealist film evokes a child's nightmare universe filled with eternal triangles, macabre slapstick, chiropractors, and tortured fantasies of birth, life and death. Accompanied by a novel experimental soundtrack. Produced by Sidney Peterson at Workshop 20 of the California School of Fine Arts.

Hausa Village
Strange preparations for a wedding in Nigeria. A unique anthropological film record.

✦ ✦ ✦ ✦ ✦ ✦

Archer Winsten, "Cinema 16 Begins Its Third Season," *New York Post*, 9/14/49

As Executive Sec'y Amos Vogel girds his 16mm. loins for his third year of adventures in the unknown world of narrow gauge films, the future looks very promising. This Cinema 16 organization has had a phenomenal growth and success since its tentative start at the Provincetown Playhouse in October of 1947. They had planned four performances of their collection of unusual 16mm. films, hoping that the public would be sufficiently interested to pay expenses. Instead, twenty performances were necessary, selling out to 8,000 spectators.

By April of the next year censorship trouble had dictated the exclusion of the general public in favor of private showings to membership only. There were too many genuinely interesting items, like "The Private Life of a Cat," that induced panic among the non-experimental members of the Board of N. Y. Censors. But the general public could still join the organization at an expense of $10.00 or less, depending on the number in a group, student status, etc. This year's program of forty-seven films at eight showings brings the average admission charge down to a very reasonable level. Inquiries should be directed to Cinema 16, 59 Park Avenue, New York 16, N. Y. (Tel. MU. 9-7288).

Programs to Be Repeated

In addition to the regular evening showings at the Central Needle Trades Auditorium on West 24th Street, the same programs will be repeated on the following Sunday mornings at the more intimate and charming Paris Theatre on 58th Street.

Judging from past programs and descriptive comment on future bills, the extreme variety of each session guarantees something of intense interest for every cinematic taste. Experimental, scientific, psychological, art, sociological abstract and unclassifiable items achieve a scatter-gun coverage that stimulates approval and criticism in wholesale quantities. The one sure result is cinema fare at an opposite pole from the rutted entertainment of the movie palaces. As such, Cinema 16 is unique and stimulating to those who have given up on the latter.

Mr. Vogel, however, is careful to point out that the venture's success (2,600 members currently) is not a manifestation without parallel. The desire for this kind of picture seems to be countrywide. Already the Cinema 16 programs are scheduled for showings in Washington, Chicago, and Los Angeles. The organization has been in touch with 150 similar groups throughout the country, some having as few as twenty members and the largest being the 600-strong group at the San Francisco Museum of Art.

The Field Expands

The field of pictures still to be brought to light expands the more it is explored. Mr. Vogel is consciously moving slowly backward through some forty years of experimental film work. One of this year's programs includes: "Early Films from the Unique Collection of Joseph Cornell." Three Melies magic shorts are among them, along with early slapstick and "unconscious avant-garde techniques." Another exciting prospect on the same December program is "Geography of the Body" by Willard Maas. This is described as "An analogical pilgrimage of the terrors and splendours of the body as the undiscovered, the mysterious continent." Extreme magnification, commentary by the British poet, George Barker, and a simple wholesome approach to the nude are said to render this picture as unacceptable to the prudish as it will be revealing to the liberated.

This department's continuing praise of Cinema 16 is not to be taken as blanket approval of all their choices. I can state positively, though, that they have never put on a program which was, for me, a total delight or a complete failure. The percentage has always stood in favor of the intellectually stimulating. But most of all, Cinema 16 offers the opportunity of seeing the best of a vast field of production of which only specialists are even aware. For every picture shown, ten have been inspected. Speaking both as professional and amateur movie-goer, I wouldn't want to miss them.

Reprinted by permission of the *New York Post*.

❖ ❖ ❖ ❖ ❖ ❖

Letter to Amos Vogel from Frank Stauffacher 10/17/49

San Francisco Museum of Art [. . .]

Oct. 17, 1949

Dear Amos,

Thank you very much for your long and informative letter. It is very gratifying to learn that Cinema 16 has really climbed up to a position of eminence in this most difficult field. I am in a position to know the enormous amount of discouraging work connected with showing out-of-the way films—even though I have always had the backing of the museum and the existence of an auditorium. But you have built Cinema 16 singlehandedly, and you are certainly to be congratulated and offered continued help, whatever it may be.

Our organization will continue to function as usual. Our successes—always doubted before a series,—and always beyond expectations after every seat is sold, and there is no more standing room—make us realize that we must continue, as this kind of an outlet is definitely needed. And it is due to this, I feel, that this area continues to be the seat of a kind of experimental film renaissance.

In spite of this, however, I personally get nothing out of the Art in Cinema showings beyond my personal expenses. It has been entirely a labor of love, and that is why, when there are no series coming up, I drop the whole project temporarily and plunge into something else. It is not my desire to show films at all. I'd rather make them. But I am so complexly bound up with the field, and with Art in Cinema, that I can't seem to get out of it completely, and turn it over to someone else. Every time we have tried that, other elements immediately come in—personal ambitions, attempts to "take over" and utilize for personal gain or partisan policies, etc.—all the elements that would be the death of this organization as a liberal, flexible, and experimental outlet.

Previously I've been in a position financially to be able to absorb the losses of my own time spent on Art in Cinema. The trip to N.Y. last year was out of my own pocket, and resulted in benefit to Art in Cinema. But this year, having gotten married, with more personal expenses, less income, I am in a rough financial position even though Art in Cinema has money in the bank. I have made arrangements to take a more substantial percentage of this money, but it really could not be a very large, steady, month-to-month income unless we put on more frequent showings, and that I don't care to do. It would involve me further in a field that is actually only of secondary interest (to me).

I am telling you all of this because it leads directly to such a seemingly insignificant subject as the distribution of my own two or three films. In other words, where I wouldn't give a damn last year about income from a couple of little films, this year it is a different matter, and I suddenly realize that I could make a certain amount of income from them. Particularly when I found that the film SAUSALITO had a very popular and favourable reaction when I showed it here a couple weeks ago. (This may be partially due to the familiarity of its subject matter with local audiences; I don't know.) At any rate, this is, very sincerely, my position: Personally in debt on all sides; having to look everywhere for a better income. Under these circumstances it is my responsibility to myself to find the most remunerative outlet for my films—small as that may be—even though I don't, naturally, expect to depend too much on that income since it can't amount to very much, no matter which way I look at it. You can see my position.

Anyway, I'll be glad to send you SAUSALITO, ZIGZAG. GOETHE IN S. F. is not yet finished, but will be, I hope, in time for this Friday evening showing—an extra program added to the series to take care of a lot of the stuff we had no room for. I can't send these, however, for about two weeks as they will be shown at several other programs in Berkeley, and besides, I want to smooth out the continuity of SAUSALITO, and make another print. It holds together beautifully, in part, other parts fall apart. It is 400', black and white, sound.

I have no stills from ZIGZAG. Stills from SAUSALITO, I think I sent you a couple. Will enclose program notes, such as they are. I will send you these films for your examination. You may find SAUSALITO a bit too esoteric for your audiences. It is a personal documentary of a place, set in a poetic form.

Thank you very much for the information sent. I am returning the sheet with the information you requested.

Let me hear your reaction to my remarks concerning this matter. My position is dictated by acute necessity.

Sincerely yours,

[hw] Frank Stauffacher

Frank Stauffacher

Reprinted by permission of Barbara Stauffacher Solomon.

✦ ✦ ✦ ✦ ✦

Letter to Frank Stauffacher from Amos Vogel, 11/15/49

November 15, 1949

Mr. Frank Stauffacher
Art in Cinema
San Francisco Museum of Art
San Francisco 2, Calif.

Dear Frank:

Your recent letter was both detailed, frank, and not altogether clear.

I fully appreciate the personal difficulties that you are involved in and I fully agree with you that you have to find the most remunerative outlet for your films that you can possibly find. What, exactly, follows?

I think it would be very unfortunate if for personal reasons you would permit one of the great many "partisan" film makers or "film aesthetes" to take over Art in Cinema. However much you may dislike being an exhibitor, I hope you will continue also in this capacity. You have done an outstanding job. Your work is recognized all over the country, and your aim to provide a "liberal, flexible and non-partisan experimental film outlet" is fully appreciated everywhere.

It seems obvious to me that without taking a "commercial attitude" toward Art in Cinema, you should take out as much as you personally need to continue and expand the project. In a society based on money, you cannot be expected to give your time and effort without the slightest remuneration. At the same time, Art in Cinema and the film artists can rely on you to take out the minimum rather than the maximum necessary for the successful continuation of the project, but I must say that I have noticed a certain modesty on your part, or rather a reluctance to take what is due you. Needless to say, just as you help the film producers, the project has to help you so that you can continue the job of making the <u>larger</u> work known to wider audiences.

You may not like me to say this, but I do think that the best development for you and the experimental film makers on the West Coast would consist of an <u>expansion</u> rather than a contraction of Art in Cinema's activities by more shows, more publicity, and more expensive promotion to be recouped by greater income. If you were not so reluctant to continue as exhibitor, perhaps some closer collaboration with Cinema 16 might be possible. What do you think ?

Please send us SAUSALITO, ZIG ZAG, FORM EVOLUTION, and GOETHE IN SAN FRANCISCO as soon as possible, as we are now setting up our programs until the summer. Please do not delay.

Will you send me Shoemaker's address and tell me about any new films you may have heard about.

VAN GOGH is now available from the Museum of Modern Art, MICHELANGELO should be available soon from Film Program Services. Also McLaren's new short, BEGONE, DULL CARE (National Film Board of Canada).

Sincerely yours,

Amos Vogel
Cinema 16
AV:MG

✦ ✦ ✦ ✦ ✦ ✦

Letter to Gregory Markopoulos from Amos Vogel, 12/15/49

December 5, 1949

Mr. Gregory Markopoulos
523 Bush St.
Toledo 11, Ohio

Dear Gregory:

I was somewhat surprised by the contents of your last letter. It contained references to a number of problems which it is very difficult to discuss in a letter, and I should have thought that you would have taken the opportunity to discuss them with me when you were in New York. However, you preferred not to.

1. Enclosed find your stills.

2. I cannot possibly send you the sound print of PSYCHE as it is too consistently booked. I am instead forwarding the only silent print we have (I cannot understand your reference to "two silent prints of PSYCHE in our possession": we do not have the print that was in England). I can send you LYSIS and CHARMIDES, but only for a limited time. Let me know from when to when you need them so that we will know to refuse bookings during this period of time. We already have bookings for them for February 18th and March 12th.

3. I am enclosing a list of addresses of renters.

4. I am enclosing statement and check through December 1st. Our usual procedure is to send statements once every three months; the only reason we didn't send one in December was because of the fact that there had been no bookings whatsoever during the summer months. Your request for monthly statements would simply entail more work for us and would be of very little help to you. I hope you will find the "once every three months" procedure acceptable.

5. As to rental rates, whether you know it or not, rental rates paid for experimental films are already far higher than rentals paid for other films. For example, GREAT EXPECTATIONS or SHOE SHINE can be rented for less money than PSYCHE. The difficulty with taking a "brief glance" at the crowded Hunter College Auditorium is that one sees the possible income but not the manifold expenses that go into putting on a show of this kind. I cannot attempt to explain the intricacies of our business to you in a letter—the exorbitant costs of mailings, advertisements, postage, etc. I can only assure you that we would be unable to pay any more for rentals than what we are paying now.

I think a misconception has arisen according to which we have an extremely profitable business operation here, which thrives on the products of individual film producers. The real situation is different. We struggled for three hard years to get to the point we have now reached, and even with our present type of operation, we would simply have to close as of today, if we had to pay higher film rentals, leaving you with nothing. When during the first year of our existence, we continued to operate at an even greater loss and at one time presented two showings for 8 people due to a blizzard, we made no attempt to cut our payment to producers, nor did the producers suggest we pay less "since rentals are based on attendance." As a matter of fact: 1. All 16mm rentals are based on flat fees and <u>not</u> on percentages. 2. The rental rate for "theatrical showings" is specified here in the contract as $30.00. #3. This rate is already higher than that paid for other experimental films of the same calibre or running time.

Nevertheless, if our method of operation should ever expand into a more successful or stable set-up than we have at present, I will have no objections to discussing a mutually satisfactory arrangement for possible future bookings.

But you should understand that we have always tried to maintain a relationship with experimental film producers which is based on close collaboration between pioneers in a field which, it appears to us, would be of interest only to idealists and not to business men. The future of the experimental film movement lies in the hands not only of the producers, but also of the distributors and exhibitors. We feel—with all due modesty—that we have done our part in publicizing and making known the work of the new avant-garde to audiences nationally that had not even been aware of their very existence. This, incidentally, is a form of intangible payment which is far more important in the long run for out-of-town bookings and other ways of increasing your revenue than a few extra dollars for a single rental.

We are looking forward to receiving THE DEAD ONES.

Very sincerely, yours,

Amos Vogel
Cinema 16
AV:MG

P.S.—The following paragraph is an excerpt from a letter of one of our subscribers, Ted Reynolds, 400 East 50 Street, New York City:

"Your November 25th showing of experimental films was an amazing experience—certainly an extraordinary collection of <u>good</u> avant-garde films. I look forward to any future repeat showings you may have of the psychological films. The first viewing of them was an almost breathtaking experience. Markopoulos' "Psyche" is the most fascinating film poem since "Blood of a Poet" and one of the few films I cannot find alterable fault with. Thank you for this wonderful showing."

✦ ✦ ✦ ✦ ✦ ✦

Program Announcement, Spring 1950

March 1950

Human Beginnings
An unprecedented experiment in sex education for the 5-year-old. Produced by Eddie Albert, this is a worthy successor to his controversial Human Growth. 5-year-olds express their conceptions of birth and their feelings about the new baby in revealing drawings, modeling clay and spirited discussions. In color.

Be Gone, Dull Care
Norman McLaren's (*Fiddle-De-Dee*) newest film unreels a fantastic fabric of brilliant colors and tumultuous patterns set to boogie-woogie music. Hand-painted on film, frame by frame; no camera was used.

The Work of Arne Sucksdorff
Cinema 16 proudly presents *A Divided World* and *Valley of Dreams,* two films by one of the most distinguished documentary film producers of our time. Academy Award Winner of 1949.

The Fable of the Peacock
An ancient Hindu fable, charmingly interpreted in classical gesture language by Lakshimi Wana Singh. A Regency Production.

A Lecture-on-Film about *Odd Man Out*
What makes a motion picture "great"? Basil Wright, famed film producer (*Song of Ceylon*) and critic discusses and analyzes—on film—Carol Reed's *Odd Man Out,* with illustrations from the motion picture. The action of the film is stopped or repeated for clarification and analysis. Third in the "Critic and Film Series" produced by the British Film Institute for film societies.

April 1950

Proem
A delightful allegorical journey into the imaginary world of a chess board, inspired by Lewis Carroll and "acted" by animated modeling clay. This is a charming new film by the producers of the widely acclaimed *No Credit.*

It Takes All Kinds
5 young people are confronted with an identical obstacle and react in 5 different ways. They then reveal similarly different behavior patterns in their relations with the other sex. Directed by Alexander Hammid (*Forgotten Village, Private Life of a Cat*).

Experiments in the Revival of Organisms
An outstanding film record of the famous studies conducted at the Voronezh Institute of Experimental Physiology, including the unique experiments in which a dog's head, severed from the body, reacts to stimuli, and an animal is revived after having been dead for 15 minutes. Complete English narration by J. B. S. Haldane.

A Discussion-on-Film of Scenes from "Great Expectations"
A. Jympson Harman, English Film Critic, discusses and analyzes on film a key sequence from *Great Expectations.* The episode is shown more than once to indicate how horror and surprise is created in the mind of the spectator. First in the "Critic and Film Series" produced by the British Film Institute.

To Hear Your Banjo Play
A captivating medley of ballads, spirituals and square dances, featuring Pete Seeger, Sonny Terry, Woodie Guthrie. Directed by Willard Van Dyke. Photographed by Richard Leacock (*Louisiana Story*). Story by Alan Lomax.

May 1950

The Lead Shoes
A surrealist exploration of two ballads, "Edward" and "The Three Ravens," scrambled in jam session style and interwoven with a boogie-woogie score. Produced by Workshop 20 at California Institute of Fine Arts.

Unconscious Motivation
Produced by Dr. Lester F. Beck of the University of Oregon, this astonishing 40-minute motion picture is an unrehearsed, authentic clinical record, showing the inducement of an artificial neurosis by hypnotic suggestion in a young man and a young woman. Upon reawakening, the subjects, by means of dream analysis, ink blot and word association tests, gradually realize first the existence of a traumatic experience and then its content by slowly reconstructing the bogus events which caused it. Their reactions, discussion and self-analysis were spontaneous, unrehearsed and unpredictable: the result is a most unusual motion picture.

The Battle of San Pietro
A master of the cinema, John Huston (*Treasure of Sierra Madre*) portrays the horror of battle and the cruelty of its aftermath in unforgettable images that make this one of the great anti-war films of all times.

The Work of Oskar Fischinger
The father of the "absolute film" and internationally famous film experimentalist is here represented by three films: *Absolute Film Study No. 11* is an abstraction set to Mozart's "Divertissement"; *Allegretto,* a non-objective color film accompanied by jazz; *Motion Painting No. 1*—hand-painted in oil on glass—won the Grand Prix 1949 at the International Experimental Film Festival in Belgium.

June 1950

Film and Reality
A history of the documentary film as shown in the works of Sergei Eisenstein, John Grierson, Andre Gide, Jean Vigo, Robert Flaherty, Jean Painleve, Pare Lorentz, Louis de Rochemont, and accompanied by an authoritative commentary. Selected by Alberto Cavalcanti (*Dead of Night*). Assembled by Ernest Lindgren (Author, *The Art of Film*). Produced by the British National Film Library.

✦ ✦ ✦ ✦ ✦ ✦

Program Notes by Arthur Knight for Arne Sucksdorff's *Valley of Dreams* and *A Divided World*, Shown in March 1950

VALLEY OF DREAMS and A DIVIDED WORLD
Two films by Arne Sucksdorff. A Svensk Filmindustri Production. (20 min.)

"The films of Arne Sucksdorff fall into no conventional category. True, all his work to date has been in the field of short subjects, but none of them can be readily defined as a documentary, experimental, educational, scientific, or even as a nature film. For these short pictures are completely Sucksdorff's own, reflecting both his special interests and his particular philosophy. In making them, Sucksdorff is at once writer, director, cameraman, editor and sound technician. If he were a musician, he would probably write their scores too. Instead, he has worked as collaborator with a number of Sweden's foremost young composers, Erland von Koch, Stig Rybrant, Yngve Sjold and Hilding Rosenberg. All the elements of film making, Sucksdorff himself moulds and synthesizes into the final picture, often spending as much as six months on a single ten-minute subject.

Sucksdorff, a modest, handsome man still in his early thirties, had studied to become a naturalist in his native Sweden, but soon abandoned this for painting and drawing. In 1937 he entered an art school in Germany, at the same time taking up photography as a hobby. Here began the imposing collection of lenses and cameras that made possible his later films. He made his first picture in 1939, A SUMMER'S TALE, which not only won him a "Charlie"—the Swedish equivalent of our "Oscar"—but also got him his job with Svensk Filmindustri, the leading Swedish film company. He has remained there ever since. Because he works slowly, his output is not large. There are to date less than a dozen Sucksdorff films. But each is distinguished in its own way.

For his pictures, Sucksdorff prepares a conventional scenario, then goes off on location—more often than not in some wild and lonely place—and there lets the country itself suggest whatever changes are to be made. With infinite patience then he photographs the material he will need, often shooting hundreds of feet of film to procure the few frames that will be right for his purposes. Sound too is recorded on location. Returning to the studio at Stockholm, he painstakingly assembles his material, shaping it to his plan, adding the finishing touches of sparse commentary and music. The completed picture may be anywhere from one to four reels long. Sucksdorff lets his material dictate its own length. And that incidentally, is the source of his greatest difficulty in American commercial distribution where a short subject is always made to a required length of either one or two reels. Cutting down a Sucksdorff film to a single reel for theatrical release is no enviable assignment, so dense is its texture and so perfectly related are all the parts to the whole.

Fortunately, neither of the pictures on this program today has had to undergo that indignity. A DIVIDED WORLD is one of the best examples of Sucksdorff's wild life studies, embodying much of his own philosophy. It begins with an organist playing a Bach fantasia, an epitome of the safety and security of the civilized world. Then, slowly, the camera moves into a snow-covered wilderness, and the music is swallowed up in the night cries of animals and birds. The cruel, ceaseless struggle for survival is shown with shocking intensity as beast eats beast and nature stands by, impassive. When the camera turns back to the snug little house on the edge of the forest, civilization takes on new meanings. The music of Bach suggests the sublimation of primitive instincts through art and man's creation.

VALLEY OF DREAMS, on the other hand, is fantasy on a child's plane, a projection of the imaginings and yearnings of a little girl who dreams of the world on the other side of her valley. It is a lyric piece, reminiscent of nothing so much as the work of Robert J. Flaherty—the little child, the wise grandparent, and nature seen with an artist's eye. In fact, the whole body of Sucksdorff's work invites comparison with Flaherty's. Like Flaherty, Sucksdorff seeks the far-off places. Like Flaherty, he shows man against nature, or records a remote pattern of life relatively untouched by civilization. The same kind of camera perception, the ferreting out of detail, the anticipation of movement—marks the work of both men.

The similarity can not be pushed too far, however: Flaherty, a moralist, shows in his films how things should be; Sucksdorff shows how things actually are. Each new film is for him a new excitement, a new challenge—and for his ever increasing audiences, a new revelation of the wonders that can be accomplished by the movie camera in the hands of a true master film maker."

—Arthur Knight

(Mr. Knight is Chairman of the Film Department of the Dramatic Workshop and Technical Institute)

✦ ✦ ✦ ✦ ✦ ✦

Program Notes by Parker Tyler for Sidney Peterson's *The Lead Shoes*, Shown in May 1950

<u>THE LEAD SHOES</u>
Produced by Workshop 20 at California Institute of Fine Arts. Directed by Sidney Peterson. Distributed by Cinema 16. (17 minutes)

"In 'The Lead Shoes' we have before us an unusually vivid and skillful example of creative-experimental film. I think no one can deny its impact on the emotions. Whatever its complete meaning, everything is on the surface of the audio-visual unit which Sidney Peterson has contrived in this work. If its attack on the nerves is shocking, its use of the emotions is deep; if it seems to mock normal vision with the special lens which has been used throughout to distort the regular optical image, that mockery has a reasonable and positive basis. A nightmare mood saturates the film, and nightmare consistently distorts reality.

The human intelligence, moreover, has always wanted to discover and utilize the meaning of dreams and the visions of entranced persons, however strange or perverse these might be. As Cocteau has usefully suggested both by word and filmic example, the poet is a kind of seer. He penetrates to the depths and brings forth images birthed there by a marriage between his deepest self and things everybody experiences in daily life, perhaps through reading. Peterson came upon two old ballads, "Edward" and "The Three Ravens," the first a Colonial popularization of the Cain-and-Abel legend, and the second concerning three birds that witnessed a fallow-deer carry off a dying knight from the field of battle. In Peterson's film, the mother's passionate hysteria when she learns of "Abel's" murder indicates that at least a symbolic incest is present, a point given more weight when we consider that "Edward" is a variation of an older Scotch ballad, "Lord Randall," about a son who confesses to his mother that he killed his <u>father.</u>

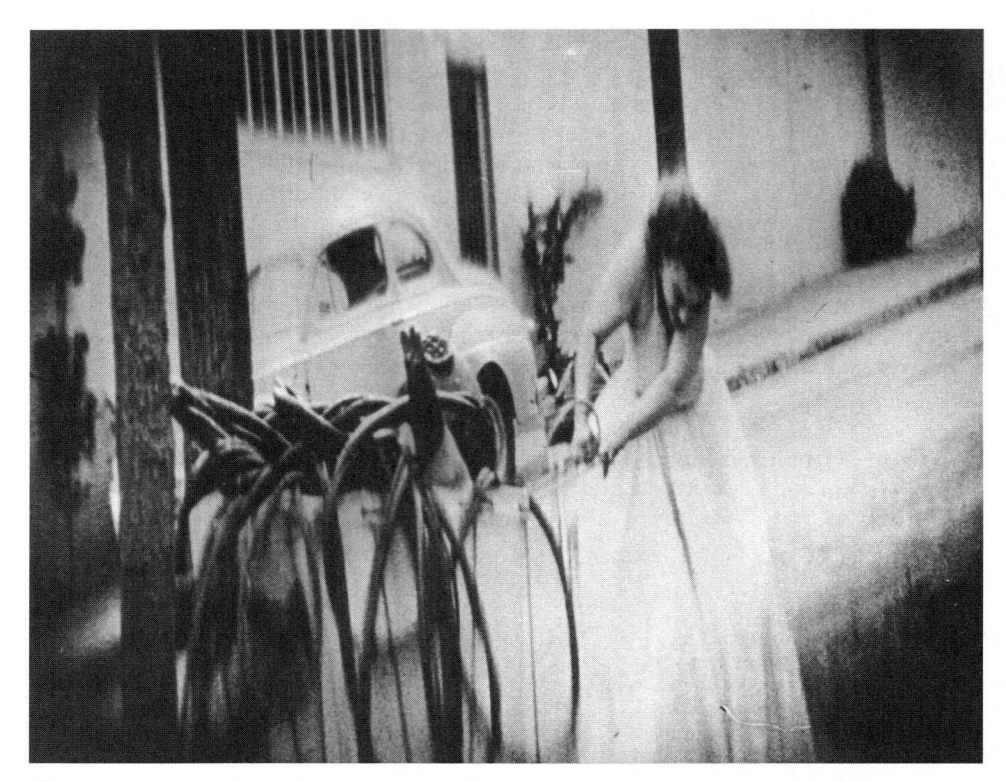

Illustration 36. *The Lead Shoes* (1949) by Sidney Peterson. Courtesy Anthology Film Archives.

In that timeless time in which the true creator does preliminary work—perhaps in a twinkle—Peterson visualized Edward, the murderous "Cain," in kilts and the corpse of "Abel" in a diving suit; thus the two ballads are fused because the diving suit substitutes for the knight's armor in "The Three Ravens." Then he must have felt the violence of a complex insight: a diver's lead shoes keep him on the seabottom, which seems equivalent to that abysmal level of instinct where anything is possible. When the frantic mother digs up her son from the sand on the shore, she is performing again the labor she had on giving birth to him; the suit itself becomes a sort of coffin. Once more, before he is consigned to the grave, she must hold him close to her. If we can assume all this, as I believe we can, we may go further to note that the tragic emotion is ingeniously modified by two devices: one is the hopscotch game seen parallel with the main action. Every mother of two sons has the problem of balancing her affections, which must be divided between them. This moral action was once anticipated in the physical terms of the hopscotch which she played as a girl: the player must straddle a line between two squares without falling or going outside them. The second device, the boogie-woogie accompaniment with is clamorous chorus, like the first, may have been instinctively rather than consciously calculated by Peterson. It operates unmistakably: the voices and music supply a savage rhythm for the ecstatic if accursed performers of the domestic catastrophe. It is the lyrical interpretation of the tragedy and suggests the historical fact that Greek tragedy derived from the Dionysian revel. Lastly we have the sinister implement and symbol of the castration rite, the knife and the bread—perhaps representing the murderer's afterthought rather than part of his deed. Even in this outstanding experimental film, a blend of tragedy and farce, all may not be perfectly integrated. But the whole effect is so compelling that I believe 'The Lead Shoes' may be called a notable event."

Parker Tyler

Reprinted by permission of Charles Boultenhouse.

❖ ❖ ❖ ❖ ❖ ❖

Letter to Amos Vogel from Parker Tyler, 5/11/50

May 11, 1950

Dear Amos:

I don't know what's to be done about these experimental film-makers. Evidently, if one is to get at the deepest meaning, or rather all the possible meanings, one has to use a microscope. The Lead Shoes takes the cake so far. I just noticed last night that a subtitle exists: "The Three Edwards," then it struck me that that part of the refrain in which Edward confesses that it is his "own true love" he has killed is not just homosexual byplay, as I originally construed it. Our experimentalist has, I would hazard, elided *three* versions of the same ballad; in other words, the whole thing is literally a nightmare with the expected lapses and unpredictable ellipses of the dream. The "three ravens" are three versions of "Edward the murderer": the first kills his sweetheart, the second kills his brother, the third kills his father. According to the visual text, this supposition is very hard to justify; therefore it is just as well the program note didn't try. To begin with, there is no differentiation of the male persons although the corpse looks blondish (that is, we can visually assume two males: Cain and Abel). It even strikes me that Peterson intends a chain murder in which Brother No. 1 kills Brother No. 2, then Brother No. 3 kills Brother No. 1. At least this would explain the last sequence of the castrating murderer. I don't see why Peterson didn't supply a gloss. Want to ask him, for the record?

Yet does it matter? Apparently a good part of the audience last night—the belligerently uneducated part—simply loathed it. And explaining such a puzzle piece-by-piece probably would only have irritated the more. On the given visual-surface of the film, I would stand by my program note as the most plausible interpretation.

Cordially,

[hw] Parker

P. S. Did I mention my Kafka-Chaplin essay is in the Spring Sewanee Rev? I enjoyed the Fischingers and also the psychiatric film. It's amusing to reflect that "The Lead Shoes" gives just as much trouble as the young man and young woman were given by their hypnosis-dream!—And so, because I'm just as tenacious as they are, though I have nothing to prompt me but my own mother wit, I'll venture to reinterpret the hop-scotch and the "erasure" (reverse movement) of the white chalk line: hopping from square to square means the change of personality from one murderer or murder to another (the three Edwards), and the disappearance of the line signifies, thus, the elimination of the line dividing one from another: they are "three in one." THE END.

Reprinted by permission of Charles Boultenhouse.

✦ ✦ ✦ ✦ ✦ ✦

Letter to Amos Vogel from Joseph Cornell, 6/3/50

Dear Mr. Vogel,

I have a particularly favorite experimental subject, of my own making, that at last is able to be projected without risk of impairing the master original(composed of at least 30 strips), and it is this last consideration which has not made it possible to offer it to you before. During the past 10 years this one reeler has had the enthusiastic endorsement of artists(Dali, Tchelitchew and many others) as well as poets and laymen. It has never had a public presentation.

There would be no complication with records as my other showing, and new music and an enlarged version make of this subject something completely fresh. The only consideration it does need is the scotch-taping of a piece of deep blue glass to the lens, or a mask could be supplied.

I'd be glad to arrange for a showing should you wish(preferably in a theatre before or after one of your showings- a small room does not do it justice at all.

Sincerely yours,

[hw] Joseph Cornell

Reprinted by permission of the Archives of American Art.

[Because of the mention of the blue glass in paragraph 2, I assume Cornell is describing Rose Hobart *(1936), which was not shown at Cinema 16.]*

✦ ✦ ✦ ✦ ✦ ✦

Letter to Amos Vogel from Gregory Markopoulos, 6/13/50

Dear Mr. Amos Vogel;

I have spoken to my attorney, in regards to my legal right of having prints made from kodachrome—originals, in your possession of the film trilogy: du sang de la volupte et de la mort; consisting of PSYCHE, LYSIS, CHARMIDES; and have been informed that that is my legal previlege.

I have written to you in regards to this twice, and without any avail.

Upon legal advice, I am sending you this letter, asking you to allow me to have prints made of my works.

If, not; a series of letters have been prepared to send to the periodicals here and abroad; exposing CINEMA 16 as a skeeming commercial venture, and what it is; and how on several occasions it has attempted to purchase films from individuals, young film experementalists for practically naught; in which case the films would have been shown at such places as HUNTERS COLLEGE, and PARIS THEATER etc., to capacity audiences; attendance being give to <u>anyone</u>, member or non-member, who payed the fee for seeing the films.

Needless to say, I should hear from you, within a relatively short period of time. Should I not hear from you, and I am away, my attorney shall proceed from there.

Sincerely yours,

[hw] Gregory J. Markopoulos

gregory j. markopoulos
523 bush
Toledo 11 Ohio
6/13/50
<u>2nd copy</u>

> Reprinted by permission of the Estate of Gregory J. Markopoulos/ Courtesy Tenemos, Inc.

✦ ✦ ✦ ✦ ✦ ✦

Letter to Gregory Markopoulos from Amos Vogel, 9/18/50

September 18, 1950

Mr. Gregory Markopoulos
c/o American Express
8 Rue Scribe
Paris, France

Dear Gregory Markopoulos:

I was shocked by the letter containing various accusations which you sent me during the summer. I was more shocked by your subsequent correspondence with me, which indicated that you simply wanted to continue your relation with me "as before."

You can't have it both ways: You will have to learn to draw the consequences. Either you consider these accusations groundless and senseless, as I do—then you must retract them; or you continue to insist on them—then you ought to break off relations, as I on my part would take all steps necessary to protect myself against these senseless charges.

Especially exasperating was your characterization of Cinema 16 as "a scheming commercial venture which has on several occasions attempted to purchase films from young film experimentalists for practically nought." I have never "attempted" to buy anything from you. On the other hand, you have attempted (after having practically insisting that I buy the trilogy) to sell me THE DEAD ONES for $180.00. I suppose if I accept your offer, I will once more be characterized as "a scheming business man".

I have no objection to your owning a print of the trilogy for your own personal use, if you will pay for the print, advance the money, and if it is understood that you will not show it or rent it to others.

On the other hand, you will understand that I cannot lend you the only print of the trilogy we have, since it is part of our rental catalog.

I have enclosed a letter "To whom it may concern". You might let me know what your production plans are.

Sincerely,

Amos Vogel

AV:MG

✦ ✦ ✦ ✦ ✦ ✦

Letter to Amos Vogel from Gregory Markopoulos, Circa 9/50

Dear Amos Vogel,

Thank you.

1: After checking into all matters; and let this be my retraction, for what I may have said in the past, ...after seeing what cut-throats there are in Paris in connection with all films, etc., I am more than pleased that you have my first three films; and henceforth, you have my complete faith in you.

2: In regards to sending my films over, upon further inquiry, I do not think it advisable, because one cannot trust the exhibitors here. You might coresspond though, with the following person, whom I trust implicitly; and who would like to show American Experemental films: Frederic Froeschel, 3 blvd. St. Michel, Paris. He wrote the scenario for Les Sange Des Btes, and is head of the Cine-Club Des Quartier Latin. He has been trying unsuccesfully for three years to obtain the experemental films; perhaps you could work something out.

3: In regards to THE DEAD ONES, if you are interested, in beginning anew, I should be very happy to make, at your suggestion any idea which would rescue my film; it is the best that I have created.

4: Thank you for assuring me that I can obtain a print of my films, and also for the TO WHOM IT MAY CONCERN. I shall try to make a new film, and upon its completion, I shall let you know.

Thank you agin, do let me know inregards to THE DEAD ONES. And forgive this typing, its rather impossible with the machine I have at the moment.

Very sincerely yours,

[hw] Gregory J. Markopoulos

gregory j. markopoulos
c/o american express
paris
france.

Reprinted by permission of the Estate of Gregory J. Markopoulos/ Courtesy Tenemos, Inc.

✦ ✦ ✦ ✦ ✦ ✦

Program Announcement, Fall 1950

October 1950

Masterspieces from the Berlin Museums
The camera explores some of the outstanding works in the famous collection: Cranach, Rubens, Botticelli, Corregio, Raphael. Commentary by Thomas Craven, noted art authority, delivered by Basil Rathbone. In color.

Ouled Nail
A charming folk dance of North Africa. A young girl dances for money to buy herself a husband.

Object Lesson
International Prize Winner: "World's Best Avant-garde Film," Venice International Film Festival, 1950. A film that will stir you by its strange imagery.

The Rose and the Mignonette
A memorable and moving French film poem. English version by Stephen Spender, spoken by the noted British actor, Emlyn Williams.

Fingers and Thumbs
Another of Julian Huxley's brilliant scientific films—a humorous and informative comment on evolution.

Ai-Ye ("Mankind")
More than any travelog could, this provocative, impressionistic account gives you a "feeling" of the atmosphere, the reality, the mysterious charms of South America. A vivid, richly colored kaleidoscope of people, textures, lush vegetation and poverty. Ozzie Smith's spectacular drum and native song accompaniment is an inspired improvisation: Entirely unrehearsed, it was composed and recorded on the spot during Smith's first viewing of the film.

November 1950

Franklin Watkins
A perceptive and moving account of a well-known modern painter at work. Close-ups and sensitive photography reveal the process of artistic creation. Bartok's String Quartets played by the Pro-Arte and the Budapest String Quartets.

Sausalito
A strongly subjective, imaginative "documentary," in which the reality and the atmosphere of a suburb of San Francisco are recalled by sounds, textures and pieces of visual experience. A very unusual experiment.

Shipyard
Paul Rotha's masterpiece of the documentary cinema welds striking images, experimental sound and skillful editing into a thoroughly engrossing film experience.

Cowboy Ambrose
The Holdup of the Pink Garter Bar; Sunny Jim Arsenic and Handsome Jack Rancid in a fearful struggle to the end. This hilarious Mack Swain comedy is a nostalgic reminder of the long-gone days of the great American film comedy.

Aqua Pure Ballet
The patterns and changing colors of water create a richly sensuous color symphony, set to a vivid jazz score.

December 1950

Japanese Family
A little-known family pattern is charmingly and intimately revealed in an absorbing film study. Produced by Julien Bryan, photographed by Minoru Konda. Accompanied by Japanese music.

Un Chien Andalou
One of the classics of surrealism. Produced by Luis Bunuel and Salvador Dali. A brilliant, violent and shocking film.

The Plow that Broke the Plains
A moving and dramatic social document, written and directed by Pare Lorentz. Outstanding musical score by Virgil Thomson. Photography by Paul Strand and Ralph Steiner. This famous film classic gave the initial impetus to the American documentary film movement.

Social Behavior of Rhesus Monkeys
The social and sexual conduct of a colony of monkeys as revealed to a scientist's hidden camera. A Psychological Cinema Register Film produced by the Pennsylvania State College. Kinds of behavior shown include maternal, reproductive, dominance, fighting, homosexual and play.

The Tear (La Larme)
A vivid pen-and-ink abstraction by Soren Melson, hand-drawn directly on film. No camera was used. Set to jazz.

Illustration 37. *The Plow That Broke the Plains* (1936) by Pare Lorenz. Courtesy Museum of Modern Art Film Stills Archive.

January 1951

A Selection of Some of the Best Recent European Documentary and Avant-Garde films collected and brought to the U.S. by Cinema 16.

The World of Paul Delvaux
A curious and poetic journey through the fantastic world of the celebrated surrealist painter Paul Delvaux. Produced by Henri Storck. Poem written and spoken by Paul Eluard, distinguished French poet. International Prize Winner, Venice International Film Festival, 1947.

Aubervilliers
Eli Lotar's searing indictment of a slum district of Paris. Lyrics by Jacques Prevert, music by Joseph Kosma. Prix International de Poesie, International Film Festival, Belgium, 1949. (English version)

Recent Danish Experimental Films:

Flugten ("Escape"): A murderer in flight. Outstanding experimental film by Albert Mertz and Jorgen Roos.

Legato: Hanning Bendtsen's delicate orchestration of exquisite, lace-like abstractions.

Eaten Horizons: Love destroyed by fulfillment: a disturbing surrealist film by Jorgen Roos and Wilhelm Freddie.

Le Sang des Bêtes (*The Blood of the Beasts*)
George Franju's tormented and controversial film, the artistic sensation of Paris and London for two years, here presented for the first time in America. A film of savage honesty and violent visual impact. Music by Kosma. (English version) "...not a scene that fails to move by the sheer beauty of its great visual style." (Jean Cocteau). Prix Jean Vigo and Grand Prix International, 3rd International Short Film Festival, France, 1950.

✦ ✦ ✦ ✦ ✦ ✦

Letter to Amos Vogel from Sidney Peterson, 10/21/50

ORBIT FILMS
DIMENSONS INCORPORATED

Seattle Studios
1737A Westlake North
Seattle 9, Washington
[. . .]

Oct 21, 1950

Dear Amos:

It was a fluke—my not getting the two letters before yours of the 18th inst. I went down to San Francisco on a trip, the letters were forwarded to me there and arrived after I had returned to Seattle. Presumably they are still sitting in San Francisco in an empty house waiting upon the return of the people whose house it is. Normally I am here in Seattle and mail gets to me in the usual way. Sorry to have caused you so much extra trouble. Trouble of one kind or another seems to be implicit in the movie business of whatever branch. I have my share of it here though gradually the situation clears. It is a lot easier to create something by simply going out by yourself and making something than it is to essay something comparable within a commercial framework and employing an organization to do it. It means an organization as an instrument or, rather, a series of instruments, and instruments too, fluent enough to meet requirements in a number of fields. Aside from various misc. we're half through a feature in 35mm which promises to be not unrevolutionary and perhaps even exciting. A kind of monodrama in a documentary (location) style. We have a couple of "discoveries" in the way of performers. Anyway, amid the trials and tribulations out here, your words were cheering. I'm inclined to agree with the European audiences about THE LEAD SHOES. It's more consistent than the others. The disturbing factor in it, I think, from the point of view of its integrity of style, is the ambiguity of genre introduced by the somewhat hammish performance of the woman in the nightgown. It's tragedy in a way with an occasional gufaw. In a way that makes it very personal. But it does have a sustained quality and it is certainly not an avant-garde repetition. Do you suppose movie audiences will ever learn to take works as experiences instead of merely as expressions, what does it mean? etc.?

Naturally I am pleased about the honorable mention at Venice. It was the first I had heard of it and even though I know enough about such things not to take them too seriously (perhaps this isn't entirely right) I'm still and I suppose always will be a pushover for a little recognition in the right places. A man has to have some encouragement, somewhere, somehow, and once, in this world and especially in this country, you depart from the ordinary fiduciary values in what you do, it's not easy to come by. I'm grateful to you for what you have done and are doing, for yr. continued efforts.

If I had a print kicking around I'd certainly send it to you for the Danish Film Museum (don't know anything about them; what do they do?) but I haven't and right now haven't got the dough to pay for one. Incidentally, do you owe me anything on rentals? Just curious. I've given the Multichrome Laboratories in San Francisco (they have the original of The Lead Shoes in their vault) an order for a print to be made and forewarded to you. They'll also foreward you a bill. The size will probably surprise you, or will if you expect a print from a negative. I've never had a dupe neg. made. The prints are all reversibles. I've forgotten what they run but seem to recall something around seven or eight cents a foot. I seem to recall that a print was something around fifty bucks. If that's going to bankrupt you let me know and we'll see what we can work out.

What is the European stuff that you arranged to bring over here? I'd like to hear about it. Sometime soon I'm slated to give a lecture here at the university along with showing them examples of experimental stuff and I'd like to arrange for something new. Incidentally, what were the hot-blooded Italians demonstrating for and against. Didn't they like jazz? Or like it? Demonstrations have a way of being irrelevant to main issues. Not that I don't like demonstrations. I approve of them thoroughly. It's about the only way that cabbage head the audience has of showing that it's alive, that and, of course, box office. As between demonstrations and box office I think for the time being we have to content ourselves with the demonstrations. At least in our more serious moments. I hope sincerely that some of the stuff I am going to be able to do in this commercial framework will be demonstration provoking.

One of these days I'll be getting to New York and one of the reasons I look foreward to it is the prospect of a long talk with you. Meanwhile,

Sincerely

[hw] Sidney Peterson

Reprinted by permission of Sidney Peterson.

✦ ✦ ✦ ✦ ✦

Letter to Amos Vogel from Frank Stauffacher, 1/6/51

San Francisco Museum of Art [. . .]

Jan. 6, 1951

Amos Vogel
Cinema 16, Inc.
59 Park Ave.
New York, 16, N. Y.

Dear Amos,

These first few weeks of the New Year have me catching up with my long-neglected correspondence pertaining to the film world. For the last two and a half months I have been virtually buried in a shooting studio and a cutting room trying to fulfill a contract with an advertising agency for nine rather elaborate TV commercials. It has been a harrowing experience because it was not only new to me, but to the advertising people as well. But now we can take a sigh of relief because we are both satisfied—the advertisers and I. Stop-action photography, under pressure, is a real back-breaker. You may catch them on the Eastern networks as they will be released all over. They advertise Starkist Tuna! So much for the reason for my prolonged silence.

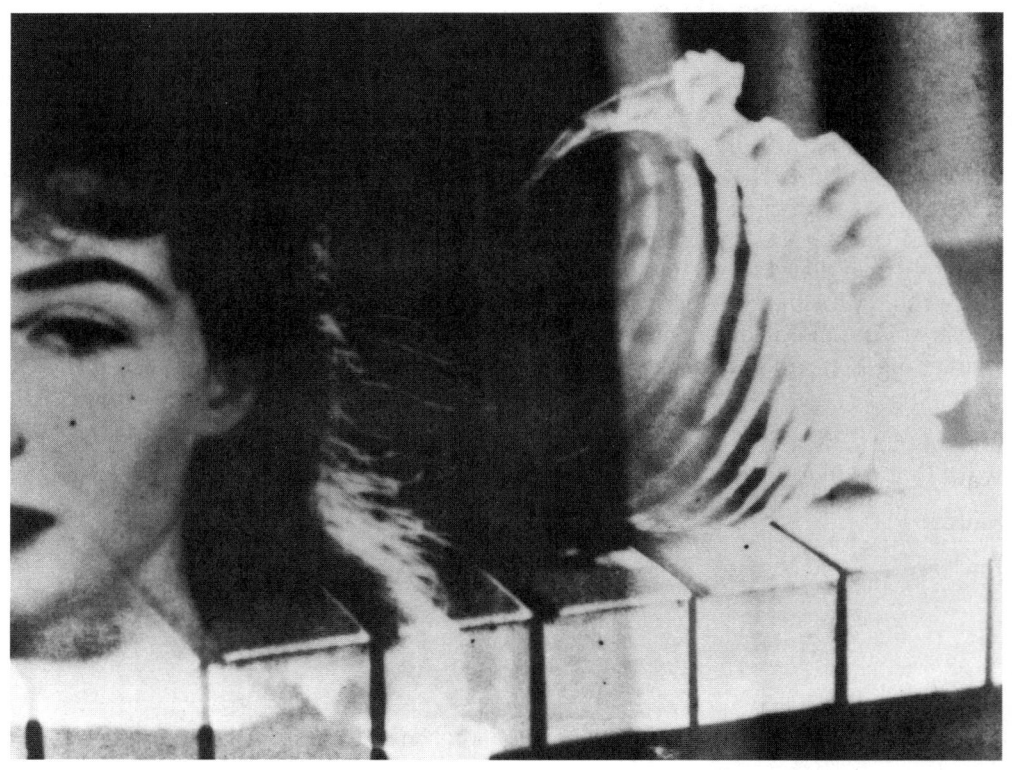

Illustration 38. *Sausalito* (1948) by Frank Stauffacher. Courtesy Anthology Film Archives.

Thank you for your interesting report on the reaction to my SAUSALITO. All of the criticisms are quite valid, and I am aware of them. I did not want to change it, however; I felt it legitimate to let it go as a truly experimental piece, with the good and bad left as they were; in the nature of a "sketch." For I feel an experimental film carried to a point of perfection can really no longer be called experimental; it then becomes a film of a particular kind, a finished film, even if the subject and treatment are bizarre. And besides, I could not feel my way accurately in saying what I wanted to say until I had said it, and then let the statement live it's own life, on its own, with audiences. What was wrong with my film then became obvious—as I expected. What I was trying to do was convey a mood, an atmosphere—but punctuated with just enough satire to prevent it's becoming pretentiously arty. So if audiences are moved to laughter, I am gratified. I find the reaction here is the same; and it was so in Los Angeles too, at the Coronet Theatre.

I was just down in Hollywood over the New Year weekend, seeing acquaintances again. I met Harry Leonard, of "Sight and Sound", and he is eager to see the collected work of our S. F. Group, so whenever you find it convenient, let me have Peterson's films so that I can prepare the whole list for him. Then I'll make a date with him, and drive down. I'll certainly have Cinema 16 mentioned. I saw Man Ray, Jay Leyda, John Whitney and Fischinger. Fischinger has built a very curious "machine" consisting of various movable screens and colored lights behind which he stands and "creates" abstract compositions to music on records. He has not made a film in conjunction with it yet, but I think it would be a riot at one of our showings, as I found last year that the "live" demonstrations—the Jim Davis plastics, and the live bop band with Harry Smith's films was a great sensation.

Here in S. F., Harry Smith is working on a three-dimensional abstract film which will require colored glasses to be worn by the spectators. So far I have not inquired into the feasibility of the scheme, but I shall do my best to present it if costs allow. Broughton is working full-time on his new film, to be called SEXTETTE, and I am about to go to work finishing up the film on San Francisco. Arledge is working spasmodically on a new dance film. Until I delve deeper into trying to get this coming series started, I have no more information for you as, aside from these items, I've been too out of touch with the field.

Which brings me to the coming series, which I tentatively have planned for these dates: March 9, 16, 23, 30. I put it ahead one month in order to allow Broughton, Smith, and myself time in which to finish our respective films. Now, those are the dates, and since I have not booked anything yet, I would like to start with the titles that you mentioned back in November: AUBERVILLIERS, PAUL DELVAUX, SANG DES BETES, LAFCADIO, ELIZABETH, the Danish films, and Rotha's SHIPYARD. You see I have just gone right down the list in your letter. Will they be available to me in March? If so, let me know at your earliest convenience, and I will be then be more organized and will have settled on their order. However, if the Berkeley Cinema Circle is going to show them before March, I would not care to show them, naturally, because it would reduce Art in Cinema's reputation for firsts, as you can readily understand.

Raymond Rohauer, in Hollywood, is running the Coronet Theatre on an every-night basis, showing a great, rather indiscriminate variety of material. However, he does seem to get his hands on some very peculiar items which he must salvage out of the dust in the back rooms of film vaults. He is disarmingly free with his sources, although some of them are so shady that he won't reveal them. However, after spending a couple of hours with him and taking notes and addresses, I have the impression that I could forage some interesting films. Since I have not organized my notes yet, or really inquired into their worth, I won't take the trouble now to hand them on, because they are in too confused a state. But I will certainly send on to you what is worthwhile in the slightest degree.

Let me hear from you as soon as possible. And let me know your future plans. I am enclosing a special delivery stamp in order to expedite your reply. Thanks again for your sincere words on SAUSALITO. I hadn't time to send a rental invoice. I'll enclose it. But the main thing I'm concerned with now is the setting up of the new series here, so let me know.

Sincerely,

[hw] Frank

Thanks for the Xmas card!

Reprinted by permission of Barbara Stauffacher Solomon.

[I have eliminated a handwritten postscript relating to the payment of an invoice. William Moritz discusses Fischinger's Lumigraph, which Stauffacher describes in paragraph 3, in "The Films of Oskar Fischinger," Film Culture, *No. 58–60 (1974), pp. 75–76.]*

✦ ✦ ✦ ✦ ✦ ✦

Program Announcement, Spring 1951

March 1951

On the Edge
Dream or reality? A dark and doom-haunted episode of desperation is acted out by two people in a setting of eerie desolation. A striking new experimental film by Curtis Harrington, producer of *Fragment of Seeking*.

The Atom Strikes
First detailed account of the effects of the atomic bomb on Hiroshima, just released: an unprecedented film document. Includes dramatic interview with a survivor.

The Work of U.P.A.
Cinema 16 proudly presents the first comprehensive compilation of the work of United Productions of America (producers of Columbia's sensational cartoon *Gerald McBoing-Boing*) whose outstanding films promise to revolutionize the American cartoon field. A representative of U. P. A. will introduce the films, which include *Trouble Indemnity, Punchy De Leon, Bungled Bungalow* and others.

Hypnotic Behavior
In a series of unstaged, authentic experiments two subjects are hypnotized and in trance experience insensibility to pain; blindness and deafness; eye and arm catalepsy; post-hypnotic amnesia. According to instructions given in the trance

state, the same photographs appear amusing to one subject, depressing to the other in a fascinating last sequence. Produced by Dr. Lester F. Beck, Department of Psychology, University of Oregon.

April 1951

Experimental Masochism
Unusual experiments with a group of rats who learn to "enjoy" electric shocks pose some provocative questions concerning the nature of masochistic behavior. A psychological Cinema Register release.

Picnic
Constant transitions from realism to phantasy reveal the anguish of an adolescent caught up in the fatality of a false love. This film by Curtis Harrington begins as a satirical comment on American middle class life and ends as tragedy. Original musical score by Ernest Gold.

The Photographer
Willard Van Dyke's (*The City, Valleytown*) important new motion picture on the outstanding American photographer, Edward Weston; a sensitive revelation of an artist's search for beauty amidst the wind-swept sand dunes, abandoned mining towns and ever-changing seascapes of the Pacific coast.

Feelings of Depression
Fourth in the "Mental Mechanisms" series, this film traces the story of a young man who because of emotional difficulties experienced as a child, is rendered incapable of enjoying a normal adult life. Produced by the National Film Board of Canada.

Room Studies
Hand-painted directly onto film by Soren Melson, Denmark's foremost experimental film producer. No camera was used. Agitated jazz accompanies the restless and phantastic images.

May 1951

Children Learning by Experience
Hidden cameras reveal an unstaged portrayal of childhood in a charming yet thought-provoking psychological film. Companion piece to the highly successful *Children Growing Up with Others*, shown by Cinema 16 in 1949.

The London Fire Raids
An authentic and terrifying newsreel record of the London "Blitz." A reminder and a warning.

Color Categorizing in Rhesus Monkeys
Unusually interesting experiments reveals the monkeys' intelligence in responding to complex test situations.

Nomads of the Jungle
A revealing glimpse into the lives of a strange tribe in the Malayan jungles. A film by Victor Jurgens.

The Idea
Based on Frans Masereel's famous woodcuts, this picture has been hailed as the first "trick" film with a serious theme: an idea is conceived by the artist, condemned by the world, and lives on forever. Outstanding musical score by the noted modern composer Arthur Honegger.

June 1951

A Drop of Water
The high-powered microscope explores the phantastic forms of the microcosmos in action and in brilliant color.

Lafcadio
Jean Beranger's films deal with problems of adjustment to the values of society—in this case, a sensitive portrayal of the experiences of a bi-sexual, culminating in real or imagined suicide. An interesting example of recent European poetic film production.

La Lettre
Jean Mallon's delightful and imaginative film exercise, set to music by Jean Wiener.

RKO's "This Is America" Series
The development and significance of this important series of documentary-informational films is traced in a full-length presentation of some of its best releases, including:

I Am an Alcoholic
The story of Alcoholics Anonymous
Street of Shadows
The Lower East Side
Love That Beauty
Slenderizing in ten easy lessons
Passport to Nowhere
The plight of the D. P.s

✦ ✦ ✦ ✦ ✦ ✦

Letter to Amos Vogel from Frank Stauffacher, 5/4 and 5/29, 1951

San Francisco Museum of Art [. . .]

May 4, 1951

Dear Amos,

Although the San Francisco series is now finished, there are still two programs to go on the Berkeley series—the 8th and the 22nd of May. However, I'll answer your letter of the 28th now.

I want to thank you for your cooperation in sending things at last minute request, and for accepting my desultory returning, with good grace. As a matter of fact, I would have sent all of the items back immediately after showing except that I could not see how I could send them all back in the original container, as you requested, unless I waited until all their playdates were over. Also, as I mentioned, this series has been a terrible drain on my already taxed energy and time, since it is no small task to handle it right without constant attention, and my outside business jumped suddenly into hectic activity. I can honestly say this time that I am glad it (the museum series) is over and finished. During its existence I am continual prey to strangers, artistic crackpots, odd visiting film-makers unknown to me (and with no films), eager, pushing film students, bores, cranks, and an army of friends whom I usually never see, but who suddenly heave into sight for free tickets. There was even a kind of maniac from Paris who claimed Art in Cinema was a greater event than anything happening in similar fields in Europe. I couldn't get rid of him. He would climb into my car with my wife and I, talking a steady stream, carrying a huge brief case filled with copious notes. And into this madhouse dropped Clarence Laughlin—no quiet person himself. I tell you it was pretty awful, even though enormously successful.

At the end of the series, last Friday, I sent out to all the audience, a check list of the films shown. I am enclosing one. The returns have been immensely revealing. I want to hand out a similar one at the Berkeley series, and on the basis of these tallies, issue a report. The audience at S. F. was around 500 per night. At Berkeley, almost 800. And they are both excellent audiences, alive and a cut above the average in intelligence.

You ask about my financial setup at the museum. This activity was started five years ago by myself and Richard Foster, neither of us members of the museum staff, and neither of us dependent upon it for financial returns. It has been a truly non-profit function. From the net of the first series came the booklet. Since then, a fund has been kept from which money is sometimes taken for certain local film makers in need. Sausalito came from that fund, part of Broughton's films, Harry Smith's, a couple of Peterson's, Deren has been given some—none of these payments were large, but they have helped people in this manner, in a small way, all in an effort to help the field in a completely selfless effort. The fund has never been really large because I have spared no expense in trying to make each series tops.

However, for several years my personal finances fell badly. I left my job as an advertising artist and set myself up free-lancing. That, you know, is a tough, competitive business, and it has taken me almost two years to get established, and added to that, of late, has been my new business of producing television films on a small scale. These outside activities are more than enough for one man, and that is why I say that the two Art in Cinema series added on top have just about killed me.

During my low period, the museum determined to compensate me on a more business-like basis by paying me one third of the net returns for a series. This didn't amount to much. I am still operating on that basis, and my one third of the net from this series will be practically non-existent. The expenses have been especially high this time, and the series has taken twice as much effort than usual. It is truly a labor of love, but I am getting quite fed up with it since it now cuts deeply into my outside activities at a time when I can't afford to have that happen.

The Berkeley series is handled differently. It also is a labor of love. They pay me a flat fee of $600.00 for which I arrange, make notes, book, and pay the rentals on the whole series. Using a majority of 35mm. film, you can readily see that I do not come out of this one very wealthy, either.

The true compensation in all of this is in the excitement, the activity, and the further awareness of actually extending the horizon of the experimental film, and the extending of the awareness of it. (I loathe calling it the "experimental film", but there is no other ready handle). Nevertheless, the compensation in this form has worn pretty thin to me personally, by now, and I would actually like to get more out of it if I put so much time into it.

As you can see by the list of films on the questionaire, I did not show all of the films rented from you. For example, I could not show but one item from each of the two reels of Danish abstract, drawn-on-film work. I was not alone in thinking them quite crude, rather unimaginative, and harrowing to look at. The technique is carried to its furthest end far more excellently by McLaren, so why show much less works? They recieved a decided negative—even the two I did show.

Lafcadio was also unshowable, although you did qualify it by saying it was rather amateurish; it was adolescent and boring. Elisabeth was also adolescent, but more interesting, and more concisely done, and the theme was both good, and simply presented. But a bit childish. Shipyard was good of its kind, but I have never been sold on Rotha as a film maker, and this one didn't change my mind any. It is full of that British stuffiness hard to describe, and unless you are interested in shipbuilding, rather dull. The only brilliant parts seems to be imitative of Grierson, or Eisenstein. To my mind, Song of Ceylon, Night Mail, and even the hoary old Drifters are far superior as wonderful contributions, or I should say, developments, of the British documentary.

Sang Des Betes was indeed the prize, and I am very sorry not to have been able to present it here at the museum, on 16mm.

Up to now, I think the best films shown on both series have been Sang Des Betes, the three Sucksdorff films, and of its kind, Pacific 231. The Loon's Necklace has been immensely popular, also.

You will no doubt meet Rohauer soon as he is planning to be in N. Y. sometime after the week of May 27. He is young, and really does not know very much about the subject of experimental films. He is a promoter, and he deals in strange sources of films, but nevertheless he is square, and can be trusted. He has no 35mm at the Coronet. He presents films quite indiscriminately, that is, without much selection. I've never been to any of his showings, so don't know what his attendance is. But he has been quite helpful to me in finding certain films, and in showing my own. He is shrewd, and no doubt makes a fair financial go of his showings.

[Frank]

May 29, 1951

As you can see by the date, I started this letter the first of the month, but didn't get to finish it until now.

Sorry there had to be this delay also in remitting the rental money. We had a change of bookeepers, and so everything is delayed. It will come through in a few days, so don't worry.

Reprinted by permission of Barbara Stauffacher Solomon.

✦ ✦ ✦ ✦ ✦ ✦

Letter to Amos Vogel from Kenneth Anger, 6/23/51

Paris, 23 June, 1951

Dear Mr. Vogel:

I hope you received satisfactorily the publicity material and photographs, which I sent to you some time ago. In regard to these photographs: it is urgent that the fourteen small ones—frame enlargements—be sent back to me <u>immediately</u> by return air mail. They are a unique set and are needed as soon as possible for inclusion in the next month's issue of "Cahiers du Cinema", a film review which is doing an article on me. I have assured them that these photos will be available to illustrate the article, and I hope you understand that it is <u>urgent</u> that I have them immediately, and that you will act accordingly. You may, if you wish, deduct the air-mail charges from my "Fireworks" income. If you need the photos again later, I can return them to you.

I am now engaged in a very interesting new project, and I will take this opportunity to outline it for you briefly.

The new film, which is now in the rehersal stage, is called MALDOROR—being my adaptation of "Les Chants de Maldoror", by Lauréamont, the famous early example of surrealist writing. I want to make the film on 16mm Kodachrome. I am first concentrating on one 15 minute section of this film, which can be released as a short film as well as be included in the entire film. This episode is called "The Hymn to the Ocean", after one of the most celebrated passages in the book. In my film adaptation I have conceived this episode as a ballet, and I am extremely fortunate to have received the full co-operation of the world famous Grand Ballet de Marquis de Cuevas, with Rosella Hightower and Serge Golovine as stars, to dance this for me. The well-known French composer, Henri Sauguet, has agreed to write the music. This obviously makes the film perfect for release as a short subject that can be shown widely, with appeal for different audiences. My plan is to photograph this during the month of August at Deauville, when the ballet company will be appearing there. I unfortunately have only the slimmest of budgets to be working on up to the present time, and the expenses are very steep for me, as you can imagine, with over forty costumes, among other items, to prepare. I am therefore forced to appeal for outside financial help, and in view of this I should like to offer to you the following proposition: If you feel that either you, personally, or Cinema 16, or several persons selected by you, could forward me an amount of 200 dollars or more, to facilitate the production of my film "The Hymn to the Ocean" I should guarantee for you the exclusive U.S. distribution rights on 16mm for this film. It would be understood that this amount would be payed back from the earnings of the film.

As I have an urgent need of a minimum of 200 dollars—preferably twice that amount—as soon as possible, I must offer this proposition to another distributor if I do not have your decision soon. I am perfectly confident that the amount could easily be covered in rentals to U.S. dance circles alone.

I am hoping that the success of "The Hymn to the Ocean" will facilitate for me the much longer and more difficult work of MALDOROR.

Please let me have your decision as soon as possible.

I would appreciate a report soon on the activity of "Fireworks". If you need any advice on the publicity material let me know.

May I again say that it is <u>urgent</u> that the fourteen frame enlargements from "Fireworks" be sent to me <u>immediately</u> by return air-mail.

Thanking you in advance—

Sincerely yours,

[hw] Kenneth Anger

Note new address: 11, Rue Jacob Paris 6^e

Reprinted by permission of Kenneth Anger.

[According to P. Adams Sitney, Maldoror, *the new film described in paragraph 3, collapsed in 1953 after rehearsals and tests. See* Visionary Film *(New York: Oxford, 1974), p. 104.]*

✦ ✦ ✦ ✦ ✦ ✦

Letter to Amos Vogel from Hans Richter, ?/?/51

The City College
Convent Avenue and 139th Street
New York 31, N. Y.

The Institute of Film Techniques
Office of the Director

[hw] <u>It will happen again!</u>

In 1925, at the Ufa Theatre Kurfuerstendamm, Berlin, Stephan Wolte was playing his piano piece to my abstract film "Rhythm 21". He was nearly lynched in a general mayhem.

In 1928, after my film "Vormittagsspuk" was shown at the International Music Festival in Baden-Baden, Germany, a little man with a green hat stepped in my way and expressed admiration for my little film "Rhythm 21" he had seen in 1925 in Berlin but "the new film Vormittagsspuk", what a pretentious and ill-advised cynical piece."

In 1948 at a party given by Hazel Mac Kinley, Peggy Guggenheim's sister, a slightly tipsy, still pretty but a bit faded British woman, probably an actrice, but certainly a friend of Iris Barry's, came over to the group I was standing with. The art dealer Sidney Janis introduced me. "Ah!" said the lady. "I know you are the one who made once such a nice film . . . . with hats and so . . . . a real gem". I was flattered and, expecting something good, added that I had made films since, my lates "Dreams That Money Can Buy".—"Oh!," exploded the lady. "I know! What a pretentious and arragant piece of cynical film". . . . and walked off to the powder room.

[hw] The same will happen again!

HR

Reprinted by permission of Ursula Lawder.

[This letter seems to have been written after Cinema 16 had made arrangements to show Dreams That Money Can Buy *as the December 1951 monthly presentation (Cinema 16 had premiered the film on April 22, 1948)].*

✦ ✦ ✦ ✦ ✦

Program Announcement, Fall 1951

October 1951

Elisabeth
A moving story of a lonely young woman whose longing for love ends in stark tragedy. Directed against authentic Parisian backgrounds.

Illustration 39. Program announcement, fall 1951.

New Work by U. P. A.
A selection of the best new cartoons by the producers of Columbia's Academy Award Winner *Gerald McBoing-Boing*, who are revolutionizing the American cartoon field. Last season's showing of their earlier work was one of Cinema 16's most popular programs.

The Steps of Age
A distinguished new motion picture by the makers of *The Quiet One*. A poignant and dramatic story of an elderly couple and their emotional unpreparedness for old age. Written and directed by Ben Maddow (who wrote *Asphalt Jungle*, *Intruder in the Dust*).

Four in the Afternoon
4 variations on the quest for love; James Broughton's provocative and lyrical visualization of four of his poems.

Power of Plants
A fascinating time lapse film study of plants pushing through layers of tinfoil, lifting weights and breaking bottles.

November 1951

Symptoms in Schizophrenia
An authentic study of schizophrenic patients and their symptoms, such as delusions, apathy, rigidity and echopraxia.

Adventures of Jimmie
Startling experiences of a confused young man in search of his "destiny"... a satire on the "psychological travelogue" so popular in contemporary literature. Jazz score arranged by Weldon Kees.

Song of Ceylon
Basil Wright's masterpiece of the documentary cinema affords a rare insight into the lives of the Singhalese, lifted to the level of film poetry by its emotional intensity and the sheer beauty of its images.

Angry Boy
A sensitive account of a deeply disturbed child. Revealing discussions with the psychiatrist and a dramatic portrayal of his family life uncover the source of his emotional disturbance. Directed by Alexander Hammid (*Private Life of a Cat*) for Affiliated Films.

Loony Tom, the Happy Lover
James Broughton's mischievous re-creation of the old-time film comedy—a hilarious account of Loony Tom's single-minded pursuit of the female.

December 1951

Hans Richter: *30 Years of the Avant-garde Film* (1921–1951)
A special event commemorating the 30th anniversary of the avant-garde film, as expressed in the work of Hans Richter, living link with the original movement. Mr. Richter, film producer, noted modern painter, and chairman of the Institute of Film

Techniques at City College, will himself introduce some of his early films (including *Ghosts Before Breakfast* and *Film Study* with music by Milhaud). He will then present a special feature-length screening of excerpts from his famous surrealist film.

Dreams That Money Can Buy
4 Dreams based on the visions of 4 noted contemporary artists:

The Girl with the Prefabricated Heart (Fernand Leger)
A satire on love in the machine age, played by two mannequins. Lyrics by John Latouche; song by Libby Holman & Josh White.

Ballet & Circus (Alexander Calder)
A ballet of the universe. Mobiles: Calder. Music by Paul Bowles & David Diamond.

Desire (Max Ernst)
A story of passion and desire. Music by Paul Bowles.

Narcissus (Hans Richter)
The discovery of the Self. Music by Louis Applebaum.

January 1952

Eternal Song
A romantic and beautifully photographed medley of folk songs and dances, made in 1941 by a young ethnologist among the peoples of Bohemia.

Deadly Females
A male scorpion, victorious over his opponent in a fight for the female, carries her off to romantic nuptials, and is promptly devoured by her.

Balzac
The story of a man becomes the story of an era in an important new art film. Based entirely on contemporary etchings and drawings, it traces his unhappy life and examines his curious writing habits.

Breakdown
The case of Anne Morton, victim of a schizophrenic breakdown, is recounted in an unusual new psychological film which pictures the operations of a mental hospital through the eyes of a patient.

Loops
Norman McLaren's (*Fiddle-De-Dee*) hand-painted new abstract film was made without a camera and is accompanied by synthetic sound.

SPECIAL EVENTS

Childbirth—Normal Delivery
and other medical and surgical films

Fireworks by Kenneth Anger
"The most exciting use of cinema I have seen." Tennessee Williams

"Despite the difficulties of 'forbidden' subject matter, the film's intensity of imagery produces an effect of imaginativeness and daring honesty which on the screen is startling." Lewis Jacobs, *Hollywood Quarterly*

"This film comes from that beautiful night from which emerge all true works. It touches the quick of the soul and this is very rare." Jean Cocteau

International Prizewinner at the Brussels, Cannes and Paris Film Festivals.

The Blood of the Beasts by George Franju
Franju's tormented and controversial masterpiece, the artistic sensation of Paris and London for 3 years, at last presented in America. A film of savage honesty and violent visual impact. Prix Jean Vigo and Grand Prix, International Film Festival, France 1950.

Fires Were Started by Humphrey Jennings
First American showing of the original version of this masterpiece of the documentary cinema—a tribute to a great director who recently died.

✦ ✦ ✦ ✦ ✦ ✦

Program Announcement, Spring 1952

March 1952

Margaret Mead: 1st Days in the Life of a New Guinea Baby
The first hour after birth: an almost incredible portrayal of motherhood among the head-hunting Latmul tribe, produced and narrated by the famed anthropologist.

Pen Point Percussion
The celebrated Canadian animator Norman McLaren (*Fiddle-De-Dee*) who makes films without a camera, now explains how to make music without instruments, and presents a fascinating camera-less, synthetic sound film.

Lascaux: Cradle of Man's Art
A cave sealed for 30,000 years is discovered by accident and reveals the most remarkable collection of prehistoric paintings yet found. William Chapman's film study explores the amazing work of Cro-Magnon artists, and their affinity to modern art.

Ordinary People
Produced by Basil Wright (*Song of Ceylon*), this documentary classic tells a moving and perceptive story of the London Blitz.

Vocalization and Speech in Champanzees
This Psychological Cinema Register film is a frequently amusing record of the famous chimp (recently featured in LIFE) who learned how to talk.

April 1952

Dance on Film: Two Experiments

Introspection
A striking cinematic experiment with the dance, differing fundamentally from stage choreography.

Lament
Winner of the Avant-Garde Film Award, Venice 1951. An intense and stirring portrayal of Jose Limon's dance classic, based on Lorca's poem.

Jackson Pollock
Intimate revelation of one of the most controversial modern artists at work, demonstrating his unorthodox technique of dripping and swirling paint onto canvas. Commentary spoken by Mr. Pollock.

Charles Chaplin: Early Work
This special survey features some of Chaplin's most hilarious 2-reelers produced before 1920, and is accompanied by a specially written evaluation of their technique and significance by Theodor Huff, author of the recent "Charles Chaplin" (Schuman).

Cell Division
These unprecedented motion pictures provide the first close-up views of chromosomes and cell division: a cinematic sample, magnified 200 times, of what occurs in the human body five billion times a day.

May 1952

Frenhofer and the Minotaur
A surrealist experiment inspired by Balzac's *The Unknown Masterpiece,* noteworthy for its poetic commentary delivered in the form of an "interior monologue." Produced by Sidney Peterson at the California School of Fine Arts.

Land Without Bread
Luis Bunuel's uncompromising social documentary—an unforgettable picture of poverty and degradation in Spain. Produced by the maker of *Un Chien Andalou* and *The Forgotten Ones.*

Transfer of Power
A difficult subject is translated into an exciting film adventure in this scientific film classic noted for its imaginativeness and clarity of exposition.

Color
A riotous and original experiment in colors, forms and textures, produced at the Chicago Institute of Design.

Pool of Contentment
A brilliant new British film producing talent explores the foibles of man in a film that introduces humor into the documentary film.

June 1952

Night Mail
One of the great masterpieces of the poetic cinema, with verse commentary by W. H. Auden and music by Benjamin Britten. Produced by John Grierson.

Eskimo Summer
A sensitive and revealing glimpse into the lives of a group of nomadic Eskimos. Accompanied by original Eskimo music and folk songs. Consultant: Robert Flaherty.

Robert Flaherty: A Rare Film Record
Discovered by Cinema 16, this is a rare camera study of the late Flaherty, father of the documentary film (*Nanook*). It recaptures his charm, humanity and ready wit, as he recounts his discovery of Sabu and other anecdotes connected with his films.

Tomorrow Is a Wonderful Day
An absorbing and beautifully executed story of the emotional rehabilitation of a young Jewish boy who, having lived through the concentration camps, is slowly freed of his suspicion and terror in a children's village in Palestine. Jewish customs and festivals are portrayed, accompanied by original Palestinian songs.

SPECIAL EVENTS (in addition to the 8 regular showings)
Free to members—attendance optional because of the nature of these films—dates to be announced.

Fireworks by Kenneth Anger
"The most exciting use of cinema I have seen." Tennessee Williams

"Despite the difficulties of 'forbidden' subject matter, the film's intensity of imagery produces an effect of imaginativeness and daring honesty which on the screen is startling." Lewis Jacobs, *Hollywood Quarterly*

"This film comes from that beautiful night from which emerge all true works. It touches the quick of the soul and this is very rare." Jean Cocteau

International Prizewinner at the Brussels, Cannes and Paris Film Festivals.

The Blood of the Beasts by George Franju
Franju's tormented and controversial masterpiece, the artistic sensation of Paris and London for 3 years, at last presented in America. A film of savage honesty and violent visual impact. Prix Jean Vigo and Grand Prix, International Film Festival, France 1950.

Fires Were Started by Humphrey Jennings
First American showing of the original version of this masterpiece of the documentary cinema—a tribute to a great director who recently died.

Forum Discussion of De Sica's *Miracle in Milan*
Conducted by Richard Griffith, curator, Museum of Modern Art Film Library, and Parker Tyler, author, "Magic and Myth of the Movies."

✦ ✦ ✦ ✦ ✦ ✦

Program Notes Compiled from Various Authors for Georges Franju's *The Blood of the Beasts* and Kenneth Anger's *Fireworks*, Shown in May 1952

THE BLOOD OF THE BEASTS

A Forees et Voix de France Production by Paul Legros (1949). Scenario and direction: Georges Franju. Camera: Marcel Fradetal. Music: Joseph Kosma. Commentary: Jean Painleve. Song by Charles Trenet. (20 min.)

Prix Jean Vigo and Grand Prix, International Film Festival, France 1950

Distributed by Cinema 16, New York.

"It may seem odd to describe the treatment of such material as this film deals with, as unsensational, but THE BLOOD OF THE BEASTS, though direct, has in fact a quiet and lyrical quality. The horror, and the pity this horror must occasion, are implicit throughout, but the emphasis in the film is on the strange phenomenon the whole activity represents, the fact that those engaged in it are not brutes but ordinary people. The sadness of the environs of Paris, the rapt, withdrawn actions of the slaughterers, the objective statements of the camera in the face of this odd surrealist atmosphere—animals seen communicating their suspicions to each other, the outrushes of blood—all this, inspite of its intense reality, gives to the film an almost dream-like quality, reinforced by Kosma's oddly gentle, poetic score."
—British Film Institute

"Most arresting of all the new films in the documentary group...a horrible, sickmaking picture... the brilliantly realized intention of its candor is simply to show what goes on behind the carefully drawn curtain of our sensibilities at our very doors."
—Bosley Crowther, The N. Y. Times

"Throughout Georges Franju's admirable documentary there is not a scene that fails to be moving, as if unintentionally, by the sheer beauty of its great visual style. To be sure, it is a distressing film; it will doubtlessly be called sadistic, for it fully comes to grips with the drama of its subject, never shirking the issue. It shows us the killers of whom Baudelaire spoke, the killers who kill without hate. It shows us the sacrifices of innocent animals. At times it reaches the heights of tragedy in the terrible surprise of their gestures, of attitudes we had never known of, brutally thrust at us by the camera. The horse, hit on the forehead, collapsing to its knees, already dead. The reflexes of beheaded calves, still struggling. In short, a world both noble and vile, that squeezes its last trickle of blood onto a white tablecloth, where the gourmet must not think of the martyrdom of the victims, into whose flesh he now plunges his fork.

Once again courageous film-makers, unhampered by considerations of success, have proven that the cinema is the vehicle for realism and lyricism, that all depends on the angle from which the scenes of life are viewed, and they have made us share their own particular vision which sharply points up the miracle of everyday happenings."
—Jean Cocteau

"The fantastic in fiction is generally obtained by giving to the artificial (decor, sets) the semblance of the real. In our film, we have tried to restore to the documentary reality its appearance of artificiality, and to nature, the aspect of cardboard decor. To do this, we photographed all buildings either head-on or from a profile view, avoiding any semblance of depth. Whether it is the passing of a barge which seems to emerge on an empty lot as a theatrical set emerges from the wings (the water having been blocked out photographically) or whether it is a tree which seems to have been borrowed from a theatrical prop shop, it is always with the constant preoccupation of expressing the plastic character of the decor that we often waited for days until the atmosphere was proper, or until objects were illuminated with that peculiarly Parisian, almost extra-solar, light. The choosing of the month of November for the interior shots was imposed on me by the fact that at that time the animals are slaughtered by electric light and that the smoking blood in the freezing cold of the slaughterhouses allowed us to compose our images properly.

Our cameraman Fradetal always worked with a portable camera and succeeded, in spite of the constant danger of being horned by an infuriated animal, in obtaining perfectly stable photographic images and smooth continuity. This was the more surprising since the light was extremely opaque and the lighting equipment necessarily inferior; the lights were suspended from the ceiling so that the animals would not trample on them. The sound, post-synchronized four months later, required both skill and audacity on the part of Verchere, our engineer, and Joseph, my assistant, who revealed remarkable subtlety in the choice of sound effects. In order to stress the almost ritualistic nature of the quartering of the animal, we supplied strange, murmuring voices in the background in a scene in which the killers, rendered almost indistinct by the smoking blood, seem to officiate like priests under a cone-directed light. And just as a defeated boxer is said to hear bells ringing in his ears, so the horse, breaking down under the shot of the gun, hears, as does the audience, the sound of the little bells in its harness. The death of the horse (who falls as if bowing in prayer) initiates the first slaughtering sequence. The dramatic beauty of the movement implied in this sequence was worth being carefully stressed and prepared.

It was for reasons of aesthetic realism that, on the exterior shots, I chose a girl's voice, child-like and confidential, to deliver Painleve's moving and ironic commentary. This voice first comments on the relatively pleasant views of the market vendors, but its subsequent contrast with the first scenes of slaughter provokes a lyrical explosion, accompanied by a violent shock, on the part of the surprised spectator. Likewise, it provokes a fit of indignation in those philistines among the audience who love domestic animals provided they are amused by them, savage beasts provided they are tamed, and who love to eat meat provided they do not see where it comes from. If they accuse us of sadism (fortunately, only few of them do), they mistake cinematographic means (which are only a factor in the looked-for artistic effect) for an end. I suspect that they do not know what sadism is. But if I were to start explaining my reasons for making this film, it would look like an attempt at self-justification to these tired, insipid souls who, while professing sympathy for these animals, are in truth pitiless."

—Georges Franju

FIREWORKS

Produced and photographed 1947 by Kenneth Anger (California). Distributed by Cinema 16. (15 min.)
Prix Henri Chomette, "Best Experimental Film"; Prix International for Best 16mm Film, Paris 1950; Special Award for Poetic Film, Belgian International Film Festival 1949; Special Awards at the Biarritz and Cannes International Film Festivals.

"The most exciting use of cinema I have seen." Tennessee Williams

"This film comes from that beautiful night from which emerge all true works. It touches the quick of the soul and this is very rare." Jean Cocteau

"This remarkable film was made by Kenneth Anger at the age of seventeen, under obvious emotional stress; in the spoken prologue he explains that the film served as a release for the obsessive desires of his dreams, and from the beginning the film is constantly startling, frightening, like a leaping electric wire. The motifs of blood and fire twist together the desired states of terror and ecstasy in unforgettable images, as irresistibly demanding as a cry of pain. In FIREWORKS Anger's fierce helplessness, his determined honesty must awake in the sensitive spectator emotions of pity and admiration." Alan Cook in Sequence Magazine.

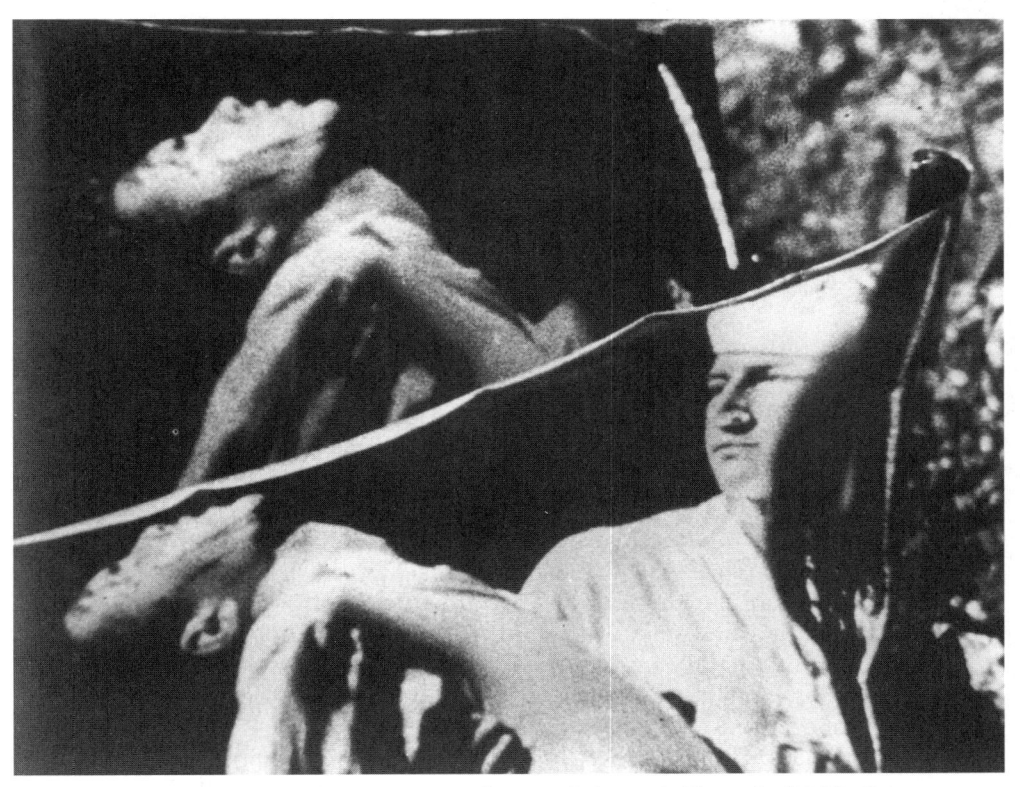

Illustration 40. Photographic evocation of Kenneth Anger's *Fireworks* (1947). Courtesy Museum of Modern Art Film Stills Archive.

"Despite the difficulties of 'forbidden' subject matter, the film's intensity of imagery, the strength and precision of its shots and continuity, produce an effect of imaginativeness and daring honesty which on the screen is startling. The objectivity of the style captures the incipient violence and perversion vividly, and the film becomes a frank and deliberate expression of personality. Consequently the film has a rare individuality which no literal summary of its qualities can communicate." Lewis Jacobs in Hollywood Quarterly

"As stream-of-consciousness in filmic terms, FIREWORKS is more a spontaneous 'dream' than a carefully structured 'dream' such as BLOOD OF A POET, Cocteau's classic film with which FIREWORKS has points of contact. Anger's film is a more or less direct attempt to deal with typical homosexual fantasies, and because his method is virtually automatic—one image or event flowing spontaneously from the previous one—the result is a film closely resembling the standard variety of wish-dream. Of course wish-dreams, as psychoanalysis has long established, are often fused with fear-dreams. The day-dreaming (and night-walking) homosexual feels towards the sex-object of the sailor, it sometimes happens, a decided ambivalence expressed in this film by the most sensational of its visual effects; the fireworks as a "human fountain." This visual pun is on gunfire, harmful, rather than pleasurable, and in turn the pun is referable to the general idea that a lover may be both friend and enemy. In the figurative explosion of the head (ingeniously conveyed by actually scratching the film) and in the Christmas-tree headdress, Mr. Anger has employed a poet's metaphoric sense to extend the central idea of fireworks. Such images are erotic, changing their kinesthetic forms in accordance with the association: if the time is Christmas, love becomes a more-than-ordinary gift, and the thrill of anticipation vibrates in the head like the star at the top of the ritual tree or assumes a tree-like form under the bedsheet. All the same, as in poetry having effective imagery but uneven writing, Anger's film is technically imperfect while its value as a poetic and psychological document is not to be gainsaid. It would have been better artistically, I believe, if such literal elements as the scene in the "Gent's Room" had been omitted; this scene provides, on the other hand, an instance of the habits of homosexuals and a possible real genesis of such a fantasy as this.

Mr. Anger informs us that psychiatrists have joined him in believing his film may be used as 'clinical therapy' in the cure of homosexual neuroses. Such a use for FIREWORKS is plausible enough; one may question, however, that it is the best approach from the viewpoint of admirers of experimental films. So it is not as a psychological document that it is presented by Cinema 16, but as an attempt to exploit the motion picture as an artistic medium. FIREWORKS has aroused high enthusiasm in Paris, where Cocteau is one of its endorsers. The chief reason for this enthusiasm, in all likelihood, is the literary cult of homosexual eroticism lately established there by Jean Genet. Yet I think the best way to approach and judge Anger's film, as an artistic organism, is to disregard the cult-nature of its content and conceive it as though it were any kind of erotic fantasy. Greater experience for Kenneth Anger as a serious artist in film should bring more smoothness and taste to his performances. The isolated beauty no less than the psychological force of many shots will register with ease. The upside-down views to symbolize emotional inversion; the stream of milk hitting the chin to signify the sailor's diaphragm muscles; the flower-like exfoliation of the entrails connecting sex with loss and suggesting love and birth as pain; the daring apparent allusion to the Pieta in the image of the youth carried by the sailor; all these have poetic intuition and human authenticity. If a more ideal artistic logic may be imagined for them, Mr. Anger is still to be congratulated for having the courage to give them any artistic status at all."

Parker Tyler

✦ ✦ ✦ ✦ ✦ ✦

Parker Tyler, "*Rashomon* as Modern Art," Cinema 16 Pamphlet (1952)

Rashomon, the new Japanese film masterpiece, is a story about a double crime: rape and homicide (or possibly suicide). The time is the Eighth Century A. D. It is told in retrospect, and in successive layers, by the three participants, the dead warrior (through a mediumistic priestess), his raped wife, and a notorious bandit perhaps

Illustration 41. Cover of *Cinema 16 Pamphlet One.*

responsible for the warrior's death as well as for his wife's violation, and by a woodcutter who alleges himself to have witnessed, accidentally, the whole episode. The quality of the film narrative is so fine than an astonishingly unified effect emerges from the conflicting stories furnished by the three principals and (following the inquest) by the lone witness. The bandit and the woman have separately fled the scene of the crimes, where the woodcutter claims, at first, to have arrived only in time to find the warrior's corpse. Nominally, the film comes under the familiar heading of stories that reconstruct crimes. However, this story does not go much beyond the presentation of each person's testimony.

The woman claims to have killed her husband in an irresponsible fit of horror after the rape took place; her husband claims to have committed hari-kiri out of grief and humiliation; the bandit claims to have killed him in honorable combat; and the woodcutter confirms the bandit's story while picturing the conduct of all participants quite differently from the ways they respectively describe it. As no trial of either of the living participants is shown, and as no consequent action reveals anything conclusive as to the crime, the decision as to the actual truth of the whole affair falls to the spectator's option. Since technically the woodcutter is the only "objective" witness, he might seem the most reliable of the four testifiers. But his integrity is *not* beyond question; the version by the warrior's ghost has contradicted his version in an important detail—one inadvertently confirmed by the woodcutter's implicit admission (in an incident following the inquest) that he stole a dagger at the scene of the crime. The ghost has testified that he felt "someone" draw from his breast the dagger with which he alleges he committed hari-kiri.

Logically, if one's aim be to establish in theory the "legal" truth of the affair, the only obvious method is to correlate all the admissible facts of the action with the four persons involved in order to determine their relative integrity as individuals—a procedure complicated necessarily not merely by the given criminal status of one participant but by the fact that all but the woodcutter have willingly assumed guilt. A further difficulty, in general, is that nothing of the background of any character is given beyond what can be assumed from his visible behavior and his social status; for example, there is only the merest hint of something unusual in the journey of the warrior and his lady through the forest. Again, even from direct observation, we have to depend a great deal on these persons as seen through the eyes of each other. So, unless one be prejudiced for one sex or another, one social class or another, it seems almost impossible to make a really plausible choice of the truth-teller (if any). Are we to conclude, in this dilemma, that *Rashomon* amounts to no more than a trick piece, a conventional mystery-melodrama, left hanging? My answer is *No*. There are several things about the movie which argue it as a unique and conscious art, the opposite of a puzzle; or at least, no more of a puzzle than those modern paintings of which a spectator may be heard to say: "But what is it? What is it supposed to mean?"

Perhaps more than one profane critic has wisecracked of a Picasso, a Dali, or an Ernst, that it demands, a posteriori, the method described by the police as "the reconstruction of the crime." My opinion is that the last thing required for the elucidation of *Rashomon's* mystery is something corresponding to a jury's verdict. Such a judgment, esthetically speaking, is as inutile for appreciating the substance of this movie as for appreciating the art of Picasso. In *Rashomon*, there is no strategic effort to conceal any more than a modern painter's purpose is to conceal instead of reveal. The basic issue, in art, must always be *what* the creator desires to reveal. Of such a painting as Picasso's *Girl Before Mirror*, it may be said that it contains an "enigma." But this enigma is merely one specific aspect of the whole mystery of being, a particular insight into human consciousness in terms of the individual, and so has that complex poetry of which all profound art partakes. So with the enigma of *Rashomon*. This great Japanese film is a "mystery story" to the extent that existence itself is a mystery as conceived in the deepest psychological and esthetic senses. As applied to a movie of this class, however, such a theory is certainly unfamiliar and therefore has to be explained.

Chagall with his levitated fantasy-world and childhood-symbols, Picasso with his creative analysis of psychological movements translated into pictorial vision—such painters set forth nude mysteries of human experience; each, in the static field of the painting, reveals multiple aspects of a single reality, whether literally or in symbols. *Rashomon*, as a time art, cinema, corresponds with multiple-image painting as a space art. The simplest rendering of time-phases in an object within the unilateral space of a single picture is, of course, in Futurist painting, such as Balla's famous dog, ambling by the moving skirts of its owner; the dachshund's legs are portrayed multiply with a fanlike, flickering kind of image similar to images as seen in the old-fashioned "bioscope" movie machine. The same dynamic principle was illustrated by Dr. Marey's original time-photography of a running horse, except that the register there was not instantaneous but successive; at least, the photographer had the cinematic idea of keeping pace with a running horse to show the pendulum-like span of its front and hind legs while its body seemed to stay in the same place (treadmill dynamics). Even in the contemporary movie camera, some movements may be so fast that one gets the sort of blur shown in Futurist images. The analogy of *Rashomon* with such procedures of stating physical movement is that, for the single action photographed, a complex action (or "episode") is substituted, and for the single viewpoint toward this action, multiple (and successive) viewpoints. The camera in this movie is actually trained four times on what theoretically is the same episode; if the results are different each time, it is because each time the camera represents the viewpoint of a different person: a viewpoint mainly different, of course, not because of the physical angle (the camera is never meant to substitute for subjective vision) but because of the psychological angle.

"Simultaneous montage" in cinema is the double-exposure of two views so that multiple actions occur in a *unilateral space visually* while existing in *separate spaces literally* and possibly—as when a person and his visual recollection are superimposed on the same film-frame—also in separate times. A remarkable aspect of the method of depicting memory in *Rashomon* is its simplicity: each person, squatting in Japanese fashion as he testifies, squarely faces the camera and speaks; then, rather than simultaneous montage, a flashback takes place: the scene shifts wholly to the fatal spot in the forest. The police magistrate is never shown and no questions addressed to the witnesses are heard. When it is the dead man's turn to testify, the priestess performs the required rite, becomes possessed by his spirit, speaks in his voice, and the scene shifts back as in the other cases. Thus we receive the successive versions of the action with little intervention between them and with the minimum of the "courtroom action."

Of course, there is a framing story, which retrospectively reveals the inquest itself. The action literally begins at the Rashomon Gate, a great ruin where the woodcutter and the priest, who has brought the woman and been present at the inquest, are sheltered during a rainstorm; joined by a tramp, these two gradually reveal everything that has taken place according to the several versions. What is important is the inherent value of the way the technique of the flashback has been variously used. The separate stories are equally straight-forward, equally forceful; no matter which version is being related, his own or another's, every participant behaves with the same conviction. As a result (it was certainly this spectator's experience) one is compelled to believe each story implicitly as it unfolds, and oddly none seems to cancel another out. Therefore it would be only from the policeman's viewpoint of wanting to pin guilt on one of the persons that, ultimately, any obligation would be felt to sift the conflicting evidence and render a formal verdict. Despite the incidental category of its form, *Rashomon* as a work of art naturally seems to call for a response having nothing to do with a courtroom.

Of an event less significant, less stark and rudimentary in terms of human behavior, the technical question of "the truth" might prove insistent enough to embarrass one's judgment. The inevitable impulse, at first sight, is to speculate on which of those who claim guilt is really guilty of the warrior's death. But whatever conclusion be tentatively reached, what eventually slips back into the spectator's mind and possesses it, is the traumatic violence of the basic pattern: that violence that is the heart of the enigma. The civilization of this medieval period is turned topsy-turvy by the bandit's strategy, in which he tricks the man, ties him up, and forces him to witness his wife's violation. It is only from this point forward that the stories differ: the woman's reaction to the bandit's assault, the husband's behavior after being freed from his bonds—everything is disputed by one version or another. But is not the heart of the confusion *within the event itself*? Is this happening not one so frightfully destructive of human poise and ethical custom that it breeds its own ambiguity, and that this ambiguity infects the minds of these people?

All the participants are suffering from shock: the warrior's agonized ghost, his hysterical wife, the bandit, when caught, seized with mad bravado. Unexpectedly—for the paths of the couple and the bandit have crossed purely by accident—three lives have been irretrievably altered after being reduced to the most primitive condition conceivable. Two men (in a manner in which, at best, etiquette has only a vestigial role) have risked death for the possession of a woman. Basically, it is a pattern that was born with the beginnings of mankind. Such an event, in civilized times of high culture, would of itself contain something opaque and even incredible. What matters morally is not how, from moment to moment, the affair was played out by its actors but that it should have been played *at all*. The illicit impulse springing up in the bandit's breast as the lady's long veil blows aside, is so violent that its consequences attack the sense of reality at its moral root. Regardless of what literally took place in the forest's depths that mild summer day, each participant is justified in reconstructing it in a manner to redeem the prestige of the moral sense, which consciously or not, is a civilized person's most precious possession. It should be emphasized that it is the Japanese people who are involved, and that to them honor is of peculiarly paramount value; even the bandit is quick to seize the opportunity to maintain—truthfully or not—that he behaved like a man of caste rather than an outlaw; he has testified that following the rape (to which, he says, the woman yielded willingly) he untied the husband and worsted him in fair swordplay.

Hence, a psychologically unilateral, indisputable perspective exists in which the tragic episode can be viewed *by the spectator:* a perspective contrary to that in which one of the persons appears technically guilty of the warrior's death. This perspective is simply the catastrophe as a single movement which temporarily annihilated the moral reality on which civilized human consciousness is based. The "legal" or objective reality of the affair (what might be called its statistics) is exactly what cannot be recovered because the physical episode, as human action, has been *self-annihilating*. Of course, then, it might be claimed that the woodcutter, not being involved except as a spectator, is a disinterested witness of the episode, and accordingly his story that the three actors in the tragedy really played a grim farce, in which two cowards were the heroes and a shrew the heroine, is the correct version. But the opening scene of the framing story makes it plain that the woodcutter's mind is in a state similar to that of the participants themselves; indeed, he is evidently dismayed and apparently by the fact that all their testimony belies what he proceeds to reveal to the priest and the tramp as "the truth." However, as the shocked witness of such a debacle of the social order—in any case a victory of evil over good—this peasant may have withheld his testimony out of superstitious timidity. If, in fact, he saw all that took place, then the added confusion that the participants contradict each other may raise bewilderment in his simple mind—may even tempt him to exploit his subconscious envy and resentment against his betters by imagining their behavior as disgraceful and ludicrous. It seems within *Rashomon's* subtle pattern to suggest that even a simple, disinterested witness should be drawn psychologically into the chaos of this incident; after all, there is no proof that he did not invent his own account in competition with the others'. This assumption would lend credit to the conclusion that the real function of each witness's story is to salvage his own sense of reality, however close his version to the event as it took place. Perhaps it would be accurate to add that the facts themselves have no true legal status since each witness is forced to draw on his subjective imagination rather than on his capacity to observe. In this case, each is in the position of the proto-artist, who uses reality only as a crude norm; the sense of invention enters *into* reality. On the other hand, there is the literal truth of the denouement, the climax of the framing story, in which the woodcutter adopts a foundling baby who has been left in the Gate's interior. The relation of this incident to the story proper strikes me as the most problematical element of all, if only because the film would have remained intact without it.

Morally, of course, this incident functions as a reinstatement of human values in the sense of good. But the specifically religious view that humanity has hopelessly degraded itself in the forest episode (the view represented by the priest) is more external than essential to the whole conception. The priest thinks in terms equivalent, logically, to the law's terms: truth or falsehood. Since some lying is self-evident, the sin of concealment is added to crime; i.e., concealment of the truth, not of the crime, for all profess crime. Ironically enough, *confession* has become a sin. What seems significant to the whole is the collective nature of the liars: they literally outnumber the truth-teller (whichever he may be). The "sin" involved has gone beyond individual performance and exists objectively as would a natural cataclysm such as a volcanic eruption. That each participant assumes guilt, including the dead man, reveals the comprehensiveness and irresistibility of the disorder. A lie, then, actually becomes the symbol of the operation by which these people mutually regain their moral identities. These identities having been destroyed as though by an objective force beyond anyone's control, any means seems fair to regain them. Since, however, they cannot separate themselves from the sense of *tragedy*, they prefer to be tragedy's heroes—its animating will rather than its passive objects. But why should the three tragedies seem as one?

To revert to our analogy with the visual media of painting and still photography, the plastic reality with which we have to deal in Rashomon is multiform rather than uniform. Within one span of time-and-space, reality (the episode in the forest) has been disintegrated. While the witnesses' stories accomplish its reintegration, they do not do so in terms of the physically unilateral except in the final esthetic sense in which the totality of a work exists all at once in a spectator's mind. The analogy is complex, but literally it is with the Futuristic image of the walking dog; like this image, the total image of Rashomon varies only in detail and degree. There is no variation on the background and origin of the tragedy; no contradiction as to the main physical patterns of the rape and the death of the warrior by a blade-wound. So the main visual aspect is held firmly, unilaterally, in place. Another image of Futurist painting renders the angles of air-displacement caused by the nose of a racing auto. Such "displacements" exist in Rashomon severally in the respective accounts of a physical action deriving from one main impetus: the desire to possess a woman.

The total psychological space in this movie, because of its complexity, is rendered in literal time as is music. A similar psychological space is rendered *simultaneously* in Picasso's *Girl Before Mirror* by the device of the mirror as well as by the double image of profile-and-fullface on the girl. Her moonlike face has a symbolic integralness as different "phases" of the same person; that is, her fullface denotes her personality as it confronts the world and her profile her personality as it confronts itself: the mirror image in which the fullface character of her aspect is diminished. To Meyer Schapiro we owe a basic observation as to this painting: it plays specifically on the body-image which each individual has of himself and others, and which is distinct from the anatomical image peculiarly available to photography. The mirror-image in Picasso's work thus asserts a psychological datum parallel with the dominantly subjective testimony of each witness in *Rashomon's* tragedy. The mirror of the movie screen is like the mirror in the painting as telescoped within the image of the total painting; successively, we see people as they think of themselves and as they are to others; for example, at one point during the woman's story, the camera substitutes for the viewpoint of her husband toward whom she lifts a dagger: we see her as conceived by herself but also as she would have been in her husband's eyes. In revealing, with such expressiveness and conviction, what novels have often revealed through first-person narratives or the interior-monologue, the film necessarily emphasizes its *visual* significance. The sum of these narratives in *Rashomon* rests on the elements of the tragedy in which all agree: one raped, one was raped, one killed, one was killed. The "variations" are accountable through something which I would place parallel with Schapiro's body-image concept: the *psychic image* that would apply especially to the memory of a past event in which the body-image is charged with maintaining, above all, its moral integrity, its ideal dignity. In a sense, Picasso's girl reconstructs and synthesizes her outer self-division within the depths of the mirror; so in the depths of each person's memory, in *Rashomon*, is recreated the image of what took place far away in the forest as consistent with his ideal image of himself.

In modern times, the human personality—as outstandingly demonstrated in the tragi-comedies of Pirandello—is easily divided against itself. But what makes a technically schizophrenic situation important and dramatically interesting is, paradoxically, the individual's sense of his former or possible unity, for without this sense he would not struggle morally against division: he would be satisfied to be "more than one person." In analytical cubism, we have a pictorial style expressing an ironic situation within the human individual's total physique, including his clothes; we do not perceive, within an individual portrayed by Picasso in this manner, a moral "split" or psychological "confusion"; rather we see the subject's phenomenal appearance portrayed formalistically in terms of its internal or "depth" elements, its overlaid facets, or complex layers of being, which—though presumably not meant to signify a conflict in the personality—correspond logically, nevertheless, to the moral dialectic within all consciousness (subjective/objective, personal/social, and so on). The same logical correspondence is seen even more plainly in the anatomical dialectic of Tchelitchew's recent paintings, where the separate inner systems are seen in labyrinthine relation to the skin-surface. Indeed, man as an internal labyrinth is common to diverse styles of modern painting, all such styles necessarily implying, as human statements, the sometimes bewildering complexity of man's spiritual being. Great beauty is justifiably found in such esthetic forms, which indirectly symbolize an ultimate mystery: that *human* mystery to which *Rashomon* so eloquently testifies in its own way and which comprises the transition from birth to death, from the organic to the inorganic, which is the individual's necessary material fate.

Against the awareness of his material fate, the individual erects many defenses: art, pleasure, ethics, God, religion, immortality—ideas, sensations, and acts whose continuity in him are preserved by constant cultivation, periodic renewal, unconscious "testimony." These constitute his moral identity in the social order. In them resides the essence of his being, the law of his contentment (such as it be), and his rational ability to function from hour to hour. In the lives of the persons of *Rashomon*, where this objective order prevailed, utter chaos was suddenly injected. Each person was shaken out of himself, became part of that blind flux which joins the intuition of the suspense-before-birth with that of the suspense-before-death and whose name is terror. This was largely because of the tragedy's physical violence, which temporarily vanquished human reason. If we look at the terror of war as depicted in Picasso's *Guernica,* we observe a social cataclysm of which the forest episode in *Rashomon* is a microcosm. Curiously enough, *Guernica* happens to be divided vertically into four main sections or panels, which Picasso has subtly unified by overlapping certain formal elements. Thus, while the great massacre is of course highly simplified here in visual terms, it is moreover synthesized by means of four stages or views. As wrenched by violence as are the individual forms, they congregate, so to speak, to make order out of confusion. Though Picasso was not recomposing from memory, he might have been; in any case, the drive of art is toward formal order and the individuals in *Rashomon,* as proto-artists, have this same drive. As gradually accumulated, the sum-total of *Rashomon* constitutes a *time mural* whose unity lies in the fact that, however different are the imaginations of the four witnesses, whatever harsh vibrations their mutual contradictions set up, the general design (as the film-makers have moulded it) remains and dominates the work's final aspect of great beauty and great truth.

Cinema 16 and the author are interested in your answers to the following questions:

Do you agree with the preceding theory as the proper way of evaluating this movie? (Yes or No)

If not, do you have a different approach of some special kind? (Yes or No)

If you have no such approach, do you think the person responsible for the warrior's death in this movie can be identified with ordinary detective methods of reasoning? (Yes or No)

If your answer to Question Two or Three is Yes, will you briefly say who, in your opinion, is the killer, and why?

please send your replies
to the address below
cinema 16 also exhibits and distributes
unusual films: for information
address

Cinema 16
175 Lexington Ave
New York 16
New York

Reprinted by permission of Diana Collier.

✦ ✦ ✦ ✦ ✦ ✦

Letter to Amos Vogel from Jean Renoir, 8/11/52

1 Via Iacopo Peri—Roma—

August 11, 1952

Mr. Amos Vogel
Cinema 16
175 Lexington Avenue
New York 16, N.Y.

Dear Mr. Vogel:

The person you may contact who would certainly know my time of arrival in New York is Harold Salemson. He is a friend and also represents my present picture in the U. S. His address is:

1501 Broadway, N/Y/ 18—Tel. Chockering 4-2395

I hope you found a print of LA REGLE DU JEU with the right cutting and good subtitles. Even so this picture is very confusing for non French audiences. I know several Americans who saw it at the Film Library in Paris and didn't like it at all. Their French companions were very much surprised. I was told of the same negative reaction in a festival in Germany, and I know that the commercial showing in the States was definitely unsuccessful. On the other hand in France the young generation places LA REGLE DU JEU much above LA GRANDE ILLUSION or LA BETE HUMAINE and I think they are right. Is this difficulty to interest foreign audiences due to the dialogue maybe impossible to translate; or the spirit of the picture (bad or good) so far away from the Anglo-Saxon spirit?

I will be very happy nevertheless to introduce my work to the members of Cinema 16 but I wanted to warn you that we must not expect a success.

With my best regards.

Sincerely,

[hw] Jean Renoir

Jean Renoir

Reprinted by permission of Alain Renoir.

✦ ✦ ✦ ✦ ✦ ✦

Program Announcement: Fall 1952/Spring 1953

October 1952

Trance and Dance in Bali (Margaret Mead)
An authentic, unstaged film record of the famous Balinese ceremonial dance drama, including the Kris ritual and actual trance seizures. A dramatic glimpse into

Illustration 42. Program announcement, fall 1952/spring 1953.

the mind of primitive man, produced and narrated by the famed anthropologist. Balinese music and chants.

Recent Work of U. P. A.
The best new cartoons by the producers of Columbia's *Gerald McBoing-Boing*, who are revolutionizing the American cartoon field, including their celebrated *Man Alive* (recently featured in *LIFE*). Last season's showing of UPA's earlier work was one of Cinema 16's most popular programs.

Images of Madness (*Images de la Folie*)
An unprecedented film document, consisting of the drawings and paintings of the insane. A moving and macabre journey through the universe of the mentally ill. Photographed at the Paris International Exposition of Psychopathic Art.

A Phantasy (Norman McLaren)
The newest creation of the famed Canadian animator. Delightful objects come to life in a surrealist landscape to disport themselves in playful rituals and grave dances. Set to jazz and synthetic sound.

November 1952

Image in the Snow
A young man's spiritual journey through the lyric landscape of a dream to a world of violence and disillusionment. This absorbing new film poem by Willard Maas is the first motion picture to use twelve-tone music... an original score by the distinguished American composer Ben Weber.

Time in the Sun
Produced by Marie Seton from Eisenstein's unfinished masterpiece *Que Viva Mexico*. Against a panorama of paganism and strange religious rituals are shown joyous and sad vignettes of Mexican life, as the people of Mexico dramatize their own moving story of love, death and oppression.

"A film of great pictorial splendor, most fascinating and enormously significant... nothing short of magnificent!"—*Herald Tribune*

"A spectacular display and magnificent account of Mexican native life which rises from mere externals to spiritual forces... the photography of Edward Tisse is so stunning and of such dramatic strength that each individual shot offers an exciting experience."—Crowther, *The N. Y. Times*

Form in Motion
The "secret" life of tableware: a mysterious film ballet, in which spoons, forks and cups reveal their subtle and delightful fascinations. By Jose Pavon.

December 1952

Ecstasy
The celebrated and much-maligned Czech poetic film presented for the first time in its uncensored, original version: a story of passion and desire, seen entirely through a woman's eyes. Produced by Gustav Machaty. With Hedy Kiesler-Lamarr, Aribert Mog. First Prize, International Film Exposition, Venice 1934.

"There can be no division of opinion as to the beauty of the photography, the artistry of the direction and the daring with which the subject of primal urge and the ecstasy of its fulfillment are portrayed. This picture puts Machaty into the front ranks of artistic directors."—*Variety* (reporting on this original version, as shown in Paris.)

"I may be wrong, but I saw nothing in any sense immoral in this picture."—Judge Learned Hand

Land of Enchantment: Georgia O'Keeffe
Henwar Rodakiewicz's masterpiece of the American documentary cinema: A beautifully photographed, poetic evocation of the Southwest, conveying the atmosphere and texture of this majestic desert and prairie country. Inspired by the life and canvases of America's foremost woman painter, it also offers an intimate and informal film portrait of O'Keeffe. The memorable sound track features Indian and Mexican native chants, myths and dances. (Restricted film)

January 1953

This Is Robert
This restricted film (not available for public showings) is here presented by special arrangement with its producer Dr. Lawrence J. Stone, Professor of Child Study, Vassar College, who will introduce and discuss it.

Entirely unstaged and unrehearsed, this unique film study was photographed over a period of five years, and traces the development of Robert, a "difficult" child, from his arrival at nursery school at two up through his first year in public school at seven.

An authentic document, the film is unprecedented in its comprehensive examination of a child's growth and problems over several years, as shown in continuing psychological and intelligence tests, unusual projective techniques (such as frustration and hostility games) and changes in behavior patterns.

Hidden cameras add to the film's authenticity. Produced by the Department of Child Study at Vassar College as part of a Series, "Studies in Normal Personality Development."

SPECIAL EVENTS 1952/1953

3 Cinema 16 Interviews: In-person appearances of noted film personalities, followed by film presentations and questions and discussion from audience:

1. Jean Renoir, director of *Grand Illusion, The River* will introduce his controversial full-length feature film *The Rules of the Game,* a grotesque commentary upon European society on the brink of collapse. Banned by the Vichy Government... panned by the American critics.

2. Archer Winsten, noted film critic of the *New York Post* will introduce and discuss Carl Dreyer's neglected film masterpiece *Day of Wrath,* a story of jealousy and passion under the shadow of religious fanaticism and superstition, set in the 17th century.

3. Sidney Meyers, director, writer, editor of *The Quiet One,* will introduce and discuss his film *The Quiet One.*" A genuine masterpiece, fashioned out of the tortured experiences of a Negro boy; a deep surge of compassion for the victims of injustice in this sad world."—Crowther, *N. Y. Times* (International Prizewinner, Venice and Edinburgh International Film Festival.)

4. Les Film Maudits: An Evening of Damned Films.
A special program of films not recommended to the squeamish, yet important in their own right:

Vampyr (The Strange Adventures of David Gray)
Carl Dreyer's eerie masterpiece—one of the greatest horror films ever made—here presented in its original, complete version, as re-discovered by Cinema 16. A startling and fantastic story, pervaded by nightmare and obsession, drawing its inspiration from the world of superstition and mysticism. Includes the complete funeral sequence, one of the most astonishing scenes ever filmed.

Fireworks (Kenneth Anger)
"Despite the difficulties of 'forbidden' subject matter, the film's intensity of imagery produces an effect of imaginativeness and daring honesty which on the screen is startling." (Lewis Jacobs, *Hollywood Quarterly*). International Prizewinner at the Brussels, Cannes and Paris Film Festivals.

Illustration 43. *The Quiet One* (1948) by Sidney Meyers. Courtesy Museum of Modern Art Film Stills Archive.

The Blood of the Beasts
Georges Franju's tormented and controversial masterpiece, the artistic sensation of Paris and London... a film of savage honesty and violent visual impact. Grand Prix Jean Vigo, International Film Festival, France 1950.

5. *Secrets of a Soul*
The first psycho-analytic film ever made: One of the most memorable of early German films, long lost, and now re-discovered by Cinema 16. Directed by G. W. Pabst, famed German director, in collaboration with Drs. Hanns Sachs and Karl Abraham, collaborators of Siegmund Freud. Based on one of Freud's case histories, it tells of a man's anxiety neurosis and its elimination by psycho-analysis. Unusual dream sequences and trick photography. Stars the noted German actor Werner Krauss.

6. Screening of the 1952 Robert Flaherty Award-Winners
This joint City College of New York–Cinema 16 program features the award presentations and screening of the best documentary films of the year, as selected by Bosley Crowther, *N. Y. Times;* Richard Griffith, Museum of Modern Art Film Library; Lewis Jacobs, Film Author; Alice Keliher, New York University; Hans Richter, City College of New York; Amos Vogel, Cinema 16; Archer Winsten, *N. Y. Post.*

7. *Childbirth: Normal Delivery*
This outstanding instruction film, used in leading medical and nursing schools nationally, is a step-by-step portrayal of the actual birth of a baby, as photographed under medical supervision. In color.

Also: *Breast Self-Examination for Cancer* and other medical-surgical films.

✦ ✦ ✦ ✦ ✦ ✦

Letter to Amos Vogel from Kenneth Anger, 12/8/52

December 8, 1952
Via Cilicia, 51
Rome

Dear Amos Vogel:

Thank you for your letter of November 21. I have been rather indisposed of late and this accounts for the delay in my reply.

As I never did receive the program notes or comment in Austria which you indicate you sent me, the fault must be placed in the mails. I am still very interested in seeing the above, so if you will be so kind as to send me other copies it will be appreciated.

I am sorry that I misunderstood the expiration date of our present contract. As my copy is in Paris I could not consult it. I am agreeable to the three year extension that you have suggested; you will find your copy signed by me, enclosed. If you need any stills or additional material for your catalogue space on FIREWORKS, please let me know. I am also enclosing a copy of an article of mine which appeared in the French revue, "Cahiers du Cinema" which takes up my personal approach to the film medium and its application in FIREWORKS. You may keep it in your files for the duration of our agreement and loan it out to critics, etc. who might desire a further orientation regarding my work. If you think it would be more helpful, or that by chance you might be able to "place" it somewhere, I can provide you with a copy in English.

I would like to amplify somewhat more the "reservation" I expressed before regarding sending the film to the West Coast. My hesitation was motivated by the fact that I have some knowledge of Rohauer's methods from the past, and therefore felt some trepidation that my film might be exploited by him as "sensational" and attract unfavorable attention. Since the police regime in that area is ever more puritanical and terroristic it is even probable that such methods would result in interference or seizure, with trouble for everyone. I assume that in New York under your special cultural set-up you do not have to contend with interference from the censor. But does this apply to other groups throughout the country? Again I would like to ask you, what protection do either of us have in the event of seizure by a public authority? I do not think that such a possibility is as "inconceivable" as you might think, taking into consideration the "neo-conservative" or "police-state" trends in the US scene. I should also like to know your attitude regarding this as it will in part influence my interest in sending other films to the US. Additionally I would like to know if you have a clause in your contract with your rentors specifically forbidding copying or reproducing the film in any form. I have learned through experience in Europe that certain individuals are not above attempting this.

On the occasion of the May Festival in Paris this year I was asked to present my works to a private assembly of some of the literary figures who assembled there. Among them was Glenway Wescott, who took a special interest in the film, expressing the opinion that he was certain the Sexual Research Institute of the Indiana University, headed by Dr. Kinsey, would want to view the film and very possibly even own a print for their collection. Of course I would be very willing to cooperate with them regarding this. However I am uncertain of Mr. Wescott's whereabouts in the US at the moment, so I am unable to write him to remind him to contact Kinsey (who he has assisted at various times with research) to arrange a screening, using the Cinema 16 copy. Since the research group is a Rockefeller grant, there should be no objection to payment either for rental or for purchase of a print. I therefore would appreciate very much if you would either write directly to the Indiana University group suggesting that the film is available, and that Mr. Wescott has indicated that it would be of interest for them to review (enclosing such material or comments on the film which you have) or else, try to contact Mr. Wescott through his publisher or other source, advising him that you have a copy of the film available should he or Dr. Kinsey wish to arrange a showing. I should imagine it worth the trouble to pursue this a little, as it might result through the contacts of this group with a series of showings. Above all I would be interested in any comments which such a group might make, and you could indicate that they could write to me directly. I think there is even a possibility that some member of the group would furnish a comment or interpretation which you could use in publicity or as a program note. If you make any progress, be sure to let me know.

I will now take up the matter of EROS EIDOLON. Its subject might be constituted, as for FIREWORKS, as a subjective "psychodrama". Again the expression is through dream symbology, upon what is certainly a more complex and interacting structure. In the arena of the disturbed personality are released the archetypal elements from the realm of collective, unconscious "myth". It is full of sweeping, patterned movement, extreme stylization of performance, atavistic violence, and "hermetic" references. It was made solely with my own "secret sharer" in mind, certainly with no thought of audience reaction. As I have stated before, I am most uncertain of what its reception might be before anything but the most select groups. Above all some acquaintance with Jung's theories would seem necessary for the fullest appreciation, though I am aware that some people can grasp these realities "intuitively". I would be interested in trying it out with your audiences if you think this advisable.

Now the problem facing me is to finish this film. The obstacle is almost entirely of a financial nature. At the present moment my credit is blocked with the Rome laboratory which is handling my work, and I have not even been able to see my most recent footage. This lamentable condition will persist until I can scrape together the amount to cover my bill there which is nearly $200. And to this moment I have been unable to find <u>from any source whatsoever</u> financial assistance for my project. I have paid for every bit out of my own living allowance, which has required considerable sacrifice on my part. Indeed, I seem to be the only one "willing" to sacrifice for the cause of my creative film work—despite verbal expressions of interest from many sources. But such so-called "interest" only increases my bitterness, I am afraid. I am very disillusioned that I have not found any patronage in Europe, where sympathy with my work is more general. Yet I certainly have tried hard enough, without any more tangible results than the US—which was nil. Under these circumstances, how can I continue in my chosen art medium? I do not look for much future improvement, though I will be willing to accept suggestions should you have any.

This impasse and the heartbreaking difficulties I have encountered in the making of EROS EIDOLON certainly account in part for my present depression and illness. It is only through occasional excursions into journalism or criticism that I can hope to supplement my present minimum income—which decidedly does not include production expenses. Since this has reached the proportions of an emergency, I would appreciate your forwarding to me at this time any income I have accrued since the September statement, as well as the amount covering the spring showing of FIREWORKS which you say Cinema 16 has scheduled. If you would consider advancing an additional amount from my future income, needless to say it would be helpful.

However difficult things may prove to be for me here, I still do not forsee a return to the US. The cultural rewards of living in Europe continue to be of immense importance to me as an artist.

I do hope that the activity of Cinema 16 is coming along well. I have not heard much news concerning the experimental film picture in the US; if any new figures or works of interest have appeared I wish you would let me know.

Again, I would appreciate hearing from you, at your convenience, concerning the matters expressed in this letter.

Most sincerely,

[hw] Kenneth Anger

Reprinted by permission of Kenneth Anger

✦ ✦ ✦ ✦ ✦ ✦

Letter to Amos Vogel from Kenneth Anger, 1/31/53

January 31, 53
Via Cilicia, 51
Rome, Italy

Dear Amos,

I have received your letter of the 26th with the enclosure of $50. I appreciate your willingness to make an advance at this time on my future earnings, and as I am truly in desperate need of funds at this time to continue my work, I hope you may be able to forward the rest without delay. I had rather hoped to have heard from you before, as it so happens that my work has been at a complete standstill for the past month due to the lack of ready cash. A hundred dollars will at least enable me to get rolling again for the time being. As I told you before, my meagre living allowance does not manage to include production expense, and I have not as yet found the outside financial help or patronage which adequate working conditions require.

If you should know of any private individual or group of individuals who might take an interest in a small amount of sponsorship of my current project, I would appreciate it immensely if you could contact them or put me in touch with them. I could send them a resumé of the scenario and stills of the completed sections. I definitely will need a minimum of four hundred more to see my way through lab costs, sound recording, and final prints. If I must depend entirely on my own resources for this sum, it could conceivably delay release of the film for another year. Naturally, I would agree to pay off the amount through my profit from rentals of that or other films.

It so happens that a newly-organized distribution organization on the West Coast is apparently interested in handling this new film; they would advance me the costs to complete it providing I would sign in advance a five-year contract. The terms of the contract are 40/60%, with the higher percentage going to the film-maker. I have made no commitments at all at the moment, but I thought it only fair that I let you know of this proposition. However I would much rather that you continue to handle exclusively my work in the U.S. The very real fact remains that I <u>need urgently</u> the money which they are apparently willing to risk, towards the film's completion.

I do believe that EROS EIDOLON will be as interesting, if not more so, than FIRE-WORKS; also that since its mainspring is mythology, that it might appeal to a wider audience. I also have an idea for a 15 minute poetic study transpiring in the fantastic gardens of the Villa d'Este at Tivoli, to be called WATERWORKS. During the past month I have sketched the scenario and I could complete it without too much difficulty. And I feel fairly certain that its appeal would be a wide one. I therefore am contemplating filming this short work within the next few weeks, as it would require only a comparatively small outlay of film and preparation, so that I could release it before EROS, which will consume some time for cutting and rather complicated sound treatment.

Concerning Rohauer, if he has had no sign of interference with showings in the past, I suppose it is acceptable to continue bookings with him. However for the next booking you might counsel him to use some discretion in advertising for the film, since it is released for cultural study purposes. I appreciate your checking into the legal questions which I raised in my last letter.

I have all my negatives with me here in Europe. However it is a simple matter for me to have another print struck off if you feel there is a need for it. The problem is how ship the print to you. Perhaps the Cinémathèque in Paris might be willing to include it in a shipment of the International Film Federation to the US which is not subject to customs. If not, perhaps I can discover a private individual returning to the US who could include it in their luggage. Or do you have any arrangements for international shipment without duty or customs inspection? This will also be an issue in shipping prints of EROS and WATERWORKS to the US.

I would be willing to sell prints to serious film study groups on the lease arrangement you mentioned. If you have any prospects, let me know. I for one am quite certain that the Kinsey research group at the University of Indiana would want a copy for their collection if they are properly contacted. I think the price might depend to some extent on the nature of the group to whom it is sold, but off-hand I would say in the neighborhood of one hundred dollars. Let me know your opinion on this. In any case I would wish to send you fresh prints from here, as I am sure duping would not be satisfactory. I will arrange for another print here immediately if you think it's indicated.

I am wondering how the print you have is holding up. I would suggest cleaning it after every rental with a velvet and carbon tetrachloride, as my experience has shown this greatly prolongs print life. Has it survived so far without any obvious breaks or scratches? If it has been damaged, I would prefer to send a fresh print for your spring showing.

In the meantime I will be investigating the best means of shipping a print to you. Please do let me hear from you at your earliest convenience.

Very truly yours

[hw] Kenneth

Reprinted by permission of Kenneth Anger.

[The film Anger calls "Waterworks" in paragraph 4 was completed in 1953 and released as Eaux d'artifice.*]*

✦ ✦ ✦ ✦ ✦ ✦

Letter to Scott MacDonald from George Stoney, 3/22/01

62A Waterloo Rd.

Dublin 4, Ireland
March 22nd, 2001

Dear Scott MacDonald,

[. . .]

When *ALL MY BABIES* was shown at Cinema 16 I was still living in Washington D.C. so attended the series only the odd time when I happened to be in town. At that time it was the only venue showing documentaries or experimental films on a regular basis so I was aware of its status and importance. The night when my film was programmed I remember in great detail.

My wife and I had invited Mrs. Mary Coley (the midwife-star of the film) to come to Washington and stay with us. It was the first time she had been north of Atlanta and the second time she had ever been a guest in the home of a white family. (The first time was when she came to Atlanta—also her first visit to that city—to stay with Sylvia Betts, the editor, when we were recording her narration for the film.) Nevertheless, she never seemed to lose her feeling of perfect calm and security. We sat together on the front row while the screening took place. It was "Miss Mary's" first time seeing the film on so big a screen and without feeling the pressure of watching it with family, friends, the white medical establishment, etc. Accordingly, she got caught up in the story to such an extent that when, in the second reel, she pours water into a pan, spilling some on the top of the stove and producing a sizzle she jumped, then, laughing, grabbed my arm and said,

"Mr. Stoney, I forgot myself so much I thought that water was going to spill on my legs."

After the screening, amid literally thunderous applause, she was asked to come to the stage and take the microphone, which she did with simple dignity and assurance. Then we retired to someone's large apartment nearby where there was a reception. Francis Flaherty was the co-honore and the two women sat together in a corner with dozens of people congratulating them, then sitting at their feet.

Certainly that screening was responsible for giving the film recognition as more than a simple training film for semi-literate Black midwives. Given the frank nature of the birth scenes I doubt that anyone else would have given the film the unrestricted screening Amos gave it.

[. . .]

Cordially,

George Stoney

[I have not been able to determine the exact date of this presentation. Since it is announced in the Fall 1952–53 schedule but not in the Spring 1953 schedule, my assumption is that the event occurred early in 1953.]

✦ ✦ ✦ ✦ ✦ ✦

Program Announcement: Spring 1953

March 1953

Christ Among the Primitives
Set to Roman Vlad's aggressive musical score, this brilliant if controversial art film uses astonishing primitive sculptures to trace the evolution of religious motives in early man. An IFE Release.

Land of the Long Day
This 1952 Robert Flaherty Award Winner is a poetic and impressionistic account of Eskimo life on Baffin Island during the short Arctic summer. A sensitive evocation of primitive life, accompanied by Eskimo songs. A NFC Release.

The Garden Spider
Undoubtedly one of the best post-war scientific films, this beautifully photographed close-up study of a spider at work reaches almost poetic intensity. An IFE Release.

Mambo
A swift and powerful color abstraction, set to the savage rhythms of a mambo. A Kinesis Production by Jordan Belson.

Images From Debussy
Restless reflections of trees, clouds and landscapes in water provide a poetic illustration of Debussy's music. An AF Films Release by Jean Mitry (*Pacific 231*).

April 1953

Van Meegeren's Faked Vermeers
This remarkable film—an artistic detective story—recounts one of the most fabulous hoaxes in the history of art and its subsequent exposure by science.

Form in Motion
The "secret life" of tableware: A mysterious film ballet, in which spoons, forks and cups reveal their subtle and delightful fascinations. By Jose Pavon.

John Gilpin
Ronald Searle, the noted British illustrator, animates a delightful 18th Century ballad by William Cowper. From the British Film Institute's Painter and Poet Series.

That the Deaf May Speak
A sensitive and compassionate film study of the emotional and educational problems confronting children deaf from birth in a "hearing" world. A Campus Film Production for Lexington School of the Deaf. "

An outstanding motion picture achievement!"—Edinburgh International Film Festival 1952.

Bop Scotch
Colorful flagstones and paving textures are syncopated with strident and restless bop music. A Kinesis Film by Jordan Belson.

May 1953

Coral Wonderland
A journey into a mysterious universe: Luxurious coral growths and startling, underwater creatures of the island reefs come to life in magnificent color under the microscope.

Song of the Prairie
A delicious satire on Westerns, enacted by Trnka's (*The Emperor's Nightingale*) charming puppets, complete with a damsel in distress and a rootin' tootin' climax.

Plague Summer
The record of a journey of six allegorical characters through landscapes brutalized by war. A hand-drawn adaptation by Chester Kessler of Kenneth Patchen's "Journal of Albion Moonlight." "Drawn with extraordinary imagination."—Lewis Jacobs, *Experiment in Film*.

Maya Through the Ages
An exploration of the most brilliant New World Civilization of Pre-Columbian times, including Healey's historic trek into the jungles of Chiapas, the discovery of the temples of Bonampak with their unique frescoes, and his unforgettable encounter with the present day descendants of the Mayas, the strange Lacandona Indians, Stone Age survivors in our time.

SPECIAL EVENTS 1953

February 25

Sidney Meyers, director, writer, editor of *The Quiet One* will introduce and discuss the film. "A genuine masterpiece." *The New York Times*. International Prize winner, Venice and Edinburgh Festivals.

March 10

Kameradschaft
Long unavailable, this masterpiece of social realism is at last presented to American audiences. Pabst's somber drama of a mine disaster on the French-German border carries a profoundly moving message of international brotherhood. "Probably the most important artistic experiment in German film history."—Manvell, *Experiment in Film*.

March 17

Secrets of a Soul

The first psycho-analytic film ever made: a memorable early German film by G. W. Pabst, re-discovered by Cinema 16. Based on one of Freud's case histories, it tells of a man's anxiety neurosis and its elimination by analysis.

April 8

Les Films Maudit: An Evening of Damned Films

A special program of films not recommended to the squeamish, yet important in their own right; introduced by Amos Vogel, Executive Secretary of Cinema 16.

Vampyr
Dreyer's eerie masterpiece, one of the greatest horror films ever made, here presented in its original version. A startling and fantastic story, pervaded by nightmare and obsession. Includes the complete funeral sequence, one of the most astonishing scenes ever filmed.

Fireworks (Kenneth Anger)
International Prize winner at the Brussels, Cannes and Paris Film Festivals. "Despite the difficulties of 'forbidden' subject matter, the film's intensity of imagery produces an effect of imaginativeness and daring honesty which on the screen is startling." (Lewis Jacobs, *Hollywood Quarterly*).

The Blood of the Beasts
Georges Franju's tormented and controversial masterpiece, the artistic sensation of Paris and London... a film of savage honesty and violent visual impact. Grand Prix Jean Vigo, International Film Festival, France 1950.

May 12

Archer Winsten, noted film critic of the New York Post will introduce and discuss Carl Dreyer's neglected masterpiece—*Day of Wrath,* a story of passion and jealousy under the shadow of religious fanaticism and superstition, set in the 17th century.

✦ ✦ ✦ ✦ ✦ ✦

Letter to Kenneth Anger from Amos Vogel, 4/23/53

4/23/53

Dear Kenneth:

As you probably know we had another showing of your film on April 8. I must say that as a result of our programming VAMPYR, BLOOD OF THE BEASTS and your film together, we had a very distinguished audience present, including practically everybody in the art and avant-garde field you can think of. The reaction to the film was very similar to the one we had last year. There was at first a sort of stunned silence, followed by scattered applause of the more intrepid among the audience and by a prolonged and pronounced "buzzing" in the audience, indicating that everybody had been in some way stimulated or provoked or disgusted or fascinated by the film. This type of reaction occurs very infrequently.

I should also add that during the showing of the film there was dead silence in the auditorium, much more pronounced than usual, indicating the close attention they paid to the film.

One young man staggered out during the beating sequence and threatened me for "provoking" him by showing such a film. I should also add that Mr. Hart was present (he is the man who runs the National Board of Review and their magazine "Films in Review", in which he acted as a censor in regard to the Markopoulos films a few years ago). I have no idea what he intends to do in relation to this showing, which I understand he thoroughly disliked. The lady with him referred to the film as "fairy propaganda." If he decides to pan the film that is his privilege as a critic, although we may disagree with this opinion. If he decides to again set himself up as a censor this is entirely a different matter and will be handled accordingly.

Enclosed are two clippings. Archer Winsten still thoroughly dislikes your film but keeps on writing about it, under the overall title "all favorable."

I have a letter from Dr. Kinsey informing us that Mr. Wescott has never been a member of the staff but merely a good friend who contributed some literary material. Kinsey does not at all refer to your film. I don't know why. I shall write to him again.

You have not as yet acknowledged receipt of the balance which I sent about a month ago.

As a result of our new catalog rentals of your film are already picking up. I shall send you a complete statement in the next few weeks.

Very sincerely yours,

[Amos]

[In paragraph 1, Vogel is referring to Anger's Fireworks.*]*

✦ ✦ ✦ ✦ ✦ ✦

Program Announcement: Fall 1953/Spring 1954

October 1953

Frustration Play Techniques: Ego Blocking Games
This restricted film demonstrates special projective techniques developed at Sarah Lawrence College for the study of ego development. Hidden cameras record unstaged psychological test situations in which various children react differently to competition, frustration and prohibition. An absorbing film record, presented by special arrangement with Dr. L. Joseph Stone (*This is Robert*) of Vassar College.

Menilmontant
This swift and uncompromising tale of love and violence in the slums of Paris—filled with delicate visual poetry—projects an intimate and astonishingly penetrat-

Illustration 44. Program announcement, fall 1953/spring 1954.

ing study of human emotions. "Unquestionably one of the most remarkable of amateur films... entitled to all and more of the praise it has elicited from European critics."—Museum of Modern Art.

Thurber's *Unicorn in the Garden* and other U. P. A. cartoons
The producers of Columbia's *Gerald McBoing-Boing*, who are revolutionizing the American cartoon field, take another significant step forward in their eagerly awaited animation of the famed James Thurber fable, proudly presented by Cinema 16 with others of their best new cartoons. "A session of Thurber's war of the sexes... simply wonderful!"—Winsten, *N. Y. Post*.

November 1953

Latuko
First and only New York showing of the complete version of the controversial Museum of Natural History production, rejected by the New York censors for public showings. Startling and oddly fascinating glimpse into the mind, witchery and violence of primitive man, as seen in tribal ceremonies, initiation rites and ritual sacrifices of the never before photographed Latuko tribe in equatorial Sudan. Remarkable on-the-spot sound (recorded by advanced experimental methods) achieves impact seldom equalled. In technicolor.

In the Street
The street as a theatre and a battleground; a somber and profoundly sensitive portrayal of the faces of Spanish Harlem, shot with concealed cameras by the makers of *The Quiet One* (Janice Loeb, James Agee and Helen Levitt). A memorable human document, full of the unexpected. "Goya's lithographs come true... a masterwork!"—*The Nation*.

Psychotherapeutic Interviewing
Complete film record of unrehearsed psychiatric interview is shown and analyzed in this restricted training film for psychiatrists. Demonstrates repression, anxiety and the role of the psychiatrist. A Psychological Cinema Register Release.

December 1953

Bells of Atlantis (Ian Hugo)
A curious and magical film voyage, at once disturbing and delightful, in search of "the lost continent" of first human memories. One of the most notable recent poetic films, based on Anaïs Nin's prose poem in her book *The House of Incest*. First orchestrated all-electronic score ever composed for film (no live sounds or instruments), created by Louis and Bebe Barron. Acted and narrated by Anaïs Nin.

Angotee
Sensitive evocation of birth, childhood and adolescence in a primitive society, filled with vivid insights into Eskimo life. A National Film Board of Canada Release.

The Crazy Ray (*Paris Qui Dort*)
Rene Clair's first film, shown in its complete version; the fantastic adventures of a group of "survivors" in a Paris paralyzed by an inventor's magical ray. A vivacious and satirical fairy tale full of cinematic tricks and serious overtones.

Neighbors (Norman McLaren)
A sardonic comment on the state of man, produced by stop-motion photography and mimed to synthetic sound. An Academy Award Winner by the famed Canadian animator (*Fiddle de Dee*).

January 1954

Grief
First showing before a non-professional audience of Dr. René A. Spitz' famed psychoanalytic study of children deprived of mother love. "These films have been a classic for those in psychiatry, but have rarely been seen by others. They are profoundly moving."—*N. Y. Times*.

Analysis-on-Film of "Great Expectations"
Unprecedented film experiment, produced by the British Film Institute: A key episode from the motion picture is shown and analyzed on film, to indicate how horror and surprise are created in the spectator.

El Dorado
A poetic evocation of the three faces of British Guiana, conveying the atmosphere and texture of a land of unexplored jungles, solitudes and primitive peoples. Accompanied by native dances and chants. A notable documentary film achievement. Released by BIS.

The Singing Street
A charming and informal medley of the traditional songs and street games of Scottish children, danced and sung by the children of Edinburgh in the streets of the city. 1952 Prize winner, Edinburgh International Film Festival.

SPECIAL EVENTS 1953/1954

October 28

1. A Symposium on "Poetry and the Film"
conducted by a group of distinguished poets, playwrights and film producers:

    Dylan Thomas, celebrated British poet
    Arthur Miller, author, *Death of a Salesman, The Crucible*
    Maya Deren, leading avant-garde film maker
    Parker Tyler, poet, film critic, author, *Magic and Myth of the Movies*
    Willard Maas, poet, film maker: chairman

November 16

2. Activity Group Therapy
This authentic film record of 65 group therapy sessions, shot with concealed cameras over a period of two years, reveals the personality changes effected in a group of emotionally disturbed children. An exciting and unstaged demonstration of one of the most important present-day group therapy practices—used in hospitals throughout the world—which permits children to "act out" their disturbances upon their environment and each other in the presence of a permissive adult. Not available for public showings, this unique film study is presented by arrangement with its producer, Dr. S. R. Slavson, who will introduce it.

January 13

3. *Bed and Sofa*
Alexander Room's famous "lost" masterpiece of the European film, cited in all histories of the cinema, at last available for scrutiny. A penetrating and forthright study of unconventional sexual mores in early Soviet Russia, set against the background of the housing shortage. "An unequalled instance of pure psychological and intimate representation of human character."—Rotha, *The Film Till Now*

February 3

4. *The Magnificent Ambersons*
Orson Welles' controversial Mercury Production for RKO, based on Booth Tarkington's Pulitzer Prize Novel. A somber tale of American magnificence and decay at the turn of the century, starring Joseph Cotten, Agnes Moorehead, Dolores Costello, Anne Baxter, Tim Holt. Especially noteworthy because of the unorthodox camera work and experimental sound track. Includes the controversial last sequence. "The finest recreation of a bygone era the movies have yet shown. . . the trouble with Welles is that he assumes too much intelligence in his audience."—Winsten, The *New York Post*.

February 24th

5. The Work of Jean Vigo
Two masterpieces by one of the few authentic geniuses of the cinema who died at 29 with less than four hours of film to his credit:

Illustration 45. *The Magnificent Ambersons* (1942) by Orson Welles. Courtesy Museum of Modern Art Film Stills Archive.

A Propos de Nice
Cinema 16 proudly introduces Vigo's first film, hitherto unavailable in America—a ferocious comment on the decadence of the French riviera.

L'Atalante
The disillusionments and tender raptures of young love, as seen in a strange and lovely film. With Michel Simon, Dita Parlo. "A masterpiece! . . . Vigo strings his episodes like pearls. . . Michel Simon gives one of the screen's greatest performances."—*Hollywood Quarterly.*

March 17

6. *The Abbey Theatre's "Juno and the Paycock"*
Sean O'Casey's great tragedy—a striking portrayal of the more squalid side of Irish life—superbly acted by the Abbey Theatre players as directed by Alfred Hitchcock. With Sara Allgood, Barry Fitzgerald, John Laurie. "Truly a remarkable film. The casting of Sara Allgood as Juno was an inspiration."—The British Film Institute.

Illustration 46. *L'Atalante* (1934) by Jean Vigo. Courtesy Museum of Modern Art Film Stills Archive.

April 21

7. Voyages Into the Subconscious
A program of films exploring facets of the subconscious by experimental cinematic techniques:

The Lead Shoes (Sidney Peterson)
Surrealist exploration of old English ballad, interwoven with boogie-woogie score. Prize winner, Venice 1950.

Mother's Day (James Broughton)
Ironic portrayal of childhood recaptures its egocentricity, sensuality and sadism in striking images.

Geography of the Body (Willard Maas)
The terrors and splendors of the human body as the undiscovered, the mysterious continent.

Glens Falls Sequence (Douglass Crockwell)
Outstanding example of "free associations" on film, hand-painted on glass by noted American illustrator.

On the Edge (Curtis Harrington)
Dream or reality? A somber episode of desperation, acted out by two people in a setting of weird desolation.

May 10

8. A Program of Restricted Nazi Propaganda Films (by special permission of the U. S. Dept of Justice)

Triumph of the Will
Leni Riefenstahl's cinema masterpiece, one of the greatest propaganda films of all time: official Nazi record of the 1934 Nuremberg Party Convention, actually staged for a vast battery of cameras like a colossal movie production. A huge and disturbing film spectacle, filled with mass scenes and ceremonies never equalled by Hollywood. Complete English sub-titles.

Also: restricted Nazi newsreels and shorts.

✦ ✦ ✦ ✦ ✦ ✦

"Poetry and the Film: A Symposium," 10/28/53

[On October 28, 1953, Cinema 16 held two sessions of a symposium with Maya Deren, Parker Tyler, Dylan Thomas, and Arthur Miller. Willard Maas acted as chairman. The following excerpts make up about one half of the symposium. Ideas repeated for the second audience and personal introductions of the panel make up, for the most part, the missing half.]

Maas: In a prepanel discussion earlier this week with the majority of the panel, we decided that maybe the best way to start this discussion would be to try to have the members of the panel outline... some of the basic aesthetic principles of the poetic film; and, therefore, I think I would like to call on Mr. Tyler first....

Tyler: Thank you. My thought was that the question, rather than the assumption, by which the symposium will proceed tonight is that of what poetry, in and outside the film, actually is. Perhaps it would be necessary, for such a demonstration, to conceive the question at the start, and honestly, as faced with the two horns of a dilemma. Now that dilemma is: On the one hand, there's the *theory* of poetry, its possibilities as such in the film medium, and on the other hand the *practice* of poetry, as concentrated in the avant-garde film. It should be hoped that we don't snag on either of these but will steer a just course between them. Now I thought we might get an over-all picture of the field to be surveyed, and to that end I'd like to give you a memorandum, so to speak, of the types of poetical expression that do appear in films today; that is, these expressions may be whole or fragmentary, they may be pure or impure, but at least they exist, and they are to be recognized as such. Now, poetical expression falls rather automatically into two groups: that is, poetry as a visual medium and poetry as a verbal medium, or, in a larger sense, as auditory, and that would, of course, include music. We might well begin with some of the shorter films that concentrate on poetry as a visual medium, and this, of course, leads right to Cocteau's *Blood of a Poet*, and to Buñuel-Dali's *Andalusian Dog*, and to Watson's *Lot in Sodom*. All these are classics now, and they emphasized a

Illustration 47. *Left to right:* Dylan Thomas, Arthur Miller, Willard Maas, Parker Tyler, Amos Vogel, and Maya Deren at the Cinema 16 symposium "Poetry and the Film," held in October 1953.

surrealist poetry of the image and gave rise to schools and styles of avant-garde all over the world. Cinema 16 patrons are familiar with some of these outstanding works—those of Maya Deren, of James Broughton, of Kenneth Anger, of Curtis Harrington. All these film-makers concentrated on what might be called pure cinema—entirely without words as a rule, although sometimes with music. Then to go back (after all, the avant-garde movement in poetry in America goes rather far back, at least to the 1920's) I know there was a type of film which got the name of cine-poem, and these films were impressionistic, but they concentrated on pictorial conceptions of city life, of nature, and importantly, they stressed abstract patterns. Then, of course, there's the poetry of painting in motion—the pure abstract film—which also has a considerable history (there are Norman McLaren, the Whitney brothers, and many others). Then, also as a candidate in this list (perhaps disputable, but at any rate certainly worth mentioning), a school of naturalistic poetry of which Robert Flaherty was the pioneer. And we presume that his films can be considered integral without the commentary. And, finally, I would include the dream and hallucination sequences, with sound effects sometimes, that appear in commercial films.

Now poetry as a visual-verbal medium: We have the fantasy films of Jean Vigo (these films are primarily visual); and we have the avant-garde films that are set to poems or to poetic prose (those of Sidney Peterson, of Willard Maas, of Ian Hugo); then there's what I would term the "severe formalism" of Sergei Eisenstein, whose montage borders on pure poetry. There are, of course, the Cocteau myth films: *Beauty and the Beast*, *The Eternal Return*, and *Orpheus*. And we might also include a special class of naturalistic poetry documents, such as *The River* and *The Blood of the Beasts*... of course they had commentary. And, then, to conclude, the fifty-fifty fusion; that is, Shakespeare's plays, Eliot's *Murder in the Cathedral*, and the numerous operas that have been filmed. Now these are, admittedly, only the main leads of a very broad field, indeed. Many definitions are required in order to isolate the poetic content and the poetic potentialities in these various manifestations... Above all, there's the indications of value that have to be made. I'm sure that the members of the panel, including myself, have a number of significant distinctions and perhaps even more important opinions on these aspects.

Maas: Well, Miss Deren, will you take over from there?

Deren: I'm going to do something I think is a bit risky, and that is to go a little bit into the question of what is poetry, and what distinguishes what we would call poetry from anything else, because I think that only if we can get this straight, can we sensibly discuss poetry in film, or the poetic film, or anything else. Now I say that it's risky, because this is a subject that has been discussed for many, many centuries, and it's been very difficult to pin down. But the reason I'm going into it is not because I think distinctions are important as formulae and as rigidities, but I think they're important in the sense that they give an audience, or any *potential* audience, a preparation, an approach, to what they're going to see. In the sense that if they're thinking they are going to see an adventure film, and if they are confronted with a poetic film, that's not going to go very well. I don't think one is always predisposed toward poetry; the whole notion of distinguishing and, if you will, labeling things is not a matter of defining them so much as a matter of giving a clue to the frame of mind you bring to them. In other words, what are you going to be watching as this unrolls? What are you going to be listening for? If you're watching for *what* happens, you might not get the point of some of the retardations because they're concerned with *how* it happens. Now poetry, to my mind, consists not of assonance; or rhythm, or rhyme, or any of these other qualities we associate as being characteristic of poetry. Poetry, to my mind, is an approach to experience, in the sense that a poet is looking at the same experience that a dramatist may be looking at. It comes out differently because they are looking at it from a different point of view and because they are concerned with different elements in it. Now, the characteristics of poetry, such as rhyme, or color, or any of those emotional qualities which we attach to the poetic work, also may be present in works which are not poetry, and this will confuse us. The distinction of poetry is its construction (what I mean by "a poetic structure"), and the poetic construct arises from the fact, if you will, that it is a "vertical" investigation of a situation, in that it probes the ramifications of the moment, and is concerned with its qualities and its depth, so that you have poetry concerned, in a sense, not with what is occurring but with what it feels like or what it means. A poem, to my mind, creates visible or auditory forms for something that is invisible, which is the feeling, or the emotion, or the metaphysical content of the movement.

Now it also may include action, but its attack is what I would call the "vertical" attack, and this may be a little bit clearer if you will contrast it to what I would call the "horizontal" attack of drama, which is concerned with the development, let's say, within a very small situation from feeling to feeling. Perhaps it would be made most clear if you take a Shakespearean work that combines the two movements. In Shakespeare, you have the drama moving forward on a "horizontal" plane of development, of one circumstance—one action—leading to another, and this delineates the character. Every once and a while, however, he arrives at a point of action where he wants to illuminate the meaning to *this* moment of drama, and, at that moment, he builds a pyramid or investigates it "vertically," if you will, so that you have a "horizontal" development with periodic "vertical" investigations, which are the poems, which are the monologues. Now if you consider it this way, then you can think of any kind of combination being possible. You can have operas where the "horizontal" development is virtually unimportant—the plots are very silly, but they serve as an excuse for stringing together a number of arias that are essentially lyric statements. Lieder are, in singing, comparable to the lyric poems, and you can see that all sorts of combinations would be possible.

It seems to me that in many films, very often in the opening passages, you get the camera establishing the mood, and, when it does that, cinematically, those sections are quite different from the rest of the film. You know, if it's establishing New York, you get a montage of images, that is, a poetic construct, after which what follows is a dramatic construct that is essentially "horizontal" in its development. The same thing would apply to the dream sequences. They occur at a moment when the intensification is carried out not by action but by the illumination of that moment. Now the short films, to my mind (and they are short because it is difficult to maintain such intensity for a long period of time), are comparable to lyric poems, and they are completely a "vertical," or what I would call a poetic construct, and they are complete as such. One of the combinations that would be possible would be to have a film that is a dramatic construct, visually, accompanied by a commentary that is essentially poetic; that is, it illuminates the moments as they occur, so that you have a chain of moments developing, and each one of them is illuminated. It's things of this sort that, I believe, occur in the work of Mr. Maas, who has done that to a certain extent in his last film, *Image in the Snow,* where the development of the film is very largely "horizontal," that is, there is a story line, but this is illuminated constantly by the poetic commentary so that you have two actions going on simultaneously. Now this, I think, is one of the great potentials of film and something that could very well be carried and developed much further, and I think that one of the distinctions of that film and also of *Geography of the Body,* is that it combines these principles. I think that this is a way of handling poetry *and* film, and poetry *in* film . . . I don't know how the other people feel about it.

Maas: Well, Mr. Thomas, being a poet, what do you feel about it?

Thomas: Well, I'm sure that all Maya Deren said was what I would have said, had I thought of it or understood it *(laughter and slight applause).* I was asked, on the side, whether that meant that I thought that the audience didn't understand what Miss Deren was saying. I'm sure they did, and I wish I was down there. But it sounds different from that side, you know. Now I'm all for (I'm in the wrong place tonight) . . . I'm all for horizontal and vertical *(laughter),* and all for what we heard about in the avant-garde. The only avant-garde play I saw in New York was in a cellar, or a sewer, or somewhere (*laughter*). I happened to be with Mr. Miller over there. We saw this play going on . . . I'm sure it was fine. And, in the middle, he said, "Good God, this is avant-garde." He said, "In a moment, the hero's going to take his clothes off . . ."

Maas: Did he?

Thomas: He did. (*Laughter.*)

Maas: All to the good.

Thomas: But I don't know. I haven't a theory to my back, as they say. But there are, all through films that I've seen all my life . . . there have always been . . . bits that have seemed to me . . . Now, this is a bit of poetry. They might have been in the UFA films or something that I saw as a child. Or somebody coming down some murderous dark, dark, silent street, apart from the piano playing. Or it might have been a little moment when Laurel and Hardy were failing to get a piano up or down a flight of stairs. That always seemed to me the poetry . . . when those moments came. Well, I have to go a step beyond those UFA films, now to the non-silent films. In the best of those moments, the words seemed to fit. They were really the right words, even though the right word might only be a grunt. I'm not at all sure that I want such a thing, myself, as a poetic film. I think films, [are] fine as they are, if only they were better! And I'm not quite sure that I want a new kind of film at all. While I'm recharging an almost empty mind with an almost empty battery, perhaps Mr. Miller would say something. (*Applause.*)

Maas: Well, I don't think I'll let it go at that, Mr. Thomas. Surely you must realize that the film is a popular medium, and you, more than anybody else, have tried to bring poetry to the public from the platform. Don't you think, in the popular art, in the way that the Elizabethan theater was a popular art, don't you think it would be possible in some way to weld poetry to the film? Do you think that it's just a verbal thing? That it would not be possible in the way that Elizabethan drama somehow welded language to the film?

Thomas: Well, just as a poem comes out . . . one image makes another in the ordinary dialectic process (somebody left out the word "dialectic," well I may as well bring it in, you know). So, as in a poem one image breeds another, I think, in a film, it's really the visual image that breeds another—breeds and breathes it. If it's possible to combine a verbal image to a visual image in this sort of horizontal way, I'd rather see horizontal films, myself. I like stories. You know, I like to see something going on *(laughter and applause).*

Maas: I shouldn't be saying anything; I'm the moderator. So, Mr. Miller, you talk about it.

Miller: Well, there've been about forty different ideas that have come across this table. It seems to me that to create a poetic film is, at bottom, the same problem as the drama presents when you contrast what is normally called naturalism with what is generally called a poetic drama. The only criticism I would have of such a discussion as this is that it is not tied to what anybody wishes to say. If I'm speaking to you now with a reasonable amount of confusion, I will sound confused, and

I will speak in this tone of voice. If, on the other hand, I was clearly imbued with something very emotionally important to me, I would start speaking in a different rhythm. I would possibly use some images and so forth, so that to speak in the blue without reference to our lives, without references really to the age in which we live, about this problem is an endless talk. Ah, that's the first place. On the question of technique, there's one obvious thing to me: The motion picture image is an overwhelming fact; it is different from any other experience we have in the arts because it is so much larger than we are. The possibility for the poet or the writer to tell a story or to transmit an emotion in their films, it seems to me, is contained within the image, so that I'm afraid, even though I'm much in sympathy with Willard's desire to join poetic speech with images, that, possibly, in the long run, it will be discovered to be a redundancy—that the poetry is in the film just as it is in the action of the play first. I was gratified to see that the poet's poet, T. S. Eliot, not long ago said as much, that, after pushing the drama around on his desk for many years, he had come to the conclusion that if the structure of the drama was not complete and beautiful, nothing he could do in the way of technical manipulation of words could get him out of the hole. I think, at bottom, that the structure of the film is the structure of the man's mind who made it, and if that is a mind that is striving for effect because it is striving for effect, the film will be empty, however interesting it happens to be on the surface. If it is a mind that has been able to organize its own experience, and if that experience is cohesive and of one piece, it will be a poetic film. Mr. Thomas has said, as Mr. Tyler has said, too, that the commercial film is full of poetic things because, at certain moments, in almost any poor structure, certain accidental qualities come into synchronization, so to speak, where, as in life sometimes, one needs only to drop a package of cigarettes, and the world explodes. Symbolic action is the point of all organization in the drama as well as in the film. To get back to the first proposition again . . . I think that it would be profitable to speak about the special nature of any film, of the fact of images unwinding off a machine. Until that's understood, and I don't know that it's understood (I have some theories about it myself), we can't begin to create, on a methodical basis, an aesthetic for that film. We don't understand the psychological meaning of images—any images—coming off a machine. There are basic problems, it seems to me, that could be discussed here. I've probably added no end to the confusion, but that's what I have to say at the moment. (*Applause.*)

Maas: Well, it seems to me that we have to start thinking about the image—the visual image and the verbal image. Can they be welded in some way?

Miller: I think that the basis for my remarks is perhaps almost physiological. I think that the reason why it seems to many of us that the silent film is the purest film and the best is because it mimics the way we dream. We mostly dream silent, black and white. A few of us claim to dream in technicolor, but that's disputed by psychologists. It's sort of a boast: Certain people want to have more expensive dreams . . . I think that the film is the closest mechanical or aesthetic device that man has ever made to the structure of the dream. In a dream, montage is of the essence, as a superimposition of images in a dream is quite ordinary. The cutting in a dream is from symbolic point to symbolic point. No time is wasted. There is no fooling around between one important situation and the most important moment in the next situation. It seems to me that if we looked at the physiology of the film, so to speak, and the psychology of the film, the way it actually turns off the machine, we begin to get the whole question of style and the whole question of aesthetics changing when one sees it that way. In other words, sound in films and speech seem, perhaps, like the redundancy they so often are in films. I'll just leave it at that for the moment; maybe somebody else will have something to say about it.

Maas: Maya, I'm sure you have something to say about it.

Deren: If everyone will forgive me, Mr. Miller has made several references to "the way it comes out of the machine," he obviously hasn't made a film because first you have to put it in the machine, and that's awfully hard. It does begin before the machine. And it begins in the mind of the creator. And your reference to montage, and so on, is, if I may be permitted to return to my "vertical"—that is, the relationship between the images in dreams, in montage, and in poetry—is . . . they are related because they are held together by either an emotion or a meaning that they have in common, rather than by the logical action. In other words, it isn't that one action leads to another action (this is what I would call a "horizontal" development), but they are brought to a center, gathered up, and collected by the fact that they all refer to a common emotion, although the incidents themselves may be quite disparate. Whereas, in what is called a "horizontal" development, the logic is a logic of actions. In a "vertical" development, it is a logic of a central emotion or idea that attracts to itself even disparate images which contain that central core, which they have in common. This, to me, is the structure of poetry, so that, for example, you could have a dramatic development, in the sense of a "horizontal" development, for a while, as I said, in Shakespeare, and let us take the monologues where, in a poetic or a "vertical" structure, he brings together all various images that relate to the feeling, let us say, of indecision. Now what I mean there by being essentially a "horizontal" development, is that it would have sufficed for Hamlet to say, "I can't make up my mind," and that's all, and that would not have affected the drama of the play, do you see? The poetic monologue there is, as it were, outside it or built upon it as a pyramid at that point as a means of intensifying that moment in the "horizontal" development. That is why film, I believe, lends itself particularly to the poetic statement, because it is essentially a montage and, therefore, seems by its very nature to be a poetic medium.

Miller: That's why I'm wondering whether the words are at all necessary, you see. Because the nature of the thing itself is so condensed. It would be like adding music to Hamlet's soliloquies.

Deren: May I answer that? The words are not necessary when they come, as in the theater, from what you see. You see, the way the words are used in films mostly derives from the theatrical tradition in which what you see makes the sound you hear. And so, in that sense, they would be redundant in film if they were used as a further projection from the image. However, if they were brought in on a different level, not issuing from the image, which should be complete in itself, but as another dimension relating to it, then it is the two things together that make the poem. It's almost as if you were standing at a window and looking out into the street, and there are children playing hopscotch. Well, that's your visual experience. Behind you, in the room, are women discussing hats or something, and that's your auditory experience. You stand at the place where these two come together by virtue of your presence. What relates these two moments is your position in relation to the two of them. They don't know about each other, and so you stand by the window and have a sense of afternoon, which is neither the children in the street nor the women talking behind you but a curious combination of both, and that is your resultant image, do you see? And this is possible in film because you can put a track on it.

Miller: I understand the process, but you see, in the drama there was a time, as you know, when action was quite rudimentary, and the drama consisted of a chorus which told the audience, in effect, what happened. Sometimes, it developed into a thespian coming forward and imitating action such as we understand action today. Gradually, the drama grew into a condition where the chorus fell away, and all of its comment was incorporated into the action. Now for good or ill, that was the development of the drama. I'm wondering now whether it's moot, whether it's to any point, to arrange a scenario so that it is necessary (and if it isn't necessary, of course it's aesthetically unwarranted) for words to be added to the organization of images, and whether that makes it more poetic. I don't think so. I can see the impulse behind it, but it seems to me that if it's a movie, it's a movie.

Maas: Well, doesn't it seem to have something to do with who is going to make this film? Is it going to be the man who has a poetical idea at the beginning, who then decides to work with a film director on this thing? Or is the poet going to work on it himself? Through words or through nothing, but just through a poetical idea, which is both visual and verbal at the same time? If he is going to work with a director he is going to have to be terribly close to that director. He may as well be the same person. Then you have to have a poet who can also make a film.

Thomas: Oh, I think that's absolutely true—or you could work very closely with someone who knew film technique to carry it out. But I think the poet should establish a scenario and a commentary that would do that as well. And he may as well star in it as well.

Maas: Miss Deren has played in her own films, and I think she played in them because she couldn't get people to do the things that a director asks people to do unless they pay them ten thousand a week. I know that for myself, because I'm working on a new poetic film with Mr. Ben Moore, another poet; we found that he had to play the leading role because nobody would go through the trouble to do it. You see, you're not going to get commercial people to do this. What I am interested in at the moment is Mr. Miller's idea about film, and I'm afraid, Mr. Miller, that I think that you think that it must always be a drama. Then if it is a drama, is there not a difference between prose drama and poetic drama? There is certainly a difference between Shakespeare and even Ibsen. Don't you think so?

Miller: I wasn't thinking only of the drama. Of course, there have been poetic pictures made, as you know, which are silent. I suppose most of them, as a matter of fact, are not dramas. But my preference is toward drama because I'm primarily interested in action. It seems to me an aesthetic impurity to introduce words into a picture of any kind. I was against, as a whole, the idea of spoken pictures, anyway. It simply attests to the poverty of imagination of screenwriters that they need the words, and to the poverty of the imagination of the audience that it demands the words. I don't think that it has anything to do remotely with real films. The words came in because the movies came after the theater, and the first people who moved into the movies were theater people, and the first commercially made films were, many of them, simply filmed plays. There's no relationship between the theater in that sense, and the films, for the simple reason I return to—a technical, physiological reason, and that is, that you're looking at an image many, many times larger than yourself, and that changes everything. It is a redundancy to add to that image, it seems to me. I just hope that your ambition to add words to film is not because you love words so much (which you should because you are a poet). I wouldn't want to interfere. I think that what you would say in words should be said instead in images.

Maas: Well, you must realize that there is a difference between Shakespeare and, let us say, any dramatist of repute. And there is a difference within poetic language, is there not?

Miller: There is, of course. The difference however, is not of the same quality as the difference between words in a movie. The whole posture of the Elizabethan drama, so to speak, is larger than life as opposed to the modern drama, which is trying to be about the same size as life. Well, the movie starts out that way. It's almost impossible, as you know, to photograph reality in pictures and make it come out reality. I know that people have tried with cameras to destroy the . . . this leads to a humorous remark. I was involved with a director once who wanted to make pictures in New York that would look real. They photographed and photographed, and it ended up looking glamorous, no matter how deep down into the East Side they went. (*Laughter.*) They tried to dirty the film and do everything they could do to it. And I kept telling him that what was required was an organization of an idea to make this look like the East Side. My point is that, in the Elizabethan drama, it takes an effort of aesthetic will to raise life larger than it is on the stage. As soon as you point a camera at anything, it's no longer real.

Maas: Mr. Tyler, I don't want to answer this. You ought to say something. You must have been thinking a lot.

Tyler: We *are* snagged on the horns of a dilemma in a way, although I'm sure we've covered a lot of ground. I think one of the most interesting things is the shape and the character of these horns—that is, Miss Deren, who is a professional artist in the poetic film, started out by using a rather complex, a rather difficult, technical vocabulary in order to describe her theory about what she does. Now that's perfectly all right. But it struck Mr. Thomas as not precisely all right, and he then proceeded to talk about his very spontaneous reactions to films in terms of what he thought was poetic in them, various little incidents, certain aspects, just points of emotion. And then Mr. Miller took over and started to talk about dreams and the pure medium of the film. Now the fact is that both these gentlemen—both of whom are professional writers, and one a professional poet—expressed the very view of life, the cinematic attitude toward life that Miss Deren and a number of other film-makers started out with and, in this primitive way, are simply reflecting, perhaps, the first stage of her development when she had the impulse to make poetic film—that is, to create meaningful images through the medium of moving photography. Now, it becomes the problem, especially here tonight, as to why she started out by using a very difficult vocabulary, a technical vocabulary, to express a sort of intellectual specialty in the way she regarded her art. As a matter of fact, the surrealists started out by excerpting parts of commercial films, jumbling them up, and making little poems out of them. It is simply a question of the editing, the montage, as Mr. Miller intelligently hinted a moment ago, a question of integrating a series of photographs, of spontaneous shots into a form, a shape, and then you have something. That is, you have a feeling about reality—which is what art is. So I think that the rudimentary ground is present; that is, poetic film means using the film as a conscious and exclusive means of creating ideas through images. As for poets and other artists collaborating with film-makers, the method of Eisenstein was one of strict collaboration in a technical sense. It was also one of literature in that he wrote out very elaborate, very detailed scripts, action for action, shot for shot, beforehand, and then, when he was in the field, since he was an artist, he remained open so that his technical advisors were always listened to. It was a question of using an original script, which was really literature, which was written as a starting point and, out of this kind of literature, creating a film. Certainly, among big film-makers and artists who created full length films, and films that were commercially distributed, Eisenstein was, in the history of films, the most conscious artist. So it seems to me just a little strange that Mr. Miller, in particular, being a dramatist, should take a purist point of view toward the film. I mean, that's his privilege, if he feels that way. But the hard part, at least to me, is that this is the way that the little film-makers, the poets of the film such as Miss Deren, feel—this is their approach to life. So now I don't know where we are! It's a question of what role literature, what role verbal poetry, should have in film. I don't know why Mr. Thomas and Mr. Miller should insist, and I'm waiting to find out if they will insist, why poetry as literature should not, or cannot, collaborate with poetry as film.

Deren: I wish mainly to say that I'm a little bit flabbergasted at the fact that people who have handled words with such dexterity as Mr. Thomas and Mr. Miller and Mr. Tyler, should have difficulty with such a simple idea as the "vertical" and the "horizontal" (*applause*).

Thomas: (*aside*) Here we go up and down again.

Deren: These seem to me the most elementary movements in the world and really quite fundamental.

Maas: I don't think you ought to get vulgar.

Deren: That has really flabbergasted me to the extent that I am unable to develop the idea any further . . . I don't see anything so difficult in the notion that what I called a "horizontal" development is more or less of a narrative development, such as occurs in drama from action to action, and that a "vertical" development such as occurs in poetry, is a part of plunging down or a construction that is based on the intent of the moment, so that, for example, from a short story, one should be able to deduce the life of the hero before and after. In other words, the chosen moment should be of such significance that one can deduce all history from it. So, in a poem, in a way, from the emotion one can particularize to the incidents that might contain it, whereas in a drama, one generalizes the emotion from the particular instant. That is, the actions of the drama may not be personally known, but one generalizes the emotion that comes from it, and then it becomes possible to identify with it as a generalized emotion. I still don't know what's so difficult about those two differences, and I think I'd like to hear something from the floor myself.

Miller: Let me just say, I didn't intend to make it so difficult; it isn't. It's just not separate. There is no separation in my mind between a horizontal story and the plumbing of its meaning in depth. (*Applause.*)

Maas: Well, surely, Mr. Miller, you must see the difference between presenting something by words or dialogue, as you do and I do and Mr. Thomas does, and presenting something by the visual image. Now Ezra Pound said, in a definition of the image, that it is an emotional and intellectual complex caught in an instant of time. It's a very direct and quick way of saying things, a lyric way of saying things, whereas the way a dramatist says things is by putting the characters that speak back and forth in conflict. We know that the sake of reaching outside the structure of the play to bring in some information. They are incorporated, completely wedded to the action. They *are* action. Now the only argument I have here at all, and the reason I have a feeling that verse, possibly, doesn't belong in the movies, is that if you have on the screen an image ... an image is a bad word because it seems static ... an action. Now it can be an action that is seemingly real or a fantastic one. And then, on top of it, you have an unseen narrator who is speaking—I'm afraid that the spoken word will be a kind of narrative, or lyrical, non-dramatic verse. And that is going to stop the motion of the motion picture. And I'm against that. I think it's an intrusion on the medium. That's all I mean, I'm speaking for an organic art, that's all. (*Applause*) ... There's a good example in the making of the movie of *Death of a Salesman*. This was a very fascinating problem, and it is right to the point here. On the stage, it seemed perfectly all right to most people that the man should move into his memories which were evoked by the action in the present. I didn't like the script of the movie, and I quarreled very much with it. One would think, offhand, that it would be much easier in a movie to dissolve the present, because the very word dissolve is so natural to the camera and simply throws the man into the past. When the present was dissolved, the meaning of what happened in the past was less. And the reason for it was that, on stage, you had the present with you all the time. We couldn't remove the set. The man had his dreams in relation to the real set that he was standing on, so there was a tension involved. There was, in other words, a reproduction of reality, because when we talk to ourselves on the street, the street is still there, and we don't vanish in thin air. But, in this movie, they made the terrible mistake of evaporating his surroundings, so that he was thrust completely into his dream. And what happened was: It became a narrative. The conflict was that this man—after all, it's not quite as bad to talk to yourself when you're alone in the desert as it is when you're standing in front of a girl at Macy's counter—that has an entirely different meaning. In one case, the man can be quite balanced; in the other case, he begins to look as though he's losing his balance. This, to my mind, is an analogy between anything that stops action, that is bad in a picture. I think, in the movie of *Death of a Salesman,* the action was stopped because the visual thing that kept the tension of those memories was evaporated. And I'm afraid that the same thing would happen with a speech in a picture.

Originally published by *Film Culture*, no. 29 (Summer 1963);
republished by the Gotham Book Mart and Gallery in 1972.

Program Notes by Amos Vogel in Response to Survey of Cinema 16 Membership, Fall 1953

CINEMA 16 FILM NOTES 1953/1954

THE INSIDE STORY
We thought you might like to know the results of the questionnaire we sent you a few months ago... to read interesting comments by your fellow-members... and to hear about improvements we have made on the basis of your suggestions:

PROGRAMMING: Your replies indicate that you would like to see a greater proportion of the programs devoted to (in order of preference): 1) documentary film classics 2) social documentaries 3) scientific films; —and a smaller proportion to 1) speakers 2) abstract films 3) psychological films.

SUGGESTIONS FOR FUTURE PROGRAMS: An astonishing number of titles were suggested proving that C16 has indeed tapped the most film-conscious audience in New York. While it would be impossible to list all titles here, many of them appear on this season's program and others are being "worked on" so that they will be available in forthcoming seasons.

SUPPLEMENTARY FILM SERIES: In addition to our regular series, a large number of members would be willing to attend (in order of preference) 1) a feature film series 2) an experimental film series 3) a film study group. Their wishes will be fulfilled when the new C16 Film Center at the New School goes into operation in December with substantial discounts from the regular course fee available to C16 members.

WINNERS OF POPULARITY CONTEST: While we fully realize the limitations of popularity contests, we nevertheless wanted to know which film our members remembered most fondly. Here is their order of preference:

Regular Programs: 1) UNICORN IN THE GARDEN 2) LATUKO 3) IN THE STREET 4) NEIGHBORS 5) IMAGES MEDIEVALES

Special Events: 1) ED MURROW—ARGUMENT IN INDIANAPOLIS 2) ALL MY BABIES 3) THE MAGNIFICENT AMBERSONS 4) ACTIVITY GROUP THERAPY 5) BED AND SOFA

The Worst Liked Film of the Year: PSYCHOTHERAPEUTIC INTERVIEWING

WHO ARE THE C16 MEMBERS?
Age: 4% under 20; 55% 21–30; 23% 31–40; 18% over 40. To put it differently, 59% of all members are below 30; 41% over 30. This provides an interesting contrast with last year's results, when 69% were below 30 and only 31% over 30.

Education: 75% are college graduates

Occupation: 41% are professionals or professionally employed; 17% the arts, advertising and publicity; 14% in business; 8% students; 8% clerical and sales; 6% skilled and technicians; and 5% housewives.

COMMENTS: It is, of course, impossible to print the several thousand comments that we received nor has it been possible to thank all of you individually. But you may be assured that your comments were analyzed and poured over (gladly or sadly) time and again... that they proved extremely helpful for our future plans... and that we are very grateful to you. Most of them were of a very positive nature (which pleased us no end), some were more or less negative, many contained excellent suggestions and ideas. (A random sampling appears on the next page... we think you will find them interesting.)

ACTION WE HAVE TAKEN AS A RESULT OF YOUR COMMENTS:

Overcrowding: The success of our recruitment drive last fall found us somewhat unprepared and we were too crowded for comfort. Next season, to correct this situation once and for all:

1) Special Events will be presented on two nights thereby doubling the seating capacity.

2) We have added a 7:15 and 9:30 PM Tuesday Series at the Central Needle Trades Auditorium. (Identical programs)

Guest Ticket Policy Liberalized: We are pleased to announce that guest tickets will be undated, valid at any performance, regular or special.

New Equipment: Those members who could not understand why we did not buy a new screen for the Central Needle Trades Auditorium will be interested to hear that we had been trying to do so for several years, but that the Board of Education did not permit the purchase of school equipment by outside groups. However we are happy to announce that an appropriation has finally been made and there will definitely be a new screen this season which will increase the illumination level and visibility.

And...

To this must be added special custom-made Bausch and Lomb lenses that we have finally been able to acquire (further improving the quality of projection) and a professional model tape recorder that will permit uninterrupted musical accompaniment to silent films; as well as special translations and English adaptation of untitled foreign films.

More Discounts at Art Theatres: We have recently made arrangements that will enable us to substantially increase the number of discounts available at art theatres in the city. (This includes the special discount ticket at the Beekman available to our members on a year-round basis).

AVOID CONTROVERSIAL FILMS? It is well to keep in mind the difference between a commercial movie theatre and a film society. The commercial movie theatre aims to entertain. The film society aims to further the appreciation of films and of new experiments in the film medium. The commercial theatre steers clear of controversy, the film society welcomes it. If the films shown by the film society are entertaining, so much the better; but entertainment value cannot be the sole criterion for film selection. The confusion between regular theatres and film societies is most clearly expressed by members who advise us to be guided in our program selections "by applause". We frankly do not feel that this can be the criterion. Neither applause nor the absence of applause can determine our program selections. The New York Philharmonic Symphony, which may be said to fulfill a similar function in music as Cinema 16 does in films, has often witnessed demonstrations when it presented contemporary music. The boos and hisses are expected by both audience and critics and while suggestions are made to drop works of this type from its program, Mr. Mitropoulos has fortunately not given in to them. We certainly do not claim that all or even the majority of the present avant-garde films are the works of a Bartok (who was roundly booded at one time or another at concerts) but we do feel that they represent significant experiments and as such worthy of exhibition at a film society.

The experiments of the French avant-garde in the twenties were much condemned at the time, the showing of L'AGE D'OR leading to a riot and fire in the theatre. Yet today many of their devices and achievements have percolated into commercial Hollywood films. It is part of the "mission" of Cinema 16 to be a showcase for such films.

Amos Vogel, Executive Secretary, Cinema 16

MEMBERS' COMMENTS

... Some utensil should be provided to stir the coffee served at the Beekman Theatre. I have seen numerous solutions to this problem, such as, stirring with the pinky finger (etiquette prescribes the use of this finger of course), the use of a fountain pen, placing much sugar into the cup and bringing along one's own utensils for the screenings. All of these solutions seem inadequate to me...

... I have found my membership in C16 has opened a whole new world for me and I'm only kicking myself that I hesitated for several years before joining...

... It was a privilege to be able to see some extremely interesting films which I would never have had the opportunity to see except through C16 membership...

... The most wasted $12 I have ever spent in New York City...

... A unique opportunity to discover the possibilities inherent in an imaginative, purposeful approach to film creation—possibilities for the most part overlooked by the large commercial companies intent upon satisfying the mass demands of an apathetic, indiscriminate audience of their own making...

... I seem to feel a deep depression in some of your programs. If it were not for my friends telling me of your past presentations, I would not know that you also have a humorous side...

... I didn't like all films equally well, neither did I expect to, nor would it be possible...

... Symposium of Poetry and the Film—one of the most boring evenings I have spent in years. Should have been titled FIVE SPEAKERS IN SEARCH OF A TOPIC...

... I enjoyed the forum on poetry. I had always thought of Miss Deren as a rather frantically disorganized person. Her complete lucidity of projecting her ideas charmed me and made Mr. Miller by comparison seem arbitrary, almost petulant. The forum was valuable if for nothing more than to encourage a reassessment of these people. I am sure I will look at Miss Deren's work with a new eye and I will be far more critical of Miller in the future. Orchids to you. May you continue to grow and grow...

... May we see some of the films made by the young, the experimenters, etc? Even if something foolish turns up (like the dialogue in BELLS OF ATLANTIS) I appreciate the compliment of being allowed to damn it on my own. In spite of the above C16 is one of the good things of life. Thanks for it...

... I think many of your films are too "off-beat" or are for very avant-garde collegiates, that you do not cater enough to those of us who are not starry-eyed and immature and a trifle decadent but just intelligent interested human beings who want to be informed or amused or touched...

... After 10 minutes of James Broughton's MOTHERS DAY I was fervantly hoping he would get himself analyzed. This past year there have been fewer films reminding me of the self-involvement of mammie boy. I could even see BELLS OF ATLANTIS again...

... I have nothing but praise to offer, thank you...

... You show more good movies than I care to see...

... I really do think something should be done about people constantly walking out during a showing. It is most annoying to those who are enjoying the films, or speakers. They never go quietly but with much noise and obviousness as if the voicing of their opinions were of the most importance to everyone. To my mind the walking out on the speakers is absolute discourteousness...

... I want American coffee at the Beekman. I don't mean this to sound chauvinistic...

... I have never before been so thoroughly pleased with a membership in any organization. I would like to take this opportunity to inquire if there are any discussion groups to act as a stimulus to a worthwhile evening. As I attend alone, I find it irritating to see a provocative film and leave it suspended, as it were, for want of a good debate. I wonder if there are enough others like myself who would care to discuss the pros and cons of the films either for enlightenment or fun...

... I am strongly in favor of a series of film "classics." Remember people of my generation rarely recall anything earlier than 1938...

... No speeches, not even the modest cute ones by Mr. Vogel-Peepers...

... I suggest that there be a ten minute intermission in the middle of the film showing. It would give me an opportunity to make the acquaintance of some of the attractive women fellow members of mine...

...Could the program notes be a little less lyrical. I can decide for myself if the film is "filled with delicate visual poetry" or is a "sensitive evocation" of something or other. We chastise you because we love you. Best wishes...

...Your program notes are highly informative and stimulating. However, their value would be enhanced if one could read them before a film showing. Granted, that mail distributions would be too costly, how about giving them out one showing in advance or printing the current and advance notes back to back thus making doubly sure they are read?...

...Heavy program notations often make me feel as if I needed an education for each presentation. Explanations should be made briefest, speakers should be forbidden...

...We would feel it a special treat to have a UPA cartoon each time. Most of the audience are serious thinkers and your UPA cartoons are very often the only intelligent humor we find for weeks at a time...

...The social documentaries which comprise the bulk of the C16 screenings may be entertaining, but they generally do not present any serious departure, technically or otherwise, from the commercial movies. Unconventional, daring and creative films assured of commercial failures should be championed by a society dedicated to the serious film...

...Show all abstract, experimental, avant-garde, etc., films in entirely separate program—for the intellectuals—I'm one of the simple minded...

...Far too many noisy "intellectual" people who rather talk than use their eyes and absorb the content. It is turning a possible service to the cinema into a "let's go down to CNTA and hiss C16" sort of thing...

...We like the Beekman Theatre: quiet, roomy, and your audience does not chatter, eat out of cellophane candy bags, or gape around to see what mutual friends are also imbibing painless culture. It's pleasant to be with people who seem to know why they are someplace...

...It is a joy to visit the beautiful Central Needle Trades Auditorium...

...I hate the Central Needle Trades Auditorium...

...Superficially you have attempted to create an esoteric social idea, but actually you have succeeded in doing nothing but to overcharge a few bewildered neurotics by making them feel like intellectuals...

...Why not attempt to make C16 more friendly by inquiring in your program notes as to membership reaction to outings, picnics, etc...

...Repeat certain films for the benefit of those who were not members at the time the films were originally shown and for those who wish to see them once again...

...I was pleased to see 3 of my last year's requests filled since the last poll...

...Watch how often you end a good description of a coming feature with the adjective "disturbing." Disturbing—that's a sales-talk?...

... I never go to the movies (C16 gives me all of the flickering screen my diet demands). If there has been something really good on television I would like to see it at Cinema 16 for I never see television firsthand (don't even own a radio much less a TV)....

... Why do you show films that I can see at the Museum of Modern Art?...

... I'm very happy you show films that I cannot see at the Museum of Moder Art since I only get out of work at 5:30 pm...

... I know you cannot please all the people all the time, but you sure do a magnificent job pleasing most of us most of the time

✦ ✦ ✦ ✦ ✦ ✦

Conversation with Robert Kelly, 12/19/00

[Robert Kelly has published more than fifty books of poetry and fiction.]

Scott MacDonald: When did you become involved with Cinema 16?

Robert Kelly: When my mother gave me a membership for Christmas; I was fifteen. My friend, Arthur Pinkerton, and I both had memberships. Going to the shows involved a long trip for us–we both lived in a remote section of Brooklyn—to the Paris Theater. But it was a wonderful occasion to get into Manhattan on Sunday mornings, when nobody else was about, and go to this elegant little movie theater. We were already getting to know all the movie theaters in the city that played art films. Events started about eleven in the morning and lasted until about one, when the regular features began, and Amos Vogel would at times—I assumed it was he; I never met him—say a few words about the program.

The film I remember most vividly of all is Willard Maas's film, *Geography of the Body* [1943], which uses a poem by George Barker that struck me as incredibly wise when I heard it, as its narration. I think Barker did the reciting. I've only seen the film once, but it's never left me. I also remember a couple early Anger films–*Fireworks* [1946], especially. Norman McLaren. And *The Lead Shoes* [1949; by Sidney Peterson]. *Mister Frenhofer and the Minotaur* [1948; by Sidney Peterson]. I remember the Sidney Peterson films very vividly. And some of Brakhage's early what he later was to call "masturbation movies"—a rather harsh name for them, I think.

Ironically, when I met Brakhage in the early Sixties, it took me a while to remember that he was one of the filmmakers I had watched with interest back at Cinema 16. His *name* had not stayed with me, unlike Willard Maas's and Peterson's and McLaren's. We met in 1963, when he came to a reading of mine in the Village; he'd just arrived in New York, sent on by Robert Duncan. Our conversations about the films I was seeing then, beginning with *Anticipation of the Night* [1959], and *Dog Star Man* [1963]—that's what he was working on at the time we were first together–had as much to do with poetry as with film. There was a lot of mutual bleeding–of his work bleeding into mine, and mine into his. I think the work of mine that is most explicitly, avowedly connected with his work is a long series of poems called *Songs 1-30*, published in the late 1960s. He and I were making our songs at the same time—two different artists going in two different directions from a common notion of song.

The Cinema 16 shows were *defining* events for me, as far as movies went. As a child, I had been condemned to watch a movie, or two movies, every day. There was something wrong with my eyes and the eye doctor from whom my parents took counsel suggested that the best thing for me was to use my eyes a lot, and the best *way* to use them, he thought, was to sit in the front row of a movie theater. That way the eyes would need to move a *lot*, would be in constant motion tracking the whole screen. I was very near-sighted. It worked out all right.

So at any rate, I had a huge fund of movies to draw on in the way of ordinary cinema, so much so that I hardly need to go to the movies anymore in my life. But the stuff I was seeing at Cinema 16 *was* very exciting and continues to be so to. It also had the wonderful property of being optically concerned. It was about being *seen*; it wasn't about transparent visual gestures and narrative.

MacDonald: Was Cinema 16 the first time you had come in contact with avant-garde film?

Kelly: It was indeed. Around the same time, I got to see some of the classics of cinema which for all practical purposes *were* avant-garde when you saw them then—things like *Potemkin*, or early Rene Clair movies, or *An Andalusian Dog*. Those things were certainly avant-garde in those days and remain so, if you're coming from the commercial cinema. Cinema 16 was my first taste of *current* avant-garde material, stuff that wasn't mentioned in the books I was reading: Jay Leyda, Paul Rotha's *The Film Till Now* . . .

MacDonald: Did the films you saw at Cinema 16 have impact on you as a poet?

Kelly: Oh very much so. God, yes! I guess the things in the visual world that spoke to me most strongly when I was a kid were the films that I saw at Cinema 16 and the paintings of Kandinsky. My trips to Cinema 16 and my trips to MoMA and to the old Guggenheim to see paintings, began more or less at the same time.

Do you remember Thomas Wilford's *Lumia*, an installation that for many years was on exhibit in the Museum of Modern Art?

MacDonald: No.

Kelly: It stood in a little closet area. You stood and watched an *incredibly* sophisticated, subtle color show. Its cycle was very long—it may have been days long—but it was one of the grandest and most instructive works of art that we had seen in those days. I think that was as profound an experience in kinetic optical art as anything I saw at Cinema 16. It was very physical, a film that did not end. It allowed you to have immediate purchase on its rhythms but also to see it as a practice: you learned the practice of watching it in a tender, relaxed, nobody's-watching way that you can't quite do in a theater with people all around you reacting.

So yes, those early experiences influenced my poetry tremendously, and still do.

The influence of film on my work is pervasive. How would we *ever* have known to abandon narrative if those few early, mad, tormented experimental filmmakers hadn't given us back to the visual world again? I'm a little bit a counter-factual historian of film, in the sense that I'm endlessly fascinated by what *would have* happened had film not taken the path of the novel and the play, but had, instead, taken the path of the painting and the photograph, had tried to displace Degas rather than Dumas.

✦ ✦ ✦ ✦ ✦ ✦

Program Notes by Dr. Rene A. Spitz for *Grief*, Shown in January 1954

A Special Cinema 16 Presentation:

GRIEF
(1947) Produced by Dr. Rene A. Spitz for the Psychoanalytic Research Project on Problems in Infancy. Restricted distribution to qualified groups only: New York University Film Library. (24 minutes)

Dr. Spitz' famed psychoanalytic study of children deprived of mother love has long been a classic in professional psychiatric circles but has only rarely been seen by others. It is here presented by special permission of the producer.

"The film GRIEF shows the consequences of long-term separation of the young infant from his mother. It was prepared as an illustration for a publication made within the framework of a large research project extending over several years, and brings examples of children and their behavior when they are separated from their mothers. The separation was studied in NURSERY, an institution in the United States, and in FOUNDLING HOME, an institution abroad.

90 children placed in FOUNDLING HOME showed striking deterioration in body and mind after a stay of several months. Our careful investigation proved that they were provided with adequate and proper food and medical attention and that the only factor which was accountable for this deterioration was the absence of the mother or a substitute. We now outline a few of the findings (For details see publications listed below).

In NURSERY babies aged 6 to 8 months reared by their own mother proved happy and healthy. Some of them suddenly became weepy and withdrawn. Investigations showed that this change was not dependent on sex or race of the afflicted infants. What distinguished the sick from the healthy infants was that they had been separated from their mother for reasons of ill health or administrative reasons. Differences in the severity of the symptoms were observed. When the separation was prolonged, deterioration progressed, loss of weight and insomnia was prevalent, previously active infants lay motionless in their bed, their expression sad and withdrawn.

The children who seemed to suffer most were those who had been deprived of a "very good" mother. Infants who had been separated from a "bad" mother showed no sign of depression. In other terms, the quality of the relation between the mother and the child prior to the separation, and the adequacy of the substitute after the separation played an important role in the extent to which a child would be affected by the separation from his mother. Therefore replacing a good mother with a motherly nurse will avert the damages of separation.

Another factor which influenced the course of the depression was the length of the mother's absence. The longer the mother stayed away, the worse became the symptoms which the infant showed. But if the mothers were reunited with their children after a period lasting not longer than 3 months, the symptoms would subside within hours of the mother's return and the children's developmental quotient would rise spectacularly. They would regain their social contact with their surroundings and would become happy youngsters again.

It remains an open question whether such an episode of deprivation in the second half of the first year of life causes permanent damage to the children's personality. Up to now it was unfortunately not possible to follow up the children observed in this research project.

However, in the other institution, FOUNDLING HOME, all the infants were permanently separated from their mothers when they reached the age of 3 to 4 months. Lack of nursing personnel limited the care of these infants to the elementary manipulations of hygiene and nourishment. Once afflicted with depression, if the mother did not return, they deteriorated progressively. In extreme cases this led to stupor, agitated idiocy and marasmus. We noted further that when separated more than 5 months, these infants were extremely susceptible to infections and showed a high mortality rate.

In both institutions all infants received the same kind of care, the same food, the same medical and hygienic attention. The only difference in treatment of these children was: some were separated from their mothers—these showed the clinical picture described. Those not separated remained free from the affliction.

This film, and others made in our research, have been widely used for the teaching of mental health in universities, colleges, hospitals, PTA's, for the training of nurses and social workers, both in our country and abroad. In some parts of the world they have led to changes in the attitude towards the hospitalization of children, and towards making it possible for parents to see their children even if hospitalized. They seem also to have had some influence on attitudes towards raising orphans. In the U. S. thanks to the child guidance movement originating in the twenties, homes for children of an institutional kind have been replaced, mostly by foster home care."

Dr. Rene A. Spitz

[...]

✦ ✦ ✦ ✦ ✦ ✦

Letter to Amos Vogel from Willard Maas, 1/6/54

Penthouse
62 Montague Street
Bklyn 1, New York

January 6th, 1954

Dear Amos,

I am glad to hear I misunderstood about the NOGUCHI and sorry if I caused any embarrassment to Jack. We must, under the circumstances, attribute it to your Christmas punch which leaves you with the honors. My impression, naturally, is the same, and I should say that something must have been said to lead me to the conclusion I stated, since such a conclusion in the beginning was far from my mind, since, after all, you had advanced the money for the soundtrack on the film, something for which Marie and I are deeply grateful, whatever other impression might be given.

If you work out the plans for the art program, and still feel you wish to show the film, you have only to contact Marie, who is, as you know, at TIME magazine.

On how films are to be financed, your guess is as good as mine, but I personally have a deep-seated lack of faith in Foundations and organizations as a whole. Believe me, this comes from MUCH experience. But this I know, any first-rate artist WILL find sponsorship of one sort or another, even if he has to go out and work or whore for it. Since I have done both, I think I speak here with authority. Maya, of course, has a right to speak there too, and since I too am a member of the advisory board of the Creative Film Foundation I shall work toward the same end as you do there, but Christ, I really wonder. I do wonder. Meanwhile my idea was that there are a good number of people who believe enough in the experimental film movement, or me personally, to be eager to contribute toward the finishing of a project which so many people have devoted energy and passion and even money. Here again, Amos, I am right. Evidently you know the wrong people, and I guess frequently I do too, but the fact remains, which may surprise you, that over 30 people, to date, have contributed $1250 toward the finishing of our film. I have a promise of several hundred more, and NARCISSUS will be finished in the next few months. I also think you underestimate Cinema 16 audiences. In fact I know you do, for one contribution came from a member who did not receive an "Appeal" but had just heard about it and sent in a check.

Well, all that's that. I seem not so often to agree with you but I am very honest which, I guess, you know better than any one else. Be grateful at least for this, as, sincerely Amos, I am grateful for the organization you have built. You have helped me a great deal. You have helped the whole experimental film movement, and I for one should not care to do anything, or say anything, which might deter its growth and influence.

Best wishes as always,

[hw] Willard

Willard

Reprinted by permission of Stephen Maas.

[*Maas lived with filmmaker Marie Menken, referred to in paragraphs 1 and 2; she made* Visual Variations on Noguchi *in 1945.* Narcissus, *by Maas and Ben Moore, was completed in 1956 and shown at Cinema 16 in 1957.*]

✦ ✦ ✦ ✦ ✦ ✦

Letter to Amos Vogel from Kenneth Anger, 2/23/54

[hw]

Pacific Palisades, Calif.

Feb. 23

Dear Amos:

Thank you for your letter of the 16th with the enclosed statement.

I'm sorry its been so long since I've written. It has been necessary for me to remain here much longer than I originally planned, to await the settlement of various family affairs. However—I have not let this time go to waste—you will be surprised to learn I have nearly completed a new film!

It is <u>by far</u> my most ambitious effort to date—and, I think, my most unusual one—

The title is "<u>Inauguration of the Pleasure Dome</u>" in color; running time 40 minutes. I am confident that it is one of the most unusual experimental films ever made. The theme is a fantastic concurrence of sorcerers and devils and figures from mythology—a Witches Sabbath. It has been arduous work—and—being in color—has cost a small fortune—luckily various friends have chipped in to help me with the film.

A San Francisco composer has done a very original score for the film, using a 43-tone scale and synthetic instruments.

It is my intention to have a 35mm print made on Eastman Color, which I will take with me to present at the Cannes Festival in about the middle of April. As you can imagine this project has taken every bit of my personal funds—and more so! To finance the final 35mm print I am counting on a donation showing which will be held in Beverly Hills next month.

Because of the great expense of the 35mm print (necessary to be well presented at the Festival) it is doubtful I will be able to afford a 16mm print at this time—even though I want one for my personal use and also would like to leave a print with you, as you probably will want to distribute it—

You are aware of the expense involved in a 16mm Kodachrome sound print running 40 minutes. What do you advise me to do? Could you make an advance to cover this print—or—do you have an account with a lab in N. Y. who can make the color print there for you, on short notice? Since I am working on a very tight schedule, I can only spend a few days in N. Y. at the most.

If you'd rather wait till I arrive in N. Y. to make your decision—let me know at once. I will have a 35mm print—perhaps it can be arranged to have a showing at

Illustration 48. Photographic evocation of Kenneth Anger's *Inauguration of the Pleasure Dome* (1954). Courtesy Museum of Modern Art Film Stills Archive.

the M. M. A. or elsewhere. However—I believe the facilities for color printing are superior here in Hollywood. I must have a lab that can print A & B rolls from commercial Kodachrome with sound from a 35mm neg. track via electrical reduction. Can Peerless or elsewhere in N. Y. do this? I would prefer working at Consolidated Labs in Hollywood where I am well acquainted for the 16mm print—if possible.

You needn't worry about "Inauguration of the Pleasure Dome" "selling"—I guarantee it will be your most unusual item! What kind of contract can you offer me for the 16mm American rights? I must hold 35mm rights plus TV rights, & 16mm foreign rights. I must say that I would be happier with a 60% arrangement for this film, in view of the extremely high production cost—and the fact that the length plus the color will allow higher rental fee. How much do you think is feasible?

I will be surprised if you aren't interested in this film—I enclose stills which suggest some of the fantastic quality of the production—yet they unfortunately cannot give an idea of the fantastic color....

I imagine Tyler would like to see this and I'm sure you must know others—can you arrange a private screening on a fairly short notice? I'll try to let you know the date of my arrival in N. Y. which will be in probability the 1st week in April—

The two new prints of "Fireworks" are waiting here and I'll bring them to you at that time, unless you feel you might need one of them before—

Please do let me hear from you at your earliest convenience—

truly yours,

Kenneth

Reprinted by permission of Kenneth Anger.

[The first version of Inauguration of the Pleasure Dome *was finished in 1954. Harry Partch is the composer referred to in paragraph 5. "Tyler" in paragraph 12 is critic Parker Tyler.]*

✦ ✦ ✦ ✦ ✦ ✦

Program Announcement: Spring 1954

March 1954

A program of "first films" to call attention to young film makers and new directions in the cinema. The emphasis is on artistic promise rather than on artistic achievement:

Psalm (Marvin Silbersher and Marvin Duckler)
The world of the orthodox Jew: his prayers, his songs, his holidays. Hebrew religious chants.

Between Two Worlds (Sam Kaner and Guy L. Cote)
A fantastic ballet notable for its striking pictorial compositions. Shown at Venice and Edinburgh Film Festivals.

Waiting (Flora Mock)
A restless color collage dealing with the anxieties of the high-tension life of today. Produced as a thesis for Motion Picture Division, University of California.

Treasure in a Garbage Can (R. Hardman and W. Perkins)
The salvaging of refuse transformed into a human interest story. (University of California)

City Without Wheels (Morton Heilig)
A poetic evocation of Venice. Exciting and authentic sound track.

Study of a Dance (Yael Woll)
A desperate love dance set against the metropolitan skyline. (City College Institute of Film Techniques)

April 1954

The Demon in Art
(Il Demoniaco Nell' Arte) First prize, International Short Film Festival, Paris 1951; Prize Winner, Woodstock Art Film Festival. A glimpse into the mind of the Middle Ages: The struggle between good and evil in the soul of man, as seen in the fantasy paintings of Brüeghel, Bosch and Grunewald, forerunners of surrealist art. A dramatic new art film from Italy released by Contemporary Films. English narration by Arthur Knight. Music by Roman Vlad.

Variety
E. A. Dupont's world-renowned melodrama of music-hall life, produced at the close of the expressionist era in German films. With Emil Jannings and Lya de Putti. Notable for its striking camera angles, photographic devices and lighting, this film exerted a profound influence on Hollywood. An UFA production supervised by Erich Pommer. Camera: Karl Freund. From a novel by Felix Hollaender.

"From all standards, a brilliant film."—Rotha, *The Film Till Now*. "A sensational success, famous for its camera tricks and its unrelieved atmosphere of sordidness and tension."—The Museum of Modern Art. "Dupont supersedes the conventional realism of the past by a realism that captures along with visible phenomena the psychological processes below their surface."—Kracauer, *From Caligari to Hitler*.

May 1954

Renoir
The painter as a man and artist: a charming camera study of the life and growth of the master of impressionist art, examining his finest canvases, many unknown in this country. A vivid glimpse of 19th Century middle class life and mores. In color. A Contemporary Films release by Jerry Winters.

Goodness Gracious
A brilliant satire on the 1914-type of stagy melodrama—made in 1914. With Clara Kimball Young and Sidney Drew.

Ballet of the Atlas
Three authentic ceremonical and love dances of the nomadic Berber tribes. Filmed in Morocco. Unusual drum score. A Film Images release.

Working and Playing to Health
A Mental Health Film Board Production by Willard Van Dyke (*The City, Valleytown*). Filmed in the form of a play, this is a sensitive dramatization of therapeutic techniques employed at a mental hospital.

Lincoln Speaks at Gettysburg
A dramatic recreation of a moment in history through contemporary engravings and drawings. A Film Images release by Paul Falkenberg and Lewis Jacobs.

[The listing of Special Events for Spring 1954 is identical to the listing of the final four Special Events in the 1953–1954 brochure: see pp. 205–8.]

✦ ✦ ✦ ✦ ✦ ✦

Letter to Cinema 16 by T.S. and Response by Amos Vogel, from May 1954 Program Notes

Sirs: We are appalled at your showing Nazi propaganda films. As democratically-minded movie-goers, we demand that you immediately drop this obscene film fare from your programs.

T. S.

As one who has himself experienced the terror of the Hitler regime, I find your complaint almost amusing. C16 examines motion pictures both from an art and a social viewpoint. There has probably been no other nation that used films as effectively for propaganda purposes as did the Nazis. It is important to study their methods and to be aware of the terrible potentialities of the cinema as a propaganda medium. This is why we are presenting what is probably one of the best and most vicious propaganda films ever made: TRIUMPH OF THE WILL.

What is disturbing about your letter is that while you describe yourself as "democratically minded people", you at the same time attempt to dictate to others in a very undemocratic fashion ("we demand that you drop this obscene... etc). In this sense, you simply align yourself with the ever growing number of groups who advocate censorship of films on the basis of political, social, religious or moral grounds.

Amos Vogel (for Cinema 16)

✦ ✦ ✦ ✦ ✦ ✦

Letter to Amos Vogel from Gerd Stern, 5/9/54

The Harry Partch Trust Fund
P.O. Box 387
Marin City, Calif.

May 9, 1954

Cinema 16
Mr. Amos Vogel
175 Lexington Ave.
New York City, N.Y.

Dear Mr. Vogel;

This letter to explain and amplify the telegram I sent for Mr. Partch earlier this week.

Kenneth Anger approached Mr. Partch four months ago in terms of using some of Mr. Partch's music in a film. No definite terms were agreed on, nor was any permission given. Mr. Anger intended to return within two weeks to discuss the problem. Three months later he returned with a completed film including an optical sound track made by dubbing from the "Plectra and Percussion Dances" record by Mr. Partch. There had been no communication whatsoever in the interval. Mr. Partch disapproves of this film entirely, and demands that neither his name or music be used with the film "Inauguration of The Pleasure Dome". Mr. Anger agreed not to use the film with the music in the presence of witnesses.

The S.F. Cinema Guild received the film with the sound track still on but Mr. Partch's name removed from the trailer. According to my information they also received a note from Mr. Anger to the effect that he would assume responsibility for any problems resulting from the use of the sound track. This film arrived in a film-box under your letterhead.

The S.F. Cinema Guild upon receiving notice from us kindly refrained using the sound-track and exhibited with a recorded substitute. I was informed by them that they had contracted for a 'world premiere'. My information has it that the film with sound-track was shown in Los Angeles for several days to paid audiences.

We consider Mr. Anger's methods and motives unfriendly and on a business level reprehensive. I fear we shall have to take legal steps against him in order to protect music rights.

Bob Greensfelder, a mutual friend of ours, assures me that you will not want to involve yourself in this kind of a situation. Would you kindly inform us, by return mail, whether you or anyone has exhibited this film (Inauguration of The Pleasure Dome) by Kenneth Anger, in the East? We also would like to know whether you have contracted to distribute this film, and if that is the case, whether Mr. Anger assured you of rights to the sound track?

We realize full well that you had no way of knowing about this problem in advance. Kindly co-operate with us in order that this matter can be settled, and consider us as fully willing to co-operate with you in turn.

Sincerely

[hw] Gerd Stern

Gerd Stern mgr.

✦ ✦ ✦ ✦ ✦ ✦

Letter to Amos Vogel from Kenneth Anger, 5/19/54

May 19 1954
Palazzo Celani
Rome

Dear Amos:

I have just arrived in Rome after visiting in Paris and Zürich so am in belated receipt of your two letters dealing with the music difficulty.

I am perfectly furious over this, and since Mr. Stern has seen fit to seriously misrepresent the situation in his insulting and libelous letter, I shall trace for you the actual facts of the case:

In January of this year, on the occasion of a visit in San Francisco at the house of the poet Robert Duncan, I first heard the private subscription recording of Partch's music. I immediately saw the possibility of using this music in connection with PLEASURE DOME which I had been working on for about one month. Mr. Duncan, who is well acquainted Mr. Partch, telephoned him, making an appointment for us to visit him and for him to see my films. Together with Mr. Duncan and a well-known San Francisco painter, Mr. Jess Collins, I went to Sausalito to Mr. Partch's quarters with copies of my films, including a 15 minute excerpt from my "work in progress", INAUGURATION OF THE PLEASURE DOME. Mr. Partch was very friendly and received the showing of my films with great interest. He particularly liked FIREWORKS, asking that it be shown a second time, while he played a portion of his music "Even Wild Horses" as an accompanyment. He and the other members of the company agreed that the combination was very effective. I then showed the sequence from PLEASURE DOME, describing before I did so the scenario and import of the film in detail. I said I hoped very much portions of his "Percussion Dances" could be used for scoring the film, as rhythmically the counterpoint with the images seemed to me very effective. In this light a portion of the music was played with the excerpt. A discussion about the use of the music with the film ensued, concluding with the <u>agreement by Mr. Partch that I could use the music with the film, that I could experiment with it or cut it in any way I wished</u>.

In other words he gave me a "carte blanche" and did not suggest or impose any restrictions whatsoever. This interview was witnessed by Mr. Duncan and Mr. Collins who will testify on my behalf. Since the agreement was a "friendly one" between artists, as one experimental artist helping and doing a favor for another, no mention was made of signing contracts, etc. I can see now that I would have been far wiser to have insisted on this, in view of later developments and the fact that Mr. Partch has "changed his mind." At the end of the evening I purchased from Mr. Partch a copy of his record that was <u>specifically</u> to be used as a master for the making of the sound-track, as we searched through a number of copies to find one without blemish. Mr. Partch also "kindly" supplied me with an old copy of the same record to be used for rehearsal purposes.

I departed from San Francisco, returning to Hollywood with full confidence in Mr. Partch's word. I plunged back feverishly into the filming of PLEASURE DOME, and subsequently the cutting and preparation of the sound-track.

When I brought the film to San Francisco expressly for Mr. Partch to see, he said he "did not like it, and could not understand it." I was quite taken aback by his attitude, when he expressed the further view that he could not see the combination involved in his music and my picture. Mr. Duncan had a long discussion with him in this regard and even drafted a preface which could be presented with the film by way of explanation.

In the meantime the film was seen by Mr. Grieg and Mr. Landberg of the Cinema Guild, who wanted very much to book it for showings in San Francisco and Berkeley. In view of the fact that I needed money for the expensive color print, I welcomed the opportunity of an early booking and accepted. Mr. Landberg further expressed his hope that an arrangement could be made with Partch, and said that he would speak to Mr. Stern, who was a personal friend of his and that he "was sure it could be worked out." It was with this understanding that I left San Francisco, flying to Indiana for my conference with Dr. Kinsey.

In addition to Mr. Landberg, at least eight other individuals of note have appealed to Mr. Partch on my behalf, who consider his treatment of me completely unfair. But it has been to no avail at all, and I have been left "holding the bag." As a neurotic whim on his part, it has cost me dearly: in addition to great personal embarrassment, the release of the film will have to be held up for at least a year, pending the preparation of a new sound track, and the raising of the funds necessary for the recording and new print, which I estimate to be $1500.

I am understandably very bitter about this. As far as your plans for the distribution of the film are concerned, they will have to wait for a new print with a new sound track. I am frank to say that the production of PLEASURE DOME has completely exhausted my finances; I will be indeed fortunate if I can find $1500 cash at my disposal even in one years time. In effect, the dispute with Harry Partch has condemned PLEASURE DOME to be shelved indefinitely. I am sorry that your plans concerning the film will have to be postponed; I do hope that before too many years have elapsed they can be set in operation.

In view of this I will of course have to shelve the print of PLEASURE DOME now in the States. I have written to the Cinema Guild to send it to me, as I will have to use it for cueing and synchronizing my new sound track.

If you care to answer Mr. Stern's letter, you may inform him that the film has been withdrawn pending the preparation of a new musical partition.

I must add that Partch & Co. have done themselves no service through this episode, and have alienated a number of people in the San Francisco area who were formerly sympathetic.

Since I can in no way guarantee how long the preparation of the new print will take, I suggest you withhold all notice concerning it until you have a new print and we have signed a contract.

I am sorry that your hopes for the film should be snuffed out so soon; I am sorry too that you have had to be concerned over such an annoying and unfortunate situation. You may be sure that I am going to be very careful in the future in regard to "collaborations" of any kind, as my sense of trust has been severely shaken.

With continued best wishes,

[hw] Kenneth Anger

Reprinted by permission of Kenneth Anger.

✦ ✦ ✦ ✦ ✦ ✦

Letter to Amos Vogel from Gerd Stern, 5/24/54

The Harry Partch Trust Fund
P.O. Box 387
Marin City, Calif.

May 24, 1954

Mr. Amos Vogel
Executive Secretary
Cinema 16
New York City 16

Dear Mr. Vogel:

In reply to yours of the 14th. You are correct in assuming that Mr. Partch's music is protected by copyright.

You state "the film has not been shown by us or anyone else". This must be to your knowledge since I know specifically that it was shown to paid audiences for one week in San Francisco and one week in Berkeley. I also know second-hand that the film was shown for several days to paid audiences in Los Angeles. I realize now, from your letter, that you were not distributing for these showings. I had assumed that you were in some wise connected with the matter because the film arrived in this area with your label affixed as return address.

In any case I wish that you would let us know, as soon as you hear from Mr. Anger, what your decision is in this matter. We would be glad to receive from you Mr. Anger's forwarding address in Europe, so we can know directly from him, what caused him to infringe on the verbal promise he made to Mr. Partch and myself to the effect that he would not show the film at all with the music.

Sincerely,

[hw] Gerd Stern

Gerd Stern
Manager

✦ ✦ ✦ ✦ ✦ ✦

Letter to Kenneth Anger from Amos Vogel, 5/24/54

5/24/54

Dear Kenneth:

This is a very unfortunate story. It is quite clear from your letter that regardless of what Mr. Partch may have said or not said, you have no contract or agreement to hold him to and that the film cannot be used as is. Long and bitter experience has finally convinced me that a legal document, however obnoxious it may look, is one's only relatively secure protection against this sort of misfortune. So in the future... be sure to get everything in writing before going ahead.

I am upset also because I had firmly counted on using the film next Fall. What do you think of these 2 possibilities?

1) To approach Mr. Partch and to ask him whether—by a payment of say, 75 or 100 Dollars, he'd be willing to let us use the film for the C 16 showing. He'd have to confirm in writing. Either you or I or both of us could write him. This isn't as crazy as it may sound to you; he may possibly be willing.

2) You work out a record score—we put it on tape (we have just acquired a very good tape recorder) and we play it in conjunction with the existing print, killing the film sound track. We've done this before, many times, and very successfully—in perfect sync with the film. In your case, there would be even less of a sync problem than usual. I consider this a very good possibility—the added advantage to you being that you'd get some immediate income to help you make the new sound version which will obviously take time to do.

This would enable me to show the film as planned.

I strongly suggest that you accept one of the two proposals. I am writing this in a hurry so you wont have the print sent to you before this reaches you.

Of course, for the records we'd use records available here, preferably LP's.

Please reply by airmail right away.

best,

Amos

✦ ✦ ✦ ✦ ✦ ✦

Letter to Gerd Stern from Amos Vogel, 6/1/54

June 1, 1954

Mr. Gerd Stern, Manager
The Harry Partch Trust Fund
P.O. Box 387
Marin City, California

Dear Mr. Stern:

I have your recent letter and appreciate the information contained in it. You are correct in assuming that we had no connection with the west coast showings.

I have no wish to get involved in this matter but I feel that a number of comments are in order.

It seems to me that you and probably Mr. Partch labor under a misconception as to the nature of the experimental film field in this country. This is a limited and poor field, peopled by producers who in all cases are young artists interested in advancing the cause of the cinema by experimentation and one or two distributors who distribute those films, not to make profits but to act as a service agency for spreading knowledge of such films.

Your telegram and letter threatening legal action may be appropriate for a large commercial film venture, but in my humble opinion seems somewhat out of place in relation to either Cinema 16 which is a non-profit, non-commercial venture, or Mr. Anger who assuredly will not and does not expect to get rich from this film.

The sum total of the story so far is simply that we will apparently be unable to show a film that we had very much wanted to show. It is this which prompts me to write this letter to ask you whether Mr. Partch would be willing to make an exception in this case. On our part, we would be willing to make a voluntary token payment in the vicinity of $75 to your Trust Fund, if permission is granted to us to exhibit the film at Cinema 16. Needless to say, this would not involve distribution rights.

Everybody is entitled to his own opinions as to the merits of any particular work of art. No matter however what one's personal reactions may be to Mr. Anger's film, I am perfectly certain that it is one of the significant recent American poetic films and will be shown and remembered many years to hence. This also was the impression of other film critics who were able to see it.

In fact, it is my humble opinion which I do not expect you to concur, that Mr. Partch's music provides an extremely effective and excellent musical counterpart to the visual images, and that just as it would not accrue Mr. Anger's film to be associated with Mr. Partch's music, the reverse is equally true. I repeat that this is quite regardless of how one might react to the subject matter of the film itself.

My deadlines are now only three weeks off and I should appreciate hearing from you before then. I trust that your decision will be a favorable one.

Mr. Anger is in no way connected with this letter.

Very sincerely yours,

Amos Vogel
Executive Secretary

AV/ao

✦ ✦ ✦ ✦ ✦ ✦

Letter to Amos Vogel from Harry Partch, 6/3/54

June 3, 1954

Amos Vogel, Executive Secretary
Cinema 16 Inc.
175 Lexington Avenue
New York, 16, N. Y.

Dear Mr. Vogel:

I have your letter of June 1st to Mr. Stern. A statement of the facts by me is now painful but absolutely necessary. Neither Mr. Stern nor I has ever been under any misapprehension as to the non-commercial nature of "experimental" films, nor can I find anything in his letter to you that suggests we were. The misconception is yours. I have been through too many years of "experimental" music to have any illusions. I never at any time suggested that there was a bank-check price on the use of my music.

All this would have been unnecessary if Kenneth Anger had availed himself of the basic courtesies and considerations that I have come to expect of dedicated creative workers. He asked no permission and I granted none. He paid exactly $7.50 for a record, and I gave him another copy. He told me that he intended to tape one copy for the purposes of experimentation and I offered no objection because I was interested.

However, and this is a very large word, the understanding was very plain to me that he intended to see me again in a matter of weeks in order to acquaint me with his progress, and I remember distinctly saying that I could not tell on the basis of five minutes of the film in question whether I thought my music was suitable.

After this very casual meeting—I had never seen the man before in my life—Kenneth Anger departed from the world for three months, as far as I was concerned, then came to San Francisco and presented me with an <u>accomplished fact</u>. Even if I had liked his film, this act alone would have prejudiced any idea of collaborating with him. Without good reason, it actually becomes repugnant, and the only reason he offered was that he was "busy."

Your statement as to the opinion of film critics regarding this film impresses me as little as do the adverse opinions of music critics over the last thirty years regarding my music. I would also point out that <u>your</u> creative work is not involved. Mine is, and I must be the judge as to whether it is injured by such associations as this.

It should be clear by now, I think, that payment of money to us has never been an issue, and as for threatening legal action, what course does one take when permission to use a copyrighted work has been denied and this denial has been immediately disregarded?

The idea that Anger's film <u>must</u> have my music in order to be shown is a prima facie case of the ridiculous. If this work of mine was so necessary to his film, why did not Anger assure himself of my willing participation? Any correlation between it and his film is non-existent. Further, it was reproduced so badly during the 45 minutes of the film that I could stand, and cut so badly, that it is even less than weak caricature of my concept in <u>Plectra and Percussion Dances</u>. The friends of my music who saw the film, even those who liked it, were a little sickened by this presentation of my music.

Again I must say, as I have wearily repeated before, Kenneth Anger does not have my permission to use my copyrighted work, <u>Plectra and Percussion Dances</u> in the showing of his film, <u>Inauguration of the Pleasure Dome</u>.

Yours sincerely,

[hw] Harry Partch

Harry Partch
P.O. Box 387
Marin City, Calif.

✦ ✦ ✦ ✦ ✦ ✦

Letter to Amos Vogel from Kenneth Anger, 7/9/54

June 9, 1954

Piazza Scanderbeg, 85
Rome Italy

Dear Amos,

I am sorry in my delay in acknowledgement of your last letter but I was invited on a trip and have been out of Rome.

Illustration 49. Kenneth Anger. Courtesy Anthology Film Archives.

As far as PLEASURE DOME is concerned, I received the copy from San Francisco some time ago. However that is all the satisfaction that I have had, as Mr. Michael Grieg has not paid me one cent of the $120. rental he owes me. Mr. Landberg of Berkeley owes me a similar sum, of which he has only put out $50., using $25. of that to ship the film to me. As it was he shipped the film by the wrong method so that it was hopelessly tied up in Italian Customs, to such an extent that I had to reforward it to Paris where the Cinematheque cleared it for me. The gentlemen of the Cinema Guild apparently feel that my absence from the country gives them the opportunity to avoid their financial obligation to me; however this is exceedingly short-sighted on their part. I have already written my family lawyer in Los Angeles to see what action should be brought against them. I should advise you to be very cautious if in the future you should have any dealings with them.

I am flying to Paris tonight to get the copy of my film from the Cinematheque and to discuss with them the matter of assistance in the rescoring of the film. During my week in Paris they want to have a retrospective showing of all my works to an invited audience, and this is the urgent matter at hand with which this letter is concerned: As you know you have the only copy of PUCE MOMENT, I would like you to send it to me via Air Parcel Post in Paris immediately. The address should be written as follows:

M. Kenneth Anger
au soins Monsieur Henri Langlois
Cinémathèque Francaise
7, Avenue de Messine
Paris.

You don't need to put the film in a can; just wrap it in heavy paper. <u>Please</u> do take care of this without delay; I <u>must</u> have the film by the 15th at the latest: I am counting on you.

When I get back to Rome from Paris I'll proceed to make the hand-painted title as we discussed, then I can send it with a friend returning to N.Y. by early fall. I'm sure you won't want to use it for anything before then.

If all goes well in Paris I may be able to get a new scored copy of PLEASURE DOME to you by next winter. But it is going to be extremely difficult at best so let's not count on anything until it is actually finished.

If I have collected any income please be so kind as to send it to my Rome address, as I need every dollar I can scrape up to help cover the huge costs of rescoring and printing.

Please do look after the PUCE MOMENT shipment right away . . .

With all best wishes,

Kenneth Anger

Reprinted by permission of Kenneth Anger.

✦ ✦ ✦ ✦ ✦ ✦

Letter to Kenneth Anger from Amos Vogel, 8/19/54

August 19, 1954

Mr. Kenneth Anger
Piazza Scanderbeg 85
Rome, Italy

Dear Kenneth:

Sorry to hear about your bad experiences with Cinema Guild. They point up the advantages of having a distributor on the spot who can get after them.

A case in point is Rohauer. I have finally obtained confirmation (in the form of one of his printed programs) of the fact that he has been using FIREWORKS without having rented it from us. I am now investigating this matter. It seems obvious that he duped a print. I will keep you informed.

Did you receive PUCE MOMENT? You gave us very little time and since the office was closed for vacation the situation was even more difficult. When can we expect to have it back? I am definitely considering putting it on one of our early 1955 programs. Please let me know.

What's new about PLEASURE DOME? Again I definitely intend to premiere this film.

I notice that you intend to return PUCE MOMENT via a friend who is to return here in the early Fall. This is a very good idea which will save quite a bit of expense—provided you can rely on the person involved.

I am enclosing a statement of your earnings from February 1st, 1954 to July 31st, 1954 and have sent you an international money order under separate cover.

How are you otherwise? How are you spending your time—you lucky man? Do you have any new film plans? Are you intending to stay in Europe?

With best personal regards,

Amos

AV/ao

✦ ✦ ✦ ✦ ✦ ✦

Letter to Amos Vogel from Kenneth Anger, 8/28/54

Rome, Aug. 28 54

Dear Amos:

I've just received your letter of the 19th with the enclosed statement. As yet the check hasn't arrived.

First of all I hasten to explain what must be the case with Rohauer. He has offered to buy from me a used copy of FIREWORKS for $100 which I left in California, for the use of his film society, excluding any form of rental or distribution or naturally duplicating of the film. I have the $100. and a letter-contract to that effect. Naturally, I did this advisably, since not only by my own experience but in the experience of Curtis and others Rohauer is not a completely trustworthy person. However, the contract limits his use of the print to his own film society showings, and I have enough friends in So. Calif. who would inform me if he tries to do anything else with it. I might add that offers to buy a print are rare indeed, and I needed the money for my rescoring of PLEASURE DOME. It is a life-of-the-print lease, and it was already a used copy. It is a fact that Curtis and others can verify that Rohauer made dupes of Broughton's films; however that's his problem if he cares to do anything about it. I believe Broughton's films are being distributed in the U. S. from more than one source. Rohauer told me he wouldn't be showing the film until some time next year; I suppose it's rather typical that he schedules a showing almost immediately after receiving the print. Aside from the two prints that you now have, and the print with Rohauer, the only other print in the U. S. is the one I sold to Kinsey at the University of Indiana.

Thanks very much for sending the print of PUCE MOMENT. I can see now that I must keep a copy of all my films with me at all times, as I never can tell when I'll have need of them for a showing. So I had better make a new print for you with titles and send that back; however that means more expense, and I don't even have enough to get half-way through the rescoring of PLEASURE DOME.

When I return to Paris in September I hope to have another "sponsor showing" of my films and I hope something will come of it. However if nothing comes of this I don't know how I'll have enough to send you extra copies back of my films. Will you be able to forward me something against either a showing or distribution income on these films? These include as well as PUCE MOMENT, my fountain film ACQUE BAROCCHE and RABBIT'S MOON, which you haven't seen, since it's on 35mm but I could have a reduction print made; and eventually PLEASURE DOME. In the latter case even assuming I manage myself the costs of scoring, the expense of a color print is roughly $270. alone, so it would be impossible for me to afford two prints, one for myself and one for Cinema 16. If you are willing to wait over a year for these films, you will probably get copies of them, but if you want them sooner, I'll have to have some help on them.

I've heard Curtis is finishing up his two last films; I suppose you're in touch with him. When I was in San Francisco I saw the rushes of an interesting film by a young man named Stan Brackhage; I gave him your address and told him to write you or send you a copy of the film when it was finished. I wonder if you've heard from him.

I'm enclosing an article that appeared in one of Rome's leading newspapers on Cinema 16; I thought you might like to see it. Also, I've seen the various articles in Saturday Review which are certainly all to the good. I wonder if Starr or someone would be interested in doing an article exclusively on U. S. experimental films; I don't believe such an article has been done, and it certainly might be beneficial. I'm sure you could suggest it to SR and make the representative selections of films available for review. I can assure you that Curtis, Broughton, and myself, among others, would appreciate it. It's ironic that more is written about our films outside of the U. S. than in it. An article by Lotte Eisner on the Avantguardia in American has recently appeared in the Italian review, Bianco e Nero.

I'll keep in touch with you as things progress, and please let me know if you have any suggestions about financing prints!

Sincerely yours,

[hw] Kenneth

Reprinted by permission of Kenneth Anger.

[I assume the "fountain film," Acque Barrocche, mentioned in paragraph 4, is Eaux d'artifice. Starr (in paragraph 6) is Cecile Starr.]

✦ ✦ ✦ ✦ ✦ ✦

Letter to Amos Vogel from Luis Buñuel, 9/17/54

Luis Bunuel
27 Cerrada Felix Cuevas
(Colonia del Valle)
MEXICO D.F.

Mexico 17 September 1954

Mr. Amos Vogel
175 Lexington Ave.
New York

Dear Mr. Vogel: First,I want to excuse my delay in answering your letter of August 19. I am the first one in criticizing my falt in punctuality. It is perhaps, my bad English, that prevents me of maintaining a correspondence.

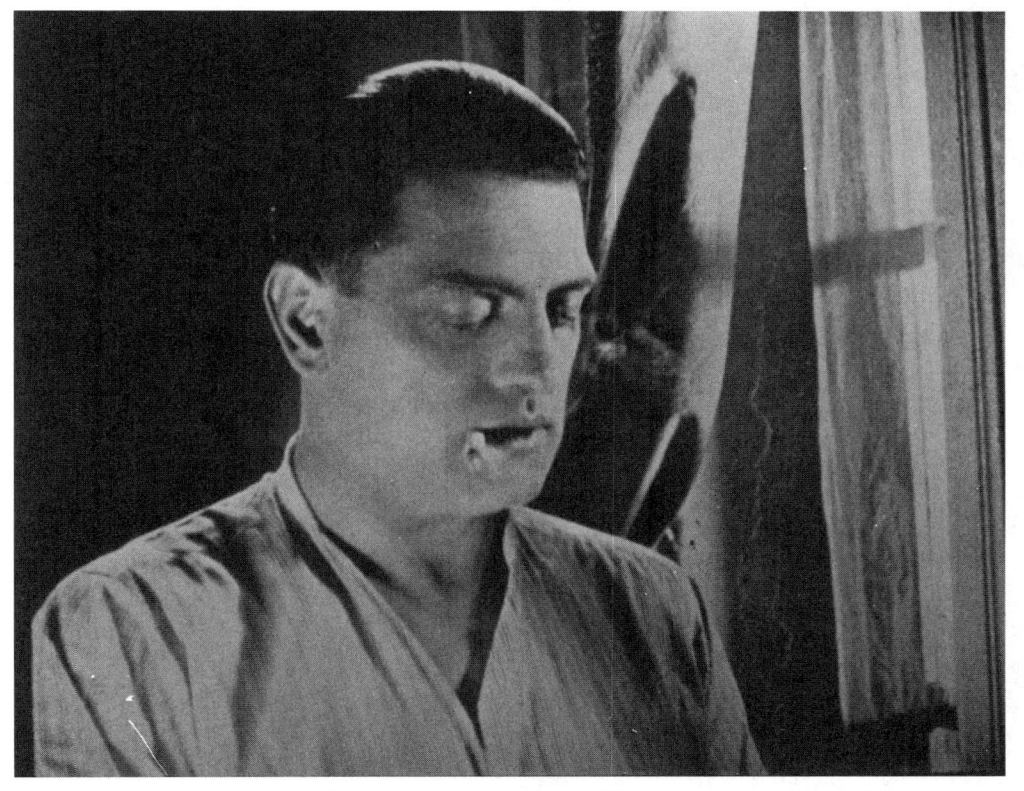

Illustration 50. Luis Buñuel in *Un Chien Andalou* (1929). Courtesy Anthology Film Archives.

It gives me great pleasure to send you some material on EL. It's a selection of articles recently written in Paris about the film, by some important critics and with whose judgement I generally agree. I suppose that, out of them, you can take some information for a better explanation of the film.

The cost of EL was about 100.000 dollars and it took me four weeks of filming. I tried to describe <u>objectively</u> a paranoiac character with delirium of interpretation. In the case of EL it is a jealous one but with a spanish or latin american kind of jealousy.

The character of Francisco is taken from real life and not from "imagination". Under a melodramatic form there is a critic of the bourgeoisie ant its fundamentals of which each spectator is allowed to interpret in his own fashion or not interpret at all.

I thank you very much for your interest.

Very truly yours

[hw] Luis Buñuel

✦ ✦ ✦ ✦ ✦ ✦

Letter to Kenneth Anger from Amos Vogel, 9/21/54

September 21, 1954

Dear Kenneth,

I was shocked at your letter re Rohauer and the very casual way in which you mention to me a clear violation of our agreement.

This agreement not only grants me exclusive distribution rights, but specifically states that you will not sell "any print or any of the rights to them to any party" and also, "no other print shall be distributed or exhibited in the US, unless it be an additional print supplied to C16 by me".

Rohauer has been one of my most active customers for this film in the past. How you took it upon yourself to make such an arrangement with him is completely beyond me. You simply took the customer out of the market, keeping, as it were, the distributor's share for yourself. How would you like it if I told you that I had failed to mention a number of rentals to you, thereby keeping your share from me?

Incidentally, $100 is a ludicrous sum, given Rohauer's set-up.

I was even more shocked by the fact that you quite obviously kept this arrangement from me, since you did not mention it during our talk concerning Rohauer in New York.

I have written Raymond and informed him that he has no rights whatsoever to show the print. I must ask you to inform him likewise and to see that it is withdrawn.

Over the years I have done my best to help you in every way; it come as a distinct {p e r s o n a l} shock to hear about this matter.

If you want our relations to continue, this type of collaboration will have to be a two-way affair.

I should like to hear from you about this.

Sincerely,

[Amos Vogel]

PS The International Postal Money Order definitely was mailed to your Rome address on August 20th. I suggest you check with your Rome post office. I've checked here and it definitely went out.

✦ ✦ ✦ ✦ ✦ ✦

Program Announcement: Fall 1954/Spring 1955

October 1954

Miramagic
A unique kaleidoscopic film technique transforms familiar objects into sensuous and startling visual fantasies. The first film of its type. With Adrianne Corri, beautiful star of Jean Renoir's *The River*. A Cinavision production by Walter Lewisohn. All electronic score by Louis and Bebe Barron.

Georges Braque
From sign painter to giant of modern art: Braque paints on transparent glass directly for the camera in this exciting film visit to the master craftsman. A subtle and adult portrayal of the mystery of artistic creation based on the scenario by the noted French art critic Stanislas Fumet. A Film Images release. Narration: Hurd Hatfield. Music by Bach.

Illustration 51. Program announcement, fall 1954/spring 1955.

The Navigator
Buster Keaton's immortal cinema farce: a grotesque and sophisticated satire on mechanized society, with semi-surrealist overtones. The imperturbable comedian—alone with a girl on a drifting ocean liner—solemnly attempts to behave normally in a world which is plainly betwitched. An MGM release directed by Donald Crisp and Buster Keaton; co-starring Kathryn Maguire. "The nightmare aspect of the familiar!"—Museum of Modern Art.

November 1954

Have You Nothing to Declare?
Rejected by the New York censors for public showings, this hilarious French farce stars the immortal Raimu in a lusty feature-length comedy featuring the Rabelaisian adventures of an absent-minded professor on a delicate mission. A young bridegroom with unforgivable inhibitions; a psychiatrist in need of psychiatric treatment; and a hypnotist who gets hypnotized are among the unusual supporting players.

Complete English titles. Dialogue by the noted French author Jean Anouilh. Based on the famous French stage hit by d'Hennequin. Starring Raimu, Pierre Brasseur, Sylvia Bataille, Saturnin-Fabre. A Brandon Films release.

"A bedroom farce in the typical French manner. Since the police haven't cracked down on de Maupassant, Boccaccio and Rabelais, there is no reason to ban this film."—*Brooklyn Eagle*.

New Cartoons by U. P. A.
Once again Cinema 16 presents a selection of the best current and forthcoming releases by the producers of Columbia's *Gerald McBoing-Boing* and *Mr. Magoo* whose work is revolutionizing the American cartoon field. The annual UPA survey has become one of Cinema 16's most popular features.

December 1954

Strange Worlds: 5 film explorations

A Study of Crystals
DDT as abstract art: Stunningly beautiful close-ups of actual crystal growth, captured by micro-cinematography in exquisite color.

Paul Delvaux
A curious journey through the celebrated painter's fantastic universe peopled by luxurious nudes in mysterious landscapes. International Prize Winner. "Probably the most beautiful film on art hitherto produced!"—UNESCO

Jazz of Lights (Ian Hugo)
The tawdriness and charm of Times Square: a personal view. Electronic score by Louis and Bebe Barron. With Anaïs Nin and Moondog.

Walkabout
Stone Age Man in our time: a fascinating study of the life, art and ceremonies of the Australian aborigines, oldest living species of man.

Treadle and Bobbin (Wheaton Galentine)
The private life of the sewing machine: a piece of delightful cinematic witchery compounded of fascination and nostalgia. A Film Images release.

January 1955

Colette
The recent death of France's most distinguished woman novelist (author of *Gigi*) makes this intimate and last camera portrait a document of historic importance. Written and spoken by Colette, it includes a romantic evocation of her past and a visit by Cocteau. English Titles. 1951 Edinburgh International Film Festival prize winner. A Brandon Films release.

The Early Chaplin Rediscovered
A rare opportunity to observe the newcomer from vaudeville (not yet the tramp) in some of his hilarious early Keystone comedies. With Fatty Arbuckle, Edna Purviance, Mack Sennett. "The clever player who takes the part of a sharper is a comedian of the first water!"—*Moving Picture World* (1914)

Neurosis and Alcohol
Cats are made neurotic and then subjected to alcohol in unusual psychological experiments designed to explore the relations between neurosis and alcohol. Produced by the Division of Psychiatry at the University of Chicago.

George F. Kennan Discusses Communism
Remarkably adult film discussion—completely unrehearsed—conducted by the noted American diplomat and authority on Russia. (By permission of the Department of Defense.)

SPECIAL EVENTS 1954/1955

October 26 and 27

1. *Chandra Lekha*
A rare opportunity to see Asia's greatest box-office success—India's first million dollar musical: a lush and charmingly unlikely tale of lavish romance and complicated adventure in old India, with delightful infusions of DeMille and Fairbanks, starring Raj Kumari, India's most famous female star. See the tender romance of Chandra and Prince Radha! Hiss the unspeakable Sasank! Thrill to the spectacular drum dance of 500 seductive maidens! By special arrangement with Hoffberg Productions. Complete English titles.

November 30 and December 1

2. *Yellow Cruise*
An astonishing Eastern Odyssey following Marco Polo's route from Beirut to Peking: this extraordinary travel film classic—the record of the 1930 Citroen-Haardt Expedition across Afghanistan, the Himalayas, the Gobi Desert to Mongolia—captures the sounds and faces of the Orient; the ruins of Palmyra; the relics of Alexander the Great; the royal road of Darius; the music of Tin Chan; the strange people of the Himalayas. Complete English narration. On-the-spot sound recording of

indigenous chants, folk melodies, street cries. "A film which the most conservative Hollywood press agent would dub colossal!"—*Newsweek*

January 25 and 26

3. *El (He)*
Bunuel, brilliant director of *The Young and the Damned* and *The Adventures of Robinson Crusoe* transforms a conventional script into a strange drama of paranoic jealousy and perversion. Only New York showing with English translation. Starring Arturo de Cordova. Photography by Gabriel Figueroa. Also: *Un Chien Andalou*, Bunuel's first film, a violent and shocking classic of pure surrealism. Scenario: Bunuel and Salvador Dali.

February 1 and 2

4. King Vidor introduces *Hallelujah*
The distinguished American director will appear in person to discuss his most famous film—a powerful drama of physical and spiritual passion on the Memphis cotton plantations. The first all-Negro film ever made, this MGM release is famous for its sound experiments and unsurpassed naturalism. "One of the four or five most important films ever made... an isolated masterpiece without posterity!"—Bardeche-Brasillach, *History of the Film*

February 15 and 16

5. *Fires Were Started*
To honor a great humanist of the cinema whose unexpected death deprives Britain of its outstanding film poet, Cinema 16 presents the first American showing of the complete version of Humphrey Jennings' masterpiece, never before available here. The common man in extreme situations: a dramatic and intense social document, richly poetic in feeling. "Without doubt the crowning achievement of the British documentary school!"—The British Film Institute. Also: Jennings' *Words for Battle*, great poems of the past as rendered by Laurence Olivier.

March 1 and 2

6. Two Legendary Masterpieces
Cited in all histories of the cinema, at last available by special arrangements with the British Film Institute, Museum of Modern Art and Dutch Film Archive.

> *Earth*
> Alexander Dovzhenko, supreme lyricist of the Soviet cimema, fashions a strange and static film of haunting beauty. Made from the only remaining negative: not shown in American since 1930. "The communication in great intensity of a personal vision. A poem, heroic and idealistic in mood."—*Sight and Sound*.

> *The General Line*
> Another hitherto unavailable masterpiece of the cinema: Eisenstein's ill-fated epic portrays man's conflict with nature and ignorance. Changed several times to fit the shifting party line, it contributed to his artistic tragedy. "Superb picto-

Illustration 52. *Earth* (1930) by Alexander Dovzhenko. Courtesy Museum of Modern Art Film Stills Archive.

rial compositions! The amazing peasant types recall Dürer and Holbein."—Rotha, *The Film Till Now*.

March 29 and 30

7. The Search for Love: 5 Variations on a theme

Fragment of Seeking (Curtis Harrington)
Mounting psychological tension explodes in a Poe-like climax in this unconventional portrayal of adolescence.

Feeling of Hostility (Robert Anderson)
The story of Clare: ambition and success as love substitutes. Unusual psychological study based on actual case history.

Four in the Afternoon (James Broughton)
A child's search for a sweetheart; an adolescent's dream of romantic love; a young girl between desire and propriety; a man longing for his past.

Mechanics of Love (Willard Maas and Ben Moore)
Another highly unorthodox film by the creator of *Geography of the Body*. Original Zither score by John Gruen.

Psyche (Gregory Markopoulos)
The noted stream-of-consciousness film poem, suggested by Pierre Louys' novel: a sensitive portrayal of a young woman's yearning and fulfillment.

2 Bonus Events

(dates to be announced . . . seating capacity limited)

An interview with Fred Zinnemann
The brilliant director of *High Noon* and *From Here to Eternity* will discuss and present his famed triumph of neo-realism, *The Search*.

An interview with Stanley Kramer
The distinguished producer of *The Caine Mutiny, High Noon, Champion*, will discuss and present exerpts from his films.

✦ ✦ ✦ ✦ ✦ ✦

Letter to Amos Vogel from Kenneth Anger, 11/26/54

21 Rue Gazan
Paris XIV
November 26, 1954

Dear Amos,

Your letter of Sept. 21 must have been one of several that were mistakenly turned back by the concierge of the apartment here, when I was down on the Cote d'Azur visiting Cocteau, as I never received it.

I have looked through all my papers here and I cannot find the copy of our original contract of March, 1951; I assume it must be in my file of papers which are still in Rome.

When I made what appears to be my mistaken arrangement with Rohauer in April of this year, I was under the decided impression that I was acting within my legal rights, i.e. that I had the right to make a sale of an individual print if it was for a personal use specifically excluding distribution. As I didn't have the contract on hand, I thought my memory was correct on this matter; that it pertained to the exclusive distribution rights for the U. S. and not the sale of a print. If the contract states, as you say, that I do <u>not</u> have the right to sell a print, even excluding distribution purposes, then I acted under a wrong impression, and I will take the steps necessary to rectify the matter.

I have enclosed a copy of the "Agreement" I made with Rohauer last April; you will see that it states that the print is for his private use only, and states specifically that it will not be rented out at any time. I sincerely thought that in so doing I was not violating my contract with you, which I had no intention of doing, I assure you.

The only reason I entered into this was that, at the time, I needed money urgently and at once to pay off my lab bills for PLEASURE DOME: Raymond offered my $100 for an old copy of FIREWORKS that I had, and as I was literally desperate for money at

Illustration 53. Fred Zinnemann (*left*) and Amos Vogel at Cinema 16, spring 1956.

that moment, I accepted. Of course I can see now I should have written you to check on the contract since I didn't have a copy with me; but I thought my memory was correct on the matter that I was free to sell a print if it was not for distribution purposes. In my overwhelming preoccupation with PLEASURE DOME, this sale of the print assumed a secondary place in my mind, as, at the time, I was confident that I was acting within my rights, and so the matter was closed. If I didn't mention the matter to you in New York, it was not because I was interested in concealing the fact from you, but that it was simply a personal matter which had been settled and closed.

The error, then, is totally mine, and I have written to Rohauer that I mistakenly entered into the agreement with him without the knowledge of the clause of the contract you have pointed out to me. I have pointed out that because of this existing clause dating from 1951 I was actually not at liberty to enter into the agreement with him, and that therefore it must be considered null and void. I have instructed him to do the following: within a week of the time that he receives my letter, he should mail the print which he has of FIREWORKS to you. When you have received the print, I will send you a check for $85 which you will then forward to him. The $15 difference is to cover the showing of several months ago, which may be considered as a rental. You may then, if you wish, deduct your half of this rental from my income for yourself. The print you will keep as an extra with the other two.

If you have another carbon of the original contract of March, 1951, I would appreciate your sending it to me. As it is, here in Paris, I have only a copy of the renewal contract of Nov. 1952, which expires, I believe, in March 1956.

I will keep in touch with you and it is my hope that this matter will be settled satisfactorily without further delay.

Yours very sincerely,

[hw] Kenneth

Reprinted by permission of Kenneth Anger.

✦ ✦ ✦ ✦ ✦ ✦

Letter to Madeline Tourtelot from Amos Vogel, 1/11/55

1/11/55

Dear Miss Tourtelot:

Of your 3 recent films, we liked one very much and want to book it—ONE BY ONE.

It is difficult to explain why RHYTHM ON CANVAS is not successful—in our humble opinion, at least, and you should never for a moment forget that it is only somebody's opinion after all. The paintings themselves are not sufficiently varied or visually striking enough to hold interest; and the fades between paintings are quite disturbing, without lending the film structure or real continuity.

SILENCE suffers from a lack of integration between the very live, excited narration and visuals that are much weaker in content and execution. The two just do not "jell". The drama (or melodrama if you wish) of the story is not "carried through" in the visuals.

You asked for frank comments—so here they are.

On the other hand, there is a simplicity about ONE BY ONE (despite a rather florid introductory statement on the sound track) that is appealing; there are beautiful images, a poetic mood that is carried through: the film makes a statement and makes it well.

We would like to show it on our annual "C 16 Discoveries" program, introducing the work of new film makers. Every year this has been one of our most popular programs. The filmmakers reply to a C 16 questionnaire, with their answers printed in the program notes, the audience responds with comment as to each film in a written questionnaire, which is then sent on to producers for their information.

The dates: April 6, 8, 11, 13, 15. (Each of our programs is shown on 5 dates). The print should reach us not later than April 1 and will be returned on the 16th. Total rental fee for the 5 dates: $ 40. This corresponds to the other rental rates paid by us; we are unable to do better. However, the real value of a C 16 screening lies in its publicity and promotional value. The press attends our screenings, releases are printed in NY newspapers and stories often are forthcoming. This in addition to our members consisting of film specialists, programming directors for civic organizations,TV programs, etc.

Of course, there should be no prior showing in the NY area either nontheatrically, theatrically or on TV. Since the programming deadline for our spring programs is only a few days off, I shall need your confirmation by return mail.

I also need a description—however brief—of the film that we can use as raw material for the printed brochure announcing the programs. This, too, I need by return mail. This can be 20 words or 200 words, just as long as it takes to cover the subject and intent of the film. Also include full credits, stills (if any).

Please continue sending us your films; we will always be interested in seeing them.

Sincerely,

Amos Vogel

✦ ✦ ✦ ✦ ✦ ✦

Transcript of Tape Recording Made by King Vidor and Played at Cinema 16 on 2/1/55 at Screening of *Hallelujah*

This is King Vidor speaking, and I send greetings to the audience at Cinema 16.

I had hoped to be with you tonight as I felt it would be an inspiration to be in close contact with those I knew to be interested in the possibilities of the motion picture as an art form; as a medium of education; of documentation or just one of pure experimentation. I regret that my assuming of the directorial chores of the Italian-American version of the three currently projected film versions of Tolstoy's WAR AND PEACE has made this impossible. It seems strange that after all these years WAR AND PEACE should suddenly evolve into a contest as to which of three similar films reaches the motion picture theatres first, but that is one of the enigmas of the business which had better be left unanswered here. It reminds me of the time Samuel Goldwyn gave me a story about U-Boats which he hoped to make into a film. While I was reading the book over the week-end, I ran into three other producers who were contemplating pictures about U-Boats. On Monday morning I told Mr. Goldwyn about the parallel stories that were being put into work. He surprised me when he said, "If three other fellows want to make the same story, that proves I am right."

I suppose it is that way with WAR AND PEACE, but it was certainly not like that with HALLELUJAH. There never had been an all-negro film made before, and no producer was receptive to the idea when I proposed it to them. It took the cataclysmic advent of sound to start the ball rolling, or rather to start me rolling with sufficient impetus to convince an executive to let me go ahead with the project. In the years preceding 1929, I had repeatedly presented the outline of the film to the studio executives. It had always met with a definite refusal. When synchronous sound recording dramatically invaded the industry in 1928, I was in Paris, but I took the first boat home and sought out a top executive of Loew's in New York. My

Illustration 54. *Hallelujah* (1929) by King Vidor. Courtesy Museum of Modern Art Film Stills Archive.

idea was still greeted with a flood of objections, but when I told them I would risk my contracted salary with their production funds the executive replied, "If that's the way you feel about it, I'll let you make a picture about whores if you want to." (Pause)

We had no portable sound equipment in those early months, and the cameras were confined to huge sound proofed booths that were completely immobile. Through the use of four wheel perambulators and counterweighted booms the American camera had only recently arrived at a state of flexibility. This sound problem was a regressive blow to this freedom of movement. The camera was being frozen because the whir and grind must not be audible to microphones. Big, icebox-like insulated booths were improvised to contain the camera and two or three operators. The lens looked through a plate glass window at the action. Cinematography had retrogressed to the nailed-down tripod of the early days. Whenever a scene could be shot silent and an open camera used, we emerged from the stuffy booths with delight. It was a period of quiet despair to those of us brought up to love the lucidity of silence. As time went on, technicians rose to the occasion and devised soundproof cases that enclosed only the camera itself.

When we started production on HALLELUJAH in Memphis in 1929 we didn't know whether it was to be a silent film or a sound film or half of each. We had no recording equipment with us during the weeks we worked on location in and around Memphis. The dialogue, if it can be called by that name, was mostly made up on the set as subtitles had been. We thought then in terms of subtitles and not in dialogue. This perhaps explains why this film is not overburdened with talk.

We tried to operate the camera at even speeds so that later sound synchronization would fit the action, and this too was a complete innovation. I won't recite here the difficulties that were encountered when this wedding between sound track and action was later accomplished. Accomplished without benefit of moviola—and fixed camera speeds, and all the appurtenances employed in present day editing of sound track and action film.

My first interests in movie direction have always been in experimenting with tempo, rhythm and music expressed in movement and dynamic composition, subject, of course, to the confines permitted by the rectangle of the flat screen. The relentless pursuit through the swamp, as I remember, seemed to accomplish some of these objectives. The scenes were staged with the use of a metronome amplified by the beat of a base drum to keep the movement of the actors precise and under control. Nina Mae McKinney, who played one of the leads, was discovered in the chorus of BLACKBIRDS, then running at a Broadway theatre. Daniel Haynes was an understudy for Jules Bledsoe in SHOWBOAT, then running at the Ziegfeld.

At the time the picture was released, we ran into a mass of resistance from the large theatre chains. In Chicago, when we could not secure a booking in a first run theatre, I was asked to go there and show the film to the local critics, who in their enthusiasm, might write reviews which would aid in getting the picture into one of the large theatres. This method uncovered a willing exhibitor who operated a small theatre on a side street, and after HALLELUJAH played for some weeks at this small theatre to capacity houses, the picture was then booked into one of the large Chicago first-run theatres. As far as I know, this is the first time that a first-run theatre has booked a film after it had played at a small second-run house.

I had hoped in appearing before you that a series of questions and answers could be developed which would bring out details in the making of this film which might prove interesting. Alas—WAR AND PEACE has come between us and it appears that we must wait until Napoleon has retreated from Moscow before this meeting can be realized. Thank you.

[Vidor seems unaware of the history of "race films"—films made exclusively or prmarily for African-American audiences, sometimes by African-American producers/directors (Oscar Micheaux, for example) and production companies. Vogel is unsure when he himself became aware of this history.]

✦ ✦ ✦ ✦ ✦ ✦

Letter to Amos Vogel from Kenneth Anger, 2/11/55

43, Paultons Sq.
Chelsea, S.W. 3.
London
Feb. 11, 1955

Dear Amos,

I am enclosing the program-note and a clipping from the London News Chronicle concerning my very successful showing at the Institute of Contemporary Arts in London.

Through an almost superhuman effort I managed to finish the new print of INAUGURATION OF THE PLEASURE DOME in time for the showing, comprising new music scored for voices and orchestra, and over 200 optical effects. I have worked myself to the point of nervous and physical collapse, but the thing is accomplished.

I am sure that you would be very impressed with the new print of PLEASURE DOME, as well as the beautiful blue-and-green toned print of EAUX D'ARTIFICE. All the films, including PUCE MOMENT, have new, very attractive hand-painted titles.

It seems to me that you should want all three of these films to add to Cinema 16 catalog. I would be very happy for you to do so, if the following conditions are agreeable to you. I would be will be willing to sign a five-year contract, if I could be given a 60% royalty, and retain the right for the sale of individual prints, for private collectors excluding distribution. This last possibility I should like left open, also in the renewal of the FIREWORKS contract, if you care to do so.

In regards to supplying the prints, it would be necessary for you to forward to me here in London a New York Draft check for $200., to assist in covering the cost of the prints. This sum would be deducted from the royalty on a New York showing for all three films, which would be $100., and subsequently covered. I think a rental of $30. for INAUGURATION OF THE PLEASURE DOME, 10. for EAUX D'ARTIFICE, and $5. for PUCE MOMENT would be suitable.

Upon the receipt of the check for $200. from you, and the agreement of conditions, I would forward the three films to you immediately. This would either be by means of a private party who is flying to N.Y. or else an air shipment of the films. A friend of mine here in London recently shipped a 1600 foot color subject to a distributor in San Francisco, via air freight, and no difficulty with the customs was reported. As there is no censorable material in these films, in a visual sense, even if an inspection is made it would not matter. But the first course would undoubtedly be preferable.

It is absolutely necessary for me to come to a final decision regards the U.S. distribution of these three films within the coming week. Since the color lab here in London is the only one capable of printing the optical effects, etc. any new prints must be made here, and I am obliged to be back on the Continent next month. I hope I may hear from you by return mail.

With sincere best wishes,

[hw] Kenneth

Reprinted by permission of Kenneth Anger.

Letter to Kenneth Anger from Amos Vogel, 2/18/55

2/18/55

Dear Kenneth:

I was happy to hear about your films. A draft check for $ 200 is enclosed, but I feel that a number of changes should be made in the conditions outlined by you.

1) Your proposal to sell prints without any participation on my part is an unusual one for distribution contracts. In addition, sales lead to precisely the type of problem we now have with Rohauer(who has not replied nor sent us the print and is now using it for his showings).

2) I suggest that you be permitted to sell any prints you want to <u>in Europe</u>—but I strongly suggest that you "sell them" on a "life of the print" lease basis with a written contract limiting use to private collection and specifically excluding exhibition. Consult a lawyer.

3) I am willing to give you the right to sell prints on such a basis also in the US, with no income to me, provided 1) we approve the sale (this will protect both of us since it would prevent illegal use of the print; you are totally unacquainted with individuals or the situations here, while I would certainly be able to advise you who NOT to sell prints to) and 2) that the division of the income is a 50/50 one. This type of division is not only true of my existing contracts but is especially fair if sales income is excluded, as far as my percentage is concerned. Distribution costs have gone up considerably in the last few years and all distributors have been forced to make the same kind of arrangements.

4) It should also be understood that if I can arrange for a print sale <u>on my own</u>, the same 50/50 provision should then obtain.

5) As per your letter, the $ 200 would be deducted from the $100 royalty for the NY showing and from the first rental incomes of the film until covered. This is perfectly agreeable.

I strongly suggest that you send the film with your friend. In fact, I dont see why import duties should be paid (as they have to, if they go thru customs, as far as I know) for what really are American goods. You should discuss this matter at your end.

Please let me hear from you at your early convenience and send the prints without delay.

Best regards,

Amos

PS Did you get my letter addressed to you in Paris—in which I asked you to again write Rohauer about your cancelling your agreement with him? Have you done so? (You would be interested to hear some of the stories current in NY about him at the moment)

❖ ❖ ❖ ❖ ❖ ❖

Letter to Amos Vogel from Kenneth Anger, 3/1/55

43, Paultons Sq.
London, S.W. 3.

March 1, 1955

Dear Amos:

This is to confirm my cable that I've received your check for $200. which has been deposited in my account here.

Your suggestions as outlined in your letter seem agreeable and we will proceed along those lines.

I will preoccupy myself this month with preparing the prints for you and seeing to their shipment. As I explained there is a distinct possibility I'll be able to arrange with a friend or acquaintance who is flying to N.Y. to bring them to you. However, I haven't got an exact date out of anyone yet. In the meantime I've asked Ada Fennell, at the British Film Institute, for advice on shipping the film to the U.S. It appears this can be done by Air Freight, once I fill out an export form here. There is of course the Customs in the States, but Ada says they've had many 16mm films go through without difficulty; also an import charge amounting to so-much-per-foot; I haven't been able to find this out exactly, as I don't know if there's a difference between new or used copies. There's also the fact that it is U.S. goods; perhaps that fact would lessen the tariff considerably. I'll do my best to find out all these things here, as quickly as possible; but perhaps you can find out the answers on the duties quicker than I can, let me know if you do.

I think it would be fine if you could have the N.Y. showing for the new films later this Spring; but I don't know how far you've arranged that in advance. I think you can reasonably count on the films being in N.Y. in five weeks time, either by one means or another. Would it then be possible for a showing in May? This will be up to you; but let me know if you have a definite date in mind.

I've begun work here on a short color film dealing with the paintings of the well-know English modern artist, Francis Bacon, who's had several shows in N.Y. and has a painting in the Museum of Modern Art. It's being sponsored by the Institute of Contemporary Arts here and the British Film Institute, which has given me the color film. The film will be decidedly "macabre" in nature and should be quite interesting. I enclose a folder on Bacon from his most recent London show and a clip from my film.

With sincere best wishes,

[hw] Kenneth

Reprinted by permission of Kenneth Anger.

✦ ✦ ✦ ✦ ✦ ✦

Program Announcement: Spring 1955

March 1955

Sunday by the Sea
Grand Prize, Venice Film Festival 1953. Warm and romantic glimpse of the pleasures of an English seaside resort, accompanied by charming music-hall ballads. Noel Meadow release.

The Elstree Story
25 years of film history are sampled in over thirty exciting excerpts from otherwise unavailable feature films produced by Britain's famed Elstree Studio, including first screen appearances of Charles Laughton, Ralph Richardson, Laurence Olivier, Stewart Granger, Ray Milland; Hitchcock's first films; and scenes with Anna May Wong, Gertrude Lawrence, Herbert Marshall, Lya de Putti, Cyril Ritchard, Richard Tauber, Madeleine Carroll, Flora Robson, Warwick Ward, Barry Fitzgerald and Annie Ondra.

Paul Tomkowicz: Street-Railway Switchman
The thoughts of an old man at work in a city street during a wintry night: poignant evocation of his feelings about his life, his job, his future. Prizewinner, Edinburgh Film Festival 1954. National Film Board of Canada release by Roman Kroitor.

Jammin' the Blues
Elusive atmosphere of "jam session" is captured in highly stylized film study by noted still photographer Gjon Mili. Not available since 1944, this rare example of experimental work financed by a major studio has just been re-released. Warner Bros.

April 1955

A Program of "First Films" to call attention to young film makers and new directions in the cinema:

Desistfilm (Stan Brakhage)
A jarring attempt to capture the frenzy of an adolescent party. Experimental sound.

Freight Stop (Allan Downs)
The re-discovery of the familiar: A poetic documentary notable for its creative editing.

Oedipus (Robert Vickrey)
A disturbing present-day version of the Oedipus legend, projected as a surrealist melodrama.

Mounting Tension (Rudolph Burckhardt)
A relaxed comedy, spoofing psychoanalysis, modern art and s-e-x. Ends happily. (All actors have since gotten married.)

In Paris Parks (Shirley Clarke)
An afternoon with the children of Paris: a joyful and nostalgic evocation of their magical diversions and amusements.

Uirapuru (Sam Zebba)
Produced as a master's thesis in Film at the University of California: a symbolic interpretation of a primitive Brazilian legend, shot among the Urubu Indians of Maranhoa. Villa-Lobos score.

Howard Street (Leslie Turner)
A new kind of social documentary explores San Francisco's skid row via candid camera and tape recorder.

May 1955

Pre-Columbian Mexican Art
An impressive portrayal of the folk art of Mexico from the astonishing creations of the primitive plateau dwellers of 3000 years ago to the expressionist and tragic art of the Aztec period. Onyx sculptures, jade masks and funeral urns reveal the myths and attitudes of vanished civilizations. Accompanied by Mexican folk melodies and synthetic "musique concrete." A Brandon Films release produced for UNESCO by Enrico Fulchignoni.

Ed Murrow's Interview With Oppenheimer: The Complete Version
The recent *See It Now* interview with the director of the Princeton Institute for Advanced Study proved both a milestone in adult television and an impressive film record of an important personality. While the original interview was cut to fit Mr. Murrow's program, the complete, hour-long version has just been made available by the Fund for the Republic. "Mr. Murrow, who has a passion for doing fine things on TV, has come along with one of his finest. A hypnotic experience... a true study in genius... the beauty and candor of the program was overwhelming." *The New Yorker*.

Blum-Blum
This charming animated trifle, based on an unpopular popular song, caused UPA to hire its producer Duane Crowther.

[The Spring 1955 Special Events were "Two Legendary Masterpieces" (March 1–2), "An Interview with Stanley Kramer" (April 19), "The Search for Love" (April 26–27): See 1954–1955 program announcement for the relevant descriptions.]

❖ ❖ ❖ ❖ ❖ ❖

Letter to Amos Vogel from Kenneth Anger, 4/27/55

April 27, 1955
21 Rue Gazan
Paris XIV

Dear Amos:

Today I have given the films INAUGURATION OF THE PLEASURE DOME and PUCE MOMENT to Mlle. Catala at the Cinémathèque, who has completed the various forms and customs declarations. She is having the films sent to you via Air France. They are both listed as being produced in the U.S. and as having been shipped from the U.S. in the course of 1954. I put the title on a "Cinema 16" label on both film cans, and the same is written on the leader of both films, as they are in effect your goods which are being returned to you.

In this way I don't think there should be any complications with the customs on your side. The case of PUCE MOMENT is simple, as you sent it to the Cinémathèque and they have the temporary admission papers for it; in the case of PLEASURE DOME the film was shipped from N.Y. to San Francisco and from there by air to Rome, in turn shipped from there to the Cinémathèque in Paris. The Cinémathèque has the temporary admission papers from Italy, but the film is still U.S. in origin.

I have ordered a new print of EAUX D'ARTIFICE from the lab in London, and will send it along as soon as I receive it. The customs form will have to be different for it, as it was not made or shipped from the U.S.

You will find enclosed your copy of the revised contract, signed by me. I have signed in spite of the fact that is still feel strongly that a 60% arrangement would have been more fair considering the high cost of these color films, but I won't pursue the matter. $15. per showing for PLEASURE DOME as my income strikes me as very little indeed, and at that rate it will be years before I have even covered my print costs, not even to mention my production costs. However, I have no illusions at all regarding the possibility of "making money" with my films, which have always been for me a losing proposition. The reality of the situation that faces an experimental film-maker is frustrating and disappointing in the extreme, and it is obvious that I will make no more films for a long, long time.

I have enclosed 10 stills and will send some others at a later date. I will also send you four large mounted stills that may be used for display purposes, which you may keep for the duration of our agreement.

I will also send you a copy of an article on my films by Roy Edwards, the critic for <u>Sight and Sound</u>, which you may either quote or paraphrase in your promotion material. I am compiling a list of comments that you may want to use, and will amplify the program note somewhat, although the one I sent you is my official note. You may possibly wish to show the films to someone like Parker Tyler who could write a note more suitable for your audiences.

Please let me know immediately upon receiving the films. I would advise you to have both prints Vaporated (or whatever process is recommended for Kodachrome) before you put them in circulation. They should be cleaned after showings with a dry clean velvet, <u>not</u> with any fluid that will cause blooping ink to run, which has been used on both prints.

Yours sincerely,

[hw] Kenneth

Reprinted by permission of Kenneth Anger.

✦ ✦ ✦ ✦ ✦ ✦

Letter to Kenneth Anger from Amos Vogel, 5/3/55

May 3, 1955

Kenneth Anger
21 Rue Gazan
Paris XIV, France

Dear Kenneth:

Thank you for the contract and for the good news concerning the films. Please check with Miss Catala as to whether they have already been sent. How soon do you expect <u>Eaux D'Artifice</u>? You should investigate whether this film too could not be considered "American goods".

Kenneth, I am fully aware of the problems of the independent film maker and in my own modest way have attempted to help them by distributing their films as widely as possible in America. I can assure you that I have not gotten "rich" on our share of the income. In fact, much more of it has been spent on overhead, clerical and booking expenses and promotion costs than you would believe possible. The important thing at the moment is to get these films and the film makers known to wider and wider audiences and to thereby bring about increased awareness of the "independent film movement". This in itself will then lead to a possible solution of the financial difficulties. For example, I am on the Board of Directors of the Creative Film Foundation which is making a serious attempt to obtain Foundation grants. I suggest that you ask them for their literature and also application blanks for a grant (although it will take some time before significant sums of money will be collected). The address is: Creative Film Foundation, 730 Fifth Avenue, Room 301, New York City.

There is also much more interest publicitywise in these films and recently The Times has begun in a very tentative way to list some of them together with their 16mm films. We will just have to remain patient and hope that the situation will open up in the near future.

Thank you for the stills. Please send others and the larger mounted stills as promised. I am also expecting the descriptive material, the Sight and Sound article, etc. I urge you again to write about Pleasure Dome in greater detail. Of course I will show it to Parker. He may do a note for it.

Can you tell me the whereabouts of the complete version of Zero de Conduit? Stan Brakhage seemed to think that you helped to put this complete version together again. How can I get this for a Cinema 16 showing? Can you give me an address or can you make the necessary connection?

Please let me hear about this.

Sincerely,

[Amos Vogel]

✦ ✦ ✦ ✦ ✦ ✦

Amos Vogel, "Cinema 16 and the Question of Programming," *Film Culture*, no. 3 (1955)

Should film societies concentrate on features or on shorts? Should they show *The Birth of a Baby* or *Rescued from an Eagle's Nest*? Are they "growing up" by turning away from educational films and toward the classics? Are they to function simply as substitutes for art cinemas in smaller communities? Is there a place on their programs for films banned by censors?

A film society functions as a viable entity only if it both expresses and satisfactorily fulfills an existing need: to provide a forum and showcase for an increased awareness and appreciation of film as a medium of art, information, and education. The [British] Federation of Film Societies states this very succinctly: "The objects of the society shall be to encourage interest in the film as an art and as a medium of information and education by means of the exhibition of films of a scientific, educational, cultural and artistic character."

This seemingly innocuous formulation leads to a number of interesting considerations:

1. It establishes as the sole criterion of programming the artistic merit, the informational-educational value, the significance of new techniques, of any given film.

2. By the same token, it excludes any moral, political, religious, ideological criteria, or objections to content and subject matter of any given film. Were content to become a criterion of programming, film societies would quickly become subject to pressure groups representing political, ideological, moral viewpoints that have no relevance to the esthetics of film. In determining to resist these pressures to the extent that they are irrelevant to a greater appreciation of the film medium and to stick closely to the criteria advanced above, the programming director or committee must take the broadest and most objective viewpoint possible. Objectivity is in itself an "education in democracy" for the group as a whole, quite applicable to other fields of human endeavor. It represents the antithesis of censorship in any form and makes the society a workshop in democracy.

Program directors must withstand attempts to prevent the showings of such films as *Triumph of the Will* (an important example of the propaganda film at its best, however vicious), *Birth of a Nation, Potemkin* (or any other Soviet films), the *Morrow-Oppenheimer Interview, Ecstasy, Oliver Twist*; likewise, some members may object to modern art and hence deplore avant-garde, expressionist, abstract, surrealist, symbolist, poetic films (including, very definitely, *Un Chien Andalou*). Others cannot bear the sight of blood (as in one of the outstanding post-war European documentaries, *Blood of the Beasts*); still others object to the portrayal of sexual problems on the screen (homosexuality in *Fireworks*).

Provided the criteria of artistic and educational value are met, all of the above films have a definite place on a film society's program. Anyone objecting to their showing has the right to absent himself from the performance; he has no right to impose his particular moral or political values on the rest of the group by asking it to withdraw the film.

3. Keeping these criteria in mind, the distinction between shorts and features becomes meaningless, a mere matter of running time. There is much film art in some shorts and little film art in many features and vice versa. Film societies that have been showing features almost exclusively, have deprived themselves of a rich and essential source of important film material. It is easy to "program" a series by mixing together one Garbo, one Eisenstein, one Marx Brothers, one Griffith and throwing in *Ecstasy* for good measure. But serious programming includes the patient search for the large mass of material available in shorts. In fact, a good case can be made for the argument that there is often more freshness, more experimentation, and a greater striving for new cinematic achievements in shorts than in features. The reason for this is quite obviously economic. The investment in commercial features is too great to permit of much experimentation. It is frequently in the short film, the "sub-standard" film, the independent film (more often a labor of love than of commerce) that we find new approaches, however halting, to the film medium. Just think of this by no means complete list of names: McLaren, Lee, Deren, Rotha, Wright, Hugo, Grierson, Peterson, Franju, Epstein, Vedrès, Bellon, Cavalcanti, Lorentz, Broughton, Van Dyke, Harrington, Ruttmann, Richter, Maas, Storck, Anger, Mitry, van der Horst, Elton, Anstey, Kirsanov, Dulac, Hammid, Emmer, Buñuel—and you will see how meaningless the separation between the short and the feature really is.

4. It is also clear that programming will vary with local conditions, the composition of the group, and other factors. In states where local censorship laws obtain, it becomes part of the function of the society to provide a showcase for otherwise unavailable films (as long as the criterion remains the inherent artistic or educational value of the film). Thus, a case can be made for both *Ecstasy*, an important early poetic film of aesthetic interest, as well as for a film on childbirth, a subject of great educational interest.

In other areas, the absence of a local art theatre will determine a concentration on foreign and art theatre-type feature films. This remains true of a large number of film society operations in the U.S.

5. To encourage interest in the cinema not only as an art form but also as a "medium of information and education" is, to the British and European ciné-clubs, a self-evident function of a film society, implicit in its very concept. This may come as a shock to some American societies. The truth of the matter seems to be that the European societies, possibly due to a broader and older cultural tradition, have never made an airtight separation between the various functions of the film medium. The important consideration is to get more and wider circles of audiences "excited" about the possibilities and achievements of the cinema. This, in addition to film classics, very definitely includes scientific films (time-lapse, high-speed, micro-cinematography); psychological studies (mental health films, psychological testing and research, candid camera approaches, such as in Slavson's *Activity Group Therapy,* or in the CBS-TV *The Search* programs); social and other documentaries; art films, be they informational (*Matisse*), poetic (*The World of Paul Delvaux*), illustrative (*Images Médiévales*), subjective-biographical (*The Tragic Pursuit of Perfection*); sound track experiments (electronic, hand-drawn, musique concrete); film-width and 3-D experiments; and finally, films made without a camera or music made without musical instruments.

In fact, while it is not within the province of this article to discuss this subject in detail, where does "education" stop and "art" begin? A truly "educational" film—in attempting to involve our emotions—often begins to assume the qualities of art. Is *Song of Ceylon* merely a work of art—or does it also convey educational, informational values without being either statistical or didactic about it? What about *Night Mail, The River, The Plow That Broke the Plains*?

6. It is well to keep in mind the difference between a commercial movie theatre and a film society. The commercial movie theatre aims to entertain; the film society aims to further the appreciation of film and of new experiments in the medium. The commercial theatre steers clear of controversy, the film society welcomes it. If the films shown by the film society are entertaining, so much the better; but entertainment value cannot be the sole criterion for film society programming, nor can audience approval or disapproval. Film societies must remain at least one step ahead of their audiences and must not permit themselves to be pulled down to the level of the lowest common denominator in the audience—a very easy, common, and dangerous occurrence in the mass media. (We could take to heart the remark made by Frederick Stock, director of the Chicago Symphony Orchestra, who after introducing Brahms to Chicago audiences for the first time said: "They do not like Brahms . . . I shall play him again.")

An historical example may be found in the works of the French avant-garde of the twenties. In spite of critical approval by a minority at the time, their efforts were frowned upon in more "respectable" circles, the showing of *L'Age d'Or,* for example, leading to a well-organized and well-publicized political riot. Yet today many of the devices and achievements of this school have not only percolated into commercial Hollywood production, but have inevitably been vulgarized as well. It is part of the function of film societies to continue as the spearhead of new experiments and talents, even at the risk of committing errors of judgment and taste. It is difficult to pick out the "greats" of tomorrow; but the film society, to remain true to itself, must never cease trying.

This, then, is a plea for more adventurous programming, for more daring, greater open-mindedness, and audacity. Perhaps the motto of the societies should be Tennessee Williams' provocative exhortation for our age when in *Camino Real* he has a somewhat tarnished Lord Byron once again setting out for unknown shores with the words: "Make voyages! Attempt them! *There is nothing else!*"

> Originally published in *Film Culture,* no. 3 (1955), as "Film Society Programming: A Challenge"; and reprinted in Cecile Starr, ed., *Film Society Primer* (Forest Hills, N.Y.: American Federation of Film Societies, 1956). Reprinted by permission of *Film Culture* and Cecile Starr.

✦ ✦ ✦ ✦ ✦ ✦

Letter to Barbara Stauffacher [Solomon] from Amos Vogel, 8/22/55

August 22, 1955

Bobbie Stauffacher
2622 Franklin Street
San Francisco, Cal.

Dear Bobbie:

I have been deeply shocked and saddened by the terrible news. There is really nothing one can say at such a time that would be truly meaningful to the ones that are left behind—but I can say this and mean it deeply: Those of us who knew Frank intimately have lost a true and rare friend, a true and rare human being. In an industry with more than the usual share of cut-throats and slick businessmen, he was the one and only person I knew who had no enemies; the only person, in fact, about whom nothing bad or negative or unpleasant was said behind his back. His integrity, devotion to his life's work and his sincerity were too transparent to be misunderstood by even the most narrow-minded. He pioneered in this field and set standards for all of us, Cinema 16 included. Art In Cinema will stand as his achievement and your contribution to it in his last months will not be forgotten either.

Being a father myself now, I know that you at least have the wonderful consolation of his continuing to live in a thousand different ways in your child.

Please let me know if I can be of any help in any way. And please be assured of my continuing friendship and love.

Marcia joins me.

Sincerely,

[Amos Vogel]

✦ ✦ ✦ ✦ ✦ ✦

Program Announcement: Fall 1955/Spring 1956

October 1955

On the Border of Life
Science tampers with creation in disquieting experiments exploring the frontiers of man: insemination by alien species, creating monsters and supermen, producing offspring without fertilization, tampering with the embryo. A film by Nicole Vedres.—Prix Louis Lumiere 1953.

Weegee's New York
The fabulous press photographer's legendary impressions of the metropolis, including his famed candid study of life and love in Coney Island. "The excitement of the sensational imagery stimulates the imagination!"—*N. Y. Times*. "Weegee has the eye of a Balzac!"—Robert Flaherty

Illustration 55. Program announcement, fall 1955/spring 1956.

When the Talkies Were Young
Clark Gable, Betty Davis, Spencer Tracey, John Barrymore, Barbara Stanwyck and James Cagney in exciting scenes from otherwise unavailable features.

Thursday's Children
Academy Award 1955. "Some of the greatest film footage ever caught by a camera... will speak to the heart of millions of people. Why it has not been snatched up by art theatres is a mystery."—Winsten, *N. Y. Post*

Go Slow on the Brighton
Startling experiment whips you from London to Brighton at 800 miles per hour.

November 1955

Disorder
The famous European comment on restless abolescence, existentialism and bohemia on Paris' Left Bank, for the first time in America. The Caves, Cocteau, Greco in a Kosma chanson, the Cafe des Deux Magots, Orson Welles.

The Scandals of Clochemerle
Previously available hereabouts only in heavily censored form, this is the first and only New York showing of the original, uncut version: A ribald and sophisticated contemplation of the morals of a French town, based on Gabriel Chevallier's celebrated book. Complete English sub-titles. "A bawdy and vastly funny film, with gusto, atmosphere and superb characterizations!"—Howard Barnes, *Herald Tribune*.

Within A Story
Reminiscent of Pirandello, this baffling psychological mystery probes the tantalizing borderland between reality and illusion. A film by Richard Bagley.

December 1955

The Letter "A"
A new idea in film making—the visual encyclopedia—permits 5 leading French film directors to "define" Alchemy, Age, Arithmetic, Automaton and Absence in unexpected and provocative visuals. Produced with cooperation of Marcel Carne, Andre Cayatte, Rene Clair, Jean Cocteau, Marcel Pagnol. A Martin J. Lewis release.

Aoi No Uye (The Lady No Uye)
Unique document, discovered among captured Japanese films, presents an authentic 11th Century Noh drama of jealousy and passion, featuring the distinguished Japanese actors K. Sakurama and S. Hohso. Complete English narration explains action, masks, gestures of Noh Theatre, one of the oldest theatre arts on record. Hypnotic musical accompaniment. By special arrangement with U. S. Dept. of Justice.

Too Much Speed
The world's most indestructible crackpots caught in extreme situations: Academy Award Winner Bob Youngson immortalizes an era of wonderful nonsense.

The Legend of St. Ursula
Renaissance life and faith is delicately suggested in Carpaccio's visualization of the tragic destiny of a medieval princess. Gregory Peck narrates.

January 1956

O Dreamland
Penetrating candid camera work and natural sounds provide a scathing and wordless comment on modern popular cultures as seen at a British amusement park by the director of *Thursday's Children*.

Duck Soup
Radiant madness, hysterical abandon and frenzied destruction are given an appalling opportunity in one of the wildest and most famous Marx Brothers comedies—a splendid satire on secret diplomacy, war and dictatorship. With Margaret Dumont, Louis Calhern, Edgar Kennedy. "All the wild, insane frenzies of humor that an entire colony of gagmen can think up over the course of several months of careful study. Magnificent in its amiable insanity!"—*N. Y. Times*

Animals in Rocket Flight
Experiences of the world's first rocket-flight passengers, photographed in actual flight 37 miles above the earth. A restricted U. S. Air Force Film.

SPECIAL EVENTS 1955/1956

November 1 and 2

1. *The White Hell of Pitz Palu*
One of the great adventure films of all time, the legendary German mountaineering classic is here presented by special arrangement in its original version. Directed by G. W. Pabst and Dr. Arnold Fanck, it has been universally acclaimed for its superb and thrilling photography. With Leni Riefenstahl, Ernst Diessel and Ernst Udet. "Wildly terrifying and astonishing... the immense grandeur and beauty, the awesomeness of nature are preserved in one of the most gripping films ever!"—James Agate.

November 29 and 30

2. Sex Education: 5 film illustrations

   Human Beginnings
   Eddie Albert's controversial experiment in sex education for 5-year-olds.

   A Normal Birth
   New film discusses "Natural Childbirth" and shows an actual delivery.

   Mollie Grows Up
   A straightforward discussion of menstruation for adolescent girls.

   The Private Life of a Cat
   Alexander Hammid's tender documentary is probably the perfect sex education film for small children. One of Cinema 16's most popular films.

   The Invader
   Remarkable study traces history of syphilis from 15th Century to today's wonder drugs through contemporary documents, prints and historic motion pictures gathered from museums all over the world. Produced by George Stoney (*All My Babies*) for Center for Mass Communication, Columbia University.

February 7 and 8

3. The Brain: Restricted medical and psychiatric films

Folie A Deux
1st Prize, Mental Hygiene Category, Venice Film Festival 1951. Unstaged film record of mother and daughter exhibiting symptoms of this psychosis.

Aphasia: Psychological Testing and Therapy
Fascinating insights into what science knows about the human brain.

Unconscious Motivation
Unique and unrehearsed psycho-analytic detective story records artificial inducement of a neurosis under hypnosis and its subsequent removal by analysis and dream interpretation.

Seizure: Social & Medical Problems of Epilepsy
First film to deal with this topic in an adult fashion.

February 28 and 29

4. *The Childhood of Maxim Gorki*
This rarely seen masterpiece of the humanist cinema weaves a rich tapestry of Russian life in the 1870's, teeming with splendid characterizations. Beautifully acted, sensitively directed, Mark Donskoi's recreation of a period is so remarkable as to resemble an unstaged documentary. "A work of art, uncompromising and beautiful in its harsh realism."—*N. Y. Post*

April 3 and 4

5. Private Visions: Harrington, Anger, Brakhage
Premieres of recent experimentals certain to evoke comment:

Reflections on Black (Stan Brakhage)
Four possible sexual dramas, visualized by a blind man. Experimental sound.

The Assignation (Curtis Harrington)
Death rides the decaying canals of Venice to claim a victim.

Puce Moment (Kenneth Anger)
Curious fragment of a sensuous evocation of the 1920's, with Yvonne Marquis.

Dangerous Houses (Curtis Harrington)
Imaginative dream voyage thrusts hero into ambiguous adventures in his search for a mysterious goal.

Inauguration of the Pleasure Dome (Kenneth Anger)
Startling and macabre portrayal of an occult ritual by the maker of *Fireworks*: a luxuriant and baroque oddity in the tradition of decadent art. With Anais Nin, Cameron Parsons, Curtis Harrington.

"Highly ingenious Chinese torment."—Jean Cocteau. "It's bright and wickedly subtle violence terrifyingly conveys the ecstasy of the eccentric few—an extraordinary, brilliant work of black art."—Paul Dehn, *London News Chronicle*

April 24 and 25

6. *Greed*
Erich Von Stroheim's immortal masterpiece of the realist cinema—a searing and ruthless study of human degradation overpowering in its grim intensity. A tragic chapter in screen history, this classic was cut to pieces for commercial release. Adapted from Frank Norris' *McTeague,* with Zazu Pitts, Gibsons Gowland, Jean Hersholt.

"The most important picture yet produced in America."—*Herald Tribune* "One of the most uncompromising films the screen has known. Stroheim is the Dostoievsky of the screen."—*N.Y. Times*

May 15 and 16

7. Horror in the Cinema: *The Cat People*
Val Lewton's offbeat shocker—an amazing boxoffice success despite mixed critical reaction—has become recognized as an important example of sophisticated horror in the cinema. With Simone Simon.

Also: climactic excerpts from Hollywood's greatest horror films.

2 Bonus Events
(dates to be announced; seating capacity limited)

An Interview with Alfred Hitchcock
In one of his rare personal appearances, the brilliant director will discuss and present excerpts from some of his most famous films.

A Weekend of Screenings
at George Eastman House, Rochester, will be organized for members interested in visiting one of the world's leading film museums and sampling its otherwise unavailable treasures at special screenings introduced by the curator Mr. James Card.

✦ ✦ ✦ ✦ ✦ ✦

Letter to Amos Vogel from Samson de Brier, 9/1/55

6026 Barton Ave.
H'Wood-38-Cal.
Sept. 1st -1955

Mr. Amos Vogel
175 Lexington Ave.
N.Y. City

Dear Mr. Vogel,

How can I express chagrin, determination to have my rights recognized, hurt pride—all at once without antagonizing you. But then I remember having been told that you are a very understanding and just person.

Illustration 56. Alfred Hitchcock and Amos Vogel at Cinema 16.

When Bebe & Louis Baron were here recently, they came to my house & I feel that they will agree that I have a certain right to your recognition in connection with the showing of "Pleasure Dome." They & Curtis (Harrington) & I agree that you probably have not been informed (Kenneth is so charmingly vague about these little "details") that almost the entire film was shot in my house. Three scenes were not:

1, Kenneth as Hecate dancing into disintegration—2, Curtis as Ceasar walking in &out of a passageway, 3, Myself as Shiva in a greek costume, lying on a couch & viewing with desultory interest the passing by of a pair of boots. With these exceptions, the entire remainder of the film was shot in my house. The furniture, decor, most of the props, all my own costumes & those of several of the others were provided by me alone. I must say in all fairness to Kenneth that he did give me most generously ten dollars towards the electricity bill!! And by the way, PUCE MOMENT was also partly shot (the boudoir scene) in an apartment belonging to me & the importantly used props were mine. This was some years ago. Kenneth & I have sustained a long & ambivalent friendship.

It was about eight years ago that Kenneth first told me about his plans for "Pleasure Dome". He has from the beginning wanted me for the part of Baron Shiva & when he returned from Europe over a year ago & saw what I had done with my house he knew at once that he must do the picture here. I played Shiva in six manifestations AND i also played the GREAT BEAST. SO you see considerable footage was devoted to me, yet i am not even mentioned in the advertising as shown to me by Curtis. Since it seemed to me only a printers proof, is it not possible to change it. Hundreds of people know me from coast to coast &as the film stands, it could scarcely have been made without my cooperation. Furthermore, i agreed to do all this with the understanding that it was to be made purely as an artistic endeavor. Now that it is being shown on a commercial basis & admission charged which goes to a private individual other than Kenneth as gain (since the initial cost of the production was paid for by showings here to which i gave consent) I feel that further showings for paid admissions are an unwarranted invasion of my privacy. As a gesture to a reluctant ego, i feel that i should at least have proper billing as both Shiva (6 manifestations) & as THE GREAT BEAST. The balcony scene with balustrade which figures prominently in several scenes was painted by BETTY VAUGHAN who also created several other effects—the gold ceiling—my white peruke—the dwarf pope etc. I will not expound any further as i do not wish to negate Kenneth's ability of which no one is more cognizant or grateful than I. No one has the ability that he has for making the ordinary extraordinary. It was for this reason that i endured several months of most trying experiences while my house was in a shamble immediately after i had had it redecorated.

Hoping that you will find a way to vindicate me by proper billing in advertisements & PROGRAMS & THAT YOU WILL ACCEPT MY INVITATION TO visit me if you come to Cal. I am

Yours truly,

SAMSON DE BRIER

[hw] Samson De Brier

SINCE i have many friends in N.Y. who would like to see me in the film will you let me know if there is any arrangement whereby they could pay to see the one film without subscribing to the series?

P.S. Awaiting your reply.

Letter to Samson de Brier from Amos Vogel, 9/12/55

September 12, 1955

Mr. Samson de Brier
6026 Barton Avenue
Hollywood 38, Cal.

Dear Mr. de Brier:

I was very sorry to receive your letter. You are quite right in assuming that I was totally unaware of this entire matter; the copy as shown to you by Curtis had been approved by Kenneth and I proceeded in good faith.

While the brochure had already been printed by the time the proof reached Curtis, it is fortunate that no other publicity or public announcement of any kind has as yet gone out.

Of course, I shall be only too happy to list your name and I hope you will bear with me in this unfortunate situation. Our film catalogue listing the film for out-of-town schools and colleges has not yet gone to press, and so it will be possible to correct this matter. This also holds true of all press releases, etc, program notes.

You need not fear that "money" is being made with this film. First, we are set up as a non-profit, non-commercial venture. Secondly, the outlets for films of this type are extremely limited, as you can imagine, and they more often than not hardly pay costs of distribution, mailing, etc. So it all remains a labor of love, for all concerned. I think Kenneth's film is an important one, and I do hope that we count on your cooperation to make it available to those few film societies or schools interested in seeing it.

The Barron's have told me much about you and I certainly will be glad to visit you if and when I will come to California.

Thank you in advance for your understanding of a situation that was not brought about intentionally.

Sincerely,

Amos Vogel

PS If you will send me a list of names and addresses of your friends, I will see what can be arranged regarding their seeing the film.

✦ ✦ ✦ ✦ ✦ ✦

Letter to Amos Vogel from Kenneth Anger, 10/15/55

[hw]
c/o Poste Restante
Cefalù-Sicily

15. Oct. 55

Dear Amos,

I would appreciate hearing from you at once concerning your plans for the New York premiere of "Puce Moment" "Eaux d'Artifice" and "Inauguration of the Pleasure Dome" and your plans as to distributing these films. I would appreciate your allowing me four passes for the premiere to present to some important personalities who would be interested in attending.

I suggest that you use at least part of the program-note I sent you from London, with references to "Master Therion" "Crowleyanity," "black magic" etc.

The reason for this being that it may result in a "tie-in" for you and possibly more publicity, as I am at present engaged in the restoration of Aleister Crowley's villa here in Cafalù, and I have promise of a spread in England's leading photo-mag, "Picture-Post" and possibly in "Life." (Aleister Crowley was the English "black magician" who inspired my film "Pleasure Dome.")

I have heard that Stan Brakhage was awarded a Fullbright in addition to being helped by the Creative Film Foundation. In the meantime I am pining away for lack of funds to continue my work. I could do an excellent film on Crowley's villa here. Could I expect any assistance from the Creative Film Foundation or other sources? I need financial help badly. This is a crucial period for me. Your advice would be appreciate.

Yours sincerely,

Kenneth

Reprinted by permission of Kenneth Anger.

❖ ❖ ❖ ❖ ❖

Letter to Madeline Tourtelot from Amos Vogel, 11/8/55

November 8, 1955

Miss Madeline Tourtelot
Gallery Studio
2719 Sheridan Road
Evanston, Ill.

Dear Miss Tourtelot:

You will perhaps understand my consternation when upon going through one of my back files, I happened to come across your correspondence—misfiled—making me realize that I had not written to you concerning your films. However regrettable an error this was due to, it is really inexcusable and I throw myself fully at your mercy.

Let us then continue as if we had never stopped corresponding. We looked at your films during the early part of the summer and found them quite interesting. They reveal a "poetic eye" a quality somewhat rare in the cinema these days.

ZAPOTECAN VILLAGE—to us–was the least interesting of the 3, primarily due to its haphazard structure. There were many very interesting and beautiful shots in CITY CONCERTO.

We were most interested in REFLECTIONS. Its overall quality is such that it may well be considered for a showing at Cinema 16. The only problem we saw was its overall length. It is quite definitely too long as it stands and would benefit greatly by being tightened. If I may make two suggestions—1) the night shots, while very beautiful, will undoubtedly be too dark for public projection; at least some could be omitted. Likewise, 2) the abstract water effects are beautiful, but there are too many and they resemble other water films, such as H2O.

Have you considered adding music to this film? If shown, it should be accompanied by a musical score.

While at present it runs close to 10 minutes, we felt that it could profitably cut to 6 or 7 for greatest impact.

Please let me know if you are interested in doing this. Quite apart from exhibition, there may also be a possibility of distribution.

Have you done any new work? Please keep me informed. . and accept, once more, my apologies. .

sincerely,

[Amos Vogel]

✦ ✦ ✦ ✦ ✦ ✦

Letter to Amos Vogel from Madeline Tourtelot, 11/11/55

Madeline Tourtelot
Gallery Studio visual-audio communication
143. E. Ontario Street
Chicago 11, Ill.

Mr. Amos Vogel
Cinema 16
175 Lexington Avenue
New York 16, N.Y.

Dear Mr. Vogel:

Thank you for your letter of Nov. 8

When you had returned my films without comment, I had simply assumed that you did not like them, and so it came as a pleasant surprise to learn that you were a bit interested.

At the moment, Reflections has been lengthened in order to more fully fill the music, 'Ma Mere L'Oye' by Ravel, for use on a TV program. I am working on a thirteen week series, correlating films to classical music for the educational channel here in Chicago. The series will begin on December 14th. Frances Flaherty asked to use the film during next summer's Seminar in order to study the problems of putting music to film, and she mentioned that several composers would work on a score, and that Rudolf Serkin and Virgil Thompson would lend their cooperation along with the Marlborough School of Music. So, Reflections will have a sound track by next Fall. I made the film for Ravel's music, but of course, it is too costly to even attempt to use this on the film.

'One By One', a Film Poem on Fall is ready. It is in color and runs approximately 13 min. 'Rhythm On Canvas', also color and 13 min. is ready. This consists of abstract paintings by Claude Bentley, and has a sound track of African drum rhythms by Jimmy Payne. 'Silence', will be out of Lab in two weeks. This is a fable by Edgar Allan Poe. The narration is done by Paul Barnes, and I filmed this in color last summer in Michigan. It runs about 11 min.

In early December I will make a b. & w. film on the sculpture of Naum Gabo in Connecticut. And my Cezanne film will be ready for release next Spring.

Very sincerely yours,

[hw] Madeline Tourtelot

Madeline Tourtelot

Reprinted by permission of Madeline Tourtelot.

[Tourtelot's Reflections *was presented at the first Robert Flaherty Seminar in the summer of 1955.*]

❖ ❖ ❖ ❖ ❖

Letter to Amos Vogel from Willard Maas, 1/9/56

Gryphon Productions
117 Greene Street
New York 12

January 9th, 1956

Dear Amos,

You must forgive me for not replying sooner, but the frantic energies we all had to put forward to finish NARCISSUS left no time for graciousness, something, as you know, I place great faith in. But finally I see my way clear: NARCISSUS will be finished in the next two weeks. I cannot tell you, make you feel, only if you had gone through the last three desperate years would you understand, how relieved I am, and how, at the minute, I am not even annoyed at your protestations about us handing out the leaflets at C16. If you had given us even one line in your program notes, it would not have been necessary, but it is so curious, Amos, though you feel quite free to plug Orson Welles' OTHELLO, one of the worst films ever made (every intelligent critic agrees there!) you would not say one word about us: Stan, Marie, Ben, and me. And when PLEASURE GARDEN was failing uptown, you did not mention one word about James but plugged in your notes a very bad French farce. These things do not go unnoticed by us. It did not occur to me, or Marie, [*hw in margin:* Marie has the right idea. She ignores the whole fucking mess including you, but she <u>did</u> help hard on the leaflets, because she is an <u>artist</u>, and believes in helping artists; call her, if you don't believe me], or Ben, that you would care about us handing out the little notices. We thought you would like it. We were mistaken, evidently. But let this be for the record: on 24th Street (or is it 23 or 25th) there was EXACTLY four of our little announcements thrown away which we picked up and deposited in the nearest garbage can. At the Beekman (and Jack is your witness!), there was not ONE announcement thrown away! So what is this talk about "littering". I have investigated this: There was NO littering. Well, after all this, I am sure, you will be happy to hear that the preview was such a great success, if we had known it, we would not have needed to circularize, C16. We turned away several hundred. I probably am doing myself in by my frank pronouncements, but you know me. Whatever happens to us now (I speak of myself but also of Stan Marie and Ben) is our own doing. If you want to go along with us, we would like that, for, Amos, I do not forget that it was you that first showed GEOGRAPHY, but if you want to reject us, we'll get along, we'll get along.

I don't know what happened along the way to make these jealousies and peculiar things happen. Why aren't you showing Maya? Why is Ian showing elsewhere? Why is Stan wishing he had not signed with you for his two films? Why am I giving you hell? Are we all wrong, Amos? You have done so much and I am the first to admit it. If you want to talk about this, I'd like to, because someway along things have gone wrong. You'll get along, for sure, and I'll get along, but good Christ, isn't there a way we could get along together?

Yours,

Will

Reprinted by permission of Stephen Maas.

[In the mid-1950s Stan Brakhage, Willard Maas, Marie Menken, and Ben Moore formed the Gryphon Film Group, which presented screenings of avant-garde film. Maas's Geography of the Body *(1943) had become an avant-garde classic.]*

✦ ✦ ✦ ✦ ✦ ✦

Program Announcement: Spring 1956

March 1956

Stained Image (*Nigoriye*) 1953
"Best Film Of The Year"—Japanese Press Critics Association

First New York showing of an important and unusual example of the contemporary Japanese realist cinema, completely unlike the classic "costume drama" that in recent years has become identified with Japanese film production. Three subtle vignettes by the brilliant woman author Ychiyo Higuchi (who died of tuberculosis at 29) offer unusual factual and psychological insights into a rigid class society and its mores, relations between the sexes, the rich and the poor, the prostitutes and their clients:

Jusanya (The Thirteenth Night): a sad and tender study of a young woman enmeshed in the feudal family order.

Otsu Gemori (The Last Day of the Year): a poignant incident in the life of an impoverished servant girl.

Nigoriye (Stained Image): Set in a brothel, the pitiful story of the Geisha O-Riki—told without sensationalism—ends in tragic violence.

Complete English titles. A Shochiku Production by Tadashi Imay, starring the leading actors of Bungaku Za, distinguished Tokyo repertory company.

April 1956

A Program of "First Films"
to call attention to new film makers and new directors in cinema:

Pattern For A Sunday Afternoon (Carmen D'Avino)
This exuberant and brilliantly colorful experiment in free self-exploration won its producer a Creative Film Foundation Grant.

Asian Earth (Michael Hagopian)
First honest effort to deal with the social and human problems of Asia on film. Venice and Edinburgh Prizewinner. Indian music and chants.

Creative Dance & The Child (L. Frank & G. Goldsmith)
Unusual psychological experiment leads children from hesitation and inhibition to emotional release by means of 'unconscious' choreography.

Communication Primer (Charles and Ray Eames)
The distinguished modern artist, furniture designer and toy maker in a striking experiment employing collage, animation, paintings and symbols.

The Towers (B. Hale)
Edinburgh and Venice Prizewinner. From tin cans, bits of tile, glass and debris, an odd and wonderful recluse builds a strange fantasy.

One By One (Madeline Tourtelot)
Fern, leaf and tree: a film poem notable for its striking photography.

May 1956

Bull Fight (Shirley Clarke)
Edinburgh and Venice Prize Winner 1955. A poetic drama fuses the reality of a Spanish bull ring with the abstraction of Anna Sokolow's creative dance. "A bold, beautiful and fluent color piece!"—*N.Y. Times*

"See It Now": Segregation in the Schools
Ed Murrow's brilliant and incisive discussion film fearlessly probes the problem through candid, unrehearsed interviews with Negroes and Whites.

A Cavalcade of American Serials
A rare and hilarious compilation of hair-raising climaxes from some of the most famous "cliff hangers" of the period complete with stunts, yawning chasms and Pearl White in miscellaneous perils.

Cubism
Aims and techniques of this controversial school of art are illustrated in a consistently provocative film survey featuring outstanding Cubist paintings from European museums unknown in this country. In color.

Microcosm (Dr. Roman Vishniak)
The world famous photographer (subject of a recent *New Yorker* profile) captures by unprecedented cine-microscopic techniques fantastic images never before seen by man. "Breathtakingly beautiful!—*N.Y. Times*

[The Spring 1956 Special Events listing included "An Interview with Alfred Hitchcock" (date to be announced), The Childhood of Maxim Gorki (February 29), "Private Visions: Harrington, Anger, Brakhage" (April 4), Greed (April 25), "Horror in the Cinema:" The Cat People (May 16), "A Weekend of Screenings at Eastman House, Rochester" (date to be announced). See 1955–1956 program announcement for relevant descriptions.]

✦ ✦ ✦ ✦ ✦ ✦

Conversation with Carmen D'Avino, 2/16/85

Scott MacDonald: From talking to people I get the sense that one of the things that was lost when Cinema 16 ended was a really sizable audience that filmmakers might have in mind when they were making their films. Cinema 16 was one of the first places to show independent and experimental animation with any kind of regularity. Norman McLaren's films were shown a lot, as were yours.

Carmen D'Avino: Cinema 16 certainly had an important effect on filmmakers and on filmmaking in general. So many things came out of it. In France there was the Annecy Film Festival, probably the most important animation festival in the world. In those years I was always sending them films. Of course, McLaren was their great hero. He had done do much. But in this country there was no such place and no real interest in experimental animation.

Illustration 57. Carmen D'Avino in his studio in New York.

I was doing some experiments in Connecticut—I'd just come back from Europe—and it happened that a friend of mine saw what I was doing and said, "You should send a few of your experiments down to Cinema 16!" That opened up a whole new possibility for me.

MacDonald: When was this?

D'Avino: Sometime between 1951 and 1956—I'm not sure exactly. Until Cinema 16 I didn't have an American audience. I was just making films for myself. I'm a painter and film gave me some new possibilities for painting. Amos and Cinema 16, and Maya Deren, got the Creative Film Foundation going, and at some point I sent a hundred feet of film down to them. When they showed my little film [D'Avino's *Pattern for a Sunday Afternoon* (1956) winner of a Creative Film Foundation grant, was shown in April, 1956], my enthusiasm took off and I started working in earnest on film after film. Being a painter it was very difficult for me to divide my time between painting and filmmaking, but I devoted more and more time to filmmaking as a result of Cinema 16.

For awhile I seemed to get an award almost every year. This brought me into New York. Cinema 16 was such a stimulus for me, and a big boost to other filmmakers too: Robert Breer, StanVanderbeek, Stan Brakhage, Bruce Conner. Getting an award was a great boost to our morale about filmmaking.

And that audience was marvelous too. They'd boo; they'd walk out; they'd scream for joy. It was a volatile and beautiful audience to present anything to. I was thrilled to have work shown at Cinema 16 [D'Avino's *Theme and Variation* (1956) was presented in January, 1957; *Motif* (1956) in November, 1957; *The Big "O"* (1959) in January, 1959; *A Trip* (1961) in January, 1961; and *Stone Sonata* (1962) in December, 1962].

Cinema 16 also distributed film. My films began to be shown to film clubs throughout the country. The rental fees were small, but it was a beginning. Now it's a different world. When Cinema 16 ended, my films went to Grove Press, which was regrettable. In the end they focused on feature films and my films were forgotten.

Today I have three-hundred feet of film here that I haven't even sent to the lab. I figure, hell, there's no sense even getting it processed, since there's not going to be an audience for it. It's discouraging.

✦ ✦ ✦ ✦ ✦ ✦

Letter to Amos Vogel from Stan Brakhage, 3/27/56

1353 West 38th Place
Los Angeles 62, Calif.
March 27, 1956

Dear Amos,

Your letter and post card were awhile arriving; for as you can see I've changed my address again. Thanks for forwarding my mail. Also, I was pleased to receive the brochure with mention of my receiving awards. I would like any other material mentioning said self you may print or run across in some publication. I would like Rushes listing of my films, for instance. I'm a ferocious egotist, you know.

Now, as to the showing of "Desistfilm" and "In Between" on the Coronet program along with my newer films, etc.—I sold Mr. Rohauer a print of "Desistfilm" over two years ago when Kenneth Anger had his "Inauguration of the Pleasure Dome" show at the Coronet. Kenneth had arranged for an after-hour showing of all my films made up to that time. "Desistfilm", of course, went over with a bang and Mr. Rohauer bought it. "In Between" was sold to him at a time when I needed money to get it printed; and I must say he was kind enough to purchase a print of that one sight unseen to help me out. This, of course, was all transacted long before I even wrote to you. My agreement with Mr. Rohauer, which was made up by his attourney, clearly states that he has the right to show the films at any time without rental charge; but he does not have any rights to distribute or rent either of the films.

I don't understand exactly what information you need on "Reflections on Black." It might be of interest to note that this was the film the actors pitched money into to help me produce it. They did this to have the experience of working with movie drama, and also for kicks. Although, I must say that I think the gory details of financial finagling might just as well be left out. I certainly hope that you aren't going to bill the production red tape behind these films like you did with "Desistfilm" last year. At least, I'll be damned if I'm going to send you lists of how many photofloods I used, etc., as I did before. As to the cast, they are all young professionals in the N. Y. acting field. "Professionals" in the sense they definitely intend to be theatrical people and have had experience at it, unlike my usual approach which is to use non-actors reinacting their own psychodramas. They read: Don Redlich, Lee Cole, Helen England, Ken Mecham, Patience Cleveland, Rita Parr. There's one called Bob whose last name I can't remember. I have no way to check as I don't have a print of the film. I guess you'll just have to run thru the titles. Everything else was, of course, done by me. This includes original music and sound. The year was '54, Winter, last Winter, and some damn cold N. Y. winter it was too. You have plenty other dope on "Reflections on Black" in your file.

My new films, "Zone Moment", "Flesh of Morning", "Nightcats", etc. are being distributed by Howard K. Smith Films, 2408 West 7th St., L. A., 57, Calif. You can contact him if you want rental rates or to arrange for program dates.

You have my okay to use the blurb on "In Between" although I won't say I like it as well as what I sent you. It's too mish-mashish. But at least it's better than what you had before.

[hw] Stan

Reprinted by permission of Stan Brakhage.

[I assume his Creative Film Foundation award mentioned In paragraph 1 was for Reflections on Black.*]*

✦ ✦ ✦ ✦ ✦

Program Notes by Stan Brakhage for *Reflections on Black*, Shown in April 1956

REFLECTIONS ON BLACK   U. S.   1954   (12 minutes)
A film by Stan Brakhage.   Sound: Mr. Brakhage.   Distribution: Cinema 16.

"The story line of the film is developed as a sexual odyssey; however, the structure of the film is that of theme and variations. Out of flickering darkness a man is created in greys. His movements are those of a blind man. The world which surrounds him are dots and streaks of light in a night scene.

The first scene realizes desire for meeting between man and woman as a sexual intrigue. The instant they meet, the blind man is handed a note. Being unable to change his part, he must move on.

The next episode is the invention of a drama which the blind man touches off but which he is not a part of. He is not even a spectator. In the creation of any drama, the creator is side-tracked a number of times by possibilities which he could investigate. He usually has to back track on these to continue developing his story line. In this sexual drama between a man and his woman who is trying to cope with the break up of their relation, I have included all the side-tracks leaving the story a continual play of possibility. These side-tracks will be thought of as hallucinations on the part of the woman, whereas they actually form the basis of the drama.

Next we see the blind man manipulated into a scene realizing the desire for mating between man and woman. In this scene he is given eyes to play the mechanical game of sex with. He passes through all the stages of manipulation, but when he gets to the bed, as these scenes can't be for real, an imaginary third party intervenes to create a cliché triangle.

In the final episode the camera becomes the eyes of the blind man for a scene of sexual observation and analysis.

<u>Stan Brakhage</u>

Reprinted by permission of Stan Brakhage.

✦ ✦ ✦ ✦ ✦ ✦

Letter to Kenneth Anger from Amos Vogel, 4/23/56

4/23/56

Dear Kenneth:

first, let me apologize for not having written you sooner. I've been in the midst of a very unfortunate and tragic family situation—my father-in-law was operated on (incurable cancer) and my mother-in-law, a severe cardiac case, had to stay at our house for several weeks since she isn't permitted to live by herself. This situation kept me away from the office for much of the time

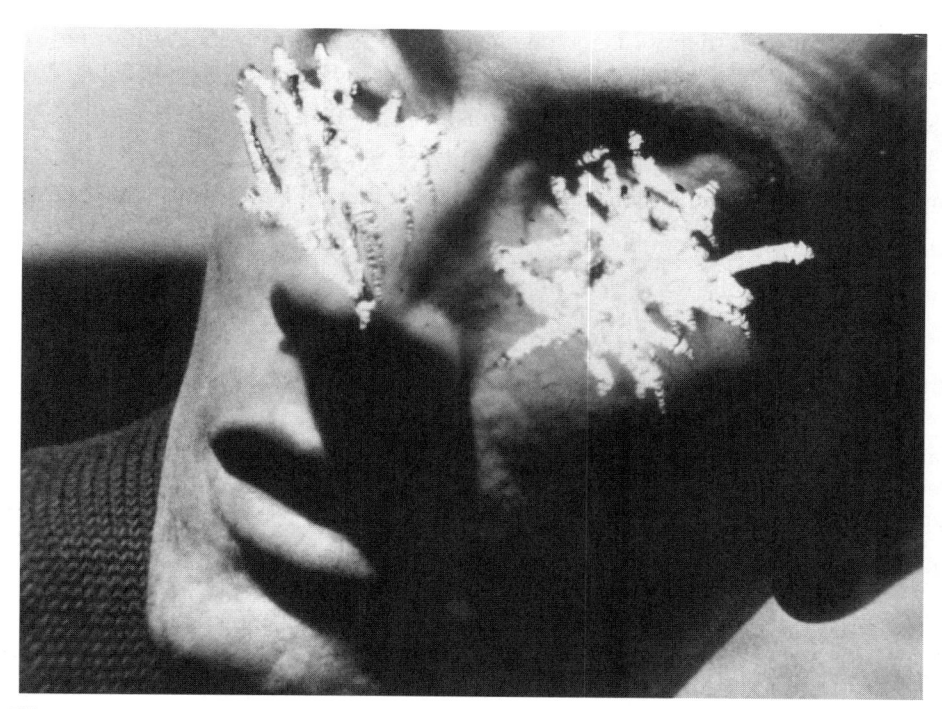

Illustration 58. *Reflections on Black* (1955) by Stan Brakhage. Courtesy Anthology Film Archives.

The screening of PLEASURE DOME was in a way more successful than I had hoped for. I had expected quite a bit of opposition to it which did not, however, materialize. It may be assumed that a spoken introduction to the films and to the types of films they were (by me) helped. In any case, there was complete attention to the film during the showing (it "held" the audience) followed by medium applause at the end. PUCE MOMENT seemed to be enjoyed, although there was only slight applause.

There was a large audience present, with a great many film and press people, as well as the real and pseudo avant-garde. But it is clear that public acceptance of films of this sort remains on a limited scale, and this very definitely includes the press, if anything more so. Apart from the usual advance notices in the Times, etc. listing the titles of the films to be shown, and the enclosed clipping, there has so far been no other review. It is unfortunately true that the field of film criticism remains dominated by the Hollywood "reviewers" and the documentary tradition, both of which are very hostile to experimental films. This is an educational job that will take years to correct.

Speaking for C 16, I have no regrets at continuing to act as the showcase for these films; all I've learned is to be patient.

All this has, of course, delayed the catalog as well. However, nothing is really lost since no bookings take place until the Fall—film societies and schools being "off" during the summer. In any case, I am sincerely sorry about the delay. Our new catalog promises to be a very exciting affair, and will make up for it.

Yes, I received the mounted and other stills, and the Picture Post articles. Brakhage's trip has been cancelled due to illness.

Any news from Europe? Any interesting "offbeat" films? Please let me hear from you!

[Amos Vogel]

✦ ✦ ✦ ✦ ✦ ✦

Letter to Amos Vogel from Fred Zinnemann, 6/6/56

Warner Bros. Pictures, Inc.
West Coast Studios
Burbank, California

June 6, 1956

Dear Mr. Vogel:

I received your very kind letter of May 23rd with some delay. I hope that this reply will reach you in time.

I can assure you that I will be in New York sometime between January and May of 1957, and if it is convenient, I believe a date could be worked out during this interval.

Until October 1st, I will be tied up with my present work on THE OLD MAN AND THE SEA. Afterwards, however, we could get together and discuss a program which might be of interest to your audience. I have always felt that I owe a tremendous debt of gratitude to Robert Flaherty, who has taught me practically everything I know about film-making. It might be of interest if I were to trace the influence which he has had on my work in sections of pictures, such as THE SEARCH, THE MEN and HIGH NOON.

Anyhow, we will be able to discuss this in ample time. Again, thank you for your very nice letter. I will be honored to accept your invitation.

Very sincerely yours,

[hw] Fred Zinnemann

FRED ZINNEMANN

Mr. Amos Vogel
Cinema 16
175 Lexington Avenue
New York 16, N. Y.

Reprinted by permission of Fred Zinnemann.

✦ ✦ ✦ ✦ ✦ ✦

Program Announcement: Fall 1956/Spring 1957

October 1956

Love in the City
Aspects of urban love not usually shown on motion picture screens are the subject of an absorbing feature-length film produced by Cesare Zavattini (*Shoeshine, Bicycle Thief, Umberto D*) and directed by six prominent Italian directors of the neo-realist school. Shown in its complete, uncensored version:

> *Paradise for Three Hours* (Dino Risi)
> Young people seek love in local dance hall in Rome. Candid cameras.
>
> *When Love Fails* (Michelangelo Antonioni)
> Attempted suicides relate and re-enact their stories in filmed interviews.
>
> *Love Cheerfully Arranged* (Federico Fellini)
> A matrimonial agency: from a preposterous premise the director of *La Strada* develops a story of unexpected heartbreak.
>
> *Paid Love* (Carlo Lizzani)
> Interviews with prostitutes, recorded without sensationalism. Will not be shown elsewhere; omitted at request of Italian government from U.S. version.
>
> *The Love of a Mother* (Maselli-Zavattini)
> An unwed mother in conflict with society; a poignant episode.
>
> *Italy Turns Around* (Alberto Lattuada)
> The beautiful girls in their summer dresses: hidden cameras record spectacular reactions of unsuspecting males.

Complete English Titles. An IFE Release

Illustration 59. Program announcement, fall 1956/spring 1957.

November 1956

The Door in the Wall
A startling experiment in a new film technique continually alters the size, shape and position of the screen image to fit the demands of this fantastic H. G. Wells story for atmosphere, tension and shock. In Technicolor.

Mambo Madness
A hectic and informal dance session, full gusto, verve and abandon.

A Conversation with Pablo Casals
NBC's memorable TV interview is a moving human document of a man of music and of principle, living in self-imposed exile. The great cellist plays a Bach bouree and a Catalonian folksong and feelingly discusses his philosophy of life.

Time Out of War
The 1955 Academy Award Winner, beset by exhibition difficulties, at last available for scrutiny. A quiet yet eloquent comment on the insanity of war.

The Elephant Will Never Forget
Pervaded with gentle sadness and humor, this is a loving last ride on London's clattering trolleys, complete with cockney music-hall ballads.

December 1956

Strange Worlds: 5 prize-winning film explorations

From Movement to Music
A paean to the mysterious grace and beauty of the human body, set to Roman Vlad's hypnotic music. Only U. S. showing of original version.

The Rival World
Recipient of Top Award at 1956 Edinburgh Film Festival: Superb scientific study—photographed in Africa—projects fierce and terrifying portrayal of pestilential insects and their alien universe. Electronic music.

Hallucinations
Twelve erotic tableaux envisioned in twilight between waking and sleeping. Unusual Swedish experiment. Musique concrète. Edinburgh 1955 Prizewinner.

The End of the Night
On the edge of the Sahara, a memorable documentary discovers a strange all-Jewish village, hundreds of years into the Middle ages. U. S. Premiere.

Maskerage
Mysterious night journey set to exotic rhythms recaptures the fearful impact of primitive art. Awards at Cannes, Venice and Edinburgh.

January, 1957

Wheat Whistle (Mugi Fuye) (1955)
The awakening to manhood, the anguish and confused sexuality of adolescence are subtly and movingly portrayed in this outstanding Japanese feature film, one of

five selected for the recent Festival of Modern Japanese Films at the University of California.

Filmed with nostalgic lyricism and keen psychological insight, it conveys the uncertainties of adolescent emotions, the discovery of friendship, love and tragedy in the story of two youths and the girl they both love.

Very different from the classic "costume drama" usually associated with Japanese productions, this adaptation of Daisei Muroo's celebrated novel *Adolescence* is a sophisticated contemporary work by the famed director Shiro Toyada, rich in local color seldom seen in Japanese movies.

Only New York showing. Complete English subtitles. A Toho Co. Production.

SPECIAL EVENTS 1956/1957

An Interview with John Huston   (date to be announced)
The creator of *Moby Dick, The Maltese Falcon, The Treasure of Sierra Madre* and *The Asphalt Jungle* in a rare public appearance.

Fred Zinnemann Introduces *The Search*   (date to be announced)
The brilliant director of *High Noon* and *From Here to Eternity* will present and discuss his famed (and otherwise unavailable) triumph of neo-realism.

October 31

Daybreak (*Le Jour Se Lève*)
Unavailable for more than a decade, this first showing of Marcel Carnè's relentless masterpiece is also its last, as the film is to be destroyed for a remake. A grim and sordid tragedy of frustration, murder and retribution, this powerful screen drama finds Jean Gabin at the peak of his art as a doomed murderer caught in a fate beyond his understanding. Screenplay by Jacques Prevert; music by Maurice Jaubert. With Arletty and Jules Berry.

"A poetic intensification of authentic human experience... few films in the history of the cinema have managed to convey human emotion and suffering so powerfully or sensitively!"—Manvell, *Experiment in Film*

November 28

This is Robert
This restricted psychological film classic (not available for public showings) presents an entirely unstaged study of a "difficult" child, photographed with hidden cameras over a period of five years. An authentic document, the film is unprecedented in its comprehensive examination of a child's growth and problems, as shown in continuing psychological and intelligence tests and unusual projective techniques (such as frustration and hostility games). Presented by special arrangement with its producer, Dr. Lawrence J. Stone, Professor of Child Study, Vassar College, who will introduce this film.

January 30

An Evening of Experimental Cinema
Co-sponsored by the Creative Film Foundation and featuring the Winners of the 1956 Creative Film Awards, as selected by a distinguished jury:

Generation (Hilary Harris)
A strident abstraction in kaleidoscope. Experimental sound.

Subject Lesson (Christopher Young)
Imaginative evocation of the inner life of man, told in symbols of strange pictorial power.

Narcissus (Ben Moore and Willard Maas)
Three somber studies of self-love in a dramatic modernization of the Greek myth. Original score by Alan Hovhaness, distinguished modern composer.

Theme and Transition (Carmen D'Avino)
Joyous and exuberant improvisation by a modern painter.

February 13th

The Italian Straw Hat
One of the most brilliant satirical comedies ever made: Rene Clair's delicious mockery of French petit-bourgeois life projects an incredible collection of absurd characters through assorted perils in pantomime and choreographic movement. "A pyramid of situations, a concatenation of exquisitely pointed characters in absurd conjunction... one of the rare masterpieces of the comic cinema."—Museum of Modern Art.

February 27

Rossellini's *The Flowers of St. Francis*
An unexpected work by the maker of *Open City* and *The Miracle*, this neglected achievement of the humanist cinema sketches subtle and haunting episodes in the life of a fervent and innocent seeker of human happiness. Scenario by Rossellini and Fellini (*La Strada*).

"A humble, poverty-stricken story, lighted only from within, conceding nothing to popular taste in entertainment."—Archer Winsten, *N. Y. Post*.

Also: *Bambini in Citta*, sensitive and poetic study of Italian slum children.

March 27

Despair and Affirmation: 2 films

No More Fleeing (Nicht Mehr Fliehen)
Possibly the most important avant-garde work of the decade, Herbert Vesely's feature-length work offers a devastating comment on the European mood in mid-century. A macabre universe of impotence and absurdity, peopled by ambiguous travellers, finally explodes into senseless violence. A paraphrase of mankind's atomic cul-de-sac (clearly influenced by existentialism), this highly

controversial film was shown at all major 1955 international film festivals. Startling 12-tone music and experimental sound.

Pleasure Garden
A comic (yet ideological) fantasy with music celebrating the victory of sensual pleasure and love over prudery and authoritarianism. By James Broughton.

April 17

Screening of 1957 Robert Flaherty Award-Winners
One of Cinema 16's most popular events co-sponsored by City College of New York—features the year's best documentary films, as selected by Bosley Crowther, *N. Y. Times;* Frances Flaherty; Richard Griffith, Museum of Modern Art; Otis Guernsey, *N. Y. Herald Tribune;* Hans Richter, City College; Cecile Starr, *Saturday Review;* Amos Vogel, Cinema 16; Archer Winsten, *N. Y. Post.*

Date to be determined

A Weekend of Screenings at George Eastman House
in Rochester will once again be organized for members interested in sampling the otherwise unavailable treasures of one of the world's great leading film museums at special screenings introduced by the curator Mr. James Card. Program includes some of the screen's greatest films and stars.

✦ ✦ ✦ ✦ ✦ ✦

Letter to Amos Vogel from Kenneth Anger, 2/19/57

21 Rue Gazan
Paris XIV

19.2.57

Dear Amos:

Thank you for forwarding the letter from the Melbourne Film Festival. I will make an effort to supply them with a new pint of INAUGURATION OF THE PLEASURE DOME so that it can take part in this year's competition, although the time limit given—March 15—is very short. However it is to my interest to have my film presented at such a festival, so I will do this even though it entails great personal financial difficulty.

I am writing you in connection with the Art Film Festival to be held this April the 27–28–29 at the Metropolitan. You must be au courant as I believe you are on the Committee.

Sidney Berkowitz is in contact with Mary Meerson of the Cinémathèque as she is advising him on selection as well as supplying some of the films. Mary is advising Sidney to take my film EAUX D'ARTIFICE, which fits into the cadre as outlined by Berkowitz, since it is a study of the greatest example of Baroque 16th Century garden architecture and "water sculptures," the Ville D'Este at Tivoli. Therefore, pending confirmation from Berkowitz, will you please reserve the print for the 27–28–29 April. There is a possibility Mary Meerson herself will be coming to New York for this manifestation.

Certainly you will agree with me as to the importance of my film being shown at this time, it it proves possible. As well as the chance for rentals there is also that of sale of copies, more interesting for me. But I do want to see my films "moving" instead of "sitting," gathering dust as seems the situation over the past year.

I do hope I can count on you to make some EFFORT in regard to my films. That is, push the catalog and advise the sources that have rented FIREWORKS that new works are now available by Kenneth Anger. Is that too much to ask?

I received notice from the Creative Film Foundation of the "honor" of the slight—very slight indeed—"Special Citation" vis-à-vis INAUGURATION OF THE PLEASURE DOME voted at the occasion of the recent awards. I assume this is to be considered Damning by Faint Praise. Do you have any illumination on this? My impression is that my work is much more appreciated abroad, than on my native shores.

Sincere regards,

[hw] Kenneth Anger

Reprinted by permission of Kenneth Anger.

✦ ✦ ✦ ✦ ✦ ✦

Program Announcement: Spring 1957

March 1957

The Prior Claim
Controversial and thought-provoking, this curious attempt to combine science and religion features some of the most extraordinary scientific film footage ever shot. Its thesis: man's ingenuity and inventions are time and again matched by the lowliest animal life, emphasizing that he has "prior claim" to nothing. A Moody Institute of Science Production.

The Back of Beyond
Shown by special arrangement, this is an unusual opportunity to view the otherwise unavailable Grand Prix winner of the 1954 Venice International Film Festival: John Heyer's remarkably photographed poetic documentary, an adventure in solitude in the heart of Australia. Told in impressionist style, it offers a vivid picture of the somber beauty of this vast wilderness and its isolated dwellers, as it takes an outback mail carrier, his incongruous truck and a raft over 300 hundred miles of sand tracks, scattered way stations, remnants of forgotten communities and inland seas. Shot under intensely difficult conditions, this film also was a prizewinner at the 1954 Edinburgh International Film Festival.

April 1957

Cops
The imperturbable Buster Keaton, never more solemn or bewildered, finds himself once more pitted against organized society in a brilliant comedy classic. "A small, serious figure bent on self-justification, caught in a series of absurd accidents. I do not think one will soon forget the exquisite close of this picture."—Gilbert Seldes

Valley of Dreams
Arne Sucksdorff's lyrical visualization of a child's fantasy, beautifully photographed in the Vestland fjord region of Norway by one of the most distinguished directors of our time. "Each of Sucksdorff's films is a new revelation of the wonders that can be accomplished by the movie camera in the hands of a true master film maker."—Arthut Knight, *Saturday Review*

Egypt
The most astonishing panorama of one of the world's greatest civilizations yet produced on film; a definitive exploration of the stupendous and unexpected range of ancient Egyptian art from the pre-historic period to the time of the Ptolomies.

Far from a textbook lecture, this is a consistently fascinating and ultimately awe-inspiring revelation of one of man's greatest achievements as it explores in full color the superb temple reliefs and tomb decorations; the papyrus caricatures and fairy tales; the legendary treasures of Karnak and Luxor; the statuary and the obelisks; the gods and their rituals; and a riotous profusion of artworks, sculptures and jewels in alabaster, gold, faience, jade and ivory.

Produced by Ray Garner under the auspices of the Archaeological Institute of America with the cooperation of the Egyptian government, the Metropolitan Museum of Art and the Museum of Fine Arts in Boston. A New York University Release.

May 1957

Distant Journey
Alfred Radok's unaccountably neglected masterpiece, an unrelenting epic of human suffering and degradation, recounts for all time the horror and the realities of the concentration camp universe. Intentionally intensified, non-realist film techniques (borrowing from both the expressionist and surrealist tradition) add to the dramatic impact of this unique work of film art.

"The most brilliant and the most powerful film on the subject ever made... departs from stark literalness into a strange, horrible, fantastic grotesqueness that truly comprehends those black barbarities... a quality of nightmare and madness builds up, until the final episode of mass destruction cause a hypnosis of insanity."—*N. Y. Times*

[The Spring 1956 Special Events were "An Interview with John Huston" (date to be announced), The Flowers of St. Francis (February 26–27), "Despair and Affirmation: 2 Films" (March 26–27), "Screening of 1957 Flaherty Award-Winners" (April 16–17), "A Weekend of Screening at George Eastman House" (date to be announced): See 1956–1957 program announcement for relevant descriptions.]

Program Notes by Amos Vogel for Roberto Rossellini's *The Flowers of St Francis*, Shown in February 1957

THE FLOWERS OF ST. FRANCIS Italy (1949/50) (80 minutes)

Directed by Roberto Rossellini. Scenario and script by Mr. Rossellini. in collaboration with Federico Fellini. Camera: Otello Martelli. Musical Background: Renzo Rossellini. English titles by Herman G. Weinberg. Released by Joseph Burstyn.

"Set in the 13th Century, this picture illustrates incidents in the life of St. Francis of Assisi, founder of the Franciscan Order. A portrait rather than a biography, it is based on the 'Fioretti de Francesco d'Assisi,' the classic collection of legends and anecdotes through which the story of Francesco has been handed down through seven centuries since his death.

At first glance, nothing could be more incongruous than to see Rossellini, one of the two architects of neo-realism and creator of those violent and tragic contemporary masterpieces, OPEN CITY and PAISAN, make a gentle and reverent film about a band of itinerant 13th Century priests. In actuality, however, the motivation in these apparently so dissimilar films is the same: a portrayal of a given social situation, a rendering of its atmosphere in both psychological and factual terms, a committed humanist approach, a search for a deeper penetration of reality. In the most profound sense of the term, all of Rossellini's films are ideological in intent.

In FLOWERS OF ST. FRANCIS, his aim was to illuminate an age by portraying a faith. Not many films have succeeded in conveying the particular atmosphere of the middle ages as well as this work has. This age is utterly alien to us; it has profoundly different values; it has a tempo of its own. In portraying it realistically, on its own grounds and as if it existed today, Rossellini has demanded more of his audience than many are willing to give. The film's tempo, structure and message is strange to us not because Rossellini has failed, but because he succeeded in his task. He has been true to his material; this is more than many of us can stand. Had he recreated this age merely in terms of its outer trappings without also revealing its mind and values, the critics might have found the film more acceptable.

Since he did not do so, he exposed himself to reviews which—while paying tribute to the film—nevertheless found it slow, disjointed or, in its religious message, too specialized. Fortified with these equivocal endorsements, the film faded quickly at the box office. A repeat viewing, several years later, only serves to re-affirm its stature as one of Rossellini's three most enduring works.

It is a film of faith, and of a humanistic faith at that, rather than 'official', organized religion. Quite possibly, on a moral level it can best be appreciated by believers in primitive religiosity, pantheists or atheists. The head of the Order is not a 'saint' but a humble human being who rejects the world for a life of poverty and piety; his followers not ordained civil servants of an established and privileged order but a tattered collection of humble, questioning, yet heroic people; the screen is filled not with miracles and institutionalized devotions, but the sounds of birds, the calm

Illustration 60. *The Flowers of St. Francis* (1950) by Roberto Rossellini. Courtesy Museum of Modern Art Film Stills Archive.

countryside, the simple acts of innocent and gentle men trying—at times desperately and with unintentionally humorous effect—to do good deeds. 'In scenes of rare and quiet grace they dance and run and sing praises to God,' said one critic. Their actions, serenity, simplicity and innocence may seem naive to people raised in our grasping and competitive age; for saintly fools that they are (unlike ourselves), they attempt to make all human suffering, all human frailties their own. The film exudes goodness, brotherhood and understanding from all its pores, as it were, without ever succumbing to sentimentality. However frail and imperfect the Brothers are, they stand up to their beliefs in fortitude and comradeship against doubts as well as brute force and conquer in the end.

In an astonishing tour-de-force Rossellini has attempted to use documentary and neo-realist techniques to convey the reality of this vanished era to us. Cold, documentary photography, stressing the greys and the blacks, evokes an image of medieval desolation. There are no actors (except for Aldo Fabrizi in the role of the tyrant), all other roles being filled anonymously by monks of the Nocere Inferiore Monastery in Rome; no sets (the film having been shot in the ancient villages of Bracciano and Soana near Rome); there is a feeling of spontaneity, an emphasis on actuality and on conveying not the popular image, but the realities, textures and smells of a particular social epoch. In its 'neo-realist' immediacy and shock impact, it recalls scenes in PAISAN and OPEN CITY and succeeds equally in revealing a living social reality. This is especially evident in the masterful handing of the action and local color in the tyrant's camp. The unthinking violence, ignorance, and brute pleasures of these half-animalistic soldiers and their camp followers is fully portrayed, as is the symbolic quality of Fabrizi's weird and horrifying armor, signifying the nature of the epoch St. Francis strove against.

The film exudes a warmth and glows with passages of lyrical and poetic flavor not found to the same extent in others of Rossellini's films but very reminiscent of Fellini's work. Fellini is credited as collaborator on the scenario of THE FLOWERS OF ST. FRANCIS and it is tantalizing to speculate on his actual contribution to this film. The moving episode with the leper comes to mind; the wordless meeting with this tattered creature, the clanging of the bells, the horror of the outcast as the middle ages must have felt it, the moving embrace. Likewise, in the splendid encounter between the half-wit monk and the heavily armored tyrant; here the worlds of war and of brotherliness clash head-on, in an oppressive and cinematically revolutionary silence, with the entire action proceeding on a subtle psychological level without words, suddenly resulting in a reversal of the antagonists' roles, with the tyrant the vanquished and the impotent priest the victor.

In referring to the film as 'semi-amateurish,' some critics fail to understand Rossellini's conception. This was a simple and artless age, says Rossellini, and this is how it must be portrayed. Far from being amateurish, it is so perfectly professional as to appear artless. Even the episodic framework must be understood in this light. The film is in the nature of a chant, a folk tale handed down through generations in a haphazard and for this very reason, culturally significant, way. It does not record the historic event in its entirety; it recalls. It remembers the highlights, those incidents that have most meaning to the collective consciousness of the race. Thus, the acting, camerawork and editing are intentionally humble, sparing and frugal; and, for once, the structure and concept of a film is perfectly wedded to its content and inner meaning.

It is interesting to view this film in the context of Rossellini's other work. Historically, it is preceded by his war trilogy, OPEN CITY, PAISAN and the less successful GERMANY, YEAR ZERO. This was followed by his ambitious and uneven two-part AMORE (LOVE) dealing, as the Italian critic Mario Gromo put it, with 'the end of earthly love' in its first part, THE HUMAN VOICE (based on Cocteau's play, starring Magnani, and never seen in America) and with 'the beginning of divine love' in its second part, THE MIRACLE. Then comes THE MACHINE THAT KILLS BAD PEOPLE, a grotesque satirical effort. Rossellini is discouraged, stops working. Finally, he emerges with his uneven 'para-Christian' trilogy, three ideological 'message' films: STROMBOLI, an artistic failure; THE FLOWERS OF ST. FRANCIS, a work of stature, curiously neglected; and EUROPE '51, in which a woman acts as the 'minstrel of God', and, ironically, is declared insane for having helped the humble and the poor.

With the great ideological themes of fascism and the resistance gone, and with his subsequent endeavors to create contemporary morality plays at a seeming impasse, Rossellini's creativity may have run its course. It is likely that with succeeding years, the topicality of PAISAN and OPEN CITY will serve to somewhat lessen their stature, while the universality of THE FLOWERS OF ST. FRANCIS will enhance its luminosity. In any event, these three films will stand as the three most mature works of this outstanding film maker.

Amos Vogel

❖ ❖ ❖ ❖ ❖ ❖

Letter to Amos Vogel from Stan Brakhage, 3/25/57

[hw] Where would you suggest I send film articles so they'll do the most good?

Stan Brakhage
2322 S. Marion St.
Denver 10, Colo.
March 25, 1957

Dear Amos,

The above is a permanent address. I have at last found a fair pay film job which I think I can handle while continuing my own work as well. Dr. has warned no more moving around for a while. I am now recovering from a case of "pernicious aenemia". Sounds frightful, but it really wasn't too bad, the worst of it being the raw liver I was forced to consume. I am now also consuming raw film stock, as always, and it looks as though I'll have at least one by summer. I'm planning on remaining here as long as I can continue my own work and still hold this job. Running around the country has been adventursome, but it has (in many ways) prevented me from mastering my own film adventures as completely as I would like to, partly from lack of funds but, I believe, more than anything else, from the rythmn of temporary and often insecure living—"spontaneous" living, if you will. Then, too, I would like to see to it I'll live long enough to bring a little maturity to my film work. In any case, I think you can count on it this time that I'll stay put for awhile at least. There's a feature film taking form in my mind and that'll take some careful planning and a steady income.

One of the reasons I'm writing is to let you know I've put you down as a Personal Reference on the security clearance papers I need for this job. I was advised to put down at least one business associate for a personal reference; and you are just about the only business associate I have who knows me well enough to vouch for me with the F. B. I. Come to think of it, you're just about the only person I've ever done business with, period. All the others were employers; and employers can't be used in this capacity. You should have seen me digging up old letters so that I could put down all the addresses I've had since 1937. I had a mountain of addresses. I'm sure one thing the government will be interested in is just what my experimental film work consists of. Maybe you have an explanation of what an experimental film is. I'm sure I don't.

I'm making arrangements so that I can get back to New York for a short period each year. This is essential for me as an artist. I must always be aware of what's going on, film-wise. And New York is the only place where just about everything goes on, or is about to. You could help me a great deal, during this period of adjusting my mind to the restrictions and the comparative isolation I'm imposing on myself and of adjusting my feelings to a healthy fear of becoming filmically dulled in this visual backwoods, by giving me some assurance that you will keep me posted on new films I should be seeing and, generally, what's happening. Is it possible I could rent certain films from time to time without paying the full devastating price if I give word of honor that they'll only be viewed by myself?

I've already made contact with the Boulder film group and was, justifiably, disturbed that they hadn't even heard of Brakhage even though they were renting from C 16. [*(hw)* When is the new brochure coming out?] Later they informed me that, when they wrote requesting prices, you only listed three films available instead of the five I'd told them you were distributing. What's the deal? Aren't you carrying the Gryphon packages? The D. U. drama department also called me wanting to rent some films and, as you already know, I referred them directly to you. My days of arranging showings are over. I did promise them I would give a short speech for the program. It'll be fun to see "In Between" again. I haven't seen it in over two years.

Till I hear from you,

[hw] Stan

Reprinted by permission of Stan Brakhage.

✦ ✦ ✦ ✦ ✦ ✦

Letter to Kenneth Anger from Amos Vogel, 4/27/57

April 27, 1957

Kenneth Anger
21 Rue Gazan
Paris XIV, France

Dear Kenneth:

At long last! Here is the catalog. I am now engaged in publicizing and mailing it, putting advertisements into film magazines, etc. Of course people will be renting for the fall and winter (they usually rent six months in advance). I am glad that we will now get started on bringing your films before a wider public.

The Film Festival, after screening several hundred films, has decided (for reasons unknown to me) to only show a total of 15 titles. Of course, what with films about famous painters, etc., this small list resulted in an automatic elimination of any other titles.

I have sent a mailing to all previous users of FIREWORKS regarding your new films and expect that it will be of some benefit.

I am not sure why you consider the "Special Citation" Damning With Faint Praise. While it is true that the jury gave awards to other films, it is equally true that many others did not receive any recognition whatsoever. Needless to say, I had only one vote on the jury. However, while I would have liked the film to win a higher award, I must say that I still felt quite pleased with the Special Citation it received.

Very sincerely yours,

Amos Vogel
Executive Secretary

AV:pg
Encl.

✦ ✦ ✦ ✦ ✦ ✦

Letter to Amos Vogel from Stan Brakhage, 5/13/57

May 13, 1957

Dear Amos,

The brochure is impressive. I haven't received a copy from C 16 yet, but Willard sent me his. You undoubtably have the most impressive display of films in the entire country, possibly in the world. I was delighted that you haven't worried about including film classics, but have concentrated upon new films. This is, of course, where distribution (even mention) is terribly needed; and you are the only one who is in any way attempting to solve the problem. I thought the write-ups exhibited remarkable taste, considering what you have to appeal to in copy in order to get them distributed at all. I, for one, was completely satisfied with the blurbs on my own films. And, believe me, after my recent experiences with the sex and sensational school of advertising in L. A. (you know whom) I appreciate your care in this matter.

I have only one boner to pick, and I guess I'll pick it so that you'll know my demanding nature hasn't gone completely to pot here in the back country. I am not very happy to discover that you feel the films you are distributing are only "Offered as significant efforts to broaden the scope of the film medium, rather than as accomplished works of art." I feel that you are underestimating the majority of the films you offer. Even within my own extremely strict criteria, I find that there are undoubtably no more accomplished works of art in the history of cinema than: Anger's "Eaux d'artifice", Maas "Geography of the Body", "Hurry, Hurry" by Marie, Peterson's "Mr. Frenhofer and the Minotaur", or Broughton's "Mothers day", or (for that matter) "Desistfilm", just to name my favorites of these, pardon the expression, "artists".

I am very curious about the films of Peter Weiss. I have never seen any of his work. I am also intrigued by "Escape", the Danish film by Mertz & Roos. Could you pick out one of the Weiss films (one you think would be the best for me to see) "Escape", and the best of the two films Soren Melson did, and send them to me for viewing? It's about time I get some idea of what's happening in European experimental film. Charge me the least you can, but the most you have to, and send them as soon as possible. I will be unendingly grateful, will handle them with gloves on (clean gate and all that), look at them privately, and return them immediately.

Even though I'm making a hell of a lot of money (for me), which is to say I'm making money, I'm up to my neck in debts and expenses. I bought a car, am taking pills and eating steaks to keep my blood from crapping out again, etc. I could use a $50.00 advance right now to get the print of my new color film. It is the one of the two lovers in the forest; and it has become so unbelievably beautiful in re-editing and re-editing that I can scarcely believe I've ever made a film before. You will, of course, have a copy for viewing as soon as the sound track is finished. I have sunk some money already into what promises to be my first feature length film. I don't want to tell you, or anyone, more about it until I know what it's going to be myself. The paradox of that statement is that once I've made the film I won't be able to talk about it because everything I have to say will have been said visually and done with.

The new German film sounds terribly exciting. When will there be a 16mm print? The new Boulder Cinema Club president is Walt Newcomb (boy in negative on "Way to Shad Gard") and I am pushing for a solid line up of C 16 films. This is personal necessity as much as philanthropy. If I have to sit through another Museum of Modern Art antique star-system film exhibition program at an experimental film club meeting, I'll simply die of boredom.

Can't think of anything else... You asked about my health—I'm feeling well enough to be very much alive and creating again. The blood is still a little low count, but then I'm charmed. If I haven't been downed yet, I don't imagine I ever will be.

Until I hear from you...

[hw] Stan

Reprinted by permission of Stan Brakhage.

[The "brochure" Brakhage mentions is a 21-page catalogue of films for rent, published by Cinema 16 in Spring 1956. It was the third of four Cinema 16 rental brochures and catalogues. The statement in the rental catalogue that Brakhage has a problem with was included in the first three catalogues; in the fourth (published in 1963), Vogel modified the statement to read: "Produced by independent film artists, these are explorations in the cinema. Offered as significant efforts to broaden the scope of the film medium and further develop its aesthetic vocabulary and potential, these films express the psychological and emotional tensions of modern life; delve into the subconscious; explore the world of color and abstract images; experiment with cinematic devices and synthetic sound" (p. 3). The film of the "two lovers in the forest," mentioned in paragraph 4, is Loving, *with filmmaker Carolee Schneemann and composer James Tenney. The film that promises to be Brakhage's "first feature" is, I assume,* Anticipation of the Night *(1958), which at forty minutes, was the longest film (by fifteen minutes) he had made until then.]*

✦ ✦ ✦ ✦ ✦ ✦

Letter to Amos Vogel from Stan Brakhage, 7/28/57

July 28, 1957

Dear Amos,

You will probably have received the three color films by now. I feel that this is a good beginning in what is essentially a new direction in film for me. The direction has been forming for the past three years, "The Wonder Ring" having been made toward the summer months of my first stay in N. Y. C., "Nightcats" have been photographed in L. A. at the same time "Flesh of Morning" was created, and "Loving" just being finished. All three have a perfection of color, form, movement, rhythm, etc. not only unparalleled in my own work but in film in general. "Nightcats", for instance, underwent over 20 complete editings to make it perfect, and "Loving" is the product of some 30 editings (that is, the films were spliced together and broken apart almost entirely that number of times). The response to "The Wonder Ring" and "Nightcats" was enthusiastic at Boulder Film Club. The S. F. Museum wants to run both this coming fall. "Loving" has been shown no where as yet.

I want all three films shown together to give each one a context they couldn't have otherwise. This is especially essential due to the shortness of the films individually. I hope you will agree with me. I must also ask for silence, as three years of intensive search in sound has produced no musical or experimental sound accompaniment for these films which is anything but destructive. The S. F. Museum bickered with me on this point by mail; but they finally agreed with my view. I think what brought them around was an attempt to find a musical accompaniment themselves and their subsequent failure.

I can send you statements on both "The Wonder Ring" and "Nightcats" by Parker Tyler. I think he has been more illuminating as to the films than I could be at this time. Parker hasn't, as yet, seen "Loving". But, those statements will have to follow later as I will retype them so that I don't lose his copy; and I want to get this letter off tonight.

I have shot 2000 ft. of color film toward the feature length night film I am at work on. It is turning out beautifully, beyond my wildest expectations. I am still, as always, in a bind to pay film expenses to get it finished. I could still use the fifty dollar advance which I asked you for so many months ago and which you never replied to either by check or letter. I have been hard-put to understand this as one of the last statements you made to me in New York was that if I needed an advance you would be happy to send it. I am not desperate for the money, however silence on a request for money is usually embarrassing to both parties concerned.

I have some addition news which will probably surprise you. I am engaged to be married and am returning to New York as soon as I can arrange for suitable employment there where my fiancee and I intend to establish our living. If you have any suggestions as to film companies I might apply to, considering the commercial aspects of my movie employment (usually "editor" as here in Denver where I am now editor in charge of the government contract with Martin Co, and occasionally "photographer", and when occasion demands, just about any occupation having to do with the making of motion pictures) please send me such advice. I am already at work on N.B.C. and am planning to advertise my abilities in the New York Times. My plan is to take two weeks in early fall for a visit to N.Y. for whatever interviews I can arrange, and then to move permanently as soon thereafter as possible.

[hw] Stan

Reprinted by permission of Stan Brakhage.

✦ ✦ ✦ ✦ ✦ ✦

Conversation with Stan Brakhage, 11/30/96

Scott MacDonald: I understand that there was a break between you and Amos Vogel because he would not show *Anticipation of the Night* (1958) at Cinema 16. Is that true? What was your experience with Cinema 16?

Stan Brakhage: Well, that's true about Amos and *Anticipation.* But it wasn't as simple as that. I mean all along, Amos was the one hope. He had an audience of five thousand people to whom he would show works that my friends and I regarded as art. That was wonderful, but he showed the films we admired in a mix with scandal movies and documentaries of various shocking subjects. In a way, Cinema 16 programs often didn't look all that different to me from the newsreels I had attended as a child during the Second World War.

Amos's main concern and consideration was to show things that you couldn't see elsewhere, and that was what attracted his audiences. They felt very special; they were seeing things that weren't allowed into the local neighborhood theaters and later that you couldn't see on television: censored things, sexual subject matter, dog heads kept alive on tables in Russian laboratories—a mix into which was stirred some of the great American independent films.

Of course, the independent filmmakers felt Amos wasn't showing enough of *their* work and other work that they felt related to, and they often felt like they were being used in a freak show environment. In fact, the book Amos finally wrote *[Film As a Subversive Art]* does show the freak show sensibility he had about film.

When the 1958 Brussels World's Fair showings of American independent film occurred, I went to Amos to get money to buy a ticket so I could go to the events. So at that point I was still friendly with Amos and Marcia, and *am* still friendly with them. I think of them *very* affectionately. And that permits me to be not too angry that Amos couldn't go as far as *Anticipation of the Night*. At that point, he just couldn't *see* it. His view was that the film would destroy my reputation. I didn't see that I was having any kind of reputation anyway, but in any case, *Anticipation* was the end for Amos. But, again in fairness to Amos, it was also the end for Parker Tyler and for many other people. They said, "Okay, that's it: Brakhage has gone completely crazy and this is just degenerate work"—not "degenerate" because of subject matter, but formally.

MacDonald: I can certainly see how Amos, audience-aware as he was, would have trouble with the film. He didn't program to make his audiences happy, but he was certainly conscious of their boredom, and *Anticipation* would have seemed, especially at that time, a long, boring film, *so* slow as to be impossible to show.

Brakhage: Oh, that's all true. It created riots in Europe and wherever it was shown. People came apart and threatened the projectionist.

But the break with Amos wasn't about his refusal to show or distribute *Anticipation*. There were other films that Amos refused to show or distribute, like Marie Menken's new work; and I told Amos, "Until you distribute Marie Menken's new work and *Anticipation of the Night*, I won't give you *any* of my new work." There were other films he wanted. So that was the break that finally led to Jane and I advertising that we would distribute films, and that we had an agreement with Bruce Conner and other people we knew about, to distribute from our home in the mountains in Colorado.

At that point, I arrived in New York to begin showing some of my work that Amos *was* distributing and some work by other people, and at that precise moment, Jonas and Adolfas were deciding to create Film-makers' Cooperative. So we more or less came to an agreement to pool our resources and that's how the New York Coop began. Jonas and Adolfas were in a better position to do distribution than Jane and I were: they were in New York and they had backing of some kind or other—

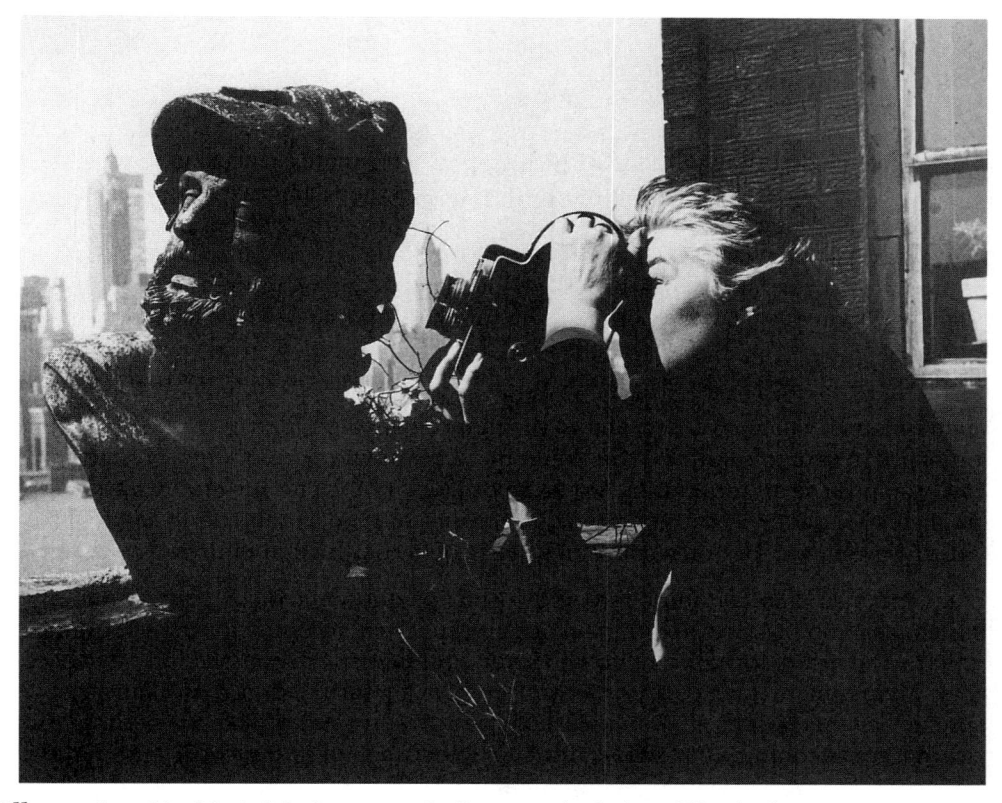

Illustration 61. Marie Menken at work. Courtesy Anthology Film Archives.

enough support for the moment, and eventually they also came to have the support of Jerome Hill. Or perhaps Jerome was already involved. So I just became part of *their* efforts.

Then gradually—and I think to Amos's bitterness—they pushed him out and occupied the Cinema 16 offices [the Cinema 16 offices were at 175 Lexington Avenue; this remained the address of Film-makers' Cooperative until 2000].

MacDonald: There were—and are—some bad feelings about that.

Brakhage: I'm sorry that it created that bitterness for Amos and Marcia, because they did a great thing: they opened the gate without which there probably would have been no American independent film movement. But Amos wasn't dedicated to the possible art of film as *we* understood it. Jonas at times wasn't either; in those days, he could be very unsteady in that respect, but by and large, Jonas has been more aesthetically inclined than Amos. Aesthetics just wasn't what Amos cared most deeply about. So as our determination became more to see what an art of film might be, Jonas became the obvious person to take over.

✦ ✦ ✦ ✦ ✦ ✦

Program Announcement: Fall 1957/Spring 1958

October 1957

A Moment in Love
A startling and lovely dream pastoral, subtly colored, unites two lovers in their moment of passion. A dance drama by Shirley Clarke. Special Citation, Creative Film Foundation; Prizewinner, Edinburgh International Film Festival 1957.

"A rare, striking fusion of movie imagery and choreography (Anna Sokolow's), beautifully designed and realized!"—*The New York Times*

The Children Are Watching Us
At last available, Vittorio de Sica's first masterpiece, preceding *Shoeshine* and *Bicycle Thief:* A delicate and intensely moving exploration of marital discord, adultery and suicide as seen through the eyes of a tortured child who becomes both the observer and protagonist of the domestic tragedy. Mingling bitterness and pity, pathos and satire, this compelling achievement clearly reveals de Sica's genius at transforming simplest emotions into deeply disturbing human experiences of universal validity. Complete English subtitles. A Brandon Films Release.

"Deals for the first time with the themes which bring out De Sica's finest talents—the fears, passions and solitude of children. In the same rank as his later masterpieces!" The British Film Institute

November 1957

Twentieth Century
John Barrymore and Carole Lombard, in one of their best and most hilarious performances, scream their way through a great screwball comedy classic of the thirties:

Illustration 62. Program announcement, fall 1957/spring 1958.

Charles MacArthur and Ben Hecht's wildly improbable travesty of show business, a sophisticated and merciless laugh riot, notable for its breathless pace and racy dialog.

Based on the celebrated stage hit, Howard Hawk's tour-de-force propels Barrymore as the frenzied impresario and Lombard as the lingerie-model-turned-star through a spectacular series of delirious complications. With Walter Connolly, Roscoe Karns, Dale Fuller.

"Give Barrymore a chance to go off his nut, and it's a pleasure. In this picture he not only goes off his nut but stays off for 91 solid minutes... the beautifully dialoged scrapping scenes between him and Lombard pave the road for some of the craziest trouping ever!"—*Variety*

Motif
This joyous new improvisation by last year's Creative Film Award recipient Carmen D'Avino is a pure visual delight.

December, 1957

Summer Love: 3 film explorations

Interplay
Peter Weiss' experimental pantomine on an erotic theme transmutes two lovers into startling compositions. (Edinburgh 1955).

A Girl in the Mist
This warm and utterly delightful summer idyl offers an unexpected and charming view of adolescence and young love in modern Japan. Romantic yet sophisticated, this Toho release is based on Yojiro Ishizaka's noted short story, tastefully directed by Hideo Suzuki. "An artistic triumph!" *Variety.*

Menschen Am Sonntag (People on Sunday)
First New York showing of legendary feature film produced by three now world-famous Hollywood directors at the start of their career: Robert Siodmak (*The Killers*), Billie Wilder (*Lost Weekend*), Fred Zinnemann (*From Here to Eternity*): A bitter-sweet metropolitan love story, casual and unsentimental, as four young people spend Sunday bathing, picnicking, making love at the shores of Berlin's Wannsee. Told with deceptive artlessness and sensual poetry. A Brandon Films Release.

January 1958

Together
Special Award Winner at the Cannes International Film Festival: a haunting and poetic study of two deaf-mutes imprisoned by silence and solitude in London's drab East End. Produced by Lorenza Mazzetti and Denis Horne, it explores with lingering simplicity their desolate existence, their sad diversions, their tender relations to each other. A neo-realist film poem of rare intensity, infused with deep emotion and melancholy. (Contemporary Films)

"A poet's film...its mood is strange and delicate; its conception, daring; its method secret, intuitive, visionary..." *Sight and Sound*

Momma Don't Allow
Candid camera excursion to the Wood Green Jazz Club in a North London pub, where shop girls, Teddy Boys and local youth meet and dance; a fresh and informal piece of urban folklore, recorded with gusto and abandon.

Glimmering (Lueur)
Extraordinary example of the European independent cinema projects an intensely dramatic account of a prisoner's harrowing escape through endless corridors to a shattering climax: a brilliant cinematic portrayal of obsessional and hallucinatory states, especially noteworthy for its advanced sound experiments. A film by Pierre Thevenard.

March 1958

Munna
One of the revelations of the 1955 Edinburgh International Film Festival, this fresh and uninhibited work completely rejects the tiresome conventions of the Indian cinema in favor of a neo-realist approach as it recounts with humor and tenderness the curious adventures of an abandoned child amidst thieves, clerks, magicians, criminals and the crowds of an Indian metropolis. Filled with unexpected plot twists, it reveals a rich cross-section of extravagantly conceived characters, nicely balancing between the farcical and the tragic. Photographed in the streets of Bombay.

"Most delightful surprise of the Edinburgh Festival... shines with gayety and imagination... reminiscent of best Italian Films!"—*Manchester Guardian*

The Praying Mantis
Alien and horrifying universe is revealed in an outstanding study of love and cruel death amidst the mysteries of nature. (Rembrandt Films)

SPECIAL EVENTS 1957/1958

November 6

The Echo (Yama No Oto)
Absorbing story of marital immaturity and frustration in post-war Japan. Peculiarly Japanese, it startles with its curious psychological subtleties, oblique editing and guilt-less recognition of unconventional sex mores. Selected for Festival of Modern Japanese Films at University of California. Only New York showing; complete English titles. Very different from the classic "costume drama" usually associated with Japanese productions, this is a sophisticated contemporary work by the famed director Mikio Naruse.

January 8

Gold Diggers of 1933
Dire consequences of tangling with show girls are temptingly catalogued in nostalgic glance at one of the most famous musicals of the thirties, long unavailable; complete with gorgeous girls, hackneyed plot and Busby Berkeley's monster production numbers in their semi-surrealist splendor. Joan Blondell, Dick Powell, Ruby Keeler, Ginger Rogers, Guy Kibbee, Aline MacMahon.

Illustration 63. *Gold Diggers of 1933* (1933) by Busby Berkeley. Courtesy Museum of Modern Art Film Stills Archive.

January 29

An Evening of Poetic & Surrealist Films

Texture of Decay
Award-winning study in fear and self-destruction (Vickrey)

House
A riot of colors, objects and designs (Eames)

The Petrified Dog
Surrealism blended with macabre slapstick (Peterson)

Autumn Fire
"the gentle and melancholy color of resigned love." (Weinberg)

Motion Painting
Grand Prix International Experimental Film Festival (Fischinger)

February 12

The Unknown Soldier
Possibly the strongest anti-war film ever made, this prize-winning Finnish masterpiece of the humanist cinema—the artistic sensation of Europe—offers a ferocious view of the horrors of modern war. Free of heroes, patriotism and sentimentality, it brings a group of foot soldiers to their breaking point in a merciless inferno of blood and death. (Tudor Films.) "A naked and wild picture, intense, rude, tumultuous, just as war itself!"—*Les Lettres Francaises*

February 26

Witchcraft Through The Ages
This exotic curio, cited in all histories of the cinema, is one of the screen's most legendary works: Banned and unavailable until now, it ruthlessly examines witchcraft, magic and diabolism under the psychologist's microscope. A record of the cruelty and dogmatism of the middle ages, it recreates the tortures of the witch courts, the orgies of the devil's mass, the hallucinations and temptations of the age.

April 2

The Brain: Restricted medical and psychiatric films

Hypnosis in Childbirth
Startling record of actual delivery without anesthetics

Brain and Behavior
What science knows about the human brain

Depressive States and Paranoid Conditions
A psychiatric study

Experiments in Perception
The season's most astonishing film

Ape and Child Reared Together
Fascinating tests and experiments

April 23

Experimental Cinema in Russia

By The Law
Three people, related by murder, trapped in an Arctic wilderness; Lev Kuleshov's extraordinary experiment, a psychological tour-de-force. Based on Jack London's "The Unexpected."

Arsenal
Dovzhenko's masterpiece of lyric symbolism, completely original in its substitution of poetic continuity and visual metaphors for the usual structure and story. Difficult and uniquely personal, this rarely seen landmark of screen experimentation is offered as tribute to the recently deceased director.

May 30 and 31

Weekend of Screenings at Eastman House
in Rochester will once again be organized for members interested in sampling the otherwise unavailable treasures of one of the word's leading film museums.

Date to be announced

Fritz Lang Introduces *M*
A city's terrifying hunt for a psychopathic child murderer, with police and underworld in ironic partnership. A rare showing of the original version of this immortal classic, notable for its relentless realism and Lorre's unsurpassed characterization of the maniac as a tortured victim of his own desires.

Date to be announced

Screening of 1958 Flaherty Award-Winners
One of Cinema 16's most popular events—co-sponsored by City College of New York—features the year's best documentary films as selected by Bosley Crowther, *N. Y. Times*, Frances Flaherty; Richard Griffith, Museum of Modern Art; Otis Guernsey, *N. Y. Herald Tribune*; Arthur Knight, *Saturday Review*; Hans Richter, City College; Cecile Starr, *Saturday Review*; Amos Vogel, Cinema 16; Archer Winsten, *N. Y. Post*.

Date to be announced

A Trip to Canada to see Chaplin's *A King in New York*
will be arranged for members wishing to see Chaplin's newest film which will not be shown in the U.S.

✦ ✦ ✦ ✦ ✦ ✦

Letter to Stan Brakhage from Amos Vogel, 10/11/57

October 11, 1957

Dear Stan,

I am terribly sorry that we took so long in having the prints returned to you. They reached here during the vacation period and stayed on to the start of our season, a very hectic and difficult period in the office. I can assure you that in the future this will not occur again. They were mailed back to you immediately upon receipt of your letter by Air Express.

I was very impressed and pleased with them and it was, again, only pressure of work connected with my new season (I'm about 200 letters behind!) that kept me from replying sooner.

They are terribly intense, and intensely personal, and intensely subjective in feeling, form and treatment. The color is outstanding and the controlled and disciplined freedom with which you handle the camera and editing is admirable. Furthermore, in each, you explore a new facet of creation, as you do in all your films—in short, you continue as a true experimenter. You are also not only one of the few film makers who keep on making films, but who also advance and open new frontiers with each new work.

THE WONDER RING is the only good film about the El I've seen. a true poetic work. NIGHT CATS is a terrifying revelation of an alien universe. LOVING intensely passionate and carefully removed from the customary vapidities surrounding the sex act in the movies.

Yes, I want to distribute them (and DAYBREAK as well, which we looked at earlier). YES, I agree that it might be best to distribute these 3 films on one reel (though this would not necessarily hold true of the showing at C 16). No, I dont really agree as to the absence of music; I can see your point very well, but long, extensive, painful experience with audiences convinces me that we are no longer attuned to the "silent" film and for this, the showing of a silent film brings about audience reactions NOT CONSONANT with their actual feelings about the work. But the final decision regarding this is, of course, up to you.

The 3 films are to run at silent speed—right? Sound speed seems much too fast.

I am hoping that you will write in detail about the feature and the other films now in the works. I am extremely anxious to see them and promise to return prints quickly.

I wrote to Rohauer regarding FLESH OF MORNING, as per your suggestion. (I want to co-distribute or at least own a print). He wrote back, saying that he had to check with you. Will you please "expedite" this.

After many delays, Willard's Gryphon promotion piece will finally be mailed out and I am hoping for good results, although it will still take some time for them to come in.

Results of the new catalog have been very good and I will send you a statement in the near future.

Can you send me the San Francisco Museum program? They have been negligent about sending me their material. Do you know who is in charge now?

I've left the most "disgusting" detail for last. A few days ago, I found, upon going through some program note material "to be filed", your letter of July 28. I had never seen this letter since I was on my vacation and it was unfortunately misfiled. Here, then, a belated response… I am enclosing $59 as requested, advance..and I am so pleased to hear about your impending marriage and your move back to NY..we need you here..and there is much we should discuss.

Please let me hear from you.

Best,

[Amos Vogel]

✦ ✦ ✦ ✦ ✦ ✦

Letter to Amos Vogel from Stan Brakhage, 10/21/57

October 21, 1957

Dear Amos,

In truth, I had begun to wonder what the hell … But then, I should have known. I've been through this with you before. There is a season, friend Amos, when you had as leave be a bear in hibernation as a correspondent. Indeed, it is as difficult during this period to gain audience from you personally as to receive communication by mail. It is, of course, that time when you are audience gaining. I remember my vexation three years ago, when I first arrived in New York, at the impossibility of either settling or, indeed, of unsettling my business with you during the fall. In order to save my, admittedly, unreasonable temper and to facilitate our relationship in the future I have determined not to attempt a correspondence with you between mid-summer and mid-winter ever again, unless it becomes absolutely necessary. However, I can't account for my tempestuous reactions should this lack of contact frustrate me during the remaining two-and-a-half seasons.

As it is, your check arrived at a more fortuitous time than it was intended for. I am bedded down, as I type this, having just been released from the hospital. I suffered the pneumonic results of the asian flu. Your letter was rather dramatically passed through the oxygen tent to me; and, indeed, I did breath easier receiving it. Conditions have altogether changed since last summer. Prospective marriage is no longer part of the dramatic structure of my life. The curtain has been rung down on that act, and I am single as ever. I am also singularly resolved not to return to New York at the present time. I have a stability here which has permitted such advancement in my work that I am determined not to wreck change in my life until I can establish a comparable livlihood elsewhere. I have shot 4000 feet of film on the prospective feature length night piece and the editing is well underway. I expect the film to be completed by the end of the year. I have also started a film workshop, the only one of its kind in the country I am sure. The activities of the workshop are centered around the The ECG group in Boulder, Colo. I will include the announcement

Illustration 64. Stan Brakhage at his home in the mountains above Boulder, Colorado. Courtesy Anthology Film Archives.

which they published at the last film showing, tho' some of the information is incorrect and the announcement itself altogether inadequate. This is because I was in the hospital at the time and unable to handle the preliminaries myself. I was also, of course, disturbed at the "blurbs" on my three films which were shown. I was unable to write them myself, and what I am quoted for was taken inappropriately from some correspondance I had with the president of the film show. However, in spite of my confinement, the workshop group had their first meeting last Saturday and, per my instruction, a young film animation technician, Stan Phillips (photographer of "Interim) lectured them on the art of animation and handed them blank and black leader to paint or scratch upon, as they desired. It's a good way to start, and the results should be interesting if not enlightening. Health permitting, I will take over this coming Saturday. Somehow the president confused the feature film I am at work upon with the workshop activities; however, I can straighten all that out on Saturday and begin the workshop activities in earnest. A laboratory in Denver, Western Cine, has agreed to give the workshop all the film they need at cost (from war-surplus stock) and I intend to let the group begin filming immediately. The exclusive emphasis of the workshop will be entirely directed toward the "experimental film" as defined by the Brussels, Belgium blurb printed on the enclosed film program. The Brussels definition, like all dealing with "experimental film" is inadequate but is still the best I have seen thus far. If possible, I would like your permission for the president of the ECG to hold all Cinema 16 rentals for the Thursday night program until Saturday morning when I can take these films through an editor with the workshop group and study them. I will take responsibility for the care given these films from Thursday night through Saturday noon and will promise that they shall not be projected or in any way shown to other groups than those members of the ECG and subsidiary workshop. I will also see to it that they are mailed promptly Saturday noon. The group cannot afford additional rental fees. Please answer immediately, as the forthcoming program includes Willard's films which I should particularly like to make available to the workshop for Saturday study, due to my familiarity with the work.

I have already signed an agreement with Rohauer to let him distribute DAYBREAK AND WHITE EYE along with FLESH OF MORNING. My principal reason for so-doing was that he agreed to distribute the two films together, which you had already refused to do when I showed them to you last winter in New York. I feel that DAYBREAK and WHITE EYE belong together, being a subjective and objective statement of the very similar emotional content which produced them. It is my feeling that WHITE EYE is by far the more important of the two, if they be taken separately; however, WHITE EYE (being more difficult to perceive, is also the film which I would have the most difficulties getting distributed at all unless it accompanied the more popular DAYBREAK.

I am glad that you agree that the three color pieces should be distributed together, and I will sign a contract to C 16 for the distribution. However, to protect myself in this respect, I would like to sign them under the title of "Three Films—The Wonder Ring, Nightcats, and Loving", stipulating (for your protection) that they may be distributed separately if so requested by the rentee. That also leaves you free to exhibit them a C16 in whatever individual manner you please. They were shot and edited to be projected at sound speed. However, I have no objection to showing them at silent speed should you, or anyone else, care to see them at a less swift pace. Similarly, I cannot absolutely force renters from playing music with them should they choose. But, it is enough to indicate my feelings in respect to my desire that they should be projected silently to say that I personally refused to let the San Francisco Museum book them from me when they insisted upon my advising them as to what music could be played with them. I realize that, once I open them through you for distribution, I can no longer exercise my demands in respect to the manner in which they will be shown. Therefore, I make no stipulations. I also want to include a statement in the paragraph to protect me from the delay in advertising which Desistfilm, Reflections on Black, and In Between suffered. I would like to stipulate that I be allowed to put out an announcement on these films, at my own expense, and to receive guarantee that this announcement will have the same benefits from your offices and mailing lists which Willard's Gryphon announcement had. I am thinking of a zinc plate sheet (possibly in two colors) with stills.

Now, I will attempt such a contract, sign it, and include it with this letter. However, if you don't find my attempt adequate, please feel free to re-write it an mail me yours.

[hw] Stan

P.S.

Can you mail me a copy of the current Film Culture which is, as I understand it, on the experimental film? I sent a lot of material to their West Coast representative, Robert Pike, who was writing me up as a West Coast Experimental Film maker. Can't get FC here.

I see, in going over my letter and yours, that there are a couple of points still to be taken care of. All of my correspondence with S. F. Museum was through my good friend, Larry Jordan in S. F. The man in charge of the Museum film shows is Baxter, I believe; but I cannot remember his first name. Jordan was in daily contact with him at the time and considered him somewhat of an ass. I cannot say that my correspondance with him gave me much different an opinion. I think you should know that Jordan is also an experimental film maker, that no one is distributing his films at present, that he has not attempted distribution, and that some overtures on your part might be worth while. I considered Larry's early work excessively immitative of my own. However, I haven't seen the long film of his which he has reportedly just finished. Jordan is also starting an experimental film theatre in S. F. and, while to start he will be showing feature classics, you should have his address for any C 16 mailings. It is : Larry C. Jordan, 1032 1/2 Kearny Street, San Francisco, Calif. I have urged Jordan, as I do all young film makers, to contact you. I suspect that he feels too insecure about his work and that that accounts for his not doing so. He can also give you more info and correct Baxter name on S. F. Museum.

I am at present at work on a series of articles on Experimental Film and would like any historical data you can send me on activities of C 16 as I intend to plug you very well both as an individual and as an organization. Send me any material on yourself you care to divulge. I am going to try Sight and Sound with the articles when finished which won't be before the first of the coming year.

Reprinted by permission of Stan Brakhage.

[The ECG group to which Brakhage refers in this letter, as well as in his letter to Vogel of 11/1/57, is the Experimental Cinema Group founded in 1957 by Bruce Conner and Gladney Oakley. The ECG exhibited film and sponsored a film production workshop which Brakhage taught for a time. Brakhage, who met Jane Brakhage at one of the ECG events, claims that the ECG—now run by Don Yannacito under the moniker, "First Person Cinema"—is the longest running, continuous exhibitor of alternative cinema in the United States.]

✦ ✦ ✦ ✦ ✦ ✦

Letter to Amos Vogel from Kenneth Anger, 10/29/57

October 29, 57

c/o Hotel Stella
133 Avenue Victor Hugo
Paris 16 France

Dear Amos,

I have just received this afternoon a letter from an experimental film-maker friend of mine in Hollywood, John Schmitz and as the contents will be of interest to you, I quote in extenso:

> "Dear Ken,
>
> Friday evening Mr. Raymond Rohauer called by phone to say that FIREWORKS and the film THE VOICES were taken by the vice squad the last evening of the weeks showing. This only affects us in Los Angeles so far; however Ray believes he must fight it in court because if he does lose they will attack other films. Later then it will mean that we can not show in New York. One other thing is that it will make experimental films difficult to show here within Film Societies. The newest one being the Creative Film Society, also on La Cienega like the Coronet. As I understand this confiscation means that we must prove that the films have merit and were not made purely to excite. This is what I am giving Ray now; letters from museums, B. F. I. etc. We have a lawyer and believe we shall win......"

That is the gist of the situation, and you will see why I am concerned and why you should be concerned also. This is the first time, to my knowledge, that there has been police interferance with a showing of experimental films in the U. S.

It is a very unhealthy, and alarming, precedent, and I strongly feel that all of us who are concerned with the experimental film in America must sit up and take notice.

I believe you will understand when I say that personally, between us, I have mixed feelings concerning the actual copy of FIREWORKS concerned and the fact that it was in the hands of Rohauer. You will remember at the time of our exchange of letters over my lease of this copy to Rohauer, and when you expressed yourself as strongly opposed to this (in spite of the fact that the copy was for use only for showings in his private film society and did not therefore interfere, as far as I could see, with my contractual engagement to you) I offered to write Rohauer saying that due to opposition from you, I wanted to purchase back the lease rights to the copy. I wrote Rohauer subsequently several times concerning this but he failed to answer. You will remember that I explained to you that I wasn't very happy about leasing him the print in the first place but I needed at the time the (fairly insignificant) sum desperately to pay off my lab debts from PLEASURE DOME which were retarding my departure for Europe.

Now insofar as this concerns you and Cinema 16, there are several matters for consideration. I must first of all warn you against accepting any rentals for FIREWORKS in the Los Angeles area, for the time being or until this case is settled. This is partly due to the fact that I do not wish for any more undue attention to be called to my film in that area at this time; also that the "rental" might in fact be "rigged" by the police and lead to confiscation. The Los Angeles police happen to be a notoriously vicious bunch, and there is no knowing where it will all lead. If they should happen to tip off the F. B. I., you should know how you stand on such matters as shipping the film from one state to another. And whereas neither of us have reason to care much for Rohauer, it could have been just as well Cinema 16 copies that were confiscated. So as a test case, it does concern you.

I do not personally care so much over the loss of one copy. (From one point of view it would even seem like a "solution" if the copy were destroyed, to the Rohauer problem.) But you will agree with me that there is a moral issue involved over the freedom of artistic expression. If FIREWORKS is condemned as "obscene" or "made to excite" and if as a result the copy is burned, there is nothing to stop the police—whether of California or New York or elsewhere—from going right down the list of American experimental films and going on a film-burning spree.

I intend writing to several American critics who have shown an interest in my film, as well as the Museum of Modern Art and "Film Culture". In regard to the latter, even though their editorial policy has not evinced much sympathy with experimental American film-making, I still feel that the editor would agree to the right of the individual film artist to make this form of personal expression. Please write me your opinions.

Yours,

[hw] Ken Anger

Reprinted by permission of Kenneth Anger.

✦ ✦ ✦ ✦ ✦ ✦

Letter to Amos Vogel from Stan Brakhage, 11/1/57

November 1, 1957

Dear Amos,

I cannot thank you enough for allowing me to hold the ECG prints over until the Saturday study period of the workshop. It was particularly wonderful that we have the Anger file for viewing. I might go so far as to say that I was enable to discover one of my major influences in the direction I am taking, to take that influence apart (visually, not physically) and to qualify my entire present direction in film thereby. If you remember, I mentioned "Concerte Baroquo", which it was called when first I saw it, as not only Kenneth Anger's most important film, but as one of the half dozen "classics" of the American experimental movement. My list is more extensive today, having added three of my own films and a number of others to it; but Anger's film still remains among the most important three or four of that list. It is ten times the films I remember it as being. While far from visually perfect, the film continually struggles to justify one of the most important conceptions ever attempted in the medium. It lives, as a work of art, on at least seven inter-related levels of comprehension—formal (the visuals) thematic-dramatic (being still within the genre of post-war American films, i.e. the solitary figure in diserted landscape enacting a drama with the surroundings) the dramatic - sexual (strict Freud) the symbolic (developing always into and out of sex symbol) the historical - evocative (being a visual paraphrase of the Baroque period itself) the evocative (through atmosphere constantly a' shift in development in and out of formal Baroque to surrealism) the musical (being rythm in by-play with the music). I am now aware that a kind of sub-conscious remembrance of the film had left an irritating vacant place in my own work, a place which I didn't discover in my own direction until "Nightcats". How wonderful that both Anger and I discover the visual formal and the possibilities of using forms in their multiple levels of expression both by way of a night film. And how understandable, the darkness acting to isolate. Out of the night comes the most fabulous undiscovered worlds of cinema imaginable.

Packer, at the Vogue Theatre here in Denver, has just given me the word. His boss, Schomann, owner of the entire chain of art theatres, will have called you by this time. And what I have struggled for years to realize has at last possibly come to pass. You will be interested in the story behind his call. I went to Packer here in Denver first to try and persuade him that the Vogue should be showing a higher quality of films to justify Art Cinema—a kind of protest, as it were. We became quite friendly in talking. Next, I approached him with the possibility of running an afternoon (Sunday) series of film classics and letting me lecture with them to enable the select audience to be more receptive to them. He, in turn, suggested I write to Schoemann (unsure of spelling), which I did. Schoemann misinterpreted the letter, probably because I included some clips on my own work, and thought Packer and I wanted to run a series of experimental films—something I would never have suggested, having given up any idea of these contemporary films reaching an audience through these means. Schoemann told Packer (long distance) that a full program of 'experimentals' would be too much for the audience but that he would consider running one classic and one experimental short. I was amazed when I heard the news, having never expected anything that good, and doubly amazed when I learned that he "wouldn't consider running the series for one theatre . . . it would have to be for the whole chain", and triply amazed when I further learned that he was going to N. Y. and would contact C16 (from the brochures I had enclosed) and investigate expenses). Five years of arguing with distributors, theatre owners, patrons, etc. and then everything suddenly becomes possible by way of a "misunderstanding". So, it looks like not only the Vogue but the entire chain is to have my originally suggested "classic" series as well as something I would never have dreamed possible, an "experimental" short. Please keep me posted on the developments from your end as I shall be waiting anxiously to see how this all develops. I will, in turn, send you any information I can get by way of Packer. I am meeting with him tonight to draw up a list of films we would like Schoemann to bargain for. Packer doesn't know 'classic' film too well nor 'experimental' film at all, and I think he will rely on my judgement to a certain extent—tho' he has, of course, his considerations to look out for commercially as well. When Schoemann gets to looking at films, I think he should definitely see the three new color works of mine. I would like them to go through your offices, that being more correct from your standpoint, than for me to send them myself. Therefore, I will return them to you as soon as I get "Loving" back from Vermont where the 'Lovers', Jim and Carolee, are seeing it for the first time.

Send me the research stuff for my article as soon as you can. In addition to that article, I am doing one at the request of Mekas for Film Culture on film sound for the January issue. The workshop is coming along fine—500 feet of student footage, some of it remarkably promising. Strange, though, how prospective film makers always start with the introspective young man or woman in midst of ruin or wilderness enacting a kind of surrealistic drama with themselves and their surroundings. Willard is the only one who's Maastered the genre, "Narcissus".

Say hello to jack and thank him for getting the card off to me—and my respects to Mrs. Vogel.

[hw] Stan

[hw] P.S. What's Anger's present address? I must write him all due praise.

Reprinted by permission of Stan Brakhage.

[The film Brakhage refers to as "Concerte Baroquo" is Eaux d'artifice.*]*

✦ ✦ ✦ ✦ ✦ ✦

Letter to Stan Brakhage from Amos Vogel, 11/4/57

November 4, 1957

Mr. Stan Brakhage
2322 S. Marion
Denver, Colorado

Dear Stan:

Thank you for your interesting letter. Jack already wrote you a few days ago agreeing to the preview procedure, provided the films are mailed back Saturday afternoon and handled very carefully.

I have carefully noted the various points mentioned in your letter, including your reference to sound speed for your new films and no music.

I am very much in need of good 8" x 10" stills of your films. I am seriously hampered by not having them, since I otherwise might be able to place material with magazines, etc. Please send me as much as you can. I will be glad to return them if they are your only copies.

I find your agreement entirely acceptable except for Paragraph 4 which had to be changed to conform with the arrangements made with Willard for his mailing. The expenses of a special mailing cannot be paid by Cinema 16 alone; they are too large. But as is true of Willard's mailing as well, I am very willing to share the expenses, the procedure being as follows: You will send me 3,500 mailing pieces printed at your expense. We will advance the cost of the mailing, said cost to be recouped from first gross income.

To signify your agreement, please <u>initial</u> my correction in Paragraph 4 (I have already done so), and return one copy to me.

As to the mailing piece itself, it should

1. <u>Definitely</u> include and very brief descriptions (possibly taken from our catalog) of your other films as well. It would be wasteful not to repeat announcing these films, since there would be no additional mailing charge for this.

2. In fact, the mailing piece could easily be more than one page, if you can stand the expense.

3. It should include excerpts from Tyler, other press comments, or statements by well known film personalities.

4. In order to fit into our envelope, the size of the announcement must not exceed 5 1/2" by 4 1/2". This means that the announcement may have to be folded by your printer.

I am enclosing material regarding Cinema 16. I don't know what autobiographical data you are interested in. Perhaps you can be more specific. I was born April 18, 1921 in Vienna. My Schooling was interrupted by Hitler. I came here in 1939, studied both at the University of Georgia and at the New School for Social Research where I obtained a BA in Economics. I started Cinema 16 in 1947. My first interest in films began with my memberships in the Vienna Film Society—an organization that attracted audiences comparable in size to Cinema 16.

Entre nous and very frankly, I am not happy about Rohauer distributing some of your films, not because of any objections to Rohauer but because in principle it is not advisable to have the work of one film maker handled by several distributors. (In fact, were I a commercial distributor I would not take your films on this basis.) There is a "closeness" that comes from having an exclusive distribution set-up which cannot be shared with other distributors.

I will also say that I have no recollection of <u>refusing</u> to distribute DAYBREAK and WHITE EYE together. My recollection is that we simply discussed the possibility of distribution and that I expressed more interest in one than in the other film. You did not tell me of your plans to give them to Rohauer. You did not indicate in your last letter if I could come to some agreement with Rohauer regarding FLESH OF MORNING. Have you been in touch with him or he with you?

Please send me the feature just as soon as it is completed, as well as any other films you may have ready.

Sorry to hear that your plans have changed and that you will not be coming East. Please keep me posted about the activities of your film workshop, a very exciting and important idea that needs duplicating in other cities. Congratulations.

Very sincerely yours,

Amos Vogel
Executive Secretary

AV:pg
Encls.

✦ ✦ ✦ ✦ ✦

Letter to Amos Vogel from Stan Brakhage, 11/8/57

November 8, 1957

Dear Amos,

Thank you for your prompt reply to my letter. I know this must have been difficult for you at this time. I am only sorry that you'd not received my letter on the prospective film series when you wrote this one. It seems that everything happens at once!

Thank you also for the clippings on C16 and the notes on yourself. Despite illness, the workshop, my feature film and now this film series (for which I must put down the films, both 'classic' and 'experimental' which I think must be included and write prospective lectures for the programs) I am going to try and have my series of articles done by Jan. It is interesting to note that none of the other articles on C16 give it, or yourself, the credit for creating an audience for a film as a work of art. That shall certainly be the emphasis of my mention of your efforts in the article, for that will certainly prove to be the most ultimately important feature of Cinema 16.

You are absolutely correct in your addition to the (4) paragraph of the contract. I was copying the provision for the mailing of the announcement from Willard's letter on the arrangements you and he had made for mailing the Gryphon pamphlet and, as Willard doesn't mention the expenses coming from first gross until later in his letter, I neglected to include it. However, as all I'm concerned with here are the same conditions granted Willard, I am quite satisfied with your addition and have signed it and included it in this letter. I shall also take all your suggestions regarding the announcement, including the possibility of extending it to two pages. This would make it possible for me to mention the Gryphon packages which would do both Willard and you an extra good turn.

I must get to bed early tonight as this damned cold is still hanging on—after a month and a half (including pneumonia), can you imagine? So, I will bring this letter to a close. I have no additional information on Schoemann deal except that he has remarked to Packer that the 'experimentals' will be impossible unless he can get them at some reduced rate. Can you take this into consideration in bargaining with him without letting him know I'm supplying you with information. I don't want him to think we're in cahoots. As I understand it, he is expecting to break even on the deal at first. If he loses money on the first series of programs, the deal will be off. Essentially he considers this a philanthropic effort on his part. It is certainly that with me. I'm spending a great deal of time on this with no reimbursement whatsoever. Now, I'm not suggesting you do the same; and I should certainly expect the film artists, as well as yourself, to receive a fair price for the showing of these films. However, I am reasonably sure that Schoemann (or however it's spelled) won't pay the full price. Hell, I shouldn't try to advise you. You know infinitely more about this than I; so I'll just pass on what information I get for what it may worth to you.

Hello to everyone. Oh—I almost forgot. Rohauer's distribution catelogue is out. He advertises "Flesh of Morning"; however, he doesn't list rental prices on any of his films but says to write for prices. I hope this doesn't mean every person will have to dicker with him personally over every film. That's the best I can do. I've written him to rent you the film. He hasn't replied with anything but the catelogue yet.

[Stan Brakhage]

Reprinted by permission of Stan Brakhage.

✦ ✦ ✦ ✦ ✦ ✦

Letter to Kenneth Anger from Amos Vogel, 11/27/57

November 27, 1957

Mr. Kenneth Anger
c/o Hotel Stella
133 Avenue Victor Hugo
Paris 16, France

Dear Ken:

The situation regarding Rohauer's showing is unfortunately not as clear cut a civil liberties case as we would like to believe. Speaking strictly for myself, there are two unfortunate aspects to Rohauer's operation in this respect.

1. His announcements definitely sensationalize this and certain other experimental films.

2. He shows films on a single admission policy to the general public. This not only means that children or teenagers can, theoretically speaking, attend the performances, but it also makes him subject to more laws and restrictions than necessary.

As you know, every rental of your film by us is carefully checked before hand so as to insure that it is shown only by adult groups and only privately. While I am of course utterly opposed to censorship of all types, it is quite obvious that in the case of a film such as this, self-restraint is necessary or else sensationalism and unscrupulous commercialism takes over—with its concommitant dangers.

The above is quite apart from my feelings regarding the fact that this is Rohauer's print. You have put the situation well in your letter. Nevertheless, I immediately contacted the American Civil Liberties Union and had a lengthy discussion with them. The outcome was that they suggested that Rohauer contact their West Coast office which alone has jurisdiction. I have no doubt that they will be of assistance to him. I have also sent them some program note material and other data.

But between me and you, I am not at all enthusiastic about this matter. In a sense, we are now all paying for the error you made in selling him the print.

Needless to say, we are watching the rental situation regarding your film very carefully until this matter is settled.

As to the "moral issue involved over the freedom of artist expression", I am of course in complete agreement, as is the American Civil Liberties Union. But first of all, I don't consider this case to be the beginning of a general attack on experimental films and secondly, even if it were, due to the circumstances involved, it would not be a particularly good case to fight. If and when a legal problem should ever arise, I would prefer it to occur at a place and time of my own choosing, if you know what I mean. For these reasons I am also not sure whether it is wise to write to the Museum of Modern Art (who are totally unsympathetic to films of this sort) and to Film Culture. I think we should watch the situation unfold before committing ourselves further.

Enclosed please find your statement covering last year's earnings.

Since our catalog was only published last spring and since rentors book six months in advance, not too much activity could have been expected, but we have already had a considerable increase in rental activity starting with the Fall of this year. This will undoubtedly be reflected in your next statement.

The reference to "special rates" on the statement refers to a new policy on our part whereby anyone renting several films for one date receives the benefit of a slight reduction in rental rates. This policy has already considerably increased the total earnings of all films.

I am handicapped by the lack of suitable stills. A number of very interesting publication projects are coming up and I cannot therefore properly "promote" your films for these publications. Can you send me any photographs?

The $74 owed you will reach you under separate cover.

With best personal regards.

Very sincerely yours,

Amos Vogel

AV:pg

P. S. I think you should explain to John Schmitz that he is wrong in mechanically applying any legal action against an open, <u>theatrical</u> showing to the general public to private showings before non-profit membership film societies. This distinction is very important.

P. P. S. Is it still possible to purchase a print of the film mentioned in one of your last letters?

✦ ✦ ✦ ✦ ✦ ✦

Letter to Amos Vogel from Stan Brakhage, 12/2/57

Dec. 2, 1957

Dear Amos,

I mailed "The Wonder Ring", "Nightcats", and "Loving" prints to you this noon. Please let me know when you receive them safely. I am always a little concerned when "Loving" travels through the mails.

The night film is now almost a third completed and I am making a print of that third. Meanwhile, editing continues on the remainder slowly but surely. I am hopeful that it may still be finished in time for the Brussels Contest; but there is no earthly way I can hurry it. You will know why when you see the film.

Outside the night film, I intend to enter the following films in the Brussels contest—"The Way To Shadow Garden", "In Between", "The Wonder Ring", "Nightcats", "Loving", "Reflections On Black", "Flesh of Morning", "Daybreak and White Eye". I would like to enter "Desistfilm", but it was finished, sound track and all, before the 1955 deadline date. The other earlier films had no sound tracks until late in 1956. Would you please send your approval of the entrance of such films as are under contract to you, if such approval is needed. Send any advice you may have on the matter. I wrote Brussels regarding the problem of censorship, having already had a lengthy correspondence with Ledoux during which I supplied him with names and addresses of all American experimental film makers known to me and advising him as to how best to invite them to enter the contest without arousing their suspicions about European film contests, and he replied kindly enough with a clearance to send the films through the Belgium embassey in Washington. I am sure that, if other film makers fear possible censorship in customs, this route for their films would be well advised. Perhaps you can pass the word along. Though I know American film makers are generally disillusioned about film contests, myself sharing the disillusionment in retrospect, I really feel that this contest will prove all it's cracked up to be and that film will perhaps really be considered as an art form for the first time in its history. My correspondence with Ledoux only serves to strengthen this belief. You might pass that along as well.

I am already making plans to attend the Festival during the last two weeks in April. If expenses can possibly be managed, that is if I can borrow the entire amount as well as what will be needed for prints and the finishing of the night film, then I shall certainly be there. At least, I have applied for passport which is a step in the right direction. It occurs to me that perhaps you might want a representative there. One of my close friends, Tone Brulin, playwrite—"Beware of Hairlip"—and director of plays at the Royal Flemish Theatre, has already promised to help me in everything from translation to introduction to people in the film world, so that I would be in a good position to deal for films.

Any word on the Shomann deal yet? I supplied Packer here in Denver with a list of films of which most of the experimentals were drawn from the C 16 catelogue.

Until I hear from you then—which I hope is soon...

[hw] Stan

Reprinted by permission of Stan Brakhage.

✦ ✦ ✦ ✦ ✦ ✦

Letter to Amos Vogel from Lindsay Anderson, 12/14/57

57, Greencroft Gardens
London NW6

December 14th 1957

Dear Amos—

A letter to you, which I wrote about ten days ago, has been lying unposted on my desk. It was rather a bad-tempered letter, so I'm glad now that I obeyed my subconscious promptings, and didn't post it... Because I received today from Thorold Dickinson a copy of the programme for the N. Y. Free Cinema show, which is certainly a very conscientious, intelligent and comprehensive document, which we couldn't have done better ourselves and we thank you for it and for all the trouble you have obviously taken to launch these films in such a sympathetic way.

What of course you couldn't know is the extent to which the whole business of Free Cinema has become here in Britain a vexed question and one which has caused on our part a certain amount of bitterness. A lot of this stems from the equivocal relationship of the whole movement with the BFI and the National Film Theatre and the Experimental Fund.... From the outside I have no doubt that this relationship looks a close and harmonious one. Unfortunately from the <u>inside</u> (as so often!) this is not so; and the success of our efforts has incurred the usual amount of resentment and jealousy and misunderstanding. To some extent this is also due to the openly radical viewpoint which we have made it a part of our policy to express, and which scares or alienates the sympathies of those who don't share it, or who are too scared to support work with an open social commitment. Always there is this tendency (and in Britain particularly) to treat films as "art" or as "experiment", socially neutral and therefore—in our present situation anyway—insignificant at best and reactionary at worst...

Now as I say, this conflict of views has led to definite tension between us and people like Stanley Reed, and the directorate of the National Film Theatre—who, in spite of all the success of Free Cinema, and the publicity prestige, new membership etc which have undoubtedly accrued from it, are perhaps slightly more resentful of the whole business than they are "for" it. The news of the New York show came as a complete surprise to Karel Reisz and myself—the first I heard of it was in fact the handout which I reseived from Thorold Dickinson, and which announced all the films as being produced by the BFI Experimental fund... Almost simultaneously, we found out (quite by <u>accident</u>) that an introduction to the programme had been recorded by Sir Michael Balcon, from a text written for him by Stanley Reed. Reed never got in touch with us to tell us that he was doing this: and the speech he wrote was, naturally, nothing to do with Free Cinema at all... He now says that Thorold Dickinson had asked him to concentrate on the Experimental Fund! Further he has said that in his view the title Free Cinema is meaningless, and that he doesn't understand what its about anyway...

To make matters worse, all this has happened at a time when the National Film Theatre has sponsored a programme, devised by Derek Prouse, its director of programmes, called CAPTIVE CINEMA—which has consisted of a string of documentary features produced by one of our commercial television companies, and which Prose has claimed represent "the most lively stimulus to British documentary since the warm and vivid work of Humphrey Jennings during the war..." (In all the publicity for the programme, and all the 'explanations' of the title which they chose for it, no allusion has been made to the aims, let alone the achievement of Free Cinema whatever). You will, no doubt, be even more perplexed when I tell you that six months ago Prose was writing in the Sunday Times that Every Day Except Christmas was "one of the best documentaries since Humphrey Jennings"!

None of this of course, is either your concern or your responsibility; but I have wanted to put you in the picture so that you can understand the peculiar relations that exist between us, as film makers, and the BFI which has been responsible for financing some of our films, and the NFT which has given us the chance of showing them—but both of which institutions remain sceptical of our aims, and only partially and sometimes reluctantly cooperative. Even Thorold, friendly though he is to experiment, is far from sharing our principles—and in Britain opposition as frequently takes the form of patronising or denying the importance of something, as it does of open hostility... I am sure that in arranging the whole affair of the Balcon recording, Thorold was in no way conscious of going behind our backs, or letting us down. He doesn't take our ideas seriously enough to realise that we believe in them... But you'll also understand that this doesn't make his attitude any the less infuriating to us...

Well anyway... that's how it is. I hope that in spite of the weight of all this opposition (and of course there's an even more positive resentment to all we've done and said in the Documentary movement proper) Free Cinema will continue... But its a hell of a fight on all fronts; and there are very few people here whom we can count on as reliable friends. The BFI will take any credit they can from the name of Free Cinema; but in doing so, they do their best to take its significance away from it, and to reduce it to just another category of experimental production. There isn't even any anxiety from them to give us another week at the NFT. It all has to be fought, for, all the time...

666666666666666

Sorry to inflict all that on you—but now you know!

How did the show go? I was definitely frightened that the evening might be too heavy a one. We found at the end of our first programme, of O Dreamland, Momma, and Together, that people had had about all they could take. But perhaps you have stronger constitutions in the U. S.! Naturally any news that you can give me of the films' reception, or of any press comment will be avidly received and digested by us all. (Thorold merely sent the programme, without comment). And if you have any spare copies of the programme, we'd love to have some. It seems to say pretty well everything. In fact as I read it, I began to feel—perhaps we really have created a Movement! It was a more encouraging feeling than you probably realise, and a real spur to carry on the battle.

I would also be very grateful on your personal comments on Every Day, particularly from an American point of view—I mean from the point of view of American audiences. I have been asked to cut it for the release by Contemporary, and to take

Illustration 65. *O Dreamland* (1953) by Lindsay Anderson. Courtesy Museum of Modern Art Film Stills Archive.

almost 10 minutes out of it, which is rather a lot... Do you think that the bits where the reliance is on overheard dialogue should go—I suppose these are largely incomprehensible to Americans... And the bit when we see the porters having tea before starting work for the night? I feel people are awfully inclined to ask for cuts without thinking whether they are going to impair the picture... (At first they wanted it cut to 20 minutes—i.e. by 50%—which I couldn't possibly do). Did you feel it was much too long?

Many thanks for the cheque for receipts on O Dreamland: every little counts! As for the other films you mention. Foot and Mouth belongs to the Central Office of Information. Frankly I don't think it would really be your cup of tea—too much an informational film, though with perhaps a few sequences in it of some impact. I have always been surprised by peoples nice reactions to it. Wakefield Express and the three little NSPCC pictures are perhaps more of a proposition for you. I'm trying at the moment to get the rights for them to be distributed by the BFI, and I'll let you know if this comes off. Thank you for your interest. It is really appreciated, believe me.

Well, forgive this grossly overlong letter—but I've felt a bit guilty about the whole thing, and, as I've said, the only thing seemed to be to try to give you some idea of the complex and not-altogether happy picture that exists here. I think Karel Reisz is the most level-headed person on our side (I am a bit impetuous i'm afraid!): but, distribution matters apart, either he or I are, I'm afraid, the only people who can speak for the idea of Free Cinema with any conviction or trustworthiness. I wish this were not so, but it is...

Thank you again for all your trouble; and I hope the reaction to the programme was such as to make you feel you hadn't wasted your time,

with all best wishes,

[hw] Lindsay

Reprinted by permission of Lindsay Anderson.

[In a letter to me (dated 4/7/89), Anderson explains, "The apprehensions I expressed about the B. F. I., the National Film Theatre, etc., proved well founded. It must have been shortly after this letter was written that we were informed by the B. F. I. (or the N. F. T.) that further Free Cinema programmes would not be automatically screened at the National Film Theatre, and this certainly played its part in our decision after six (I think) programmes, to bring the series to an end. The same reluctance to be associated with any-thing 'radical' was behind the decision of the Editorial Board of Sight and Sound *not to accept my idea of contributing a regular Notebook feature to the magazine. Of course not many people in Britain today have ever heard of Free Cinema."]*

✦ ✦ ✦ ✦ ✦ ✦

Letter to Amos Vogel from Kenneth Anger, 1/8/58

Quai de Bourbon
Paris4e
8 January 1958

Dear Amos,

This is just a brief note. I've received a letter from Rohauer requesting me to ask you to send a print of FIREWORKS to his attorney, so that the attorney can show the film to the defense witnesses, who want to see it before they appear at the trial on January 13th. These witnesses include Ray Bradbury, Dr. Zeifferstein, Kenneth Patchen and others.

I have reflected on the matter and in view of the quality of the witnesses, I for my part would agree to send a print (the oldest one) for this purpose. Since you have two prints, I assume this will not in any way interfere with your bookings.

Rohauer would pay shipping both ways. Under the circumstances I feel no further charge should be made to him.

I do not feel any risk is involved for the print in this one private showing. Since there is going to be a trial, I at least want the witnesses who have agreed to defend my work (and they are people I respect) to be well informed about it; since they have requested a screening I feel obligated to comply; so I forward the request to you. The attorney's address is:

ATTORNEY STANLEY FLEISHMAN

1741 IVAR AVENUE

Hollywood, Calif.

I hope you will be able to ship it immediately C.O.D. Air when you receive this. There is scant time, but I believe enough time to arrive the day before the trial which would allow time for the screening. In spite of my reluctances of which you are aware, I think this screening to these important witnesses is in my interest, so hope you will comply with the shipment.

Truly yours,

[hw] Kenneth

Reprinted by permission of Kenneth Anger.

✦ ✦ ✦ ✦ ✦ ✦

Letter to Lindsay Anderson from Amos Vogel, 2/3/58

February 3, 1958

Mr. Lindsay Anderson
57, Greencroft Gardens
London N. W. 6, England

Dear Lindsay:

I am terribly sorry about not having written you sooner, but a number of very difficult organizational and administrative problems and decisions occupied me completely for the past few weeks and prevented me from attending to my mail. Please accept my apologies.

We had a thoroughly successful and exciting evening at the Free Cinema's screening. A list of "VIPs" consisting of independent critics, film producers, the regular press, film society leaders and other film professionals had been very carefully compiled, and I am glad to say that most of them appeared to attend what turned out to be one of the most unusual recent film events in New York.

With this one evening, we (or rather you) managed to stir up more discussion, delight and controversy than had been true of most other film evenings in the recent past. The event served to forcibly inject the Free Cinema movement and ideology into the American film field and the results were entirely as anticipated: delight, excitement and affirmation on the one side—disagreement and opposition on the other. In short, we undoubtedly succeeded in duplicating the reactions to Free Cinema in Great Britain. However, it must be stated in all fairness that the "oppositionists" find themselves in a small circle. The large majority were deeply impressed and moved by the honesty, commitment and the "breath of fresh air" contained in these films.

I and my co-sponsors, Contemporary Films, feel privileged to have been able to bring this new movement to the attention of American audiences. I had no other motive in arranging for the screening at the Museum. I have no financial interest in or connection with Contemporary Films distribution.

I am very pleased to enclose program note and other material regarding this screening. Should you need additional copies, please let me know.

Under separate cover I am sending you a tape of Dr. Arnheim's introductory remarks. You will be able to ascertain their content and quality when you receive it. They will also be reprinted in a forthcoming symposium on Free Cinema in FILM CULTURE.

As a direct result of the evening, two additional developments have taken place:

> 1. Tony Richardson is appearing under the auspices of the New York Film Council, the American Federation of Film Societies and Cinema 16 at a special event devoted entirely to the "philosophy" and work of the Free Cinema movement. This is set for February 13th.

> 2. Plans are underway to start an American counterpart to the Experimental Production Committee. A recent meeting included John Housman, Dick Griffith (who unfortunately dislikes Free Cinema intensely), Mrs. Flaherty, Jonas Mekas, myself, Dickinson, and Bob Hughes, president of the American Federation of Film Societies.

I very much appreciated your lengthy letter of December 14th which for the first time clarified a number of puzzling facets of the BFI versus Free Cinema situation that had never been clear to us here in America. This is the kind of frankness we need, and it would have helped considerably had I heard from you earlier regarding this matter. I had suspected that difficulties of a sort existed between you and BFI, but it is only now that I am more fully cognizant of the situation as a whole. I shall certainly bear it in mind for the future.

You will note that we corrected the error regarding the sponsorship of the films in our program notes. This error appeared only in our original announcement and was caused first by the fact that we did not know that O DREAMLAND had been privately sponsored and secondly by the fact that EVERY DAY EXCEPT CHRISTMAS was added to the program only at the very last moment, at a time when the type for the entire announcement had already been set and when it had already been designed, so that to change the layout of the covering page would have involved a great deal of additional expense and work.

I apologize for this error. To us, it was a relatively minor matter which we fully intended to correct in the program note, but I can well understand why you and Karel Reisz would have felt differently, given the situation of which I had no inkling.

I am also sending you a number of the comments received in writing after the showing. These comments came only from a few people and are therefore not fully representative of the generally very favorable reaction to the films.

I am also enclosing a clipping from the New York Times. It is extremely rare for films not in commercial release to receive a listing of this sort, given the general backwardness and conservatism of the newspapers here. Therefore this announcement is doubly welcome and doubly important.

I agree that the program was somewhat too long, but unfortunately we had a choice of either doing this or not showing some of the films. This is due to the fact that the expenses for this evening ran much higher than you might imagine. In fact, they ran to almost $700, what with mailings, printed announcements, etc.; a sum that came both out of Contemporary Films and our pockets. Again, it is unfortunate that no official sponsorship for these films could be found here, given the general lethargy in the American film field. To give you one example, Richard Griffith of the Museum of Modern Art dislikes the film thoroughly and says so openly, although I would prefer you not to broadcast my telling you about this. As to Balcon's speech, although it dealt only with the Experimental Production Committee, it was entirely apropos since we "surrounded" it not only by the program notes but also by an introduction by myself which dealt with the Free Cinema movement in detail, and by Dr. Arnheim's speech.

As to Thorold, I have taken note of your remarks. Frankly, I found that quite regardless of his actual views regarding the Free Cinema movement, he was the one person here who was most helpful and cooperative in every respect in getting this program underway, obtaining biographical material from London, etc.

As to EVERY DAY EXCEPT CHRISTMAS, my personal view originally was that it could stand as is, although it did seem to be a bit long—possibly by American standards, whatever that means. However, on seeing it a number of times and also bearing in mind the problems of distribution here and the possibilities of getting a somewhat shorter version into either a theatre or on to TV, I agree that it perhaps could be cut by approximately ten minutes, the actual nature of the cuts being up to you. The overheard dialogue is rather hard to follow for Americans. On the other hand, "the porters having tea" I found to be extremely useful and interesting. I do not feel that I can make any more concrete suggestions.

Please let me know if and when we can expect WAKEFIELD EXPRESS and the other films mentioned by you.

I have succeeded in writing an even longer letter than you wrote me, but I hope that all this will lead to closer collaboration and understanding between us in the future. I for one am extremely interested in the progress of your "movement" and would appreciate any information about new films and new developments as soon as you can let me have them.

At some future date I also hope to be able to write a piece for SIGHT AND SOUND which will deal more fully with the issues of "commitment", etc., as raised in your various articles. I find myself very much in agreement with much of what you say, but on the other hand I also think that there are a number of unfortunate implications to what you say which should be very fully discussed in film circles. I hope that time will allow me to do this.

I am also enclosing some information about a children's series which we have just embarked on.

With best personal regards.

Very sincerely yours,

Amos Vogel

AV:pg
Encls.

cc: Karel Reisz

✦ ✦ ✦ ✦ ✦ ✦

Program Notes by Gideon Bachmann for Benjamin Christensen's *Witchcraft Through the Ages*, Shown in February 1958

WITCHCRAFT THROUGH THE AGES ("HÄXAN")
Produced by Svenska Filmindustri, 1919–21. Directed by Benjamin Christensen. Story and scenario: Benjamin Christensen. Photographed by Johan Ankerstjerne. Edited by Richard Louw.

Cast: Benjamin Christensen (the director, playing the role of the devil); Holst-Jorgensen, Maren Pedersen, J. Andersen, Aage Hertel, Ib Schønberg, Elith Pio, Tora Teje, Clara Pontoppidan, Elisabeth Christensen, Ella La Cour, Kate Fabian, Astrid Holm and others.

PLEASE NOTE
Tonight's screening represents the first showing of this legendary film in New York for more than twenty-five years. The print is one of the few remaining prints anywhere, and the only print available in the United States. It carries the original Swedish titles (more than 250 of them). Since it proved impossible to obtain the owner's permission to substitute English titles (this would have damaged the print), Mr. Mac Lindahl laboriously translated all titles into English while Mr. Robert Carter will provide a "live" narration. We are indebted to both of them for their invaluable help.

It is unfortunately technically impossible for present-day projectors to project this film at its original speed and close attention is therefore sometimes required to catch the fast-moving action edited for a slower projection speed.

We have reason to believe that this print is not entirely complete. A number of scenes involving nudity, further details of the witches' sabbath and the various disguises of the devil seem to be missing. It proved impossible to verify if these omissions are due to action by the customs office or by the Swedish owners of the print. We are still attempting to obtain this additional material and if and when we do, we shall show it to satisfy our more historically-minded (or depraved) members.

Illustration 66. *Witchcraft Through the Ages* (1922) by Benjamin Christensen. Courtesy Museum of Modern Art Film Stills Archive.

* * *

"The traditional obstacles to the filming of a controversial subject—especially if that subject could easily lend itself to sensational exploitation if mis-handled—all occurred during the stormy history of HÄXAN, one of those cinematic legends that have gone down as 'film classics' in all the anthologies, but which, paradoxically, very few writers have ever seen. Unavailability for decades, however, is only one of the items on the list; commercial reluctance, censorship, distributor resistance and—surprisingly—public apathy, complete the roster. From 1929 and until today, there is no record of this film having been shown commercially in its original version anywhere in the world. The only public showing, before this Cinema 16 're-unveiling', took place at the non-commercial London National Film Theatre in 1956.

Unlike other individual creative efforts in cinema, like Bunuel's L'AGE D'OR and Anger's FIREWORKS, with which it shares, besides artistic fame, a certain notoriety, HÄXAN was a <u>commissioned</u> film, and thus avoided the conventional first hurdle: producer resistance. But once the Danish director Benjamin Christensen had accepted the challenge of the newly-formed Svenska Filmindustri Company to come to Sweden to make a film on an original theme, the difficulties began.

To find his original material, Christensen for almost two years went through hundreds of medieval documents, judicial manuscripts and ancient books, some of them the rare single copies in existence. Determined, unlike the native Swedish directors of the period who took their stories from Scandinavian literature, to create something freshly filmic, Christensen rejected the temptations of Selma Lagerlof, Henrik Ibsen and Strindberg, refused to hitch his wagon to an accepted success, and instead undertook the labor of love which resulted in this extraordinary film.

The obsession with witchcraft has haunted the history of all religions. Witches have been burnt as recently as 1872 (in the evangelical Canton of Glarus in Switzerland). In 1585, for example, all inhabitants of two villages near the German town of Trier, except two, were burnt in a mass auto-da-fe, and even in a small village like Quedlinburg, a single day saw 133 people burnt at the stake as witches and 'werewolves.' Altogether it is estimated that over 5 million men and women fell victim to the persecution of religious zealots. It is no wonder, therefore, that a film tracing the history of witchcraft was bound to arouse large-scale public interest.

On re-seeing the film today, one is struck immediately by the extraordinarily cinematic presentation of the images, the excellent photography, the true-to-life atmosphere in the reconstructed medieval settings, the great attention to detail, the sincerity in the first-person titles, the extremely precise cutting. During the two years (1918-1920) that he worked on the research, Christensen discarded more than one version of the scenario; in the beginning, he felt hampered by the conflict between Svenska's demand that he make a 'documentary' and his own traditional-feature background. Eventually he decided, partly malgre-soi, against a traditional story line, but instead illustrated in the film various episodes that his research revealed as typical. As a concession to himself, and also as a dramatic device, he used the same actors and, in fact, the same characters in many of the episodes, so that the finished film is really neither a feature nor a documentary, but a form of hybrid.

Christensen not only acted one of the main roles in this film (the devil), but used first-person sub-titles, in which he becomes a sort of Dostoevskian 'first-person singular', a narrator who presents to the viewer his own ideas about witchcraft (not without sounding, at times, a propagandistic note). The 'introduction' consists of facsimiles of important medieval drawings, painstakingly collected and photographed lecture-style with intercut explanations.

His second method for 'getting his point across' is his constant harking back to the present (or, rather, to his present; obviously, the days before Freudian terminology became common property), by juxtaposing his medieval documents and reconstructions of situations in the past with situations perfectly understandable (if irrational) in the light of the discoveries of science. We see all manner of neurotic and a-social behavior chalked up to 'hysteria', which in the middle ages would have meant bewitchment or proof of consorting with the devil.

And lastly, Christensen's propagandistic vein is highlighted in his attitude towards the Church. Throughout, the Holy inquisitors are worse than the devils they purport to fight, but at the same time (and perhaps without Christensen's conscious intent) there is also an element of humanity in the depravity portrayed.

The cast consists of a mixture of professional actors and non-professionals. Christensen, the director, plays the Devil. Two poor old women, discovered in a Copenhagen crowd, play the witch and the old woman suspected of being a witch, respectively. From the Swedish stage comes Tora Teje in the role of the war widow in the modern sequence; the well-known Danish comedian Oscar Stribolt plays the part of the monk seduced by his housekeeper. Mrs. Clara Pontoppidan, one of Denmark's foremost actresses, acts the part of the nun. The hysterical, blaspheming sister is played by Alice Fredrikson, a painter. The famous Danish critic, Mr. Westermann, plays the part of the hangman. Denmark's 'most beautiful model' of the day is prettily displayed in the witches' sabbath.

Considering the type of interest that this film aroused, and the type of material that Christensen did not hesitate to include in it, it is to his credit that the film did not become an 'exploitation' item. Christensen was a sincere man, and like his predecessors in another art, Breughel and Callot, he knew how to convey the greater meaning of the whole and to obliterate the crass effect of individual scenes. Working in close collaboration with his cameraman, Johan Ankerstjerne, Christensen created fantastic images: with the help of exaggerated make-up, papier-mache masks and decor, dramatic lighting, innumerable authentic witchcraft props such as snakes, lizards, frogs, worms, and what appear to be fragments of a hanged man's body, he formed a mythical atmosphere, where nothing was impossible. At the same time, all these images are constructed with great attention to composition, so that many of them remain in the mind like a Bosch painting. In fact, the influence of the Flemish masters is apparent throughout the film, especially in the design of the frame. And this was a film shot for the editing board: no other film before, and none until Dreyer's PASSION OF JEANNE D'ARC, was so effectively mounted and rhythmically constructed in relation to the content of its frame-images. All the more it is to be regretted (and one wonders what the reasons might be) that this obviously talented director never again made a film of equal value or impact.

HÄXAN was released in its native Sweden in 1922, and a year later in the other European countries. It was not a financial success. Although produced at the height of the flowering of the 'Golden Age of Swedish Cinema,' HÄXAN, like other masterpieces of its time, was a success d'estime only. In fact, the film was no great financial success anywhere, which may have partially caused its disappearance for almost 30 years. The 'Film Daily', which reviewed it when it first came to this country in 1929, said 'the subject matter is too grim for most picture houses', and as a result it never went on from its initial Fifth Avenue Playhouse opening in New York.

When HÄXAN was revived in London's National Film Theatre in the 1955-56 season, while it was 'roared through as a farce' by the audience there, the reviews that reappraised it at that time found it still a remarkable film. Sight and Sound said, 'WITCHCRAFT THROUGH THE AGES (1920)—magic, superstition, diabolism, etc., ruthlessly examined under the psychologist's microscope, remains a remarkable film by any standards.' It is obvious on re-seeing the film today, that Christensen was far ahead of his time when he made this film. He had an uncanny understanding of the character of his audience: the macabre darkness that pervades WITCHCRAFT was directly related to the sombre tenor of the literature of the Scandinavian lands, where the long winter nights create the fatalism of the Northern character—that feeling of the inevitability of fate which, by implication, is part of the message of this film. Man cannot escape the responsibility for his actions, is the repeated message of much of the literature of the North. And in this film Christensen again and again reiterates the common guilt for this mass-crime of centuries. In scene after scene we are shown avarice, weakness, vindictiveness and smallness of mind as the causes for all that suffering. In tracing witchcraft, Christensen in a wider perspective traces the history of man's cruelty and weakness.

THE DIRECTOR
Born 1879 in Viborg, Denmark, Benjamin Christensen, after beginning his professional career as a medical student, turned to acting and soon obtained one of the coveted Royal Theatre Academy scholarships. After acting in major Danish, German and French productions and with a promise of international fame before him, Christensen decided in 1908 to quit the theatre and devote himself to film.

In rapid succession he opened two film studios of his own in Denmark and also appeared in a number of obscure Danish films. In 1913 he directed his first film, THE MYSTERIOUS X, in which he also played a major role. In this film, with its chiaroscuro lighting effects, its macabre atmosphere and its episodic editing, can be seen the roots of Christensen's later film work: his preoccupation with mystery, his ability to infuse his actors with an air of the unreal, and, not least, his flair for melodrama. His next film, made for the Danks Biografkompani in 1915, was HAEVNENS NAT, a dramatic story of circus life in which he again played a major role.

As a result of the success of HÄXAN, Christensen in 1923 accepted an UFA offer to direct a film in Germany, SEINE FRAU, DIE UNBEKANNTE, with two of UFA's top stars, Lil Dagover and Willi Fritsch. In 1926, he went to Hollywood and made six films, almost all mystery thrillers: MGM's DEVIL'S CIRCUS (Norma Shearer);

MOCKERY (Lon Chaney); and the First National releases, HAUNTED HOUSE, HAWK'S NEST, SEVEN FOOTPRINTS TO SATAN and HOUSE OF HORRORS. The coming of sound finished him and there is no record of any production until 1939, when he re-appears in Denmark with his SKILSMISSENS BORN (Children of Divorce) followed in 1940 by THE CHILD, in 1941 by GAA MED MIG HJEM and in 1942 by DANSEN MED DE LYSE HANDSKER, all in Denmark for Nordisk Film.

None of the films made by him before or after HÄXAN approached the sincerity and talent displayed in the extraordinary WITCHCRAFT THROUGH THE AGES."

Gideon Bachmann

Additional material supplied by Andrew MacKay

(Mr. Bachmann, who has written extensively on film history, is the editor of *Cinemages*, the widely praised film publication, as well as director and moderator of the weekly WFUV-FM radio show Film Forum, 9 pm Sunday.)

✦ ✦ ✦ ✦ ✦ ✦

Program Announcement: Spring 1958

March 1958

Munna
One of the revelations of the 1955 Edinburgh International Film Festival, this fresh and uninhibited work completely rejects the tiresome conventions of the Indian cinema in favor of a neo-realist approach as it recounts with humor and tenderness the curious adventures of an abandoned child amidst thieves, clerks, magicians, criminals and the crowds of an Indian metropolis. Filled with unexpected plot twists, it reveals a rich cross-section of extravagantly conceived characters, nicely balancing between the farcical and the tragic. Photographed in the streets of Bombay.

"Most delightful surprise of the Edinburgh Festival... shines with gayety and imagination... reminiscent of the best Italian Films!"—*Manchester Guardian*

The Praying Mantis
Alien and horrifying universe is revealed in an outstanding study of love and cruel death amidst the mysteries of nature. (Rembrandt Films)

April 1958

Frances Flaherty Introduces *Man of Aran*
This rare and seldom seen masterpiece of the documentary cinema has lost none of its intensity and drama, as a great film maker offers an unmatched portrayal of man against nature.

Brilliantly photographed on the barren island of Aran, off the coast of Ireland, and enacted by the inhabitants, this sensitive and poetic work records the struggle of a poverty-stricken and proud people with a desperate environment.

Illustration 67. *Man of Aran* (1934) by Robert Flaherty. Courtesy Museum of Modern Art Film Stills Archive.

Original Irish folk songs. Contemporary Films release, produced, directed and photographed by Robert J. Flaherty, assisted by Frances and David Flaherty.

"A motion picture of consummate beauty, with an overwhelming climax!" *The New York Times*

"A decided visual masterpiece... has an epic quality!" *N. Y. Herald Tribune*

Frances Flaherty, who worked alongside her husband on this and other films (*Nanook of the North, Louisiana Story, Moana*) will introduce and discuss the film.

May 1958

A Bouquet of Prize-Winning Shorts

Every Day Except Christmas
Grand Prix, Venice International Film Festival 1957. The humble night workers of London's flower markets; a provocative attempt to restore poetry and humanity to the documentary cinema. By Lindsay Anderson (Academy Award, *Thursday's Children*)

Dance of the Shells
Diploma of Merit, Edinburgh International Film Festival of 1956. Alfred Ehrhardt's experimental essay transforms innocent sea vegetation into precision-built monsters mysteriously moving in deep space.

The Case of the Mukkinese Battle-Horn
Filmed in the wonder of schizophrenoscope (The New Split Screen), this hair-raising satire on Scotland Yard records the utter destruction of a dangerous gang of international Mukkinese battle-horn smugglers, complete with echoes of Bunuel, Mack Sennet and D.W. Griffith. A brilliantly inconsequential film.

N. U.
American premiere. Michelangelo Antonioni's outstanding neo-realist classic focuses mordantly on an unexpected corner of urban life.

[The Spring 1958 Special Events listing includes The Unknown Soldier (February 12), Witchcraft Through the Ages (February 26), "The Brain" (April 2), "Experimental Cinema in Russia" (April 23), "Weekend of Screenings at Eastman House" (May 30 and 31), "Fritz Lang Introduces M" (date to be announced), "Screening of 1958 Flaherty Award-Winners" (March 22), "A Trip to Canada to see Chaplin's A King in New York (date to be announced). See 1957–1958 program announcement for relevant descriptions.]

✦ ✦ ✦ ✦ ✦ ✦

Letter to Amos Vogel from Agnes Varda, 6/30/58

June 30, 1958

Dear Amos Vogel,

It is altogether my fault if I answer your letter of May 20 this late; and already it is a little bit the fault of Rosalie-Felicite-Agnes-Justine, born May 28, much to my joy. Please excuse both of us, we were very busy getting acquainted. Now, this little animal is a month old and I answer my letters.

Do not feel embarassed I am certain of your honesty; I therefore agree to the $100 in advance for the distribution.

I have no photographs (or almost none) of the lover's sequence. It was so difficult to film, I forgot to touch the Rolleiflex, I shall send you the two or three that I have.

I shall also take care of "la Pointe-Court": translation and price.

May I remind you that the French title is "L'Opera-Mouffe" (and not "Opera Mouffe").

Enclosed you will find a signed copy of the contract letter

I did not understand all the details well (my assistant is away), but I am sure that it is all right.

Here are the songs of the "l'Opera-Mouffe".

Illustration 68. Amos Vogel (*center*) with Agnes Varda (*to right of Vogel*), Richard Roud (*to left of Vogel*), and others.

1. Sequence of the market

Opera-Mouffe
At first sight
At first thought
It's "chow"

2. Sequence of the Lovers

"Between silence and the cat
In your arms
You are here

Your dream elsewhere
I am elsewhere
I dream here..."

3. of the feelings of nature

"It was the beach
And the sun shone down
  on it"

4. of the pregancy

"It's the fish in its egg
It's the burgeoning under
  the skin
And the dove
The dove in the water"

5. Some people

"They were new born
Somebody
Somebody else
Some people"

6. Happy Holydays

"It is MotherCarnival
It is Santa-Claus
Love in its choldhood
And Saint Valentine"

7. of drunkenness

"The sleep of love
Flirts with Death
He who sleeps dines
He who dines sleeps".

8. of desires

"Between disgust
And desire
Between putrifaction
And life"

*of anguish
none

Again, please excuse this delay. Now, I am beginning to work (2 films to order, to pay for the debts...)

With friendship,

(signed) Agnes Varda

Reprinted by permission of Agnes Varda.

✦ ✦ ✦ ✦ ✦ ✦

Amos Vogel, "The Angry Young Film Makers," *Evergreen Review*, November/December 1958

In Brussels, in the spring of 1958: a huge, glimmering, high-priced, chromium-plated concoction of artificialities, the World's Fair, in which the world's governments propagandistically project antiseptic and idealized self-images. The revelations of national character are present; but they are unintentional.

The U.S.S.R. and the U.S. pavilions: the deadly earnestness, the massive mediocrity of the Russian effort; the flippant sophistication, the open, democratic purposelessness of the American. To ascend to the Russian pavilion, one must mount an imposing row of stairs—(as Man Ray puts it, similar to the Aztec pyramids, which the victim is forced to ascend—only to be sacrificed at the top). The American pavilion: at ground level, behind a charming and incongruous lagoon, its many glass doors wide and invitingly open; while at the Russian pavilion, only 2 or 3 of the doors are open at any one time, the others forbiddingly and inexplicably closed. The American pavilion: an ornate message from a rich planet in outer space, delivered at the wrong wave length: "Look how happy and rich we are," with no means of space transportation offered to the earth-bound Europeans to arrive at similar bliss. The Russian pavilion: "Look what hard-working, backward peasants we are"—solemnity, puritanism, pompousness, the stuffy odor of bureaucratism and a truly spectacular display of mid-Victorian *kitsch* in its art and interior décor sections: the ornate lamps with the glass beads, the rugs, the colored glass animals, the horrendous cups and saucers with the flowers. A wall to wall painting, stupendous in size, of a young girl waking through the fields with a bouquet in her arms, entitled, of course, "Spring." The usual paintings of happy workers parading through the streets, perhaps to celebrate Nagy's execution. In the American pavilion, the subtle satire of Steinberg's murals, totally lost on all but the European sophisticates; and the emaciated, sterile, coldly beautiful models walking down a ramp into an ethereal indoor pool that has the visitors transfixed. "Atmospheric" differences between the two giants are clearly noticeable; the sheer and deadly "weight," the authoritarian whiff of the Russians, and the free, disordered casualness of the Americans, modern, sunlit, but quite cool and inaccessible except to the native-born. There is humor and some self-deprecation here; there is none in the Russian pavilion. The Russians relate to the Europeans, if only in a perverse way: "This is what you, too, could be like, if only—," while the Americans lack any ideological message except to say "This is who we are." And the ugly barrenness of the American soda fountain type "restaurant"—complete with slow service and 65¢

milk shakes, is perhaps the exact counterpart of the plush, mid-19th century Russian restaurant, in which a complaint concerning the loudness of their "Muzak" system is met with a terrifying symbolic statement, pronounced in measured voice by the headwaiter: "The level-of-the-music-is-not-controlled-by-us-only-the-center-can-change-it...."

In Brussels, in the spring of 1958: an unruly red wig slithers across a table, envelops a glass, sips the liquid it contains through a straw and then crushes it in an octopus-like grip. A troupe of restlessly agitated abstract forms, scratched onto film without the intervention of a camera, nervously pulsates to the rhythms of African tribal chants. An occult ritual moves hypnotically across three screens, while the producer sprinkles incense across the front of the theatre. A series of harrowing documentary shots of concentration camps are set to the strains of a popular rock and roll ballad. And a reverent religious procession, led by a bearded priest, suddenly moves into 2-step and then into spasmodic reverse motion, heading into nothingness.

Such is an indication of the range of the International Experimental Film Festival held this spring in Brussels in conjunction with the World's Fair under the auspices of the Belgian Cinemateque. Spurred on by the totally unexpected promise of $15,000 in prizes (donated by Gevaert and SIBIS), the international experimental film movement, glorious and impoverished stepchild of a huge industry, responded by spewing forth 400 entries, from 1 to 80 minutes in length, of which 130 were found worthy of final consideration by the pre-screening jury.

Among these 130 final contestants are synthetic sound experiments, poetic, expressionist, dadaist, surrealist, symbolist works, abstract color animations, hand-drawn films, films shot in negative color, with musique concrete, or sound tracks produced optically without musical instruments, films made with the oscillograph, experiments with light, prisms and distortion lenses.

For an entire week, an enthusiastic audience of critics, intellectuals, film nuts, and film makers, watched these experiments parade across the screen at the rate of 9 hours per day, applauding, hooting, whistling, while an illustrious international jury tried determinedly to keep eyes open to the films and ears closed to the noise around them.

On the jury were, unexpectedly, Grierson, legendary ideologue of documentary; McLaren, the eminent animator, in danger of becoming a saint in his own lifetime, dazedly observing a parade of imitators of his own style; Oertel, producer of *Michelangelo;* Varèse, the noted contemporary composer; Man Ray, link to the classic postwar I avant-garde; Alexeyeff, producer of the unparalleled *Night on Bald Mountain;* Pierre Prévert, director of *Oh Leonard* and *Voyage Surprise.* Ensconced (expenses paid) and strangely out of place at one of Brussels' luxury hotels, they argued for hours after each of the exhausting screenings, only to be confronted with yet another 20 aural and visual attacks on the audience the morning after.

For "attacks" these films are most decidedly. Far removed from the innocuous placebos served up by the commercial theatres to passive consumers of mass culture, these poverty-stricken little films literally aim to explode the filmic frame itself. They explore in technique, treatment, style and form, the limits of the cinematic medium, revealing both its and their own potential and limitations.

Crude, exuberant, antidiplomatic, highly original or highly derivative, they display the vitality, the uncompromising violence, the unorderedness and anarchic freedom of youth. Unhampered by considerations of box-office or worldly success, they attack the (to them) false gods of puritanism, commerce, religion, mass culture and conformity, often missing the mark, yet at least aware of its existence. At times precious and jejune, they nevertheless attempt to hew to values far removed from those of the marketplace and to emulate, in their own field, the best creative efforts of the avant-garde in other media. Theirs is the desperate, last-ditch sincerity of the stepchildren and outcasts, with nothing to lose and hence a willingness to say it all.

Of the 130 titles shown, 50 came from the U.S., 20 from France, 12 from England, 9 from Germany, 7 from Poland; but surprisingly enough, unusual films were also entered by such countries as Sweden, Argentina, Israel, Japan, Austria and Yugoslavia. Quite apart from having the largest number of entries, the Americans also walked off with 6 out of 11 prizes. While this pre-eminence of the U.S. is noteworthy, the real revelation of the festival was the existence of a contemporary avant-garde in Poland.

From amongst the morass of so-called "socialist realism" of the East—the most sterile and conservative artistic tendency of our day—comes, not one lone experiment (that in itself would have been sensational), but an entire school, an avant-garde movement. The Polish October that brought Gomulka to power expressed itself also in the cinema. Seven films were entered, produced and paid for by the state film monopoly Film Polski, in 35mm and in color, representing surrealism, dadaism, abstract art, poetic and expressionist techniques. To be sure, there are derivative and jejune elements (apparently every new avant-garde movement needs to go through similar stages without being acquainted with the works of other countries); to be sure, the welcome state subsidy works both ways and may be withheld on the morrow just as it was granted yesterday (Poland's limited artistic freedoms are today once more in jeopardy); the fact remains that behind the Iron Curtain there exists, at least in one country, youth exposed to and responsive to contemporary art, slowly groping its way amidst dictatorial ukases to a grater freedom of expression.

The two best Polish works deservedly won prizes: *Dom*, the Grand Prix; *Two Men and a Chest*, a Bronze Medal. This writer would have reversed the awards.

Dom (The House) defies description. It is a work clearly in the surrealist and dadaist tradition, derivative, but thoroughly refreshing, thoroughly "free," combining cutouts, live action, drawings. In it, the "red wig" makes its triumphant entry; in it, the compulsive restatements, so effectively used by the "classic" postwar I Western avant-garde, appear to full advantage; a man enters a room, backwards, and places his hat on a rack; this action is repeated almost ten times. Directed by Walerian Borowczyk and Jan Lenica, the film, in the words of the jury, "shows an attempt to make use of the possibilities inherent in cinematographic art, which is a purely visual art."

Two Men and A Chest (by Raymond Polansky) succeeds, by means of brilliant images and a truly poetic conception, in the impossible: to blend what superficially appears as a light and fantastic comedy with a social comment of the most profound severity. Two men emerge from the sea with a dilapidated wardrobe, symbolic of a mysterious treasure. They attempt to interest organized society in it, but to no avail. While they lightheartedly pursue their task (accompanied by a lilting jazz accompaniment), hooligans, pickpockets, murderers and drunks crowd the edges of the frame. Society has no room for ambiguous and possibly dangerous treasures, and prefers to pursue its own set and corrupt ways; and appropriate conclusions are drawn by the two protagonists in a brilliant and provocative ending to a memorable work.

No other East European country had entries, except Yugoslavia, which sent an unusual art film based on the woodcuts of a noted Yugoslav artist portraying the last minutes in a man's life. Very well-substantiated rumor has it that the Russians entered ten documentaries in the mistaken notion that they were "experimentals."

Of the remaining prizes (all of the prize-winning films, including the Polish ones, will be shown by Cinema 16 this season), 6 were garnered by the Americans, the Second Prize of the festival ($5,000) falling to Len Lye's *Free Radicals*. With beautiful and exemplary economy of means, this long-neglected precursor of McLaren and UPA, undoubtedly one of the most original living talents in his field, creates a perfectly controlled work that surpasses in its simplicity and form most of the other, more elaborate works shown at the festival. The abstract designs are directly engraved on plain black leader film in a "direct" film technique without the intervention of a camera. As the jury put it, "'Direct' film animation gives an image of extreme kinetic tension. The imagery of *Free Radicals* exploits this. A 'Free Radical' is a fundamental particle of matter which contains the energy of all chemical change, very much like a compressed spring before release. The film gives an artistically symbolic portrayal of fundamental energy." There was also a special award by the selection jury to "all of the films of Stan Brakhage," one of the most talented and radical of the young American experimenters, whose originality and filmic explorations have finally brought him to his most extreme and most controversial work, the 50-minute color film *Anticipation of the Night,* which created a near riot in Brussels; and Bronze Medals were awarded to Francis Thompson's semi-abstract fantasy of New York from dawn to dusk, *N.Y., N.Y.,* a dazzling and stunning display of cinematic trickery and ingenuity, leading to some of the most breathtakingly poetic images of the city ever captured on film (this also won the Award of Exceptional Merit at the 1958 Creative Film Foundation Competition in the U.S.); to Hilary Harris' *Highway,* a restless and overpowering visualization of the American "road," set to rock-and-roll and photographed mostly from vehicles moving at high speed; to Hy Hirsh's *Gyromorphosis,* an "animation" of Nieuwenhuys' constructivist sculptures, with jazz; and finally, the special "L'Age D'Or" Award presented by the Belgian film critics to Kenneth Anger's study in black magic, *Inauguration of the Pleasure Dome,* an ornate re-creation of occult rituals in the best traditions of decadent art.

The three remaining prize winners came from Isreal (Yoram Gross' *Chansons sans paroles,* an animation of newspaper sheets and match sticks); from the Argentine (Rudolfo Kuhn's *Symphony in No B-flat*); and from France (Agnes Varda's *L'Opéra mouffe*).

Symphony in No B-flat, a mordant little satire, takes place the day after an atomic bomb has been dropped. Mutations have been created; two choir boys officiating at a wedding get married to each other instead; and memory has been erased, compelling young people to go to school once more to relearn the emotions of love.

L'Opéra mouffe, winner of the International Federation of Film Societies Award, is a film of haunting and profound originality, with a love sequence of such erotic fervor as to send the censorious screaming to the exits. It is a poetic documentary "in depth" of an impoverished section of Paris, with vivid and often terrifying images of the poor, the anxious, the old, the children, the lovers—and, as a framing theme, obsessional in power, images of pregnancy and fertility.

But there were other films of interest, which may well have deserved prizes too.

There was the work of the bold Herbert Vesely, *Nicht Mehr Fliehen* (No More Fleeing), winner of the highest 1957 Creative Film Foundation Award; a beautifully photographed and hypnotic paraphrase on mankind's atomic cul-de-sac, with two ambiguous travelers trapped in a desolate landscape that suddenly erupts in violence; followed by Vesely's newest, *Prelude,* a poetically conceived impression of a pause during a ballet rehearsal, with dancers and theatre personnel grouped in casual and evocative incidents. There was Hulten-Nordenstrom's *A Day in Town* (winner of the 1958 Creative Film Foundation Award for exceptional merit) a wild, dadaist explosion that starts as a typical Fitzpatrick travelogue of Stockholm and ends in the city's total destruction by fire and dynamite in one of the most hilarious and anarchic film experiments on record.

There was Maya Deren's celestial ballet, *The Very Eye of Night,* a mysterious and mystical transformation of space and human forms, photographed mostly in negative; *Nice Time,* Goretta and Tanner's somber account of the empty and heartbreaking pleasures of Piccadilly by night; Christopher Young's *Subject Lesson* (Creative Film Foundation Winner 1957), symbolic tracing of the development of man's consciousness, with startling juxtapositions of familiar objects and incongruous backgrounds; Vanderbeek's *What, Who, How,* a comedy of "the unexpected that lies beneath the real," a surrealist mélange of paper cutouts, with country houses, young men, terrible animals, jewelry emerging from the heads of beautiful New York models.

There were several original animation efforts: Pintoff's and Whitney's painless and charming introductions to the abstract film, *Performing Painter* and *Blues Pattern,* made for UPA; Pintoff's *Flebus,* a cartoon with a theme not usually dealt with in entertainment productions; John Hubley's *The Adventures of Asterisk,* a highly original attempt to deal with the concepts and values of modern art purely visually (produced in cooperation with the Guggenheim Museum and James Johnson Sweeney); Richard Williams' surprising *The Little Island,* one of the "discoveries" of the festival, an animated morality play, visualizing (without a single word spoken) atomic war, neutralism, power politics, moral crusades—and doing so with both humor and foreboding; there was the exuberance and utter charm of Carmen D'Avino's work, displayed in *The Big "O"* and *Motif* (1957 Creative Film Foundation Award); the impish and sophisticated visual puns and sallies of the highly original Robert Breer (*Cats, Jamestown Baloos* and *A Man and His Dog Out for Air*).

Shirley Clarke's *Moment in Love* is a poetic love ballet, choreographed by Anna Sokolow; Willard Maas' and Ben Moore's *Narcissus,* a re-creation of the classic myth in modern terms (Creative Film Foundation Award 1957).

Five other films deserve special mention. Two from France: Jean Dasque's spoof, *Cinesumac,* a very unusual portrayal of a "sound" from the time it escapes from a singer's gaping mouth (in close-up, with both tonsils showing) to the time it is captured on a film strip; and Jean-Daniel Pollet's *Pourvu qu'on ait l'ivresse,* which in its cold-blooded and pitiful portrayal of an adolescent dancehall as a sexual jungle leaves the similar *Marty* sequence at the post. From Spain, *La Gran Siguriya* (by José Val del Omar), a dark, explosive, somber, cruel and unpredictable work of the deepest passion, which in its best sections combines the heightened realism of Bunuel's *Land without Bread* with the surrealism of his *Un Chien Andalou.* From Sweden, Peter Weiss' *According to Law* (embroiled with censorship laws in several countries), an unsentimental yet passionate, poetic yet factual investigation of a Swedish prison and its inmates. Finally from Mexico, Carlos Toussaint's *La Canción de Jean Richepin.* Asked by his beloved to bring his mother's heart for her dog, a hopeless lover tears it out, stumbles with it, lets it fall. Rolling across the floor, the heart gasps out: "Are you hurt, my son?"

Polyvision, Circarama, the Czech experiment and "Impressions of Speed" deserve mention as four experiments in screen and projection techniques. Polyvision, connected with the name of the French film pioneer Abel Gance, consists of the projection of 3 images upon one huge cinemascope-type screen; no attempt is made to join the 3 images as in Cinerama; in fact, different actions proceed on each of the 3 panels and at times only the center one is utilized; the effect, at least as shown at the festival, must be considered a failure artistically. It does not blend into one visual experience, and we are reminded jarringly of the mechanical contrivance employed. This time we are taken not on *one* rollercoaster ride as in Cinerama, but on *three*—simultaneously. The effect is totally self-defeating; the human eye simply cannot correlate these three disparate images into one joined subretinal experience.

Circarama, Walt Disney's totally unexpected (to this observer) success: a 360-degree film, projected onto joined screens spaning the entire circumference of a circular theatre, in the center of which the audience stands. The film was photographed by 12 cameras mounted in circular fashion on one truck, reproducing one "continuous" image on 12 film strips, spanning 360 degrees. The effect is startling, stunning; you are "in the midst" of Times Square, "surrounded by" Times Square (complete with stereophonic sound); and even the blatant patriotism of the images, complete with Statue of Liberty and the Grand Canyon, cannot obliterate the physio-psychological impact.

In the Czech pavilion, an intimate, small "theatre" features about 8 or 9 discontinuous screens, placed at various heights and angles and at some distance apart. The audience is seated on low, irregularly placed divans. Some of the screens tilt upward from the floor, others are placed at varying depths. The film—a record of a music and dance festival in Prague—proceeds on all, most, or only one panel and consists of separate film strips, ingeniously synchronized to provide an encompassing visual poetic whole. It succeeds, in part; the assembled experimental film makers watch in awe, hoping for similar state subsidies in their own countries, one may presume.

"Impressions of Speed": in a special pavilion, a thoroughly engrossing experiment, for only 25 spectators at a time: the audience is seated as if in the cab of a simulated railroad engine, with a full view of the landscape not only in front but also on both sides of the train; a continuous all-encompassing image is projected through the simulated windows; stereophonic sound is used; the landscape flashes by, in perfect synchronization and in color, the total impression so vivid as to approach the actual experience. The jury is stumped: Has this film left behind the "illusion of art" and become "reality" itself?

Not many of the films shown at the festival can lay claim to greatness or completeness; and far less complimentary comments must be made regarding the majority of the other films shown and not mentioned in this article; for, much too often, freshness takes the place of originality, technique substitutes for meaning, form for content. Embarrassment is caused by purely derivative works, and by the adolescent preciousness of some of the others. But when all is said and done, there remains a feeling of vitality and promise, of scope and sincerity. To find even 25 unusual works among 130 is not too poor a percentage.

What binds these disparate and diverse works together? It is not merely their daring (at least as compared to the creations of the commercial cinema); it is primarily their emphasis on film as a *VISUAL* medium. This is a self-evident truth which today is being trampled to death in the mad scramble for wider screens and a more total approximation of reality, with the camera reduced to the level of a recording instrument. The contemporary cinema, more often than not, is literary in origin and form, tightly bound to (or rather emasculated by) a naturalistic sound track, dialogue and wide screens which have practically succeeded in destroying the true heart of cinematic art, the image, and its creative ordering into sequences of associative and hypnotic power via montage (editing). These experimental films restore the visual to the cinema. They remember Eisenstein, not Shakespeare. The sound track is utilized as a subsidiary component or as a creative counterpoint to the image, and not as a substitute for visual action and filmic progression (as occurs, for example, in such contemporary creations as *The Long Hot Summer* which is not a film but a literary artifact and can be reasonably well followed with eyes shut).

Duplicating, if decades late, contemporary art's break with realism and naturalism, they attempt to introduce into the film medium nonrealist storytelling, stream-of-consciousness, imagist, or symbolist techniques, surrealism, dada or, more modestly, poetic continuity and semi-abstract animation. If, in Hans Richter's words, the contemporary commercial cinema represents 19th-century realist art, theirs is a desperate effort to break through to the 20th century, regardless of the incubus of the five million dollar mass market creations of Hollywood. In these poverty-stricken works, there is an effort at pushing film to its limits, technically, thematically and aesthetically.

Thematically, the search for "self" continues to predominate—and why not? The exploration and documentation of the soul is every whit as valid as that of the outer world. It is only through the understanding and mastery of both inner and outer realities that we can hope to control our environment and thereby our own fates. In the majority of these films, the "self" is explored either directly (via symbolist, poetic, expressionist techniques) or as it expresses itself in art (abstractions, collages, automatic painting). In the former, it is either the adjustment of the self to society and its values, or its self-realization and self-knowledge that matters. In the latter, it is the free flow of artistic imagination, the magic of artistic creation. Both are "relevant" to the social situation, notwithstanding the common accusations of preciousness, of ivory towerishness, often leveled against these films. Problems of alienation and atomization of the individual, problems of sex and love, problems of adjustment and conformity are eminently social in character. The works of the modern artist, even in their most abstract and nonrepresentational forms, are but a filtering and refraction of reality through the very contemporary subconscious of its maker.

In the narrower sense, direct social relevance is found in the ideological films shown at the festival, the "political" works, such as the antibourgeois spirit found in *A Day in Town, Cuckoo Waltz, What Who How,* the sharp social satire of *Life Is Beautiful* and *Symphony in No B-flat,* the social critique of *According to Law, Two Men and a Chest, Nice Time* and *No More Fleeing.*

They display a preoccupation with the H-bomb, with totalitarianism, mass culture, concentration camps, commercialism, bureaucratism. In all, there is a concern for the body politic, an attitude of commitment. For the makers of these films, in truth, are the Angry Young Men of the contemporary cinema. They may not express their anger in the "approved" realistic and naturalistic traditions of the early (and still uncompromised) documentary movement of the thirties or the works of the British Free Cinema movement of the middle fifties—but the anger is there, expressed in the vocabularies and often oblique techniques of contemporary art. Paralleling the Angry Young Men and the Beat Generation, their anger remains on a subpolitical plane; it is an expression of generalized anguish and tension vis-à-vis organized society, not a call to action.

Perhaps the most "experimental" episode of the festival was the reception for the film makers given by the president of Gavaert (roughly, the European counterpart of Eastman-Kodak). It was held at his chateau, an authentic anachronism complete with moat, with 22 servants feeding champagne and sumptuous dainties to the "Hungry Young Men" of all nations. Candelabras, period furniture and woodwork, the high ceilings of European aristocracy blended into an incongruous and unforgettable whole, with the flaming West European Communist film maker, the pale Polish intellectual, the restless American outsider, the young fellow in fatigue jacket with only ten cents and a thoroughly original film to his name. A more experimental gathering Gevaert never did see. Finally, inebriated and exhausted, thoroughly corrupted by continental bourgeois munificence, the film makers were herded into special buses and driven thirty miles through the silent Belgian night back to the reality of their dingy rooms.

For the reality and future of the film avant-garde, as always, is precarious, its problems profound and continuing. The fundamental obstacle, of course, resides in these courageous artists' working in possibly the most expensive existing art medium. Even the relatively paltry sums involved in experimental productions are far higher than the out-of-pocket expenses of the aspiring painter, the young writer or poet. The "tools" of cinematic art are too expensive.

Now that the festival is over, the question remains: how will future productions be financed? The assembled film makers, needless to say, were deeply impressed by the fact that the Polish films were completely financed by the state; and, while it is true that such official munificence carries its own dangers of political control over the artist, it seems very attractive to people who have nothing to lose. Likewise, certain German experimentals have been partly subsidized by state or local governments out of the proceeds of the commercial film industry, and a similar method of financing has been used by the important British Film Institute's Experimental Production Committee. Yet, this state financing or subsidy cannot be hoped for in the U.S. in the foreseeable future. In the present climate of opinion, any production of surrealist films under Mr. Eisenhower's aegis would be considered "creeping socialism." Nor, it should be added, can such films expect to find any more favor under an administration headed by that sensible, well-ordered antidadaist and tortured standard-bearer of the semi-liberal phrase, Mr. Stevenson.

There remain private sources and here the work of the Creative Film Foundation opens unusual opportunities. Organized a few years back by a group of leading intellectuals and artists in several fields of endeavor (under the guidance of the energetic Maya Deren), the foundation exists to further the production and appreciation of works exploring the creative potential of the film medium. It has only recently been granted official nonprofit status by the government and is now approaching the large foundations for support. If such is forthcoming, grants will be offered to individual film makers.

There remains the exhibition and distribution of experimental films. In America, it was Miss Deren on the East Coast and Frank Stauffacher's Art in Cinema society on the West Coast which pioneered the public showing of experimental films, shortly followed by Cinema 16 which, over the past 12 years, has provided continuity and stability to the movement, enabling it to show all contemporary experimental works of interest. It has also established the most comprehensive library of the avant-garde for distribution to film societies, art museums, schools and interested individuals. This distribution is continuously growing (unlike the distribution of documentary and other types of films, which seem to suffer more profoundly from the impact of TV); yet, neither exhibition nor distribution have so far solved the financial problem of the avant-garde. The income remains—so far—too limited.

The result has been a lack of continuity in the movement, a passing from its ranks of its most talented members, only to be replaced, in each generation, by newcomers, who start afresh, from a low and derivative plane (as shown in the works of some of the new young West Coast film makers at Brussels). On the other hand, some of the "greats" of the movement are unable to continue their work. Peterson, the surrealist, has not made a film in years. Anger moved to Paris. Harrington is fashioning a Hollywood career. Broughton has left the movement, disillusioned. To continue, a film maker must be able to keep production costs minimal (this determines choice of subject matter and treatment) or he must have independent means.

Ultimately, the fate of this movement is tied to the fate of the cinema as a whole, to the fate of all art in a commercial society. The values of mass culture dominate in all media, but in none as much as in the medium of "family entertainment"—

the cinema. The art of the moving image (already surely buffeted by the introduction of sound, the development of the large screens, the rise of television) may never be able to develop its full potential and may possibly be referred to by future generations as the art that never was. If so, perhaps the historians of tomorrow will fish out from a rusty time capsule some of the dilapidated, courageous films of this festival and exclaim: "Here, gentlemen, is a little example of what might have been."

Reprinted by permission of Amos Vogel.

❖ ❖ ❖ ❖ ❖ ❖

Program Announcement: Fall 1958/Spring 1959

October 1958

Three Women
Inexplicably banned by the New York and British censors, this is a delicate and beautiful feature-length evocation of a trio of de Maupassant's stories, each centering around the emotions and fate of a woman. Richly textured, ironical and romantic, they reflect the famed author's lighthearted and pitiless critique of moral hypocrisy, human weakness and philistinism:

> *Zora:* A tender portrayal of a love affair between a French soldier and a young Negress; a comment on prejudice.

Illustration 69. Program announcement, fall 1958/spring 1959.

Coralie: A cheerfully cynical and amoral tale of a young wife who will inherit a fortune only if she has a child within three years.

Mouche: A romantic period piece of the affectionate and overgenerous Mouche who retains the loyalty of a quintet of lovers.

Selected as French entry at Cannes International Film Festival. Complete English titles. Only New York showing.

Abseits
Water, wind, sunlight and seagulls: the sounds and lonely grandeur of ebb tide on a North Sea beach.

November 1958

Poverty, Chastity and Obedience
Unrehearsed interviews with Anglican monks elicit (in frequently poetic or mystical terms) their views on God, sex, wealth and the meaning of freedom. Factual, not reverential in treatment, this is a most provocative example of adult television, produced by the BBC and shown by special arrangement.

Another Sky
Gavin Lambert's haunting and luminescent film propels a puritanical young woman on a compulsive quest for love into the desert of North Africa; this mysterious and lyrical film—a remarkable portrayal of civilized people engulfed and destroyed by the primitive power of an alien culture—abounds in rich insights into the relations between Arabs and Westerners, and is acted out against the exotic and moral atmosphere of the African landscape.

Reminiscent of Paul Bowles' somber novels, it provides a subtle confrontation of the two civilizations as reflected in the terrifying story of the young girl's sojourn into nothingness.

Award, 1958 Stratford International Film Festival. A Minotaur Production by Gavin Lambert, noted film critic and editor of the internationally famous film magazine *Sight and Sound*. Camera: Walter Lasally (*Thursday's Children, The Girl in Black*). Shown by courtesy of Edward Harrison.

December 1958

Award Winners at the International Experimental Film Festival, Brussels, 1958 selected by a distinguished international jury from 400 entries representing 29 countries, and premiered by special arrangement:

Dom
Grand Prix: a major surprise from Poland, in the surrealist tradition.

L'Opera Mouffe
Faces of the poor, fervors of erotic love, gestures of the aged, innocence of the children; a film of dark and compelling originality. (France)

Highway
Exhilirating visualization of the American "road," set to strident rock-and-roll. Poetic, startling, beautiful. (U. S.)

Symphony in No B-Flat
Mordant satire on—the atom bomb. (Argentine)

Loving
Poetic exploration of a moment in love (U. S.)

Chansons sans Paroles
Israel's first experimental film.

Gyromorphosis
Hypnotic animation of constructivist sculptures. (Holland)

Two Men and a Wardrobe
The revelation of the Festival: farcical fantasy projects disturbing parable of the modern world. (Poland)

January 1959

The General
In the funniest of all silent feature comedy classics, the imperturbable Buster Keaton is cast as a daring Federal Spy with an outlandish plan to change the course of the Civil War. This sophisticated and grotesque screen farce—eloquently touching, uproariously hilarious—is a perfect example of Keaton's art. Engulfed by switches, stolen engines, valves and other mechanical contrivances, the immortal comedian—an engine driver literally on the wrong side of the tracks—solemnly attempts to behave normally in world which is plainly bewitched.

"A one track mind near the track's end of insanity... deep below that, giving a disturbing tension and grandeur to the foolishness, a freezing whisper not of pathos but of melancholy." James Agee, *Life*

The Third Avenue El as seen by 3 film artists
A trio of unusual films offer contrasting views of a beloved memento of New York's past: *The Wonder Ring*, an intensely subjective impression of an "El" ride, by Stan Brakhage; *Echo of An Era*, the early days of the "El" as seen in charming and often humorous engravings and old photographs, by Henry Freeman; *Third Avenue El*, a romantic and colorful documentary in the realist tradition, by Kit Davidson. A nostalgic backward glance.

March 1959

Strange Worlds: 4 film explorations

Lourdes and its Miracles
George Rouquier's (*Farrebique*) astonishing revelation of the ambiguous reality of Lourdes; neither travelog nor religious apologia, but a coldly factual dissection of Lourdes as a social and psychological phenomenon, thought-provoking for both sceptic and believer. "An uncompromising and sometimes fearful reportage. Its objectivity is deeply disturbing." British Film Institute

Seifriz on Protoplasm
Highest Award, Edinburgh International Film Festival. Protoplasm is torn, gassed, poisoned, electrocuted, dissected. "Possibly the most exciting science film to be produced in the U. S." Cecile Starr, *Saturday Review*

Nice Time
Saturday Night in London's Time Square: The empty pleasures, the restless temptations of Piccadily, caught with compassion by the candid camera.

SPECIAL EVENTS 1958/1959

November 5

The Eternal Jew
Nazi propaganda at its most vicious—and most accomplished; by special arrangement with the Netherland Film Archives, the only American showing of an unprecedented feature-length "indictment" of World Jewry, composed entirely of documentary footage perverted by editing and narration. An unforgettable insight into totalitarian propaganda techniques and myths, fully analyzed in program notes.

December 3

Rituals, Tensions, Myths: The World of the Child

Maternal Deprivation
Moving psychological study of disturbed children in French nursing home who have been deprived of parents.

Frustrating Fours & Fascinating Fives
A captivating and informative film.

One Potato, Two Potato
Paperboats, chestnuts, jumping games and nonsense rhymes; London's children's games through the seasons.

A Society of Children
Fascinating Vassar study of the magic and ritual, superstition and charms of the tribal, anti-parental society of the growing child.

Willie The Kid
UPA's spoof of Westerns blends child's real and fantasy worlds.

January 21

The 1958 Creative Film Award Winners
selected by a distinguished jury; co-sponsored by Creative Film Foundation.

N. Y., N. Y.
Francis Thompson's stunning fantasy of the city, a dazzling display of film magic and artistic originality. "A genuine masterpiece!" *N. Y. Times*

A Day in Town
One of the most surprising films of the season; a wild and hilarious dadaist explosion from Sweden. (P. Hulten and H. Nordenstroem).

The Big O
Joyous variations on the letter "O" (Carmen D'Avino)

On These Evenings
Inner and outer reality blend in a Kafka-like cine-poem.

Illustration 70. *The Big "O"* (1959) by Carmen D'Avino. Courtesy Carmen D'Avino.

What, Who, How
Grotesque and animated collage comments acidly on "the unexpected beneath the real." (Stan Vanderbeek)

Round and Square
The Poetry of nightdriving, set to country music. (W. Rudy)

February 4

Tokyo Twilight
A very remarkable example of adult film making from Japan. Against neo-realist images of urban landscape, Yasujiro Ozu tells of sadness, tragic adolescent love, alienation and lack of communication between people. Most interesting are the strangely elliptic and laconic style and the delicate psychological insights into relations between the sexes and generations. A major work.

February 25

Are You Really Against Censorship?
Your "limits" are probed as we show clips from extreme types of films (some banned) that may offend because of their erotic, political, sacrilegious, racist content. Also: premiere of important Columbia University film on movie censorship, featuring an unusual recreation and discussion of the historic "The Miracle" case.

Speaker: Ephraim London, well-known civil liberties lawyer of "The Miracle" case fame, currently arguing "Lady Chatterley's Lover" before the courts.

March 25

Strike
An event of the greatest importance: Eisenstein's ill-fated first film, hitherto completely unavailable and only recently "re-discovered" in Soviet archives; a major piece of cinema, a brilliant orchestration of film devices and creative editing. Originally banned in several countries, renounced by Eisenstein himself under Stalin's regime, this explosive blend of realism with grotesque stylization achieves an almost surrealist intensity.

"Never has the entry of a new talent into the cinema been heralded with such brilliance and one is not at all sure if this is not a greater film than *Potemkin*." British Film Institute

April 15

The Lower Depths
Consummate performances by Jean Gabin and Louis Jouvet, and Jean Renoir's masterful direction characterize this distinguished humanist work, based on Gorky's famed play. A drama of the loss of human dignity, of the degradation of a class, the film moves amidst the felons, prostitutes, misers, outcasts and gamblers of the slums. French Critics Award, "Best Film of the Year."

"A mature, impressive, extraordinarily fascinating production!" *The N.Y. Times*

April 29

The Erotic Cinema: *Lulu*
At last, Pabst's hitherto unavailable milestone of the German Cinema, much beset by censorship difficulties: "Wedekind's violent obsession with sexual hunger provided Pabst with a subject for his flair for abnormal psychology. Lulu, epitome of sexual voracity, destroys others and is herself ultimately destroyed. This clinical dissection of an irrational world is carried out by Pabst with the greatest success. Louise Brooks' performance is one of the phenomena of the cinema." British Film Institute. With Fritz Kortner, Franz Lederer, Gustav Diessl.

May 20

Activity Group Therapy
By request, a repeat of a most popular event: Not available for public showings, this authentic film record of 65 group therapy sessions, shot with concealed cameras over a period of two years, reveals the personality changes effected in a group of emotionally disturbed children. An exciting demonstration of one of the most important present-day group therapy practices which permits children to "act out" their disturbances in the presence of a permissive adult. The producer, Dr. S. R. Slavson, will introduce it.

Federico Fellini, director of *La Strada* and *Cabiria,* has agreed to appear at Cinema 16 this season, barring a last-minute change in his production plans.

Illustration 71. *Pandora's Box—Lulu,* in Cinema 16 program announcement—(1929) by G. W. Pabst. Courtesy Museum of Modern Art Film Stills Archive.

✦ ✦ ✦ ✦ ✦ ✦

Program Notes by Siegfried Kracauer for Fritz Hippler's *The Eternal Jew,* Shown in November 1958

11/4/58

THE ETERNAL JEW   Germany   (80 minutes)
A. D. F. G. Production, based on an idea by Dr. E. Taubert. Director: Fritz Hippler. Camera: A. Endrejat, A. Hafner, E. Stoll, H. Cluth, R. Hartmann, F. C. Heere. Music: F. R. Friedl. Editing: H. D. Schiller and A. Baumeister.

By special arrangement with the Netherland Film Archives

Only New York presentation

English adaptation: Amos Vogel; Narrated by: Robert Carter

Film will be introduced by Amos Vogel, Exec. Sec'y, Cinema 16

This program note is compiled from a recording of remarks made by Dr. Siegfried Kracauer after a screening of the film as well as from his studies of the Nazi propaganda film, "The Conquest of Europe on the Screen" (Social Research, September 1943) and "Propaganda and the Nazi War Film" in his book From Caligari to Hitler (Princeton University Press, 1947).

Dr. Kracauer, well-known in this country as the author of the just-mentioned book and a social scientist, was an editor of "Frankfurter Zeitung" in 1920–1933. He was the recipient of two Rockefeller grants and a Guggenheim Fellowship for his research on the history and philosophy of the German cinema. Presently he is completing a book on the aesthetics of film which will be published by the Oxford University Press.

"This is the only full-length Nazi documentary against the Jews I know of. One thing is sure: it was made after the Polish campaign (which gave the Nazis an opportunity to shoot scenes in the Jewish ghettoes). But it might as well have been compiled only at a time when the war took a bad turn for the Nazis. There is one fact which makes me assume that much. The film amounts to a wholesale condemnation of the Jews and all that is Jewish, yet achieves this goal in a very forced and artificial way. In fact, this film is much weaker in technique and power of conviction than previous Nazi documentaries, such as TRIUMPH OF THE WILL and BAPTISM OF FIRE. This tends to show that it was, so to speak, a conscience-saving propaganda message issued at a moment when the Nazis prepared the death camps in Poland or had already begun to set them up. The film's intention of justifying some sinister anti-Jewish measures stands out glaringly. I have the distinct feeling that this film served to rekindle hatred against the Jews in a period when many Germans were wavering and entertaining heretic thoughts.

The weakness of the film shows in the predominance, unusual for the Nazis, of the spoken word. In their great propaganda films, the Nazis always tried to let the pictures speak, keeping the commentary subdued or only using it as a means of further increasing the impact of the imagery.

This was a truly cinematic procedure, for film differs from other arts in that it reflects the visible world to a hitherto unknown extent. Everyday life, with its infinitesimal movements, its multitude of transitory actions, can be disclosed nowhere but on the screen.

While the pre-Hitler Germans availed themselves of these techniques to conquer more and more provinces of the visible world, the Nazis used them with quite another intention. In emphasizing the role of the visuals, they tried to suppress the intellect and affect directly emotional life. Hence the predominance of pictures over verbal explanations in the bulk of Nazi newsreels and propaganda films. The pictures themselves are so selected that they work primarily on the instincts, on unavowed drives. Taylor has said of the Nazi propaganda tracts that they supersede rational argumentation by 'pictures and symbols'. Nazi speeches, too, dwell upon metaphoric turns, for the spell of the image smothers the interest in motivations and reasons. Instead of appealing to the understanding of their audiences, the Nazis attempted to weaken the faculty of understanding which might have undermined the basis of the entire system. Rather than suggesting through information, Nazi propaganda withheld information or degraded it to a further means of propagandistic suggestion. This propaganda was tantamount to psychological manipulation in grand style. Accordingly, the Nazi film propagandists were not in the least concerned with conveying reality through their candid-camera work. On the contrary.... But they did everything they could to drive home the fact that their films consisted of unadulterated newsreel and documentary material and to evoke the impression that, in consequence, reality itself was moving across the screen. This accounts for the disquiet and uneasiness which Nazi propaganda films arouse in unbiased minds. Before our eyes palpable reality becomes a sham—a transformation all the more upsetting as it was to exert its impact on a whole people.

In contradistinction to the earlier Nazi propaganda films, THE ETERNAL JEW is a spoken lecture or, if you wish, a massive editorial which in crude anti-semitic language assembles all the well-known and worn-out arguments against the Jews. The pictures are often degraded to sheer illustrations of the spoken text or do not relate to it at all. You see the Polish Jews in their homes and on the streets of the ghetto; while the narrator abuses them as swindlers and parasites, concerned with money only, many faces just give the lie to these accusations. Thus the image of a tired Jew, stooped over his wares, flagrantly contradicts the synchronized verbal insinuation. In other words, the commentary does not succeed in providing the stimuli needed for the hoped-for effects of the pictures.

This is particularly manifest in passages where the film makers visibly overdo their job. One is the long list of hateworthy Jews, which includes world-renowned figures like Einstein and Chaplin (a Jew, according to the Nazis). I can hardly believe that, even among the Nazis, many were willing to accept such a sweeping verdict. And this, in turn, would confirm my original assumption that the whole film was designed to justify terrible actions in preparation or already under way. There is something desperate about this late effort of the Nazis to turn the tide of public opinion in their favor.

Let me just indicate the main areas which this propaganda film covers. A large part is filled with pictures and descriptions of the Polish Jews for the purpose of impressing upon the audience the racial differences between them and the rest of the world. Some of the ghetto scenes give the impression that they were re-enacted by the Jews under pressure during the German occupation of Poland. For instance, the bodily movements of the students in the Talmud school seem grossly exaggerated; and the shots which first show Polish Jews with their beards and all, and then as clean-shaved, normally clothed Europeans, cannot have been obtained voluntarily either.

After having exhausted this theme, the film turns to a large-scale historical retrospect which deals with the migrations of the Jews in a pseudo-objective way. Then the film elaborates on the parasitic role of the Jews in Western life and culture, business and industry, stubbornly insisting that the assimilated West European Jews are but descendants of the strange and ugly looking Polish Jews. The strongest point is made toward the end with a series of alleged documentary shots focusing on the ritual killing of animals by Jews. These pictures are horrifying indeed, but they are not any more gruesome than the images of Franju's BLOOD OF THE BEASTS. The necessity of having to eat is a bad business after all.

In spite of the fatal prevalence and omnipresence of the spoken word, however, the film still utilizes certain effective pictorial devices, rarely applied in Anglo-Saxon propaganda films. Take, for instance, the animated diagrams which picture the spread of the Jews from the Orient to Poland and from there back to Germany, etc: the maps and figures representing the latter migration spread octopus-like, reminiscent of an army of cockroaches. No sooner has the allusive diagram been shown than the speaker compares the Jews with rats. He has already prepared us for this drastic comparison by pictures anticipating it. After a while, another diagram appears on the screen which, through a rapidly increasing maze of lines, illustrates the infiltration of the Jews in international commerce and finance all over the world. These lines resemble a spider, as they grow and interpenetrate each other.

Another cunning pictorial device is to show the Jews smiling—particularly when the worst things are being said about them. The Jewish butchers smile while animal life is ebbing away. When deceiving the tax collector or cheating in the bazaar, or doing anything that is made to appear as wicked, the Jews invariably have a smile on their face. This, of course, is to suggest to the spectator that the Jew lies eternally in ambush, always prompted by a desire of defrauding his innocent neighbor.

Also, here as elsewhere, the Nazis work by way of pictorial contrasts. In order to cater to physiognomical preferences and prejudices, they contrast close-ups of Jews with German faces. Whenever they want to show that the Jews 'feed' on their host people without doing any productive work, shots of Jews trading and enjoying themselves are juxtaposed with shots of toiling German miners, peasants and the like. And the terrible slaughter scenes are immediately followed by the apotheosis common to all Nazi documentaries: Hitler haranguing the masses; jubilant youngsters in the crowd hailing the Fuehrer; and endless columns marching toward new victories.

To sum up, behind this film you feel the concern of the Germany propaganda ministry over the German state of mind. Hence the excessive recourse to words, the over-argumentation, the inadequacy of the pictures. At the bottom of it all lurks despair and fatigue. One is inclined to believe that the film at least partially defeated its purpose."

—Siegfried Kracauer

✦ ✦ ✦ ✦ ✦ ✦

Conversation with Melvin Van Peebles, 1/18/01

Van Peebles: Cinema 16 was a pivotal element in my career—and I mean *pivotal*.

MacDonald: Really?

Van Peebles: At the time when I made my first short films, most independent, short films were very avant-garde in their use of light and color and sound. But I had always been interested in telling stories. My early films were short stories. I took these three short stories [*A King* (1958), *Sunlight* (1958), *Three Pickup Men for*

Herrick (1959)] to Hollywood, hoping to get hired to write, direct, etcetera. The racial climate being what it was at the time, I was told I really didn't have the qualities necessary for a director. They didn't say this *directly*, but they made it clear.

One of the more insidious sidebars of racism is that people will not only convince themselves (of course, sometimes they won't even bother to convince themselves), but even more destructive, they'll convince the *artist* that he does not have the necessary attributes for whatever job he's applying for. I was discouraged by what they said, and decided to go back to my second love, which was astronomy. I was interested in what's now called celestial mechanics. Sputnik had just gone up, and I thought satellites and trajectories were going to be the future and, as it turns out, I was absolutely on the mark. I was a veteran, so I decided to use my veterans benefits to go and get my Ph.D. in astronomy. One university that offered celestial mechanics was in Holland: I wrote to them and they accepted me. So I booked a trip to Holland.

Jump cut. To go to Holland, you took a boat from New York, so I came to New York, and while in New York, I heard about this gentleman who did mini-festivals of short films and showed other kinds of film that weren't in the mainstream.

MacDonald: Amos Vogel?

Van Peebles: Yes, Amos Vogel. So I found my way to Amos Vogel. And Amos Vogel took *Three Pick-up Men for Herrick* and *Sunlight*–each ran about nine minutes—and put them into his rental film collection [The films are listed in Cinema 16's 1963 film rental catalogue; also *Three Pickup Men for Herrick* was shown on February 24th, 1960, with Edward Bland's *The Cry of Jazz* (1958) as a special event: the screening was followed by a panel discussion with James Baldwin, Marshall Stearns, Mark Kennedy, and Nat Hentoff]. Amos was *very* kind; he and his wife, Marcia, were very sweet people. So they took my films, and I went off to Holland.

Jump cut. About a half year later, I come in from school one day, and there's a letter from the Cinematheque Francaise. They had found me in Holland, and they had seen my short films. It turns out they had invited Vogel, who was really the flag-bearer for the independent filmmakers in the U.S., to come to France with some of the films shown and distributed by Cinema 16.

MacDonald: Do you remember what year this was?

Van Peebles: It's got to be 1959. And among those films were my two shorts. Well, the Cinematheque saw these films and apparently they were blown away. I guess Amos must have explained to them that I was an astronomy student and where I was. So here was this postcard in an envelope, asking, "What are you doing in astronomy? You're made for cinema. Your work is cinema." Of course, this was the complete opposite of what White America had told me, and at that time there was no Black America I could turn to for approbation or analysis.

There was the Cinematheque, thanks to Amos Vogel, giving me words of encouragement. And with those words of encouragement, I went to France and the rest is history.

✦ ✦ ✦ ✦ ✦

Program Announcement: Spring 1959

March 1959

Strange Worlds: 3 film explorations

Lourdes and its Miracles
George Rouquier's (*Farrebique*) astonishing revelation of the ambiguous reality of Lourdes; neither travelog nor religious apologia, but a coldly factual dissection of Lourdes as a social and psychological phenomenon, thought-provoking for both sceptic and believer. "An uncompromising and sometimes fearful reportage. Its objectivity is deeply disturbing." British Film Institute

Seifriz on Protoplasm
Highest Award, Edinburgh International Film Festival. Protoplasm is torn, gassed, poisoned, electrocuted, dissected. "Possibly the most exciting science film to be produced in the U. S." Cecile Starr, *Saturday Review*

Nice Time
Saturday Night in London's Times Square: The empty pleasures, the restless temptations of Piccadilly, caught with compassion by the candid camera.

April 1959

A Program of Folk Art and Americana

Big Bill Blues
The only film record of the recently deceased, legendary American folk singer Big Bill Broonzy, in a moving rendition of four of his blues.

Toccata for Toy Train
Charles Eames, famed designer, fashions an exuberant and curious universe of fantasy from exquisite toys and miniature trains. (George K. Arthur)

Big Business (A tribute to Laurel and Hardy)
A brilliant farce comedy propels two mildly ineffectual Christmas tree vendors (goaded by inexplicable failure) into a cataclysmic attack on property.

3 Films from the Unique Walter Lewisohn Collection

Mississippi Steamboatin'
The folklore of the River: a most colorful era romantically recreated in old river songs and beautifully tinted visual mementos.

Prophet of Taos
D. H. Lawrence's reflections on the wisdom and religion of the American Indians, narrated by Aldous Huxley.

Clipper Ship Days
A robust and delightful view of the temptations of the Barbary Coast. Authentic, contemporary illustrations, miners' songs and sea chanties.

May 1959

Adventures of Asterisk
Brilliant, witty and highly original attempt to explain the philosophy of modern art not by narrative, but by purely visual means. Vibraphone: Lionel Hampton.

Pacific 321
The nervous rhythm of Arthur Honegger's celebrated symphonic poem fully captured in a masterpiece of editing and photography.

The Room
A destitute room, transmuted by the startling magic of stop-motion photography into a luxuriant explosion of color. A new work by D'Avino (*The Big O*).

Integration: The Unsolved Problem

> *Crisis in Levittown*
> Unrehearsed and often startling interviews with residents, filmed during disturbances following arrival of first Negro family.
>
> *Brotherhood of Man*
> Based on Dr. Benedict's "races of Mankind", this triumphant work of film art has already become a contemporary classic.
>
> *The Face of the South*
> A thoroughly fascinating and unorthodox discussion of controversial issues, conducted by a latter-day Will Rogers.

[The Spring 1959 Special Events listing is identical to the one included in the 1958–1959 program announcement from February 25th on. See pp. 351–53.]

❖ ❖ ❖ ❖ ❖ ❖

Archer Winsten, "Rages and Outrages," *New York Post*, 3/2/59

A definitive session on censorship, sponsored and organized by Cinema 16, took place last Tuesday and Wednesday evenings, with results both theoretical and applied. The stated purpose of the show was not merely to repeat the usual arguments against censorship but to explore this particular audience's own limits of acceptance by means of "extreme types of films (some banned) that may offend because of their political, erotic, sacrilegious, or racist content."

Ephraim London, leading law specialist on civil liberties, introduced the program with some remarks touching the important Supreme Court shift of 1952, in which the Constitutional guarantee of freedom of the press, specifically denied to the movies for some 30 years, was at that time regarded as applicable to the movies also. In dealing with the New York State censorship, he cited the law prohibiting among other things any scene that might inspire lust in a normal adult and then permitted himself to question the censorial thinking process that banned, on those grounds, a shot in "The Bicycle Thief" showing a six-year-old boy relieving himself against a wall. The burden of his statement was that all censorship, being a prior restraint, is bad because no one is qualified to administer it properly, and, as a rule only the least qualified to undertake such work.

Then came the picture and the audience trial by celluloid. Sacrilege ("The Miracle"), politics (a union film supposedly pro-Communist), racist ("Birth of a Nation"), and erotic material (possibly "Geography of the Body") failed to drive out a single weakling. Apparently it takes something really basic to torture the strongminded, something like blood and guts. A medical view of a caesarean operation sent weak males tottering into the fresh air. One had to be carried from the prone position he had assumed in the aisle. It is noteworthy that no females collapsed at this film, according to Cinema 16's presiding genius Amos Vogel. The picture, which is prefaced with a warning to the squeamish, "The Blood of the Beasts," Franju's famous documentary of the Paris slaughterhouse, was the one that sped both men and women elsewhere. Practically everyone can eat meat, but few can enjoy the process by which it is procured, or even view this with equanimity.

But the point of censorship to be made is simply this: how remarkably easy it is for anyone who is offended to get up and leave, how little damage is done, how unnecessary censorship is!

Cinema 16 came through with a 10-strike this past week again. I cannot recall a year in which that venerable and indispensable organization has dug up so many items that might otherwise have been unavailable. Its "Lourdes and its Miracles" was made by Georges Rouquier, the genius of "Farrebique." This is not a return to greatness, but it is an exceedingly penetrating look at the dismal sickness abounding at the holy shrine. By word of mouth a story of miraculous cure is given. But to the eye, the sick come out of the blessed water as withered and crippled as they went in. Rouquier is careful to draw no conclusions, but his camera eye is merciless.

The other item, "Little Island," is a 30-minute cartoon riotous with originality and thought. Its designs deal with three small creatures in the grip of Truth, Beauty and Good. How they are affected and what battles they have are something much too delightful to be described in words. This is a short that should reach the theaters when someone can figure out what theater would welcome the truly original and how to fit in the odd length, which is neither a feature nor a short.

Audiences still do want to see good things. That is a cornerstone of belief.

Creators are still making new, fresh films. Those have been seen.

But between the two there are roadblocks, deceptive directions, all kinds of discouragements. If a critic doesn't stand up and fight occasionally, who will?

Reprinted by permission of the *New York Post*.

❖ ❖ ❖ ❖ ❖ ❖

Jonas Mekas, "Movie Journal," *Village Voice*, 9/16/59

For eight years now I have been faithfully attending the screenings of Cinema 16. I have been going even to those programs which I did not particularly care for—just out of a sheer sense of solidarity. For I have always felt—and feel so today—that Cinema 16 is providing a most useful service to all those who care for cinema. It has served continuously as an antidote to the boredom of commercial cinema—a place where you can see some of the best dramatic films from all over the world, and, in uncensored versions, such works as Mahaty's ECSTASY, Eisenstein's STRIKE, Bunuel's EL, or the modern Japanese movies.

Open to Experiment

Its most important aspect, however, is that Cinema 16 is a place where the young experimentalists and film poets can still introduce their work to the general public, even at a time when people laugh at any sensitive attempt at poetry. While most of the other film societies and movie theaters stick to the accepted, the recognized, the official, Cinema 16 has always been open to experiment, to the breaking of frontiers, at times even to the point of anti-cinema (as in the many psychiatric films shown there). This, then, might be my credo: I believe in Cinema 16 because it trickles little drops of uncomfortable poison into the fat and plump veins of our commercial cinema; because it never states or accepts what cinema is or what it should be; because with all due respect to the dead, to the past, it always manages to keep one foot in the cradle. So I accept Cinema 16 as my Sunday-morning and Wednesday-evening church.

This year Cinema 16 continues its untraditional tradition. For all those to whom cinema is full of constant excitement, this season has many surprises. The three Polish movies, EVA WANTS TO SLEEP (a political satire), EROICA (a satire of heroism), and THE LAST DAY OF SUMMER (a tender love story), are worth that excitement alone. Then there is Bunuel's savage parody of the psychological murder drama, THE CRIMINAL LIFE OF ARCHIBALDO DE LA CRUZ; Tod Browning's horror classic, THE FREAKS; and the world premiere of two new films, John Cassavetes' long awaited SHADOWS, and PULL MY DAISY, by Alfred Leslie, Robert Frank, and Jack Kerouac. You will also see the controversial CRY OF JAZZ (with a discussion evening on jazz); the 1959 Creative Film Foundation Award winners; the disturbing documentary LIGHT FOR JOHN; more of the Brussels Film Festival winners, etc., etc. (Yearly subscription for 16 screenings is $15.50. For information write to Cinema 16, 175 Lexington Avenue, New York, N. Y.)

If you look for cinema in New York, you have only two choices today: Ingmar Bergman and Cinema 16...

Reprinted by permission of *The Village Voice*.

✦ ✦ ✦ ✦ ✦ ✦

Program Announcement: Fall 1959/Spring 1960

October 1959

End of Innocence
One of the major surprises of the 1958 Cannes International Film Festival, Leopoldo Nilsson's controversial Argentinian prizewinner offers a delicate psychological exploration of a young girl's sensual awakening in the stifling puritanical milieu of aristocratic Buenos Aires society in the 'twenties. Here, in a strange, almost medieval atmosphere of sexual repression and dogmatic religiosity, Anna, confused and turbulent in her transition from girl to woman, becomes the victim of a disastrous seduction by an older man, himself the victim of environment and tradition. Delicate yet corrosive, with a romantic density seldom encountered in the cinema, this is a subtle work of psychological insight and social criticism. Shown by courtesy of Kingsley International Pictures.

"An atmosphere of prurience and moral decay is evoked with such authority as to leave no doubt of a rare and uncompromising talent."—*London Times*

Blue Jeans
On the beaches of Cannes, a vivacious French short—with a very American title—accompanies two youths on Vespas in a never-ending search for girls "without middle-class prejudices." The pretty girls in bikinis, with Bardot hairdos, the dubious Don Juans in James Dean sweatshirts, provide a charming view of adolescent awkwardness, verve—and loneliness. South American rock-and-roll music.

Illustration 72. Program announcement, fall 1959/spring 1960 season.

November 1959

Eva Wants to Sleep
In a strange city dominated by Keystone Cops and wicked crooks, guileless Eva, fresh from the provinces, looks for a place to sleep in a bizarre, night-long search. This wild and daring social satire from Poland—filled with the irreverence of Rene Clair, the abandon of the Marx Brothers—propels safe-crackers, prostitutes, thugs, bureaucrats and corrupt police through a hilarious series of misadventures to an explosive climax, as it joyfully ridicules authority, planning, red tape and shortcomings of an over-controlled life. A wonderfully absurd mixture of satire, slapstick, fantasy and surrealism.

"Methods of Mack Sennet applied to a serious theme." *Manchester Guardian*

Grand Prix, San Sebastian and Edinburgh International Film Festival. A Film Polski Production by Tadeusz Chmielewski. Complete with English titles.

Virtually unknown here, the Polish cinema over the past three years achieved international acclaim and numerous festival awards with films of unusual artistry, dealing courageously with social issues and utilizing the full resources of modern art. This is Program 1 of a three-program Festival of Polish Films, organized with the University of California and Polish State Film Company.

December 1959

The Last Day of Summer
Grand Prix, Venice International Film Festival 1958. On a deserted and wildly beautiful beach, a man and a woman, haunted by the experience of war and terror, find love, and then despair, in an almost intolerably poignant, profoundly humanistic work. Beautifully photographed, this haunting love story moves on the highest levels of cinema art, as it offers a symbolic and ultimately despairing comment on humanity at the end of the road. A Film Polski Production by Tadeusz Konwicki and Jan Laskowski.

"One of the most moving, most compassionate, most humanly understanding works I have seen in a long time. This is a whole film." Paul Rotha

Un Autre Monde
This official French entry at the major 1959 International Film Festivals is visually one of the most beautiful films ever shown at Cinema 16: A stunning revelation of a secret world of unbelievable beauty and mysterious landscapes. The creator of this film is light; its protagonists: the interior structures of crystallizing chemicals in extraordinary full-color magnification.

Fable for Friendship
Told as a puzzle, this is a highly sophisticated and imaginative attempt to utilize the techniques of modern art for a "message" film. Winner of the International Unesco Competition, by the renowned Czech animator Jiri Trnka.

January 1960

The Seven Bridges of Koenigsberg
simply cannot be crossed in one continuous walk, said Swiss mathematician Euler in his famed theorem... and this charming, irreverent film proves why.

The Captive Cinema
What our TV could do but doesn't: Fascinating, unrehearsed British TV interviews—'captive films', made for a single showing—with all the immediacy and impact of real people in their true surroundings: in a sewer, a sewerman in laughing control of his kingdom; in a Gypsy camp, bitterness and pride; in Robert Morley's dressing room, a satire on "This Is Your Life"; in a dustman's condemned flat, an unexpected revelation. First American showing of this historic National Film Theatre program in London also includes hilarious satire on American tourists, and *Fan Fever*, merciless, surprising interviews of promoters, psychiatrists, passionate girls and less passionate parents.

The World of the Microbes: In Quest of the Tubercle Bacilli
Grand Prix, 1958 Venice International Film Festival. Possibly the most sensational film of the season, this eerie masterpiece easily surpasses Hollywood's science fiction thrillers in tension and horror. Unique full color, time-lapse motion pictures taken under an electron microscope at 12,000 magnification, record unbelievable seventy hour struggle between tubercle bacillus and white blood corpuscles. A Tokyo Cinema Production by Tensor Onuma.

March 1960

Khajurajo
Deification of beauty and sex; humanization of the Gods; destruction of aesthetic barriers characterize the sublime, grotesque, erotic and massive scultpures and imagery of Khajurajo, 10th Century capital of the great Hindu kings. Five of the unsurpassed temples in this empty city of the Gods are scrutinized in a beautifully photographed comment on Buddhist philosophy.

All My Babies
Robert Flaherty Award: a milestone of cinema art, George Stoney's legendary masterpiece, profoundly humanistic, deeply moving, portrays the wonder and pain of childbirth in unforgettable images, as it accompanies a Negro midwife in the deep South. Center for Mass Communication, Columbia University Press. "An enobling human experience. Since it includes the actual delivery of a baby, it cannot be shown except on a carefully restricted basis; but a great film has been made, ready to be seen when the public is ready to see it on a mature basis." Cecile Starr, *Saturday Review*

A Night at the Peking Opera
A stunning and memorable visit to one of the world's greatest spectacles: a flamboyant blend of exquisite pantomime, circus, comedy, ballet and acrobatics, resplendent with exotic costumes, masks and hypnotic music.

Illustration 73. *All My Babies* (1952) by George Stoney. Courtesy Museum of Modern Art Film Stills Archive.

SPECIAL EVENTS 1959/1960

November 11

The Cinema of Improvisation

> *Shadows*
> The most important American independent film of the decade, already a legend: John Cassavetes' pulsating revelation of the demi-world of the night people; floaters, chicks, jazz musicians and hipsters in the neon-lit desert of Times Square. Overpowering in its immediacy, this brilliant return to improvisation in the cinema etches a compassionate, violent portrayal of pick-ups and brawls, loneliness, casual affairs and search for identity. Notably adult treatment of an interracial love story reveals Negroes not as liberal cliches but as human beings in all their complexities.
>
> Winner of Film Culture's Independent Film Award.
>
> *Pull My Daisy*
> Jack Kerouac, Robert Frank and Alfred Leslie's brilliant tragi-comedy, a new direction in film making, complies with James Agee's request for "works of pure fiction, played against, into, and in collaboration with unrehearsed reality." With Kerouac's spontaneous dialog, Allen Ginsberg's and Gregory Corso's performances, it evokes an image of a heroic and bedraggled circle.

December 2

Eroica
In two scathing episodes of high psychological sophistication, a remarkably defiant work from Poland sardonically debunks the concept of heroism: the first deprives the Warsaw rebellion of sentimentality in a macabre tale of a con man who becomes a hero in spite of himself; the second deals with Polish prisoners in a Nazi camp who join their oppressors in ironic partnership to maintain a false myth so as not to destroy their own morale. The humanism of this revealing post-Stalinist work transcends national boundaries.

Also: a selection of outstanding Polish shorts.
Program 3 in a Festival of Contemporary Polish Films.

January 6

The 1959 Creative Film Award Winners
selected by a distinguished jury; co-sponsored by Creative Film Foundation

> *Have I Told You Lately That I Love You*
> Dehumanization indicted (Hanisch)
>
> *Dance Chromatic*
> Astonishing fusion of dance and paintings (Emshwiller)
>
> *Bridges-Go-Round*
> Sensuous patterns of bridges in space (Clarke)

Handwritten
A sparkling tour-de-force in vertical montage (Boltenhouse)

Dwightiana
Frivolous motion study made to entertain a friend (Mencken)

The City
A disquieting message of pessimism (Ramsbott)

The Rose Window
Bouncy, fast, colorful; a sumptuous experiment (Rubington)

January 27

Horror In The Cinema: *Freaks*
Rare showing of Hollywood's most famous "film noir", one of the most unusual works in the history of the cinema: Tod Browning's hallucinatory collection of human monsters in a macabre and bizarre tale with surrealist overtones.

Speaker: Mr. James Card, Curator of Motion Pictures, Georges Eastman house.

"This gem stands in a class by itself as a venture into the grisly and the grotesque." *The New Yorker.*

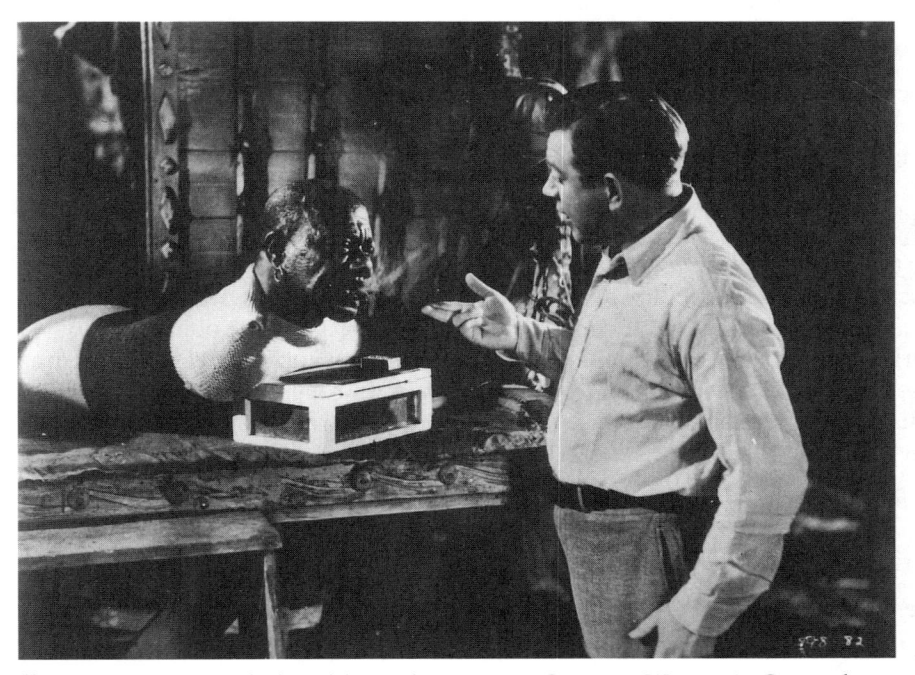

Illustration 74. *Freaks* (1932) by Tod Browning. Courtesy Wisconsin Center for Film and Theater Research.

February 10

The Best in Scientific Films

Living in a Reversed World
Fascinating psychological experiments with subjects who for several weeks wear glasses reversing right and left.

Studies in Human Fertility
Scientific investigation of relative merits of various contraceptive practices and some of the newer techniques.

Psychotic Illness in Childhood
Father's movies of baby become unique record of origins of her psychosis 10 years later. London Institute of Psychiatry.

Seifriz on Proplasm
Highest Award, Edinburgh International Film Festival. Protoplasm is torn, gassed, poisoned, electrocuted and dissected.

February 24

The Cry of Jazz
The Negro talks back: extremist and openly provocative, the most controversial film of the season (made by young Negro intellectuals in Chicago) explodes in a series of passionate outbursts regarding the death of jazz at the hands of the Whites and the suffering of the Negroes in America.

Also 3 *Pickup Men for Herrick,* film by the young Negro director Melvin Van.

Discussion: James Baldwin, distinguished Negro author; Marshall Stearns, Professor, Hunter College, President, Institute of Jazz Studies; Mark Kennedy, scenarist of film; Nat Hentoff, Scope of Jazz, WBAI, Co-editor, *The Jazz Review.*

May 18

The Criminal Life of Archibaldo de La Cruz
Luis Bunuel, unquestionably one of the greatest directors of our day, continues his remarkable investigation of psycho-sexual aberrations in one of his most daring works: a brilliant and uniquely disturbing satire on psychological murder dramas, based on the "confessions" of a would-be mass murderer, complete with sex, sadism and a sardonic "happy end" a la Bunuel. The sensation of Paris and London in its first American presentation.

"A macabre comedy, loaded with shock portions and erotic symbolism." *Variety*

April 20

The Victim Is Man

Cartier-Bresson's "Le Retour"
The greatest human document to come out of the war; an almost intolerably moving film by the master still-photographer.

The Skilled Worker
A man defeated by automation.

It is Good To Live
Unprecedented Japanese film record of Hiroshima survivors examines, a decade later, their lives and camaraderie. U. S. premiere.

Light For John
Documentary of mentally retarded newsboy, told by his mother.

March 30

Best Brussels Festival Experimentals (2)

Cine Sumac
Disastrous journey of an electronic gremlin; a satire (Dasque)

Autumn Spectrum
Sensuous reflections in Amsterdam canals (Hirsh)

Flesh of Morning
Daring evocation of sexual fantasy and self-love (Brakhage)

Cats Et Al
Outrageous visual assaults by ultra-rapid montage (Breer)

Etude
Electic current produces surprise on oscilloscope (Puttemans/Jespers)

Song of Richepin
Savage, erotic surrealist shocker from Mexico (Toussaint)

Prelude
Ballet dancers pause in a darkened theatre; a dream moment (Vesely)

✦ ✦ ✦ ✦ ✦ ✦

Conversation with Ed Emshwiller, 1/4/85

Ed Emshwiller: In those early days, Vogel was, along with Maya Deren, the real champion of off-beat films; and for awhile in the fifties Cinema 16 was the only place in New York you could find something other than Hollywood movies. I was a regular subscriber year after year. I first heard about Cinema 16 in 1951 when I was living in the city. Then I moved out to Long Island, but I came in religiously on Wednesday nights to Cinema 16. You bought a season subscription and if you were like me, if you paid for it, you wanted to go.

I think in the end that's what killed Cinema 16. Toward the end there were a number theaters—the Bleecker Street, the New Yorker, and so forth—showing a variety of work, including some of the kinds of things that in the late forties and early fifties you could only get from Amos. And you didn't have to subscribe for a whole year. Enough of a taste developed, partly *because* of Cinema 16, that exhibitors were encouraged to start importing and showing a wider variety of movies. So Amos's own success was his downfall. Of course, I'm speaking as an outsider, but that's how it seemed.

He did support types of film that an individual could make. During the fifties I did what I called "doodles." I would go to Cinema 16 and see some animation or some surrealist movie, and I would go home and try the same thing. Later on, I decided I was going to make a real movie. I took it to Amos and said I'd like this to be considered for one of the annual experimental awards he and Maya Deren did. The film was considered by the group, and it got the top award [Emshwiller's *Dance Chromatic* (1959) was presented in a January, 1960 program of Creative Film Foundation Award-winning films]. I was so delighted: it just started me.

I had been led to filmmaking through attendance at Cinema 16, though earlier I had been an art student in Paris, and later at a college in Michigan, where I belonged to cine clubs. But none of them seemed to have the programming strength Vogel had. He was a master programmer. Sometimes you'd be bored out of your skull and sometimes you'd never seen anything like it, but each time you went to Cinema 16 was an *adventure.* It was the *uncertainty* I liked so much.

Scott MacDonald: One of the things that's really startling now, when you go through the Cinema 16 materials, is the numbers of people that came to screenings. Do you have a memory of the mood of those events?

Emshwiller: Oh yeah! There was always a huge crowd and a lot of excitement. I remember Vogel telling me one time that he could predict how audiences at the various screenings would respond to things. There was a seven o'clock crowd and a nine o'clock crowd on Wednesday nights, and then there was the eleven o'clock crowd on Sunday mornings. Each crowd had its own personality. Even though he'd be showing the same program, the seven o'clock crowd, who went to Cinema 16 right from work (they might have a drink first), had a very different response than the nine o'clock crowd, who would have had supper first. Of course, the thing about a theater is that when you get a lot of people together, mob psychology plays a big role.

MacDonald: One of the unusual things about Cinema 16 is that it functioned in a public sphere to a degree that independent film exhibition now doesn't. It's hard to imagine the experience of seeing experimental films with a thousand people. Do you remember particular programs as being especially memorable?

Emshwiller: I do recall one evening that struck me as extraordinary. Amos, who's an Austrian Jew, presented a Nazi propaganda film that showed Jews as rats, deformed idiots, degenerates, as if to say: "These people *should be* exterminated." It was made at the height of the Final Solution type of thinking [In November 1958 Vogel showed Fritz Hippler's *The Eternal Jew* (1940)] It was such hideous propaganda that you had to wonder whether by showing these films you were encouraging socially undesirable behavior. I thought it was a terrific program because you didn't leave feeling, "Oh sure, I'm against censorship": you really were conflicted about where one draws the line. That kind of programming had educational value: pat attitudes were challenged, and without anybody preaching—just by showing films and asking the question.

And I always liked the annual Creative Film Awards night, because it centered on the kind of movies that I personally was most interested in making.

MacDonald: When Cinema 16 ended, did the ending seem abrupt, or could you feel it coming during the last year or two?

Emshwiller: It was petering out—that's my sense of it.

MacDonald: Near the end of Cinema 16, there was a big rift, or what now looks in retrospect like a rift, between Amos and the New American Cinema Group.

Emshwiller: Oh boy, I'll say! It was happening when I first came on the scene. I think that in many cases it really didn't have much to do with art, though the argument took place in the guise of art. There were constant ego battles. I wrote a piece (it was published in *Filmmakers' Newsletter*) because I was frustrated about the tendency of experimental filmmakers and others in our small field to stab one another in the back. We were in a ghetto, beating one another up, and I thought we ought to direct that energy to the outside. Someone took me aside after I wrote that letter and said, "Ed, don't be naive. Artists have always been the greatest enemies of other artists."

What I sense happened was that when Vogel said, "I will show *this* film of yours, but I won't show *that* one," some of the filmmakers were offended. They felt, "Who is this guy to decide which of my works is of value and should be shown?" A real battle seemed to take place. I was very unhappy with it myself. I felt a great sense of obligation and loyalty to Vogel for all he had done for me.

✦ ✦ ✦ ✦ ✦ ✦

Letter to John Cassavetes from Amos Vogel, 11/17/59

November 17, 1959

Mr. John Cassavetes
13630 Sunset Blvd.
Pacific Palisades, Calif.

Dear John Cassavetes:

It is very unfortunate that you were unable to be present at our showing. The reception of your film exceeded all expectations: the event, far from merely being an excellent showing of an excellent film, turned into a personal and artistic triumph for you, the dimensions of which were truly astonishing. The house was packed for all performances; a large number of leading critics and film specialists were present, too numerous to mention (for example, Paddy Chayefsky, Kenneth Tynan of the New Yorker, Professor Meyer Schapiro, Arthur Knight, and many others); the audience was "with" the film throughout, and at the end, there was a long and pronounced ovation that continued for a longer time than I have witnessed at Cinema 16 in many a year.

Most of the cast were present, several of your collaborators; they can tell you in greater detail what a tremendous success the screening was.

The immediate result, of course, was that very strong interest was evinced in the film by several of the commercial distribution firms here; Cassel must have told you about this; suffice it to say that I had lengthy telephone conversations with both Kingsley, whose interest was rekindled by the reception; and also with Irving Shapiro of Films Around the World, one of the largest distributors in the country, who was particularly interested in the foreign rights.

Thus, as expected, the screening may well lead to a commercial release of the film, which it so richly deserves.

Two days prior to the showing, Gideon Bachmann informed me of Louis Malle's interest in seeing the film and I arranged, at my expense, for a 35mm screening which Seymour attended. Malle is the director of THE LOVERS, one of the foremost leaders of the French Young Wave; a man who today is "on top" in the French industry and can do anything he wants. He was extremely impressed and enthusiastic and suggested that the film be sent to Europe and that he would personally intervene in terms of distribution. Cassel knows about this and should follow it through. It is a wonderful contact for you.

I am enclosing the payment as per our agreement. I would appreciate your keeping the amount of the rental in confidence, since it is much higher than what we usually pay, and was due entirely to the nature and quality of the film.

There remains a serious problem, of which you already know. I refer to the fact that a number of people—including Jonas Mekas and Gideon Bachmann—feel that the second version, as shown by us, is totally inferior and a 'commercial compromise.' I have spent hours with them, attempting to convince them that they are wrong. Jonas intended to make a public attack on the film at our showing, but I convinced him to first write you, since he also plans to write in SIGHT AND SOUND and elsewhere about the new version.

There now does exist a controversy in New York regarding the film, and a confusion as to what is the "proper" version. I have discussed this with Cassel and assume he has told you about it. I cannot discuss it in detail in a letter, except to say that you must have a very clear-cut stand on the issue, as shown, for example, in your decision to send this new version to the various festivals and to have this be the version that will be distributed.

You will further confuse the issue, were you to decide to permit the earlier version to be shown. The result will be that you will compete with yourself and create a confusion in people's mind, so that they will think there are two SHADOWS in existence.

For example, it is now being stated by certain people that Kingsley financed the new version; that it was done in accord with his wishes, and that thus it constitutes a commercial "betrayal." You and I know that Kinsley stepped out of the deal at a very stage; and that, in fact, the changes are due to your desire to strengthen the film, not to commercially compromise it.

Nevertheless, you will have to take a very strong stand, it seems to me, in favor of the new version being "the" film. I realize that this is none of my business; I am simply giving you my opinion; in fact, I do not wish to become involved in this matter and prefer my name be kept out of it completely especially since the decision rests entirely with you. But my opinion stands.

I would like to hear from you as to how you intend to handle this problem. My own position is clear; I showed this version both because I knew that this was "the film" as far you and your coproducers were concerned; and because I personally feel, that while both versions have strong points and weaknesses, the new one is the better one for reasons too complex to discuss in a letter.

Illustration 75. *Shadows* (1959) by John Cassavetes. Courtesy Museum of Modern Art Film Stills Archive.

I think it is important for you to clarify Kingsley's role in all this to people like Jonas, as well as possible in public statements, say, in SIGHT AND SOUND, should Jonas come out with a statement in that magazine. This will be especially important if Kingsley actually decides to become the distributor (or Columbia).

I also would like you to let me know what decisions were made as regards the distribution; the reason being that I will be in Europe this spring, both as a juror at an International Film Festival (with John Grierson) as well as to lecture with outstanding American films at film museums and film societies in Western Europe. I may have some interesting plans regarding your film, which I would like to discuss further with you as soon as I hear from you;—plans which would further contribute to the commercial success of the film.

In any event, it would be essential to subtitle the film as soon as possible in at least one foreign language (preferably French).

Please let me hear from you at your early convenience.

Again, my thanks and gratitude for permitting me to introduce this outstanding film to audiences and critics here. You have made a film that will live a very long time: a permanent contribution to film history and film art.

With best personal regards,

Amos Vogel
Executive Secretary

[*In paragraph 7 Vogel mentions a controversy over the two versions of* Shadows. *Jonas Mekas's version of the controversy is reprinted in* Movie Journal *(New York: Collier, 1972), pp. 10–11.]*

✦ ✦ ✦ ✦ ✦ ✦

Letter to John Cassavetes from Amos Vogel, 11/20/59

November 20, 1959

Mr. John Cassavetes
13630 Sunset Blvd.
Pacific Palisades, Cal.

Dear John Cassavetes:

Despite the fact that Jonas Mekas promised me not to write anything about the film until after having spoken to you, you will see by the enclosed that he rushed into print with his first attack on the film.

By referring to a "commercialized version," "in no way to be confused with the original," which was shown at Cinema 16, and then urging people to see the presumably "un-commercialized" version elsewhere, he has compounded the confusion which I warned you would exist if two versions of what is only one film continue to circulate.

It is clearer now than ever that the "other version" should never have been publicized and certainly should not continue to circulate.

Retroactively, he cheapens our showing and your artistic integrity. While as a critic he has a perfect right to his opinion, we are both harmed by this.

For this reason, I have already sent a strong letter to Village Voice and urge you to immediately send them a strong statement of your own, upholding the version shown as "the film." Perhaps it would be good to even wire them, asking them to be sure to print your statement.

My letter to the Village Voice reads as follows:

"In response to Jonas Mekas' statements in his November 18th column regarding Shadows, permit me to state Cinema 16's position:

1. Last year, John Cassavetes, the director of the film, privately showed it to a number of people, was dissatisfied and reshot some of it and then arranged for a Cinema 16 premiere of the film as finally completed to his own satisfaction.

2. I am in full agreement with John Cassavetes about this final version. I consider it an improvement in terms of clarify and character motivation. The plot, ideology and mood of the film remain the same.

3. It is one thing to deplore the mutilation of Stroheim's "Greed" at the hands of a third party; it is another thing to attack the artist for himself attempting to improve upon a film to the best of his ability.

Mekas has not sufficiently pondered the fact that the same C 16 audience which was perceptive and sophisticated enough to fully respond to "Pull My Daisy" (which Mekas considers a subtle, great but difficult film), then proceeded to accord "Shadows" a tumultuous ovation.

It saddens me that in all this Mekas has failed to take into account the past history of Cinema 16 and what it stands for. For 13 years, Cinema 16 has been fighting the battle of the commercially unprofitable, the untried and experimental, the new and controversial.

Jonas himself refers to his "unrealistic anger" about the film. He is right. Unrealistic it is."

I had hoped to discuss this letter with you before sending it and to perhaps have you co-sign it. However, I was unable to reach you by phone prior to their printer's deadline.

In any case, it would not be logical for me to carry the ball in this matter, since what is being attacked, essentially, is more your film than my showing.

I hope you will not underestimate the importance of your making a statement regarding this matter.

Please let me know what you plan to do; if necessary, please phone me.

Sincerely,

Amos Vogel

✦ ✦ ✦ ✦ ✦ ✦

Letter to Amos Vogel from John Cassavetes, 1/19/60

January 19, 1960

Mr. Amos Vogel
175 Lexington Avenue
New York 16, New York

Dear Amos:

Not being a terribly organized fellow and not being terribly proud of it, but simply wishing to underline the importance of your interest in "Shadows," I would like to thank you for your continued support. I received several offers for festivals for the picture which were very generous to say the least. Your letters regarding the reception that the film received at Cinema 16, along with the many that were sent to me because of the screening, certainly helped to fill the expectations that we all had for the film when we originally started.

Due to a misunderstanding that has arisen between Dave Horne and myself regarding his status in the film, I feel that I am unable at this time to send the picture anywhere, and therefore, it is at present in limbo. However, I screened "Shadows" for Cecil Smith, who is international editor of the Los Angeles Times in California, and he was heartily in favor of the film and deeply moved by its intention. He will have a piece on "Shadows" appearing in the Times (Los Angeles, that is) on January 24th. I will get copies of the article and send them to you.

Albert Johnson of the Film Quarterly Magazine of the University of California, who is the American correspondent of the British Quarterly, Sight and Sound, is doing a review in the Quarterly out March 1st and also doing an article in Sight and Sound mainly concerned with "Shadows." On May 4th, I would like to show "Shadows" as part of a campus lecture program. I am to call him to give him more information and I will not forget to send you copies of his comments.

You mentioned that Louis Malle had seen "Shadows" and stated that he would be helpful in the French distribution of the picture. Could you enlighten me further as to that conversation, as Seymour Castle at times is quite uncommunicative. There have been numerous requests in California for a screening and I am in a quandary as to how to proceed. I know that you are interested in "Shadows" and I certainly would appreciate your advice as to how to best distribute the picture in a non-commercial way that would benefit the purposes of experimental film.

As to the festivals and their interest, since we have been invited by some 10, namely, Vancouver, West German, Melbourne, Toronto, San Francisco, and several lesser festivals, I would like your opinion as to the possibilities of gaining entry into a festival such as Venice or Cannes. I feel very much, and have always felt, that the Venice Film Festival was far and above the most extraordinary. I feel also that this film would have the greatest empathy with the judges at Venice, since "Shadows" contains, in my opinion, much of that neo realistic influence.

Please advise me as to your feelings on the subject and thank you once more for your continued interest.

Sincerely,

[hw] John Cassavetes

John Cassavetes

Reprinted by permission of Gena Rowlands Cassavetes.

✦ ✦ ✦ ✦ ✦ ✦

Program Announcement: Spring 1960

March, 1960

Khajurajo
Deification of beauty and sex; humanization of the Gods; destruction of aesthetic barriers characterize the sublime, grotesque, erotic and massive scultpures and imagery of Khajurajo, 10th Century capital of the great Hindu kings. Five of the unsurpassed temples in this empty city of the Gods are scrutinized in a beautifully photographed comment on Buddhist philosophy.

All My Babies
Robert Flaherty Award: a milestone of cinema art, George Stoney's legendary masterpiece, profoundly humanistic, deeply moving, portrays the wonder and pain of childbirth in unforgettable images, as it accompanies a Negro midwife in the deep South. Center for Mass Communication, Columbia University Press.

"An enobling human experience. Since it includes the actual delivery of a baby, it cannot be shown except on a carefully restricted basis; but a great film has been made, ready to be seen when the public is ready to see it on a mature basis." Cecile Starr, *Saturday Review*

A Night at the Peking Opera
A stunning and memorable visit to one of the world's greatest spectacles: a flamboyant blend of exquisite pantomime, circus, comedy, ballet and acrobatics, resplendent with exotic costumes, masks and hypnotic music.

April 1960

Side Street Story
Cannes International Film Festival Prizewinner: This sophisticated comedy from Italy—a blend of sardonic humor and philosophical sadness—satirizes the unending victimization (and resilience) of the "little man" under successive regimes ranging from Mussolini to the German and Western occupation. Richly human and colorful, it examines in humorous episodes the cynicism of the rulers, the deceits of the ruled, illicit sex, illicit trade, and survival through hilarious elasticity. Farcical and wistful in turn, it offers the Chaplinesque sadness of de Filippo, the eloquent wordlessness of Toto (Italy's top comedians) and surpasses the more famous neo-realist films in its sophisticated ambiguities and lack of sentimentality.

"An excellent, strikingly original, richly ironic and vital picture! It is in its rejection of trite story lines and conclusions that the film most clearly defines its unique contributions." Archer Winsten, *New York Post*

Music Studio: Harry Partch
Abandoning conventional music and musical instruments, one of this generation's most original and iconoclastic artists invents his own instruments and music annotation (43-tone-to-the-octave) and in this first study (by Madeline Tourtelot) plays his startling and wondrous compositions on Cloud Chamber Bowls, Diamond Marimba, Boo, Harmonic Canons and Surrogate Kithara.

May 1960

Midvinterblot
A ritual of human sacrifice in primeval Sweden, somber and mysterious. A brilliant piece of imaginative anthropology by Sweden's eminent Gosta Werner.

Radha and Krishna
Highest Award, 1959 San Francisco International Film Festival. A delicate Indian legend evokes the tender love of the beautiful milkmaid and the cowherd God, the divine lover, in the magnificent color miniatures of the Pahari painters.

Folkdances of India
This spectacular and sumptuous panorama, one of the season's most beautiful films, overwhelms the Westerner with riotous colors, sensuous rhythms, the beauty of men and women, the unbelievable multiplicity of races, faces and landscapes. Original folk dances of Rajastan, Manipur, Koli, Punjab, Kerala, Assam, Darjeeling are exuberantly performed in their natural surroundings.

Metrographic
Gulls, gladiators, cocks, suns and mysterious strangers: a charmingly cryptic improvisation, dreamt by the Swiss Vittorio Speich in Holland.

Les Bain de Mer
A hilarious, pitiless, candid satire, directed by Tati's gagwriter Jean L'Hote.

[The Spring 1960 Special Events listing includes The Cry of Jazz *(February 24),* "Screening of 1960 Flaherty Award Winners" *(March 16),* "Best Brussels Festival Experimentals (2)" *(March 30),* "The Victim as Man" *(April 20), and* The Criminal Life of Archibaldo de la Cruz *(May 18). See 1959–1960 program announcement for relevant descriptions.]*

❖ ❖ ❖ ❖ ❖ ❖

Program Announcement: Fall 1960/Spring 1961

October 1960

She Done Him Wrong
Rare opportunity to see the complete version of Mae West's controversial comedy that led to the establishment of the Hollywood Code. With violet eyes, swaying hips, platinum coiffure, the Great American Institution—a puritanical country's image of impermissible eroticism—triumphantly slinks through a robust double entendre comedy, replete with racy songs, white slavery, Cary Grant as preacher, swan beds, and melodrama. Based on Miss West's notorious 'Diamond Lil', it provides a first-rate example of her style (including her tendentious delivery of innocuous songs) and totally destroyed Hollywood's confession-tale heroine in its cynical view of life and lust.

"It's not the men in my life that worry me, it's the life in my men." Mae West

How to Marry a Princess
This flamboyant and hilarious parody of a medieval fairytale, an unexpected surprise from Rumania, created a sensation at the major 1960 Film Festivals. Pre-release showing by special arrangement with George K. Arthur.

A Place in the Sun
Brilliant achievement from Czechoslovakia—a multiple international prize winner—employs relentless rhythm, delightful humor and primitive visual symbols to convey a most complex message. Pre-release showing by special arrangement with George K. Arthur.

Illustration 76. Program announcement, fall 1960/spring 1961.

November 1960

A Festival of International Prizewinners from France, presented in cooperation with Unifrance.

Simenon
This absorbing first documentary of the famed novelist alternates scenes of his unorthodox, compulsive work habits with filmed sequences of the novel he is writing, enacted by Michael Simon and others.

Lovers and Clowns
An enchanting pantomime, evoked by Brassai, one of the world's leading photographers. A George K. Arthur release.

Journey to Boscavia
The gentle adventures of mythical Boscavian soldiery, satirized by renowned French cartoonist Bosc (*New Yorker, Punch*)

Dragon of Komodo
On an inaccessible island, a terrifying prehistoric monster in discovered is solitude and hunger in a tense and wordless film.

Forbidden Bullfight
The terror and beauty of the 'corrida' evoked in an hallucinatory film poem.

The Struggle against the Frost
Completely mad, semi-surrealist parody by Frances's most original animator. A splendid, nonsensical farce.

December 1960

The Criminal Life of Archibaldo de La Cruz
Luis Bunuel, one of the greatest directors of our day, continues his investigation of psycho-sexual aberrations and false moral values in one of his most daring works: a uniquely disturbing satire on psychological murder dramas, based on the 'confessions' of a would-be mass murderer, complete with sex, sadism and a sardonic 'happy ending'. The sensation of Paris and London, this black comedy is one of the strangest ever released by a commercial studio. Ridiculing both its characters and its audience, the film's sophisticated ambiguities and serio-comic morbidity have so far prevented its commercial release: its critical fame, however, is already assured.

"A macabre comedy, loaded with shock portions and erotic symbolism, carried out with a successful tongue-in-cheek attitude." *Variety*

American premiere of subtitled version, prepared by Mr. Bunuel for Cinema 16.

The Murderers of Anne Frank
Controversial East German documentary featurette, banned in several countries, proclaims—by means of sensational hidden camera sequences and documents—that Anne Frank's murderers are prospering in West Germany today.

January 1961

A Festival of International Prizewinners from Germany, in cooperation with Federation of German Film Producers.

Fashion in the City
Slick, erotic, stylish, filled with beautiful girls; the magic world of fashion as pretext for stunning avant-garde pyrotechnics.

Who Wants to Be a Soldier?
A symptomatic, anti-militarist plea.

Carl Orff: Music for Children
Exciting experiment in progressive education—creative self-realization through free rhythm and melodic improvisation—moves hypnotically on the level of subconscious revelation.

The Magic Tape
Six 1960 International Awards; a dazzling film achievement offers constant visual excitement and startling experimental techniques.

Patience
Erotic 'Kitsch' postcards, satirically used, offer self-critique of German conformism and petty bourgeois values.

Salinas
Harvest of salt: Incisive, almost lyrical film of severe classic beauty and form; a model of creative film making.

Rhythm of the Port
Restless tour-de-force of realistic images in rhythmic montage concentrates movement, color and sound into 'visual music.'

Key Around the Neck
A critique of the Swedish welfare state, debatable, stimulating and, for America, disquieting.

March 1961

Butterflies Do Not Live Here
A poignant and harrowing study of the paintings and poems of Jewish children in the Terecin concentration camp, produced in illegal art classes during their imprisonment and accidentally recovered after the war, years after their youthful creators had perished in the gas chambers. An authentic document of our age. A Rembrandt Films release.

The Council of the Gods
This hard-hitting propaganda film, generally considered East Germany's most important production to date, provides a memorable glimpse into Communist mentality and world view, as it probes in compelling plot developments the moral and human dilemmas of a German scientist under Hitler and the Occupation; raises the question of individual responsibility; and indicts German Big Business for its collaboration with Hitler and America. Despite its propagandistic one-sidedness, the film manages to raise disquieting questions.

Complete with English subtitles. A DEFA production by Kurt Maetzig, based on a story by the noted German author Friedrich Wolf. Music by Hans Eisler.

SPECIAL EVENTS 1960/1961

November 9

Bed and Sofa
Alexander Room's legendary 'lost' masterpiece of the European film, cited in all histories of the cinema, in one of its rare showings. A penetrating and forthright study of unconventional sexual mores in early Soviet Russia, set against the background of the housing shortage. Because of its subject matter, this film suffered from even more restricted distribution than other Soviet films. "An unequalled instance of pure psychological and intimate representation of human character." Rotha, *The Film Till Now*

December 7

Festival of French Prizewinners: Program 2

The Statues Also Die
First opportunity to view Alan Resnais' (*Hiroshima, Mon Amour*) long-banned documentary of the achievements and the degradation, under colonialism, of African Negro art. Exclusive U. S. presentation.

Ballade Chromo
Two children transported into the exotic world of 19th Century lithographs and then into Miro's iridescent universe.

Diagnostic CIV
Unbelievable complexity of a modern open-heart operation, seen as profoundly human achievement. A work of film art.

The Forgotten Man
Acute and often shocking ethnographic study does not flinch in its uncompromising portrayal of Stone Age men in our time.

My Jeanette and My Friends
Folksongs frame warm vignette of lives, loves and celebrations of poor impoverished peasants working in mines near Avignon.

January 25

The 1960 Creative Film Award Winners
selected by a distinguished jury; co-sponsored by Creative Film Foundation

Inner and Outer Space
A magical and immense journey. (Breer)

Odds and Ends
Eminent rationalist talks himself into a corner. (Belson-Conger)

A Movie
A pessimistic comedy of executions, catastrophes and sex. (Connor)

A Trip
Cows, trains, tunnels, birds—but no camera. Irresistible. (D'Avino)

Life Lines
Abstract art and nude in dynamic counterpoint. (Emshwiller)

Science Friction
Non-verbal political satire, ominous and comical. (Vanderbeek)

Transformation
Colorful evolutions of spontaneous abstractions. (Emshwiller)

May 2, 1960
Caryl Chessman's execution. (Preston)

February 1

Der Untertan (The Vassal)
American Premiere. The subtle psychological and emotional evolution of a subservient young man into a full-fledged reactionary leader, ruthless and slightly ludicrous, provides Wolfgang Staudte with an opportunity to savagely attack German Super-Patriotism, military ideals and authoritarian values. A highly revealing and interesting work, this East German production is based on a novel by Heinrich Mann (author of *The Blue Angel*). Complete English titles. "The direction is powerful, biting and sustained; the acting and photography on a very high level indeed!" The British Film Institute

February 15

Four Families
Japan, France, Canada, India: Provocative anthropological discussion film, with Margaret Mead, contrast identical episodes in child rearing—bathing and feeding, attitudes toward physical affection, parental authority, religious rituals—in 4 diver-

Illustration 77. *A Movie* (1958) by Bruce Conner. Courtesy Bruce Conner.

gent cultures, as recorded in authentic documentary footage; and discusses their possible psychological effects on individual personality and national characteristics.

Also: *I Was a 90-Pound Weakling:* Unwittingly hilarious, unrehearsed interviews with muscle builders, Yogis, vibrating equipment manufacturers and assorted faddists offer delicious self-expose and perceptive social comment.

March 1

The Late Mattia Pascal
Rare screening of the legendary prototype of highbrow cinema, L'Herbier's bizarre adaptation of Pirandello's story of a man who—searching for absolute freedom—is unexpectedly given an opportunity to exercise it. Mad and mysterious, filled with Chaplinesque humor and semi-surrealist tragedy, this utterly unpredictable adventure in ambiguous freedom, conceived by an arch-skeptic, erupts in a paradoxical denouement.

March 29

Screening of 1961 Flaherty Award Winners
One of our most popular events, co-sponsored by City College: 1961's best documentaries, chosen by a distinguished jury.

April 26

Restricted Medical and Scientific Films

Frisian Conjoined Twins
The famed study of Siamese twins.

Red River of Life
A memorable film full of visual excitement and mystery, records—for the first time, live—the inside of a human heart.

Thinking Machines
Mechanical mouse learns by trial and error; IBM computer plays chess; machine recognizes shapes.

Warning in the Dark
How the blind 'see' obstacles without touching them.

Intra-Uterine Movements of Foetus
Unprecedented Japanese scientific film photographs the live embryo within the mother.

May 17

Robert Wise Introduces *The Setup*
The distinguished director of *I Want to Live, Odds Against Tomorrow, Executive Suite, The Day the Earth Stood Still*, and the forthcoming *West Side Story*, analyzes one of his best works, a masterpiece of film realism, noteworthy for its visual strength and complex editing. Despite its brutal fight sequences, this chillingly accurate work emerges primarily as a dramatic paraphrase of human aspirations and illusions, as it follows the tragedy of an aging prizefighter in a world of corruption, non-feeling and squalor. Based on Joseph Moncure March's noted poem of the Jazz Age, the entire film covers the space of an hour. With Robert Ryan, Audrey Totter.

Date to be determined

Chartered Plane Excursion to Venice Film Festival
is being organized for August at approximately half the usual fare. For members only.

✦ ✦ ✦ ✦ ✦ ✦

Program Notes Compiled by Amos Vogel for the 1960 Creative Film Awards Presentation, in January 1961

THE 1960 CREATIVE FILM AWARD WINNERS
an evening of experimental cinema, co-sponsored by the Creative Film Foundation and Cinema 16

THE CREATIVE FILM FOUNDATION, the co-sponsor of tonite's event, was organized in 1955 as a non-profit corporation. Directors of the Foundation who also served as jury of the Creative Film Awards are: Rudolf Arnheim, Louis Barron, Joseph Campbell, Maya Deren, Clement Greenberg, Alexander Hammid, Lewis Jacobs, Arthur Knight, James Merrill, Barney Rosset, Meyer Schapiro, Kurt Seligman, Albert Stadler, James Johnson Sweeney, Parker Tyler and Amos Vogel. According to its Statement of Purpose, "the Foundation shall give assistance to film-makers whose primary aim is creating artistic achievement, and who are particularly concerned with exploring the new filmic medium, experimenting with its techniques and altogether contributing to the enlargement of the expressive range and scope of filmic vocabulary and to the development of film form."

TRANSFORMATION   Special Citation   (5 minutes)
A film by Ed Emshwiller.   Distribution: Cinema 16.

"Having no preconception except a sense of constant change and continuity and rhythm, I painted and drew a series of visual abstractions letting each development suggest what followed. Varied techniques in art and animation were used to see how they would work together. 'Finding' a film in this way is more exciting for me than 'finding' a painting. Music taken from the second movement of a string quartet by Gunther Schuller."

Ed Emshwiller

MAY 2, 1960   Special Citation   (3 minutes)
A film by Richard Peterson.   Distribution: Cinema 16

"The attitude to, and content of my films is a direct product of my reflections on the human condition and my limitations, technical and financial.

First, the human condition. As I see it, man exists in a metaphorical pillory. His actions are severely limited, his eyes blinded with the muck that is thrown at him. His only freedom of action is in the dream world and then, like Camus' Sisyphus, he only obtains these sublime moments when his attackers tire of their sport, when momentarily he ceases to be an object of pure function.

I have been in the pillory for years, but now, with the aid of film, I have managed to wriggle one arm free. With this good arm, I can catch and hurl back some of the garbage which has been thrown at me. And by garbage I mean the lies, the distortions, the hypocrisies which are the manipulators' weapons. In short, through film I have discovered power.

The will to have power is good only when it is directed to power over things... steel, stones, paint, film. It is evil when directed to the control and manipulation of other men.

MAY 2, 1960 is an attempt to present, in chronological order, the events which led to the execution of Caryl Chessman. All cuttings are taken from various New York newspapers of that day, and the whole film tries to show a synthesis of the appalling 'Remedy' of capital punishment and the journalistic image of a small world at large.

Working on a homemade animation table makes considerable limitations on what can be done, particularly when compared with that which my imagination tells me should be done. However, the worst limitation of all is financial. Even though this film cost me less than $100, every cent represents a unit of time which had to be spent in creatively unproductive labour."

Richard Peterson

METROGRAPHIC   Special Citation   (3 minutes)
A Martin Toonder Films Production by Vittorio Speich.   Camera: Antei Bolchorst.
Music: Jan Walhoben.   Distribution: Cinema 16.

Gulls, gladiators, cocks, suns, mysterious strangers and a portmanteau theater—a charming and cryptic phantasy, not based on any definite theme; but simply a "dream" in which the designer has been guided only by associations of colors and forms. The shapes and objects he pictures are supplied with strange adaptive power and are subject to continuous transformations.

INNER AND OUTER SPACE   Award of Distinction   (7 minutes)
A film by Robert Breer.   Distribution: Cinema 16.

"This film was drawn and photographed one frame at a time. I developed a special technique for the production of this film which besides permitting me to see in advance what effect the individual drawings were going to give when combined on film also greatly simplified this cumbersome process in general. I was free to work spontaneously and directly in the same spirit of research and play I formerly applied to painting.

This film is essentially abstract, the inner space of the title referring to a kind of kinesthetic space and the outer space referring to space as we imagine it."

Robert Breer

ODDS AND ENDS   Award of Distinction   (5 minutes)
A film by Jane Belson Conger.   Distribution: Cinema 16.

Live action and animation are compiled into a total abstract structure. The accompanying narration is a tongue-in-cheek dissertation on poetry and jazz, in which an anonymous, eminent and indefatigable rationalist talks himself into a corner. "I don't know just what to say other than that I have been extremely impressed with the works of other film makers and 'I just got high and put it together.'"

Jane Belson Conger

A TRIP   Award of Distinction   (1 minute)
A film by Carmen D'Avino.   Distribution: Cinema 16.

"When my motion picture camera broke down and the painting on the easel reached an impasse, I grabbed some old exposed and discarded film and threw it into the bath tub. For good measures I sprinkled different color dyes in the water and waited. When the stew seemed gooey enough, I marinated it with a dash of alcohol. (Cognac was all I had. But I left a sufficient amount in the bottle for other purposes.) After scraping all the muck from the film, I mangled it a little more by stomping and sandpapering the emulsion side. Then I hung it up to dry. Finally I cut it up into two feet lengths and began to draw directly on the film with ink. When I glanced at what I had done under a viewer, I was shocked!!! I had made a film!!! So... I titled it A TRIP and ran out to find some music to fit, only to find I had the music I needed right here in the studio, a beat up old dusty record... somewhat scratched. After distorting the music by speeding up the turntable, I had it put on a soundtrack, cut the film to fit and had them married in one print. The whole production with three finished prints cost me the enormous sum of Twenty-Five Dollars!!! Hollywood could do it all for a slightly larger budget."

Carmen D'Avino

A MOVIE   Award of Distinction   (7 minutes)
A film by Bruce Conner.   Distribution: Cinema 16

"What you're about to see is not anarchic humor but a pun on anarchic humor—not a free laugh but the reconstruction of human depth, achievement and emotion through the pendulous beauty of breasts swaying glabrous and sexual or sunlit; explosions, contradictions and juxtapositions, THE ELEPHANT CHARGES, the horrors of war, the Ego of the Artist hanging over you in the huge letters of his name projected. Anything I can say about this movie is stupid. Read Countess Julie by Strindberg after seeing A MOVIE. Compare them for yourself. I laugh myself half sick with big laughs each time I see this beginning. I am confronted with abominable crimes. I become restive and despondent and rise at the end like the diver. Nothing has happened! I have been through a reconstruction and am bare again. What can I say about A MOVIE. It is a comedy. The opposite of tragedy. Dante's Comedy. Bruce Conner hanging in space over your heads.

If you've forgotten the meaning of Chagall, Modigliani, Klee, the men with a radiance thrown tightly over what they do and the absolute revolution of Pollock remember it for a minute. A MOVIE is a pun on virtual associations. I say that for the gentleness of it—think of what is restrained by the artist's belief."

Michael McClure

LIFE LINES   Award of Distinction   (8 minutes)
A film by Ed Emshwiller. Distribution: Cinema 16

"In this film I have tried to express various aspects of the title, using animated lines, a hand, and a nude model. The main problems to solve were to strike a balance in the use of symbols having quite different impact so that they worked together (a live figure often tends to dominate over the artwork), and to use the symbolism effectively in an abstract form. Although still primarily interested in abstract film-making, I enjoyed the attempt, in this work, to incorporate more literal meaning.

All optical effects were done in the camera, a Bolex. Music was composed for film by Gunther Schuller."

Ed Emshwiller

SCIENCE FRICTION   Award Distinction   (9 minutes)
A film by Stan Vanderbeek.   Distribution: Cinema 16.

"SCIENCE FRICTION is a satire on the over-infatuation with rockets today. . . a spoof at the rocket stage of life. . .

The purpose of 'poetic-politic' satire in my films is to attack some of the aspects of the super-reality that has been so hastily and carelessly built around us. It seems desperate and peculiar that today we have so few comic and comic-tragic spokesmen to jibe at the massive involuntary joke on living in a monolithic society and statistical age. If this film has a social ambition, it is to help disarm the social fuse of people living with anxiety, to point out the insidious folly of competitive suicide (by way of rockets).

In this film and others I am trying to evolve a 'litera-graphic' image, an international sign language of fantasy and satire. There is a social literature through filmic pantomine, that is, non-verbal comedy-satire; a 'comic-ominous' image that pertains to our times and interests which Hollywood and the commercial film are ignoring.

Juxtaposition and mistaken identity are two important factors in experimental comedy; what is the comic image? what is the comic catalyst? what about experimental comedy along the borders of dream and reality?

Animation art as it is practised today, has deliberately kept itself at the 8-year old level of image and symbol, designed for children who can tirelessly watch a indestructible cat chasing an endless mouse. Film animation is a profoundly rich art form waiting to be used."

Stan Vanderbeek

✦ ✦ ✦ ✦ ✦ ✦

Conversation with Robert Breer, 12/19/00

Scott MacDonald: You didn't know about Cinema 16 until you came back from Europe, right?

Robert Breer: I guess that's true. You know the story about Henri Langlois at the Cinematheque Francaise sending a letter to Richard Griffith at MoMA on my behalf. When I got back, I had lunch with Griffith, and left the films. There was a long silence so I went back to retrieve them and one of Griffith's assistants handed them to me, and I kind of shrugged and wondered aloud if Griffith had had a reaction of any kind, and the assistant looked at me and said, "Well, Mr. Griffith really prefers Westerns." I still don't know whether that was a facetious comment. I took my films and left.

I can't remember the sequence here, but at some point I showed films to Margareta Akermark, also at MoMA, and she was relatively negative about them, too. She drew a blank and sent me to this woman who ran an educational film program. I can't remember exactly which films I had in those days, but probably *Recreation*

[1956] and some pretty wild ones, at least according to them. And this woman got very agitated after seeing *Recreation* and went flying around in her office and said she couldn't tell whether it was very good or very bad. And finally decided they were very bad, I guess.

So I was being sloughed off everywhere, but somebody put me onto Amos. I went to Amos at 175 Lexington Avenue. It was a kind of grim looking office. He had a big desk, and I have the impression that I sat in a much smaller chair in front of the desk. Amos played the impresario a little bit, as I remember. He had a sense that I didn't have any other choice but to sign up with him. Which, of course, was true. I think he *was* positive about the films—I know he was later—but even at the beginning he was willing to give them a shot.

At some point he showed me Bruce Conner's *A Movie* [1958] and I expressed interest. Amos said he was considering distributing it but had told Bruce that it wasn't funny enough and that he should go back and do something more to it.

I don't want to betray Amos, but that's what I remember.

MacDonald: Did you go to Cinema 16 screenings? Were you a member?

Breer: No. I did go to a screening at the Fashion Industries Auditorium—I was in a program there. Actually in several of those programs. I remember seeing a photograph of a whole bunch of us (ten people: Maya Deren, Ed Emshwiller, me . . .) sitting up on the stage. It might have been connected with Maya Deren's Creative Film Foundation Awards. But I didn't go to screenings on any sort of regular basis, no.

Amos had parties in his apartment, and I remember him showing *Blazes* [1961]; he had a screen propped up on a pillow in his bedroom. He might have shown films by other people too, but I only have eyes for my own.

MacDonald: Was he your only distributor at that point?

Breer: In those days, yeah. Langlois kept a couple of my films—without asking, so I wouldn't call him a *distributor*. Thief, maybe. But yeah, Amos was the only act in town. He tried to tie everything up with exclusive contracts, but it was kind of silly because there wasn't any competition around anyhow. When Amos sold his films to Barney Rosset at Grove, and Rosset's lawyer got into the act, they made appointments with each of us separately to sign an exclusive contract with Grove. They promised that big things were going to happen for the films.

The only person that got suckered into that was Carmen D'Avino. As "underground filmmakers" we didn't consult each other a lot. It's not like we all hung out together. We knew each other, but we didn't compare notes on career moves, except in that case. Several of us realized the danger of exclusive contracts. But nobody had alerted Carmen and the consequence was that he couldn't show his own films, and Grove never showed them. That was a bummer—they just sat on those films.

Somebody somewhere mentioned that my dog, Amos, was named after Amos Vogel; and that's true in a way. But it sounds derogatory and it wasn't at all: we liked the name and we liked Amos. It certainly wasn't meant as a put-down.

You know, I was there when Jonas offered himself up to Amos.

MacDonald: What do you mean "offered himself up"?

Breer: Well, he wanted to join with Amos. This is *so* long ago. I have this perfect vision in my brain, but I'm not sure that it isn't just a fantasy. It is pretty clear to me and I've mentioned it before for no good reason. It was in Jonas's office on Sixth Avenue. I remember that Gregory Markopoulos was sleeping on a cot in the back. Amos was sitting on a bench with Jonas next to him, proposing to join forces. This is before Jonas put together his Coop [the Film-makers' Cooperative] and Amos shrugged and said, "Why should I?" and right after that sold everything to Grove. That was one of the things that triggered Jonas to start the Coop. Amos was descriminating among our films, and Jonas had the brilliant idea *not* to descriminate, to let *us* decide which of our films to put into distribution.

✦ ✦ ✦ ✦ ✦ ✦

Letter to Amos Vogel from Joseph Campbell, 10/10/61

[hw]
136 Waverly Place
New York 14, N.Y.
October 10, 1961

Dear Amos—

Once again, my thanks to you for a Cinema 16 Press Pass. This year we are going to use it; for I finally finished the book that has glued me to my desk for the last three years, and though another is about to be initiated, the pressure this time will not be as great as last. Moreover, Jean is insisting that I crawl out of my cell this year and meet the contemporary world. What better salon, than Cinema 16.

And I want to thank you, also, for that wonderful party and film-showing in your apartment last spring. It was a delightful evening—and I am considerably ashamed of the length of time it has taken me to let you learn of my appreciation.

The book that I blame for everything is now in press and will be out in February—and as a token of my otherwise undemonstrated appreciation, admiration, and warm regard, there will be a copy in the mail to you, right away.

Jean joins me in best wishes, from house to house—and we look forward to participation this year in your "festival."

Yours ever

Joe

Reprinted by permission of Russell & Volkening, agents for Joseph Campbell.

✦ ✦ ✦ ✦ ✦ ✦

Program Announcement: Spring 1961

March 1961

Butterflies Do Not Live Here
A poignant and harrowing study of the paintings and poems of Jewish children in the Terecin concentration camp, produced in illegal art classes during their imprisonment and accidentally recovered after the war, years after their youthful creators had perished in the gas chambers. An authentic document of our age. A Rembrandt Films release.

The Council of the Gods
This hard-hitting propaganda film, generally considered East Germany's most important production to date, provides a memorable glimpse into Communist mentality and world view, as it probes in compelling plot developments the moral and human dilemmas of a German scientist under Hitler and the Occupation; raises the question of individual responsibility; and indicts German Big Business for its collaboration with Hitler and America. Despite its propagandistic one-sidedness, the film manages to raise disquieting questions.

Complete with English subtitles. A DEFA production by Kurt Maetzig, based on a story by the noted German author Friedrich Wolf. Music by Hans Eisler.

April 1961

New Talent
A perennial favorite. this program introduces new film makers of promise:

Tokyo 1958
Japan's first experimental film, made by a group of young film intellectuals: a savage, sardonic comment on the Americanization of Japanese life, sex and commerce—and its clash with the equally spurious values of old Japan. Premiere.

Krushchev
Irreverent portrayal of Ike's and K's (short-lived) love affair. "The cleverest film of the new film genre of anarchic satires based on photomontage" Richard Griffith, Museum of Modern Art Film Library. (Lebar & Kaplan)

Broadway Express
Compassion, sadness and humanism pervade one of the few genuine recent American social documentaries, photographed with concealed cameras on New York subways. (Michael Blackwood)

The End of Summer
A satire on avant-garde cliches and experimental films. (Ralph Hirshorn)

The End of the Line
Folksongs, nostalgia, interviews and unexpected warmth permeate this charming—and thought-provoking—tribute to the steam locomotive. (Macartney-Filgate)

Black And White Burlesque
Follies of the flesh and of politics satirized in a mad film collage. (Richard Preston)

May 1961

Fury
One of Hollywood's most controversial films which created a sensation upon its initial release: Fritz Lang's dark study of mob violence and lynch law, starring Spencer Tracy and Sylvia Sidney, in which the famed German film maker directs his jaundiced, coldly dispassionate eye toward American reality in as unusual a first Hollywood film as has ever been made by a foreigner. The existence of evil in society; the hypocrisy of law and order, the transformation of men into mobs are sharply edged in this fast and brilliantly executed warning which remains a daringly conceived contribution to the American social cinema, as relevant today as when it was made.

"A grim and purposeful attack on mob violence, as unsparing and relentless in its method as the subject it treats. Bitingly written, superbly directed; it is the finest original drama of the year. Director, writer, cast—they all have a share in the glory of this film." *The New York Times*

"Conceived with an intellectual rigor quite uncharacteristic of American 'problem' pictures; realized with extraordinary and gripping subtlety; systematically and inhumanly forceful; masterfully planned: an unmistakable allusion to the insensate, destructive urge to mass-power that has so often obsessed Lang." Gavin Lambert, *Sight and Sound.*

[The Spring 1961 Special Events listing includes The Late Mattia Pascal *(March 1),* "Screening of 1961 Flaherty Award Winners *(March 29),* "Restricted Medical and Scientific Films" *(April 26),* "Robert Wise Introduces The Setup" *(May 17), and a "Chartered Plane Excursion to Venice Film Festival." See 1960–1961 program announcement for relevant descriptions.]*

✦ ✦ ✦ ✦ ✦ ✦

Program Announcement: Fall 1961/Spring 1962

October 1961

The Sun's Burial
This sensational film—a paroxysm of violence and eroticism—is the work of Japan's foremost 'New Wave' director, Nagisa Ohshima. Signalling the emergence of a new generation in Japanese films, it explodes with the anger and fury of their rebellion, and reveals, beneath its squalor and brutality, a deep—and hopeless—humanism. Bunuel himself seems challenged in this inexorable tale of terror, murder and depravity, enacted by racketeers, whores, robbers, agitators and thugs amidst the slums and industrial wastelands of Tokyo. Elliptical continuity, disjointed editing and haunting images both express and reinforce its basic themes: societal decline; corruption by money, power and poverty; perversion of the innocent; victimization of the guilty.

Illustration 78. Program announcement, fall 1961/spring 1962.

Illustration 79. *The Sun's Burial* (1960) by Oshima Nagisa. Courtesy Museum of Modern Art Film Stills Archive.

"A film of intense beauty and color.... Like Goya, Ohshima depicts the horror because he values gentleness." *The Japan Times*

Cinemascope and Eastman Color. Complete English titles. By special arrangement with Shochiku Films.

Lines Horizontal
Norman McLaren's first film in Cinemascope; a beautiful experiment in pure design. Music: Pete Seeger. Highest Award, Edinburgh and Venice 1960.

November 1961

An Angel Has Fallen
A very unexpected film from Poland about a woman lavatory attendant ends on a sublimely magical note; a new work by Raymond Polanski, whose *Two Men And a Wardrobe* created a sensation at its 1958 Cinema 16 premiere.

La Maternelle
The first screening in over 15 years of Jean Benoit-Levy's unforgettable study of the children of the poor in a Paris day nursery. Pathetic and humorous, tragic and full of warmth, it relates the story of an abandoned child, her insatiable need for motherly love, transposed to a compassionate adult. A Contemporary Films release. Complete English titles.

"A film of extraordinary insight, tenderness and tragic beauty; of great subtlety and almost unbearable power; a film whose profound sincerity and humanity raise it to heights that the screen seldom attains." *The New York Times*

The Dream of Wild Horses
A beautiful work of the poetic cinema. Highest Award, Edinburgh 1960. A film by Denys Colomb de Daunant.

December 1961

The New American Cinema: I

The Sin of Jesus
The eagerly awaited premiere of Robert Frank's (*Pull My Daisy*) controversial new film which blends extreme realism and lyrical fantasy. Adapted from the short story by Isaac Babel. With Julie Bovasso and Robert Blossoms.

The Time of the Heathen
Amidst solitude and desolation, a major new talent projects a psychological drama of guilt and violence, culminating in a daring denouement. As in *The Sin of Jesus*, naturalism and avant-garde techniques are surprisingly linked in this modern morality tale by Peter Kaas, Ed Emshwiller and Peg Santvoord.

With Hollywood 'independents' assuming the role of the defunct major studios, 1961 has seen the emergence of a new group of "true" independents dissimilar in style, but united in their determination to break through to commercial distribution despite the unorthodox financing, production methods and subject matter. This is Program I of two programs devoted to their works.

January 1962

The Fall (La Caida)
A young girl's search for moral values in a puritanical environment; a band of wild irresistible, prurient and eccentric children; a mysterious uncle who speaks from a gramophone record, promising gifts and wonders. Sudden flashes of strange originality illuminate this curious film by Leopoldo Torre-Nilsson (*End of Innocence*), evoked in an impressionistic narrative style.

"The most personal work of the festival, one of the most eagerly discussed among the films shown. Its mood is one of malevolent sexuality and clastrophobic disquiet; its theme, the impact of a hypocritical society on innocence. It confirms Tore-Nilsson as Argentine's most individual talent, producing films of a unique fascination." *Sight and Sound*

Actua-Tilt
Grand Prix, Tours 1961. A savage attack on dehumanization, spurious eroticism, and monstrous progress, cut to a barrage of staccato visuals.

Magritte
Curious souvenirs of a voyage into the universe of the famed Belgian surrealist painter. "Reality is a word devoid of meaning; space is not certain; the world has lost all consistency. My task is to evoke the mystery."

March 1962

Two Timid Souls
Rene Clair's hitherto unavailable triumph of the comic cinema—a hilarious, jubilant celebration—abounds in mad chases, timid lawyers, masked bandits, damsels in distress, with predictably wonderful results. Revealing Clair's skill in combining irony, comedy, sentiment and fantasy, it achieves its effects by purely visual means.

"The richest example of Clair as caricaturist and a freer surrender of his genius to the film medium than *The Italian Straw Hat*." The British Film Institute

April 1962

A Generation
The only New York showing of the first film in Andrezj Wajda's trilogy of Polish youth, which includes *Kanal* and *Ashes and Diamonds*; a powerful, ragged, political work, diffused with lyricism and melancholy, this is a story of youth forced into manhood by war, terror and the heat of experience. A major work, selected for special presentation at the Cannes and Venice International Film Festivals.

SPECIAL EVENTS 1961/1962

November 8

The Girl With The Golden Eyes
A mysterious, perverse Gothic tale, derived from Balzac and transposed to a deceptively contemporary Paris, probes the secret of a bizarre love in an atmosphere of

sophisticated decadence. Opulent in its artificiality, the film is especially noteworthy for its visual pyrotechnics, luxuriant imagination and unexpected continuity. Official 1961 French entry at Venice, this work by Jean-Gabriel Albicocco offers a provocative counterpoint to the films of the 'New Wave.' A special preview, courtesy Kingsley International Pictures.

December 6

The New American Cinema: II

Sunday
Dan Drasin's spontaneous camera captures the folksingers riot in Washington Square, an ominous confrontation of youth and authority.

Guns Of The Trees
This first feature by Jonas Mekas, *Village Voice* critic, *Film Culture* editor—a cry of anguish—represents an attempt at a new film form: a plotless mosaic of 5 protagonists at a crucial period of their lives. The best-loved or most-hated film on this year's program. Poetry written and spoken by Allen Ginsberg. With Ben Carruthers, Argus Speare Julliard, Frances Stillman, Adolfas Mekas. An Emile de Antonio release.

January 24

American Propaganda Films

Operation Abolition
The most famous propaganda film of the decade.

Boycott
Boycott as economic weapon in America today; an anti-Catholic film.

Message From Mississippi
A proud defense of segregation.

Language of Faces
Witnesses of peace, harbingers of war; a pacifist film.

February 7

The 1961 Creative Film Award Winners

The year's best avant-garde films, selected by a distinguished jury. Co-sponsored by Creative Film Foundation.

February 21

Stars
From Bulgaria, a moving love story of a Greek Jewess on her way to Auschwitz and a German soldier guarding the transport. Counterposing the idealism of the one to the pessimistic cynicism of the other, the film refuses to oversimplify either. Second Prize, Cannes 1959. Award at Edinburgh.

"Brilliant for its pathos, restraint, delicacy and originality." *Films and Filming*

March 21

Good Morning (Ohayo)
A delightful comedy of Tokyo's 'suburbia,' filled with odd Western touches, Eastern customs, rebellious children, TV sets and a broad humor startling by American standards. This is the 49th film of Yasujiro Ozu, an undisputed master of the screen who is entirely unknown here. A Shochiku Films release.

March 28

Screening of 1962 Flaherty Award Winners

One of our most popular annual events, co-sponosred by City College; 1962's best documentaries as selected by a distinguished jury.

April 25

The Beats and the Outs: Two Views

The Flower Thief
This frantic, crude, splendiferous riot provides the closest filmic approximation of the beat philosophy so far. Beneath its flamboyant tableaux and aggressive madness lurks a deadly serious rejection of organized society. (Ron Rice)

The Mirage
This European view of an outsider's odyssey offers a singular counterpoint to *The Flower Thief* in its almost classic serenity and Kafkaesque flavor. (Peter Weiss)

May 16

The Crowd
Only New York showing of King Vidor's classic of American naturalism, a story of regimentation and poignant attempts of two young people, ultimately compromised, to rise from "the crowd." With the negative gone, this is the only existing print. "One of the greatest films to have come from Hollywood." Rotha, *The Film Till Now*.

Speaker: Mr. James Card, Curator of Motion Pictures, George Eastman House.

✦ ✦ ✦ ✦ ✦ ✦

Dwight Macdonald, "Some Animadversions on the Art Film," *Esquire*, 4/62

I have been looking through the old programs of Cinema 16, a New York film society with some four thousand members which is now in its fifteenth year, and I have been viewing some of its current offerings and it occurs to me it is time to cast a cold eye on what is known as "the art film." Its ideals are high and it is dedicated to truth—no escapism, no box office. I am in favor of high ideals, but why are they so seldom entertaining in art films? I am also in favor of Truth and Realism, but why are they here always depressing? Above all, why are most art films pooh? Cinema

16 describes itself as "the Off-Broadway of the cinema" and "the Little Mag of the film world," adding that its "only ambition is to search out the creative, the artistic, the experimental; its only goal is to be the showcase for new directions in the cinema." But almost all the creative and new-directional films it has shown in its fifteen years—there haven't been many—have not been art films but rather films produced in the ordinary course of commercial (or Communist) moviemaking. Although I think Cinema 16 could have done much better with its programming, this isn't entirely its fault. From Griffith to Antonioni, all the great films—with only a few exceptions, such as Cocteau's *Blood of a Poet* and Vigo's *Zero de Conduite*—have been aimed directly at the box office. Cinema 16 is not analogous to Off-Broadway and the little magazines because (1) their level has been higher than that of the commercial theatre and press; and (2) they have often first presented writers who later became famous (as Joyce and Eliot in *The Little Review* and O'Neill at the Provincetown Playhouse). Neither of these statements can be made about the art film, which has remained through the decades a stagnant little back eddy.

Cinema 16 must be given credit for first showing such films—all but one non-art—as Torre-Nilsson's *End of Innocence,* Eisenstein's *Strike,* Cassavetes' *Shadows,* and Resnais' *Night and Fog,* and for reviving such films—all non-art—as Renoir's *The Rules of the Game,* Lang's *M,* Dovzhenko's *Arsenal* and *Earth,* Donskoi's *The Childhood of Gorki,* Welles' *The Magnificent Ambersons* and Clair's *The Italian Straw Hat.* But these plums were sparsely distributed through a vast pudding of dullness, nor was I lucky as a Jack Horner. The dullness is spiced with *Angst.* The more distressing aspects of life are so frequently on view at Cinema 16 that I have often wondered just who its four thousand devotees are. Masochists? Psychiatric social workers on a busman's holiday? Whoever they are, they have taken a lot of punishment. Typical Cinema 16 documentary films of past seasons:

Images of Madness ("macabre journey through the universe of the mentally ill").... *Frustration Play Techniques: Ego Blocking Games* ("special projective techniques developed at Sarah Lawrence College.... Hidden cameras record test situations in which various children react differently to competition, frustration and prohibition").... *Neurosis and Alcohol* ("cats are made neurotic and then subjected to alcohol").... *The Invader* ("traces history of syphilis from fifteenth century").... *The Praying Mantis* ("alien and horrifying universe... love and cruel death").... *The Unknown Soldier* ("merciless inferno of blood and death").... *Witchcraft Through the Ages* ("cruelty and dogmatism of the Middle Ages, tortures of the witch courts, orgies of the devil's mass").... *Depressive States and Paranoid Conditions.... Maternal Deprivation* ("disturbed children at a French nursing home").... *The World of the Microbes* ("in quest of tubercle bacilli").... *The Murderers of Anne Frank* ("controversial East German featurette banned in several countries... proclaims that Anne Frank's murderers are prospering in West Germany today").... *Psychotic Illnesses in Childhood....May 2, 1960* ("Caryl Chessman's execution").

There is a lot of *Angst* in the art films too. Some typical shorts have been: *Bells of Atlantis,* by Ian Hugo and Anais Nin, a paradigm of corny *avant-gardism....* *Together,* a British "free cinema" film which I found tedious and dreary, or, as translated into Cinema 16 copywriting: "a study of two deaf mutes imprisoned by silence and solitude... explores with lingering simplicity their desolate existence, their sad diversions".... *Actua-Tilt,* a recent French offering which is ballyhooed as "a savage attack on dehumanization, spurious eroticism and monstrous progress"; the attack is indeed savage, so much so that it becomes indistinguishable from the brutalitarian tendencies attacked.... *Abseits,* which is described as "water, wind, sunlight, and seagulls; the sounds and lonely grandeur of ebb tide on a North Sea beach." It's always ebb tide at Cinema 16.... To be fair, there are two shorts in the current season which are very good: one on the Belgian surrealist painter, Magritte; and *Sunday,* Dan Drasin's sound-camera reportage on last summer's folk-singer demonstration in New York's Washington Square.

During 1961–62, Cinema 16 has shown or will show four new feature films. I have already reviewed here (unfavorably) Robert Frank's *The Sin of Jesus.* Notes on the other three follow.

The Time of the Heathen
"Amidst solitude and desolation, a major new talent projects a psychological drama of guilt and violence," is Cinema 16's hard sell for this one. Well, as I have observed before, there is art-film cliché as well as Hollywood cliché and here Peter Kass, Ed Emshwiller and Peg Santvoord, with the loftiest intentions, have created a little anthology of the genre. The two protagonists are a seamy-faced wanderer who is not quite right in the head, and a Negro boy who is, one discovers without surprise halfway through the film, a deaf mute. There is the obligatory opening sequence of the man walking endlessly through a depressing landscape, the obligatory rape-murder scene, the obligatory chase through tangled wood (Griffith did it better in *Birth of a Nation*), the obligatory locations—ruined houses, desolate beach. There is also a long color sequence of montages about the bombing of Hiroshima which may be fruitfully compared with the similar montages in Resnais' film; it is the difference between the artistic and the artsy. This sequence is justified, plotwise, by the revelation that the psychotic wanderer has been reduced to his sad state by his guilt-feeling because he helped drop the bomb on Hiroshima. This is conveyed, with elephantine subtlety, by a shot of the Distinguished Flying Cross falling out of his nerveless hand as he dies on the beach. He has been shot by a proto-fascist character who has been gunning for him and the Negro boy because they are the only witnesses to the killing of the boy's mother by the proto-fascist's weakling son. However, it all ends happily: the proto-fascist is killed by the cops and the boy finds the love and protection he needs in the person of a nice old country doctor. In short, a TV fable tarted up with camera effects and the kind of "advanced" cutting that is designed to convince a Cinema 16 audience they are getting their money's worth. It lasted eighty minutes but seemed longer than *Ben Hur.* It got "top award" at the Bergamo (Italy) Film Festival, one more reason for steering clear of those unfestive festivities.

The Sun's Burial
This was introduced by Cinema 16's publicity man with his usual restraint: "a paroxysm of violence and eroticism... the work of Japan's foremost New Wave director, Nagisa Ohshima... explodes with the anger and fury of their rebellion and reveals, beneath its squalor and brutality, a deep—and hopeless—humanism." I didn't catch the humanism or the eroticism—both concepts I'm sympathetic to—

because I couldn't find anything underneath the squalor and brutality. It seemed to me a monotonous series of beatings up slung together without either motivation or cinematic form; the cutting was as arbitrary as in a "blue" movie, the only object being to get on to the next scene of mayhem; when two people met, one's only curiosity was as to which would smash the other to the ground first. Eroticism was represented by (a) the master of a brothel pushing the padded armrest of his crutch—he's crippled, natch—against the throat of a whore who had been so foolish as to get herself pregnant, slowly throttling her as everybody, including the neophyte boy who is presented as the innocent Candide of the film passively listens to her strangled screams; and (b) two young toughs (one of them Candide) robbing a lovemaking couple in a park—Candide crashes a club down on the man's skull and his companion (he's *really* bad) rapes the girl after having stifled her screams by stuffing her mouth with a clod of grass (that's quite a close-up). There are several other scenes of deep (and hopeless) humanism. Candide, trying to go straight, is delivering a load of tripes on his bicycle; he is waylaid by the gang, who slug him to the ground, kick him senseless and then belabor him with assorted lights and livers. It all winds up—or so I've been told, I left shortly after the intestinal attack—with most of the cast, stunned or wounded by a grenade, dying in agony as they try to crawl out of the ensuing conflagration. *The Sun's Burial* is all in color. Blood does make such a nice red.

Guns of the Trees
Jonas Mekas is the film critic of *The Village Voice,* a Greenwich Village weekly that had Norman Mailer as a contributing member and that first printed the cartoons of Jules Feiffer. Mr. Mekas is also the editor-publisher of a magazine called *Film Culture* which is, as Herbert Hoover once remarked of Prohibition, "an experiment noble in purpose." Sympathetic as I am to Mr. Mekas' purpose, which is simply to present with the utmost intransigence the true aims of cinema, I must confess I rate dedication lower than acumen and enthusiasm lower than talent. The proof of pudding is in the eating and much of *Film Culture* and of Mr. Mekas' column strikes me as not very nutritious. Now we have his first movie, *Guns of the Trees,* which Cinema 16 bills as "controversial... the best-loved or most-hated film on this year's program." I detect a note of desperation here: when an entrepreneur so advertises a cultural product, one suspects the first reactions have been hostile, as in the case of *Les Liaisons Dangereuses* ... which got adverse notices—Brendan Gill's rave in *The New Yorker* is currently displayed in lonely splendor in front of the theatre—and whose promoters were reduced to running one of those pro-and-con ads with an exhortations to the public to decide for themselves. Flattering, but why don't they ever ask us to decide about hits?

Guns of the Trees got off to a good start with an impassioned leaflet by its creator which I read with nervous appreciation (will I dig it? am I a square?) before the house lights went down. It was headed, with a jaunty echo of dry-cleaning establishments, "WHILE-U-WAIT," and its text raised considerable expectations. In the interests of cultural history, I reproduce the salient passages:

> You may ask yourself, what is *Guns of the Trees* all about, what's the story?
>
> There is no story. Telling stories is for peaceful and content people. And at this juncture in my life I am neither content nor peaceful. I am deeply and totally dis-

Illustration 80. *Guns of the Trees* (1960) by Jonas Mekas. Courtesy of Anthology Film Archives.

content. Do I have to list the reasons why? Haven't you read your *Times* and *Pravda* today? Why do you wonder, then, that poets are beginning to get uneasy?

Yes, the artists are abandoning the beautiful, happy, entertaining, self-glorifying stories. They are beginning to express their anxiety in a more open and direct manner. They are searching for freer form, one which permits them a larger scale of emotional statements, explosions of truths, outcries of warnings, accumulations of images—not to carry out an amusing story but to fully express the tremblings of the consciousness of man, to confront us eye-to-eye with the soul of modern man. . . .

It's not through the mind and order that I create. I create through my ignorance and chaos. Order doesn't interest me. I know that through my chaos I have a chance of arriving somewhere, of catching some secret movements of subconscious, of Life, of Man. . . .

It is from this anxiety that my discontent grows. And I am throwing it against all those who are for death. It is not that I believe in changing them. They are perhaps not even worth saving, not worth the breath of a single flower trampled under their Power. It's only that my patience has run out. It's only that I had to make this gesture of solidarity for those who think and feel the same way I do, are angry about the same things I am—for all the others my film will have no meaning. My film is only a letter of solidarity to the friends of an existential discontent, no matter in what continent, what country—a letter from the mad heart of the insane world, WHILE-U-WAIT."

Then the film began. George Jean Nathan once wrote a piece about the opening of the Paramount Theatre in New York circa 1926. He described in detail the platoons of epauletted, cloaked, shakoed, ushers, the spotlights and the red carpets, the hand-painted oil paintings that lined the walls (they still do), the Baroque profusion of the gold-leafed interior, the stupendous obligato on the mighty Wurlitzer organ, and then—I quote from memory—"the great golden curtains parted and we saw a movie in which a floozy seduced a bond salesman." Such, *toute proportion gardée*, was my reaction to *Guns of the Trees* after reading Mr. Mekas' eloquent leaflet.

I expected something profound and difficult. What I got was two contrasting love stories which were all too easily followed (once one got used to *avant-garde* cutting) since they represented Good and Bad, Creative and Destructive, Life and Death, or, existentially speaking, Authentic and Inauthentic. The Creative, Authentic, etc., couple was colored, the Destructive, etc., couple was white. "The small people don't learn," says the Negro girl, who was embarrassingly smug, to the tense white girl, who later kills herself, "but people like you and me should learn from everything." (This is the Salinger complex, the We Happy Few syndrome.) This labored fable takes place in a welter of *"avant-garde"* effects that don't come off, as in the stylized mimes that open and close the film. The settings were grimly "realistic," in the mode that I remember from similar art-film efforts in the Thirties: railroad yards, city dumps, crumbling walls and alley ways, frowzy parks, kitchens that could do with a little dishwashing. Shot 210 is described in the script as: "Somewhere in the Bronx. A field of broken glass, junk, sun—Gregory walks across the junkyard, slowly, looking down, black." Meanwhile, back at the dump....

All that is spontaneous in *Pull My Daisy* is self-conscious here; Ginsberg is inferior to Kerouac as a narrator because he is really rhetorical while Kerouac is mock-rhetorical; here Ginsberg alternates with folk songs, the last refuge of the American left; he is too pompous and they are too simple. All those MacLeishian questions: "What is man?" "Perhaps just to be." "Will it ever change?" No reply from Ben Carruthers' co-star, Adolfas Mekas, Jonas' brother, who is perhaps the most stolid movie actor since Francis X. Bushman.

The symbol of police brutality is some cops timidly pushing around folk-singers in Washington Square—maybe Eleanor Roosevelt or the New York *Post* will object; in the Thirties the cops were, with not too much hyperbole, called "Cossacks" and they really roughed up Communist demonstrators in Union Square; a clear gain in civil liberties, but not much of a symbol of Power trampling underfoot those Flowers of Life. Sorry, forgot the climactic expression of rebellion: Carruthers pissing on my bank—Manufacturers Hanover Trust Company branch at Fifth Avenue and 43rd Street—or, to be accurate, *almost* pissing on it; he gets his fly open, but he is drunk and his pals lead him away before the awful deed is done.

Gregory (Francis X. Mekas) has a big scene with a "social worker"—the quotes are in the script, perhaps to imply that the "social worker" is not a social worker really though why it's not bad enough to be actually a social worker I don't see—which runs as follows: (Gregory speaking) "There is nothing wrong with Fidel Castro." "You compare yourself with Fidel Castro?" "No, I identify with him." "You realize

Fidel Castro is a revolutionary. Are you revolting against something?" "Yes I am." "What are you revolting against?" (TV scripts run on this way but at least it's from hunger.) "Against dishonesty, corruption." "What do you want? To change the world? Is that your idea?" "I think everybody wants to change the world, no?" There then comes a blank white screen, which is Mr. Mekas' ingenious transition device, after which we hear the portentous tones of Mr. Ginsberg:

"What do you think of America? You who run America, vote hypocrite, edit school books, make foreign wars, appoint aldermen and football coaches?

"You who therefore are America, the land that opens its mouth to speak with four hundred billion dollars of armaments and two cents' worth of measly foreign aid [anybody checked these figures?] all for bombs and horror, fraud, dope fiends, Syngman Rhee, Batista, Chiang Kai-shek, madmen, Franco—who else God knows. I refuse to read the paper."

This is cut into (shot 187): "Frances, somewhere in the fields, standing by a pile of burning autumn leaves." So even that most charming and nostalgic ceremony of American life is twisted into an emblem of our allegedly death-oriented society.

Instead of transitional music, Mr. Mekas uses an electronic squeak of varying pitch. Very *avant-garde* but after a while it gets on one's nerves just like Hollywood's mood music. But he does score one coup: he has dug up from somewhere a line that still haunts me: "Where are the snows of yesteryear?" Now where could he have found *that*?

Reprinted by permission of *Esquire Magazine* © 1962, the Hearst Corporation.

✦ ✦ ✦ ✦ ✦ ✦

Amos Vogel, "Riposte from Cinema 16," *Esquire*, 9/62

It would be nice to begin with some profound observations, but I am afraid your cataclysmic criticisms [in the April issue] of Cinema 16 are largely based on lack of acquaintance with our programs and on 'tendentious selection.' I cannot prove this charge in 500 words: but from about 250 programs presented during fifteen years, you arbitrarily concentrated on films of 'Angst' (omitting large numbers of joyous programs), review in detail three programs you hated (while barely mentioning twenty programs you liked), and criticize so-called 'typical documentaries' (actually representing less than ten percent of our total programs and including feature-length fiction films and animations).

To say that Cinema 16's films are inferior to Off-Broadway, and have not led to the revelation of substantial talents, is quaint, considering that we were the first to introduce to American audiences the films of Antonioni, Robert Bresson, Norman McLaren, Robert Breer, John Cassavetes, Robert Frank, Shirley Clarke, Georges Franju, Bert Haanstra, Hilary Harris, Andrzej Munk, Leopoldo Torre-Nilsson, Yasujiro Ozu, Karel Reisz, Tony Richardson, Arne Sucksdorff, Lindsay Anderson, Stan Vanderbeek, Agnes Varda. As to the classics, how, exactly are Dreyer, Welles, Eisenstein, Lang, Dovzhenko, Vigo, Vidor, De Sica, Rossellini inferior to Off-Broadway revivals?

You dislike the anxiety in some of our films. 'I am in favor of truth, but why is it always depressing?' Because nowadays, Dwight, it is often is. Why attack *us* for this? You seem to have left this kind of anxiety far behind, to be reasonably at peace with a world going insane. But others aren't. Instead of analyzing why so many films are being made about human alienation, race relations, atomic war, you 'deplore' Angst, express your 'opposition' to it and then attack—not its source, but the artist who portrays it and the exhibitor who shows it.

As to the experimental films, we frankly prefer the honest, however imperfect, exploration 'from passion' to the lifeless, technically perfect commercial works made 'to order.' By definition, this also assures that (in searching out the new) we will commit errors of judgement. We prefer the risk of error to the revealed truth of the already established.

You accuse us of not being entertaining enough. Art and experimentation, whether 'committed' or subjective, are only incidentally 'entertaining' and we have never claimed to exist for the sake of entertaining our members; we leave this to the neighborhood houses.

The most saddening aspect of your attack is the realization of your own entrapment in the values of the commercial cinema. Without qualification, you claim that 'almost all creative films have been produced in the ordinary course of commercial moviemaking.' This is untrue, or, at best, misleading. Equally revealing is your insistence on 'entertainment' values (that discredited criterion) and your horror at the new *avant-garde* (you do not realize that it is no longer 'daring' to 'recognize' *Blood of a Poet* as an *avant-garde* masterpiece; things have been happening since). And to deplore, of all things, 'Angst' today, Dwight, is socially conservative. Your position implies a (however ambiguous) defense of the commercial cinema and the deprecation of many valuable, creative efforts outside it, of which, I am proud to say, Cinema 16 forms a part.

—Amos Vogel

Dear Amos: Well, you did your best. Your main complaint—that I commented on only a few of the programs you've presented in the last ten years—reminds me of the editor of the new edition of Webster's unabridged dictionary owlishly noting that the reviews, almost all of which (including mine in *The New Yorker*) were hostile, had dealt with less than one percent of the 450,000 definitions in his tome. The reason I reviewed in detail a mere three (out of 250) programs you have presented was, of course, that I naturally concentrated on your current season, in which you present just four feature films, all of which I thought terrible (I'd already paid my respects to the fourth). As to Angst v. Entertainment, this is a false antithesis; art must be entertaining, that is pleasurable, or it isn't art; I have already recorded the pleasure I got from the artistic representation of Angst in such films as *Hiroshima, Mon Amour, The Four Hundred Blows,* and *L'Aventura*. No foe, I, of Angst. But it's got to be aesthetically enjoyable or it just ain't art. "After an evening of art films," Pauline Kael has remarked somewhere, "I often want to see a movie." Me too.

—Dwight.

Reprinted by permission of *Esquire Magazine* © 1962, the Hearst Corporation.

✦ ✦ ✦ ✦ ✦ ✦

Conversation with P. Adams Sitney, 5/20/00

P. Adams Sitney: I slowly began to realize that there was a kind of rivalry between Jonas's Charles Cinema and Cinema 16. I would stay in New York till Sunday in order to attend the Cinema 16 screenings, which were set up long in advance. They were designed as a kind of smorgasbord of genres so you wouldn't see a lot of the same thing. You might see an exotic documentary (I remember one about people walking on fire) and an avant-garde film from America, and maybe something from the Polish Film School, and an extraordinary scientific film… There seemed to be a division of filmmakers. Certain of the more established avant-garde filmmakers—Breer, Emshwiller, Vanderbeek—would be more likely to be seen at Cinema 16 than at the Charles Cinema, at first. But by the end of the Charles Cinema screenings, it was clear that a major shift had occurred and *all* of those people were showing at the Charles.

At the beginning I really didn't understand this division, in part because neither of the principals ever spoke directly about it. I would go over to Cinema 16, where I rented and borrowed a lot of films. I had become very friendly with Jack Goelman.

Scott MacDonald: He mentioned he used to let you take films home.

Sitney: Eventually I had seen the entire library of films Cinema 16 distributed.

Illustration 81. P. Adams Sitney (*with glasses*) at press conference at Overseas Press Club in December 1963, with (*from left*) Jack Smith, George Fenin (secretary of Overseas Press Club), Gregory Markopoulos, Andy Warhol. Photo Jonas Mekas.

Cinema 16 underwrote the Maya Deren issue of *Filmwise* [No. 2 (1962)], which also received help from the Film-makers' Cooperative. I first realized there *was* a problem when Amos was annoyed with me for not telling him that the Film-makers' Cooperative was involved. Then one evening I overheard Vanderbeek talking with Jonas and some other people and saying, "Now that we're doing this, we have to go tell Amos." They were going to be distributing their films through the Film-maker's Cooperative and if Amos insisted on exclusive distribution, they were going to leave him. Again, since I wasn't a filmmaker, and since I was a kid [Sitney was 16 in 1961], I was standing on the outside trying to feel my way around all this. My sense was that Jonas thought that he was doing his own thing and didn't feel that he was in competition with Cinema 16. Amos and Jack felt that they had carefully built up something that had a very delicate, minimal economy and that this new development was disruptive and bad for the field. And there was the real ideological difference: Amos and Jack seemed to think that if films like *Anticipation of the Night* were shown, people would stop being interested in avant-garde films, and of course *that* position fueled the moral polemic of Jonas and all the people who were wild about Brakhage.

MacDonald: Menken was involved in this, too, right? Brakhage told me that he was frustrated when Amos wouldn't show a new Menken film.

Sitney: You know, in favor of Amos, a Menken screening was always a problem. Willard would come storming in, often in a belligerent mood, often inebriated, demanding that someone show something of Marie's. Of course, the film in question wasn't even glued together at the time. Amos and Jack ran a business of sorts, and wanted to see films before they agreed to show them. They programmed six or seven months in advance. And they might say yes or no to a particular Menken film. If Willard came in with half a film and said that Teji Ito was going to do a soundtrack for it, Amos and Jack would remind Willard that that wasn't the way it was done at Cinema 16, and he would get into a terrible huff.

However, for Jonas, that kind of interaction was fine. He went ahead and scheduled a Menken show, and I believe about a third of her films were made the evening before that show [the Charles Theater presented a Menken Retrospective in two programs—Finished Works and Works-in-Progress—at midnight on December 29 and 30, 1961]. She was up all night putting them together. Some had soundtracks, some didn't. Gerard Malanga was making titles; Willard was running around screaming and cursing out everybody. This is a mode of operation that Jonas could handle: midnight at the Charles—no announced program. Cinema 16 simply didn't operate that way.

MacDonald: Were you a member of Cinema 16?

Sitney: Well, for years I couldn't afford it. It cost something like fifteen dollars, which in those days was a fabulous amount of money. Then as I got to know Jack and Amos, they let me in free. In fact, one evening I absolutely saved a show for them. They discovered late that a film that had come from out of town, perhaps from Europe, was on cores, not on reels. I went running to Adolfas Mekas's editing room and grabbed all the split 35mm reels I could get and I rushed back down to the Needle Trades Auditorium so they could project the film. I made myself useful whenever I could. That was one of the ways in which I earned some free tickets.

MacDonald: What do you remember about Cinema 16 screenings?

Sitney: The more radical Cinema 16 shows were the Wednesday night shows down at the Needle Trades Auditorium. It was harder for me to get in from high school on a Wednesday night coming from so far away (though when I think about how often I played hooky and how often I managed to get to New York, I'm rather astonished now), so my memories of Cinema 16 are colored by my experiences on Sunday mornings uptown.

I grew up as a Catholic, and we went to church on Sunday. The Sunday Cinema 16 screenings were at eleven o'clock in the morning in, what was then, posh new uptown theaters, like the Beekman. It felt like going to church. All these people were dressed up in jackets and ties, coming to see the latest Japanese film or a collection of short films from the Polish Film School. The people looked very interesting but it was a little like going to the New York Philharmonic: there was no contact among people who didn't arrive together. There wasn't a lobby life. Of course, Amos and some of the older people, composers and writers and so on, knew each other, but these were the kind of people who had enough money that they would just go to a restaurant together after the show. If I knew someone, I would end up going out with them somewhere, but at those screenings one didn't have the sense of being part of a vital fresh community. Of course, it turns out that many, many fascinating people were there.

While Cinema 16 was Lincoln Center, the Charles was a clubhouse. Down at the Charles, people who didn't have enough money to go to Stanley's for beer hung out in the lobby. These were the days of the Horn & Hardarts. You could wander in there and spend nothing, or buy one cup of tea and re-soak the bag in hot water and get free lemon slices for it—or if you were really daring, make yourself a lemonade with lemon, sugar, and water—and sit for hours. In those days, it was possible to live in New York with no money. New York was a dying city. No one wanted to live there. You could get an apartment. George Landow's apartment cost about nine dollars a month! The toilet was in the hall. There was a whole culture in New York of people living on next to nothing, and the Charles was *their* alternative movie theater.

❖ ❖ ❖ ❖ ❖ ❖

Program Announcement: Fall 1962/Spring 1963

October 1962

Paris Belongs To Us
This enigmatic "thriller"—subject of an unusual manifesto by all French New Wave directors—has become the center of an international controversy. Abrupt, elliptic, paranoid, it enmeshes suspects, victims and seekers alike in a shadowy mystery of

Illustration 82. Program announcement, fall 1962/spring 1963.

murder and suicide, possibly linked to a secret world-wide conspiracy and creates a sense of almost cosmic disaster. The film's hallucinatory power and ideological preoccupations have been widely compared to Resnais' *Marienbad*. An AJYM Films-Films du Carosse Production by Jacques Rivette. A Merlyn Films release.

"The fruit of an astonishing persistence over several years to bring to the screen a personal vision of the world today; a universe of anguished confusion and conspiracy. It is the fusion of poetic vision and realist impression which makes it a film of foremost importance to us." Claude Chabrol, Jacques Demy, Jean Luc Godard, Pierre Kast, Jean-Pierre Melville, Alain Resnais, Francois Truffaut, Agnes Varda.

"Perhaps the most brilliant and absorbing statement yet made of the pressures which the human mind has to bear in this mid-century of fear. It is difficult to convey the peculiar hypnotic quality of the direction, the extraordinary density of this film." British Film Institute

November 1962

International Prizewinners From Abroad

Rupture
Hilarious, disastrous attempt to break off with girl by mail (Etaix)

Bodega Bohemia
Macabre, disturbing human document (Schamoni)

Alpha Omega
Man's ridiculous progress from cradle to grave (Bozzetto)

The Fat and The Lean
Grotesque parable in pantomime (Polanski)

Mint Tea
A brilliant and somber film about youth in a Paris Cafe (Kafian)

La Cadeau
Something about a horn that moos; season's funniest film

Palladini
Beautiful Biancofiore Rescued From Sarazen Rodomonte's Dungeon

Don Quixote
Boldest experiment of the year, from Yugoslavia (Kristi; Herts-Lion)

December 1962

The Happiness of Us Alone
1962 International Prizewinner. Amidst the chaos of a defeated Japan, a haunting film explores with lingering simplicity the story of two deaf-mutes and their attempts to establish a normal life together. Delicate and acute, the film is notable for its intensity of feeling. Directed by Zenzo Matsuyama, one of Japan's leading avant-garde writers. A Toho Release. Cinemascope.

January 1963

The Innocent Sorcerers
Jazz, sex, ennui, a lack of values and youthful anti-heroes are surprisingly dealt with in Andrzej Wajda's newest film, an example of the new Polish sophistication. Beneath its pseudo-intellectual posturing lurks a very contemporary pathos and scepticism. Cannes 1961.

"Re emphasizes the skill and versatility of the director of *Ashes and Diamonds, Kanal* and *A Generation,* by confining the bulk of its action to a repartee between a young surgeon and a sophisticated student, who devote most of a flirtatious night to a game of strip poker." *New York Times*

"Like some sophisticated French bedroom comedy situation, but mordantly turned upon itself. The airy love game culminates in an extraordinarily complex moment of guilt and shame, when the soul stands naked instead of the body." *Sight and Sound*

also: *Waiting,* Grand Prix, Short Films, Cannes 1962 and *Pictures of Our Village,* new Polish experimental film.

March 1963

Trance, Ritual and Hypnosis

La Taranta
Unique ethnological document, photographed in Italy, records maniacal dances and seizures of women in religious ecstasy. Commentary by Salvatore Quasimodo, Nobel Prize poet. A film by Gianfranco Mengozzi.

Sainthood and Sanity
Are the "visions" of saints different from those of the insane? BBC's Christopher Mayhew (*Poverty, Chastity and Obedience*) interviews a psychiatrist, a priest, a

Hindu mystic and a mental patient in a discussion program impossible on American TV.

Cosmic Ray
A daring, hypnotic visual experience by Bruce Conner (*A Movie*)

The Fire Walkers
Roussos Condouros' documentary record of Greek rite: walking barefeet on charcoal without pain or burning. "One of the rare, perfectly authentic film records of possession." UNESCO

L'Ondomane
Splendiferous adventures of suggestible TV addict (Arcady)

Unconscious Motivation
Unrehearsed psychoanalytic experiment records inducement of neurosis under hypnosis and its subsequent removal by analysis.

Thanatopsis
Throbbing intensity of life experienced by totally passive protagonist. A film by Ed Emshwiller.

April 1963

If The Wind Frightens You
This very modern film by Belgian director Emile Degelin created much comment at Cannes. Two beautiful young people, brother and sister, vacationing on North Sea beaches, come to realize an erotic tension between them which they can neither conceive nor acknowledge. Subtle, lyrical, assured, the film evokes the sensousness and mystery of youth. The subject is handled without sensationalism. Spiral films. "Risks to enlist against itself the unanimous condemnation of hypocrites and libertines." *Peuple*

May 1963

Los Golfos (*The Hooligans*)
Carlos Saura's pitiless Spanish "New Wave" film catches the criminal violence and empty bravado of its youthful protagonists in an ironic criticism of totalitarianism. Cannes and London Film Festivals 1960.

"The film's depiction of a Spain rarely seen on the screen clearly hints at a new movement. The feeling for its grimy milieu and its sordid, anti-romantic view communicate a real passion." *Sight and Sound*

also: *Brutality in Stone* Premiere of German "New Wave" anti-Nazi film.

SPECIAL EVENTS 1962/1963

November 7

Pickpocket
Premiere of Robert Bresson's (*Diary of a Country Priest, A Man Escaped*) hypnotic study of a kleptomaniac, revealing theft as an act of high art and sexual gratifica-

tion, in sequences of poetic passion. An existentialist 'Crime and Punishment;' set in a non-moral world. Agnes Delahaie Production, with Martin Lassalle.

"Bresson reaches a peak in his career with a film whose brilliantly executed technical display, personal idiom and preoccupations all coalesce into total self-fulfillment." The British Film Institute

also: *Ed and Frank*—the values of an American suburban family and an American artist are counterposed in direct, unrehearsed interviews by noted British filmmaker Dennis Mitchell. NET-BBC Production.

December 5

The Best New American Independent Films

The Cross-Country Runner
Satire on a man who cannot stop running.

Stone Sonata
Gamboling, Tumb-e-ling Boulders In The Greenery! (D'Avino)

Millions In Business As Usual
Faces, buildings, girls, crowds, NY! (Burckhardt)

Horse Over Teakettle
Challenge, proudly flung against the bomb (Breer)

Metanoia
Dark vision of classic simplicity by noted painter (Bolotowski)

Smoke
Irreverent, ribald comedy, full of wild visual puns (Kramer)

The Gift
Herbert Danska's much-discussed, ironic comment on the human and esthetic predicament of the modern artist tenderly counterposes the story of an aging painter to the first love experience of a young couple. Music by Gunther Schuller.

January 30

Cockeyed Luck
Chaplinesque satire concerning a bumbling opportunist who vainly tries to 'adjust' to a succession of political regimes in Poland and becomes variously suspected as Fascist, Resistance Fighter, Collaborator, Jew, Anti-Communist and Foreign Spy. Last film of the the great Andrzej Munk (*Eroica*) who died this year at 43. "Ruthless satire on bureaucracy, Stalinism, and Polish character in general; one of the most extraordinary films to come out of Poland in recent years." British Film Institute

February 13

Tomorrow I Shall Be A Fire Tree
With a scenario by Kurosawa, this notable first film by Hiromichi Horikawa explores with keen psychological insight the growing into manhood of a Japanese

boy, in episodes reflecting his uncertain discoveries of friendship, ambition, tragedy and love. Despite the universality of the emotions portrayed, unexpected actions and psychological overtones lend an exotic, appealing flavor to the film. A Toho release.

February 27

Prince Bajaja
This most beautiful film, a medieval folktale by Czech master puppeteer Jiri Trnka resembles sumptuous 15th Century illuminated manuscripts in its exquisite colors and sophisticated naivete. The mood is romantic, the folk music of melodic beauty, the puppets oddly wistful. (Rembrandt Films)

March 20

Screening of 1963 Flaherty Award Winners
One of our most popular events, co-sponsored by City College; 1963's best documentaries as selected by a distinguished jury.

April 17

The Street By The Sea
Seleuk Bakkalbasi's Turkish feature is probably the season's oddest film: the story of a middle-aged solitary, unable to make contact with life and people around him. Already a "cult" film, its laconic style, desolate mood and curious psychology has been likened by Alain Robbe-Grillet and others to Antonioni.

"Weaves a spell akin to the one cast by primitive painters." *Tribune de Lausanne.*

"I did not follow those who left early and my patience was rewarded. A strange spell emanates from this film; the figure of this man, embarassed with himself and with life, haunts me." Georges Sadoul.

May 16

Garbo and Fairbanks: Two Hollywood Myths

The Kiss
Garbo in her last silent film, at the height of her power, in a murder mystery interestingly directed by Jacques Feyder. With Lew Ayres.

When The Clouds Roll By
Delightful feature-length satire on dubious 'psychoanalysts' fully reveals Fairbanks' lighthearted charm and physical prowess.

✦ ✦ ✦ ✦ ✦ ✦

Letter to Friends of Cinema 16 from Amos Vogel, 2/63

exhibition and distribution of documentary and experimental films **CINEMA 16** incorporated

175 Lexington Avenue   New York 16, New York   Murray Hill 9-7288 and 9-7289

Amos Vogel
Executive Secretary

Committee of Sponsors:
Erica Anderson
Kenneth Anger
W. H. Auden
Paul Ballard
Jean Benoit-Levy
Leonard Bernstein
Van Wyck Brooks
Henry Seidel Canby
Eddie Cantor
Theodore R. Conant
Robert Delson
John Dos Passos
Ernestine Evans
James T. Farrell
David Flaherty
Robert J. Flaherty +
Waldo Frank
John Gassner
Robert Gessner
John Grierson
Richard Griffith
John Gunther
Oscar Hammerstein, II
Natalie Hays Hammond
Curtis Harrington
Walter E. Harris
Robert P. Heller
Bryn J. Hovde
Elizabeth Hudson
John Huston
Horace M. Kallen
Arthur Knight
Dr. Siegfried Kracauer
Albert Lewin
Roy Lockwood
Mary Losey
Len Lye
Arthur L. Mayer
Allan McNab
Yehudi Menuhin
Gjon Mili
Pierre Monteux
Seymour Peck
Erwin Piscator
Carl Pryer, Jr.
Philip Rahv
Man Ray
C. R. Reagan +
Jean Renoir
Elmer Rice
Hans Richter
Paul Rotha
Juliet Barrett Rublee
Edward R. Sammis
Gilbert Seldes
Elie Siegmeister
Mark Starr
Frank Stauffacher
Roy E. Stryker
Deems Taylor
Francis Thompson
Parker Tyler
Margaret Valiant
Helen Van Dongen
Gordon R. Washburn
Herman Weinberg
Eli Willis
Archer Winsten
Basil Wright

This letter will come as an unhappy surprise. I address it to you as one of our loyal friends.

Cinema 16 is faced with a grave problem. For the past 15 years, we have achieved what no other cultural, non-profit venture in New York has even attempted; to run on a self-sustaining basis. All existing cultural projects depend on heavy subsidies from wealthy individuals or organizations. In contrast, Cinema 16 has so far derived its income entirely from memberships.

While the years have seen our transformation from a struggling venture into an institution, the financial tide has been running against us. Our costs, as has been true of other cultural projects, have risen faster than our income which has also been adversely affected by factors more fully explored in the enclosed report.

To keep ahead of increases in theatre and film rentals, printing, advertising and mailing costs, we raised membership fees slightly on three occasions, but have finally reached the point where they can be raised no further. We are thus caught in a financial squeeze.

As a result, a cumulative deficit which we had hoped to eliminate, has instead grown into a sum which threatens our existence.

I have never before approached you for help. Now I must.

This is an appeal for $20,000. Your contribution will be deeply appreciated whatever its size; perhaps you are willing to become a 'Patron' of Cinema 16 by contributing $100, or a 'Sponsor' by contributing $500. This appeal is also directed to the one unknown individual who could solve the problem single-handedly; by any realistic standards, our needs are modest.

In all simplicity, as of this moment Cinema 16 is in your hands. You will decide whether we will continue or suspend operations at the end of this season.

Very sincerely yours,

Amos Vogel
Executive Secretary

Illustration 83. Opening page of Amos Vogel's letter asking the Cinema 16 membership for financial assistance. *(Letter continues on pg. 412.)*

THE PROBLEM

Cinema 16 has been able to exist for sixteen years solely because it fills the need for a pioneer who is one step ahead of the commercial cinemas, not subject to box-office or censorship pressures, oriented toward the art, rather than the commerce of film; a pioneer who continuously opens up new areas that are unacceptable, unavailable or even unknown to the commercial cinemas. But we are encountering serious problems.

Cost: In the past five years, our costs have risen over 30%. The brochure cost is now over $3000; a Sunday Times advertisement $500; the recent postal increase adds $1000 annually. Our importation of features, while assuring you films not available elsewhere, has added $300 customs and transportation costs per title, exclusive of the high rental fee required to lure films across the ocean.

On the other hand, our salaries remain at a modest $360 for 3 people (some unpaid at present); and our average membership income of $14.50 for 15 shows represents a 90 cents admission charge per program. Though this seems modest, we feel that we cannot ask you to pay more without losing in numbers. This gap between rising costs and stationary membership fees is one decisive factor in our crisis.

Thousands of Members, but: While we maintain the proud distinction of being the world's largest film society, membership totals fluctuate too close to our constantly increasing minimum requirements and have at times fallen below them.

The right to be controversial: By refusing to reject unpopular but meritorious films which meet with a measure of resistance even from our own membership (avant-garde works, controversial social films, etc.); by refusing to show films of questionable value but of popular appeal, we suffer financially, while fulfilling our true function.

Newspaper coverage: We have been clearly told by the newspapers that we cannot expect as much publicity as we deserve, their space being reserved primarily for the commercial cinema, a prime advertising source. Nor can we disregard the 'undischarged responsibility' of most mass circulation film critics toward our venture, their routine support or genteel indifference. These factors add to the advertising costs necessary to make our activities known to the public.

Advances in the Commercial Film Field: In the last decade, all exhibitors, Cinema 16 included, have to some extent been affected by film showings on television. There has also been more adventurous programming by some art theatres, partly caused by 'product' shortage, partly by Cinema 16's success, which indicated to the ever timid commercial exhibitors that it may have become 'safe' to show certain new kinds of films. This is both a testimonial to our pioneering and a contributory cause of our difficulties.

THE CONTINUING NEED FOR CINEMA 16

The Limitations of the Art Theatres: Even the more adventurous art theatres, however, cannot show most of the films seen at Cinema 16. They are directly subject to box-office pressures, go out of business if their programming is too esoteric, immediately drop a film or new policy when it becomes unprofitable. This is true even of the 'repertory theatres' which have given up some of their interesting programming experiments and have fallen back on the safer American star vehicles of the 30's or double bills of all too familiar classics. These art theatres cannot rely on 'prepaid' membership incomes; cannot afford to show (far less, import) programs consisting exclusively of shorts; nor can they show non-theatrical scientific, psychological and medical studies.

There is need for a showcase—

—for foreign films not in American distribution: Many films of artistic value are not bought by American distributors due to their presumably dubious box-office appeal. While these films therefore cannot be shown in theatres, we are readily able to obtain them for Cinema 16.

—for new film makers: the 'talents of tomorrow' are frequently discovered and premiered at Cinema 16. We were the first to show Shirley Clarke, Norman McLaren, Tony Richardson, Carmen D'Avino, Robert Breer, Michelangelo Antonioni, Robert Frank, Stan Vanderbeek, John Cassavetes, Robert Bresson.

—for film talk in New York, where film makers, creative artists, critics and audiences can meet face to face. Our speakers have included Dali, Flaherty, Hitchcock, Tennessee Williams, Renoir, Archer Winsten, Arthur Miller, Dylan Thomas.

—for experimental films, an area of high significance for the future of film art; we have successfully pioneered in the exhibition and distribution of such films not only in New York, but also nationally to art museums, film societies and universities.

—for controversial social documentaries, propaganda and political films.

—for short films, to us an often freer sampling of the potentialities of film art, because cheaper to produce than features. In theatres the short is an appendage to the feature; at Cinema 16, it holds a place of honor. More than 300 shorts, many of them prizewinners, have been shown by us in the last decade; most have not been commercially released and were seen only at Cinema 16.

—for censorable films: censorship, especially as to sex, violence, blasphemy, is still with us; and so are legal restrictions on psychological and medical studies. These restrictions do not apply to our screenings.

Cinema 16 thus remains the only continuing showcase for important films whose unconventional and unfashionable qualities at present deny them a commercial showing—a function of much significance for both audience and film maker. However, it has also finally become clear that a venture as unorthodox as ours cannot fully pay its own way; its deficits must be underwritten by those most concerned with its programs and activities.

We need your help. If it is not forthcoming, Cinema 16 will suspend operations at the end of the present season.

Cinema 16 Income and Expenses for the year ending August 31, 1963

Expenses:
Salaries—Office (3 people)	$18,600.00
Theatre & Projection	2,400.00
Film Rentals	4,200.00
Film Distribution Royalties	4,000.00
Film Import, Preparation, Customs	5,700.00
Advertising	5,800.00
Mailings (including postage)	5,700.00
Printing	7,100.00
Theatre and Office Rent	5,200.00
Office Expenses and Overhead	5,300.00
Legal, Accounting and Payroll Taxes	1,900.00
Insurance, Repairs, Previews, misc.	2,800.00
	$68,700.00
Receipts:	$59,000.00
Net Loss (Sept. 1, 1962–August 31, 1963)	9,700.00
Net Loss (Sept. 1, 1961–August 31, 1962)	8,370.00
Net Loss (Sept. 1, 1960–August 31, 1961)	1,900.00
Accumulated Net Loss (August 31, 1963)	$19,970.00

✦ ✦ ✦ ✦ ✦ ✦

Nat Hentoff, "Last Call for Cinema 16," *Village Voice*, 2/21/63

Cinema 16 is about to fold. For sixteen years Amos Vogel's persistently independent venture has been entirely self-sustaining. No foundation bread. No substantial private patrons. Costs rose, but membership fluctuated at a level about 1000 below the number needed to break even. Now Cinema 16 needs $15,000 to stay alive.

I expect the news of this imminent demise will surprise most of you. There have been no overt signs of sinking in recent years. Every fall that messianic ad has appeared in the papers, followed by proselytizing columns by Archer Winsten in the Post and Jonas Mekas here. (The rest of the press has been exceedingly chary of space for Cinema 16 although the news values of many of the premieres there have been considerable. The press is uninterested because it is a business office dictum that in the entertainment section, space goes to them what pay by way of ads. Furthermore, the reviewers aren't interested in discovery, self or otherwise.)

Difficult Stance

In any case, the end is indeed near. Amos Vogel has never asked his membership for extra help before. He probably should have, but the stance of a pleader is difficult for him. In the mail this week, however, is a letter to his 3000 members telling them the score. Unless those members are radically different from most of the citizenry, the percentage of returns will not be enough for survival. There is always the chance of one or two wealthy members who will rescue our Wednesday nights and Sunday mornings, but it's only the edge of a chance.

Dwight Macdonald to the contrary, Cinema 16 has been of immense value. The actual viewing and feeling kicks have been enormously variegated and unpredictable. I can't think of anything I've ever belonged to which was less concerned with saving itself by establishing a homogeneity of membership. Vogel exacerbates every member at least six or seven times a season, but at the same time other members are surprised into intensity by the same feature or short. There is a safe way of operating Cinema 16, of keeping Dwight Macdonald entertained, but that isn't Vogel's groove, and he's about to pay for having had so much respect for Cinema 16's audience.

Cumulative Impact

For me, the major importance of Cinema 16 has been what its pictures have told me of other countries and how their people deal with the basics of being. For the "cinema" as a whole, the club has done a great deal to help broaden and perhaps even deepen national awareness of what can be done with a camera and an open eye. Vogel was the first to show Antonioni, Vanderbeek, Bresson, McLaren, and a good many others. A Cinema 16 showing has often led to later, wider distribution of a key film; and after sixteen years there has been a cumulative Cinema 16 impact on timid distributors which convinced them that it was "safe" to show certain kinds of exploratory films.

Simply on the level of straight knowledge, many of the medical and other scientific shorts in Cinema 16's history would never have been available to most of us laymen if the club hadn't existed. Legal restrictions which prevent showing of these films in profit-making theatres don't apply to Cinema 16.

Not Ready

There are many more reasons why Cinema 16 is much more necessary than say, a group of buildings such as Lincoln Center. But our cultural explosion seems to be much more involved with contractors than with alarmingly alive art. In culture, as in sex and work, we get what we deserve in the sense that we only get what we're ready for. And unless Vogel's members do respond in numbers that would contradict all statistical charts of fund-raising campaigns—and unless some of you feel moved to contribute—the death of Cinema 16 will indicate that we're not ready for it. We've had an accidental grant of sixteen years because of one stubborn, resourceful man; and now we're on our own, left with the revivals and the art houses and the intermittent centers for the new such as the late Charles Theatre. But the Bleecker Street Cinema and the New Yorker and any future Charles can't begin to fill Cinema 16's particular scope of spurs to self-awareness.

New York, in short, is indeed the cultural center of the country. A depressing fact of life and of Cinema 16's death. The address, by the way, is 175 Lexington Avenue.

Reprinted by permission of *The Village Voice*.

✦ ✦ ✦ ✦ ✦ ✦

Conversation with Jonas Mekas, 5/24/85

Scott MacDonald: I remember you telling me that you started to go to Cinema 16 screenings as soon as you got to this country.

Jonas Mekas: Yes, it was very prominent at that time. Sunday morning was Cinema 16—from eleven o'clock until I don't know what time, at the Paris Theater and later at the Central Needle Trades Auditorium. We [Jonas and his brother Adolfas] joined immediately and attended absolutely every Cinema 16 screening. For some time, it was the only place you could see the American avant-garde cinema. Of course, it affected my whole life; I consider it one of my universities.

MacDonald: You were involved with a group that formed during the later years of Cinema 16.

Mekas: The New American Cinema Group began meeting in 1959. In 1960, the group decided that it should become more active in fighting censorship, in exploring new production avenues, and in distribution. At the time, there were only two or three distribution possibilities for the independents: Brandon, Contemporary Films, and Cinema 16. All three were run by people who had their own particular tastes. They chose one film and rejected another, and they often rejected our favorite works. We thought that the idea of a distribution center that would be run by filmmakers and would serve the filmmakers' wishes should be explored. Three or four filmmakers got appointed to explore those possibilities—I was one; Ed Bland was another. We decided that we definitely should create our own cooperative distribution center. . .

MacDonald: I've heard people say that those developments occurred because of Brakhage's *Anticipation of the Night* [1958].

Mekas: No. That was only one instance that made some filmmakers, Stan especially, very angry. It became crucial only at the meeting at which Film-makers' Cooperative was officially created. Amos was there. This was decades ago and memories can be wrong, but as I remember, Amos said that he liked the work of the New American Cinema filmmakers and that we didn't need a cooperative because he would always distribute our work. It was at that point that Stan said, "But my new work you refused!"

But Cinema 16 was not the key reason we formed the Film-makers' Cooperative. The filmmakers that belonged to the New American Cinema Group were not all avant-garde filmmakers. Cinema 16 was only interested in distributing avant-garde, or "experimental" as it was then called, film, and there were filmmakers in the group interested in other kinds of films. Brandon, Contemporary Films, and Cinema 16—each was interested in a slightly different kind of film. No matter how open Amos would have been, he could not have accommodated all the filmmakers in the group. We needed an outlet controlled by ourselves, where no film would be rejected and all would be available. And so the Film-makers' Cooperative came into existence.

As I remember, Amos said at that meeting, "If you create this, it is the end of the independent cinema, because I'm doing my best and nobody else is going to do more." Of course, for us that could be no argument. At that time already, questions were raised about whether this was being done in opposition to Cinema 16. Amos has always taken that position. But our purpose was simply to bring some new activity to film—to expand it, not to shrink it, which proved to be what happened.

MacDonald: So this all came to a head, at least between Vogel and the New American Cinema Group, at this particular meeting?

Mekas: It was not such a big clash, really. I don't think what we did had an impact on Cinema 16. Cinema 16 was ending. The record shows that there were financial problems and it had to end. But remember, it accomplished a lot. It went for more than a decade *very* strongly indeed, but like other undertakings it reached a very natural end. Nothing would have saved it except a lot of money, but that was not available to independent distributors and exhibitors at that time. It's fantasy to think that if Film-makers' Cooperative had not come into existence, Cinema 16 would have survived and continued.

MacDonald: So you think that Amos took something personally that he shouldn't have taken personally?

Mekas: Times had changed. Something wasn't there anymore or something different was there. The Cinema 16 crowd was a very specific group. It was not like any audience that you would see today at, let's say, The Collective or Millennium or Anthology. It was the Madison Avenue world and the fine arts crowd. It was not, I would say, the lower middle classes. But *whatever* it was exhausted itself after a decade and attendance naturally began falling off.

Also, after the Beat Generation and their democratization of the arts, a new, completely different, sloppier audience began developing and going to different places to see films. To them Cinema 16 was too clean, too official. And, of course, around that time avant-garde film itself began changing, on both coasts. With Ron Rice and Robert Frank, and others, a sloppier film came in.

MacDonald: For years the Film-makers Cooperative was in the same building Cinema 16 had used for its offices. How did that happen?

Mekas: Just by accident. It became available several years after Cinema 16 ended in 1963. Until 1966 we were at 414 Park Avenue South. It's also possible—actually I don't remember—that Cinema 16 kept it during those years and then, when it became available, called us.

When Amos got into film distribution, there were people who blamed him because they felt he stepped over them. But I think that the time comes when somebody simply steps in and does what has to be done. Amos did that, and I feel the New American Cinema group did that too.

✦ ✦ ✦ ✦ ✦

Archer Winsten, "Rages and Outrages," *New York Post*, 3/11/63

It came as a chock to learn a couple of weeks ago that Cinema 16 had gotten itself into a financial hole during the past three years and would have to quit if it couldn't make up a $20,000 deficit before April 1.

First reaction was that letting this valuable institution founder would be unthinkable. It performs several unique functions. To put it simply, Cinema 16 is a forerunner, an artistic plow, a device for getting pictures from all over the world shown in New York, pictures that could not make their own way by reason of predicted box-office strength.

By definition a function of this sort is not apt to be self-sustaining. However, Cinema 16 did sustain itself for a dozen years because there were so many different groups in NYC who had absolutely no place to see what they wanted, whether it was avant-garde, scientific oddities, sociology, psychology, art experimental, foreign whatnots, films guaranteed not to be popular, even the censorable, or the very shocking.

* * *

Eventually, especially in the past three years, some of these groups have gotten themselves more organized. Many more theaters have opened to foreign films, and they have broadened their scope because the general public has been educated to accept far-out fodder. The avant-garde has its own places and groups where their kind of thing can be oohed and ahed in sympathetic surroundings. And finally, the very catholicity of Cinema 16 has worked against it, since every program had something that could be disliked as well as something unique. It is a sad fact of human nature that among intellectuals, art lovers and cinemaddicts anger is more dynamic than approval. More people quit Cinema 16 in pique than bought two subscriptions because they liked it so much.

Attendance reached a stationary plateau, or declined a little as other cinema avenues opened.

Costs of printing, advertising, postage, customs fees, and film rental all rose while income had been raised only a little through subscription increases. And that's how Cinema 16 got into its hole.

* * *

This reviewer has for many years mingled praise with a note of caution in writing about Cinema 16. But these have been pieces of general appreciation. There has been little space devoted to the fact that in Amos Vogel, Cinema 16's founder, there has been a cinematic critical intelligence so all-encompassing in taste, so devoted to the proposition that controversy is the breath of life, so keen and tireless in seeking quality work from all over the world that the sum-total of product shown is incomparable.

Foundations spend thousands of dollars on talents highly speculative, hundreds of thousands on institutions of dubious worth. They gamble with their millions. Here is a sure thing they could support.

Philanthropists spend their millions on those who are adept in getting their ears and purses, too, frequently pouring the golden flood down a rathole.

* * *

Cinema 16's talent and that of Amos Vogel, alas, stop short of money-raising wizardry. Had he been a self-seeker from the start, he would have had his own theater and shrine by now, magnificently endowed, and with his footprints, hand-shape and facial bas-relief permanently set in the lobby. But his programs would have been less interesting.

It is clear that someone should form immediately NAAAV (National Association for the Advancement of Amos Vogel), but in default of such a sensible procedure, which this department cannot undertake on account of a deficiency in arithmetic, let me state that the address of Cinema 16 is 175 Lexington Avenue. To show you how strongly I feel, if anyone will send them $10, I will match it, once. If someone has $100 to give, he becomes a Patron. I should think that would be tax deductible (not this year) since Cinema 16 is most obviously a non-profit venture.

Reprinted by permission of the *New York Post*.

✦ ✦ ✦ ✦ ✦ ✦

Final Cinema 16 Distribution Catalog Film Listings, 1963

Introduction

Since the publication of our first listing of experimental films in 1950, the independent and avant-garde cinema in America has come into its own. In 1950, we were the first to pioneer in both the exhibition and distribution of such films at a time when their very purpose, integrity and seriousness were openly questioned by many; step-child of the industry, they were at times considered scandalous, fraudulent, or irrelevant. Their distribution was limited to hardy individuals and stubborn public institutions unwilling to join in the prevailing lack of celebration.

Today these films are used by hundreds of universities, public libraries, churches, civic groups, film societies, art institutes and individuals across the nation. They have become curriculum-integrated in cinema, art, or English literature departments. They are exhibited at church conventions; at special festivals, on television and in theatres; discussed in magazines; used by art galleries, advertising agencies and coffee houses for their own nefarious purposes; purchased by international film archives. The basic question asked is no longer why such films are being made but rather (and rightly so) an investigation of the quality and originality of a particular title or tendency in the field.

Illustration 84. The four Cinema 16 distribution brochures.

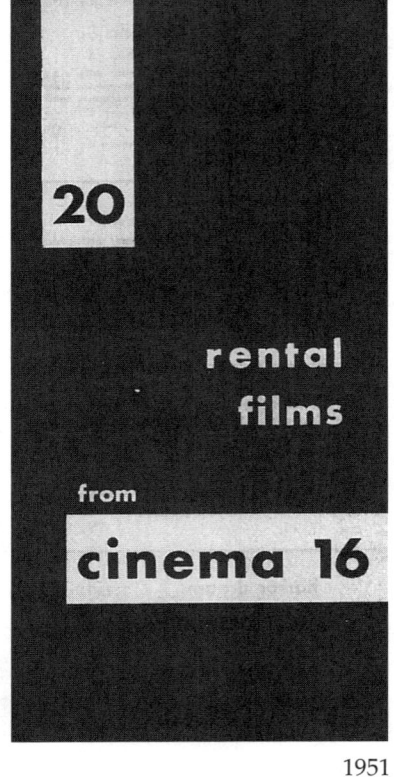

1951

1956

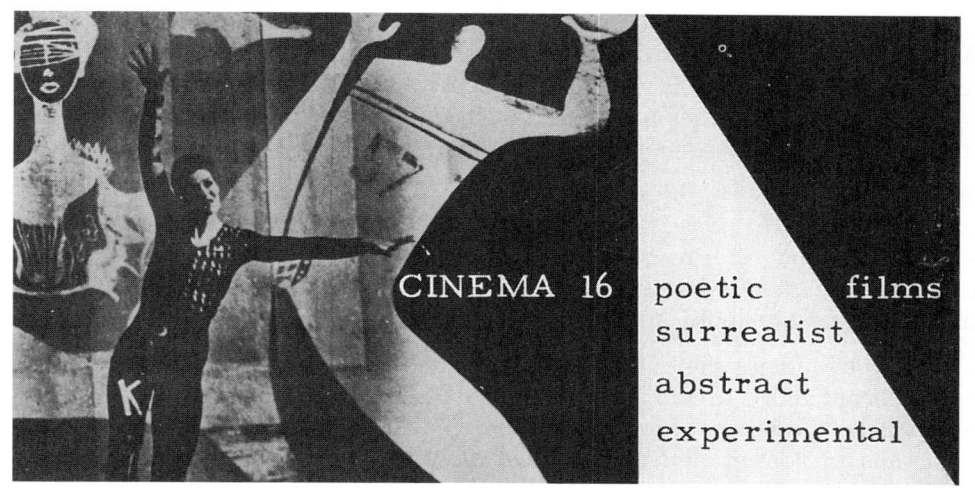

CINEMA 16 poetic films
surrealist
abstract
experimental

1953

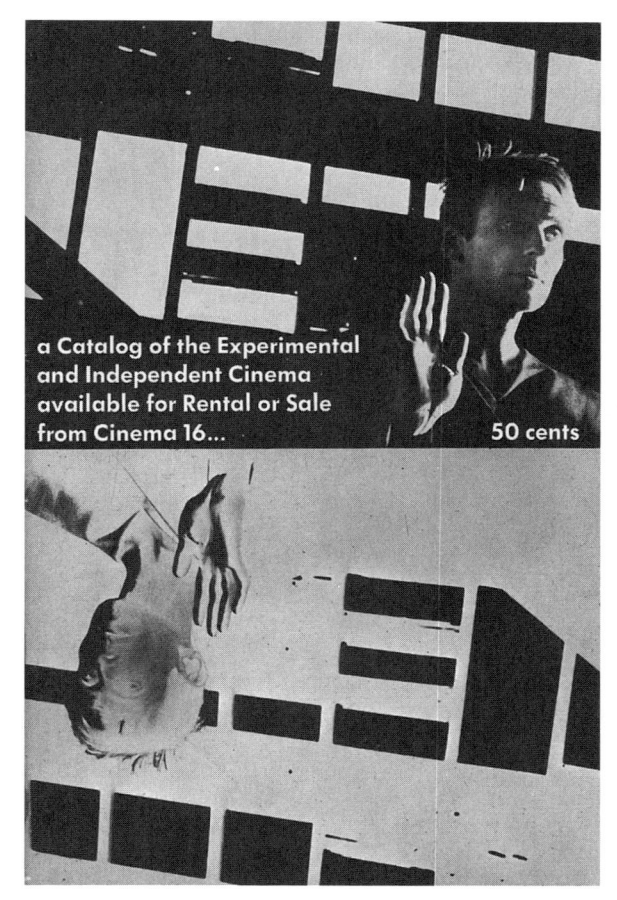

a Catalog of the Experimental and Independent Cinema available for Rental or Sale from Cinema 16...

50 cents

1963

It is our fond conviction that our activities have significantly contributed to this happy development. There is also no doubt that the publication of this new catalog—the most comprehensive listing of experimental cinema published anywhere in the world—will further contribute to a more rapid opening up of the field and a more general appreciation of the efforts and achievements of the film avant-garde.

With the appearance of this catalog listing over 240 films and representing more than 140 filmmakers, there now exists a central international source for the poetic, independent and experimental cinema. New titles are continuously added to the collection. No attempt is made to duplicate the work of distributors in the documentary, educational or feature film field.

Produced by independent film artists, these are explorations in the cinema. Offered as significant efforts to broaden the scope of the film medium and further develop its aesthetic vocabulary and potential, these films express the psychological and emotional tensions of modern life; delve into the subconscious; explore the world of color and abstract images; experiment with cinematic devices and synthetic sound.

They were produced primarily for adult audiences and are therefore not subject in either content or treatment to the vicissitudes of a "production code" or of pressure groups; nor do they necessarily abide by so-called community standards (or prejudices) in regard to sex, violence, religion or politics. A few of the titles are most definitely suggested for adult audiences only: these are clearly designated and care should be exercised in programming them.

Practically all of the titles are "pre-tested" by having been successfully exhibited at Cinema 16 in New York; a large number are international prizewinners; and a great many have already been shown widely and successfully at film societies, colleges, art museums, universities and civic groups nationally.

No attempt is made in this catalog to either include all independent film makers or to include all the work of any one particular filmmaker; quality and originality remain the sole criteria of selection. However, if we err at times, as we must, we hope to do so long the lines of encouraging the new rather than the safe and already accepted.

We wish to express our gratitude to both the filmmakers and the users of these films for having made this catalog possible.

—Amos Vogel, Cinema 16

[Alphabetical listing of film titles (with filmmakers) presented in the catalogue (in the catalogue only proper names are capitalized; we have used conventional capitalization):]

The Adventures of Asterisk	John Hubley
Adventures of Jimmie	James Broughton
A la Mode	Stan Vanderbeek
And So to Work	Richard Massingham
Anticipation of the Night	Stan Brakhage
Appointment with Darkness	Robert Vickrey

At Land	Maya Deren
The Atom Strikes	
Barney Oldfield's Race for Life	Mack Sennett
The Battle of Wangapore	John Daborn
Be Gone Dull Care	Norman McLaren
Between Two Worlds	Sam Kaner and Guy L. Cote
Bharatnatyam	
Big Business	J. W. Horne
The Big "O" and other films	Carmen D'Avino
Le Bijou	Francis Lee
Black and White Burlesque	Richard Preston
The Blood of the Beasts	Georges Franju
Bonjour Paris	
Brussels Experimental Festival Packages	
Brutality in Stone	Peter Schamoni and Alexander Kluge
The Cage	Sidney Peterson
Cat's Cradle	Stan Brakhage
A Cavalcade of American Serials	
Charmides	Gregory Markopoulos
Cinesumac	Jean Dasque
The City	Wolfgang Ramsbott
City Without Wheels	Morton Heilig
Clinic of Stumble	Sidney Peterson
Color Designs #1	Hugo Lateltin
Coming Shortly	Tony Rose
Cosmic Ray	Bruce Conner
The Cross-Country Runner	Mark McCarty
The Cry of Jazz	Edward Bland
Cubism	Pierre Alibert
Cuckoo Waltz	E. van Moerkerken
The Cure	Charles Chaplin
Dance Chromatic	Ed Emshwiller
Daybreak and Whiteye	Stan Brakhage
The Dead	Stan Brakhage
Desistfilm	Stan Brakhage
Dime Store	Dorsey Alexander
Double Whoopee	James Parrott
Do You Remember	Tony Thompson
Easy Street	Charles Chaplin
Eaux d'Artifice	Kenneth Anger
The Elephant Will Never Forget	John Krish
Elisabeth	Jean Beranger
The End of Summer	Ralph Hirshorn
Escape	Albert Mertz and Jorgen Roos
Etude	Pierre Puttemans and Paul Jespers
Experiments in Perception	
Faces in the Shadows	Peter Weiss
Fiddle De Dee	Norman McLaren
Film Exercises #4 and 5	John and James Whitney

Fireworks	Kenneth Anger
Footballs as It Is Played Today	Joseph Anderson
Form in Motion	Jose Pavon
Fotodeath	Al Kouzel
Four in the Afternoon	James Broughton
Freight Stop	Allen Downs
Geography of the Body	Willard Maas
Glens Falls Sequence	Douglass Crockwell
Glimmering	Pierre Thevenard
Good Night, Nurse	Henry George
Go Slow on the Brighton	Donald Smith
The Griffith Report	Tony Davies
Guernica	Alain Resnais
Hallucinations	Peter Weiss
Handwritten	Charles Boultenhouse
Harlem Wednesday	John Hubley
Have I Told You Lately that I Love You	Stuart Hanisch
His Marriage Wow	Harry Edwards
Homage to Jean Tinguely	Robert Breer
Hoppity Pop	Norman McLaren
Horror Dream	Sidney Peterson
Horse Over Teakettle and other films	Robert Breer
Hotel Apex	Weldon Kees
Hurry Hurry and other films	Marie Menken
The Idea	Berthold Bartosch
The Idyl	Francis Lee
Image in the Snow	Willard Maas
The Immigrant	Charles Chaplin
Inauguration of the Pleasure Dome	Kenneth Anger
In Between	Stan Brakhage
Interim	Stan Brakhage
Interplay	Peter Weiss
Introspection	Sara Kathryn Arledge
It Is Good to Live	Fumio Kamei
The Juggler of Our Lady	Al Kouzel
Krushchev	Robert Lebar and Howard Kaplan
Lafcadio	Jean Beranger
Laughing Gravy	James Horne
The Lead Shoes	Sidney Peterson
Life and Death of a Hollywood Extra	Vorkapich and Florey
Lifelines	Ed Emshwiller
Light for John	Warren Brown
Little Phantasy on a 19th Century Painting	Norman McLaren
Living in a Reversed World	
Lizzies of the Field	Eddie Cline
Loony Tom, the Happy Lover	James Broughton
Loving and other films	Stan Brakhage
Lysis	Gregory Markopoulous

Magritte	Luc de Heusch
Man and Dog Out for Air, etc.	Robert Breer
The Man He Might Have Been	
Mankinda	Stan Vanderbeek
The Maze	Richard Preston
The Mechanics of Love	Willard Maas and Ben Moore
Meditation on Violence	Maya Deren
Meshes of the Afternoon	Maya Deren
Metal Dimensions: Bertoia	Madeline Tourtelot
Metanoia	Ilya Bolotowsky
Metrographic	Vittorio Speich
Millions in Business As Usual	Rudolph Burckhardt
The Mirage	Peter Weiss
Mr. Frenhofer and the Minotaur	Sidney Peterson
Monkey into Man	Stuart Legg
Moonbird	John Hubley
Mothers Day	James Broughton
Motion Picture	Frank Paine
Mounting Tension	Rudolph Burckhardt
A Movie	Bruce Conner
The Music Box	James Parrott
Music Studio: Harry Partch	Madeline Tourtelot
Narcissus	Ben Moore and Willard Maas
Neighbors	Norman McLaren
Next Stop 28th	Ed Corley
1941	Francis Lee
Nightscapes	Richard Preston
No Credit	Leonard Tregillus and Ralph Luce
No More Fleeing	Herbert Vesely
N. U.	Michelangelo Antonioni
Object Lesson	Christopher Young
Odds and Ends	Jane Belson Conger
O Dreamland	Lindsay Anderson
Oedipus	Robert Vickrey
One by One	Madeline Tourtelot
On These Evenings	Herbert Vesely
L'Opera Mouffe	Agnes Varda
Operation Abolition	
Operation Correction	
Pacific 231	Jean Mitry
Paris Belongs to Us	Jacques Rivette
The Path	Richard Myers
Pat's Birthday	Robert Breer
Pattern for a Sunday Afternoon	Carmen D'Avino
Paul Tomkowicz, Street-Car Switchman	Roman Kroitor
Peep Show	Ken Russell
The Petrified Dog	Sidney Peterson
Pickpocket	Robert Bresson

Poem 8	Emlen Etting
The Potted Psalm	Sidney Peterson
Power of Plants	
Prelude: Dog Star Man	Stan Brakhage
The Private Life of a Cat	Alexander Hammid
Psyche	Gregory Markopoulos
Puce Moment	Kenneth Anger
Rare Early French Hand-colored Films	
Reflections	Madeline Tourtelot
Reflections on Black	Stan Brakhage
Relief	Peter Weiss
Ritual in Transfigured Time	Maya Deren
La Rose et le Reseda	Andre Michel
Rotate the Body	Madeline Tourtelot
Science Friction	Stan Vanderbeek
The Searching Eye	Madeline Tourtelot
The Seven Bridges of Koenigsberg	Bruce Cornwall
Shipyard	Paul Rotha
Short Spell	S. W. Jones
Simon	Peter Zadek
The Sin of Jesus	Robert Frank
Sirius Remembered	Stan Brakhage
Six Films by Maya Deren	
Skullduggery	Stan Vanderbeek
The Sluice	Wolfgang Ramsbott and Harry Kramer
Smoke	Joseph Kramer
The Song of Jean Richepin	Carlos Toussaint
Songs Without Words	Yoram Gross
Stone Sonata, Motif and *A Trip*	Carmen D'Avino
The Studio of Dr. Faust	Peter Weiss
A Study in Choreography for Camera	Maya Deren
A Study of Crystals	
Subject Lesson	Christopher Young
Summer	Madeline Tourtelot
Sunlight	Melvin Van [Peebles]
Swain	Gregory Markopoulos
Symphony in No B Flat	Rudolfo Kuhn
The Tear and other films	Soren Melson and Henning Bendtsen
The Tender Game	John Hubley
10,000 Talents	Don Levy
Texture of Decay	Robert Vickrey
Thanatopsis	Ed Emshwiller
Thigh Line Lyre Triangular	Stan Brakhage
This Day	Leonard Stark
Three Abstract Film Exercises	John and James Whitney
Three Pickup Men for Herrick	Melvin Van [Peebles]
3:10 to Yuma	Hazel Wilkinson
Time Out of War	Denis and Terry Sanders

The Train	Gosta Werner
Transformation	Ed Emshwiller
23 Avant-Garde Film Makers	
Two Tars	James Parrott
Uirapuru	Sam Zebba
Van Meegeren's Faked Vermeers	G. E. Magnel
The Very Eye of Night	Maya Deren
The Visit	Jack Gold
Visual Variations on Noguchi	Marie Menken
The Voyeur	Angel Hurtado
Waiting	Flora Mock
Warning in the Dark	
Watch the Birdie	Bob Godfrey and Keith Learner
The Way to Shadow Garden	Stan Brakhage
Wedlock House: An Intercourse	Stan Brakhage
Weegee's New York	Weegee
What Who How	Stan Vanderbeek
Window Water Baby Moving	Stan Brakhage
The World of Paul Delvaux	Henri Storck
You're Darn Tootin'	Edgar Kennedy

[A description accompanied each listing in the catalog. The catalog was also liberally illustrated with photographs from the films.]

✦ ✦ ✦ ✦ ✦ ✦

Letter to Amos Vogel from Stan Brakhage, 11/66

[hw]
Mid-Nov. '66

Dear Amos and Marcia,

Your letter is practically a historical document proclaiming the end of an era: but then, too, I know it is for you rather simply a relief to be out from under a burden become too great considering each of you holds full time jobs <u>other</u> than C16 responsibilities. And I want to take this opportunity to thank both of you for sustaining that difficulty until you could find someone else to assume it. A less dedicated pair of people might have made less thoughtful arrangements in some spur-of-the-moment thru which C16 could have disappeared altogether: but you have both acted with some careful consideration for all concerned. All the same, I shall miss (as I already do) the long discussions with you, Amos, and the personal touch which Marcia, you, can manage to give even to an economic statement. I hope, therefor, we shall remain in some touch with each other and that I shall be able to see you from the time-to-time I get to New York and shall hear from you each occasionally by letter.

Blessings,

Stan

P.S.

I do have one question—I guess for you, Marcia...Western Cine did recently inform me you'd ordered one print each of 2 films (I don't have the exact titles now) to be sent to U. of Calif. in San Diego (I assume for print sale): and as there was no indication in the new statements about this, I wonder if you would be so good as to let me know what it was all about, etc?

(I did okay the order with Western Cinema; and I assume the prints were mailed).

Reprinted by permission of Stan Brakhage.

[The occasion of this letter was Cinema 16's decision to cease distributing films and to let Grove Press take over the distribution of those films filmmakers did not want to distribute independently.]

✦ ✦ ✦ ✦ ✦ ✦

Amos Vogel, "Thirteen Confusions," *Evergreen Review*, 6/67

After two decades of obscurity, poverty, ignorant rejection, and dogged persistence, the American film avant-garde suffers today, for the first time in its history, from an ominous new ailment: over-attention without understanding, over-acceptance without discrimination. Crime of crimes, it has become fashionable. Its gurus and artists are in danger of becoming the avant-garde establishment; its growing fame hides only imperfectly an inner weakness. The following observations, aimed at the removal of confusions, represent a criticism from within, fully cognizant of the movement's many achievements.

These lie not merely in the many talents and works it has discovered and championed, but in its continuing creative "desecration" of the medium, leaving nothing undisturbed, taking nothing for granted. In the hands of the movement's foremost practitioners, film is sacked, atomized, caressed, and possessed in a frenzy of passionate love; neither emulsion, exposure, lighting, film speeds, developing, nor rules of editing, camera movement, composition, or sound are safe from the onslaught of these poetic experimentalists who have irrevocably invaded the medium. While most commercial films can safely be followed with one's eyes closed, these works force spectators to open them wide, thereby rendering them defenseless against the magic powers of the medium.

The American avant-garde is part of a strong international trend toward a more visually-oriented, freer, more personal cinema. This movement expresses a revolt against the ossifications of institutions and the conservatism of the old. It represents a cinema of passion.

By restoring the primacy of the visual element, this movement brings us face to face with the essence of the medium, the profound and inexplicable mystery of the image.

Thematically, stylistically, and ideologically, the films belonging to this tendency reflect and prefigure an era of social change, disorientation, and decline, and are suffused with an existentialist humanism devoid of certainty or illusion. Liberated from nineteenth-century art, they increasingly displace realistic narrative structures, clearly defined plots, and well-delineated characters by visual ambiguity and poetic complexity, exploring ideas and forms vertically instead of illustrating events horizontally. There are strong influences of surrealism, neo-Dadaism, Pop Art, the "absurd" theatre and the Theatre of Cruelty, Robbe-Grillet and the new novel. Textbook rules of filmmaking have been abandoned. Editing is explosive, elliptic, unpredictable; camera movements fluid, frequent, and free; time and space are telescoped, destroyed, or obliterated and memory, reality, and illusion fused, until, in a flash of revelation, we realize that the totality of these uncertainties and discontinuities reflect nothing less than the modern world view in philosophy, science, art, and politics. These questioning, white-hot filmmakers—themselves anguished configurations of the anxieties and limited wisdoms they portray—are the committed artists of the sixties, the true explorers of our day.

But the American avant-garde seems to have arrived at a crossroads. On the one hand, the seeds planted by Frank Stauffacher's "Art in Cinema" series and Maya Deren's screenings in the forties, as well as Cinema 16's programs of 1947–1963, have been transformed into a full-blown, highly visible movement. There are unceasing, voluminous productions; new exhibition outlets; schools, art centers, and civic groups clamoring for the "underground"; discotheques and coffeehouses utilizing film-oriented mixed-media techniques; mass circulation magazines and television providing widespread publicity. This new state remains the undeniable achievement of Jonas Mekas and the "New American Cinema" Group.

On the other hand, however, there now exists a certain wariness concerning the movement even among its friends and supporters. Too many of the films are unsatisfactory, even with the greatest of efforts at a sympathetic magnification of their small virtues. In film circles, it is no secret that, after all the growth and publicity, audiences at the Film-Makers Cinematheque in New York are leveling off. To this must be added the paradox of voluminous productivity and little new talent; the growing credibility gap between the movement's house organs and observed filmic quality; the absence, despite new and laudable attempts, of any real resolution to the crucial distribution and exhibition problem. As the faint odor of trouble becomes more noticeable, the evangelical ardor of the movement's leaders becomes more insistent, the manifestos and exorcisms less circumspect.

To begin the process of an informed critique of the American avant-garde (and more specifically, the ideology and style of the New American Cinema tendency within it) is an act of the highest and most necessary loyalty to the movement. The time has come to rescue it from the blind rejection of commercial reviewers and the blind acceptance of its own apostles; both posing as critics and neither subjecting it to dispassionate, informed analysis.

1. Confusing Times Square with Manhattan

The New American Cinema (NAC) and the American film avant-garde are *not* synonymous. The NAC group is the dominant, but not the only factor within the American independent film movement today. Because of its vociferousness and quantity of production, it impresses its values and style on the entire movement, and is frequently and erroneously equated with it. This leads to the convenient omission of Bruce Baillie and the Canyon Cinema Cooperative, other East coast filmmakers; George Manupelli and Richard Myers in the Midwest; and Hilary Harris, Carmen D'Avino, Francis Thompson, Len Lye, and others in New York.

2. Confusing a Producers' Cooperative with a School

The New American Cinema is neither ideologically, stylistically, nor otherwise a unified movement or tendency. In its manifestos, it elevates eclectic aestheticism and undifferentiated enthusiasm into a principle, instead of admitting that the group—ranging the spectrum from Anger to Breer to Warhol to Brakhage—is an economic and not an aesthetic unit.

3. Confusing Historical Continuity with Immaculate Conception

It is necessary to situate the NAC within history—the past, the present, the speculative future. As to the past, the American film avant-garde has its roots in the European surrealist and expressionist avant-garde of the twenties and the American experimentalists of the forties and fifties. The current NAC leaders, for obvious and indefensible reasons, prefer to draw a veil of silence and disregard over the past, thereby contributing to the provincialism of its adherents. It is only recently and because of internal criticism of the kind perpetrated here in public that a few of the works or writings of the "forerunners" have begun to appear on some Cinematheque programs or in *Film Culture*. Nevertheless, it is safe to say that the crucial importance of such filmmakers as Sidney Peterson, the Whitney Brothers, Ralph Steiner, Oscar Fischinger, Watson-Webber, Maya Deren, Curtis Harrington, and James Broughton remain unknown or unanalyzed trivia in the ideological development of the new generation. A resemblance to a certain type of history rewriting is not entirely out-of-place. It evinces the customary narrowness and demagoguery, but is fortunately unaccompanied by effective control over the information media. One shudders at what might happen if some of our present-day proponents of total liberty became Commissars of Film Culture.

As to the present, the NAC is undeniably and inevitably part of the worldwide movement toward a more visual cinema, all their protestations to the contrary. It is impossible to remain neutral when confronted with the astonishing provincialism of the NAC's ideologues in dismissing, disregarding, or exorcising Antonioni, Godard, Resnais, Skolimowski, Bellocchio, and Lester; and as their field of vision narrows, magnifying every object in it, until pygmies loom like giants.

The NAC will transcend its present dilemmas only by studying carefully the techniques and achievements of these experimenters; and by fully acknowledging that this international "pro-visual" movement is neither an exclusive club nor a dogmatic sect, but include both Emshwiller and Antonioni, VanDerBeek and Godard. No film or filmmaker can be read out of this movement by papal decree.

Jonas Mekas's statement at the recent Museum of Modern Art "New Cinema" symposium ("Old cinema, even when it is successful, is horrible; New Cinema, even when it fails, is beautiful") is provocative and untenable. Bertolucci's *Before the Revolution*, Rivette's *Paris Belongs to Us*, Dreyer's *Gertrud*, Skolimowski's *Walkover*,

Schorm's *Courage for Every Day,* Teshigahara's *Woman in the Dunes,* Rocha's *Black God and Blond Devil,* Jancso's *The Round-Up,* Paradjhanov's *Shadows of Forgotten Ancestors,* Antonioni from *L'Avventura* to *Blow-Up,* Resnais from *Hiroshima* to *La Guerre Est Finie,* Godard's *Breathless* to whatever his latest—*all of these were created within what Mekas calls the "old" cinema*—are avant-garde works. They are not merely more important than the failures, but often more important than even the successes of the independent avant-garde. Some day soon an interesting discussion will be begun as to the relative degree of experimentation, achievement, subversion, and political or artistic daring in these works on the one hand and the NAC films on the other. In any case, the creations of these so-called "commercial" directors can be disregarded only by hopeless dogmatists.

4. Confusing Freedom with Formlessness

Lack, failure, and disregard of form is the over-riding weakness of today's avant-garde. Current tendencies in all the arts toward improvisation, fluidity, and chance are mistaken for a total absence of form, and the temptation is to disregard the fact that it is precisely the achieved works of this kind that reveal an inner structure and logic.

This inner coherence is "felt" rather than explicable. It is totally lacking in so many current efforts, which could go on equally well for fifteen minutes or for fifty, and in which the succession or duration of shots remains totally irrelevant or mutable in terms of the total construct of the work. They lack surprise, mystery, and that inexorable form and flow that are the characteristics of all great art.

Film, both as a plastic and time art, involves considerations of tempo, length, progression, editing, camera positioning. These considerations, even in experimental works, are not and can never be suspended. They operate quite independently of the artist's announced intentions on the deepest psychological levels, and they determine the work's value as art. A strong sense of form, structure, and tempo are inevitably present in the best works of the American avant-garde movement, quite regardless of their specific and differing aesthetic commitments.

5. Confusing Content with Quality

Thematic liberation is no guarantee of quality. Nor is the use of five simultaneously-operating projectors, extreme nudity, unexceptionable anti-Vietnam sentiments, hand-held cameras, portrayals of transvestism. Said Cocteau ironically, when first confronted with Cinemascope: "The next time I write a poem, I shall use a larger piece of paper."

6. Confusing Non-Selectivity with Art

The NAC's proudly proclaimed policy of showing, distributing, and praising every scrap of film is self-defeating. Every new person who gets a camera and thereupon "completes" a "work," immediately obtains a public showing and distribution. In this manner several hundred titles are added to the yearly "oeuvre" of the American avant-garde. Under the circumstances, it is easier to discover epigones of Brakhage than new Brakhages.

It may be essential to show every single film to filmmakers at internal, workshop screenings so that they can see each other's work; it is suicidal if this is done with general audiences. Given the present volume and level of "production"—miles of new films—this gluts the market and inundates the viewer in a morass of mediocrity or worse. Sooner or later, the audience refuses to accept the frequent ratio of five minutes of promising footage to two hours of tedium. Unable to judge the works in advance or to rely on somebody else's judgment (since no selection takes place), they ultimately decide to stay away or to stop renting films, their frustrated interest supplanted by hostile irritation. How could they have known, amidst the welter of unknown new productions and a total absence of critical writing, that *Metanomen, Lost in Cuddahy, Oh Dem Watermelons,* and *Relativity* were most eminently worth seeing and four hundred other recent films were not?

There is therefore a need for a new showcase for the avant-garde, not under the control of one faction within the movement, however important, but presenting the best new avant-garde films, as carefully selected by a group of avant-garde—including NAC—critics and writers. Selectivity is a function of taste and of proper growth.

Any criticism of this method of selection as an impermissible "directing" of public taste is hypocritical. First, wherever there is exhibition, there is prior exercise of judgment. Second, this criticism applies, if anywhere, to the *present* system of control by one faction.

7. Confusing Good with Bad

It is time for the NAC to admit that there is such a thing as a bad avant-garde film; that in fact there are more bad avant-garde films than good ones; that at least half of the films presently exhibited or distributed are bad; that one must be able to point out why some are bad or why others are good; and that to do so, it is necessary to establish critical standards and to develop critical writing and taste.

It is time to admit that not all that is good is avant-garde; that not all that is avant-garde is good; and that even a good avant-garde filmmaker can make a bad film.

Ultimately, there is only good and bad art, within the framework of one's particular value system. Our real interest in avant-garde art resides not in its being avant-garde, but in its implicit promise of quality as against the exhaustion of the commercial cinema. There is nothing inherently superior or automatically supportable in the concept of avant-garde cinema as against the "old" cinema, unless it proves its superiority in practice.

8. Confusing Propagandists with Critics

It is quite correct to say that publicists and propagandists were eminently essential to the creation of this so often unjustly maligned and disregarded movement. No one will deny their success in contributing to the creation and visibility of the movement.

In the process, however, they have unperceptively blurred all distinction between propaganda and criticism, until their "reviews" and house organs have begun to resemble the literary vanity presses, with an appropriately hallucinatory inflection.

Today, when the avant-garde is entering a dangerous new stage, analysis must take precedence over publicity and the two must be clearly distinguished from each other.

Publicists are hyperbolical, particularly where the client's products are concerned. For this reason, the following formulations, continually posing as critical evaluations in published articles and essays, should properly be labeled publicity or advertising copy: "A work of beauty," "a beautiful work," "it is beautiful." Particular care must be taken with such phrases as "one of the . . ." (e.g., "This is one of the most beautiful works of the American avant-garde"). Finally, the continuous procession, week after week, of new masters, geniuses, and giants quickly becomes an object of suspicion or ridicule.

We need proponents, not fetishists, of avant-garde cinema. We must rigorously insist on the same standards of judgement for avant-garde films as we apply to any other works of art. This concern with standards must not be equated with authoritarian strictures regarding style or content. On the contrary, it is when we coddle the experimenters with misplaced tolerance, when we talk of "achievement" where there are only attempts, of "attempts" where there is nothing, of "retrospectives" after two years of production, that we profoundly weaken the movement.

9. Confusing Publicity with Achievement

Publicity is no proof of quality; large-scale attention by the mass media is no guarantee of achievement. It merely denotes that the avant-garde film has reached the level of a marketable commodity; it has become "copy." This is because the avant-garde's aggressively antiestablishment stance expresses itself frequently in well-advertised taboo subjects: eroticism, "deviations," drugs; charmingly offbeat acts and disturbances; publicizable new techniques (mixed media, "creative" tedium); and interesting visual gestures of a vaguely oppositional nature.

Since this limited radicalism is, by virtue of nonselective programming, drowned in endless reams of innocuous films, it is the more easily subsumed by the establishment, which, by publicizing it, robs the underground of its cult appeal while simultaneously deriding it ideologically. In this sense, the latitude granted to these isolated showcases for exhibiting whatever they wish implies that they serve as a safety valve for the draining off of radical impulses and that the avant-garde, at the very moment of its acceptance by the establishment, is faced with the possibility of imminent emasculation or absorption.

10. Confusing One Swallow with a Summer

The commercial success of a single film, *The Chelsea Girls,* must not blind us to the realization that the distribution and exhibition problems of the avant-garde remain unresolved. The reviews and word-of-mouth publicity regarding this film's presumed depravity and sexual daring automatically provide a ready-made audience for it. No pejorative comment is intended; the saleability of sex in a sexually repressed society is inevitable.

11. Confusing One Generation with Another

It is a significant comment on the stagnation for the American avant-garde that most of those who are by common consent considered today's best directors are members of the middle generation first seen at Cinema 16: Anger, Brakhage, Breer, Clarke, Conner, D'Avino, Emshwiller, Harris, Frank, Markopoulos, Menken, Maas,

Rice, VanDerBeek. Of the younger generation, among the few to approach the above in promise or interest are Warhol, Bruce Baillie, Peter Goldman, and, possibly, Tony Conrad and Sheldon Rochlin.

Among the welter of new works and new directors there will undeniably be found new talents, and, in this sense, the present explosion of filmmaking is to be welcomed. But after more than six years of this activity, it is today equally legitimate to speculate as to the paucity of significant new talents and to wonder, when they do arise, about the influence of unquestioning acceptance and the dismissal of world cinema on the later development of such new talents.

To this query must be added the threatening- or already-accomplished exhaustion of some of the middle generation talents and their inability to progress beyond earlier achievement.

12. Confusing Literary with Visual Critics

The movement needs not merely critics as such; it needs visually-oriented critics. Most of the current reviewers and critics come out of a literary or journalistic tradition. Their commitments are to clear narratives, realism or naturalism, noble and identifiable sentiments, with the visual serving as illustration of an underlying literary thesis. This is criticism oriented toward sociology, literature, psychology, not toward the visual essence of cinema.

Art critics and historians, such as Amberg, Arnheim, Hauser, Langer, Panofsky, Read, Richter, Schapiro, and Tyler, have always concerned themselves with the aesthetics of film; and the recent incursion of new art critics and historians into film criticism (Battcock, Cohen, Geldzahler, Kepes, Kirby, Meyer, Michelson, O'Doherty, Sontag) is therefore to be welcomed and encouraged. Visually oriented, their special sensibilities and commitments, their openness to the techniques and philosophy of modern art, could significantly contribute to the elaboration of an aesthetic for the visual cinema. This new aesthetic must include an investigation of the differences between film and the other plastic arts (the element of time, the illusionary portrayal of motion and reality on a two-dimensional surface, the use of sound, the cinema as a palace of dreams). These "filmic" characteristics, at least in the case of Happenings, Environments, and mixed-media works, are now, in any case, becoming more closely related to the other arts.

The NAC could do worse than to concern itself with these questions and to study the writings of these new critics, as well as the works of Balázs, Nilsen, Cocteau, Eisenstein, and Pudovkin.

13. Confusing Popes with Free Men

Ultimately, the growing ability to "see" implies the ability to see oneself. Growth occurs through mistakes recognized as such, criticism realized as valid, the exposure of the self to new and alien influences, interaction with a hostile yet changing world. Blind adulation and hermeticism are the enemies of growth and lead to the repetition of what has already been achieved; the rise of epigones and mediocrities; the progressive narrowing of vision and the cumulative deterioration of taste. What the American avant-garde is confronted with is sectarianism parading as freedom, flattery as criticism, sterile eclecticism as artistic philosophy, anti-intellectual know-nothingness as liberation. Dogmas, myths, and popes are inevitable stages in human pre-history; a higher state will be reached when they are superseded by men of free will.

Reprinted by permission of Amos Vogel.

✦ ✦ ✦ ✦ ✦ ✦

Amos Vogel, "The Eternal Subversion," from *Film As a Subversive Art* (New York: Random House, 1974)

In the last analysis, every work of art, to the extent that it is original and breaks with the past instead of repeating it, is subversive. By using new form and content, it opposes the old, if only by implication, serves as an eternally dynamic force for change, and is in a permanent state of "becoming." It is therefore the triumph, the irony and the inevitable fate of the subversive creator, as he succeeds, immediately to supersede himself; for at the moment of victory, he is already dated.

Art can never take the place of social action, and its effectiveness may indeed be seriously impaired by restrictions imposed by the power structure, but its task

Illustration 85. Amos Vogel with John Lennon and Yoko Ono.

remains forever the same: to change consciousness. When this occurs, it is so momentous an achievement, even with a single human being, that it provides both justification and explanation of subversive art.

The subversive artist performs as a social being. For if it is true that developments in philosophy, politics, physics, and cosmology have affected the evolution of modern art, and if the subversion of the contemporary filmmaker is thus fed by art itself, it is also directly related to society as a whole. Here the artist finds himself at odds with its unplanned and cancerous growth in the service of the profit motive and its heedless disregard of human values. Wherever he turns, he sees exploitation and magnificent wealth, heartrending poverty and colossal waste, the destruction of races and entire countries in the name of democracy or a new order, the denial of personal liberties on a global scale, the corruption of power and privilege, and the growing international trend toward totalitarianism. He sees control of all communication by the few and the rise of new media (television and cable TV) that hold the technological potential of more repression. He sees the blighted cities, the polluted rivers and oceans, the unbridled exploitation of natural resources, the succession of economic crises, inflation, depressions, and ever more destructive wars, and the rise—as permanent and monstrous institutions—of war economies and their intolerable burden upon society as a whole. He witnesses the phenomenon of manipulated democracy and an electorate whose voting power is increasingly denuded of meaning, since real control rests elsewhere.

All this explains why so many of the most serious international filmmakers find themselves in varying degrees of revolt or opposition to their respective establishments—and also find an affinity to the emerging third world cinema and the new pro-democratic forces in the East. It is here that the Czechoslovak film renaissance of the Dubček era assumes its profound international significance and acquires the historical weight that the Russians, despite their destruction of this movement, have not been able to eliminate. There have not yet been any oppositional films from Russia or China; perhaps they exist, though control over the means of film production makes this unlikely. One can only surmise that at some date Sinyavskys and Solzhenitsyns of cinema will arise in these countries, to join filmmakers all over the world, whose task, by definition, constitution, and by virtue of the repressive societies within which they operate, must forever remain subversive.

Forever? Forever. For it is clear that even a post-revolutionary society, based on the ideals the subversives hold dear, will carry within itself new potentials of corruption, new bureaucracies, and new institutions which, at first progressive, will degenerate into ossified structures to be overcome in turn. It was Marx who, when asked in an interview to characterize the meaning of life in a single word, unhesitatingly replied: "Struggle." Was it a slip of the tongue that prevented him from limiting this definition to life "under capitalism," thus giving it the historical dimension he gave to every other phenomenon? Or was it not rather his realization, so often expressed in his philosophical writings, that the essence of life, under all circumstances and in all societies, was eternal change, the constant transformation of all forms and systems?

It is in this sense that the subject of this book will always remain on the agenda, and that these pages are but a rough draft; for the subject of this book is human freedom, and its guardians, at all times and under all conditions, are the subversives.

Reprinted by permission of Amos Vogel.

✦ ✦ ✦ ✦ ✦ ✦

Amos Vogel, "Foreword" to the New German Edition of *Film As a Subversive Art* (Vienna: Hannibal Verlag, 1997)

Though my book was written in English, my native language is German. It therefore gives me much pleasure to note that the first republication of the book occurs in the German language.

It is an additional source of pleasure for me—this time, a perverse one—that it occurs in Austria, the country which, under Hitler, almost succeeded in killing me. Obviously, a new wind is blowing in my native country, though its purity is somewhat impaired by odors wafting from the direction of Jorg Haider, the hope of the New Austrian Right.

But I, in my new country, should not complain too much about others; we have our own noxious right-wing and its power, too, is growing.

In fact, contemporary America—a late capitalist colossus, owned by large corporations while parading as a democracy and dominated by rabid commercialism and consumerism—is now attempting to dominate the world via trans-nationals, Hollywood cinema and television, the export of American cultural "values," the Disneyfication of the globe. It's not the dinosaurs and extra-terrestrials that the rest of the world ought to be afraid of; it is the commodification of all spheres of human existence, the seemingly unstoppable commercialization of human life and society, the growing international blight of the theme parks, the all-pervasive malling of the world. Our fate seems to be the homogenization of culture—an universal leveling down, an anesthetizing, pernicious blandness.

The space in which this infantilization of the human race is most clearly revealed is in the monstrous structures of American television; for the first time in history, the most powerful mass medium of a society is totally controlled and dominated by advertisers and the market, totally driven by commercial imperatives, saturated by ubiquitous commercials that deliver audiences to advertisers (not programs to audiences); and an ever larger spectrum of channels delivering primarily garbage 365 days a year. Thus has the marvelous potential of this medium been betrayed.

And the American cinema—today the most powerful in the world—is not far behind in its successful stultification of audiences. We are inundated by meretricious stories, a failure to explore the marvelous aesthetic potential of this medium, a pandering to the lowest common denominator, a truly horrifying concentration on the most cruel violence, a smirking perversion of sex hobbled by hoary prohibitions. This is topped by an obscene (profit-driven) blockbuster obsession leading to more and more films in the 100 million dollar range.

For those who still have resources of personal identity—an increasingly difficult and perilous endeavor—there exists no more important obligation than to attempt to counteract these tendencies. Otherwise, future generations may accuse us of having been "good Germans" all over again; cooperating with evil not by our deeds but by our silence. Silence, under such circumstances, is complicity.

There were moments in our blood-drenched century, when there seemed to be hope; the equalitarian impulses behind the 1917 Russian revolution (perverted within less than ten years); the Kibbutz movement's attempts in Israel to establish socialist communes (today they exploit Arab/Third World labor); the promise of the 1960s (eventuating in the current world situation). As we approach the Millennium, these humanist impulses are now behind us.

And yet, everything in past human history teaches that these attempts to transform us into humans will inevitably continue. In terms of cinema, this explains the very large importance of independent showcases and independent festivals; it explains the "exceptions" (from the Hollywood drivel); both those that constitute the content of my book as well as, even more importantly, those that continue to be made today. Not those fake "independent films" whose makers only aspire to become the next Hollywood stars—but those true iconoclasts and independents—feature, avant-garde or documentary filmmakers—who even under today's bleak circumstances audaciously continue to "transgress" (i.e. subvert) narrative modes, themes, structures, and the visual/aural conventions of mainstream cinema.

What a pleasure, then, for a man of cinema, to help discover and support these "exceptions." Though I am 76, my search continues unabated; I attend film festivals, museum series, the special showcases, serve on juries and selection committees, write articles and reviews, inform potential distributors and exhibitors and compose supporting letters to foundations and governmental institutions for grants and subsidies.

Momentous changes have occurred since the original edition of this book, among them the disappearance of the USSR and the GDR, the dissolution of Yugoslavia, the triumph, globally, of American commercial cinema and television. Yet I find no reason to modify or change any of the basic theses or structures put forth in the original.

For me, the most important conclusion I came to then remains as true today. Realizing its significance, I had stealthily placed it at the very end of my book, neither highlighting nor situating it in a separate paragraph, thus making sure that the real message of the work would be appreciated fully only by those who had kept on reading to the very end. There is therefore no better way for me to conclude this forward than by once again not drawing my new readers' attention to it [See "The Eternal Subversion," pp. 437–39].

Reprinted by permission of Amos Vogel.

Index

Page numbers in *italics* indicate illustrations

Abbas, Khwaja Ahmad, *Munna,* in Spring 1958 program, 302, 332
The Abbey Theatre's "Juno and the Paycock" (Hitchcock), in Fall 1953/Spring 1954 special event, 200
Abel, Richard, on ciné-club audiences, 2
Abseits (Hart), in Fall 1958/Spring 1959 program, 346
Absolute Films No. 2-4, and first program, 84
Absolute Film Study No. 11 (Fischinger), in Spring 1950 program, 143
According to Law (Weiss), at International Experimental Film Festival, 341
ACLU (American Civil Liberties Union), on confiscation of *Fireworks* (Anger), 317–18
Activity Group Therapy (Slavson): popularity of, with members, 213; special event presentation of, 199, 350
Actua-Tilt, in Fall 1961/Spring 1962 program, 393
The Adventures of Asterisk (Hubley): at International Experimental Film Festival, 340; in Spring 1959 program, 357
Adventures of Jimmie (Broughton), in Fall 1951 program, 166
Affiliated Films, Jack Goelman at, 71
A.F. Films: distribution by, 82–83, 118–19, 120–21. *See also* Kossoff, Rosalind
Agee, James: Cinema 16 reviewed by, 107–8; *In the Street* (with Levitt and Loeb), 35*n.* 36, 197, 213
Ai-Ye (Mankind), in Fall 1950 program, 151
Albert, Eddie: *Human Beginnings,* 141, 265; *Human Growth,* in Spring 1949 program, 113
Albicocco, Jean-Gabriel, *The Girl with the Golden Eyes,* in Fall 1961/Spring 1962 special event, 393–94
Alexander, Dorsey: *Birth of a Sphere,* availability of, 123; *Dime Story,* in Fall 1949 program, 134
Alexandrov, Grigori: *Romance Sentimentale* (with Eisenstein), sources for, 77, 79; *Time in the Sun* (with Seton and Eisenstein), 75, 184
Alexeyeff, Alexander, on International Experimental Film Festival jury, 337
Alibert, Pierre, *Cubism,* in Spring 1956 program, 276
Allegretto (Fischinger), in Spring 1950 program, 143
Allen, Lewis, New American Cinema Group formed by, 18, 33*n.* 23
Allen, Steve, attendance of, 23, 75
All My Babies (Stoney), *363;* popularity of, with members, 213; presentation of, 192; Robert J. Flaherty Award for, 34*n.* 31; in Spring 1960 program, 362, 375
All the News, and first program, 84
Alpha Omega (Bozzetto), in Fall 1962/Spring 1963 program, 406
Alvey, Glen H., Jr., *The Door in the Wall, 50;* in Fall 1956/Spring 1957 program, 284; presentation of, 50
Amateur Cinema League, distribution through, 79
American Civil Liberties Union. *See* ACLU
American Federation of Film Societies: meetings of, 83; work of, with New American Cinema Group, 33*n.* 23
"American Propaganda Films" special event (Fall 1961/Spring 1962), 394
America Today, Soviet film guild presentation of, 31*n.* 12
An Angel Has Fallen (Polanski), in Fall 1961/Spring 1962 program, 392
The Andalusian Dog. See Un Chien Andalou
Anderson, Lindsay: *Every Day Except Christmas,* 321–22, 333; *Foot and Mouth,* distribution of, 322; *O Dreamland,* 265, 321, 322, *322; Wakefield Express,* distribution of, 322, 326
Anderson, Robert: *Breakdown,* in Fall 1951 program, 167; *The Feeling of Hostility,* 12, 111, 245
And So They Live (Ferno), in second program, 9, 93
Anger, Kenneth, *235;* in Cinema 16 canon, 25; in *Cinema* magazine, 40; distribution of films of, 98; *Drastic Demise,* 90, 98; *Eaux d'artifice* (*see Eaux d'artifice*); *Eros Eidolon,* financing of, 189–90; *Escape Episode,* 90, 98, 102; *Fireworks* (*see Fireworks*); *Inauguration of the Pleasure Dome* (*see Inauguration of the Pleasure Dome*); income from distribution of, 76; *Maldoror,* making of, 163; and poetic cinema, 203; *Puce Moment,* 236, 252–54, 257, 266, 281; *Scorpio Rising,* influence of *Weegee's New York* on, 20; Stan Brakhage recommended by, 238
Angotee, in Fall 1953/Spring 1954 program, 198
Angry Boy (Hammid), in Fall 1951 program, 166
"The Angry Young Film Makers" (Vogel) (article), 336–45
Animals in Rocket Flight, in Fall 1955/Spring 1956 program, 265
Animation: importance of Cinema 16 to, 276–78; *vs.* film, 49
Annecy Film Festival, importance of, to animation, 276
Annenberg School of Communications, University of Pennsylvania, Amos Vogel at, 26
Another Sky (Lambert), in Fall 1958/Spring 1959 program, 346

Anstey, Edgar, *Housing Problems* (with Elton), in Fall 1948 program, 111
Anthology Film Archives Film Preservation, Cecile Starr honored by, 81
Anthology Film Archives Selection Committee, 61; vs. Collective for Living Cinema, 62
Anticipation of the Night (Brakhage): filming of, 307; inception of, 296; in International Experimental Film Festival, 319; presentation of, controversy over, 298, 404, 416; Robert Kelly impression of, 218
Antonioni, Michelangelo: as commercial avant-garde, 58; *N. U.*, in "A Bouquet of Prize-Winning Shorts" (Spring 1958), 334; *When Love Fails*, in Fall 1956/Spring 1957 program, 283
Aoi No Uye (The Lady No Uye), in Fall 1955/Spring 1956 program, 264
Aparajito (Ray), Robert J. Flaherty Award for, 34n. 31
Ape and Child Reared Together, in "The Brain" special event (Spring 1958), 305
Aphasia: Psychological Testing and Therapy, in "The Brain" special event (Fall 1955/Spring 1956), 266
Apollo Theater, 66, 71
A Propos de Nice (Vigo), in Fall 1953/Spring 1954 special event, 199–200
Aqua Pure Ballet, in Fall 1950 program, 152
"Are You Really Against Censorship?" special event (Fall 1958/Spring 1959), 11, 349–50; reviewed by Archer Winsten, 357–58
Argus Films, 51
Aristide Maillol (Lods), in Fall 1948 program, 111
Arledge, Sara Kathryn: dance film by, 157; *Introspection*, 16, 114, 169
Arsenal (Dovzhenko): audience reaction to, 123; in "Experimental Cinema in Russia" special event (Spring 1958), 305; sources for, 77, 79
"Art and the Experimental Film" program, rental of, 80
Art Film Festival, *Eaux d'artifice* (Anger) in, 287–88
Art house movement, 3
Art in Cinema: audiences of, 4, 123, 161; catalog of, 84–86; distribution by, 78; *Escape Episode* (Anger) presented at, 90; financial organization of, 78, 79–80, 137, 139, 161; presentations of, 3–4, 122; programming for, 123. *See also* Stauffacher, Frank
Art theaters, competition from, 22, 412
Art vs. entertainment, 15, 395–402
Asian Earth (Hagopian), in Spring 1956 program, 275
The Assassination of King Alexander of Yugoslavia, in Fall 1949 program, 133
The Assignation (Harrington), in "Private Visions" special event (Spring 1956), 266
At Land (Deren), Provincetown Playhouse screening of, 4
The Atom Strikes (U.S. Government): distribution of, 16; in Spring 1951 program, 158
Aubervilliers (Lotar): Art in Cinema interest in, 157; in Fall 1950 program, 153
Auden, W. H.: sponsorship of, 5; work on *Night Mail* (Watt and Wright), 37

Audience(s): building, 58, 68; influence of, on programming, 14, 47, 161, 213–18; reactions of, 47, 75, 121, 195–96, 278, 368 (*see also specific films*); regional differences in, 122–23. *See also* Members and membership
Austria, Nazi occupation of, 38
Automatic Drawing (McLaren), discussion of, in Fall 1948 program, 111
The Automatic Moving Co., in Fall 1949 program, 135
Autumn Fire (Weinberg), in "An Evening of Poetic and Surrealist Films" special event (Fall 1957/Spring 1958), 304
Autumn Spectrum (Hirsh), in Fall 1959/Spring 1960 special event, 367
Avant-garde films: audience preference for, 47; Cinema 16 and, 24, 25; commercial, 58–60; as component of programming, 40; distribution of, 16, 17–19; focus of, 342–43; future of, 343–45; as ghetto, 369; predisposed openness to, 48; in relation to documentary films, 2; vs. modern painting, 47–48; vs. popular films, 60
Avant-garde movement: critique of, 428–35; development of, 44; disappointments of, 55; enthusiasm for, 47; hostility to, 58; social context of, 55–56; survival of, 62; vs. New American Cinema Group, 429–30; waning of, 29
Avery, Ralph, in Cinema 16 incorporation, 4–5
Avery, Rene, in Cinema 16 incorporation, 4–5

Bachmann, Gideon, *Witchcraft Through the Ages* (Christensen) program notes, 327–32
The Back of Beyond (Heyer), in Spring 1957 program, 288
Bagley, Richard, *Within a Story*, in Fall 1955/Spring 1956 program, 264
Bakkalbasi, Seleuk, *The Street By the Sea*, in Fall 1962/Spring 1963 special event, 410
Ballade Chromo, in Fall 1960/Spring 1961 special event, 379
Ballet & Circus (Calder), in Fall 1951 program, 167
Ballet mécanique (Murphy and Leger): ciné-club presentation of, 2; Film Guild presentation of, 31n. 11
Ballet of the Atlas, in Spring 1954 program, 226
Balloons: Aggression and Destruction Games (Vassar College), in first membership program, 103
Balzac, in Fall 1951 program, 167
Barr, Alfred H., in MoMA Film Library creation, 3
Barry, Iris, as MoMA Film Library curator, 3
Bartosch, Berthold, *The Idea*, in Spring 1951 program, 160
Batista, Fulgencio, Cuban government under, 38
The Battle of Plants (British Instructional Films), London Film Society presentation of, 32n. 19
The Battle of San Pietro (Huston), in Spring 1950 program, 143
Beat generation, 55–56; membership of, 44
"The Beats and the Outs: Two Views" special event (Fall 1961/Spring 1962), 395
Beatty, Tally, *A Study in Choreography for Camera* (with Deren): in first membership program, 103; Provincetown Playhouse screening of, 4
Beauty and the Beast. See *La Belle et La Bete*

Beck, Lester F.: *Hypnotic Behavior,* 135, 158–59; *Unconscious Motivation,* 143, 408
Bed and Sofa (Room): in Fall 1953/Spring 1954 special event, 199; in Fall 1960/Spring 1961 special event, 379; popularity of, with members, 213
Beekman Theater: children's series at, 20–21; programs at, 76, 82, 405
Begone, Dull Care (McLaren): availability of, 139; in Spring 1950 program, 142
Bell Labs, film rentals by, 76
Bells of Atlantis (Hugo), in Fall 1953/Spring 1954 program, 198
Belson, Jordan: Art in Cinema screenings of, 4; *Bop Scotch,* in Spring 1953 program, 194; distribution of films of, 117; and Guggenheim Foundation, 117; *Improvisation No. 1,* 16, 117, *118; Mambo,* in Spring 1953 program, 193; *Transmutation,* 79, 84, 85, 123
Belson-Conger, Jane, *Odds and Ends:* Creative Film Award for, 34*n.* 30, 384; in Fall 1960/Spring 1961 special event, 380
Bendtsen, Hanning, *Legato,* in Fall 1950 program, 154
Benoit-Levy, Jean: *La Maternelle,* in Fall 1961/Spring 1962 program, 392; sponsorship of, 130
Beranger, Jean: *Elisabeth,* Art in Cinema interest in, 157; *Lafcadio,* 157, 160, 162
Bergman, Ingmar, early work of, 37
Bernstein, Leonard, sponsorship of, 5
Bertolucci, Bernardo, as commercial avant-garde, 58
"The Best in Scientific Films" special event (Fall 1959/Spring 1960), 366
Between the Tides (Keene), Robert J. Flaherty Award for, 34*n.* 31
Between Two Worlds (Kaner and Cote), in Spring 1954 program, 225
Beyond All Law (Griffith), London Film Society presentation of, 32*n.* 19
Bharatnatyam, in Fall 1949 program, 133
Bhownagary, J. S., *Radha and Krishna,* in Spring 1960 program, 375
Big Bill Blues (Delire), in "A Program of Folk Art and Americana" (Spring 1959), 356
Big Business (Horne and McCarey), in "A Program of Folk Art and Americana" (Spring 1959), 356
The Big "O" (D'Avino), *349;* Creative Film Award for, 34*n.* 30; in Fall 1958/Spring 1959 special event, 278, 348; at International Experimental Film Festival, 340
Billy's Bible (Cricks and Martin), London Film Society presentation of, 32*n.* 19
Birth of a Sphere (Alexander), availability of, 123
Black and White Burlesque (Preston), in "New Talent" program (Spring 1961), 389
Blackwood, Michael, *Broadway Express,* in "New Talent" program (Spring 1961), 389
Bland, Edward: *The Cry of Jazz,* in Spring 1960 special event, 366; New American Cinema Group membership of, 33*n.* 23
Blazes (Breer), private showing of, 387
Blood of a Poet (Cocteau): as art, 15; as poetic cinema, 202–3

The Blood of the Beasts (Franju), *12;* Art in Cinema interest in, 157; distribution of, 16; in Fall 1950 program, 153; Film Forum presentation of, 35*n.* 36; Frank Stauffacher opinion of, 162; in "Les Films Maudits: An Evening of Damned Films" special event (Spring 1953), 187, 195; as poetic cinema, 204; program notes for, 171–72; special events presentation of, 11, 168, 170; and Spring 1951 program, 51
"The Blue Book of 16mm Films," as distribution source, 130
Blue Jeans (Rozier), in Fall 1959/Spring 1960 program, 360
Blues Pattern (Pintoff and Whitney), at International Experimental Film Festival, 340
Blum-Blum (Crowther), in Spring 1955 program, 256
Bodega Bohemia (Schamoni), in Fall 1962/Spring 1963 program, 406
Bogdanovich, Peter, New American Cinema Group membership of, 33*n.* 23
Bolotowsky, Ilya, *Metanoia,* in Fall 1962/Spring 1963 special event, 409
Boltenhouse, Charles, *Handwritten:* Creative Film Award for, 34*n.* 30; in Fall 1959/Spring 1960 special event, 365
Boogie Doodle (McLaren), discussion of, in Fall 1948 program, 111
Bop Scotch (Belson), in Spring 1953 program, 194
Borowczyk, Walerian, *Dom:* in Fall 1958/Spring 1959 program, 346; International Experimental Film Festival prize for, 338
Bosc, Jean, *Journey to Boscavia,* in Fall 1960/Spring 1961 program, 377
Boulton, Laura, *Eskimo Summer,* in Spring 1952 program, 170
Boundarylines (Stapp): in first program, 9, 85, 89; program notes for, 89
"A Bouquet of Prize-Winning Shorts," in Spring 1958 program, 333–34
Boycott, in "American Propaganda Films" special event (Fall 1961/Spring 1962), 394
Bozzetto, Bruno, *Alpha Omega,* in Fall 1962/Spring 1963 program, 406
Bradbury, Ray, as witness in *Fireworks* confiscation case, 323
Brain and Behavior, in "The Brain" special event (Spring 1958), 304
"The Brain" special event: Fall 1955/Spring 1956, 266; Spring 1958, 304
Brakhage, Stan, 278, *308;* and Amos Vogel, 32*n.* 20, 67–68; *Anticipation of the Night (see Anticipation of the Night);* in Cinema 16 canon, 25; *Daybreak,* 306, 309, 315, 319; *Desistfilm,* 255, 279; distribution by, 299; distribution of films of, 279, 294, 314–15; *Dog Star Man,* Robert Kelly impression of, 218; Experimental Cinema Group workshop by, 307–9; *Flesh of the Morning,* 306, 309, 315, 319, 367; government employment of, 293; Gryphon Film Group, 273–74, 306; *In Between,* 279, 319; influence of *Eaux d'artifice* (Anger) on, 312–13; interest of, in European experimental films, 295; International Experimental Film Festival prize for, 339; Kenneth Anger recommendation of, 238; at Literarisches Colloquium event, *51;*

Brakhage, Stan (*continued*)
Loving, 7, 296, 297, 306, 319, 347; *Mothlight,* Marcia Vogel appreciation for, 68; *Nightcats,* 297, 306, 319; on programming, 298; *Reflections on Black,* 34n. 30, 266, 279, 280, 281, 319; Robert Kelly impression of, 218; *The Way to Shadow Garden,* in International Experimental Film Festival, 319; *White Eye,* 309, 315, 319; *The Wonder Ring,* 14, 35n. 36, 297, 306, 319, 347
Brando, Marlon, attendance of, 23
Brandon, Tom, distribution by, 79, 82, 83
Brandon Films, distribution through, 79, 82, 83
Brassai, *Lovers and Clowns,* in Fall 1960/Spring 1961 program, 377
Breakdown (Anderson), in Fall 1951 program, 167
Breast Self-Examination for Cancer, in Fall 1952/Spring 1953, 187
Breer, Robert, 82, 278; on Amos Vogel, 32n. 20; *Blazes,* private showing of, 387; *Cats,* at International Experimental Film Festival, 340; *Cats Et Al,* in Fall 1959/Spring 1960 special event, 367; distribution of films of, 386–88; *Horse Over Teakettle,* in Fall 1962/Spring 1963 special event, 409; *Inner and Outer Space,* 34n. 30, 380, 384; *Jamestown Baloos,* at International Experimental Film Festival, 340; *A Man and His Dog Out for Air,* at International Experimental Film Festival, 340; presentation of, 8; *Recreation,* 34n. 30, 35n. 36
Brentano, Felix, *What is Modern Art,* in Spring 1949 program, 112
Bresson, Robert: as commercial avant-garde, 58; *Pickpocket,* 16, 408–9
Bridges-Go-Round (Clarke): Creative Film Award for, 34n. 30; in Fall 1959/Spring 1960 special event, 364
Britain, control over Palestinian immigration, 39
British Federation of Film Societies, 2
British Film Institute: program notes by, for *The Blood of the Beasts* (Franju), 171; relation to Free Cinema, 320–23
British Instructional Films, *The Battle of Plants,* London Film Society presentation of, 32n. 19
British Polychromide, *Selections Illustrating the British Polychromide Colour Process,* London Film Society presentation of, 32n. 19
Broadway Express (Blackwood), in "New Talent" program (Spring 1961), 389
Brooks, Bob, work on *The Film Society Primer,* 83
Brooks, Van Wyck, sponsorship of, 5
Brotherhood of Man (Cannon): audience reaction to, 123; in "Integration: The Unsolved Problem" (Spring 1959), 357
Broughton, James: *Adventures of Jimmie,* in Fall 1951 program, 166; Amos Vogel enthusiasm for, 47; on Anthology Film Archives Selection Committee, 61, 62; in Cinema 16 canon, 25; in *Cinema* magazine, 40; distribution of films of, 83, 118–19, 120–21; *Four in the Afternoon,* 12, 16, 166, 245; *Loony Tom, the Happy Lover,* 16, 166; membership of, 67; *Mother's Day (see Mother's Day); Pleasure Garden,* 274, 287; and poetic cinema, 203; *The Potted Psalm* (with Peterson) *(see The Potted Psalm); Sextette,* work on, 157

Brown, Warren, *Light for John,* in "The Victim is Man" special event (Spring 1960), 367
Browning, Tod, *Freaks,* in "Horror in the Cinema" special event (Fall 1959/Spring 1960), 11, 365
Brutality in Stone (Kluge and Schamoni), in Fall 1962/Spring 1963 program, 408
Bryan, Julien, *Japanese Family,* in Fall 1950 program, 152
Bucher, Jules, *The Window Cleaner:* audience reaction to, 123; in Spring 1949 program 113
Bull Fight (Clarke), in Spring 1956 program, 276
Bungled Bungalow (U.P.A.), in Spring 1951 program, 158
Buñuel, Luis, 239; *The Criminal Life of Archibaldo de La Cruz,* 366, 378; *El,* 239–40, 244; *Land Without Bread,* 113, 113, 169; lecture by, at Columbia University, 3; *Un Chien Andalou* (with Dali) *(see Un Chien Andalou)*
Burckhardt, Rudolph: *Millions in Business as Usual,* in Fall 1962/Spring 1963 special event, 409; *Mounting Tension,* in Spring 1955 program, 255
Butterflies Do Not Live Here, in Spring 1961 program, 379, 389–90
By the Law (Kuleshov): in "Experimental Cinema in Russia" special event (Spring 1958), 305; sources for, 78

The Cage (Peterson): censorship issues with, 91; distribution of, 16; editing of, 95; and first program, 84; *The Potted Psalm* (Broughton and Peterson) compared to, 91; prints of, for Belgium, 125; sources for, 78, 79
Cahier du Cinema (magazine), article about *Fireworks* (Anger) in, 188
Calder, Alexander, *Ballet & Circus,* in Fall 1951 program, 167
California Institute of the Arts, Ed Emshwiller as dean of, 25
California School of Fine Arts, documentary for, by Sidney Peterson, 106
Cameo Theater, Film Guild programming at, 3, 31n. 11
Campbell, Joseph: attendance of, 23, 388; Creative Film Award presented by, 21, 24
Canada, film society movement in, 2–3
Canadian Film Board, *The Feeling of Rejection,* in second program, 9, 92
Canadian Filmmakers Distribution Centre, avant-garde film distribution by, 17–18
Cannon, Robert: *Brotherhood of Man,* 123, 357; *Gerald McBoing-Boing,* in Fall 1951 program, 166; *Willie the Kid,* in "Rituals, Tensions, Myths: The World of the Child" special event (Fall 1958/Spring 1959), 348
Cantor, Eddie, sponsorship of, 5
Canyon Cinema, avant-garde film distribution by, 17
The Captive Cinema, in Fall 1959/Spring 1960 program, 362
Card, James: as curator of George Eastman House, 20; in "Horror in the Cinema" special event (Fall 1959/Spring 1960), 365
Carl Orff: Music for Children, in Fall 1960/Spring 1961 program, 378

Carné, Marcel, *Daybreak (Le Jour Se Lève)*, in Fall 1956/Spring 1957 special event, 285
Carruthers, Ben, New American Cinema Group membership of, 33n. 23
Cartier-Bresson's "Le Retour," in "The Victim is Man" special event (Spring 1960), 366
C.A.S.A. (Club des amis du septième art), 1–2
Casals, Pablo, *A Conversation with Pablo Casals*, in Fall 1956/Spring 1957 program, 284
The Case of the Mukkinese Battle-Horn (Sterling), in "A Bouquet of Prize-Winning Shorts" (Spring 1958), 334
Casino de Grenelle, Club des Amis de Spartacus programming at, 30n. 3
Cassavetes, John: Louis Malle interest in, 370; presentation of, 8; *Shadows (see Shadows)*
The Cat People (Lewton), in "Horror in the Cinema" special event (Spring 1956), 267
Cats (Breer), at International Experimental Film Festival, 340
Cats Et Al (Breer), in Fall 1959/Spring 1960 special event, 367
"A Cavalcade of American Serials," in Spring 1956 program, 276
Cavalcanti, Alberto: *Film and Reality*, in Spring 1950 program, 143; *Rien que les heures*, Film Guild presentation of, 31n. 11; work on *Night Mail* (Watt and Wright), 37
Cell Division, in Spring 1952 program, 169
Censorship regulations, and membership film societies, 7, 42, 91, 317
Central Needle Trades Auditorium, 73; programs at, 11, 43, *43*, 82
Central Theater, Film Guild programming at, 31n. 11
Chandra Lekha (Vasan), in Fall 1954/Spring 1955 special event, 11, 243
Chansons sans paroles (Gross): in Fall 1958/Spring 1959 program, 347; International Experimental Film Festival prize for, 339
Chaplin, Charles: *The Early Chaplin Rediscovered*, in Fall 1954/Spring 1955 program, 243; early work of, in Spring 1952 program, 169; *Easy Street*, distribution of, 16; *The Face on the Bar Room Floor* (with Sennett), London Film Society presentation of, 32n. 19; *The Immigrant*, distribution of, 16–17; *A King in New York*, excursion to see (Spring 1958), 20, 305; *One A.M.*, London Film Society presentation of, 32n. 19
Chapman, William, *Lascaux: Cradle of Man's Art*, in Spring 1952 program, 168
Charles Cinema vs. Cinema 16, 403, 405. See also Film-makers' Cooperative
Charmides (Markopoulos): availability of, 108–9, 140; distribution of, 16; legal rights to, 148–49; meaning of, 109
Chenal, Pierre, *The Scandals of Clochemerle*, in Fall 1955/Spring 1956 program, 264
Childbirth-Normal Delivery: in Fall 1952/Spring 1953 special event, 187; in Spring 1952 special event, 11, 167
The Childhood of Maxim Gorki (Donskoi), in Spring 1956 special event, 265
The Children Are Watching Us (de Sica), in Fall 1957/Spring 1958 program, 300
Children Growing Up with Others, in Fall 1949 program, 135
Children Learning by Experience, in Spring 1951 program, 159
Children's Cinema, 20–21, *21*
Chmielewski, Tadeusz, *Eva Wants to Sleep*, in Fall 1959/Spring 1960 program, 361
Christ Among the Primitives, in Spring 1953 program, 193
Christensen, Benjamin, *Witchcraft Through the Ages*, 328; program notes for, by Gideon Bachmann, 327–32; in Spring 1958 special event, 11, 304
Ciné-club movement, 1–4, 30n. 3
Cinema (magazine), influence of, on Amos Vogel, 40
"The Cinema of Improvisation" special event (Fall 1959/Spring 1960), 364
Cinema 16: certificate for filmmakers from, 74; compared to commercial cinema, 15; competition of, 22–23; components of, 40; in cultural mainstream, 5; dissatisfaction with programs of, 53, 369; distribution by, 16–17, 54, 419–27, *420, 421*; educational mission of, 8, 12; end of, 22, 69, 76, 367, 368–69; financial organization of, 5–7, 41, 63, 65, 140–41; financial straits of, 22, 53–54, 69, 76, 411–14; first program of, 43, 84; impact of, 415; importance of, to avantgarde film, 24–25, 34n. 35, 412–13; incorporation of, 4–5; influence of, on film societies, 25, 83; invitations to, 59; politics of, 13; press coverage of, 14–15, 412; purpose of, 1, 4–5, *6*, 52, 107; social context of, 55–56; social importance of, 41; sponsors of, 5; vs. Charles Cinema, 403, 405
Cinesumac (Dasque): in Fall 1959/Spring 1960 special event, 367; at International Experimental Film Festival, 341
Circarama, at International Experimental Film Festival, 341
The City (Ramsbott): Creative Film Award for, 34n. 30; in Fall 1959/Spring 1960 special event, 365
The City (Van Dyke-Steiner): in first membership program, 103; presentation of, at Cecile Starr film society, 81
City Concerto (Tourtelot), critique of, 272
City of Gold (Low and Koenig), Robert J. Flaherty Award for, 34n. 31
City Without Wheels (Heilig), in Spring 1954 program, 225
Clair, Rene: in avant-garde cinema, 219; *The Crazy Ray*, in Fall 1953/Spring 1954 program, 198; *The Italian Straw Hat*, in Fall 1956/Spring 1957 special event, 286; *Two Timid Souls*, in Fall 1961/Spring 1962 program, 393
Clampitt, Amy, in Cecile Starr film society, 81
Clarke, Bert, work on *The Film Society Primer*, 83
Clarke, Shirley: *Bridges-Go-Round*, 34n. 30, 364; *Bull Fight*, in Spring 1956 program, 276; at Literarisches Colloquium event, *51*; membership of, 67; *A Moment in Love*, 300, 341; New American Cinema Group membership of, 33n. 23; *In Paris Parks*, in Spring 1955 program, 256; presentation of, 8

Clinic of Stumble (Peterson): explanation of, 124–25; income from showing of, 124
Clinton, Germaine, on Canadian film societies, 2
Clipper Ship Days, in "A Program of Folk Art and Americana" (Spring 1959), 356
Club des Amis de Spartacus, 30*n*. 3
Club des amis du septième art (C.A.S.A.), 1–2
Club Français du cinéma, formation of, 2
Cockeyed Luck (Munk), in Fall 1962/Spring 1963 special event, 409
Cocteau, Jean: *Blood of a Poet,* 15, 174, 202–3; *The Eternal Return,* as poetic cinema, 204; *La Belle et La Bete,* 123, 204; *Orpheus,* as poetic cinema, 204; program notes by, 171, 173
Cohan (George M.) Theater, Film Guild programming at, 31*n*. 11
Colette, in Fall 1954/Spring 1955 program, 243
Collective for Living Cinema *vs.* Anthology Film Archives Selection Committee, 62, *62*
College courses, Cinema 16 and, 21, 22, *22*
Colomb de Daunant, Denys, *The Dream of Wild Horses,* in Fall 1961/Spring 1962 program, 392
Color (Metal): financing for, 127; in Spring 1952 program, 169
Color Categorizing in Rhesus Monkeys, in Spring 1951 program, 159
Color Designs No. 1 (Latletin), distribution of, 16, 128
Columbia University: Cecile Starr at, 81–82; film courses at, 3
Commercial cinema: avant-garde, 58–60; Cinema 16 compared to, 15; competition from, 23, 412; consumerism in, 58; poetry in, 206–7; as reflection of society, 13; *vs.* membership film societies, 45, 108, 214–15. *See also* Hollywood film industry; Popular film
Communication Primer (Eames and Eames), in Spring 1956 program, 275
Condouros, Roussos, *The Fire Walkers,* in "Trance, Ritual and Hypnosis" program (Fall 1962/Spring 1963), 408
Conner, Bruce, 278; *Cosmic Ray,* in "Trance, Ritual and Hypnosis" program (Fall 1962/Spring 1963), 408; at Literarisches Colloquium event, *51*; *A Movie,* 34*n*. 30, 380, *381*, 385; presentation of, 8
Consumerism, in commercial film, 58
Contemporary Films, distribution by, 76, 82, 83
A Conversation with Pablo Casals, in Fall 1956/Spring 1957 program, 284
Cook, Alan, program notes by, for *Fireworks* (Anger), 173
Cooper, Karen, 25, 63
Cooperative distribution, of avant-garde films, 18–19, 33*n*. 23; disadvantages of, 55; Stan Brakhage on, 299–300
Cops (Keaton), in Spring 1957 program, 289
Coralie, in Fall 1958/Spring 1959 program, 346
Coral Wonderland, in Spring 1953 program, 194
Cornell, Joseph: presentation of, 8, 99, 104–5, 119–20, 135; *Rose Hobart,* 148
Cornwall, Bruce, *The Seven Bridges of Koenigsberg,* in Fall 1959/Spring 1960 program, 362
Coronet Theatre: *Escape Episode* (Anger) premiere at, 90; *Fireworks* (Anger) and, 188, 191; variety of material presented at, 157–58

Corso, Gregory, in *Pull My Daisy* (Frank), 56
Cosmic Ray (Conner), in "Trance, Ritual and Hypnosis" program (Fall 1962/Spring 1963), 408
Cote, Guy L., *Between Two Worlds* (with Kaner), in Spring 1954 program, 225
The Council of the Gods (Maetzig), in Spring 1961 program, 379, 389
Cowboy Ambrose (Swain), in Fall 1950 program, 152
Crawley, F. R., *The Loon's Necklace,* Frank Stauffacher opinion of, 162
The Crazy Ray (Clair), in Fall 1953/Spring 1954 program, 198
Creative Dance & the Child (Frank and Goldsmith), in Spring 1956 program, 275
Creative Film Associates, distribution by, 106
Creative Film Awards: presentation of, 21, *23*, 34*n*. 30; program notes for, 382–86; winners of presented at special events, 12, 21, 364, 380, 394. *See also* Creative Film Foundation
Creative Film Foundation: founding of, 4, 34*n*. 30; grants from, 258, 271, 278. *See also* Creative Film Awards
The Criminal Life of Archibaldo de La Cruz (Buñuel): in Fall 1960/Spring 1961 program, 378; in Spring 1960 special event, 366
Crisis in Levittown, in "Integration: The Unsolved Problem" (Spring 1959), 357
Crockwell, Douglas, *Glens Falls Sequence. See Glens Falls Sequence*
The Cross-Country Runner (McCarty), in Fall 1962/Spring 1963 special event, 409
Crossroads of America (Research Institute of America), in Spring 1949 program, 114
The Crowd (Vidor), in Fall 1961/Spring 1962 special event, 11, 395
Crowley, Aleister, as subject of *Inauguration of the Pleasure Dome* (Anger), 271
Crowther, Bosley: hostility of, to avant-garde film, 52; program notes by, for *The Blood of the Beasts* (Franju), 171
Crowther, Duance, *Blum-Blum,* in Spring 1955 program, 256
The Cry of Jazz (Bland), in Spring 1960 special event, 366
Crystallization, in Spring 1949 program, 114
Cuba, Amos Vogel residence in, 38
Cubism (Alibert), in Spring 1956 program, 276
Cuckoo Waltz (Moerkerken), Creative Film Award for, 34*n*. 30
Czechoslovakia, "Impressions of Speed" experiments of, at International Experimental Film Festival, 341–42

Dali, Salvador: Creative Film Award winner presented by, 21, *23*; *Un Chien Andalou* (with Buñuel) *(see Un Chien Andalou)*
Dance Chromatic (Emshwiller): Creative Film Award for, 34*n*. 30, 368; in Fall 1959/Spring 1960 special event, 364; influence of Cinema 16 on, 25
Dance of the Shells (Ehrhardt), in "A Bouquet of Prize-Winning Shorts" (Spring 1958), 334
Dangerous Houses (Harrington), in "Private Visions" special event (Spring 1956), 266

Danska, Herbert, *The Gift*, in Fall 1962/Spring 1963 special event, 409
Dasque, Jean, *Cinesumac:* in Fall 1959/Spring 1960 special event, 367; at International Experimental Film Festival, 341
Davidson, Kit, *Third Avenue El*, in Fall 1958/Spring 1959 program, 347
D'Avino, Carmen, *277; The Big "O,"* 34*n*. 30, 278, 340, 348, *349;* on Cinema 16 audiences, 14; in Cinema 16 canon, 25; Creative Film Award presented to, *23;* distribution of films by, by Grove Press, 33*n*. 22, 278; at Literarisches Colloquium event, *51;* membership of, 67; *Motif*, 278, 301, 340; *Pattern for a Sunday Afternoon*, 275, 278; *The Room*, 34*n*. 30, 35*n*. 36, 357; *Stone Sonata*, 278, 409; *Theme and Transition*, 34*n*. 30, 278, 286; *A Trip*, 34*n*. 30, 278, 380, 384–85
Davis, Jim, live compositions of, 157
Davis, Richard, *New Faces Come Back*, in Fall 1948 program, 111
Daybreak (Brakhage): distribution of, 306, 309, 315; in International Experimental Film Festival, 319
Daybreak (Le Jour Se Lève) (Carné), in Fall 1956/Spring 1957 special event, 285
A Day in Town (Hulten and Nordenstroem): Creative Film Award for, 34*n*. 30, 340; in Fall 1958/Spring 1959 special event, 348; at International Experimental Film Festival, 340
Day of Wrath (Dreyer), in Spring 1953 special event, 185, 195
Deadly Females, in Fall 1951 program, 167
The Dead Ones (Markopolous): distribution of, 150–51; financing of, 126; interest of Cinema 16 in, 141; sale of, 150
De Antonio, Emile, New American Cinema Group membership of, 33*n*. 23
Death Day (Eisenstein), in first membership program, 103
Death of a Salesman (Miller) (play), filmed version of, 212
De Filippo, Eduardo, *Side Street Story*, in Spring 1960 program, 375
Degelin, Emile, *If The Wind Frightens You*, in Fall 1962/Spring 1963 program, 408
Delannoy, Jean, *Symphonie Pastorale*, audience reaction to, 123
Delire, Jean, *Big Bill Blues*, in "A Program of Folk Art and Americana" (Spring 1959), 356
Delson, Robert, in Cinema 16 incorporation, 4–5
De Mille, Agnes, attendance of, 23
The Demon in Art, in Spring 1954 program, 225
DePalma, Brian, presentation of, 8
Depressive States and Paranoid Conditions, in "The Brain" special event (Spring 1958), 304
Deren, Maya: Creative Film Award for, 34*n*. 30; and Creative Film Foundation, 21; in Film Artists Society, 33*n*. 30–34*n*. 30; in first membership program, 103; influence of, 4, 40; *At Land*, Provincetown Playhouse screening of, 4; membership of, 67; *Meshes of the Afternoon* (with Hammid), 4, *41*, 103; in "Poetry and the Film" symposium (Fall 1953), 11, 199, 202–12, *203; The Private Life of a Cat* (with Hammid), 42, 111, 135, 265; *Ritual in Transfigured Time*, in first membership program, 103; *A Study in Choreography for Camera* (with Beatty), 4, 103; symposia sponsored by, 82; *The Very Eye of Night*, at International Experimental Film Festival, 340
Der Untertan (The Vassal) (Staudte), in Fall 1960/Spring 1961 special event, 380
De Sica, Vittorio: *The Children Are Watching Us*, in Fall 1957/Spring 1958 program, 300; *Miracle in Milan*, special events forum on, in Spring 1952 program, 170
Desire (Ernst), in Fall 1951 program, 167
Desistfilm (Brakhage): Raymond Rohauer purchase of, 279; in Spring 1955 program, 255
"Despair and Affirmation" special event (Spring 1957), 286–87
A Detective's Tour of the World, in Fall 1949 program, 135
Development of the Chick Embryo (Huxley), in Fall 1949 program, 133
Diagnostic CIV, in Fall 1960/Spring 1961 special event, 379
Dialectic programming, 10; in International Film Seminars, 25; at Proctor's Pleasure Palace, 32*n*. 19
Diener, David: in Cinema 16 incorporation, 4–5; and Cinema 16 publicity, 67
Diener, Marcia. *See* Vogel, Marcia
Dime Story (Alexander), in Fall 1949 program, 134
Disney, Walt, Circarama, at International Experimental Film Festival, 341
Disorder, in Fall 1955/Spring 1956 program, 264
Distant Journey (Radok), in Spring 1957 program, 289
Distribution, 16–19; by A.F. Films, 82; by Art in Cinema, 78; attitudes about, 106; of Carmen D'Avino films, 278; cooperative, 18–19, 33*n*. 23, 55, 299–300; by Creative Film Associates, 106; of *Eros Eidolon* (Anger), 190; to film societies, 131; financial considerations in, 95–96; of *Inauguration of the Pleasure Dome* (Anger), 224; inception of, 54; Jack Goelman involvement with, 76; by Joseph Cornell, 99, 104–5; of Lindsay Anderson films, 322, 326; methods of operation for, 17–19; of *Mother's Day* (Broughton), 118–19; of Robert Breer films, 386–88; of *Shadows* (Cassavetes), 370, 374; sources of, 77–78, 130–31; by Stan Brakhage, 299; of Stan Brakhage films, 279, 294, 306, 309, 314–15; *vs.* programs, 118, 121. *See also* Rental fees
Distribution catalog, 419–27, *420, 421*
A Divided World (Sucksdorff): Film Forum presentation of, 35*n*. 36; program notes for, 143–45; in Spring 1950 program, 142
Documentary films: distribution of, 16; emphasis on, at Cinema 16, 8; importance of *Night Mail* (Watt and Wright) in, 37; in relation to avant-garde films, 2
Dog Star Man (Brakhage), Robert Kelly impression of, 218
Dom (Borowczyk): in Fall 1958/Spring 1959 program, 346; International Experimental Film Festival prize for, 338
Don Quixote (Kristi and Herts-Lion), in Fall 1962/Spring 1963 program, 407

Donskoi, Mark, *The Childhood of Maxim Gorki,* in Spring 1956 special event, 265
The Door in the Wall (Alvey), in Fall 1956/Spring 1957 program, 50, *50,* 284
Dos Passos, John, sponsorship of, 5
Dots (McLaren), discussion of, in Fall 1948 program, 111
Dovzhenko, Alexander: *Arsenal,* 77, 79, 123, 305; *Earth,* 244, *245;* importance of, to Jack Goelman, 71
Downs, Alan, *Freight Stop,* in Spring 1955 program, 255
Dragon of Komodo, in Fall 1960/Spring 1961 program, 377
Drasin, Dan, *Sunday,* in "The New American Cinema" special event (Fall 1961/Spring 1962), 394
Drastic Demise (Anger), 90, 98
Dratfield, Leo, distribution by, 76, 82, 83
The Dream of Wild Horses (Colomb de Daunant), in Fall 1961/Spring 1962 program, 392
Dreams That Money Can Buy (Richter), *46;* audience reaction to, 123, 165; distribution difficulties with, 46; in Fall 1951 program, 167; in first membership program, 43, 92, 102–4
Dreyer, Carl, 82; *Day of Wrath,* in Spring 1953 special event, 185, 195; *Vampyr (The Strange Adventures of David Grey),* in "Les Films Maudits: An Evening of Damned Films" special event (Spring 1953), 186, 195
Drifters (Grierson), Frank Stauffacher opinion of, 162
A Drop of Water, in Spring 1951 program, 160
Duchamp, Marcel, membership of, 67
Duckler, Marvin, *Psalm* (with Silbersher), in Spring 1954 program, 225
Duck Soup (McCarey), in Fall 1955/Spring 1956 program, 265
Dufaux, Georges, *I Was a 90-Pound Weakling* (with Koenig), in Fall 1960/Spring 1961 special event, 381
Dulac, Germaine, Federation Française des Ciné-Clubs formed by, 2
Dupont, E. A., *Variety,* in Spring 1954 program, 226
Dutch Film Museum, *The Eternal Jew* (Hippler) imported from, 45
Dwightiana (Menken): Creative Film Award for, 34*n.* 30; in Fall 1959/Spring 1960 special event, 365

Eames, Charles: *Communication Primer* (with Eames), in Spring 1956 program, 275; *House,* in "An Evening of Poetic and Surrealist Films" special event (Fall 1957/Spring 1958), 304; *Toccata for Toy Train,* in "A Program of Folk Art and Americana" (Spring 1959), 356
Eames, Ray, *Communication Primer* (with Eames), in Spring 1956 program, 275
The Early Chaplin Rediscovered, in Fall 1954/Spring 1955 program, 243
Earth (Dovzhenko), *245;* in "Two Legendary Masterpieces" special event (Spring 1955), 244
The Earth Is Born (Schwartz), Robert J. Flaherty Award for, 34*n.* 31

Eastman (George) House, weekend screenings at, 20, 267, 287, 305
Easy Street (Chaplin), distribution of, 16
Eaten Horizons (Roos and Freddie), in Fall 1950 program, 153
Eaux d'artifice (Anger), 191; in Art Film Festival, 287–88; distribution of, 252–54; influence of, on Stan Brakhage, 312–13; prints for, 257
The Echo (Yama No Oto) (Naruse), in Fall 1957/Spring 1958 special event, 303
Echo of an Era (Freeman), in Fall 1958/Spring 1959 program, 347
Ecstasy (Machaty), in Fall 1952/Spring 1953 program, 184–85
Ed Murrow-Argument in Indianapolis, popularity of, with members, 213
Ed Murrow's Interview with Oppenheimer: The Complete Version, in Spring 1955 program, 256
"The Educational Film Guide," as distribution source, 130–31
Educational Film Library Association, film evaluations from, 131
Educational Screen, 16mm reviews in, 131
"The Educator's Guide to Free Films," as distribution source, 131
Eggeling, Viking: sources for films of, 77; *Symphonie Diagonale,* 32*n.* 19, 79
Egypt (Garner), in Spring 1957 program, 289
Ehrhardt, Alfred, *Dance of the Shells,* in "A Bouquet of Prize-Winning Shorts" (Spring 1958), 334
8th Street Playhouse, Film Guild programming at, 31*n.* 11
Eisenstein, Sergei: *Death Day,* in first membership program, 103; dialectic editing of, 10; *The General Line,* in "Two Legendary Masterpieces" special event (Spring 1955), 244–45; importance of, to Jack Goelman, 71; and poetic cinema, 204; *Potemkin,* 2, 30*n.* 3, 31*n.* 11, 219; *Romance Sentimentale* (with Alexandrov), sources for, 77, 79; *Strike,* in Fall 1958/Spring 1959 special event, 350; *Time in the Sun* (with Seton and Alexandrov), 75, 184
El (Buñuel), 239–40; in Fall 1954/Spring 1955 special event, 244
El Dorado, in Fall 1953/Spring 1954 program, 198
The Elephant Will Never Forget, in Fall 1956/Spring 1957 program, 284
Eliot, T. S., *Murder in the Cathedral,* as poetic cinema, 204
Elisabeth (Beranger): Art in Cinema interest in, 157; in Fall 1951 program, 165; Frank Stauffacher opinion of, 162
The Elstree Story, in Spring 1955 program, 255
Elton, Arthur, *Housing Problems* (with Anstey), in Fall 1948 program, 111
Emshwiller, Ed: on audiences, 368; *Dance Chromatic,* 25, 34*n.* 30, 364, 368; on end of Cinema 16, 367, 368–69; *Life Lines,* 34*n.* 30, 380, 385; at Literarisches Colloquium event, *51; Thanatopsis,* in "Trance, Ritual and Hypnosis" program (Fall 1962/Spring 1963), 408; *The Time of the Heathen* (with Kaas and Santvoord), 392, 397; *Transformation,* 34*n.* 30, 380, 383–84

End of Innocence (Nilsson), in Fall 1959/Spring 1960 program, 360
The End of St. Petersburg (Pudovkin), presented at Club des Amis de Spartacus, 30*n*. 3
The End of Summer (Hirshorn), in "New Talent" program (Spring 1961), 389
The End of the Line (MacCartney-Filgate), in "New Talent" program (Spring 1961), 389
The End of the Night, in "Strange Worlds" (Fall 1956/Spring 1957), 284
Entertainment *vs.* art, 15, 395–402
Ernst, Max, *Desire*, in Fall 1951 program, 167
Eroica (Munk), in Fall 1959/Spring 1960 special event, 364
Eros Eidolon (Anger), 189–90, 190
"The Erotic Cinema" special event (Fall 1958/Spring 1959), 350
Escape (Mertz and Roos), interest of Stan Brakhage in, 295
Escape Episode(Anger), 90; interest of Cinema 16 in, 98, 102
Eskimo Summer (Boulton), in Spring 1952 program, 170
Esquire (magazine), quality of Cinema 16 questioned in, 15, 395–402
Essays, Cinema 16 publication of, 12–13
The Essential Cinema (Sitney) (book), 62
The Eternal Jew (Hippler): audience reaction to, 368; in Fall 1958/Spring 1959 special event, 11, 45, 348, 368; program notes for, by Siegfried Kracauer, 45, 351–54
The Eternal Return (Cocteau), as poetic cinema, 204
Eternal Song, in Fall 1951 program, 167
"The Eternal Subvserion" (Vogel), 435–37
Etting, Emlen: *Oramunde*, audience reaction to, 123; *Poem 8*, 16, 128, 133
Etude (Puttemans and Jespers), in Fall 1959/Spring 1960 special event, 367
Eva Wants to Sleep (Chmielewski), in Fall 1959/Spring 1960 program, 361
"An Evening of Experimental Cinema" special event (Fall 1956/Spring 1957), 286
"A Evening of Poetic and Surrealist Films" special event (Fall 1957/Spring 1958), 304
Evergreen Review, "The Angry Young Film Makers" (Vogel) (article), 336–45
Everson, William K., program notes by, 12
Every Day Except Christmas (Anderson), 321–22; in "A Bouquet of Prize-Winning Shorts" (Spring 1958), 325, 333
Exhibitors, network of, 17
Experimental Cinema Group, Stan Brakhage workshop at, 307–9
"Experimental Cinema in Russia" special event (Spring 1958), 305
Experimental films. *See* Avant-garde films
An Experimentally Produced Social Problem in Rats (Yale University), in Spring 1949 program, 115
Experimental Masochism (Psychological Cinema Register), in Spring 1951 program, 159
Experiments in Perception, in "The Brain" special event (Spring 1958), 304
Experiments in the Revival of Organisms, in Spring 1950 program, 142

Explosions on the Sun (Menzel), in Fall 1949 program, 133

Fable for Friendship (Trnka), in Fall 1959/Spring 1960 program, 361
The Fable of the Peacock (Singh), in Spring 1950 program, 142
The Face of the South, in "Integration: The Unsolved Problem" (Spring 1959), 357
The Face on the Bar Room Floor (Sennett and Chaplin), London Film Society presentation of, 32*n*. 19
Falkenberg, Paul, *Lincoln Speaks at Gettysburg* (with Jacobs), in Spring 1954 program, 226
The Fall (La Caida) (Nilsson), in Fall 1961/Spring 1962 program, 393
The Fall of the House of Usher (Watson and Webber), Film Guild Playhouse screening of, 3
Fanck, Arnold, *The White Hell of Pitz Palu* (with Pabst), in Fall 1955/Spring 1956 special event, 265
Fassbinder, Rainer Werner, as commercial avant-garde, 58
The Fat and the Lean (Polanski), in Fall 1962/Spring 1963 program, 406
Faulkner, William, *The Sound and the Fury* (novel), 48
Federation Française des Ciné-Clubs, formation of, 2
Feeling All-Right, in Fall 1949 program, 133
The Feeling of Hostility (Anderson): in Fall 1948 program, 111; in "The Search for Love" special event (Spring 1955), 12, 245
The Feeling of Rejection (Canadian Film Board), in second program, 9, 92
Feelings of Depression, in Spring 1951 program, 159
Fellig, Arthur. *See* Weegee
Fellini, Frederico: in Fall 1958/Spring 1959 special event, 350; *Love Cheerfully Arranged*, in Fall 1956/Spring 1957 program, 283
Fenin, George, 403
Ferno, John, *And So They Live*, in second program, 9, 93
Feyder, Jacques, *The Kiss*, in "Garbo and Fairbanks: Two Hollywood Myths" special event (Fall 1962/Spring 1963), 410
Fiddle De Dee (McLaren): distribution of, 16; in first membership program, 103
Fifth Avenue Playhouse, first program at, 43
Film(s), poetic, 202–12
"The Film and Its Related Arts" (course), 21
Film and Reality (Cavalcanti), in Spring 1950 program, 143
"Film and Reality" (course), 21
Film Artists Society, 33*n*. 30–34*n*. 30
Film as a Subversive Art (Vogel) (book), 25, 435–37, 437–38
Film Classic Exchange, distribution through, 79
Film Comment (journal), Amos Vogel writing in, 25
Film Council of America, work with film societies, 83
Film courses, Cinema 16 and, 21, 22, 22
Film Culture (magazine), 310
Film Exercises No. 4 & 5 (Whitney and Whitney), distribution of, 16

Film Forum, 25, 35*n*. 36, 63
Film Forum Review: Cecile Starr at, 81; Institute for Adult Education sponsorship of, 82; 16mm reviews in, 131
Film Guild Playhouse, opening of, 3, 31*n*. 11
Film Liga (journal), 2
Filmmakers, as speakers, 48
Film-makers' Cooperative: competition with Cinema 16, 18–19, 404; disadvantages of, 55; distribution through, 17; formation of, 416–17; Stan Brakhage on, 299–300. *See also* Charles Cinema
Filmmaking, financial considerations in, 95–96, 123, 126–27
Film News, 16mm reviews in, 131
Film society(ies): advice for running, 130–32; Cecile Starr project, 81; censorship regulations and, 7, 42, 91, 317; at colleges, 76; financial organization of, 42, 78, 79–80, 161–62; importance of, as venues, 34*n*. 35; influence of Cinema 16 on, 25, 83; influence of, on Amos Vogel, 37–38; presentation in, importance of, 132; professionalism in, 132; *vs.* commercial cinema, 45, 108, 214–15
Film society movement: in Europe, 2, 32*n*. 19; in United States, 3. *See also* Ciné-club movement
Film Society Primer (Starr) (book), 25, 83
Film *vs.* animation, 49
Film World, 16mm reviews in, 131
Fingers and Thumbs (Huxley), in Fall 1950 program, 151
The Fire Walkers (Condouros), in "Trance, Ritual and Hypnosis" program (Fall 1962/Spring 1963), 408
Fires Were Started (Jennings): in Fall 1951 special event, 168; in Fall 1954/Spring 1955 special event, 244; in Spring 1952 special event, 170
Fireworks (Anger), 90; audience reaction to, 65, 195–96; censorship of, 188, 191; compared to *Blood of a Poet* (Cocteau), 174; confiscation of, 311–12, 323–24; customs issues in shipping, 191; distribution of, 16, 240–41, 246–48; explicit content of, 7, 45; in Fall 1951 program, 167–68; Film Forum presentation of, 35*n*. 36; interest of Cinema 16 in, 102; in "Les Films Maudits: An Evening of Damned Films" special event (Spring 1953), 186, 195; necessity of membership showing for, 98; popularity of, 17; program notes for, 173–75; publicity for, 163, 164, 187–88; Raymond Rohauer purchase of, 237, 240–41, 246–48; Robert Kelly impression of, 218; Sexual Research Institute interest in, 188–89; special events presentation of, 11; in Spring 1952 program, 170
First Steps (House), in first membership program, 103
Fischinger, Oscar: *Absolute Film Study No. 11,* in Spring 1950 program, 143; *Allegretto,* in Spring 1950 program, 143; and first program, 84; and Guggenheim Foundation, 117; Lumigraph machine, 157; *Motion Painting No. 1,* 143, 304; sources for films of, 77, 79
Five Abstract Film Exercises (Whitney and Whitney), in second program, 9
Five for Four (McLaren), in second program, 9, 92

Flaherty (Robert J.) Awards, winners of presented at special events, 12, 287, 305, 381, 395, 410
Flaherty, Frances, in Spring 1958 program, 332–33
Flaherty, Robert: as Committee of Sponsors chair, 5, 67, 97, *101*; compared to Arne Sucksdorff, 145; *Man of Aran,* in Spring 1958 program, 332–33, *333*; *Moana,* 30*n*. 3, 31*n*. 11; *Nanook of the North,* Film Guild presentation of, 31*n*. 11; and poetic cinema, 203; sponsorship of, 130
Flaherty (Robert) Seminar, dialectic diversity of, 25
Flebus (Pintoff), at International Experimental Film Festival, 340
Fleming, Victor, *When the Clouds Roll By* (with Reed), in "Garbo and Fairbanks: Two Hollywood Myths" special event (Fall 1962/Spring 1963), 410
Flesh of the Morning (Brakhage): distribution of, 306, 309, 315; in Fall 1959/Spring 1960 special event, 367; in International Experimental Film Festival, 319
The Flowers of St. Francis (Rossellini), *291*; in Fall 1956/Spring 1957 special event, 286; program notes for, 290–93
The Flower Thief (Rice), in "The Beats and the Outs: Two Views" special event (Fall 1961/Spring 1962), 18, 395
Flugten ("Escape") (Mertz and Roos), in Fall 1950 program, 153
Folie A Deux, in "The Brain" special event (Fall 1955/Spring 1956), 266
Folkdances of India, in Spring 1960 program, 376
Foot and Mouth (Anderson), distribution of, 322, 326
Forbidden Bullfight, in Fall 1960/Spring 1961 program, 377
The Forgotten Man, in Fall 1960/Spring 1961 special event, 380
Form Evolution (Metal), 127, 139
Form in Motion (Pavon), in Spring 1953 program, 75, 184, 193
Foster, Richard, and Art in Cinema screenings, 3–4
Four Families (Mead), in Fall 1960/Spring 1961 special event, 380–81
Four in the Afternoon (Broughton): distribution of, 16; in Fall 1951 program, 166; in "The Search for Love" special event (Spring 1955), 245
Fragment of Seeking (Harrington), in "The Search for Love" special event (Spring 1955), 12, 245
Franju, Georges: *The Blood of the Beasts (see The Blood of the Beasts);* presentation of, 8; program notes by, for *The Blood of the Beasts* (Franju), 172
Frank, Robert: New American Cinema Group membership of, 33*n*. 23; *Pull My Daisy,* in "The Cinema of Improvisation" special event (Fall 1959/Spring 1960), 55, 364; *The Sin of Jesus,* in "The New American Cinema" program (Fall 1961/Spring 1962), 18, 392
Franklin Watkins, in Fall 1950 program, 152
Freaks (Browning), in "Horror in the Cinema" special event (Fall 1959/Spring 1960), 11, 365
Freddie, Wilhelm, *Eaten Horizons* (with Roos), in Fall 1950 program, 153
Free Cinema, 320–23; New York screening of, 321–22, 324–26

Freeman, Henry, *Echo of an Era*, in Fall 1958/Spring 1959 program, 347
Free Radicals (Lye), International Experimental Film Festival prize for, 339
Freight Stop (Downs), in Spring 1955 program, 255
Frisian Conjoined Twins, in "Restricted Medical and Scientific Films" special event (Fall 1960/Spring 1961), 382
Froeschel, Frederic, interest of in experimental film, 150
From Movement to Music, in "Strange Worlds" (Fall 1956/Spring 1957), 284
Frustrating Fours & Fascinating Fives, in "Rituals, Tensions, Myths: The World of the Child" special event (Fall 1958/Spring 1959), 348
Frustration Play Techniques: Ego Blocking Games (Stone), Fall 1953/Spring 1954 program, 196
Fulchignoni, Enrico, *Pre-Columbian Mexican Art*, in Spring 1955 program, 256
Funding: government, 29–30, 44, 58; through Creative Film Foundation, 258, 271, 278; through Guggenheim Foundation, 117
Fury (Lang), in Spring 1961 program, 390

Galentine, Wheaton, *Treadle and Bobbin*, in "Strange Worlds" (Fall 1954/Spring 1955), 243
"Garbo and Fairbanks: Two Hollywood Myths" special event (Fall 1962/Spring 1963), 410
The Garden Spider, in Spring 1953 program, 193
Gardner, Robert, presentation of, 8
Garner, Ray, *Egypt*, in Spring 1957 program, 289
Garrison Films, Soviet revolutionary films distributed by, 31n. 12
Gaspell, Susan, Provincetown Playhouse established by, 4
Gehr, Ernie, *Serene Velocity*, vs. *The Sound and the Fury* (Faulkner) (novel), 48
The General (Keaton), in Fall 1958/Spring 1959 program, 347
The General Line (Eisenstein), in "Two Legendary Masterpieces" special event (Spring 1955), 244–45
General Motors, film rentals by, 76
Generation (Harris): Creative Film Award for, 34n. 30; in "An Evening of Experimental Cinema" special event (Fall 1956/Spring 1957), 286
A Generation (Wajda), in Fall 1961/Spring 1962 program, 393
Geography of the Body (Maas): distribution of, 16, 128; in Fall 1949 program, 134; Film Forum presentation of, 35n. 36; as poetic cinema, 205; Robert Kelly impression of, 218; in "Voyages into the Subconscious" special event (Spring 1954), 12, 201
George Braque, in Fall 1954/Spring 1955 program, 241
George Eastman House, weekend screenings at, 20, 267, 287, 305
George F. Kennan Discusses Communism, in Fall 1954/Spring 1955 program, 243
George M. Cohan Theater, Film Guild programming at, 31n. 11

Gerald McBoing-Boing (Cannon), in Fall 1951 program, 166
The Gift (Danska), in Fall 1962/Spring 1963 special event, 409
Gillin, Don, New American Cinema Group membership of, 33n. 23
Ginsberg, Allen: membership of, 44; in *Pull My Daisy* (Frank), 56
Girl Before a Mirror (Picasso) (painting), *Rashomon* (Kurosawa) compared to, 177, 180–81
A Girl in the Mist (Suzuki), in "Summer Love" program (Fall 1957/Spring 1958), 301
The Girl with the Golden Eyes (Albicocco), in Fall 1961/Spring 1962 special event, 393–94
The Girl with the Prefabricated Heart (Leger), in Fall 1951 program, 167
Glens Falls Sequence (Crockwell): distribution of, 16; in first membership program, 92; in first program, 9, 85, 89; program notes for, 86; in "Voyages into the Subconscious" special event (Spring 1954), 201
Glimmering (Lueur) (Thevenard), in Fall 1957/Spring 1958 program, 302
Goelman, Jack: in programming, 44, 72–74; work at Cinema 16, 71–72
Goethe in San Francisco (Stauffacher): distribution of, 138; interest of Cinema 16 in, 139
Go! Go! Go! (Menken), influence of *Weegee's New York* on, 20
Gold Diggers of 1933 (LeRoy), in Fall 1957/Spring 1958 special event, 11, 303, *303*
Good Morning (Ohayo) (Ozu), in Fall 1961/Spring 1962 special event, 395
Goodness Gracious (Young), in Spring 1954 program, 226
Goretta, Claude, *Nice Time* (with Tanner): at International Experimental Film Festival, 340; in "Strange Worlds" (Spring 1959), 348, 356
Go Slow in Brighton (Smith), in Fall 1955/Spring 1956 program, 264
Gould, Symon: in art house movement, 3; Film Guild founded by, 31n. 11
Government funding, 29–30, 44, 58
Graham, Martha, in *Lamentations*, 9
Grand Illusion (Renoir). See *La Grande Illusion*
Great Expectations: discussion-on-film about, 142, 198; rental rates for, 140
Greed (Stroheim), in Spring 1956 special event, 11, 267
Grief (Spitz): in Fall 1953/Spring 1954 program, 198; program notes for, 220–21
Grierson, John: on documentary theory, 129–30; *Drifters*, Frank Stauffacher opinion of, 162; on International Experimental Film Festival jury, 337; sponsorship of, 100
Griffith, D. W.: *Beyond All Law*, London Film Society presentation of, 32n. 19; at Museum of Modern Art, 82
Griffith, Richard: program notes by, 12; in sponsorship drive, 67; sponsorship of, 130
Gross, Yoram, *Chansons sans paroles*: in Fall 1958/Spring 1959 program, 347; International Experimental Film Festival prize for, 339

Grove Press, film distribution through, 17, 33*n*. 22, 278, 428
Gryphon Film Group, promotion of, 274, 306
Guggenheim Foundation, funding through, 117
Gunning, Tom, on Filmliga programs, 2
Guns of the Trees (Mekas), *399*; Dwight MacDonald review of, 398–401; in "The New American Cinema" special event (Fall 1961/Spring 1962), 394
The Guns of the Trees (Mekas), presentation of, 18
Gutman, Walter, New American Cinema Group membership of, 33*n*. 23
Gyromorphosis (Hirsh): in Fall 1958/Spring 1959 program, 347; International Experimental Film Festival prize for, 339

Haanstra, Bert, *The Rival World,* in "Strange Worlds" (Fall 1956/Spring 1957), 284
Hagopian, Michael, *Asian Earth,* in Spring 1956 program, 275
Hale, B., *The Towers,* in Spring 1956 program, 275
Hallelujah (Vidor), *250*; in Fall 1954/Spring 1955 special event, 11, 244, 249–51
Hallucinations (Weiss), in "Strange Worlds" (Fall 1956/Spring 1957), 284
Hammerstein, Oscar, II, sponsorship of, 5
Hammid, Alexander: at Affiliated Films, 71; *Angry Boy,* in Fall 1951 program, 166; *It Takes All Kinds,* in Spring 1950 program, 142; *Meshes of the Afternoon* (with Deren), 4, *41,* 103; *The Private Life of a Cat* (with Deren), 42, 111, 135, 265
Hands (Simon), Film Guild Playhouse screening of, 3
The Hands of Orlac (Weine), London Film Society presentation of, 32*n*. 19
Handwritten (Boltenhouse): Creative Film Award for, 34*n*. 30; in Fall 1959/Spring 1960 special event, 365
Hanisch, Stuart, *Have I Told You Lately That I Love You:* Creative Film Award for, 34*n*. 30; in Fall 1959/Spring 1960 special event, 364
Hanky Panky Cards, in Fall 1949 program, 135
The Happiness of Us Alone (Matsuyama), in Fall 1962/Spring 1963 program, 407
Harman, A. Jympson, *Great Expectations* discussion-on-film, in Spring 1950 program, 142
Harper's (magazine), Spring 1949 program reviewed in, 128–30
Harrington, Curtis: *The Assignation,* in "Private Visions" special event (Spring 1956), 266; in Cinema 16 canon, 25; *Dangerous Houses,* in "Private Visions" special event (Spring 1956), 266; *On the Edge,* 12, 158, 202; *Fragment of Seeking,* in "The Search for Love" special event (Spring 1955), 12, 245; *Picnic,* in Spring 1951 program, 159; and poetic cinema, 203
Harris, Hilary: *Generation,* 34*n*. 30, 286; *Highway,* 339, 346; *Organism,* influence of *Weegee's New York* on, 20
Hart, Wolf, *Abseits,* in Fall 1958/Spring 1959 program, 346
Harvard University, Amos Vogel at, 26
Hauduroy, Jean-François, Simenon, in Fall 1960/Spring 1961 program, 377

Hausa Village, in Fall 1949 program, 135
Have I Told You Lately That I Love You (Hanisch): Creative Film Award for, 34*n*. 30; in Fall 1959/Spring 1960 special event, 364
Haversham College, Amos Vogel at, 39
Have You Nothing to Declare, in Fall 1954/Spring 1955 program, 242
Häxan. See Witchcraft Through the Ages
He. See El
Hecht, Ben, *Twentieth Century* (with MacArthur), in Fall 1957/Spring 1958 program, 300–301
Heilig, Morton, *City Without Wheels,* in Spring 1954 program, 225
Hen Hop (McLaren), in second program, 9, 92
Henig, Carolyn, editorial work on *The Film Society Primer,* 83
Henry Moore (Sweeney), in Fall 1948 program, 111
Hentoff, Nat, Cinema 16 covered by, 414–15
Herskowitz, Richard, International Film Seminars presidency of, 25
Heusch, Luc de, *Magritte,* in Fall 1961/Spring 1962 program, 393
Heyer, John, *The Back of Beyond,* in Spring 1957 program, 288
High Noon (Zinnemann), influence of Robert Flaherty on, 282
High School of Fashion Industries Auditorium, presentations at, 71
Highway (Harris): in Fall 1958/Spring 1959 program, 346; International Experimental Film Festival prize for, 339
Hippler, Franz, *The Eternal Jew:* audience reaction to, 368; in Fall 1958/Spring 1959 special event, 11, 45, 348, 368; program notes for, by Siegfried Kracauer, 45, 351–54
Hiroshima, bombing of, 40
Hirsh, Hy: *Autumn Spectrum,* in Fall 1959/Spring 1960 special event, 367; *Gyromorphosis,* 339, 347; *Horror Dream* (with Peterson) *(see Horror Dream)*
Hirshorn, Ralph, *The End of Summer,* in "New Talent" program (Spring 1961), 389
Hitchcock, Alfred, *268*; *The Abbey Theatre's "Juno and the Paycock,"* in Fall 1953/Spring 1954 special event, 200; lecture by, at Columbia University, 3; *The Man Who Knew Too Much,* in Spring 1956 special event, *60,* 267; membership of, 67; presentation of, 11, 60
Hoellerer, Walter, at Literarisches Colloquium event, *51*
Hoffa and the Unions (Wasserman), Robert J. Flaherty Award for, 34*n*. 31
Hollywood AFL Film Council, *Poverty in the Valley of Plenty,* in Fall 1948 program, 111
Hollywood film industry: consumerism in, 58; domination of, 47–48; and film society development, 3, 129. *See also* Commercial cinema; Popular film
Hollywood Quarterly, program notes for *Fireworks* (Anger) from, 173
The Hooligans (Los Golfos) (Saura), in Fall 1962/Spring 1963 program, 408
Hoppity Pop (McLaren), discussion of, in Fall 1948 program, 111
Horak, Jan-Christopher, *Lovers of Cinema* (book), 29

Horikawa, Hiromichi, *Tomorrow I Shall Be a Fire Tree*, in Fall 1962/Spring 1963 special event, 409–10
Horne, Denis, *Together* (with Mazzetti), in Fall 1957/Spring 1958 program, 302, 321
Horne, James W., *Big Business* (with McCarey), in "A Program of Folk Art and Americana" (Spring 1959), 356
Horror Dream (Hirsh and Peterson): distribution of, 16; and first program, 84; interest of Cinema 16 in, 92, 95, 106; in Spring 1949 program, 114
"Horror in the Cinema" special event: Fall 1959/Spring 1960, 365; Spring 1956, 267
Horse Over Teakettle (Breer), in Fall 1962/Spring 1963 special event, 409
House (Eames), in "An Evening of Poetic and Surrealist Films" special event (Fall 1957/Spring 1958), 304
House, Frederick, *First Steps*, in first membership program, 103
House Un-American Activities Committee, era of, 13
Housing Problems (Elton and Anstey), in Fall 1948 program, 111
Howard Street (Turner), in Spring 1955 program, 256
How to Marry a Princess, in Fall 1960/Spring 1961 program, 376
Hubley, John: *The Adventures of Asterisk*, 340, 357; presentation of, 8
Hugo, Ian: *Bells of Atlantis*, in Fall 1953/Spring 1954 program, 198; distribution of films of, 83; *Jazz of Lights*, in "Strange Worlds" (Fall 1954/Spring 1955), 242; and poetic cinema, 204
Hulten, Pontus, *A Day in Town* (with Nordenstroem): Creative Film Award for, 34*n*. 30, 340; in Fall 1958/Spring 1959 special event, 348; at International Experimental Film Festival, 340
Human Beginnings (Albert): in "Sex Education" special event (Fall 1955/Spring 1956), 265; in Spring 1950 program, 141
Human Growth (Albert), in Spring 1949 program, 113
Humes, Harold, New American Cinema Group membership of, 33*n*. 23
The Hunters (Marshall), Robert J. Flaherty Award for, 34*n*. 31
Huston, John: *The Battle of San Pietro*, in Spring 1950 program, 143; sponsorship of, 5, 130; in Spring 1957 special event, 285
Huxley, Julian: in Cinema 16 canon, 25; *Development of the Chick Embryo*, in Fall 1949 program, 133; *Fingers and Thumbs*, in Fall 1950 program, 151; *Monkey into Man* (with Legg and Zuckerman) *(see Monkey into Man)*
The Hymn to the Ocean (Anger), financing for, 163–64
Hypnosis in Childbirth, in "The Brain" special event (Spring 1958), 304
Hypnotic Behavior (Beck): in Fall 1949 program, 135; in Spring 1951 program, 158–59

I Am an Alcoholic (RKO), in Spring 1951 program, 160
The Idea (Bartosch), in Spring 1951 program, 160
The Idyll (Lee): distribution of, 16; in first membership program, 103
If the Wind Frightens You (Degelin), in Fall 1962/Spring 1963 program, 408
Image in the Snow (Maas): audience reaction to, 75; in Fall 1952/Spring 1953 program, 184; as poetic cinema, 205
Images From Debussy (Mitry), in Spring 1953 program, 193
Images Medievales, popularity of, with members, 213
Images of Madness (Images de la Folie), in Fall 1952/Spring 1953 program, 184
The Immigrant (Chaplin), distribution of, 16–17
"Impressions of Speed," at International Experimental Film Festival, 341–42
Improvisation No. 1 (Belson), distribution of, 16, 117, 118
Inauguration of the Pleasure Dome (Anger), 224; Coronet Theater presentation of, 279; Creative Film Award for, 34*n*. 30, 288, 294–95; credit for, 268–70; distribution of, 224, 252–54; income from, 235; International Experimental Film Festival prize for, 339; prints for, 223–24, 257; in "Private Visions" special event (Spring 1956), 266, 281; rescoring of, 229–30, 237–38, 246–47; San Francisco Cinema Guild presentation of, 227; soundtrack of, 227–39, 246–47
In Between (Brakhage): in International Experimental Film Festival, 319; Raymond Rohauer purchase of, 279
Independent Film Makers Association Inc., 33*n*. 30–34*n*. 30
Independent screening spaces, as Cinema 16 competition, 22–23
Independent Television Service, Ed Emshwiller on board of, 25
Indiana University Sexual Research Institute, interest in *Fireworks* (Anger), 188–89
Indonesia Calling (Ivens), in Spring 1949 program, 113
Inner and Outer Space (Breer): Creative Film Award for, 34*n*. 30, 384; in Fall 1960/Spring 1961 special event, 380
The Innocent Sorcerers (Wajda), in Fall 1962/Spring 1963 program, 407
In Paris Parks (Clarke), in Spring 1955 program, 256
Institute for Adult Education, *Film Forum Review* sponsored by, 82
Institute of Film Techniques at City College, education of Jack Goelman at, 71
"Integration: The Unsolved Problem," in Spring 1959 program, 357
International Center for Photography, Roman Vishniak exhibit at, 49
International Experimental Film Festival, 337–45; Stan Brakhage entries in, 319; winners of, in Spring 1960 special event, 367
International Film Festival, *The Potted Psalm* (Broughton and Peterson) in, 125
International Film Seminars, dialectic diversity of, 25
Interplay (Weiss), in "Summer Love" program (Fall 1957/Spring 1958), 301

In the Street (Levitt, Loeb, and Agee): in Fall 1953/Spring 1954 program, 197; Film Forum presentation of, 35n. 36; popularity of, with members, 213

Intra-Uterine Movements of Foetus, in "Restricted Medical and Scientific Films" special event (Fall 1960/Spring 1961), 382

Introspection (Arledge): distribution of, 16; in Spring 1949 program, 114; in Spring 1952 program, 169

The Invader (Stoney), in "Sex Education" special event (Fall 1955/Spring 1956), 265

Israel, ideological basis of, 10

The Italian Straw Hat (Clair), in Fall 1956/Spring 1957 special event, 286

Italy Turns Around (Lattuada), in Fall 1956/Spring 1957 program, 283

It Is Good to Live (Kamei), in "The Victim is Man" special event (Spring 1960), 367

It Takes All Kinds (Hammid), in Spring 1950 program, 142

Ivens, Joris: on Filmliga, 30n. 5; *Indonesia Calling*, in Spring 1949 program, 113; lecture by, at Columbia University, 3; *New Earth*, in Fall 1949 program, 133, *134*

Ives, Burl, attendance of, 23, 75

Ivory, James, short films of, with Ismail Merchant, 82–83

I Was a 90-Pound Weakling (Dufaux and Koenig), in Fall 1960/Spring 1961 special event, 381

Jackson Pollock, in Spring 1952 program, 169

Jacobs, Lewis: and Creative Film Foundation, 34n. 30; *Lincoln Speaks at Gettysburg* (with Falkenberg), in Spring 1954 program, 226; program notes by, for *Fireworks* (Anger), 174

Jacoby, Irving, at Affiliated Films, 71

Jamestown Baloos (Breer), at International Experimental Film Festival, 340

Jammin' the Blues (Mili), in Spring 1955 program, 255

Japanese Family (Bryan), in Fall 1950 program, 152

Jazz of Lights (Hugo), in "Strange Worlds" (Fall 1954/Spring 1955), 242

Jennings, Humphrey, *Fires Were Started:* in Fall 1951 special event, 168; in Fall 1954/Spring 1955 special event, 244; in Spring 1952 special event, 170

Jespers, Paul, *Etude* (with Puttemans), in Fall 1959/Spring 1960 special event, 367

JFK (Stone), influence of video on, 61

John Gilpin (Searle), in Spring 1953 program, 193

Johnnes, Peretz, children's series co-developed by, 20–21

Journey to Boscavia (Bosc), in Fall 1960/Spring 1961 program, 377

Juilliard, Argus Speare, New American Cinema Group membership of, 33n. 23

Jurgens, Victor, *Nomads of the Jungle* (Jurgens), in Spring 1951 program, 159

Jusanya (The Thirteenth Night), in Spring 1956 program, 275

Kaas, Peter, *The Time of the Heathen* (with Emshwiller and Santvoord): Dwight MacDonald review of, 397; in "The New American Cinema" program (Fall 1961/Spring 1962), 392

Kaleidescopio, sources for, 78, 79

Kamei, Fumio, *It Is Good to Live*, in "The Victim is Man" special event (Spring 1960), 367

Kameradschaft (Pabst), in Spring 1953 special event, 194

Kaner, Sam, *Between Two Worlds* (with Cote), in Spring 1954 program, 225

Kaplan, Howard, *Krushchev* (with Lebar), in "New Talent" program (Spring 1961), 389

Keaton, Buster: *Cops*, in Spring 1957 program, 289; *The General*, in Fall 1958/Spring 1959 program, 347; *The Navigator*, in Fall 1954/Spring 1955 program, 242

Keene, Ralph, *Between the Tides*, Robert J. Flaherty Award for, 34n. 31

Kelly, Robert, influence of Cinema 16 on, 218–20

Kelman, Ken, on Anthology Film Archives Selection Committee, *61, 62*

Kenton, Erle, *Picking Peaches*, in Spring 1949 program, 114

Kessel, Norman, as projectionist, 72

Kessler, Chester, *Plague Summer*, in Spring 1953 program, 194

Key Around the Neck, in Fall 1960/Spring 1961 program, 379

Khajurajo, in Spring 1960 program, 362, 374

Kiesler, Frederick, Film Guild Playhouse designed by, 3, 31n. 11

Kimberly-Clark, film rentals by, 76

King: A Filmed Record, Montgomery to Memphis, 53

A King in New York (Chaplin), excursion to see (Spring 1958), 20, 305

Kinsey, Alfred, interest in *Fireworks* (Anger), 188–89

The Kiss (Feyder), in "Garbo and Fairbanks: Two Hollywood Myths" special event (Fall 1962/Spring 1963), 410

Kluge, Alexander: *Brutality in Stone* (with Schamoni), in Fall 1962/Spring 1963 program, 408; presentation of, 8

Knight, Arthur: and Creative Film Foundation, 34n. 30; film courses taught by, 21, *22*; films reviewed by, 82; program notes for *Valley of Dreams* and *A Divided World*, 12, 143–45; sponsorship of, 130

Koenig, Wolf: *City of Gold* (with Low), Robert J. Flaherty Award for, 34n. 31; *I Was a 90-Pound Weakling* (with Dufaux), in Fall 1960/Spring 1961 special event, 381

Konwicki, Tadeusz, *The Last Day of Summer* (with Laskowski), in Fall 1959/Spring 1960 program, 361

Kossoff, Rosalind, 82–83; meeting with James Broughton, 118–19. *See also* A.F. Films

Kracauer, Siegfried: on Hollywood cinema, 129; on importance of Cinema 16, 24; membership of, 67; program notes by, 12, 45, 351–54; sponsorship of, 130

Kramer, Stanley: in Fall 1954/Spring 1955 special event, 11, 246; *Smoke*, in Fall 1962/Spring 1963 special event, 409
Kroitor, Roman, *Paul Tomkowicz: Street-Railway Switchman*, in Spring 1955 program, 255
Kruschev (Lebar and Kaplan), in "New Talent" program (Spring 1961), 389
Kubelka, Peter, on Anthology Film Archives Selection Committee, 61, 62
Kuhn, Rudolfo, *Symphony in No B-Flat*, 339, 340, 347
Kuleshov, Lev, *By the Law*: in "Experimental Cinema in Russia" special event (Spring 1958), 305; sources for, 78
Kurosawa, Akira, *Rashomon*, Parker Tyler essay on, 13, *175*, 175–82

La Belle et la Bete (Cocteau): audience reaction to, 123; as poetic cinema, 204
La Bete Humaine (Renoir), *La Grande Illusion* compared to, 183
Labor unions, for projectionists, 43
La Cadeau, in Fall 1962/Spring 1963 program, 407
La Canción de Jean Richepin (Toussaint): in Fall 1959/Spring 1960 special event, 367; at International Experimental Film Festival, 341
The Lady No Uye (Aoi No Uye), in Fall 1955/Spring 1956 program, 264
Lafcadio (Beranger): Art in Cinema interest in, 157; Frank Stauffacher opinion of, 162; in Spring 1951 program, 160
La Grande Illusion (Renoir), compared to *La Regle du Jeu* (Renoir), 183
La Gran Siguriya (Val del Omar), at International Experimental Film Festival, 341
Laine, Edvin, *The Unknown Soldier*, in Spring 1958 special event, 304
La Lettre (Mallon), in Spring 1951 program, 160
La Maternelle (Benoit-Levy), in Fall 1961/Spring 1962 program, 392
Lambert, Gavin, *Another Sky*, in Fall 1958/Spring 1959 program, 346
Lament, in Spring 1952 program, 169
Lamentations: in first program, 9, 85, 89; program notes for, 88
Land of Enchantment: Georgia O'Keefe (Rodakiewicz), in Fall 1952/Spring 1953 program, 185
Land of the Long Day (Spencer), in Spring 1953 program, 193
Land Without Bread (Buñuel): in Spring 1949 program, 113, *113*; in Spring 1952 program, 169
Landau, Ely: financial help from, 53–54; *King: A Filmed Record, Montgomery to Memphis* produced by, 53
Lang, Fritz: *Fury*, in Spring 1961 program, 390; *M*, in Spring 1958 special event, 305
Language of Faces, in "American Propaganda Films" special event (Fall 1961/Spring 1962), 394
La Regle du Jeu (Renoir), 183; in Fall 1952/Spring 1953 special event, 185

La Rose et la Reseda (Michel), distribution of, 16
Lascaux: Cradle of Man's Art (Chapman), in Spring 1952 program, 168
Laskowski, Jan, *The Last Day of Summer* (with Konwicki), in Fall 1959/Spring 1960 program, 361
The Last Day of Summer (Konwicki and Laskowski), in Fall 1959/Spring 1960 program, 361
The Last Day of the Year (Otsu Gemori), in Spring 1956 program, 275
L'Atalante (Vigo), in Fall 1953/Spring 1954 special event, 199–200
La Taranta (Mengozzi), in "Trance, Ritual and Hypnosis" program (Fall 1962/Spring 1963), 407
The Late Mattia Pascal (L'Herbier), in Fall 1960/Spring 1961 special event, 381
Latletin, Hugo, *Color Designs No. 1*, distribution of, 16, 128
Lattuada, Alberto, *Italy Turns Around*, in Fall 1956/Spring 1957 program, 283
Latuko (McQueeny): in Fall 1953/Spring 1954 program, 11, 197; popularity of, with members, 213
Laurot, Edouard de, New American Cinema Group membership of, 33n. 23
Leacock, Ricky, at Affiliated Films, 71
The Lead Shoes (Peterson), *146*; audience reaction to, 147, 154–55; availability of, 155; distribution of, 16, 54; Parker Tyler on, 147–48; program notes for, by Parker Tyler, 145–47; Robert Kelly impression of, 218; in Spring 1950 program, 143; in "Voyages into the Subconscious" special event (Spring 1954), 12, 201
Lebar, Robert, *Krushchev* (with Kaplan), in "New Talent" program (Spring 1961), 389
Le Bijou (Lee): distribution of, 16; in Fall 1949 program, 134
Le Chien Andalou (Buñuel and Dali), in Fall 1948 program, 111
Lee, Francis: *The Idyll*, 16, 103; *Le Bijou*, 16, 134; *1941*, distribution of, 16
Legato (Bendtsen), in Fall 1950 program, 153
The Legend of St. Ursula, in Fall 1955/Spring 1956 program, 264
Leger, Fernand: *Ballet méchanique* (with Murphy), 2, 31n. 11; *The Girl with the Prefabricated Heart*, in Fall 1951 program, 167
Legg, Stuart: *Monkey into Man* (with Huxley and Zuckerman) *(see Monkey into Man)*; *Round Trip*, in first membership program, 103
Le Jour Se Lève (Daybreak) (Carné), in Fall 1956/Spring 1957 special event, 285
Lenica, Jan, presentation of, 8
Lennon, John, 435
Lenya, Lotte: attendance of, 23; Creative Film Award winner presented by, 21
Leonard, Harry, interest in Art in Cinema of, 157
LeRoy, Mervyn, *Gold Diggers of 1933*, in Fall 1957/Spring 1958 special event, 11, 303, *303*
Lerski, Helmar, *Tomorrow Is a Wonderful Day* (Lerski), in Spring 1952 program, 170

Les Amis de Spartacus, 30n. 3
Le Sang des Bêtes. See The Blood of the Beasts
Les Bain de Mer (L'Hote), in Spring 1960 program, 376
"Les Films Maudits: An Evening of Damned Films" special event (Spring 1953), 186–87, 195
Leslie, Alfred, New American Cinema Group membership of, 33n. 23
Lester, Henry M., *One Second in the Life of a Humming Bird,* in first membership program, 103
Lester, Richard, presentation of, 8
The Letter "A," in Fall 1955/Spring 1956 program, 264
Levitt, Helen, *In the Street* (with Loeb and Agee): in Fall 1953/Spring 1954 program, 197; Film Forum presentation of, 35n. 36; popularity of, with members, 213
Lewisohn, Walter: collection of, in "A Program of Folk Art and Americana" (Spring 1959), 356; *Miramagic,* in Fall 1954/Spring 1955 program, 241
Lewton, Val, *The Cat People,* in "Horror in the Cinema" special event (Spring 1956), 267
Leyda, Jay, 157
L'Herbier, Marcel, *The Late Mattia Pascal,* in Fall 1960/Spring 1961 special event, 381
L'Hote, Jean, *Les Bain de Mer,* in Spring 1960 program, 376
Life Lines (Emshwiller): Creative Film Award for, 34n. 30, 385; in Fall 1960/Spring 1961 special event, 380
Light for John (Brown), in "The Victim is Man" special event (Spring 1960), 367
Light Reflections, in Fall 1949 program, 133
Lincoln Center, film department of, 26, 69
Lincoln Speaks at Gettysburg (Falkenberg and Jacobs), in Spring 1954 program, 226
Lines Horizontal (McLaren), in Fall 1961/Spring 1962 program, 392
The Little Island (Williams), at International Experimental Film Festival, 340
Living in a Reversed World: in "The Best in Scientific Films" special event (Fall 1959/Spring 1960), 366; Film Forum presentation of, 35n. 36
Lizzani, Carlo, *Paid Love,* in Fall 1956/Spring 1957 program, 283
Lods, Jean, *Aristide Maillol,* in Fall 1948 program, 111
Loeb, Janice, *In the Street* (with Levitt and Agee): in Fall 1953/Spring 1954 program, 197; Film Forum presentation of, 35n. 36; popularity of, with members, 213
Logan, Joshua, attendance of, 23
L'Ondomane (Arcady), in "Trance, Ritual and Hypnosis" program (Fall 1962/Spring 1963), 408
London, Ephraim, in "Are You Really Against Censorship?" special event (Fall 1958/Spring 1959), 11, 349–50
London Film Society, 2, 32n. 19
The London Fire Raids, in Spring 1951 program, 159
The Loon's Necklace (Crawley), Frank Stauffacher opinion of, 162
Loony Tom, the Happy Lover (Broughton): distribution of, 16; in Fall 1951 program, 166

Loops (McLaren): discussion of, in Fall 1948 program, 111; in Fall 1951 program, 167
L'Opera Mouffe (Varda): distribution of, 51, 334; in Fall 1958/Spring 1959 program, 346; International Experimental Film Festival prize for, 339, 340; International Federation of Film Societies Award for, 340; songs for, 335
Lorentz, Pare: *The Plow that Broke the Plains,* 152, 153; *The River,* 115, 129, 204
Losey, Mary, sponsorship of, 130
Los Golfos (The Hooligans) (Saura), in Fall 1962/Spring 1963 program, 408
Lotar, Eli, *Aubervilliers:* Art in Cinema interest in, 157; in Fall 1950 program, 153
Lot in Sodom (Watson), as poetic cinema, 202–3
Lourdes and Its Miracles (Rouquier), in "Strange Worlds" (Spring 1959), 347, 356
Love Cheerfully Arranged (Fellini), in Fall 1956/Spring 1957 program, 283
Love in the City (Zavattini), in Fall 1956/Spring 1957 program, 283
The Love of a Mother (Maselli and Zavattini), in Fall 1956/Spring 1957 program, 283
The Love of Zero, sources for, 77, 79
Lovers and Clowns (Brassai), in Fall 1960/Spring 1961 program, 377
Lovers of Cinema (Horak) (book), 29
Love That Beauty (RKO), in Spring 1951 program, 160
Loving (Brakhage), 297; censorship and, 7; distribution of, 306; in Fall 1958/Spring 1959 program, 347; financing for, 296; in International Experimental Film Festival, 319
Low, Colin, *City of Gold* (with Koenig), Robert J. Flaherty Award for, 34n. 31
The Lower Depths (Renoir), in Fall 1958/Spring 1959 special event, 350
Luce, Ralph, *No Credit* (with Tregillus), in Fall 1949 program, 133
Lueur (Glimmering) (Thevenard), in Fall 1957/Spring 1958 program, 302
Lulu (Pabst), in "The Erotic Cinema" special event (Fall 1958/Spring 1959), 350, *351*
Lumia (Wilford) (optical art), influence on Robert Kelly, 219
Lumigraph machine, 157
Lye, Len, *Free Radicals,* International Experimental Film Festival prize for, 339
Lysis (Markopoulos): availability of, 108–9, 125, 127, 140; distribution of, 16; legal rights to, 148–49; meaning of, 109

M (Lang), in Spring 1958 special event, 305
Maas, Willard: Creative Film Award presented by, 24; *Geography of the Body* (see *Geography of the Body*); Gryphon Film Group, 273–74, 306; *Image in the Snow,* 75, 184, 205; *The Mechanics of Love* (with Moore), in "The Search for Love" special event (Spring 1955), 12, 245; *Narcissus* (with Moore) *(see Narcissus);* and poetic cinema, 204; in "Poetry and the Film" symposium (Fall 1953), 11, 199, 202–12, *203;* public behavior of, 67, 75–76, 82, 404

MacArthur, Charles, *Twentieth Century* (with Hecht), in Fall 1957/Spring 1958 program, 300–301
MacCartney-Filgate, Terrence, *The End of the Line,* in "New Talent" program (Spring 1961), 389
MacDonald, Dwight, quality of Cinema 16 questioned by, 15, 395–402
Machaty, Gustav, *Ecstasy,* in Fall 1952/Spring 1953 program, 184–85
Maddow, Ben, *The Steps of Age,* in Fall 1951 program, 166
Maetzig, Kurt, *The Council of the Gods,* in Spring 1961 program, 379, 389
The Magic Tape, in Fall 1960/Spring 1961 program, 378
Magnel, G. E., *Van Meegeren's Faked Vermeers,* in Spring 1953 program, 193
The Magnificent Ambersons (Welles), 200; in Fall 1953/Spring 1954 special event, 11, 199; popularity of, with members, 213
Magritte (Heusch), in Fall 1961/Spring 1962 program, 393
Mailer, Norman, attendance of, 23
Mailing lists, for publicity, 131, 309, 314–15, 316
Makavejev, Dusan, student films of, 51
Maldoror (Anger), making of, 163
Malle, Louis, interest in John Cassavetes, 370
Mallon, Jean, *La Lettre,* in Spring 1951 program, 160
Mambo (Belson), in Spring 1953 program, 193
Mambo Madness, in Fall 1956/Spring 1957 program, 284
A Man and His Dog Out for Air (Breer), at International Experimental Film Festival, 340
Man of Aran (Flaherty), in Spring 1958 program, 332–33, 333
The Man Who Knew Too Much (Hitchcock), presentation of, 60, 267
Margaret Mead: 1st Day in the Life of a New Guinea Baby (Mead), in Spring 1952 program, 168
Markopoulos, Gregory, 403; *Charmides,* 16, 108–9, 140, 148–49; *The Dead Ones,* 126, 141, 150–51; *Lysis (see Lysis);* New American Cinema Group membership of, 33n. 23; *Psyche (see Psyche);* relationship with Cinema 16, 93; rental fees for works of, 108; *Un Deuil Perpetuel,* 109
Mars (McMahon), sources for, 78, 79
Marshall, John, *The Hunters,* Robert J. Flaherty Award for, 34n. 31
Maskerage, in "Strange Worlds" (Fall 1956/Spring 1957), 284
Masterpieces from the Berlin Museums, in Fall 1950 program, 151
Maternal Deprivation, in "Rituals, Tensions, Myths: The World of the Child" special event (Fall 1958/Spring 1959), 348
Mathieson, Muir, *Steps of the Ballet,* in Spring 1949 program, 113
The Mating of Birds, London Film Society presentation of, 32n. 19
Matsuyama, Zenzo, *The Happiness of Us Alone,* in Fall 1962/Spring 1963 program, 407
May 2, 1960 (Preston): Creative Film Award for, 34n. 30; in Fall 1960/Spring 1961 special event, 380

Maya Through the Ages, in Spring 1953 program, 194
Mayhew, Christopher: *Poverty, Chastity and Obedience,* in Fall 1958/Spring 1959 program, 346; *Sainthood and Sanity,* in "Trance, Ritual and Hypnosis" program (Fall 1962/Spring 1963), 407–8
Mazzetti, Lorenza, *Together* (with Horne), in Fall 1957/Spring 1958 program, 302, 321
McCarey, Leo: *Big Business* (with Horne), in "A Program of Folk Art and Americana" (Spring 1959), 356; *Duck Soup,* in Fall 1955/Spring 1956 program, 265
McCarthy hearings, era of, 13
McCarty, Mark, *The Cross-Country Runner,* in Fall 1962/Spring 1963 special event, 409
McLaren, Norman: *Automatic Drawing,* discussion of, in Fall 1948 program, 111; *Begone, Dull Care,* 139, 142; *Boogie Doodle,* discussion of, in Fall 1948 program, 111; in Cinema 16 canon, 25; *Dots,* discussion of, in Fall 1948 program, 111; in Fall 1948 program, 111; *Fiddle De Dee,* 16, 103; *Five for Four,* in second program, 9, 92; *Hen Hop,* in second program, 9, 92; *Hoppity Pop,* discussion of, in Fall 1948 program, 111; importance of Cinema 16 venue to, 276; on International Experimental Film Festival jury, 337; *Lines Horizontal,* in Fall 1961/Spring 1962 program, 392; *Loops,* 111, 167; *Neighbors,* 198, 213; *Pen Piont Percussion,* in Spring 1952 program, 168; *A Phantasy,* in Fall 1952/Spring 1953 program, 184; and poetic cinema, 203; presentation of, 8; Robert Kelly impression of, 218; special event presentation of, 11; *Synthetic Sound Experiments,* discussion of, in Fall 1948 program, 111
McMahon, Reginald, *Mars,* sources for, 78, 79
McQueeny, Edgar, *Latuko:* in Fall 1953/Spring 1954 program, 197; popularity of, with members, 213; special events presentation of, 11
Mead, Margaret: *Four Families,* in Fall 1960/Spring 1961 special event, 380–81; *Margaret Mead: 1st Day in the Life of a New Guinea Baby,* in Spring 1952 program, 168; *Trance and Dance in Bali,* in Fall 1952/Spring 1953 program, 183–84
The Mechanics of Love (Maas and Moore), in "The Search for Love" special event (Spring 1955), 12, 245
Mekas, Adolfas: cooperative distribution through, 299–300; on membership of Cinema 16, 68–69; New American Cinema Group membership of, 33n. 23
Mekas, Jonas: on Anthology Film Archives Selection Committee, 61, 62; attack on Amos Vogel in *Village Voice,* 54; *Guns of the Trees,* 394, 398–401, 399; *The Guns of the Trees,* presentation of, 18; influence of Cinema 16 on, 416; membership to Cinema 16, 24; New American Cinema Group formed by, 18, 33n. 23, 52, 416; presentation of, 8; relationship with Amos Vogel, 52, 68–69, 403; supported by, in print, 18; *Village Voice* column of, 18, 54, 359, 372–73
Melson, Soren: *Room Studies,* in Spring 1951 program, 159; Stan Brakhage interest in, 295; *The Tear (La Larme),* in Fall 1950 program, 152

Members and membership: comments from, 215–18; cost of, 13, 22, 69; demographics of, 13–14, 44, 74–75, 130, 213–14; growth of, 129, 130, 136; invitations to, 59; *New York Times* ads and, 13. *See also* Audience(s)
Membership film society (ies). *See* Film society (ies)
The Men (Zinnemann), influence of Robert Flaherty on, 282
Men Against Money (United Electrical Workers, CIO), in Spring 1949 program, 114
Mengozzi, Gianfranco, *La Taranta,* in "Trance, Ritual and Hypnosis" program (Fall 1962/Spring 1963), 407
Menilmontant, Fall 1953/Spring 1954 program, 196–97
Menken, Marie, 299; *Dwightiana,* 34n. 30, 365; *Go! Go! Go!,* influence of *Weegee's New York* on, 20; Gryphon Film Group, 273–74, 306; membership of, 67; problems with screenings of, 404; *Visual Variations on Noguchi,* presentation of, 222
Menotti, Gian-Carlo, attendance of, 23
Menschen Am Sonntag (People on Sunday) (Siodmak, Wilder, and Zinnemann), in "Summer Love" program (Fall 1957/Spring 1958), 302
Menuhin, Yehudi, sponsorship of, 5
Menzel, D. H., *Explosions on the Sun,* in Fall 1949 program, 133
Merchant, Ismail, short films of, with James Ivory, 82–83
Mertz, Albert: *Eaten Horizons* (with Roos), in Fall 1950 program, 153; *Escape* (with Roos), 153, 295
Meshes of the Afternoon (Deren and Hammid), 41; in first membership program, 103; in Provincetown Playhouse screening of, 4
Message From Mississippi, in "American Propaganda Films" special event (Fall 1961/Spring 1962), 394
Meta, and first program, 84
Metal, Martin: *Color,* 127, 169; *Form Evolution,* interest of Cinema 16 in, 127, 139
Metamorphosis, in Fall 1949 program, 135
Metanoia (Bolotowsky), in Fall 1962/Spring 1963 special event, 409
Metrographic (Speich): Creative Film Award for, 34n. 30, 384; in Spring 1960 program, 376
Meyers, Sidney, *The Quiet One,* 186; in Spring 1953 special event, 186, 194
Michel, Andre, *La Rose et la Reseda:* distribution of, 16; in Fall 1950 program, 151
Michelangelo (Oertel), availability of, 139
Microcosm (Vishniak), in Spring 1956 program, 276
Microphotography, presentation of, 20
Midvinterblot (Werner), in Spring 1960 program, 375
Mili, Gjon, *Jammin' the Blues,* in Spring 1955 program, 255
Miller, Arthur: Creative Film Award winner presented by, 21; *Death of a Salesman* (play), filmed version of, 212; in "Poetry and the Film" symposium (Fall 1953), 11, 199, 202–12, 203
Millions in Business As Usual (Burckhardt), in Fall 1962/Spring 1963 special event, 409

Mint Tea (Kafian), in Fall 1962/Spring 1963 program, 407
The Miracle (Rossellini), Ephraim London defense of, 11
Miracle in Milan (De Sica), special events forum on, in Spring 1952 program, 170
The Mirage (Weiss), in "The Beats and the Outs: Two Views" special event (Fall 1961/Spring 1962), 395
Miramagic (Lewisohn), in Fall 1954/Spring 1955 program, 241
Mississippi Steamboatin', in "A Program of Folk Art and Americana" (Spring 1959), 356
Mitry, Jean: *Images From Debussy,* in Spring 1953 program, 193; *Pacific 231,* 162, 357
Moana (Flaherty): Club des Amis de Spartacus presentation of, 30n. 3; Film Guild presentation of, 31n. 11
Mock, Flora, *Waiting,* in Spring 1954 program, 225
Moerkerken, E. van, *Cuckoo Waltz,* Creative Film Award for, 34n. 30
Mollie Grows Up, in "Sex Education" special event (Fall 1955/Spring 1956), 265
MoMA. *See* Museum of Modern Art
A Moment in Love (Clarke): in Fall 1957/Spring 1958 program, 300; at International Experimental Film Festival, 341
Momma Don't Allow (Reisz), in Fall 1957/Spring 1958 program, 302, 321
Monkey into Man (Legg, Huxley, and Zuckerman), 49; in first program, 9, 85, 89–90; in *New York Post* review, 14–15; program notes for, 88
Moore, Ben: Creative Film Award presented to, 24; Gryphon Film Group, 273–74, 306; *The Mechanics of Love* (with Maas), in "The Search for Love" special event (Spring 1955), 12, 245; *Narcissus* (with Maas) *(see Narcissus)*
Morgan, Henry, attendance of, 23, 75
Moss, Paul F., *Power of Plants* (with Schnee): distribution of, 16; in Fall 1951 program, 166
Mother (Pudovkin): Club des Amis de Spartacus presentation of, 30n. 3; Soviet film guild presentation of, 31n. 12
Mother's Day (Broughton), 122; audience reaction to, 118, 122, 128; distribution of, 16, 118–19, 120–21; program notes for, 115–16; in Spring 1949 program, 114; in "Voyages into the Subconscious" special event (Spring 1954), 12, 201
Mothlight (Brakhage), Marcia Vogel appreciation for, 68
Motif (D'Avino): Creative Film Foundation award for, 340; in Fall 1957/Spring 1958 program, 278, 301; at International Experimental Film Festival, 340
Motion Painting No. 1 (Fischinger): in "An Evening of Poetic and Surrealist Films" special event (Fall 1957/Spring 1958), 304; in Spring 1950 program, 143
Mouche, in Fall 1958/Spring 1959 program, 346
Mounting Tension (Burckhardt), in Spring 1955 program, 255
Moussinac, Leon, Club Français du cinéma formed by, 2

A Movie (Conner), *381*; Creative Film Award for, 34*n*. 30, 385; in Fall 1960/Spring 1961 special event, 380
"Movie Journal" (column), Cinema 16 described in, 18
Movie previews, influence of video on, 61
Mr. Frenhofer and the Minotaur (Peterson), 125; distribution of, 16; Robert Kelly impression of, 218; in Spring 1952 program, 169
Mr. Motorboat's Last Stand, sources for, 78, 79
MTV, influence of, on film, 61
Mugi Fuye (Wheat Whistle) (Muroo), in Fall 1956/Spring 1957 program, 284–85
Munk, Andrzej: *Cockeyed Luck*, in Fall 1962/Spring 1963 special event, 409; *Eroica*, in Fall 1959/Spring 1960 special event, 364
Munna (Abbas), in Spring 1958 program, 302, 332
The Murderers of Anne Frank, in Fall 1960/Spring 1961 program, 378
Murder in the Cathedral (Eliot), as poetic cinema, 204
Muroo, Daisei, *Wheat Whistle (Mugi Fuye)*, in Fall 1956/Spring 1957 program, 284–85
Murphy, Dudley, *Ballet méchanique* (with Leger), 2, 31*n*. 11
Murray Hill Theater, programs at, 76
Murrow, Edward: *Ed Murrow-Argument in Indianapolis*, popularity of, with members, 213; *Ed Murrow's Interview with Oppenheimer: The Complete Version*, in Spring 1955 program, 256; *"See It Now": Segregation in the Schools*, in Spring 1956 program, 276
Museum of Modern Art: distribution through, 79; film presentations at, 3, 66, 71; receptions at, 82
Museum of Modern Art Film Library: creation of, 3; distribution by, 80, 131
Music Studio: Harry Partch (Tourtelot), in Spring 1960 program, 375
Musso, Jeff, *The Puritan*, in Fall 1948 program, 111
Myers, Sidney, at Affiliated Films, 71
My Jeanette and My Friends, in Fall 1960/Spring 1961 special event, 380

Nanook of the North (Flaherty), Film Guild presentation of, 31*n*. 11
Narcissus (Maas and Moore): Creative Film Award for, 34*n*. 30, 341; in "An Evening of Experimental Cinema" special event (Fall 1956/Spring 1957), 50, 286; financing of, 222; finishing of, 273–74; at International Experimental Film Festival, 341
Narcissus (Richter), in Fall 1951 program, 167
Naruse, Mikio, *The Echo (Yama No Oto)*, in Fall 1957/Spring 1958 special event, 303
The Nation (magazine), Cinema 16 reviewed in, 107–8
National Endowment for the Arts, 29
National Endowment for the Humanities, 29
National Film Society of Canada, 2–3
National Film Theatre (Britain), relation to Free Cinema, 320–21
Natural Born Killers (Stone), influence of video on, 61

The Navigator (Keaton), in Fall 1954/Spring 1955 program, 242
Nazi regime: Austrian occupation by, 38; propaganda films of, 45, 202, 226–27
Neighbors (McLaren): in Fall 1953/Spring 1954 program, 198; popularity of, with members, 213
Neurosis and Alcohol, 49; in Fall 1954/Spring 1955 program, 243; in Spring 1949 program, 112
New American Cinema Group: criticism of, 428–35; dissatisfaction of, with Cinema 16, 53, 369; distribution and, 18–19; financial stability of, 53–54; formation of, 18, 416; members of, 33*n*. 23; mission of, 33*n*. 23, 52; *vs.* avant-garde movement, 429–30
"The New American Cinema" special event (Fall 1961/Spring 1962), 392, 394
New cinema *vs.* old cinema, 430–31. See also New American Cinema Group
New Earth (Ivens), in Fall 1949 program, 133, *134*
New Faces Come Back (Davis), in Fall 1948 program, 111
"New Frontiers for Film" (course), 21, 22
New School for Social Research, 21, 22, 39
"New Talent" program (Spring 1961), 389–90
New York City Foster Grandparent Program, Marcia Vogel directorship of, 64–65
New Yorker Films, 52
New York Film Council: Cecile Starr and, 81; function of, 83
New York Film Festival: filmmakers at, 48; founding of, 26
New York Post (newspaper): "Are You Really Against Censorship?" special event (Fall 1958/Spring 1959) reviewed in, 357–58; on end of Cinema 16, 418–19; first program reviewed in, 14–15, 89–90; second program reviewed in, 92–93
New York State Censorship Office, in early programming, 41
New York Times (newspaper): advertisements in, 74; lack of coverage in, 52; program announcements in, 13
New York University, 21, 22, 26
Nice Time (Goretta and Tanner): at International Experimental Film Festival, 340; in "Strange Worlds" (Spring 1959), 348, 356
Nicht Mehr Fliehen (Vesely): Creative Film Award for, 34*n*. 30, 340; in "Despair and Affirmation" special event (Spring 1957), 286–87; at International Experimental Film Festival, 340
A Night at the Peking Opera, in Spring 1960 program, 362, 375
Nightcats (Brakhage), 297; distribution of, 306; in International Experimental Film Festival, 319
Night Mail (Watt and Wright), *115*; audience reaction to, 65; Frank Stauffacher opinion of, 162; influence of, on Amos Vogel, 37; in Spring 1949 program, 114; in Spring 1952 program, 170; at Vienna film society, 37
Nigoriye (Stained Image), in Spring 1956 program, 275
Nilsson, Leopoldo: *End of Innocence*, in Fall 1959/Spring 1960 program, 360; *The Fall (La Caida)*, in Fall 1961/Spring 1962 program, 393

Nin, Anaïs, membership of, 67
1941 (Lee), distribution of, 16
No Credit (Tregillus and Luce), in Fall 1949 program, 133
Nomads of the Jungle (Jurgens), in Spring 1951 program, 159
No More Fleeing (Vesely): Creative Film Award for, 34n. 30, 340; in "Despair and Affirmation" special event (Spring 1957), 286–87; at International Experimental Film Festival, 340
Nonfiction films: audience preference for, 47; as component of programs, 40. *See also* Documentary films
Nordenstroem, Hans, *A Day in Town* (with Hulten): Creative Film Award for, 34n. 30, 340; in Fall 1958/Spring 1959 special event, 348; at International Experimental Film Festival, 340
A Normal Birth, in "Sex Education" special event (Fall 1955/Spring 1956), 265
N. U. (Antonioni), in "A Bouquet of Prize-Winning Shorts" (Spring 1958), 334
N.Y., N.Y. (Thompson): Creative Film Award for, 34n. 30, 339; in Fall 1958/Spring 1959 special event, 348; influence of *Weegee's New York* on, 20; International Experimental Film Festival prize for, 339

Object Lesson (Young), in Fall 1950 program, 151
Odd Man Out (Reed), lecture-on-film about, in Spring 1950 program, 142
Odds and Ends (Belson-Conger): Creative Film Award for, 34n. 30, 384; in Fall 1960/Spring 1961 special event, 380
O Dreamland (Anderson), 322; in Fall 1955/Spring 1956 program, 265, 321, 325; income from, 322
Oelen, Evelyn, on New York Film Council, 81
Oertel, Curt: on International Experimental Film Festival jury, 337; *Michelangelo*, availability of, 139
Office of War Information Group, presentation of films of, at Cecile Starr film society, 81
Ohayo (Good Morning) (Ozu), in Fall 1961/Spring 1962 special event, 395
The Old Man and the Sea (Zinnemann), 282
One A.M. (Chaplin), London Film Society presentation of, 32n. 19
One by One (Tourtelot): availability of, 273; in Spring 1956 program, 248–49, 275
O'Neill, Eugene, Provincetown Playhouse established by, 4
One Potato, Two Potato, in "Rituals, Tensions, Myths: The World of the Child" special event (Fall 1958/Spring 1959), 348
One Second in the Life of a Humming Bird (Lester), in first membership program, 103
Ono, Yoko, 435
On the Border of Life (Veders), in Fall 1955/Spring 1956 program, 263
On the Edge (Harrington): in Spring 1951 program, 158; in "Voyages into the Subconscious" special event (Spring 1954), 12, 202
On These Evenings (Vesely): Creative Film Award for, 34n. 30; in Fall 1958/Spring 1959 special event, 348

Onuma, Tensor, *The World of the Microbes: In Quest of the Tubercle Bacilli*, in Fall 1959/Spring 1960 program, 362
Operation Abolition, in "American Propaganda Films" special event (Fall 1961/Spring 1962), 394
Oramunde (Etting), audience reaction to, 123
Ordinary People (Wright), in Spring 1952 program, 168
Orff, Carl, *Carl Orff: Music for Children*, in Fall 1960/Spring 1961 program, 378
Organism (Harris), influence of *Weegee's New York* on, 20
Orpheus (Cocteau), as poetic cinema, 204
Oshima, Nagisa: as commercial avant-garde, 58; presentation of, 8; *The Sun's Burial*, 51, 390–92, *391*, 397–98
Othello (Welles), 274
Otsu Gemori (The Last Day of the Year), in Spring 1956 program, 275
Ouled Nail, in Fall 1950 program, 151
Over Dependency, in Fall 1949 program, 133
Overture (Polidoro), Robert J. Flaherty Award for, 34n. 31
Ozu, Yasujiro: *Good Morning (Ohayo)*, in Fall 1961/Spring 1962 special event, 395; presentation of, 8; *Tokyo Twilight*, in Fall 1958/Spring 1959 special event, 349

Pabst, G. W.: *Kameradschaft*, in Spring 1953 special event, 194; *Lulu*, in "The Erotic Cinema" special event (Fall 1958/Spring 1959), 350, *351*; *Secrets of a Soul*, in Spring 1953 special event, 187, 194–95; *The White Hell of Pitz Palu* (with Fanck), in Fall 1955/Spring 1956 special event, 265
Pacific 231 (Mitry): Frank Stauffacher opinion of, 162; in Spring 1959 program, 357
Paid Love (Lizzani), in Fall 1956/Spring 1957 program, 283
Painting, modern, *vs.* film, 47–48
Palestine, British immigration policy in, 39
Palladini, in Fall 1962/Spring 1963 program, 407
Pandora's Box. See Lulu
Paradise for Three Hours (Risi), in Fall 1956/Spring 1957 program, 283
Paris Belongs to Us (Rivette), in Fall 1962/Spring 1963 program, 405–6
Paris Theater, 11; Sunday programs at, 76, 82, 136
Partch, Harry: *Music Studio: Harry Partch* (Tourtelot), in Spring 1960 program, 375; "Plectra and Percussion Dances" (musical composition), on *Inauguration of the Pleasure Dome* soundtrack, 227–34
Passport to Nowhere (RKO), in Spring 1951 program, 160
Patchen, Kenneth, as witness in *Fireworks* confiscation case, 323
Patience, in Fall 1960/Spring 1961 program, 378
Pattern for a Sunday Afternoon (D'Avino): Creative Film Foundation grant for, 278; in Spring 1956 program, 275
Paul Delvaux: Art in Cinema interest in, 157; in "Strange Worlds" (Fall 1954/Spring 1955), 242

Paul Tomkowicz: Street-Railway Switchman (Kroitor), in Spring 1955 program, 255
Pavon, Jose, *Forms in Motion,* in Spring 1953 program, 75, 184, 193
Peller, Rene, in sponsorship drive, 67
Pen Piont Percussion (McLaren), in Spring 1952 program, 168
People on Sunday (Menschen am Sonntag) (Siodmak, Wilder, and Zinnemann), in "Summer Love" program (Fall 1957/Spring 1958), 302
Performing Painter (Pintoff and Whitney), at International Experimental Film Festival, 340
Perlman, Jack, New American Cinema Group membership of, 33n. 23
Petersen, Rene, in sponsorship drive, 67
Peterson, Sidney, 96; Amos Vogel enthusiasm for, 47; in avant-garde programming, 44; *The Cage (see The Cage);* California School of Fine Arts documentary by, 106; in Cinema 16 canon, 25; in *Cinema* magazine, 40; *Clinic of Stumble,* 124–25; *Horror Dream* (with Hirsh) *(see Horror Dream); The Lead Shoes (see The Lead Shoes); Mr. Frenhofer and the Minotaur,* 16, 125, 169, 218; *The Petrified Dog,* 16, 124, 135, 304; and poetic cinema, 204; *The Potted Psalm* (with Broughton) *(see The Potted Psalm);* presentation of, 8
The Petrified Dog (Peterson): in "An Evening of Poetic and Surrealist Films" special event (Fall 1957/Spring 1958), 304; distribution of, 16; in Fall 1949 program, 135; proceeds from showing of, 124
A Phantasy (McLaren), in Fall 1952/Spring 1953 program, 184
The Photographer (Van Dyke), in Spring 1951 program, 159
Picasso, Pablo, *Girl Before a Mirror* (painting), *Rashomon* (Kurosawa) compared to, 177, 180–81
Picking Peaches (Kenton), in Spring 1949 program, 114
Pickpocket (Bresson): distribution of, 16; in Fall 1962/Spring 1963 special event, 408–9
Picnic (Harrington), in Spring 1951 program, 159
Picture in Your Mind (Stapp), in Fall 1949 program, 133
Pintoff, Ernst: *Blues Pattern* (with Whitney), at International Experimental Film Festival, 340; *Flebus,* at International Experimental Film Festival, 340; *Performing Painter* (with Whitney), at International Experimental Film Festival, 340
A Place in the Sun, in Fall 1960/Spring 1961 program, 376
Plague Summer (Kessler), in Spring 1953 program, 194
Pleasure Garden (Broughton), 274; in "Despair and Affirmation" special event (Spring 1957), 287
"Plectra and Percussion Dances" (Partch) (musical composition), on *Inauguration of the Pleasure Dome* soundtrack, 227–34
The Plow that Broke the Plains (Lorentz), in Fall 1950 program, 152, 153
Poem 8 (Etting): distribution of, 16, 128; in Fall 1949 program, 133

"Poetry and the Film" symposium (Fall 1953), 11, 199, 203; transcript of, 202–12
Poirier, Léon, *Yellow Cruise* (with Sauvage), in Fall 1954/Spring 1955 special event, 73, 243–44
Polanski, Roman: *An Angel Has Fallen,* in Fall 1961/Spring 1962 program, 392; *The Fat and the Lean,* in Fall 1962/Spring 1963 program, 406; presentation of, 8; student films of, 51; *Two Men and a Wardrobe,* 51, 338–39, 347
Polidoro, Jean Louis, *Overture,* Robert J. Flaherty Award for, 34n. 31
Political films, distribution of, 83
Pollet, Jean-Daniel, *Pourvu qu'on ait l'ivresse,* at International Experimental Film Festival, 341
Polyvision, at International Experimental Film Festival, 341
Pool of Contentment, in Spring 1952 program, 169
Popular film *vs.* avant-garde, 60. *See also* Commercial cinema; Hollywood film industry
Post-censorship, and membership film societies, 42
Potemkin (Eisenstein): in avant-garde cinema, 219; Club des Amis de Spartacus presentation of, 2, 30n. 3; Film Guild presentation of, 31n. 11
The Potted Psalm (Broughton and Peterson): *The Cage* (Peterson) compared to, 91; distribution of, 16; in first program, 9, 85, 89; prints of, for International Film Festival, 125; program notes for, 88–89; reaction to, 95
Pound, Ezra, on images, 212
Pourvu qu'on ait l'ivresse (Pollet), at International Experimental Film Festival, 341
Poverty, Chastity and Obedience (Mayhew), in Fall 1958/Spring 1959 program, 346
Poverty in the Valley of Plenty (Hollywood AFL Film Council), in Fall 1948 program, 111
Power of Plants (Moss and Schnee): distribution of, 16; in Fall 1951 program, 166
Pratt Institute, Amos Vogel at, 26
The Praying Mantis, in Spring 1958 program, 302, 332
Pre-Colombian Mexican Art (Fulchignoni), in Spring 1955 program, 256
Prelude (Vesely): in Fall 1959/Spring 1960 special event, 367; at International Experimental Film Festival, 340
Press, coverage of Cinema 16 by, 14–15, 412
Preston, Richard: *Black and White Burlesque,* in "New Talent" program (Spring 1961), 389; *May 2, 1960,* 34n. 30, 380
Prévert, Pierre, on International Experimental Film Festival jury, 337
Prince Bajaja (Trnka), in Fall 1962/Spring 1963 special event, 410
Prior censorship, and membership film societies, 7
The Prior Claim, in Spring 1957 program, 288
The Private Life of a Cat (Deren and Hammid): censorship of, 42, 135; in Fall 1948 program, 111; in "Sex Education" special event (Fall 1955/Spring 1956), 265
"Private Visions" special event (Spring 1956), 266
Proctor's Pleasure Palace, dialectical programming at, 32n. 19
Proem, in Spring 1950 program, 142

Program(s) and presentation(s): managing, 132; members' comments on, 215–18; press coverage of, 14–15, 412; selecting (see Programming); Stan Brakhage on, 298; *vs.* distribution, 118, 121

Program announcement(s): for Fall 1948, 111–12; for Fall 1949, 133–39; for Fall 1950, 151–54; for Fall 1951, 165–68; for Fall 1952/Spring 1953, *183*, 183–87; for Fall 1953/Spring 1954, 196–202, *197;* for Fall 1954/Spring 1955, *241*, 241–46; for Fall 1955/Spring 1956, *263*, 263–67; for Fall 1956/Spring 1957, *283*, 283–87; for Fall 1957/Spring 1958, 300–305, *301;* for Fall 1958/Spring 1959, *345*, 345–50; for Fall 1959/Spring 1960, 360–67; for Fall 1960/Spring 1961, 376–82, *377;* for Fall 1961/Spring 1962, 390–95, *391;* for Fall 1962/Spring 1963, 405–10, *406;* for first program, *87;* in publicity, 131; for second program, *94;* for Spring 1949, 112–15; for Spring 1950, 141–43; for Spring 1951, 158–60; for Spring 1952, 168–70; for Spring 1953, 193–95; for Spring 1954, 225–26; for Spring 1955, 255–56; for Spring 1956, 275–76; for Spring 1957, 288–89; for Spring 1958, 332–34; for Spring 1959, 356–57; for Spring 1960, 374–76; for Spring 1961, 389–90; for third program, *100*, 102–4

Programming: audience influence on, 14, 47, 131, 213–18; criteria for, 44, 47, 259–62; dialectic format of, 10; Jack Goelman in, 72–74; Marcia Vogel in, 65; method for, 44, 72–74; structure and design for, 9–10, 131–32; viability of format for, 57

Program notes: on audience survey responses, 213–18; authors of, 12–13; for *The Blood of the Beasts* (Franju), 171–72; for Creative Film Awards, by Amos Vogel, 382–86; for *A Divided World* (Sucksdorff), by Arthur Knight, 143–45; for *The Eternal Jew* (Hippler), by Siegfried Kracauer, 45, 351–54; for *Fireworks* (Anger), 173–75; for first program, 86–89; for *The Flowers of St. Francis* (Rossellini), by Amos Vogel, 290–93; for *Grief* (Spitz), 220–21; for *The Lead Shoes* (Peterson), by Parker Tyler, 145–47; members' comments on, 217; for *Mother's Day* (Broughton), 115–16; on *Reflections on Black* (Brakhage), 280; uniqueness of, 45–46; for *Valley of Dreams* (Sucksdorff), by Arthur Knight, 143–45; for *Witchcraft Through the Ages* (Christensen), by Gideon Bachmann, 327–32

"A Program of Folk Art and Americana," in Spring 1959 program, 356

"Projecting Mothion Pictures in the Class Room," 132

Projectionists: importance of, 132; unionized, 43, 72

"The Projectionist's Manual," 132

Prophet of Taos, in "A Program of Folk Art and Americana" (Spring 1959), 356

Provincetown Playhouse: Maya Deren screenings at, 4; programs at, 40–41; second program at, 97

Psalm (Silbersher and Duckler), in Spring 1954 program, 225

Psyche (Markopoulos): availability of, 140; distribution of, 16; in Fall 1948 program, 111; legal rights to, 148–49; and *Lysis*, 109; proceeds from showing of, 109; rental rates for, 140; in "The Search for Love" special event (Spring 1955), 12, 246; silent print of, 93

Psychological Cinema Register: distribution by, 49, 131; *Experimental Masochism*, in Spring 1951 program, 159; *Psychotherapeutic Interviewing*, 198, 213; *Vocalization and Speech in Chimpanzees*, in Spring 1952 program, 168

Psychotherapeutic Interviewing (Psychological Cinema Register): in Fall 1953/Spring 1954 program, 198; popularity of, with members, 213

Psychotic Illness in Childhood, in "The Best in Scientific Films" special event (Fall 1959/Spring 1960), 366

Publicity: cost of, 412; David Diener in, 67; for early programs, 41, 66–67, 85, *87*, *94*, *100;* mailing lists in, 131, 309, 314–15, 316; necessity of, 57–58, 84, 131

Puce Moment (Anger): audience reaction to, 281; Cinematheque presentation of, 236; distribution of, 252–54; prints for, 257; in "Private Visions" special event (Spring 1956), 266

Pudovkin, Vsevolod: *The End of St. Petersburg*, presented at Club des Amis de Spartacus, 30*n*. 3; *Mother*, 30*n*. 3, 31*n*. 12

Pull My Daisy (Frank), in "The Cinema of Improvisation" special event (Fall 1959/Spring 1960), 55, *56*, 364

Punchy De Leon (U.P.A.), in Spring 1951 program, 158

The Puritan (Musso), in Fall 1948 program, 111

Puttemans, Pierre, *Etude* (with Jespers), in Fall 1959/Spring 1960 special event, 367

Queens College, Marcia Vogel at, 40

The Quiet One (Meyers), *186;* in Spring 1953 special event, 185, 194

Quotas, in U.S. immigration, 38

Radha and Krishna (Bhownagary), in Spring 1960 program, 375

Radok, Alfred, *Distant Journey*, in Spring 1957 program, 289

Rain, sources for, 77, 79

Ramsbott, Wolfgang, *The City:* Creative Film Award for, 34*n*. 30; in Fall 1959/Spring 1960 special event, 365

Rashomon (Kurosawa): compared to *Girl Before a Mirror* (Picasso) (painting), 177, 180–81; Parker Tyler essay on, 13, *175*, 175–82

Ray, Man, 157; on International Experimental Film Festival jury, 337

Ray, Satyajit, *Aparajito*, Robert J. Flaherty Award for, 34*n* 31

Rebay, Hilla, at Guggenheim Foundation, 117

Recreation (Breer): Creative Film Award for, 34*n*. 30; Film Forum presentation of, 35*n*. 36

Red River of Life, in "Restricted Medical and Scientific Films" special event (Fall 1960/Spring 1961), 382

Reed, Carol, *Odd Man Out,* lecture-on-film about, in Spring 1950 program, 142
Reed, Theodore, *When the Clouds Roll By* (with Fleming), in "Garbo and Fairbanks: Two Hollywood Myths" special event (Fall 1962/Spring 1963), 410
Reflections (Tourtelot): interest of Cinema 16 in, 272; soundtrack for, 273
Reflections on Black (Brakhage), *281;* Creative Film Award for, 34*n.* 30; in International Experimental Film Festival, 319; in "Private Visions" special event (Spring 1956), 266; program notes on, 279, 280
Reinhardt, Ad, attendance of, 23
Reisz, Karel, *Momma Don't Allow,* in Fall 1957/Spring 1958 program, 302
Renoir (Winters), in Spring 1954 program, 226
Renoir, Jean: *La Regle du Jeu,* 183, 185; *The Lower Depths,* in Fall 1958/Spring 1959 special event, 350; sponsorship of, 130
Rental fees: for experimental films *vs.* other films, 140; financial considerations in, 95–96, 123, 140–41; setting, 99, 105, 108, 117; for small groups, 91–92. *See also* Distribution
Research Institute of America, *Crossroads of America,* in Spring 1949 program, 114
Resnais, Alain: presentation of, 8; *The Statues Also Die,* in Fall 1960/Spring 1961 special event, 379
"Restricted Medical and Scientific Films" special event (Fall 1960/Spring 1961), 382
Rhythm of the Port, in Fall 1960/Spring 1961 program, 378
Rhythm on Canvas (Tourtelot): availability of, 273; critique of, 248
Rhythmus 21 (Richter): audience reaction to, 164; London Film Society presentation of, 32*n.* 19; sources for, 79
Rice, Ron, *The Flower Thief,* in "The Beats and the Outs: Two Views" special event (Fall 1961/Spring 1962), 18, 395
Richardson, Tony, presentation of, 8
Richter, Hans: in Cinema 16 canon, 25; *Dreams That Money Can Buy (see Dreams That Money Can Buy);* at Institute of Film Techniques at City College, 71; membership of, 67; *Narcissus,* in Fall 1951 program, 167; *Rhythmus 21,* 32*n.* 19, 79, 164; sources for films of, 77, 79; sponsorship of, 130; *30 Years of the Avant-Garde,* in Fall 1951 program, 166–67; *Vormittagsspuk,* audience reaction to, 164
Riefenstahl, Leni, *Triumph of the Will:* audience reaction to, 226–27; in Spring 1954 program, 202
Rien que les heures (Cavalcanti), Film Guild presentation of, 31*n.* 11
Risi, Dino, *Paradise for Three Hours,* in Fall 1956/Spring 1957 program, 283
Ritual in Transfigured Time (Deren), in first membership program, 103
"Rituals, Tensions, Myths: The World of the Child" special event (Fall 1958/Spring 1959), 348
The Rival World (Haanstra), in "Strange Worlds" (Fall 1956/Spring 1957), 284

The River (Lorentz): as poetic cinema, 204; in Spring 1949 program, 115, 129
Rivette, Jacques: *Paris Belongs to Us* (Rivette), in Fall 1962/Spring 1963 program, 405–6; presentation of, 8
Robbins, Jerome, attendance of, 23
Robert Flaherty: A Rare Film Record, in Spring 1952 program, 170
Robert Flaherty Seminar, dialectic diversity of, 25
Robert J. Flaherty Awards, winners of presented at special events, 12, 21, 187, 287, 305, 381, 395, 410
Rochlin, Sheldon, New American Cinema Group membership of, 33*n.* 23
Rodakiewicz, Henwar, *Land of Enchantment: Georgia O'Keefe,* in Fall 1952/Spring 1953 program, 185
Rogosin, Lionel: New American Cinema Group membership of, 33*n.* 23; presentation of, 8
Rohauer, Raymond: confiscation of films from, 311–12, 317–18, 323–24; Coronet Theatre presentations by, 157–58, 162; *Daybreak* (Brakhage) distributed by, 309; *Desistfilm* (Brakhage) purchased by, 279; *Fireworks* (Anger) presented by, 237; *Fireworks* (Anger) purchased by, 237, 240–41, 246–48; *Flesh in the Morning* (Brakhage) distributed by, 309; *In Between* (Brakhage) purchased by, 279; *White Eye* (Brakhage) distributed by, 309
Romance Sentimentale (Alexandrov and Eisenstein), sources for, 77, 79
The Room (D'Avino): Creative Film Award for, 34*n.* 30; Film Forum presentation of, 35*n.* 36; in Spring 1959 program, 357
Room, Alexander, *Bed and Sofa:* in Fall 1953/Spring 1954 special event, 199; in Fall 1960/Spring 1961 special event, 379; popularity of, with members, 213
Room Studies (Melson), in Spring 1951 program, 159
Roos, Jorgen: *Eaten Horizons* (with Freddie), in Fall 1950 program, 153; *Escape* (with Mertz), 153, 295
The Rose and the Mignonette (Michel): distribution of, 16; in Fall 1950 program, 151
Rose Hobart (Cornell), 148
The Rose Window (Rubington): Creative Film Award for, 34*n.* 30; in Fall 1959/Spring 1960 special event, 365
Rossellini, Roberto: *The Flowers of St. Francis,* 286, 290–93, *291; The Miracle,* Ephraim London defense of, 11
Rosset, Barney, film distribution through, 17
Rotha, Paul: *Shipyard,* 16, 152, 157, 162; sponsorship of, 130; *The World is Rich,* in first membership program, 103
Roud, Richard, 26, *335*
Round and Square (Rudy), in Fall 1958/Spring 1959 special event, 349
Round Trip (Legg), in first membership program, 103
Rouquier, George, *Lourdes and its Miracles,* in "Strange Worlds" (Spring 1959), 347, 356
Rozier, Jacque, *Blue Jeans,* in Fall 1959/Spring 1960 program, 360

Rudy, W., *Round and Square*, in Fall 1958/Spring 1959 special event, 349
The Rules of the Game (Renoir). *See La Regle du Jeu*
Rupture (Etaix), in Fall 1962/Spring 1963 program, 406
Russia, World's Fair pavilion of, 336–37
Rybczynski, Zbigniew, videos of, 61

Sainthood and Sanity (Mayhew), in "Trance, Ritual and Hypnosis" program (Fall 1962/Spring 1963), 407–8
Salinas, in Fall 1960/Spring 1961 program, 378
Sanders, Denis and Terry: New American Cinema Group membership of, 33n. 23; *Time Out of War*, in Fall 1956/Spring 1957 program, 284
San Francisco Cinema Guild, *Inauguration of the Pleasure Dome* (Anger) presented by, 227, 235
San Francisco Museum of Art, Art in Cinema presentations at, 3–4
Santvoord, Peg, *The Time of the Heathen* (with Kaas and Emshwiller): Dwight MacDonald review of, 397; in "The New American Cinema" program (Fall 1961/Spring 1962), 392
Sarris, Andy, on animation, 49
Sashascopes (Stewart), London Film Society presentation of, 32n. 19
Saturday Review: Amos Vogel in, 130–32; Cecile Starr at, 83; 16mm reviews in, 81–82, 131
Saura, Carlos: *Los Golfos (The Hooligans)*, in Fall 1962/Spring 1963 program, 408; presentation of, 8
Sausalito (Stauffacher), *156*; audience reaction to, 137, 157; availability of, 128; distribution of, 137–38; in Fall 1950 program, 152; interest of Cinema 16 in, 139
Sauvage, André, *Yellow Cruise* (with Poirier), in Fall 1954/Spring 1955 special event, 73, 243–44
The Scandals of Clochemerle (Chenal), in Fall 1955/Spring 1956 program, 264
Schamoni, Peter: *Bodega Bohemia*, in Fall 1962/Spring 1963 program, 406; *Brutality in Stone* (with Kluge), in Fall 1962/Spring 1963 program, 408
Schmitz, John, *The Voices*, confiscation of, 311–12
Schnee, Thelma, *Power of Plants* (with Moss): distribution of, 16; in Fall 1951 program, 166
School of Visual Arts, Amos Vogel at, 26
Schwartz, Zachary, *The Earth Is Born*, Robert J. Flaherty Award for, 34n. 31
Science Friction (Vanderbeek): Creative Film Award for, 34n. 30, 386; in Fall 1960/Spring 1961 special event, 380
Scorpio Rising (Anger), influence of *Weegee's New York* on, 20
Screen Guild, screenings for, in art house movement, 3
Screening spaces, independent, as competition, 22–23
The Search (Zinnemann): in Fall 1956/Spring 1957 special event, 285; influence of Robert Flaherty on, 282
"The Search for Love" special event (Spring 1955), 12, 245–46

Searle, Ronald, *John Gilpin*, in Spring 1953 program, 193
Secrets of a Soul (Pabst), in Spring 1953 special event, 187, 194–95
"See It Now": Segregation in the Schools (Murrow), in Spring 1956 program, 276
Seifriz on Protoplasm: in "The Best in Scientific Films" special event (Fall 1959/Spring 1960), 366; in "Strange Worlds" (Spring 1959), 347, 356
Seizure: Social & Medical Problems of Epilepsy, in "The Brain" special event (Fall 1955/Spring 1956), 266
Seldes, Gilbert, sponsorship of, 5
Selections Illustrating the British Polychromide Colour Process (British Polychromide), London Film Society presentation of, 32n. 19
Seligman, Kurt, Creative Film Award winner presented by, 21
Sendak, Maurice, Children's Cinema program announcement and ticket by, *21*
Sennett, Mack, *The Face on the Bar Room Floor* (with Chaplin), London Film Society presentation of, 32n. 19
Sequence Magazine, program notes from, for *Fireworks* (Anger), 173
Serene Velocity (Gehr), vs. *The Sound and the Fury* (Faulkner) (novel), 48
Seton, Marie, *Time in the Sun* (with Eisenstein and Alexandrov), in Fall 1952/Spring 1953 program, 75, 184
The Setup (Wise), in Fall 1960/Spring 1961 special event, 382
The Seven Bridges of Koenigsberg (Cornwall), in Fall 1959/Spring 1960 program, 362
"Sex Education" special event (Fall 1955/Spring 1956), 265
Sextette (Broughton), work on, 157
Sexual Research Institute, interest in *Fireworks* (Anger), 188–89
Shadows (Cassavetes), *371*; audience reaction to, 369; in "The Cinema of Improvisation" special event (Fall 1959/Spring 1960), 364, 369; controversy over versions of, 370–71, 372–73; distribution of, 370, 374
Shapiro, Meyer: attendance of, 23; lectures of, on modern art, 40
She Done Him Wrong (Sherman), in Fall 1960/Spring 1961 program, 376
Sherman, Lowell, *She Done Him Wrong* (Sherman), in Fall 1960/Spring 1961 program, 376
Shipyard (Rotha): Art in Cinema interest in, 157; distribution of, 16; in Fall 1950 program, 152; Frank Stauffacher opinion of, 162
Shoe Shine, rental rates for, 140
Side Street Story (de Filippo), in Spring 1960 program, 375
Silbersher, Marvin, *Psalm* (with Duckler), in Spring 1954 program, 225
Silence (Tourtelot): availability of, 273; critique of, 248
Simenon (Hauduroy), in Fall 1960/Spring 1961 program, 377

Simon, Stella, *Hands,* Film Guild Playhouse screening of, 3
Singh, Lakshimi Wana, *The Fable of the Peacock,* in Spring 1950 program, 142
The Singing Street, in Fall 1953/Spring 1954 program, 198
The Sin of Jesus (Frank), in "The New American Cinema" program (Fall 1961/Spring 1962), 18, 392
Siodmak, Robert, *People on Sunday (Menschen am Sonntag)* (with Wilder and Zinnemann), in "Summer Love" program (Fall 1957/Spring 1958), 302
Sitney, P. Adams, *403;* on Anthology Film Archives Selection Committee, *61, 62; The Essential Cinema* (book), 62; films borrowed by, 75, 403; membership of, 24, 404–5
16 mm format, democratizing potential of, 9
The Skilled Worker, in "The Victim is Man" special event (Spring 1960), 366
Slavson, S. R., *Activity Group Therapy:* in Fall 1953/Spring 1954 special event, 199; in Fall 1958/Spring 1959 special event, 350; popularity of, with members, 213
Smith, Donald, *Go Slow in Brighton,* in Fall 1955/Spring 1956 program, 264
Smith, Harry: Art in Cinema screenings of, 4; three-dimensional film by, 157
Smith, Jack, *403*
Smoke (Kramer), in Fall 1962/Spring 1963 special event, 409
Social Behavior of Rhesus Monkeys, in Fall 1950 program, 152
A Society of Children, in "Rituals, Tensions, Myths: The World of the Child" special event (Fall 1958/Spring 1959), 348
Song of Ceylon (Wright), *66;* audience reaction to, 65; in Fall 1951 program, 166; Frank Stauffacher opinion of, 162; importance of, to Amos Vogel, 37
Song of Richepin. See *La Canción de Jean Richepin*
Song of the Prairie (Trnka), in Spring 1953 program, 194
Sontag, Susan, attendance of, 23
The Sound and the Fury (Faulkner) (novel), *vs.* avant-garde film, 48
Soviet revolutionary films, 31*n.* 12; distribution of, 83
Soviet Union, under Stalin, 39
Special events, 11–12. *See also specific events*
Speich, Vittorio, *Metrographic:* Creative Film Award for, 34*n.* 30, 384; in Spring 1960 program, 376
Spencer, Michael, *Land of the Long Day,* in Spring 1953 program, 193
Spitz, Rene, *Grief:* in Fall 1953/Spring 1954 program, 198; program notes for, 220–21
Sponsors, 5, 67, 130; soliciting, 97, *101,* 110
Stabovoy, Grigori, *Two Days,* 3, 31*n.* 11
Stained Image (Nigoriye), in Spring 1956 program, 275
Stalin, Josef, Soviet Union under, 39
Stapp, Philip: *Boundarylines,* 9, 85, 89; *Picture in Your Mind,* in Fall 1949 program, 133

Stark, Leonard, *This Day:* distribution of, 16; in Fall 1948 program, 111
Starr, Cecile: attendance of, 82; distribution through, 81; experience of, with film societies, 83; *Film Society Primer* (book), 25, 83; honored by Anthology Film Archives Film Preservation, 81
Stars, in Fall 1961/Spring 1962 special event, 394
Statement of Purposes, 4–5, *6,* 52
The Statues Also Die (Resnais), in Fall 1960/Spring 1961 special event, 379
Staudte, Wolfgang, *The Vassal (Der Untertan),* in Fall 1960/Spring 1961 special event, 380
Stauffacher, Barbara, and Art in Cinema screenings, 4
Stauffacher, Frank: and Art in Cinema screenings, 3–4; death of, 262; finances of, 137–38, 139, 161; *Goethe in San Francisco,* 138, 139; *Sausalito* (see *Sausalito*); as social agent, 56. *See also* Art in Cinema
Steiner, Ralph: *The City* (with Van Dyke), 81, 103; on Soviet revolutionary film audiences, 31*n.* 12
The Steps of Age (Maddow), in Fall 1951 program, 166
Steps of the Ballet (Matheison), in Spring 1949 program, 113
Sterling, Joseph, *The Case of the Mukkinese Battle-Horn,* in "A Bouquet of Prize-Winning Shorts" (Spring 1958), 334
Stern, Bert, New American Cinema Group membership of, 33*n.* 23
Stewart, Alex, *Sashascopes,* London Film Society presentation of, 32*n.* 19
Stone, David C., New American Cinema Group membership of, 33*n.* 23
Stone, Joseph L., in Cinema 16 canon, 25
Stone, Lawrence J.: *Frustration Play Techniques: Ego Blocking Games,* Fall 1953/Spring 1954 program, 196; *This Is Robert,* 185, 285
Stone, Oliver, influence of video on, 61
Stone Sonata (D'Avino), in Fall 1962/Spring 1963 special event, 278, 409
Stoney, George: *All My Babies* (see *All My Babies*); *The Invader,* in "Sex Education" special event (Fall 1955/Spring 1956), 265
Storck, Henri, *The World of Paul Delvaux,* in Fall 1950 program, 153
The Story of Bees, in Fall 1948 program, 111
"Strange Worlds": in Fall 1954/Spring 1955 program, 242–43; in Fall 1956/Spring 1957 program, 284; in Spring 1959 program, 347, 356
The Street By the Sea (Bakkalbasi), in Fall 1962/Spring 1963 special event, 410
Street of Shadows (RKO), in Spring 1951 program, 160
Strike (Eisenstein), in Fall 1958/Spring 1959 special event, 350
Strizhevski, M. V., *Taras Bulba,* London Film Society presentation of, 32*n.* 19
Stroheim, Erich von, *Greed,* in Spring 1956 special event, 11, 267
The Struggle against the Frost, in Fall 1960/Spring 1961 program, 377
Studies in Human Fertility, in "The Best in Scientific Films" special event (Fall 1959/Spring 1960), 366

A Study in Choreography for Camera (Deren and Beatty): in first membership program, 103; Provincetown Playhouse screening of, 4
Study of a Dance (Woll), in Spring 1954 program, 225
A Study of Crystals, in "Strange Worlds" (Fall 1954/Spring 1955), 242
Subject Lesson (Young): Creative Film Award for, 34*n.* 30, 340; in "An Evening of Experimental Cinema" special event (Fall 1956/Spring 1957), 286; at International Experimental Film Festival, 340
Sucksdorff, Arne: background of, 143–45; *A Divided World,* 35*n.* 36, 142, 143–45; Frank Stauffacher opinion on films of, 162; presentation of, 8; Robert Flaherty compared to, 145; *A Summer's Tale,* 144; *Valley of Dreams,* 142, 143–45, 289; *Wind from the West,* in first membership program, 103
Suite No. 2, and first program, 84
"Summer Love" program (Fall 1957/Spring 1958), 301
A Summer's Tale (Sucksdorff), 144
Sunday (Drasin), in "The New American Cinema" special event (Fall 1961/Spring 1962), 394
Sunday by the Sea, in Spring 1955 program, 255
The Sun's Burial (Oshima), *391;* Dwight MacDonald review of, 397–98; in Fall 1961/Spring 1962 program, 51, 390–92
Suzuki, Hideo, *A Girl in the Mist,* in "Summer Love" program (Fall 1957/Spring 1958), 301
Swain, Mack, *Cowboy Ambrose,* in Fall 1950 program, 152
Sweeney, James Johnson, *Henry Moore,* in Fall 1948 program, 111
Symphonie Diagonale (Eggeling): London Film Society presentation of, 32*n.* 19; sources for, 79
Symphonie Pastorale (Delannoy), audience reaction to, 123
Symphony in No B-Flat (Kuhn): in Fall 1958/Spring 1959 program, 347; International Experimental Film Festival prize for, 339, 340
Symptoms in Schizophrenia, in Fall 1951 program, 166
Synthetic Sound Experiments (McLaren), discussion of, in Fall 1948 program, 111

Talbot, Daniel, New American Cinema Group membership of, 33*n.* 23, 52
Tanner, Alain, *Nice Time* (with Goretta): at International Experimental Film Festival, 340; in "Strange Worlds" (Spring 1959), 348, 356
Taras Bulba (Strizhevski), London Film Society presentation of, 32*n.* 19
The Tear (La Larme) (Melson), in Fall 1950 program, 152
Television: as Cinema 16 competition, 22; homogenization of culture through, 437
Texture of Decay (Vickrey), in "An Evening of Poetic and Surrealist Films" special event (Fall 1957/Spring 1958), 304
Thanatopsis (Emshwiller), in "Trance, Ritual and Hypnosis" program (Fall 1962/Spring 1963), 408
That the Deaf May Speak, in Spring 1953 program, 193–94

Theme and Transition (D'Avino): Creative Film Award for, 34*n.* 30; in "An Evening of Experimental Cinema" special event (Fall 1956/Spring 1957), 278, 286
Thevenard, Pierre, *Glimmering (Lueur),* in Fall 1957/Spring 1958 program, 302
Thinking Machines, in "Restricted Medical and Scientific Films" special event (Fall 1960/Spring 1961), 382
Third Avenue El (Davidson), in Fall 1958/Spring 1959 program, 347
"The Third Avenue El," in Fall 1958/Spring 1959 program, 347
The Thirteenth Night (Jusanya), in Spring 1956 program, 275
30 Years of the Avant-Garde (Richter), in Fall 1951 program, 166–67
This Day (Stark): distribution of, 16; in Fall 1948 program, 111
"This Is America" series (RKO), in Spring 1951 program, 160
This Is Robert (Stone): in Fall 1952/Spring 1953 program, 185; in Fall 1956/Spring 1957 special event, 285
Thomajan, Guy, New American Cinema Group membership of, 33*n.* 23
Thomas Benton ... The Making of a Mural, in Fall 1949 program, 135
Thomas, Dylan: membership of, 67; in "Poetry and the Film" symposium (Fall 1953), 11, 199, 202–12, *203*
Thompson, Francis, *N.Y., N.Y.:* Creative Film Award for, 34*n.* 30, 339; in Fall 1958/Spring 1959 special event, 348; influence of *Weegee's New York* on, 20; International Experimental Film Festival prize for, 339
3 Abstract Film Exercises (Whitney and Whitney): distribution of, 16; in second program, 92
3 Pickup Men for Herrick (Van Peebles), in Fall 1959/Spring 1960 special event, 355, 366
Three Women, in Fall 1958/Spring 1959 program, 345–46
Thurber, James, *Unicorn in the Garden:* in Fall 1953/Spring 1954 program, 197; popularity of, with members, 213
Thursday's Children, in Fall 1955/Spring 1956 program, 264
Time in the Sun (Seton, Eisenstein, and Alexandrov), in Fall 1952/Spring 1953 program, 75, 184
The Time of the Heathen (Kaas, Emshwiller, and Santvoord): Dwight MacDonald review of, 397; in "The New American Cinema" program (Fall 1961/Spring 1962), 392
Time Out of War (Sanders and Sanders), in Fall 1956/Spring 1957 program, 284
Tjurunga, in Spring 1949 program, 114
Toccata for Toy Train (Eames), in "A Program of Folk Art and Americana" (Spring 1959), 356
Toeplitz, Jerzy, 51
Together (Mazzetti and Horne), in Fall 1957/Spring 1958 program, 302, 321
To Hear Your Banjo Play (Van Dyke), in Spring 1950 program, 142

Tokyo 1958, in "New Talent" program (Spring 1961), 389
Tokyo Twilight (Ozu), in Fall 1958/Spring 1959 special event, 349
Tomorrow I Shall Be a Fire Tree (Horikawa), in Fall 1962/Spring 1963 special event, 409–10
Tomorrow Is a Wonderful Day (Lerski), in Spring 1952 program, 170
Too Much Speed (Youngson), in Fall 1955/Spring 1956 program, 264
Tourtelot, Madeline: *City Concerto,* critique of, 272; *Music Studio: Harry Partch,* in Spring 1960 program, 375; *One by One,* 248–49, 273, 275; *Reflections,* 272, 273; *Rhythm on Canvas,* 248, 273; *Silence,* 248, 273; *Zapotecan Village,* critique of, 272
Toussaint, Carlos, *La Canción de Jean Richepin:* in Fall 1959/Spring 1960 special event, 367; at International Experimental Film Festival, 341
The Towers (Hale), in Spring 1956 program, 275
Trailers, influence of video on, 61
Trance and Dance in Bali (Mead), in Fall 1952/Spring 1953 program, 183–84
"Trance, Ritual and Hypnosis" program (Fall 1962/Spring 1963), 407
Transfer of Power, in Spring 1952 program, 169
Transformation (Emshwiller): Creative Film Award for, 34n. 30, 383–84; in Fall 1960/Spring 1961 special event, 380
Transmutation (Belson): availability of, 123; and first program, 84; Frank Stauffacher involved in, 79, 85
Treadle and Bobbin (Galentine), in "Strange Worlds" (Fall 1954/Spring 1955), 243
Treasure in a Garbage Can (Hardman and Perkins), in Spring 1954 program, 225
Tregillus, Leonard, *No Credit* (with Luce), in Fall 1949 program, 133
A Trip (D'Avino): Creative Film Award for, 34n. 30, 384–85; in Fall 1960/Spring 1961 special event, 278, 380
Triumph of the Will (Riefenstahl): audience reaction to, 226–27; in Spring 1954 program, 202
Trnka, Jiri: *Fable for Friendship,* in Fall 1959/Spring 1960 program, 361; *Prince Bajaja,* in Fall 1962/Spring 1963 special event, 410; *Song of the Prairie,* in Spring 1953 program, 194
Trouble Indemnity (U.P.A.), in Spring 1951 program, 158
Truffaut, Francois, presentation of, 8
Turner, Leslie, *Howard Street,* in Spring 1955 program, 256
Twentieth Century (MacArthur and Hecht), in Fall 1957/Spring 1958 program, 300
Two Days (Stabovoy): Film Art Cinema screening of, 31n. 11; Film Guild Playhouse screening of, 3, 31n. 11
"Two Legendary Masterpieces" special event (Spring 1955), 244
Two Men and a Wardrobe (Polanski): in Fall 1958/Spring 1959 program, 51, 347; International Experimental Film Festival prize for, 338
Two Timid Souls (Clair), in Fall 1961/Spring 1962 program, 393

Tyler, Parker: and Creative Film Foundation, 34n. 30; on *The Lead Shoes,* 147–48; membership of, 67; in "Poetry and the Film" symposium (Fall 1953), 11, 199, 202–12, *203;* program notes by, 12, 46, 145–47, 174–75; *Rashomon* (Kurosawa) essay by, 13, *175,* 175–82; in Spring 1949 program, 114, 121

Uirapuru (Zebba), in Spring 1955 program, 256
Un Autre Monde, in Fall 1959/Spring 1960 program, 361
Un Chien Andalou (Buñuel and Dali): in avant-garde cinema, 219; in Fall 1950 program, 152; as poetic cinema, 202–3; sources for, 77, 79
Unconscious Motivation (Beck): in Spring 1950 program, 143; in "Trance, Ritual and Hypnosis" program (Fall 1962/Spring 1963), 408
Underground, sources for, 78, 79
Un Deuil Perpetuel (Markopoulos), 109
Unicorn in the Garden (Thurber): in Fall 1953/Spring 1954 program, 197; popularity of, with members, 213
Unions, for projectionists, 43
United Electrical Workers, CIO, *Men Against Money,* in Spring 1949 program, 114
United Productions of America: in Fall 1951 program, 166; in Fall 1952/Spring 1953 program, 184; in Fall 1953/Spring 1954 program, 197; in Fall 1954/Spring 1955 program, 242; in Spring 1951 program, 158
United States: immigration to, 38; World's Fair pavilion of, 336–37
United States government: *The Atom Strikes,* 16, 158; funding from, 29–30, 44, 58
University of Georgia, Amos Vogel at, 39
University of Pennsylvania, Amos Vogel at, 25, 26
The Unknown Soldier (Laine), in Spring 1958 special event, 304

Val del Omar, José, *La Gran Siguriya,* at International Experimental Film Festival, 341
Valley of Dreams (Sucksdorff): program notes for, 143–45; in Spring 1950 program, 142; in Spring 1957 program, 289
Valley Town (Van Dyke), in Fall 1949 program, 135
Vampyr (The Strange Adventures of David Grey) (Dreyer), in "Les Films Maudits: An Evening of Damned Films" special event (Spring 1953), 186, 195
Vancouver Film Society, 2
Vanderbeek, Stan, 278; at Literarisches Colloquium event, *51;* presentation of, 8; *Science Friction,* 34n. 30, 380, 386; *What, Who, How,* 34n. 30, 340, 349
Van Dyke, Willard: at Affiliated Films, 71; in Cinema 16 canon, 25; *The City* (with Steiner), 81, 103; in first membership program, 103; *To Hear Your Banjo Play,* in Spring 1950 program, 142; *The Photographer,* in Spring 1951 program, 159; presentation of films of, at Cecile Starr film society, 81; *Valley Town,* in Fall 1949 program, 135; *Working and Playing to Health,* in Spring 1954 program, 226
Van Gogh, availability of, 139

Van Meegeren's Faked Vermeers (Magnel), in Spring 1953 program, 193

Van Peebles, Melvin: importance of Cinema 16 to, 354–55; presentation of, 8; *3 Pickup Men for Herrick,* in Fall 1959/Spring 1960 special event, 355, 366

Varda, Agnes, *335; L'Opera Mouffe,* 51, 334, 339, 340, 346; presentation of, 8

Varèse, Edgard, on International Experimental Film Festival jury, 337

Variety (Dupont), in Spring 1954 program, 226

Vasan, S. S., *Chandra Lekha,* in Fall 1954/Spring 1955 special event, 11, 243

The Vassal (Der Untertan) (Staudte), in Fall 1960/Spring 1961 special event, 380

Vassar College, *Balloons: Aggression and Destruction Games,* in first membership program, 103

Veders, Nicole, *On the Border of Life,* in Fall 1955/Spring 1956 program, 263

Venice Film Festival, excursion to, 382

The Very Eye of Night (Deren), at International Experimental Film Festival, 340

Vesely, Herbert: in Cinema 16 canon, 25; *No More Fleeing,* 34n. 30, 286–87, 340; *Prelude,* 340, 367; *On These Evenings,* 34n. 30, 348

Vickrey, Robert, *Texture of Decay,* in "An Evening of Poetic and Surrealist Films" special event (Fall 1957/Spring 1958), 304

"The Victim is Man" special event (Spring 1960), 366–67

Video, 60–61

Vidor, King: *The Crowd,* 11, 395; *Hallelujah,* 11, 244, 249–51, *250;* presentation of, 60

Vienna, film society of, 32n. 19, 37–38

Vigo, Jean: *L'Atalante,* in Fall 1953/Spring 1954 special event, 199–200; and poetic cinema, 204; *A Propos de Nice,* in Fall 1953/Spring 1954 special event, 199–200; *Zero de conduite,* 15, 259

Village Voice (newspaper): Amos Vogel writing in, 25, 372–73; Cinema 16 covered in, 414–15; Jonas Mekas column in, 18, 54, 359, 372–73

Vishniak, Roman: *Microcosm,* in Spring 1956 program, 276; presentation of, 20, 49

Visual sensibility, as criteria for programs, 47

Visual Variations on Noguchi (Menken), presentation of, 222

Vocalization and Speech in Chimpanzees (Psychological Film Register), in Spring 1952 program, 168

Vogel, Amos, *64, 335, 435;* "The Angry Young Film Makers" (Vogel) (article), 336–45; and cigars, 32n. 20; in Cinema 16 incorporation, 4–5; in completion of *Weegee's New York,* 20, 33n. 25; Creative Film Awards program notes by, 382–86; early influences on, 37–38; education of, 39, 315; educational mission of, 8, 12, 13; *Film as a Subversive Art* (book), 25, 435–38; *The Flowers of St. Francis* (Rossellini) program notes by, 290–93; ideological opposition to Jewish state, 10; Lincoln Center film department directorship of, 26, 69; at Literarisches Colloquium event, *51;* marriage of, 40, 65–66; New York Film Festival founded by, 26; at "Poetry and the Film" symposium (Fall 1954), *203;* relationship with Jonas Mekas, 52, 68–69; teaching career of, 26

Vogel, Marcia, *64;* appreciation of avant-garde films by, 65; in Cinema 16 incorporation, 4–5; importance of, to Cinema 16, 63–64; marriage of, 40, 65–66; public involvement of, 63

Vogel, Samuel, in Cinema 16 incorporation, 4–5

Vogue Theater, experimental film presentations at, 313

The Voices (Schmitz), confiscation of, 311–12

Vormittagsspuk (Richter), audience reaction to, 164

"Voyages into the Subconscious" special event (Spring 1954), 12, 201–2

Waiting (Mock), in Spring 1954 program, 225

Wajda, Andrezj: *A Generation,* in Fall 1961/Spring 1962 program, 393; *The Innocent Sorcerers,* in Fall 1962/Spring 1963 program, 407

Wakefield Express (Anderson), distribution of, 322, 326

Walkabout, in "Strange Worlds" (Fall 1954/Spring 1955), 242

Warhol, Andy, *403*

Warning in the Dark, in "Restricted Medical and Scientific Films" special event (Fall 1960/Spring 1961), 382

Wasserman, Al, *Hoffa and the Unions,* Robert J. Flaherty Award for, 34n. 31

Watson, James Sibley: *The Fall of the House of Usher* (with Webber), Film Guild Playhouse screening of, 3; *Lot in Sodom,* as poetic cinema, 202–3

Watt, Harry, *Night Mail* (with Wright). See *Night Mail*

Waxworks, sources for, 77, 79

The Way to Shadow Garden (Brakhage), in International Experimental Film Festival, 319

Webber, Melville, *The Fall of the House of Usher* (with Watson), Film Guild Playhouse screening of, 3

Weegee (Arthur Fellig): in first membership program, 103; *Weegee's New York,* 20, 33n. 25, 263

Weegee's New York: completion of, with Amos Vogel, 20, 33n. 25; in Fall 1955/Spring 1956 program, 263; in first membership program, 103

Weinberg, Herman G., *Autumn Fire,* in "An Evening of Poetic and Surrealist Films" special event (Fall 1957/Spring 1958), 304

Weine, Robert, *The Hands of Orlac,* London Film Society presentation of, 32n. 19

Weiss, Peter: *According to Law,* at International Experimental Film Festival, 341; *Hallucinations,* in "Strange Worlds" (Fall 1956/Spring 1957), 284; *Interplay,* in "Summer Love" program (Fall 1957/Spring 1958), 301; *The Mirage,* in "The Beats and the Outs: Two Views" special event (Fall 1961/Spring 1962), 395; presentation of, 8; Stan Brakhage interest in, 295

Welles, Orson: *The Magnificent Ambersons,* 11, 199, *200,* 213; *Othello,* 274

Werner, Gosta, *Midvinterblot,* in Spring 1960 program, 375

Wescott, Glenway, and *Fireworks* (Anger), 188–89

West, Mae, *She Done Him Wrong*, in Fall 1960/Spring 1961 program, 376
What Is Modern Art (Brentano), in Spring 1949 program, 112
What, Who, How (Vanderbeek): Creative Film Award for, 34*n*. 30; in Fall 1958/Spring 1959 special event, 349; at International Experimental Film Festival, 340
Wheat Whistle (Mugi Fuye) (Muroo), in Fall 1956/Spring 1957 program, 284–85
When Love Fails (Antonioni), in Fall 1956/Spring 1957 program, 283
When the Clouds Roll By (Fleming and Reed), in "Garbo and Fairbanks: Two Hollywood Myths" special event (Fall 1962/Spring 1963), 410
When the Talkies Were Young (Youngson), in Fall 1955/Spring 1956 program, 264
White Eye (Brakhage): distribution of, 309, 315; in International Experimental Film Festival, 319
The White Hell of Pitz Palu (Pabst and Fanck), in Fall 1955/Spring 1956 special event, 265
Whitney, James, 157; *Film Exercises No. 4 & 5* (with Whitney), distribution of, 16; and first program, 84; *Five Abstract Film Exercises* (with Whitney), in second program, 9; and poetic cinema, 203; sources for films of, 77, 79; *3 Abstract Film Exercises* (with Whitney), 16, 92
Whitney, John, 157; *Blues Pattern* (with Pintoff), at International Experimental Film Festival, 340; *Film Exercises No. 4 & 5* (with Whitney), distribution of, 16; and first program, 84; *Five Abstract Film Exercises* (with Whitney), in second program, 9; *Performing Painter* (with Pintoff), at International Experimental Film Festival, 340; and poetic cinema, 203; sources for films of, 77, 79; *3 Abstract Film Exercises* (with Whitney), 16, 92
Who Wants to Be a Soldier?, in Fall 1960/Spring 1961 program, 378
Wilder, Billy, *People on Sunday (Menschen am Sonntag)* (with Siodmak and Zinnemann), in "Summer Love" program (Fall 1957/Spring 1958), 302
Wilenski, Eli (Eli Wilentz), influence of, on Amos Vogel, 40
Wilford, Thomas, *Lumia* (optical art), influence on Robert Kelly, 219
Williams, Richard, *The Little Island*, at International Experimental Film Festival, 340
Williams, Tennessee: Creative Film Award winner presented by, 21; program notes by, for *Fireworks* (Anger), 173
Willie the Kid (Cannon), in "Rituals, Tensions, Myths: The World of the Child" special event (Fall 1958/Spring 1959), 348
Willis, Eli, sponsorship of, 5
Wilson, Armine T., on film societies' relationships to Cinema 16, 34*n*. 35
Wind from the West (Sucksdorff), in first membership program, 103
The Window Cleaner (Bucher): audience reaction to, 123; in Spring 1949 program, 113

Winsten, Archer: "Are You Really Against Censorship?" reviewed by, 357–58; on end of Cinema 16, 418–19; first program reviewed by, 14–15, 89–90; second program reviewed by, 92–93; in Spring 1953 special event, 185, 195; third season reviewed by, 135–36
Winters, Jerry, *Renoir*, in Spring 1954 program, 226
Wise, Robert, *The Setup*, in Fall 1960/Spring 1961 special event, 11, 382
Witchcraft Through the Ages (Christensen), *328*; program notes for, by Gideon Bachmann, 327–32; in Spring 1958 special event, 11, 304
Within a Story (Bagley), in Fall 1955/Spring 1956 program, 264
Woll, Yael, *Study of a Dance*, in Spring 1954 program, 225
The Wonder Ring (Brakhage), 297; audience reaction to, 14; distribution of, 306; in Fall 1958/Spring 1959 program, 347; Film Forum presentation of, 35*n*. 36; in International Experimental Film Festival, 319
Workers Film and Photo League, 31*n*. 12
Working and Playing to Health (Van Dyke), in Spring 1954 program, 225
The World Is Rich (Rotha), in first membership program, 103
The World of Paul Delvaux (Storck), in Fall 1950 program, 153
The World of the Microbes: In Quest of the Tubercle Bacilli (Onuma), in Fall 1959/Spring 1960 program, 362
World's Fair of 1958, American *vs.* Russian pavilions at, 336–37
World War II, Amos Vogel during, 38–40
Wright, Basil: *Night Mail* (with Watt) (*see Night Mail*); *Odd Man Out* lecture-on-film, in Spring 1950 program, 142; *Ordinary People*, in Spring 1952 program, 168; *Song of Ceylon*, 37, 65, 66, 162, 166

Yale University, *An Experimentally Produced Social Problem in Rats*, in Spring 1949 program, 115
Yama No Oto (The Echo) (Naruse), in Fall 1957/Spring 1958 special event, 303
Yellow Cruise (Poirier and Sauvage), in Fall 1954/Spring 1955 special event, 73, 243–44
Young, Christopher: *Object Lesson*, in Fall 1950 program, 151; *Subject Lesson*, 34*n*. 30, 286, 340
Young, James, *Goodness Gracious*, in Spring 1954 program, 226
Youngson, Bob: *Too Much Speed*, in Fall 1955/Spring 1956 program, 264; *When the Talkies Were Young*, in Fall 1955/Spring 1956 program, 264

Zapotecan Village (Tourtelot), critique of, 272
Zavattini, Cesare: *Love in the City*, in Fall 1956/Spring 1957 program, 283; *The Love of a Mother* (with Maselli), in Fall 1956/Spring 1957 program, 283
Zebba, Sam, *Uirapuru*, in Spring 1955 program, 256
Zero de conduite (Vigo): as art, 15; availability of, 259
Zigzag, 128, 138, 139

Zinnemann, Fred: in Fall 1954/Spring 1955 special event, 11, 246; *High Noon*, influence of Robert Flaherty on, 282; *The Men*, influence of Robert Flaherty on, 282; *The Old Man and the Sea*, 282; *People on Sunday (Menschen am Sonntag)* (with Siodmak and Wilder), in "Summer Love" program (Fall 1957/Spring 1958), 302; *The Search*, 282, 285

Zionist movement, and Amos Vogel, 39

Zora, in Fall 1958/Spring 1959 program, 345

Zuckerman, S., *Monkey into Man* (with Huxley and Legg). *See Monkey into Man*